D.F. SKERTCHLY   2011

✝ YOUR **M**SUNDAY**ISSAL**

YOUR SUNDAY MISSAL

General Editor:
Denis McBride C.Ss.R.

Editors:
Peter Edwards
Andrew Lyon

Your Sunday Missal
Published by
Redemptorist Publications
Alphonsus House, Chawton, Hampshire, GU34 3HQ UK
Tel. +44 (0)1420 88222, Fax +44 (0)1420 88805
Email rp@rpbooks.co.uk www.rpbooks.co.uk
A Registered Charity limited by guarantee.
Registered in England 3261721

© Redemptorist Publications, 2011

First published November 2011

Cover and layout design: Rosemarie Pink
Illustrations: Roger Smith
Music typesetting: Michael Bennett

ISBN 978-0-85231-397-8

Concordat cum originali: Paul Moynihan
Imprimatur: + Kieran Conry
9 September 2011

The publisher gratefully acknowledges permission to use the following
copyright material in this missal:
Excerpts from the English translation and chants of *The Roman Missal*
© 2010, International Commission on English in the Liturgy Corporation.
All rights reserved.

Excerpts from THE JERUSALEM BIBLE, copyright © 1966 by Darton,
Longman & Todd, Ltd and Doubleday, a division of Random House, Inc.
Reprinted by permission.

Psalms from the Grail Psalter reprinted by permission of HarperCollins
Publishers Ltd © 1963.

Printed and bound in Italy by: L.E.G.O. S.p.A. Italy

WELCOME FROM THE EDITOR

Introduction

It all began when Jesus asked his disciples to remember him: remember him not by brooding on their shared past but by continuing to celebrate what they were doing at that moment: "Do *this* in memory of me." Those arresting, haunting words of Jesus have defined the Christian community for two thousand years. We meet together to hallow the memory of the Lord by doing *this*: celebrating the Eucharist.

At the Last Supper, before Jesus is handed over into the hands of his enemies, he hands himself over into the hands of his friends. He, literally, gives *himself* away in the breaking of bread; he puts himself into the safekeeping of his followers. The gift of Jesus is the gift of himself, *Corpus Christi*. He will be lifted up by the hands of his persecutors, but he will also be lifted up by the hands of his loving friends. And that will happen throughout history.

In following Jesus' command we hope not only that we will be consumers of the bread of life but also that we will become bread, one for another. We are charged to *become* the memory, to bring it into the present tense. This is summarised in the prayer of St Augustine: "We pray that we might become what we eat, the Body of Christ."

When we look at the shape of the Mass, we see four parts, each essential to the unfolding drama:

The Introductory Rites

When we assemble together to meet Jesus in word and sacrament, we are greeted with a blessing, then invited to be realistic about ourselves and acknowledge our sins. This is not a place for fantasy or self-delusion; neither is it a place for destructive self-recrimination. Before the God of all mercies we confess that we stand in need of God's grace and compassion. That acknowledgement is met by the absolution by the priest and leads into the "Lord, have mercy", when we plead together for the mercy of the Lord.

The Liturgy of the Word

We are now invited to attend to God's word in the scriptures. So many stories are told in the readings. We hear from all kinds of people: from warrior kings; stammering prophets; determined luminaries; aggrieved parents; ambitious children; brilliant storytellers; mumbling stargazers; people stunned in wonder at their healing. As well as heroes and heroines, we meet people who are weak and bewildered and distraught, for whom faith provides a shelter. We attempt to connect their story to our own.

But there is one Word that, above all, speaks in God's true accent: that Word is Jesus. We meet him in Gospel, this God in our skin. Thus we stand to greet this sacred Word, and in formal liturgies the book is carried in procession, accompanied by acolytes carrying lighted candles, and then is incensed. This Word is different: this Word is Good News – a Word that deserves opening up and considering in the homily. Following that reflection, we stand to profess our belief; and since no one can believe for us, each of us now prays, "I believe..." The Liturgy of the Word concludes when we petition God for the needs of the Church and the world; our faith now reaches out to specific situations in our world today.

The Liturgy of the Eucharist

While the Liturgy of the Word focuses upon the table of the Lord's word – the ambo – the Eucharistic liturgy centres upon the altar of the Lord – both a place of sacrifice and the table from which we are fed. The themes of sacrifice, thanksgiving and meal will prevail: the action will be on taking, blessing, breaking and sharing.

The gifts of bread and wine are taken to the altar and blessed by the priest. The Eucharistic Prayer begins by praising God for his great deeds of creation and redemption, and moves into asking the Spirit to transform these gifts of the earth into the sacred Body and Blood of the Lord. As the words of Jesus at the Last Supper are solemnly recalled, the action of the Holy Spirit effects the real presence of the Body and Blood of Christ.

We call to mind the saving death and resurrection of the Lord; we pray for unity in the Holy Spirit, for all the members of the Church, for our departed brothers and sisters. In praise of God, we affirm our assent to all that has been proclaimed, in the great "Amen". In the Communion Rite we pray the prayer of Jesus, hallowing the name of the Father and pleading for forgiveness. Before we share the bread of life, we exchange the peace of Christ, an act of reverence to our neighbour. The Liturgy of the Eucharist comes to a close when we have the opportunity to unite ourselves with the Lord, in personal communion with the one who said, "Do this in memory of me."

The Concluding Rites

The Mass concludes when we are sent out, commissioned to carry beyond the door of the church what we have been doing. As we have prayed, so we are invited to live.

In thanks

If the Eucharist is about giving thanks, I would like to thank my two co-editors, Peter Edwards and Andrew Lyon, for their wholehearted commitment in producing this missal; Rosemarie Pink, who, with her enduring equanimity, set everything in typescript; my confrère Richard Reid, for assembling a selection of prayers by St Alphonsus; and everyone at Redemptorist Publications for their steadfast support. Our single hope is that this missal will be a faithful and constant companion in worshipping the God of all kindness, in whom there is plentiful redemption.

Denis McBride cssr

Denis McBride C.Ss.R.
Feast of the Most Holy Redeemer, 2011

CONTENTS
THE ORDER OF MASS

THE SUNDAY MASSES

PRINCIPAL CELEBRATIONS DURING THE YEAR

Year	Cycle	Epiphany [*]	Ash Wed.	Easter	Ascension [**]	Pentecost
2012	B	8 Jan	22 Feb	8 Apr	20 May	27 May
2013	C	6 Jan	13 Feb	31 Mar	12 May	19 May
2014	A	5 Jan	5 Mar	20 Apr	1 June	8 June
2015	B	4 Jan	18 Feb	5 Apr	17 May	24 May
2016	C	3 Jan	10 Feb	27 Mar	8 May	15 May
2017	A	8 Jan	1 Mar	16 Apr	28 May	4 June
2018	B	7 Jan	14 Feb	1 Apr	13 May	20 May
2019	C	6 Jan	6 Mar	21 Apr	2 June	9 June
2020	A	5 Jan	26 Feb	12 Apr	24 May	31 May
2021	B	3 Jan	17 Feb	4 Apr	16 May	23 May
2022	C	2 Jan	2 Mar	17 Apr	29 May	5 June
2023	A	8 Jan	22 Feb	9 Apr	21 May	28 May
2024	B	7 Jan	14 Feb	31 Mar	12 May	19 May
2025	C	5 Jan	5 Mar	20 Apr	1 June	8 June
2026	A	4 Jan	18 Feb	5 Apr	17 May	24 May
2027	B	3 Jan	10 Feb	28 Mar	9 May	16 May

[*] In Ireland, the Epiphany is celebrated on 6 January.
[**] In Scotland, the Ascension is celebrated on the Thursday after the sixth Sunday of Easter (three days earlier than the date listed here).

Body and Blood of Christ	Sacred Heart of Jesus	Ordinary Weeks of the Year				First Sunday of Advent	Year
		Before Lent		After Pentecost			
		Until	Week	From	Week		
10 June	15 June	21 Feb	7	28 May	8	2 Dec	2012
2 June	7 June	12 Feb	5	20 May	7	1 Dec	2013
22 June	27 June	4 Mar	8	9 June	10	30 Nov	2014
7 June	12 June	17 Feb	6	25 May	8	29 Nov	2015
29 May	3 June	9 Feb	5	16 May	7	27 Nov	2016
18 June	23 June	28 Feb	8	5 June	9	3 Dec	2017
3 June	8 June	13 Feb	6	21 May	7	2 Dec	2018
23 June	28 June	5 Mar	8	10 June	10	1 Dec	2019
14 June	19 June	25 Feb	7	1 June	9	29 Nov	2020
6 June	11 June	16 Feb	6	24 May	8	28 Nov	2021
19 June	24 June	1 Mar	8	6 June	10	27 Nov	2022
11 June	16 June	21 Feb	7	29 May	8	3 Dec	2023
2 June	7 June	13 Feb	6	20 May	7	1 Dec	2024
22 June	27 June	4 Mar	8	9 June	10	30 Nov	2025
7 June	12 June	17 Feb	6	25 May	8	29 Nov	2026
30 May	4 June	9 Feb	5	17 May	7	28 Nov	2027

FIRST SUNDAY OF ADVENT – A

Be prepared!
During Advent we prepare ourselves for the birth of Christ. We make
ourselves ready as the new homes into which he will come. The long hours of
waiting are nearly over and the dawn of our salvation is about to break. Soon
we will walk in the light of the Lord.

Entrance Antiphon
To you, I lift up my soul, O my God.
In you, I have trusted; let me not be put to shame.
Nor let my enemies exult over me;
and let none who hope in you be put to shame.　　cf. Psalm 24:1-3

The Gloria is not said or sung.

Collect
Grant your faithful, we pray, almighty God,
the resolve to run forth to meet your Christ
with righteous deeds at his coming,
so that, gathered at his right hand,
they may be worthy to possess the heavenly Kingdom.
Through our Lord Jesus Christ, your Son,
who lives and reigns with you in the unity of the Holy Spirit,
one God, for ever and ever.

First Reading　　　　　　　　　　　　　　　　　Isaiah 2:1-5
The Lord gathers all nations together into the eternal peace of
God's kingdom.
The vision of Isaiah son of Amoz, concerning Judah and Jerusalem.

In the days to come
the mountain of the Temple of the Lord
shall tower above the mountains
and be lifted higher than the hills.
All the nations will stream to it,

peoples without number will come to it; and they will say:

"Come, let us go up to the mountain of the Lord,
to the Temple of the God of Jacob
that he may teach us his ways
so that we may walk in his paths;
since the Law will go out from Zion,
and the oracle of the Lord from Jerusalem."

He will wield authority over the nations
and adjudicate between many peoples;
these will hammer their swords into ploughshares,
their spears into sickles.
Nation will not lift sword against nation,
there will be no more training for war.
O House of Jacob, come,
let us walk in the light of the Lord.

Psalm   Psalm 121

R. **I rejoiced when I heard them say:
     "Let us go to God's house."**

1. I rejoiced when I heard them say:
    "Let us go to God's house."
    And now our feet are standing
    within your gates, O Jerusalem. R.

2. It is there that the tribes go up,
    the tribes of the Lord.
    For Israel's law it is,
    there to praise the Lord's name.
    There were set the thrones of judgement
    of the house of David. R.

3. For the peace of Jerusalem pray:
    "Peace be to your homes!
    May peace reign in your walls,
    in your palaces, peace!" R.

4. For love of my brethren and friends
   I say: "Peace upon you!"
   For love of the house of the Lord
   I will ask for your good. R.

Second Reading   **Romans 13:11-14**
Our salvation is near.

You know "the time" has come: you must wake up now: our salvation is even nearer than it was when we were converted. The night is almost over, it will be daylight soon – let us give up all the things we prefer to do under cover of dark; let us arm ourselves and appear in the light. Let us live decently as people do in the daytime: no drunken orgies, no promiscuity or licentiousness, and no wrangling or jealousy. Let your armour be the Lord Jesus Christ.

Gospel Acclamation
Alleluia, alleluia!
Let us see, O Lord, your mercy
and give us your saving help.
Alleluia!   **Psalm 84:8**

Gospel   **Matthew 24:37-44**
Stay awake so that you may be ready.

Jesus said to his disciples: "As it was in Noah's day, so will it be when the Son of Man comes. For in those days before the Flood people were eating, drinking, taking wives, taking husbands, right up to the day Noah went into the ark, and they suspected nothing till the Flood came and swept all away. It will be like this when the Son of Man comes. Then of two men in the fields one is taken, one left; of two women at the millstone grinding, one is taken, one left.

"So stay awake, because you do not know the day when your master is coming. You may be quite sure of this that if the householder had known at what time of the night the burglar would come, he would have stayed awake and would not have allowed anyone to break through the wall of his house. Therefore, you too must stand ready because the Son of Man is coming at an hour you do not expect.

The Creed is said.

Prayer over the Offerings
Accept, we pray, O Lord, these offerings we make,
gathered from among your gifts to us,
and may what you grant us to celebrate devoutly here below,
gain for us the prize of eternal redemption.
Through Christ our Lord.

Preface I of Advent, p. 490.

Communion Antiphon
The Lord will bestow his bounty,
   and our earth shall yield its increase.   Psalm 84:13

Prayer after Communion
May these mysteries, O Lord,
in which we have participated,
profit us, we pray,
for even now, as we walk amid passing things,
you teach us by them to love the things of heaven
and hold fast to what endures.
Through Christ our Lord.

The Solemn Blessing for Advent may be used, p. 508.

SECOND SUNDAY OF ADVENT – A

Prepare a way for the Lord!
We prepare ourselves for the coming of Christ through repentance. We are
called to change the pattern of our lives in order to be ready when he comes.
John the Baptist calls us to look again at our lives, to make sure that the Lord
will have no obstacle in his path.

Entrance Antiphon
O people of Sion, behold,
the Lord will come to save the nations,
and the Lord will make the glory of his voice heard
in the joy of your heart.   cf. Isaiah 30:19. 30

The Gloria is not said or sung.

Collect
Almighty and merciful God,
may no earthly undertaking hinder those
who set out in haste to meet your Son,
but may our learning of heavenly wisdom
gain us admittance to his company.
Who lives and reigns with you in the unity of the Holy Spirit,
one God, for ever and ever.

First Reading   Isaiah 11:1-10
He judges the wretched with integrity.
A shoot springs from the stock of Jesse,
a scion thrusts from his roots:
on him the spirit of the Lord rests,
a spirit of wisdom and insight,
a spirit of counsel and power,
a spirit of knowledge and of the fear of the Lord.
(The fear of the Lord is his breath.)
He does not judge by appearances,
he gives no verdict on hearsay,
but judges the wretched with integrity,
and with equity gives a verdict for the poor of the land.

His word is a rod that strikes the ruthless;
his sentences bring death to the wicked.

Integrity is the loincloth round his waist,
faithfulness the belt about his hips.

The wolf lives with the lamb,
the panther lies down with the kid,
calf and lion cub feed together
with a little boy to lead them.
The cow and the bear make friends,
their young lie down together.
The lion eats straw like the ox.
The infant plays over the cobra's hole;
into the viper's lair
the young child puts his hand.
They do no hurt, no harm,
on all my holy mountain,
for the country is filled with the knowledge of the Lord
as the waters swell the sea.

That day, the root of Jesse
shall stand as a signal to the peoples.
It will be sought out by the nations
and its home will be glorious.

Psalm   Psalm 71

R. **In his days justice shall flourish
and peace till the moon fails.**

1. O God, give your judgement to the king,
to a king's son your justice,
that he may judge your people in justice
and your poor in right judgement. R.

2. In his days justice shall flourish
and peace till the moon fails.
He shall rule from sea to sea,
from the Great River to earth's bounds. R.

3. For he shall save the poor when they cry
and the needy who are helpless.

He will have pity on the weak
and save the lives of the poor. R.

4. May his name be blessed for ever
and endure like the sun.
Every tribe shall be blessed in him,
all nations bless his name. R.

Second Reading   Romans 15:4-9
Christ is the saviour of all men.

Everything that was written long ago in the scriptures was meant to teach us something about hope from the examples scripture gives of how people who did not give up were helped by God. And may he who helps us when we refuse to give up, help you all to be tolerant with each other, following the example of Christ Jesus, so that united in mind and voice you may give glory to the God and Father of our Lord Jesus Christ.

It can only be to God's glory, then, for you to treat each other in the same friendly way as Christ treated you. The reason Christ became the servant of circumcised Jews was not only so that God could faithfully carry out the promises made to the patriarchs, it was also to get the pagans to give glory to God for his mercy, as scripture says in one place: For this I shall praise you among the pagans and sing your name.

Gospel Acclamation
Alleluia, alleluia!
Prepare a way for the Lord,
make his paths straight,
and all mankind shall see the salvation of God.
Alleluia!   Luke 3:4. 6

Gospel   Matthew 3:1-12
Repent, for the kingdom of heaven is close at hand.

In due course John the Baptist appeared; he preached in the wilderness of Judaea and this was his message: "Repent, for the kingdom of heaven is close at hand." This was the man the prophet Isaiah spoke of when he said:

A voice cries in the wilderness:
Prepare a way for the Lord,
make his paths straight.

This man John wore a garment made of camel-hair with a leather belt round his waist, and his food was locusts and wild honey. Then Jerusalem and all Judaea and the whole Jordan district made their way to him, and as they were baptised by him in the river Jordan they confessed their sins. But when he saw a number of Pharisees and Sadducees coming for baptism he said to them, "Brood of vipers, who warned you to fly from the retribution that is coming? But if you are repentant, produce the appropriate fruit, and do not presume to tell yourselves, 'We have Abraham for our father,' because, I tell you, God can raise children for Abraham from these stones. Even now the axe is laid to the roots of the trees, so that any tree which fails to produce good fruit will be cut down and thrown on the fire. I baptise you in water for repentance, but the one who follows me is more powerful than I am, and I am not fit to carry his sandals; he will baptise you with the Holy Spirit and fire. His winnowing-fan is in his hand; he will clear his threshing-floor and gather his wheat into the barn; but the chaff he will burn in a fire that will never go out."

The Creed is said.

Prayer over the Offerings
Be pleased, O Lord, with our humble prayers and offerings,
and, since we have no merits to plead our cause,
come, we pray, to our rescue
with the protection of your mercy.
Through Christ our Lord.

Preface I of Advent, p. 490.

Communion Antiphon
Jerusalem, arise and stand upon the heights,
and behold the joy which comes to you from God.   Baruch 5:5; 4:36

Prayer after Communion
Replenished by the food of spiritual nourishment,
we humbly beseech you, O Lord,
that, through our partaking in this mystery,
you may teach us to judge wisely the things of earth
and hold firm to the things of heaven.
Through Christ our Lord.

The Solemn Blessing for Advent may be used, p. 508.

THIRD SUNDAY OF ADVENT – A

Rejoice, the Lord is coming soon!
God sends his own Son to save us. Joy and gladness
are ours, and the time for sorrow and lamenting is over.
Christ is standing at the gates and we know he is
the one for whom we have been waiting. Do not lose heart.
Take courage! Your God is coming!

Entrance Antiphon
Rejoice in the Lord always; again I say, rejoice.
Indeed, the Lord is near.

Philippians 4:4-5

The Gloria is not said or sung.

Collect
O God, who see how your people
faithfully await the feast of the Lord's Nativity,
enable us, we pray,
to attain the joys of so great a salvation
and to celebrate them always
with solemn worship and glad rejoicing.
Through our Lord Jesus Christ, your Son,
who lives and reigns with you in the unity of the Holy Spirit,
one God, for ever and ever.

First Reading   Isaiah 35:1-6. 10
God himself is coming to save you.

Let the wilderness and the dry-lands exult,
let the wasteland rejoice and bloom,
let it bring forth flowers like the jonquil,
let it rejoice and sing for joy.

The glory of Lebanon is bestowed on it,
the splendour of Carmel and Sharon;

they shall see the glory of the Lord,
the splendour of our God.

Strengthen all weary hands,
steady all trembling knees
and say to all faint hearts,
"Courage! Do not be afraid.

"Look, your God is coming,
vengeance is coming,
the retribution of God;
he is coming to save you."

Then the eyes of the blind shall be opened,
the ears of the deaf unsealed,
then the lame shall leap like a deer
and the tongues of the dumb sing for joy;
for those the Lord has ransomed shall return.

They will come to Zion shouting for joy,
everlasting joy on their faces;
joy and gladness will go with them
and sorrow and lament be ended.

Psalm   Psalm 145

R. **Come, Lord, and save us.**

or

R. **Alleluia!**

1. It is the Lord who keeps faith for ever,
    who is just to those who are oppressed.
    It is he who gives bread to the hungry,
    the Lord, who sets prisoners free. R.

2. It is the Lord who gives sight to the blind,
    who raises up those who are bowed down,
    the Lord, who protects the stranger
    and upholds the widow and orphan. R.

3. It is the Lord who loves the just
   but thwarts the path of the wicked.
   The Lord will reign for ever,
   Zion's God, from age to age. R.

Second Reading   James 5:7-10

Do not lose heart for the Lord's coming will be soon.

Be patient, brothers, until the Lord's coming. Think of a farmer:
how patiently he waits for the precious fruit of the ground until it
has had the autumn rains and the spring rains! You too have to be
patient; do not lose heart, because the Lord's coming will be soon.
Do not make complaints against one another, brothers, so as not to
be brought to judgement yourselves; the Judge is already to be seen
waiting at the gates. For your example, brothers, in submitting with
patience, take the prophets who spoke in the name of the Lord.

Gospel Acclamation

Alleluia, alleluia!
The spirit of the Lord has been given to me.
He has sent me to bring good news to the poor.
Alleluia!   Isaiah 61:1 (Luke 4:18)

Gospel   Matthew 11:2-11

Are you the one who is to come, or have we got to wait for someone
else?

John in his prison had heard what Christ was doing and he sent his
disciples to ask him, "Are you the one who is to come, or have we
got to wait for someone else?" Jesus answered, "Go back and tell
John what you hear and see; the blind see again, and the lame walk,
lepers are cleansed, and the deaf hear, and the dead are raised to
life and the Good News is proclaimed to the poor; and happy is the
man who does not lose faith in me."

As the messengers were leaving, Jesus began to talk to the people
about John: "What did you go out into the wilderness to see? A reed
swaying in the breeze? No? Then what did you go out to see? A man
wearing fine clothes? Oh no, those who wear fine clothes are to be
found in palaces. Then what did you go out for? To see a prophet?

Yes, I tell you, and much more than a prophet: he is the one of whom scripture says: Look, I am going to send my messenger before you; he will prepare your way before you. I tell you solemnly, of all the children born of women, a greater than John the Baptist has never been seen; yet the least in the kingdom of heaven is greater than he is."

The Creed is said.

Prayer over the Offerings
May the sacrifice of our worship, Lord, we pray,
be offered to you unceasingly,
to complete what was begun in sacred mystery
and powerfully accomplish for us your saving work.
Through Christ our Lord.

Preface I or II of Advent, pp. 490-491.

Communion Antiphon
Say to the faint of heart: Be strong and do not fear.
Behold, our God will come, and he will save us.   cf. Isaiah 35:4

Prayer after Communion
We implore your mercy, Lord,
that this divine sustenance may cleanse us of our faults
and prepare us for the coming feasts.
Through Christ our Lord.

The Solemn Blessing for Advent may be used, p. 508.

FOURTH SUNDAY OF ADVENT – A

God is with us!
God our Father sent his only Son to be born on earth of human stock. His
name is Jesus and his mother's name is Mary. He is the Saviour of all the
world, and through him we are called to holiness of life.

Entrance Antiphon
Drop down dew from above, you heavens,
and let the clouds rain down the Just One;
let the earth be opened and bring forth a Saviour.   cf. Isaiah 45:8

The Gloria is not said or sung.

Collect
Pour forth, we beseech you, O Lord,
your grace into our hearts,
that we, to whom the Incarnation of Christ your Son
was made known by the message of an Angel,
may by his Passion and Cross
be brought to the glory of his Resurrection.
Who lives and reigns with you in the unity of the Holy Spirit,
one God, for ever and ever.

First Reading   Isaiah 7:10-14
The maiden is with child.
The Lord spoke to Ahaz and said, "Ask the Lord your God for a
sign for yourself coming either from the depths of Sheol or from
the heights above." "No," Ahaz answered "I will not put the Lord to
the test."
    Then Isaiah said:

    "Listen now, House of David:
    are you not satisfied with trying the patience of men
    without trying the patience of my God, too?
    The Lord himself, therefore,

will give you a sign.
It is this: the maiden is with child
and will soon give birth to a son
whom she will call Emmanuel,
a name which means 'God-is-with-us'."

Psalm   Psalm 23

R. **Let the Lord enter!**
   He is the king of glory.

1. The Lord's is the earth and its fullness,
   the world and all its peoples.
   It is he who set it on the seas;
   on the waters he made it firm. R.

2. Who shall climb the mountain of the Lord?
   Who shall stand in his holy place?
   The man with clean hands and pure heart,
   who desires not worthless things. R.

3. He shall receive blessings from the Lord
   and reward from the God who saves him.
   Such are the men who seek him,
   seek the face of the God of Jacob. R.

Second Reading   Romans 1:1-7
Jesus Christ, descendant of David, Son of God.
From Paul, a servant of Christ Jesus who has been called to be an
apostle, and specially chosen to preach the Good News that God
promised long ago through his prophets in the scriptures.

   This news is about the Son of God, who, according to the human
nature he took, was a descendant of David: it is about Jesus Christ
our Lord who, in the order of the spirit, the spirit of holiness that
was in him, was proclaimed Son of God in all his power through
his resurrection from the dead. Through him we received grace and
our apostolic mission to preach the obedience of faith to all pagan
nations in honour of his name. You are one of these nations, and

by his call belong to Jesus Christ. To you all, then, who are God's beloved in Rome, called to be saints, may God our Father and the Lord Jesus Christ send grace and peace.

Gospel Acclamation

Alleluia, alleluia!
The virgin will conceive and give birth to a son
and they will call him Emmanuel,
a name which means "God-is-with-us".
Alleluia!   Matthew 1:23

Gospel   Matthew 1:18-24

Jesus is born of Mary who was betrothed to Joseph, son of David.

This is how Jesus Christ came to be born. His mother Mary was betrothed to Joseph; but before they came to live together she was found to be with child through the Holy Spirit. Her husband Joseph, being a man of honour and wanting to spare her publicity, decided to divorce her informally. He had made up his mind to do this when the angel of the Lord appeared to him in a dream, and said "Joseph son of David, do not be afraid to take Mary home as your wife, because she has conceived what is in her by the Holy Spirit. She will give birth to a son and you must name him Jesus, because he is the one who is to save his people from their sins." Now all this took place to fulfil the words spoken by the Lord through the prophet:

> The virgin will conceive and give birth to a son
> and they will call him Emmanuel,

a name which means "God-is-with-us". When Joseph woke up he did what the angel of the Lord had told him to do: he took his wife to his home.

The Creed is said.

Prayer over the Offerings

May the Holy Spirit, O Lord,
sanctify these gifts laid upon your altar,
just as he filled with his power the womb of the Blessed Virgin Mary.
Through Christ our Lord.

Preface II of Advent, pp. 490-491.

Communion Antiphon
Behold, a Virgin shall conceive and bear a son;
and his name will be called Emmanuel.   Isaiah 7:14

Prayer after Communion
Having received this pledge of eternal redemption,
we pray, almighty God,
that, as the feast day of our salvation draws ever nearer,
so we may press forward all the more eagerly
to the worthy celebration of the mystery of your Son's Nativity.
Who lives and reigns for ever and ever.

The Solemn Blessing for Advent may be used, p. 508.

The liturgies for Christmas time begin on p. 49.

FIRST SUNDAY OF ADVENT – B

Stay awake!
Advent is a time of waiting and watching for the coming of the Lord Jesus.
The Holy Spirit is our constant help so that we may always be alert and
prepared for the last day. The best preparation is a life lived in the knowledge
that God is our Father and we are the work of his hands.

Entrance Antiphon
To you, I lift up my soul, O my God.
In you, I have trusted; let me not be put to shame.
Nor let my enemies exult over me;
and let none who hope in you be put to shame.   cf. Psalm 24:1-3

The Gloria is not said or sung.

Collect
Grant your faithful, we pray, almighty God,
the resolve to run forth to meet your Christ
with righteous deeds at his coming,
so that, gathered at his right hand,
they may be worthy to possess the heavenly Kingdom.
Through our Lord Jesus Christ, your Son,
who lives and reigns with you in the unity of the Holy Spirit,
one God, for ever and ever.

First Reading   Isaiah 63:16-17; 64:1. 3-8
Oh, that you would tear the heavens open and come down.
You, Lord, yourself are our Father,
Our Redeemer is your ancient name.
Why, Lord, leave us to stray from our ways
and harden our hearts against fearing you?
Return, for the sake of your servants,
the tribes of your inheritance.
Oh, that you would tear the heavens open and come down
– at your Presence the mountains would melt.

No ear has heard,
no eye has seen
any god but you act like this
for those who trust him.
You guide those who act with integrity
and keep your ways in mind.
You were angry when we were sinners;
we had long been rebels against you.
We were all like men unclean,
all that integrity of ours like filthy clothing.
We have all withered like leaves
and our sins blew us away like the wind.
No one invoked your name
or roused himself to catch hold of you.
For you hid your face from us
and gave us up to the power of our sins.
And yet, Lord, you are our Father;
we the clay, you the potter,
we are all the work of your hand.

Psalm   Psalm 79

R. **God of hosts, bring us back;**
    let your face shine on us and we shall be saved.

1. O shepherd of Israel, hear us,
    shine forth from your cherubim throne.
    O Lord, rouse up your might,
    O Lord, come to our help. R.

2. God of hosts, turn again, we implore,
    look down from heaven and see.
    Visit this vine and protect it,
    the vine your right hand has planted. R.

3. May your hand be on the man you have chosen,
    the man you have given your strength.

And we shall never forsake you again:
give us life that we may call upon your name. R.

Second Reading   1 Corinthians 1:3-9
We are waiting for our Lord Jesus Christ to be revealed.
May God our Father and the Lord Jesus Christ send you grace and
peace.

I never stop thanking God for all the graces you have received
through Jesus Christ. I thank him that you have been enriched in so
many ways, especially in your teachers and preachers; the witness
to Christ has indeed been strong among you so that you will not be
without any of the gifts of the Spirit while you are waiting for our
Lord Jesus Christ to be revealed; and he will keep you steady and
without blame until the last day, the day of our Lord Jesus Christ,
because God by calling you has joined you to his Son, Jesus Christ;
and God is faithful.

Gospel Acclamation
Alleluia, alleluia!
Let us see, O Lord, your mercy
and give us your saving help.
Alleluia!   Psalm 84:8

Gospel   Mark 13:33-37
Stay awake, because you do not know when the master of the house
is coming.
Jesus said to his disciples: "Be on your guard, stay awake, because
you never know when the time will come. It is like a man travelling
abroad: he has gone from home, and left his servants in charge,
each with his own task; and he has told the doorkeeper to stay
awake. So stay awake, because you do not know when the master
of the house is coming, evening, midnight, cockcrow, dawn; if he
comes unexpectedly, he must not find you asleep. And what I say to
you I say to all: Stay awake!"

The Creed is said.

Prayer over the Offerings
Accept, we pray, O Lord, these offerings we make,
gathered from among your gifts to us,
and may what you grant us to celebrate devoutly here below,
gain for us the prize of eternal redemption.
Through Christ our Lord.

Preface I of Advent, p. 490.

Communion Antiphon
The Lord will bestow his bounty,
    and our earth shall yield its increase.   Psalm 84:13

Prayer after Communion
May these mysteries, O Lord,
in which we have participated,
profit us, we pray,
for even now, as we walk amid passing things,
you teach us by them to love the things of heaven
and hold fast to what endures.
Through Christ our Lord.

The Solemn Blessing for Advent may be used, p. 508.

SECOND SUNDAY OF ADVENT – B

Prepare a way for the Lord!
We prepare each day of our lives for the coming of the Lord. We are called to straighten out those things in our behaviour and attitudes that prevent us from living holy and saintly lives. The Lord promises a new heaven and new earth, where he will reign for ever. This is the source of our joy.

Entrance Antiphon
O people of Sion, behold,
the Lord will come to save the nations,
and the Lord will make the glory of his voice heard
in the joy of your heart.   cf. Isaiah 30:19. 30

The Gloria is not said or sung.

Collect
Almighty and merciful God,
may no earthly undertaking hinder those
who set out in haste to meet your Son,
but may our learning of heavenly wisdom
gain us admittance to his company.
Who lives and reigns with you in the unity of the Holy Spirit,
one God, for ever and ever.

First Reading   Isaiah 40:1-5. 9-11
Prepare a way for the Lord.
"Console my people, console them"
says your God.
"Speak to the heart of Jerusalem
and call to her
that her time of service is ended,
that her sin is atoned for,
that she has received from the hand of the Lord
double punishment for all her crimes."

A voice cries, "Prepare in the wilderness
a way for the Lord.

Make a straight highway for our God
across the desert.
Let every valley be filled in,
every mountain and hill be laid low,
let every cliff become a plain,
and the ridges a valley;
then the glory of the Lord shall be revealed
and all mankind shall see it;
for the mouth of the Lord has spoken."

Go up on a high mountain,
joyful messenger to Zion.
Shout with a loud voice,
joyful messenger to Jerusalem.
Shout without fear,
say to the towns of Judah,
"Here is your God."
Here is the Lord coming with power,
his arm subduing all things to him.
The prize of his victory is with him,
his trophies all go before him.
He is like a shepherd feeding his flock,
gathering lambs in his arms,
holding them against his breast
and leading to their rest the mother ewes.

Psalm   Psalm 84

R. **Let us see, O Lord, your mercy
and give us your saving help.**

1. I will hear what the Lord God has to say,
a voice that speaks of peace,
peace for his people.
His help is near for those who fear him
and his glory will dwell in our land. R.

2. Mercy and faithfulness have met;
justice and peace have embraced.

Faithfulness shall spring from the earth
and justice look down from heaven. R.

3. The Lord will make us prosper
and our earth shall yield its fruit.
Justice shall march before him
and peace shall follow his steps. R.

Second Reading　　　　　　　　　　　　　　　2 Peter 3:8-14
We are waiting for the new heavens and new earth.

There is one thing, my friends, that you must never forget: that with
the Lord, "a day" can mean a thousand years, and a thousand years
is like a day. The Lord is not being slow to carry out his promises,
as anybody else might be called slow; but he is being patient with
you all, wanting nobody to be lost and everybody to be brought to
change his ways. The Day of the Lord will come like a thief, and
then with a roar the sky will vanish, the elements will catch fire and
fall apart, the earth and all that it contains will be burnt up.

Since everything is coming to an end like this, you should be
living holy and saintly lives while you wait and long for the Day of
God to come, when the sky will dissolve in flames and the elements
melt in the heat. What we are waiting for is what he promised: the
new heavens and new earth, the place where righteousness will be
at home. So then, my friends, while you are waiting, do your best
to live lives without spot or stain so that he will find you at peace.

Gospel Acclamation
Alleluia, alleluia!
Prepare a way for the Lord,
make his paths straight,
and all mankind shall see the salvation of God.
Alleluia!　　　　　　　　　　　　　　　　　　Luke 3:4. 6

Gospel　　　　　　　　　　　　　　　　　　Mark 1:1-8
Make his paths straight.

The beginning of the Good News about Jesus Christ, the Son of God.
It is written in the book of the prophet Isaiah:

Look, I am going to send my messenger before you;
he will prepare your way.

A voice cries in the wilderness:
Prepare a way for the Lord,
make his paths straight,

and so it was that John the Baptist appeared in the wilderness, proclaiming a baptism of repentance for the forgiveness of sins. All Judaea and all the people of Jerusalem made their way to him, and as they were baptised by him in the river Jordan they confessed their sins. John wore a garment of camel-skin, and he lived on locusts and wild honey. In the course of his preaching he said, "Someone is following me, someone who is more powerful than I am, and I am not fit to kneel down and undo the strap of his sandals. I have baptised you with water, but he will baptise you with the Holy Spirit."

The Creed is said.

Prayer over the Offerings
Be pleased, O Lord, with our humble prayers and offerings,
and, since we have no merits to plead our cause,
come, we pray, to our rescue
with the protection of your mercy.
Through Christ our Lord.

Preface I of Advent, p. 490.

Communion Antiphon
Jerusalem, arise and stand upon the heights,
and behold the joy which comes to you from God.   Baruch 5:5; 4:36

Prayer after Communion
Replenished by the food of spiritual nourishment,
we humbly beseech you, O Lord,
that, through our partaking in this mystery,
you may teach us to judge wisely the things of earth
and hold firm to the things of heaven.
Through Christ our Lord.

The Solemn Blessing for Advent may be used, p. 508.

THIRD SUNDAY OF ADVENT – B

Be happy at all times!
Happiness is our birthright as Christians. We give thanks to God for the Holy
Spirit who lives in us and makes us aware of our wonderful mission to spread
the Good News of redemption. The Spirit brings us deep peace, because the God
who called us will not fail us.

Entrance Antiphon
Rejoice in the Lord always; again I say, rejoice.
Indeed, the Lord is near.

Philippians 4:4-5

The Gloria is not said or sung.

Collect
O God, who see how your people
faithfully await the feast of the Lord's Nativity,
enable us, we pray,
to attain the joys of so great a salvation
and to celebrate them always
with solemn worship and glad rejoicing.
Through our Lord Jesus Christ, your Son,
who lives and reigns with you in the unity of the Holy Spirit,
one God, for ever and ever.

First Reading   Isaiah 61:1-2. 10-11
I exult for joy in the Lord.
The spirit of the Lord has been given to me,
for the Lord has anointed me.
He has sent me to bring good news to the poor,
to bind up hearts that are broken;

to proclaim liberty to captives,
freedom to those in prison;
to proclaim a year of favour from the Lord.

"I exult for joy in the Lord,
my soul rejoices in my God,
for he has clothed me in the garments of salvation,
he has wrapped me in the cloak of integrity,
like a bridegroom wearing his wreath,
like a bride adorned in her jewels.

"For as the earth makes fresh things grow,
as a garden makes seeds spring up,
so will the Lord make both integrity and praise
spring up in the sight of the nations."

Psalm   Luke 1

R. **My soul rejoices in my God.**

1. My soul glorifies the Lord,
   my spirit rejoices in God, my Saviour.
   He looks on his servant in her nothingness;
   henceforth all ages will call me blessed. R.

2. The Almighty works marvels for me.
   Holy his name!
   His mercy is from age to age,
   on those who fear him. R.

3. He fills the starving with good things,
   sends the rich away empty.
   He protects Israel, his servant,
   remembering his mercy. R.

Second Reading   1 Thessalonians 5:16-24
May you all be kept safe, spirit, soul and body, for the coming of
the Lord.
Be happy at all times; pray constantly; and for all things give thanks
to God, because this is what God expects you to do in Christ Jesus.
    Never try to suppress the Spirit or treat the gift of prophecy with
contempt; think before you do anything – hold on to what is good
and avoid every form of evil.

May the God of peace make you perfect and holy; and may you all be kept safe and blameless, spirit, soul and body, for the coming of our Lord Jesus Christ. God has called you and he will not fail you.

Gospel Acclamation
Alleluia, alleluia!
The spirit of the Lord has been given to me.
He has sent me to bring good news to the poor.
Alleluia!   Isaiah 61:1 (Luke 4:18)

Gospel   John 1:6-8. 19-28
There stands among you, unknown to you, the one who is coming after me.

A man came, sent by God.
His name was John.
He came as a witness,
as a witness to speak for the light,
so that everyone might believe through him.
He was not the light,
only a witness to speak for the light.

This is how John appeared as a witness. When the Jews sent priests and Levites from Jerusalem to ask him, "Who are you?" he not only declared, but he declared quite openly, "I am not the Christ." "Well then," they asked "are you Elijah?" "I am not" he said. "Are you the Prophet?" He answered, "No." So they said to him, "Who are you? We must take back an answer to those who sent us. What have you to say about yourself?" So John said, "I am, as Isaiah prophesied:

a voice that cries in the wilderness:
Make a straight way for the Lord."

Now these men had been sent by the Pharisees, and they put this further question to him, "Why are you baptising if you are not the Christ, and not Elijah, and not the prophet?" John replied, "I baptise with water; but there stands among you – unknown to you – the one who is coming after me; and I am not fit to undo his sandal-strap." This happened at Bethany, on the far side of the Jordan, where John was baptising.

The Creed is said.

Prayer over the Offerings
May the sacrifice of our worship, Lord, we pray,
be offered to you unceasingly,
to complete what was begun in sacred mystery
and powerfully accomplish for us your saving work.
Through Christ our Lord.

Preface I or II of Advent, pp. 490-491.

Communion Antiphon
Say to the faint of heart: Be strong and do not fear.
Behold, our God will come, and he will save us.   cf. Isaiah 35:4

Prayer after Communion
We implore your mercy, Lord,
that this divine sustenance may cleanse us of our faults
and prepare us for the coming feasts.
Through Christ our Lord.

The Solemn Blessing for Advent may be used, p. 508.

FOURTH SUNDAY OF ADVENT – B

Mary, you have won God's favour.
The Lord is always faithful to his promises. From before the time of David
right up to the birth of Jesus there is no doubt that the Lord is with his people.
That which has been hidden for endless ages is revealed in Jesus Christ, the son
of the Virgin Mary.

Entrance Antiphon
Drop down dew from above, you heavens,
and let the clouds rain down the Just One;
let the earth be opened and bring forth a Saviour.   cf. Isaiah 45:8

The Gloria is not said or sung.

Collect
Pour forth, we beseech you, O Lord,
your grace into our hearts,
that we, to whom the Incarnation of Christ your Son
was made known by the message of an Angel,
may by his Passion and Cross
be brought to the glory of his Resurrection.
Who lives and reigns with you in the unity of the Holy Spirit,
one God, for ever and ever.

First Reading   2 Samuel 7:1-5. 8-12. 14. 16
The kingdom of David will always stand secure before the Lord.
Once David had settled into his house and the Lord had given him
rest from all the enemies surrounding him, the king said to the
prophet Nathan, "Look, I am living in a house of cedar while the
ark of God dwells in a tent." Nathan said to the king, "Go and do all
that is in your mind, for the Lord is with you."

But that very night the word of the Lord came to Nathan:

"Go and tell my servant David, 'Thus the Lord speaks: Are
you the man to build me a house to dwell in? I took you from

the pasture, from following the sheep, to be leader of my people Israel; I have been with you on all your expeditions; I have cut off all your enemies before you. I will give you fame as great as the fame of the greatest on earth. I will provide a place for my people Israel; I will plant them there and they shall dwell in that place and never be disturbed again; nor shall the wicked continue to oppress them as they did, in the days when I appointed judges over my people Israel; I will give them rest from all their enemies. The Lord will make you great; the Lord will make you a House. And when your days are ended and you are laid to rest with your ancestors, I will preserve the offspring of your body after you and make his sovereignty secure. I will be a father to him and he a son to me. Your House and your sovereignty will always stand secure before me and your throne be established for ever."

Psalm   Psalm 88

R. **I will sing for ever of your love, O Lord.**

1. I will sing for ever of your love, O Lord;
    through all ages my mouth will proclaim your truth.
    Of this I am sure, that your love lasts for ever,
    that your truth is firmly established as the heavens. R.

2. "I have made a covenant with my chosen one;
    I have sworn to David my servant:
    I will establish your dynasty for ever
    and set up your throne through all ages." R.

3. He will say to me: "You are my father,
    my God, the rock who saves me."
    I will keep my love for him always;
    for him my covenant shall endure. R.

Second Reading   Romans 16:25-27
The mystery, which was kept secret for endless ages, is now made clear.
Glory to him who is able to give you the strength to live according to the Good News I preach, and in which I proclaim Jesus Christ,

the revelation of a mystery kept secret for endless ages, but now so clear that it must be broadcast to pagans everywhere to bring them to the obedience of faith. This is only what scripture has predicted, and it is all part of the way the eternal God wants things to be. He alone is wisdom; give glory therefore to him through Jesus Christ for ever and ever. Amen.

Gospel Acclamation
Alleluia, alleluia!
I am the handmaid of the Lord:
let what you have said be done to me.
Alleluia!   Luke 1:38

Gospel   Luke 1:26-38
Listen! You are to conceive and bear a son.
The angel Gabriel was sent by God to a town in Galilee called Nazareth, to a virgin betrothed to a man named Joseph, of the House of David; and the virgin's name was Mary. He went in and said to her, "Rejoice, so highly favoured! The Lord is with you." She was deeply disturbed by these words and asked herself what this greeting could mean, but the angel said to her, "Mary, do not be afraid; you have won God's favour. Listen! You are to conceive and bear a son, and you must name him Jesus. He will be great and will be called Son of the Most High. The Lord God will give him the throne of his ancestor David; he will rule over the House of Jacob for ever and his reign will have no end." Mary said to the angel, "But how can this come about, since I am a virgin?" "The Holy Spirit will come upon you" the angel answered "and the power of the Most High will cover you with its shadow. And so the child will be holy and will be called Son of God. Know this too: your kinswoman Elizabeth has, in her old age, herself conceived a son, and she whom people called barren is now in her sixth month, for nothing is impossible to God." "I am the handmaid of the Lord," said Mary "let what you have said be done to me." And the angel left her.

The Creed is said.

Prayer over the Offerings
May the Holy Spirit, O Lord,
sanctify these gifts laid upon your altar,
just as he filled with his power the womb of the Blessed Virgin Mary.
Through Christ our Lord.

Preface II of Advent, pp. 490-491.

Communion Antiphon
Behold, a Virgin shall conceive and bear a son;
and his name will be called Emmanuel.   Isaiah 7:14

Prayer after Communion
Having received this pledge of eternal redemption,
we pray, almighty God,
that, as the feast day of our salvation draws ever nearer,
so we may press forward all the more eagerly
to the worthy celebration of the mystery of your Son's Nativity.
Who lives and reigns for ever and ever.

The Solemn Blessing for Advent may be used, p. 508.

The liturgies for Christmas time begin on p. 49.

FIRST SUNDAY OF ADVENT – C

Your liberation is near at hand.
We have no reason to fear the second coming of Christ if we allow God to
teach us how to grow in holiness. We ask God to help us to love one another
with generosity and integrity. In this way we can hold our heads high and have
the strength to survive all that will happen in our lives; and so when the time
comes we will be able to stand with confidence before Christ and his saints.

Entrance Antiphon
To you, I lift up my soul, O my God.
In you, I have trusted; let me not be put to shame.
Nor let my enemies exult over me;
and let none who hope in you be put to shame.   cf. Psalm 24:1-3

The Gloria is not said or sung.

Collect
Grant your faithful, we pray, almighty God,
the resolve to run forth to meet your Christ
with righteous deeds at his coming,
so that, gathered at his right hand,
they may be worthy to possess the heavenly Kingdom.
Through our Lord Jesus Christ, your Son,
who lives and reigns with you in the unity of the Holy Spirit,
one God, for ever and ever.

First Reading   Jeremiah 33:14-16
I will make a virtuous Branch grow for David.
See, the days are coming – it is the Lord who speaks – when I am
going to fulfil the promise I made to the House of Israel and the
House of Judah:

"In those days and at that time,
I will make a virtuous Branch grow for David,
who shall practise honesty and integrity in the land.

In those days Judah shall be saved
and Israel shall dwell in confidence.
And this is the name the city will be called:
The Lord-our-integrity."

Psalm   Psalm 24

R. **To you, O Lord, I lift up my soul.**

1. Lord, make me know your ways.
   Lord, teach me your paths.
   Make me walk in your truth, and teach me:
   for you are God my saviour. R.

2. The Lord is good and upright.
   He shows the path to those who stray,
   he guides the humble in the right path;
   he teaches his way to the poor. R.

3. His ways are faithfulness and love
   for those who keep his covenant and will.
   The Lord's friendship is for those who revere him;
   to them he reveals his covenant. R.

Second Reading   1 Thessalonians 3:12 – 4:2
May the Lord confirm your hearts in holiness when Christ comes.
May the Lord be generous in increasing your love and make you
love one another and the whole human race as much as we love you.
And may he so confirm your hearts in holiness that you may be
blameless in the sight of our God and Father when our Lord Jesus
Christ comes with all his saints.

   Finally, brothers, we urge you and appeal to you in the Lord Jesus
to make more and more progress in the kind of life that you are
meant to live: the life that God wants, as you learnt from us, and as
you are already living it. You have not forgotten the instructions we
gave you on the authority of the Lord Jesus.

Gospel Acclamation
Alleluia, alleluia!
Let us see, O Lord, your mercy
and give us your saving help.
Alleluia!   Psalm 84:8

Gospel   Luke 21:25-28. 34-36
Your liberation is near at hand.

Jesus said to his disciples: "There will be signs in the sun and moon and stars; on earth nations in agony, bewildered by the clamour of the ocean and its waves; men dying of fear as they await what menaces the world, for the powers of heaven will be shaken. And then they will see the Son of Man coming in a cloud with power and great glory. When these things begin to take place, stand erect, hold your heads high, because your liberation is near at hand.

"Watch yourselves, or your hearts will be coarsened with debauchery and drunkenness and the cares of life, and that day will be sprung on you suddenly, like a trap. For it will come down on every living man on the face of the earth. Stay awake, praying at all times for the strength to survive all that is going to happen, and to stand with confidence before the Son of Man."

The Creed is said.

Prayer over the Offerings
Accept, we pray, O Lord, these offerings we make,
gathered from among your gifts to us,
and may what you grant us to celebrate devoutly here below,
gain for us the prize of eternal redemption.
Through Christ our Lord.

Preface I of Advent, p. 490.

Communion Antiphon
The Lord will bestow his bounty,
    and our earth shall yield its increase.   Psalm 84:13

Prayer after Communion
May these mysteries, O Lord,
in which we have participated,
profit us, we pray,
for even now, as we walk amid passing things,
you teach us by them to love the things of heaven
and hold fast to what endures.
Through Christ our Lord.

The Solemn Blessing for Advent may be used, p. 508.

SECOND SUNDAY OF ADVENT – C

Christ is the joy we await.
God will bring to completion the work he has begun in us. Our love for one
another will help us to be blameless when Christ comes again. Our lives on
earth are a preparation for the day when the Lord comes, and so we can be full
of joy and expectancy.

Entrance Antiphon
O people of Sion, behold,
the Lord will come to save the nations,
and the Lord will make the glory of his voice heard
in the joy of your heart.   cf. Isaiah 30:19. 30

The Gloria is not said or sung.

Collect
Almighty and merciful God,
may no earthly undertaking hinder those
who set out in haste to meet your Son,
but may our learning of heavenly wisdom
gain us admittance to his company.
Who lives and reigns with you in the unity of the Holy Spirit,
one God, for ever and ever.

First Reading   Baruch 5:1-9
God means to show your splendour to every nation.
Jerusalem, take off your dress of sorrow and distress,
put on the beauty of the glory of God for ever,
wrap the cloak of the integrity of God around you,
put the diadem of the glory of the Eternal on your head:
since God means to show your splendour to every nation under heaven,
since the name God gives you for ever will be,
"Peace through integrity, and honour through devotedness".
Arise, Jerusalem, stand on the heights

and turn your eyes to the east:
see your sons reassembled from west and east
at the command of the Holy One, jubilant that God has
    remembered them.
Though they left you on foot,
with enemies for an escort,
now God brings them back to you
like royal princes carried back in glory.
For God has decreed the flattening
of each high mountain, of the everlasting hills,
the filling of the valleys to make the ground level
so that Israel can walk in safety under the glory of God.
And the forests and every fragrant tree will provide shade
for Israel at the command of God;
for God will guide Israel in joy by the light of his glory
with his mercy and integrity for escort.

Psalm   Psalm 125

R. **What marvels the Lord worked for us!**
    Indeed we were glad.

1. When the Lord delivered Zion from bondage,
    it seemed like a dream.
    Then was our mouth filled with laughter,
    on our lips there were songs. R.

2. The heathens themselves said: "What marvels
    the Lord worked for them!"
    What marvels the Lord worked for us!
    Indeed we were glad. R.

3. Deliver us, O Lord, from our bondage
    as streams in dry land.
    Those who are sowing in tears
    will sing when they reap. R.

4. They go out, they go out, full of tears,
    carrying seed for the sowing:
    they come back, they come back, full of song,
    carrying their sheaves. R.

Second Reading   Philippians 1:3-6. 8-11
Be pure and blameless for the day of Christ.

Every time I pray for all of you, I pray with joy, remembering how
you have helped to spread the Good News from the day you first
heard it right up to the present. I am quite certain that the One who
began this good work in you will see that it is finished when the
Day of Christ Jesus comes. God knows how much I miss you all,
loving you as Christ Jesus loves you. My prayer is that your love for
each other may increase more and more and never stop improving
your knowledge and deepening your perception so that you can
always recognise what is best. This will help you to become pure
and blameless, and prepare you for the Day of Christ, when you
will reach the perfect goodness which Jesus Christ produces in us
for the glory and praise of God.

Gospel Acclamation
Alleluia, alleluia!
Prepare a way for the Lord,
make his paths straight,
and all mankind shall see the salvation of God.
Alleluia!   Luke 3:4. 6

Gospel   Luke 3:1-6
All mankind shall see the salvation of God.

In the fifteenth year of Tiberius Caesar's reign, when Pontius Pilate
was governor of Judaea, Herod tetrarch of Galilee, his brother
Philip tetrarch of the lands of Ituraea and Trachonitis, Lysanias
tetrarch of Abilene, during the pontificate of Annas and Caiaphas,
the word of God came to John son of Zechariah, in the wilderness.
He went through the whole Jordan district proclaiming a baptism
of repentance for the forgiveness of sins, as it is written in the book
of the sayings of the prophet Isaiah:

A voice cries in the wilderness:
Prepare a way for the Lord,
make his paths straight.
Every valley will be filled in,
every mountain and hill be laid low,
winding ways will be straightened
and rough roads made smooth.
And all mankind shall see the salvation of God.

The Creed is said.

Prayer over the Offerings
Be pleased, O Lord, with our humble prayers and offerings,
and, since we have no merits to plead our cause,
come, we pray, to our rescue
with the protection of your mercy.
Through Christ our Lord.

Preface I of Advent, p. 490.

Communion Antiphon
Jerusalem, arise and stand upon the heights,
and behold the joy which comes to you from God.   Baruch 5:5; 4:36

Prayer after Communion
Replenished by the food of spiritual nourishment,
we humbly beseech you, O Lord,
that, through our partaking in this mystery,
you may teach us to judge wisely the things of earth
and hold firm to the things of heaven.
Through Christ our Lord.

The Solemn Blessing for Advent may be used, p. 508.

THIRD SUNDAY OF ADVENT – C

The Lord is very near.
We have no need to worry, and if we ask the Lord for anything he will not
refuse us. We can look to the future with confidence and without fear,
because the Lord is with us. He is the cause of our happiness.
We are a people of hope and joy.

Entrance Antiphon
Rejoice in the Lord always; again I say, rejoice.
Indeed, the Lord is near.   Philippians 4:4-5

The Gloria is not said or sung.

Collect
O God, who see how your people
faithfully await the feast of the Lord's Nativity,
enable us, we pray,
to attain the joys of so great a salvation
and to celebrate them always
with solemn worship and glad rejoicing.
Through our Lord Jesus Christ, your Son,
who lives and reigns with you in the unity of the Holy Spirit,
one God, for ever and ever.

First Reading   Zephaniah 3:14-18
The Lord will dance with shouts of joy for you as on a day of festival.
Shout for joy, daughter of Zion,
Israel, shout aloud!
Rejoice, exult with all your heart,
daughter of Jerusalem!
The Lord has repealed your sentence;
he has driven your enemies away.
The Lord, the king of Israel, is in your midst;
you have no more evil to fear.

When that day comes, word will come to Jerusalem:
Zion, have no fear,
do not let your hands fall limp.
The Lord your God is in your midst,
a victorious warrior.
He will exult with joy over you,
he will renew you by his love;
he will dance with shouts of joy for you
as on a day of festival.

Psalm   Isaiah 12

R. **Sing and shout for joy
    for great in your midst is the Holy One of Israel.**

1. Truly, God is my salvation,
   I trust, I shall not fear.
   For the Lord is my strength, my song,
   he became my saviour.
   With joy you will draw water
   from the wells of salvation. R.

2. Give thanks to the Lord, give praise to his name!
   Make his mighty deeds known to the peoples!
   Declare the greatness of his name. R.

3. Sing a psalm to the Lord
   for he has done glorious deeds,
   make them known to all the earth!
   People of Zion, sing and shout for joy
   for great in your midst is the Holy One of Israel. R.

Second Reading   Philippians 4:4-7

The Lord is very near.

I want you to be happy, always happy in the Lord; I repeat, what I want is your happiness. Let your tolerance be evident to everyone: the Lord is very near. There is no need to worry; but if there is anything you need, pray for it, asking God for it with prayer and thanksgiving, and that peace of God, which is so much greater than we can understand, will guard your hearts and your thoughts, in Christ Jesus.

Gospel Acclamation

Alleluia, alleluia!

The spirit of the Lord has been given to me.

He has sent me to bring good news to the poor.

Alleluia!   Isaiah 61:1 (Luke 4:18)

Gospel   Luke 3:10-18

What must we do?

When all the people asked John, "What must we do, then?" he answered, "If anyone has two tunics he must share with the man who has none, and the one with something to eat must do the same." There were tax collectors too who came for baptism, and these said to him, "Master, what must we do?" He said to them, "Exact no more than your rate." Some soldiers asked him in their turn, "What about us? What must we do?" He said to them, "No intimidation! No extortion! Be content with your pay!"

A feeling of expectancy had grown among the people, who were beginning to think that John might be the Christ, so John declared before them all, "I baptise you with water, but someone is coming, someone who is more powerful than I am, and I am not fit to undo the strap of his sandals; he will baptise you with the Holy Spirit and fire. His winnowing-fan is in his hand to clear his threshing-floor and to gather the wheat into his barn; but the chaff he will burn in a fire that will never go out." As well as this, there were many other things he said to exhort the people and to announce the Good News to them.

The Creed is said.

Prayer over the Offerings
May the sacrifice of our worship, Lord, we pray,
be offered to you unceasingly,
to complete what was begun in sacred mystery
and powerfully accomplish for us your saving work.
Through Christ our Lord.

Preface I or II of Advent, pp. 490-491.

Communion Antiphon
Say to the faint of heart: Be strong and do not fear.
Behold, our God will come, and he will save us.

cf. Isaiah 35:4

Prayer after Communion
We implore your mercy, Lord,
that this divine sustenance may cleanse us of our faults
and prepare us for the coming feasts.
Through Christ our Lord.

The Solemn Blessing for Advent may be used, p. 508.

FOURTH SUNDAY OF ADVENT – C

Mary, mother of the Lord.
Mary does the will of God perfectly. When God speaks to her she is quick to
obey, and in her flesh God's Word becomes incarnate. Of all women Mary is
the most blessed because she believed that God's promises would be fulfilled in
the humblest of his creatures. She was for Elizabeth the cause of her joy.
She is the same for us.

Entrance Antiphon
Drop down dew from above, you heavens,
and let the clouds rain down the Just One;
let the earth be opened and bring forth a Saviour.   cf. Isaiah 45:8

The Gloria is not said or sung.

Collect
Pour forth, we beseech you, O Lord,
your grace into our hearts,
that we, to whom the Incarnation of Christ your Son
was made known by the message of an Angel,
may by his Passion and Cross
be brought to the glory of his Resurrection.
Who lives and reigns with you in the unity of the Holy Spirit,
one God, for ever and ever.

First Reading   **Micah 5:1-4**
Out of you will be born the one who is to rule over Israel.
The Lord says this:

    You, Bethlehem Ephrathah,
    the least of the clans of Judah,
    out of you will be born for me
    the one who is to rule over Israel;
    his origin goes back to the distant past,
    to the days of old.

The Lord is therefore going to abandon them
till the time when she who is to give birth gives birth.
Then the remnant of his brothers will come back
to the sons of Israel.
He will stand and feed his flock
with the power of the Lord,
with the majesty of the name of his God.
They will live secure, for from then on he will extend his power
to the ends of the land.
He himself will be peace.

Psalm   Psalm 79

R. **God of hosts, bring us back;**
    let your face shine on us and we shall be saved.

1. O shepherd of Israel, hear us,
    shine forth from your cherubim throne.
    O Lord, rouse up your might,
    O Lord, come to our help. R.

2. God of hosts, turn again, we implore,
    look down from heaven and see.
    Visit this vine and protect it,
    the vine your right hand has planted. R.

3. May your hand be on the man you have chosen,
    the man you have given your strength.
    And we shall never forsake you again:
    give us life that we may call upon your name. R.

Second Reading   Hebrews 10:5-10
Here I am! I am coming to obey your will.
This is what Christ said, on coming into the world:

    You who wanted no sacrifice or oblation,
    prepared a body for me.
    You took no pleasure in holocausts or sacrifices for sin;

then I said,
just as I was commanded in the scroll of the book,
"God, here I am! I am coming to obey your will."

Notice that he says first: You did not want what the Law lays down as the things to be offered, that is: the sacrifices, the oblations, the holocausts and the sacrifices for sin, and you took no pleasure in them; and then he says: Here I am! I am coming to obey your will. He is abolishing the first sort to replace it with the second. And this will was for us to be made holy by the offering of his body made once and for all by Jesus Christ.

Gospel Acclamation
Alleluia, alleluia!
I am the handmaid of the Lord:
let what you have said be done to me.
Alleluia!   Luke 1:38

Gospel   Luke 1:39-45
Why should I be honoured with a visit from the mother of my Lord?
Mary set out and went as quickly as she could to a town in the hill country of Judah. She went into Zechariah's house and greeted Elizabeth. Now as soon as Elizabeth heard Mary's greeting, the child leapt in her womb and Elizabeth was filled with the Holy Spirit. She gave a loud cry and said, "Of all women you are the most blessed, and blessed is the fruit of your womb. Why should I be honoured with a visit from the mother of my Lord? For the moment your greeting reached my ears, the child in my womb leapt for joy. Yes, blessed is she who believed that the promise made her by the Lord would be fulfilled."

The Creed is said.

Prayer over the Offerings
May the Holy Spirit, O Lord,
sanctify these gifts laid upon your altar,
just as he filled with his power the womb of the Blessed Virgin Mary.
Through Christ our Lord.

Preface II of Advent, pp. 490-491.

Communion Antiphon
Behold, a Virgin shall conceive and bear a son;
and his name will be called Emmanuel.   Isaiah 7:14

Prayer after Communion
Having received this pledge of eternal redemption,
we pray, almighty God,
that, as the feast day of our salvation draws ever nearer,
so we may press forward all the more eagerly
to the worthy celebration of the mystery of your Son's Nativity.
Who lives and reigns for ever and ever.

The Solemn Blessing for Advent may be used, p. 508.

The liturgies for Christmas time begin on p. 49.

THE NATIVITY OF THE LORD: VIGIL MASS – ABC

Welcome the newborn Saviour!
We come in spirit to Bethlehem, to the crib, to celebrate the birth of Jesus,
Emmanuel. With Mary and Joseph we give thanks for this birth which is the
fulfilment of God's ancient promises. Now we can know that truly God is
with us, and we rejoice with great joy.

Entrance Antiphon

Today you will know that the Lord will come, and he will save us,
and in the morning you will see his glory.   cf. Exodus 16:6-7

The Gloria is said or sung.

Collect

O God, who gladden us year by year
as we wait in hope for our redemption,
grant that, just as we joyfully welcome
your Only Begotten Son as our Redeemer,
we may also merit to face him confidently
when he comes again as our Judge.
Who lives and reigns with you in the unity of the Holy Spirit,
one God, for ever and ever.

First Reading   Isaiah 62:1-5

The Lord takes delight in you.
About Zion I will not be silent,
about Jerusalem I will not grow weary,
until her integrity shines out like the dawn
and her salvation flames like a torch.
The nations then will see your integrity,
all the kings your glory,
and you will be called by a new name,
one which the mouth of the Lord will confer.

You are to be a crown of splendour in the hand of the Lord,
a princely diadem in the hand of your God;
no longer are you to be named "Forsaken",
nor your land "Abandoned",
but you shall be called "My Delight"
and your land "The Wedded";
for the Lord takes delight in you
and your land will have its wedding.
Like a young man marrying a virgin,
so will the one who built you wed you,
and as the bridegroom rejoices in his bride,
so will your God rejoice in you.

Psalm   Psalm 88

R.   **I will sing for ever of your love, O Lord.**

1. "I have made a covenant with my chosen one;
   I have sworn to David my servant:
   I will establish your dynasty for ever
   and set up your throne through all ages." R.

2. Happy the people who acclaim such a king,
   who walk, O Lord, in the light of your face,
   who find their joy every day in your name,
   who make your justice the source of their bliss. R.

3. "He will say to me: 'You are my father,
   my God, the rock who saves me.'
   I will keep my love for him always;
   for him my covenant shall endure." R.

Second Reading   Acts 13:16-17. 22-25
Paul's witness to Christ, the son of David.
When Paul reached Antioch in Pisidia, he stood up in the synagogue,
held up a hand for silence and began to speak:
    "Men of Israel, and fearers of God, listen! The God of our nation
Israel chose our ancestors, and made our people great when they were

living as foreigners in Egypt; then by divine power he led them out.

"Then he made David their king, of whom he approved in these words, 'I have selected David son of Jesse, a man after my own heart, who will carry out my whole purpose'. To keep his promise, God has raised up for Israel one of David's descendants, Jesus, as Saviour, whose coming was heralded by John when he proclaimed a baptism of repentance for the whole people of Israel. Before John ended his career he said, 'I am not the one you imagine me to be; that one is coming after me and I am not fit to undo his sandal.'"

Gospel Acclamation
Alleluia, alleluia!
Tomorrow there will be an end to the sin of the world
and the saviour of the world will be our king.
Alleluia!

Gospel   Matthew 1:1-25
The ancestry of Jesus Christ, the son of David.
A genealogy of Jesus Christ, son of David, son of Abraham:
Abraham was the father of Isaac,
Isaac the father of Jacob,
Jacob was the father of Judah and his brothers,
Judah was the father of Perez and Zerah, Tamar being their mother,
Perez was the father of Hezron,
Hezron the father of Ram,
Ram was the father of Amminadab,
Amminadab the father of Nahshon,
Nahshon the father of Salmon,
Salmon was the father of Boaz, Rahab being his mother,
Boaz was the father of Obed, Ruth being his mother,
Obed was the father of Jesse;
and Jesse was the father of King David.

David was the father of Solomon, whose mother had been Uriah's wife,
Solomon was the father of Rehoboam,
Rehoboam the father of Abijah,
Abijah the father of Asa,
Asa was the father of Jehoshaphat,

Jehoshaphat the father of Joram,
Joram the father of Azariah,
Azariah was the father of Jotham,
Jotham the father of Ahaz,
Ahaz the father of Hezekiah,
Hezekiah was the father of Manasseh,
Manasseh the father of Amon,
Amon the father of Josiah;
and Josiah was the father of Jechoniah and his brothers.
Then the deportation to Babylon took place.

After the deportation to Babylon:
Jechoniah was the father to Shealtiel,
Shealtiel the father of Zerubbabel,
Zerubbabel was the father of Abiud,
Abiud the father of Eliakim,
Eliakim the father of Azor,
Azor was the father of Zadok,
Zadok the father of Achim,
Achim the father of Eliud,
Eliud was the father of Eleazar,
Eleazar the father of Matthan,
Matthan the father of Jacob;
and Jacob was the father of Joseph the husband of Mary; of her
was born Jesus who is called Christ.

The sum of generations is therefore: fourteen from Abraham to
David; fourteen from David to the Babylonian deportation; and
fourteen from the Babylonian deportation to Christ.

This is how Jesus Christ came to be born. His mother Mary
was betrothed to Joseph; but before they came to live together
she was found to be with child through the Holy Spirit. Her
husband Joseph, being a man of honour and wanting to spare her
publicity, decided to divorce her informally. He had made up his
mind to do this when the angel of the Lord appeared to him in
a dream and said, "Joseph son of David, do not be afraid to take
Mary home as your wife, because she has conceived what is in her
by the Holy Spirit. She will give birth to a son and you must name
him Jesus, because he is the one who is to save his people from

their sins." Now all this took place to fulfil the words spoken by the Lord through the prophet:

> The Virgin will conceive and give birth to a son
> and they will call him Emmanuel,

a name which means "God-is-with-us". When Joseph woke up he did what the angel of the Lord told him to do: he took his wife to his home and, though he had not had intercourse with her, she gave birth to a son and he named him Jesus.

The Creed is said.
All kneel at the words *and by the Holy Spirit was incarnate.*

Prayer over the Offerings
As we look forward, O Lord,
to the coming festivities,
may we serve you all the more eagerly
for knowing that in them
you make manifest the beginnings of our redemption.
Through Christ our Lord.

Preface I, II or III of the Nativity of the Lord, pp. 491-492.

Communion Antiphon
The glory of the Lord will be revealed,
and all flesh will see the salvation of our God.   cf. Isaiah 40:5

Prayer after Communion
Grant, O Lord, we pray,
that we may draw new vigour
from celebrating the Nativity of your Only Begotten Son,
by whose heavenly mystery we receive both food and drink.
Who lives and reigns for ever and ever.

The Solemn Blessing for the Nativity of the Lord may be used,
pp. 508-509.

THE NATIVITY OF THE LORD: MASS DURING THE NIGHT – ABC

This night a Saviour is born!
In the stillness of the night God enters human history through the birth of his only Son. He is our joy, our peace and our hope. We praise the Lord for his goodness to us in giving us so great a gift.

Entrance Antiphon
The Lord said to me: You are my Son.
It is I who have begotten you this day.   Psalm 2:7

or

Let us all rejoice in the Lord, for our Saviour has been born in the world.
Today true peace has come down to us from heaven.

The Gloria is said or sung.

Collect
O God, who have made this most sacred night
radiant with the splendour of the true light,
grant, we pray, that we, who have known the mysteries
    of his light on earth,
may also delight in his gladness in heaven.
Who lives and reigns with you in the unity of the Holy Spirit,
one God, for ever and ever.

First Reading   Isaiah 9:1-7
A son is given to us.
The people that walked in darkness
has seen a great light;
on those who live in a land of deep shadow
a light has shone.
You have made their gladness greater,
you have made their joy increase;

they rejoice in your presence
as men rejoice at harvest time,
as men are happy when they are dividing the spoils.
For the yoke that was weighing on him,
the bar across his shoulders,
the rod of his oppressor,
these you break as on the day of Midian.
For all the footgear of battle,
every cloak rolled in blood,
is burnt,
and consumed by fire.
For there is a child born for us,
a son given to us
and dominion is laid on his shoulders;
and this is the name they give him:
Wonder-Counsellor, Mighty-God,
Eternal-Father, Prince-of-Peace.
Wide is his dominion
in a peace that has no end,
for the throne of David
and for his royal power,
which he establishes and makes secure
in justice and integrity.
From this time onwards and for ever,
the jealous love of the Lord of hosts will do this.

Psalm   Psalm 95

R. **Today a saviour has been born to us;**
    he is Christ the Lord.

1. O sing a new song to the Lord,
    sing to the Lord all the earth.
    O sing to the Lord, bless his name. R.

2. Proclaim his help day by day,
    tell among the nations his glory
    and his wonders among all the peoples. R.

3. Let the heavens rejoice and earth be glad,
   let the sea and all within it thunder praise,
   let the land and all it bears rejoice,
   all the trees of the wood shout for joy
   at the presence of the Lord for he comes,
   he comes to rule the earth. R.

4. With justice he will rule the world,
   he will judge the peoples with his truth. R.

Second Reading   Titus 2:11-14

God's grace has been revealed to the whole human race.

God's grace has been revealed, and it has made salvation possible for the whole human race and taught us that what we have to do is to give up everything that does not lead to God, and all our worldly ambitions; we must be self-restrained and live good and religious lives here in this present world, while we are waiting in hope for the blessing which will come with the Appearing of the glory of our great God and saviour Christ Jesus. He sacrificed himself for us in order to set us free from all wickedness and to purify a people so that it could be his very own and would have no ambition except to do good.

Gospel Acclamation
Alleluia, alleluia!
I bring you news of great joy:
today a saviour has been born to us, Christ the Lord.
Alleluia!   Luke 2:10-11

Gospel   Luke 2:1-14

Today a saviour has been born to you.

Caesar Augustus issued a decree for a census of the whole world to be taken. This census – the first – took place while Quirinius was governor of Syria, and everyone went to his own town to be registered. So Joseph set out from the town of Nazareth in Galilee and travelled up to Judaea, to the town of David called Bethlehem, since he was of David's House and line, in order to be registered together with Mary, his betrothed, who was with child. While they were there the time came for her to have her child, and she gave birth to a son, her first-born. She wrapped him in swaddling clothes, and laid him in a manger because there was no room for them at the inn. In the countryside close by there were shepherds who lived in the fields and took it in turns to watch their flocks during the night. The angel of the Lord appeared to them and the glory of the Lord shone round them. They were terrified, but the angel said, "Do not be afraid. Listen, I bring you news of great joy, a joy to be shared by the whole people. Today in the town of David a saviour has been born to you; he is Christ the Lord. And here is a sign for you: you will find a baby wrapped in swaddling clothes and lying in a manger." And suddenly with the angel there was a great throng of the heavenly host, praising God and singing:

"Glory to God in the highest heaven,
and peace to men who enjoy his favour".

The Creed is said.
All kneel at the words *and by the Holy Spirit was incarnate.*

Prayer over the Offerings
May the oblation of this day's feast
be pleasing to you, O Lord, we pray,
that through this most holy exchange
we may be found in the likeness of Christ,
in whom our nature is united to you.
Who lives and reigns for ever and ever.

Preface I, II or III of the Nativity of the Lord, pp. 491-492.

Communion Antiphon
The Word became flesh, and we have seen his glory.   John 1:14

Prayer after Communion
Grant us, we pray, O Lord our God,
that we, who are gladdened by participation
in the feast of our Redeemer's Nativity,
may through an honourable way of life become worthy
of union with him.
Who lives and reigns for ever and ever.

The Solemn Blessing for the Nativity of the Lord may be used, pp. 508-509.

25 December

THE NATIVITY OF THE LORD: DAWN MASS – ABC

The new light of the world!
God takes pity on us and sends us his only Son to be our Saviour. Jesus Christ is born for us as the new light of the world. In the stable of Bethlehem with the shepherds we discover in this human baby the measure of God's compassionate love for us.

Entrance Antiphon
Today a light will shine upon us, for the Lord is born for us;
and he will be called Wondrous God,
Prince of peace, Father of future ages:
and his reign will be without end.   cf. Isaiah 9:1. 5; Luke 1:33

The Gloria is said or sung.

Collect
Grant, we pray, almighty God,
that, as we are bathed in the new radiance of your incarnate Word,
the light of faith, which illumines our minds,
may also shine through in our deeds.
Through our Lord Jesus Christ, your Son,
who lives and reigns with you in the unity of the Holy Spirit,
one God, for ever and ever.

First Reading   Isaiah 62:11-12
Look, your saviour comes.
This the Lord proclaims
to the ends of the earth:

> Say to the daughter of Zion, "Look,
> your saviour comes,
> the prize of his victory with him,
> his trophies before him".

They shall be called "The Holy People",
"The Lord's Redeemed".
And you shall be called "The-sought-after",
"City-not-forsaken".

Psalm   Psalm 96

R. **This day new light will shine upon the earth:**
    the Lord is born for us.

1. The Lord is king, let earth rejoice,
   the many coastlands be glad.
   The skies proclaim his justice;
   all peoples see his glory. R.

2. Light shines forth for the just
   and joy for the upright of heart.
   Rejoice, you just, in the Lord;
   give glory to his holy name. R.

Second Reading   Titus 3:4-7
It was for no reason except his own compassion that he saved us.
When the kindness and love of God our saviour for mankind were
revealed, it was not because he was concerned with any righteous
actions we might have done ourselves; it was for no reason except
his own compassion that he saved us, by means of the cleansing
water of rebirth and by renewing us with the Holy Spirit which he
has so generously poured over us through Jesus Christ our saviour.
He did this so that we should be justified by his grace, to become
heirs looking forward to inheriting eternal life.

Gospel Acclamation
Alleluia, alleluia!
Glory to God in the highest heaven,
and peace to men who enjoy his favour.
Alleluia!   Luke 2:14

Gospel   Luke 2:15-20

The shepherds found Mary and Joseph and the baby.

Now when the angels had gone from them into heaven, the shepherds said to one another, "Let us go to Bethlehem and see this thing that has happened which the Lord has made known to us." So they hurried away and found Mary and Joseph, and the baby lying in the manger. When they saw the child they repeated what they had been told about him, and everyone who heard it was astonished at what the shepherds had to say. As for Mary, she treasured all these things and pondered them in her heart. And the shepherds went back glorifying and praising God for all they had heard and seen; it was exactly as they had been told.

The Creed is said.
All kneel at the words and by the Holy Spirit was incarnate.

Prayer over the Offerings
May our offerings be worthy, we pray, O Lord,
of the mysteries of the Nativity this day,
that, just as Christ was born a man and also shone forth as God,
so these earthly gifts may confer on us what is divine.
Through Christ our Lord.

Preface I, II or III of the Nativity of the Lord, pp. 491-492.

Communion Antiphon
Rejoice, O Daughter Sion; lift up praise, Daughter Jerusalem:
Behold, your King will come, the Holy One and Saviour of the world.
                                                      cf. Zechariah 9:9

Prayer after Communion
Grant us, Lord, as we honour with joyful devotion
the Nativity of your Son,
that we may come to know with fullness of faith
the hidden depths of this mystery
and to love them ever more and more.
Through Christ our Lord.

The Solemn Blessing for the Nativity of the Lord may be used,
pp. 508-509.

25 December

THE NATIVITY OF THE LORD: MASS DURING THE DAY – ABC

The Word was made flesh!
Jesus Christ is God's Son. God gives us the most precious of all Christmas gifts in Jesus. Through his birth we are reborn, and now for the rest of our days we will live in him who is the radiant light of God's glory. Christ makes it possible for us to share God's life.

Entrance Antiphon
A child is born for us, and a son is given to us;
his sceptre of power rests upon his shoulder,
and his name will be called Messenger of great counsel.

cf. Isaiah 9:5

The Gloria is said or sung.

Collect
O God, who wonderfully created the dignity of human nature
and still more wonderfully restored it,
grant, we pray,
that we may share in the divinity of Christ,
who humbled himself to share in our humanity.
Who lives and reigns with you in the unity of the Holy Spirit,
one God, for ever and ever.

First Reading   Isaiah 52:7-10
All the ends of the earth shall see the salvation of our God.
How beautiful on the mountains,
are the feet of one who brings good news,
who heralds peace, brings happiness,
proclaims salvation,
and tells Zion,
"Your God is king!"
Listen! Your watchmen raise their voices,

they shout for joy together,
for they see the Lord face to face,
as he returns to Zion.
Break into shouts of joy together,
you ruins of Jerusalem;
for the Lord is consoling his people,
redeeming Jerusalem.
The Lord bares his holy arm
in the sight of all the nations,
and all the ends of the earth shall see
the salvation of our God.

Psalm   Psalm 97

R. **All the ends of the earth have seen
    the salvation of our God.**

1. Sing a new song to the Lord
    for he has worked wonders.
    His right hand and his holy arm
    have brought salvation. R.

2. The Lord has made known his salvation;
    has shown his justice to the nations.
    He has remembered his truth and love
    for the house of Israel. R.

3. All the ends of the earth have seen
    the salvation of our God.
    Shout to the Lord all the earth,
    ring out your joy. R.

4. Sing psalms to the Lord with the harp,
    with the sound of music.
    With trumpets and the sound of the horn
    acclaim the King, the Lord. R.

Second Reading   Hebrews 1:1-6

God has spoken to us through his Son.

At various times in the past and in various different ways, God spoke to our ancestors through the prophets; but in our own time, the last days, he has spoken to us through his Son, the Son that he has appointed to inherit everything and through whom he made everything there is. He is the radiant light of God's glory and the perfect copy of his nature, sustaining the universe by his powerful command; and now that he has destroyed the defilement of sin, he has gone to take his place in heaven at the right hand of divine Majesty. So he is now as far above the angels as the title which he has inherited is higher than their own name.

God has never said to any angel: You are my Son, today I become your father, or: I will be a father to him and he a son to me. Again, when he brings the First-born into the world, he says: Let all the angels of God worship him.

Gospel Acclamation

Alleluia, alleluia!

A hallowed day has dawned upon us.

Come, you nations, worship the Lord,

for today a great light has shone down upon the earth.

Alleluia!

Gospel   John 1:1-18

The Word was made flesh, and lived among us.

In the beginning was the Word:
the Word was with God
and the Word was God.
He was with God in the beginning.
Through him all things came to be,
not one thing had its being but through him.
All that came to be had life in him
and that life was the light of men,
a light that shines in the dark,
a light that darkness could not overpower.

A man came, sent by God.
His name was John.
He came as a witness,
as a witness to speak for the light,
so that everyone might believe through him.
He was not the light,
only a witness to speak for the light.

The Word was the true light
that enlightens all men;
and he was coming into the world.
He was in the world
that had its being through him,
and the world did not know him.
He came to his own domain
and his own people did not accept him.
But to all who did accept him
he gave power to become children of God,
to all who believe in the name of him
who was born not out of human stock
or urge of the flesh
or will of man
but of God himself.
The Word was made flesh,
he lived among us,
and we saw his glory,
the glory that is his as the only Son of the Father,
full of grace and truth.

John appears as his witness. He proclaims:
"This is the one of whom I said:
He who comes after me
ranks before me
because he existed before me."

Indeed, from his fullness we have, all of us, received –
yes, grace in return for grace,

since, though the Law was given through Moses,
grace and truth have come through Jesus Christ.
No one has ever seen God;
it is the only Son, who is nearest to the Father's heart,
who has made him known.

The Creed is said.
All kneel at the words *and by the Holy Spirit was incarnate.*

Prayer over the Offerings
Make acceptable, O Lord, our oblation on this solemn day,
when you manifested the reconciliation
that makes us wholly pleasing in your sight
and inaugurated for us the fullness of divine worship.
Through Christ our Lord.

Preface I, II or III of the Nativity of the Lord, pp. 491-492.

Communion Antiphon
All the ends of the earth have seen the salvation of our God.
cf. Psalm 97:3

Prayer after Communion
Grant, O merciful God,
that, just as the Saviour of the world, born this day,
is the author of divine generation for us,
so he may be the giver even of immortality.
Who lives and reigns for ever and ever.

The Solemn Blessing for the Nativity of the Lord may be used,
pp. 508-509.

THE HOLY FAMILY OF JESUS, MARY AND JOSEPH – A

Christ in the human family.
God sets before us the Holy Family of Nazareth as the model for all families.
The family unit is the basic structure upon which human society is built.
A Christian family life is a powerful witness to our world of God's love for
us revealed in Christ.

Entrance Antiphon
The shepherds went in haste,
and found Mary and Joseph and the Infant lying in a manger.

Luke 2:16

The Gloria is said or sung.

Collect
O God, who were pleased to give us
the shining example of the Holy Family,
graciously grant that we may imitate them
in practising the virtues of family life and in the bonds of charity,
and so, in the joy of your house,
delight one day in eternal rewards.
Through our Lord Jesus Christ, your Son,
who lives and reigns with you in the unity of the Holy Spirit,
one God, for ever and ever.

First Reading   Ecclesiasticus 3:2-6. 12-14
He who fears the Lord respects his parents.
The Lord honours the father in his children,
and upholds the rights of a mother over her sons.
Whoever respects his father is atoning for his sins,
he who honours his mother is like someone amassing a fortune.
Whoever respects his father will be happy with children of his own,
he shall be heard on the day when he prays.

Long life comes to him who honours his father,
he who sets his mother at ease is showing obedience to the Lord.
My son, support your father in his old age,
do not grieve him during his life.
Even if his mind should fail, show him sympathy,
do not despise him in your health and strength;
for kindness to a father should not be forgotten
but will serve as reparation for your sins.

Psalm   **Psalm 127**

R. **O blessed are those who fear the Lord
    and walk in his ways!**

1. O blessed are those who fear the Lord
    and walk in his ways!
    By the labour of your hands you shall eat.
    You will be happy and prosper. R.

2. Your wife like a fruitful vine
    in the heart of your house;
    your children like shoots of the olive,
    around your table. R.

3. Indeed thus shall be blessed
    the man who fears the Lord.
    May the Lord bless you from Zion
    all the days of your life! R.

Second Reading   Colossians 3:12-21
Family life in the Lord.
You are God's chosen race, his saints; he loves you, and you should
be clothed in sincere compassion, in kindness and humility,
gentleness and patience. Bear with one another; forgive each other
as soon as a quarrel begins. The Lord has forgiven you; now you
must do the same. Over all these clothes, to keep them together and
complete them, put on love. And may the peace of Christ reign in

your hearts, because it is for this that you were called together as parts of one body. Always be thankful.

Let the message of Christ, in all its richness, find a home with you. Teach each other, and advise each other, in all wisdom. With gratitude in your hearts sing psalms and hymns and inspired songs to God; and never say or do anything except in the name of the Lord Jesus, giving thanks to God the Father through him.

Wives, give way to your husbands, as you should in the Lord. Husbands, love your wives and treat them with gentleness. Children, be obedient to your parents always, because that is what will please the Lord. Parents, never drive your children to resentment or you will make them feel frustrated.

Gospel Acclamation
Alleluia, alleluia!
May the peace of Christ reign in your hearts;
let the message of Christ find a home with you.
Alleluia!   Colossians 3:15. 16

Gospel   Matthew 2:13-15. 19-23
Take the child and his mother and escape into Egypt.
After the wise men had left, the angel of the Lord appeared to Joseph in a dream and said, "Get up, take the child and his mother with you, and escape into Egypt, and stay there until I tell you, because Herod intends to search for the child and do away with him." So Joseph got up and, taking the child and his mother with him, left that night for Egypt, where he stayed until Herod was dead. This was to fulfil what the Lord had spoken through the prophet:

I called my son out of Egypt.

After Herod's death, the angel of the Lord appeared in a dream to Joseph in Egypt and said, "Get up, take the child and his mother with you and go back to the land of Israel, for those who wanted to kill the child are dead." So Joseph got up and, taking the child and his mother with him, went back to the land of Israel. But when he learnt that Archelaus had succeeded his father Herod as ruler of Judaea he was afraid to go there, and being warned in a dream he left for the region of Galilee. There he settled in a town called

Nazareth. In this way the words spoken through the prophets were to be fulfilled:

He will be called a Nazarene.

The Gospels for Year B (pp. 72-73) or Year C (pp. 77-78) may be read as alternatives.

The Creed is said when this feast is celebrated on a Sunday.

Prayer over the Offerings
We offer you, Lord, the sacrifice of conciliation,
humbly asking that,
through the intercession of the Virgin Mother of God and
     Saint Joseph,
you may establish our families firmly in your grace and your peace.
Through Christ our Lord.

Preface I, II or III of the Nativity of the Lord, pp. 491-492.

Communion Antiphon
Our God has appeared on the earth, and lived among us.

Baruch 3:38

Prayer after Communion
Bring those you refresh with this heavenly Sacrament,
most merciful Father,
to imitate constantly the example of the Holy Family,
so that, after the trials of this world,
we may share their company for ever.
Through Christ our Lord.

The Solemn Blessing for the Nativity of the Lord may be used,
pp. 508-509.

THE HOLY FAMILY OF JESUS, MARY AND JOSEPH – B

Christ in the human family.
God sets before us the Holy Family of Nazareth as the model for all families.
The family unit is the basic structure upon which human society is built.
A Christian family life is a powerful witness to our world of God's love for us revealed in Christ.

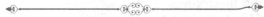

Entrance Antiphon
The shepherds went in haste,
and found Mary and Joseph and the Infant lying in a manger.

Luke 2:16

The Gloria is said or sung.

Collect
O God, who were pleased to give us
the shining example of the Holy Family,
graciously grant that we may imitate them
in practising the virtues of family life and in the bonds of charity,
and so, in the joy of your house,
delight one day in eternal rewards.
Through our Lord Jesus Christ, your Son,
who lives and reigns with you in the unity of the Holy Spirit,
one God, for ever and ever.

The first and second readings for Year A (see pp. 66-69) may be used as an alternative.

First Reading   Genesis 15:1-6; 21:1-3
Your heir shall be of your own flesh and blood.
The word of the Lord was spoken to Abram in a vision, "Have no fear, Abram, I am your shield; your reward will be very great."

"My Lord," Abram replied "what do you intend to give me? I go childless..." Then Abram said, "See, you have given me no descendants; some man of my household will be my heir". And then this word of the Lord was spoken to him, "He shall not be your heir; your heir shall be of your own flesh and blood". Then taking him outside he said, "Look up to heaven and count the stars if you can. Such will be your descendants" he told him. Abram put his faith in the Lord, who counted this as making him justified.

The Lord dealt kindly with Sarah as he had said, and did what he had promised her. So Sarah conceived and bore a son to Abraham in his old age, at the time God had promised. Abraham named the son born to him Isaac, the son to whom Sarah had given birth.

Psalm   Psalm 104

R. **He, the Lord, is our God.**
   He remembers his covenant for ever.

1. Give thanks to the Lord, tell his name,
   make known his deeds among the peoples.
   O sing to him, sing his praise;
   tell all his wonderful works! R.

2. Be proud of his holy name,
   let the hearts that seek the Lord rejoice.
   Consider the Lord and his strength;
   constantly seek his face. R.

3. Remember the wonders he has done,
   his miracles, the judgements he spoke.
   O children of Abraham, his servant,
   O sons of the Jacob he chose. R.

4. He remembers his covenant for ever,
   his promise for a thousand generations,
   the covenant he made with Abraham,
   the oath he swore to Isaac. R.

Second Reading   Hebrews 11:8. 11-12. 17-19

The faith of Abraham, Sarah and Isaac.

It was by faith that Abraham obeyed the call to set out for a country that was the inheritance given to him and his descendants, and that he set out without knowing where he was going.

It was equally by faith that Sarah, in spite of being past the age, was made able to conceive, because she believed that he who had made the promise would be faithful to it. Because of this, there came from one man, and one who was already as good as dead himself, more descendants than could be counted, as many as the stars of heaven or the grains of sand on the seashore.

It was by faith that Abraham, when put to the test, offered up Isaac. He offered to sacrifice his only son even though the promises had been made to him and he had been told: It is through Isaac that your name will be carried on. He was confident that God had the power even to raise the dead; and so, figuratively speaking, he was given back Isaac from the dead.

Gospel Acclamation

Alleluia, alleluia!

At various times in the past

and in various different ways,

God spoke to our ancestors through the prophets;

but in our own time, the last days,

he has spoken to us through his Son.

Alleluia!   Hebrews 1:1-2

Gospel   Luke 2:22-40

The child grew, filled with wisdom.

When the day came for them to be purified as laid down by the Law of Moses, the parents of Jesus took him up to Jerusalem to present him to the Lord

– observing what stands written in the Law of the Lord: Every first-born male must be consecrated to the Lord – and also to offer in sacrifice, in accordance with what is said in the Law of the Lord, a pair of turtledoves or two young pigeons. Now in Jerusalem there was a man named Simeon. He was an upright and devout man; he looked forward to Israel's comforting and the Holy Spirit rested on him. It had been revealed to him by the Holy Spirit that he would not see death until he had set eyes on the Christ of the Lord. Prompted by the Spirit he came to the Temple; and when the parents brought in the child Jesus to do for him what the Law required, he took him into his arms and blessed God; and he said:

> "Now, Master, you can let your servant go in peace,
> just as you promised;
> because my eyes have seen the salvation
> which you have prepared for all the nations to see,
> a light to enlighten the pagans
> and the glory of your people Israel."

As the child's father and mother stood there wondering at the things that were being said about him, Simeon blessed them and said to Mary his mother, "You see this child: he is destined for the fall and for the rising of many in Israel, destined to be a sign that is rejected – and a sword will pierce your own soul too – so that the secret thoughts of many may be laid bare."

There was a prophetess also, Anna, the daughter of Phanuel, of the tribe of Asher. She was well on in years. Her days of girlhood over, she had been married for seven years before becoming a widow. She was now eighty-four years old and never left the Temple, serving God night and day with fasting and prayer. She came by just at that moment and began to praise God; and she spoke of the child to all who looked forward to the deliverance of Jerusalem.

When they had done everything the Law of the Lord required, they went back to Galilee, to their own town of Nazareth. Meanwhile the child grew to maturity, and he was filled with wisdom; and God's favour was with him.

The Creed is said when this feast is celebrated on a Sunday.

Prayer over the Offerings
We offer you, Lord, the sacrifice of conciliation,
humbly asking that,
through the intercession of the Virgin Mother of God and
    Saint Joseph,
you may establish our families firmly in your grace and your peace.
Through Christ our Lord.

Preface I, II or III of the Nativity of the Lord, pp. 491-492.

Communion Antiphon
Our God has appeared on the earth, and lived among us.

Baruch 3:38

Prayer after Communion
Bring those you refresh with this heavenly Sacrament,
most merciful Father,
to imitate constantly the example of the Holy Family,
so that, after the trials of this world,
we may share their company for ever.
Through Christ our Lord.

The Solemn Blessing for the Nativity of the Lord may be used,
pp. 508-509.

THE HOLY FAMILY OF JESUS, MARY AND JOSEPH – C

Christ in the human family.
God sets before us the Holy Family of Nazareth as the model for all families.
The family unit is the basic structure upon which human society is built.
A Christian family life is a powerful witness to our world of God's love for
us revealed in Christ.

Entrance Antiphon
The shepherds went in haste,
and found Mary and Joseph and the Infant lying in a manger.

Luke 2:16

The Gloria is said or sung.

Collect
O God, who were pleased to give us
the shining example of the Holy Family,
graciously grant that we may imitate them
in practising the virtues of family life and in the bonds of charity,
and so, in the joy of your house,
delight one day in eternal rewards.
Through our Lord Jesus Christ, your Son,
who lives and reigns with you in the unity of the Holy Spirit,
one God, for ever and ever.

The first and second readings for Year A (see pp. 66-69) may be
used as an alternative.

First Reading   1 Samuel 1:20-22. 24-28
Samuel is made over to the Lord for the whole of his life.
Hannah conceived and gave birth to a son, and called him Samuel
"since" she said "I asked the Lord for him."
    When a year had gone by, the husband Elkanah went up again
with all his family to offer the annual sacrifice to the Lord and to

fulfil his vow. Hannah, however, did not go up, having said to her husband, "Not before the child is weaned. Then I will bring him and present him before the Lord and he shall stay there for ever."

When she had weaned him, she took him up with her together with a three-year-old bull, an ephah of flour and a skin of wine, and she brought him to the temple of the Lord at Shiloh; and the child was with them. They slaughtered the bull and the child's mother came to Eli. She said, "If you please, my lord. As you live, my lord, I am the woman who stood here beside you, praying to the Lord. This is the child I prayed for, and the Lord granted me what I asked him. Now I make him over to the Lord for the whole of his life. He is made over to the Lord."

There she left him, for the Lord.

Psalm   Psalm 83

R.   **They are happy who dwell in your house, O Lord.**

1. How lovely is your dwelling place,
   Lord, God of hosts.
   My soul is longing and yearning,
   is yearning for the courts of the Lord.
   My heart and my soul ring out their joy
   to God, the living God. R.

2. They are happy, who dwell in your house,
   for ever singing your praise.
   They are happy, whose strength is in you;
   they walk with ever growing strength. R.

3. O Lord, God of hosts, hear my prayer,
   give ear, O God of Jacob.
   Turn your eyes, O God, our shield,
   look on the face of your anointed. R.

Second Reading   1 John 3:1-2. 21-24

We are called God's children; and that is what we are.
Think of the love that the Father has lavished on us,
by letting us be called God's children;
and that is what we are.
Because the world refused to acknowledge him,

therefore it does not acknowledge us.
My dear people, we are already the children of God
but what we are to be in the future has not yet been revealed,
all we know is, that when it is revealed
we shall be like him
because we shall see him as he really is.

My dear people,
if we cannot be condemned by our own conscience,
we need not be afraid in God's presence,
and whatever we ask him,
we shall receive,
because we keep his commandments
and live the kind of life that he wants.
His commandments are these:
that we believe in the name of his Son Jesus Christ
and that we love one another
as he told us to.
Whoever keeps his commandments
lives in God and God lives in him.
We know that he lives in us
by the Spirit that he has given us.

Gospel Acclamation
Alleluia, alleluia!
Open our heart, O Lord,
to accept the words of your Son.
Alleluia!   cf. Acts 16:14

Gospel   Luke 2:41-52
Jesus is found by his parents sitting among the doctors.
Every year the parents of Jesus used to go to Jerusalem for the feast
of the Passover. When he was twelve years old, they went up for the
feast as usual. When they were on their way home after the feast, the
boy Jesus stayed behind in Jerusalem without his parents knowing
it. They assumed he was with the caravan, and it was only after a
day's journey that they went to look for him among their relations
and acquaintances. When they failed to find him they went back to
Jerusalem looking for him everywhere.

Three days later, they found him in the Temple, sitting among the doctors, listening to them, and asking them questions; and all those who heard him were astounded at his intelligence and his replies. They were overcome when they saw him, and his mother said to him, "My child, why have you done this to us? See how worried your father and I have been, looking for you." "Why were you looking for me?" he replied. "Did you not know that I must be busy with my Father's affairs?" But they did not understand what he meant.

He then went down with them and came to Nazareth and lived under their authority. His mother stored up all these things in her heart. And Jesus increased in wisdom, in stature, and in favour with God and men.

The Creed is said when this feast is celebrated on a Sunday.

Prayer over the Offerings
We offer you, Lord, the sacrifice of conciliation,
humbly asking that,
through the intercession of the Virgin Mother of God and
    Saint Joseph,
you may establish our families firmly in your grace and your peace.
Through Christ our Lord.

Preface I, II or III of the Nativity of the Lord, pp. 491-492.

Communion Antiphon
Our God has appeared on the earth, and lived among us.
                                                              Baruch 3:38

Prayer after Communion
Bring those you refresh with this heavenly Sacrament,
most merciful Father,
to imitate constantly the example of the Holy Family,
so that, after the trials of this world,
we may share their company for ever.
Through Christ our Lord.

The Solemn Blessing for the Nativity of the Lord may be used,
pp. 508-509.

1 January

SOLEMNITY OF MARY,
THE HOLY MOTHER OF GOD – ABC

God sent his Son, born of a woman.
Mary is the mother of Christ and the mother of the Church. By the power of
the Holy Spirit she is linked to God in a unique way. She is also our spiritual
mother who encourages us to say "yes" to God, just as she did.

Entrance Antiphon
Hail, Holy Mother, who gave birth to the King,
who rules heaven and earth for ever.

or

Today a light will shine upon us, for the Lord is born for us;
and he will be called Wondrous God,
Prince of peace, Father of future ages:
and his reign will be without end.   cf. Isaiah 9:1. 5; Luke 1:33

The Gloria is said or sung.

Collect
O God, who through the fruitful virginity of Blessed Mary
bestowed on the human race
the grace of eternal salvation,
grant, we pray,
that we may experience the intercession of her,
through whom we were found worthy
to receive the author of life,
our Lord Jesus Christ, your Son.
Who lives and reigns with you in the unity of the Holy Spirit,
one God, for ever and ever.

First Reading   Numbers 6:22-27

They are to call down my name on the sons of Israel, and I will bless them.

The Lord spoke to Moses and said, "Say this to Aaron and his sons: 'This is how you are to bless the sons of Israel. You shall say to them:

May the Lord bless you and keep you.
May the Lord let his face shine on you and be gracious to you.
May the Lord uncover his face to you and bring you peace.'

This is how they are to call down my name on the sons of Israel, and I will bless them."

Psalm   Psalm 66

R. **O God, be gracious and bless us.**

1. God, be gracious and bless us
   and let your face shed its light upon us.
   So will your ways be known upon earth
   and all nations learn your saving help. R.

2. Let the nations be glad and exult
   for you rule the world with justice.
   With fairness you rule the peoples,
   you guide the nations on earth. R.

3. Let the peoples praise you, O God;
   let all the peoples praise you.
   May God still give us his blessing
   till the ends of the earth revere him. R.

Second Reading   Galatians 4:4-7

God sent his Son, born of a woman.

When the appointed time came, God sent his Son, born of a woman, born a subject of the Law, to redeem the subjects of the Law and to enable us to be adopted as sons. The proof that you are sons is that God has sent the Spirit of his Son into our hearts: the

Spirit that cries, "Abba, Father", and it is this that makes you a son, you are not a slave any more; and if God has made you son, then he has made you heir.

Gospel Acclamation
Alleluia, alleluia!
At various times in the past
and in various different ways,
God spoke to our ancestors through the prophets;
but in our own time, the last days,
he has spoken to us through his Son.
Alleluia!   Hebrews 1:1-2

Gospel   Luke 2:16-21
They found Mary and Joseph and the baby... When the eighth day came, they gave him the name Jesus.
The shepherds hurried away to Bethlehem and found Mary and Joseph, and the baby lying in the manger. When they saw the child they repeated what they had been told about him, and everyone who heard it was astonished at what the shepherds had to say. As for Mary, she treasured all these things and pondered them in her heart. And the shepherds went back glorifying and praising God for all they had heard and seen; it was exactly as they had been told.

When the eighth day came and the child was to be circumcised, they gave him the name Jesus, the name the angel had given him before his conception.

The Creed is said.

Prayer over the Offerings
O God, who in your kindness begin all good things
and bring them to fulfilment,
grant to us, who find joy in the Solemnity of the holy Mother of God,
that, just as we glory in the beginnings of your grace,
so one day we may rejoice in its completion.
Through Christ our Lord.

Preface I of the Blessed Virgin Mary, p. 504.

Communion Antiphon
Jesus Christ is the same yesterday, today, and for ever.

Hebrews 13:8

Prayer after Communion
We have received this heavenly Sacrament with joy, O Lord:
grant, we pray,
that it may lead us to eternal life,
for we rejoice to proclaim the blessed ever-Virgin Mary
Mother of your Son and Mother of the Church.
Through Christ our Lord.

A Solemn Blessing may be used, pp. 508-509, 515.

SECOND SUNDAY AFTER THE NATIVITY – ABC

God chose us in Christ.
God's only Son was made flesh and lived among us so that we who believe
in him might become the adopted sons and daughters of the Father. Before the
world was made, God chose us in Christ, and for this
we give thanks to the Father.

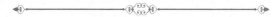

Entrance Antiphon

When a profound silence covered all things
and night was in the middle of its course,
your all-powerful Word, O Lord,
bounded from heaven's royal throne.   Wisdom 18:14-15

The Gloria is said or sung.

Collect

Almighty ever-living God,
splendour of faithful souls,
graciously be pleased to fill the world with your glory,
and show yourself to all peoples by the radiance of your light.
Through our Lord Jesus Christ, your Son,
who lives and reigns with you in the unity of the Holy Spirit,
one God, for ever and ever.

First Reading   Ecclesiasticus 24:1-2. 8-12

The wisdom of God has pitched her tent among the chosen people.

Wisdom speaks her own praises,
in the midst of her people she glories in herself.
She opens her mouth in the assembly of the Most High,
she glories in herself in the presence of the Mighty One;

"Then the creator of all things instructed me,
and he who created me fixed a place for my tent.

He said, 'Pitch your tent in Jacob,
make Israel your inheritance.'
From eternity, in the beginning, he created me,
and for eternity I shall remain.
I ministered before him in the holy tabernacle,
and thus was I established on Zion.
In the beloved city he has given me rest,
and in Jerusalem I wield my authority.
I have taken root in a privileged people,
in the Lord's property, in his inheritance."

Psalm   Psalm 147

R. **The Word was made flesh,
    and lived among us.**

or **Alleluia!**

1. O praise the Lord, Jerusalem!
    Zion, praise your God!
    He has strengthened the bars of your gates,
    he has blessed the children within you. R.

2. He established peace on your borders,
    he feeds you with finest wheat.
    He sends out his word to the earth
    and swiftly runs his command. R.

3. He makes his word known to Jacob,
    to Israel his laws and decrees.
    He has not dealt thus with other nations;
    he had not taught them his decrees. R.

Second Reading   Ephesians 1:3-6. 15-18
He determined that we should become his adopted sons through
Jesus.
Blessed be God the Father of our Lord Jesus Christ, who has blessed
us with all the spiritual blessings of heaven in Christ. Before the
world was made, he chose us, chose us in Christ, to be holy and

spotless, and to live through love in his presence, determining that we should become his adopted sons, through Jesus Christ, for his own kind purposes, to make us praise the glory of his grace, his free gift to us in the Beloved.

That will explain why I, having once heard about your faith in the Lord Jesus, and the love that you show towards all the saints, have never failed to remember you in my prayers and to thank God for you. May the God of our Lord Jesus Christ, the Father of glory, give you a spirit of wisdom and perception of what is revealed, to bring you to full knowledge of him. May he enlighten the eyes of your mind so that you can see what hope his call holds for you, what rich glories he has promised the saints will inherit.

Gospel Acclamation
Alleluia, alleluia!
Glory be to you, O Christ, proclaimed to the pagans;
Glory be to you, O Christ, believed in by the world.
Alleluia!   cf. 1 Timothy 3:16

Gospel   John 1:1-18
The Word was made flesh, and lived among us.

In the beginning was the Word:
the Word was with God
and the Word was God.
He was with God in the beginning.
Through him all things came to be,
not one thing had its being but through him.
All that came to be had life in him
and that life was the light of men,
a light that shines in the dark,
a light that darkness could not overpower.

A man came, sent by God.
His name was John.
He came as a witness,
as a witness to speak for the light,
so that everyone might believe through him.

He was not the light,
only a witness to speak for the light.

> The Word was the true light
> that enlightens all men;
> and he was coming into the world.
> He was in the world
> that had its being through him,
> and the world did not know him.
> He came to his own domain
> and his own people did not accept him.
> But to all who did accept him
> he gave power to become children of God,
> to all who believe in the name of him
> who was born not out of human stock
> or urge of the flesh
> or will of man
> but of God himself.
> The Word was made flesh,
> he lived among us,
> and we saw his glory,
> the glory that is his as the only Son of the Father,
> full of grace and truth.

John appears as his witness. He proclaims:
"This is the one of whom I said:
He who comes after me
ranks before me
because he existed before me."

Indeed, from his fullness we have, all of us, received –
yes, grace in return for grace,
since though the Law was given through Moses,
grace and truth have come through Jesus Christ.
No one has ever seen God;
it is the only Son, who is nearest to the Father's heart,
who has made him known.

The Creed is said.

Prayer over the Offerings
Sanctify, O Lord, the offerings we make
on the Nativity of your Only Begotten Son,
for by it you show us the way of truth
and promise the life of the heavenly Kingdom.
Through Christ our Lord.

Preface I, II or III of the Nativity of the Lord, pp. 491-492.

Communion Antiphon
To all who would accept him,
he gave the power to become children of God.   cf. John 1:12

Prayer after Communion
Lord our God, we humbly ask you,
that, through the working of this mystery,
our offences may be cleansed
and our just desires fulfilled.
Through Christ our Lord.

The Solemn Blessing for the Nativity of the Lord or for
The Beginning of the Year may be used, pp. 508-509.

THE EPIPHANY OF THE LORD – ABC

Christ is revealed to all peoples.
Wise men from the east, guided by a star, come to worship Christ. In them we
see the homage of the nations to Christ, who is for ever the light of the world.
We too are called to become an epiphany — a revealing — of God, by letting the
light of Christ shine in our lives.

Entrance Antiphon
Behold, the Lord, the Mighty One, has come;
and kingship is in his grasp, and power and dominion.

cf. Malachi 3:1; 1 Chronicles 29:12

The Gloria is said or sung.

Collect
O God, who on this day
revealed your Only Begotten Son to the nations
by the guidance of a star,
grant in your mercy,
that we, who know you already by faith,
may be brought to behold the beauty of your sublime glory.
Through our Lord Jesus Christ, your Son,
who lives and reigns with you in the unity of the Holy Spirit,
one God, for ever and ever.

First Reading   Isaiah 60:1-6
Above you the glory of the Lord appears.
Arise, shine out Jerusalem, for your light has come,
the glory of the Lord is rising on you,
though night still covers the earth
and darkness the peoples.

Above you the Lord now rises
and above you his glory appears.

The nations come to your light
and kings to your dawning brightness.

Lift up your eyes and look round:
all are assembling and coming towards you,
your sons from far away
and daughters being tenderly carried.

At this sight you will grow radiant,
your heart throbbing and full;
since the riches of the sea will flow to you,
the wealth of the nations come to you;

camels in throngs will cover you,
and dromedaries of Midian and Ephah;
everyone in Sheba will come,
bringing gold and incense
and singing the praise of the Lord.

Psalm   Psalm 71

R. **All nations shall fall prostrate before you, O Lord.**

1. O God, give your judgement to the king,
   to a king's son your justice,
   that he may judge your people in justice
   and your poor in right judgement. R.

2. In his days justice shall flourish
   and peace till the moon fails.
   He shall rule from sea to sea,
   from the Great River to earth's bounds. R.

3. The kings of Tarshish and the sea coasts
   shall pay him tribute.
   The kings of Sheba and Seba
   shall bring him gifts.
   Before him all kings shall fall prostrate,
   all nations shall serve him. R.

4. For he shall save the poor when they cry
   and the needy who are helpless.
   He will have pity on the weak
   and save the lives of the poor. R.

Second Reading   Ephesians 3:2-3. 5-6

It has now been revealed that pagans share the same inheritance.

You have probably heard how I have been entrusted by God with
the grace he meant for you, and that it was by a revelation that I
was given the knowledge of the mystery. This mystery that has now
been revealed through the Spirit to his holy apostles and prophets
was unknown to any men in past generations; it means that pagans
now share the same inheritance, that they are parts of the same
body, and that the same promise has been made to them, in Christ
Jesus, through the gospel.

Gospel Acclamation

Alleluia, alleluia!
We saw his star as it rose
and have come to do the Lord homage.
Alleluia!   Matthew 2:2

Gospel   Matthew 2:1-12

We saw his star and have come to do the king homage.

After Jesus had been born at Bethlehem in Judaea during the reign
of King Herod, some wise men came to Jerusalem from the east.
"Where is the infant king of the Jews?" they asked. "We saw his star
as it rose and have come to do him homage." When King Herod
heard this he was perturbed, and so was the whole of Jerusalem. He
called together all the chief priests and the scribes of the people, and
enquired of them where the Christ was to be born. "At Bethlehem
in Judaea," they told him "for this is what the prophet wrote:

And you, Bethlehem, in the land of Judah,
you are by no means least among the leaders of Judah,
for out of you will come a leader
who will shepherd my people Israel."

Then Herod summoned the wise men to see him privately. He

asked them the exact date on which the star had appeared, and sent them on to Bethlehem. "Go and find out all about the child," he said "and when you have found him, let me know, so that I too may go and do him homage." Having listened to what the king had to say, they set out. And there in front of them was the star they had seen rising; it went forward and halted over the place where the child was. The sight of the star filled them with delight, and going into the house they saw the child with his mother Mary, and falling to their knees they did him homage. Then, opening their treasures, they offered him gifts of gold and frankincense and myrrh. But they were warned in a dream not to go back to Herod, and returned to their own country by a different way.

The Creed is said.

Prayer over the Offerings
Look with favour, Lord, we pray,
on these gifts of your Church,
in which are offered now not gold or frankincense or myrrh,
but he who by them is proclaimed,
sacrificed and received, Jesus Christ.
Who lives and reigns for ever and ever.

Preface of the Epiphany of the Lord, p. 493.

Communion Antiphon
We have seen his star in the East,
and have come with gifts to adore the Lord.   cf. Matthew 2:2

Prayer after Communion
Go before us with heavenly light, O Lord,
always and everywhere,
that we may perceive with clear sight
and revere with true affection
the mystery in which you have willed us to participate.
Through Christ our Lord.

The Solemn Blessing for the Epiphany of the Lord may be used,
p. 510.

THE BAPTISM OF THE LORD – A

You are my Son, the Beloved.
The Holy Spirit came down upon Jesus, the beloved Son of God, at his baptism in the River Jordan. The same Holy Spirit comes down on each one of us and helps us to live our lives so that we are faithful to our baptismal calling.

Entrance Antiphon
After the Lord was baptised, the heavens were opened,
and the Spirit descended upon him like a dove,
and the voice of the Father thundered:
This is my beloved Son, with whom I am well pleased.

cf. Matthew 3:16-17

The Gloria is said or sung.

Collect
Almighty ever-living God,
who, when Christ had been baptised in the River Jordan
and as the Holy Spirit descended upon him,
solemnly declared him your beloved Son,
grant that your children by adoption,
reborn of water and the Holy Spirit,
may always be well pleasing to you.
Through our Lord Jesus Christ, your Son,
who lives and reigns with you in the unity of the Holy Spirit,
one God, for ever and ever.

or

O God, whose Only Begotten Son
has appeared in our very flesh,
grant, we pray, that we may be inwardly transformed
through him whom we recognise as outwardly like ourselves.
Who lives and reigns with you in the unity of the Holy Spirit,
one God, for ever and ever.

First Reading   Isaiah 42:1-4. 6-7

Here is my servant in whom my soul delights.

Thus says the Lord:

Here is my servant whom I uphold,
my chosen one in whom my soul delights.
I have endowed him with my spirit
that he may bring true justice to the nations.

He does not cry out or shout aloud,
or make his voice heard in the streets.
He does not break the crushed reed,
nor quench the wavering flame.

Faithfully he brings true justice;
he will neither waver, nor be crushed
until true justice is established on earth,
for the islands are awaiting his law.

I, the Lord, have called you to serve the cause of right;
I have taken you by the hand and formed you;
I have appointed you as covenant of the people and light of the
    nations,
to open the eyes of the blind,
to free captives from prison,
and those who live in darkness from the dungeon.

Psalm   Psalm 28

R. **The Lord will bless his people with peace.**

1. O give the Lord you sons of God,
    give the Lord glory and power;
    give the Lord the glory of his name.
    Adore the Lord in his holy court. R.

2. The Lord's voice resounding on the waters,
    the Lord on the immensity of waters;
    the voice of the Lord, full of power,
    the voice of the Lord, full of splendour. R.

3. The God of glory thunders.
    In his temple they all cry: "Glory!"
    The Lord sat enthroned over the flood;
    the Lord sits as king for ever. R.

Second Reading   Acts 10:34-38
God anointed him with the Holy Spirit.

Peter addressed Cornelius and his household: "The truth I have now come to realise" he said "is that God does not have favourites, but that anybody of any nationality who fears God and does what is right is acceptable to him.

"It is true, God sent his word to the people of Israel, and it was to them that the good news of peace was brought by Jesus Christ – but Jesus Christ is Lord of all men. You must have heard about the recent happenings in Judaea; about Jesus of Nazareth and how he began in Galilee, after John had been preaching baptism. God had anointed him with the Holy Spirit and with power, and because God was with him, Jesus went about doing good and curing all who had fallen into the power of the devil."

Gospel Acclamation
Alleluia, alleluia!
The heavens opened and the Father's voice resounded:
"This is my Son, the Beloved. Listen to him."
Alleluia!   cf. Mark 9:8

Gospel   Matthew 3:13-17
As soon as Jesus was baptised he saw the Spirit of God coming down on him.

Jesus came from Galilee to the Jordan to be baptised by John. John tried to dissuade him. "It is I who need baptism from you," he said, "and yet you come to me!" But Jesus replied, "Leave it like this for the time being; it is fitting that we should, in this way, do all that righteousness demands." At this, John gave in to him.

As soon as Jesus was baptised he came up from the water, and suddenly the heavens opened and he saw the Spirit of God descending like a dove and coming down on him. And a voice spoke from heaven, "This is my Son, the Beloved; my favour rests on him."

The Creed is said.

Prayer over the Offerings

Accept, O Lord, the offerings
we have brought to honour the revealing of your beloved Son,
so that the oblation of your faithful
may be transformed into the sacrifice of him
who willed in his compassion
to wash away the sins of the world.
Who lives and reigns for ever and ever.

Preface

It is truly right and just, our duty and our salvation,
always and everywhere to give you thanks,
Lord, holy Father, almighty and eternal God.

For in the waters of the Jordan
you revealed with signs and wonders a new Baptism,
so that through the voice that came down from heaven
we might come to believe in your Word dwelling among us,
and by the Spirit's descending in the likeness of a dove
we might know that Christ your Servant
has been anointed with the oil of gladness
and sent to bring the good news to the poor.

And so, with the Powers of heaven,
we worship you constantly on earth,
and before your majesty
without end we acclaim:
Holy, Holy, Holy Lord God of hosts…

Communion Antiphon

Behold the One of whom John said:
I have seen and testified that this is the Son of God.   John 1:32. 34

Prayer after Communion
Nourished with these sacred gifts,
we humbly entreat your mercy, O Lord,
that, faithfully listening to your Only Begotten Son,
we may be your children in name and in truth.
Through Christ our Lord.

Ordinary Time now begins and continues until the Season of Lent.
For the Sundays of Ordinary Time, Year A, turn to p. 560.

THE BAPTISM OF THE LORD – B

You are my Son, the Beloved.
The Holy Spirit came down upon Jesus, the beloved Son of God, at his
baptism in the River Jordan. The same Holy Spirit comes down on each one
of us and helps us to live our lives so that we are faithful to our baptismal
calling.

Entrance Antiphon
After the Lord was baptised, the heavens were opened,
and the Spirit descended upon him like a dove,
and the voice of the Father thundered:
This is my beloved Son, with whom I am well pleased.

cf. Matthew 3:16-17

The Gloria is said or sung.

Collect
Almighty ever-living God,
who, when Christ had been baptised in the River Jordan
and as the Holy Spirit descended upon him,
solemnly declared him your beloved Son,
grant that your children by adoption,
reborn of water and the Holy Spirit,
may always be well pleasing to you.
Through our Lord Jesus Christ, your Son,
who lives and reigns with you in the unity of the Holy Spirit,
one God, for ever and ever.

or

O God, whose Only Begotten Son
has appeared in our very flesh,
grant, we pray, that we may be inwardly transformed
through him whom we recognise as outwardly like ourselves.
Who lives and reigns with you in the unity of the Holy Spirit,
one God, for ever and ever.

The first and second readings for Year A (see pp. 93-94) may be used as an alternative.

First Reading   Isaiah 55:1-11

Come to the water. Listen and your soul will live.

Oh, come to the water all you who are thirsty;
though you have no money, come!
Buy corn without money, and eat,
and, at no cost, wine and milk.
Why spend money on what is not bread,
your wages on what fails to satisfy?
Listen, listen to me, and you will have good things to eat
and rich food to enjoy.
Pay attention, come to me;
listen, and your soul will live.

With you I will make an everlasting covenant
out of the favours promised to David.
See, I have made of you a witness to the peoples,
a leader and master of the nations.
See, you will summon a nation you never knew,
those unknown will come hurrying to you,
for the sake of the Lord your God,
of the Holy One of Israel who will glorify you.

Seek the Lord while he is still to be found,
call to him while he is still near.
Let the wicked man abandon his way,
the evil man his thoughts.
Let him turn back to the Lord who will take pity on him,
to our God who is rich in forgiving;
for my thoughts are not your thoughts,
my ways not your ways – it is the Lord who speaks.
Yes, the heavens are as high above earth
as my ways are above your ways,
my thoughts above your thoughts.

Yes, as the rain and the snow come down from the heavens and do not return without watering the earth, making it yield and giving growth to provide seed for the sower and bread for the eating, so the word that goes from my mouth does not return to me empty, without carrying out my will and succeeding in what it was sent to do.

Psalm   Isaiah 12:2-6

R. **With joy you will draw water
    from the wells of salvation.**

1. Truly, God is my salvation.
   I trust, I shall not fear.
   For the Lord is my strength, my song,
   he became my saviour.
   With joy you will draw water
   from the wells of salvation. R.

2. Give thanks to the Lord, give praise to his name!
   Make his mighty deeds known to the peoples!
   Declare the greatness of his name. R.

3. Sing a psalm to the Lord
   for he has done glorious deeds,
   make them known to all the earth!
   People of Zion, sing and shout for joy
   for great in your midst is the Holy One of Israel. R.

Second Reading   1 John 5:1-9
The Spirit and water and blood.
Whoever believes that Jesus is the Christ
has been begotten by God;
and whoever loves the Father that begot him
loves the child whom he begets.
We can be sure that we love God's children
if we love God himself and do what he has commanded us;
this is what loving God is –
keeping his commandments;
and his commandments are not difficult,
because anyone who has been begotten by God
has already overcome the world;

this is the victory over the world –
our faith.
Who can overcome the world?
Only the man who believes that Jesus is the Son of God:
Jesus Christ who came by water and blood,
not with water only,
but with water and blood;
with the Spirit as another witness –
since the Spirit is the truth –
so that there are three witnesses,
the Spirit, the water and the blood,
and all three of them agree.
We accept the testimony of human witnesses,
but God's testimony is much greater,
and this is God's testimony,
given as evidence for his Son.

Gospel Acclamation

Alleluia, alleluia!
John saw Jesus coming towards him, and said:
This is the Lamb of God who takes away the sin of the world.
Alleluia!   cf. John 1:29

Gospel   Mark 1:7-11

You are my Son, the Beloved; my favour rests on you.

In the course of his preaching John the Baptist said, "Someone is
following me, someone who is more powerful than I am, and I
am not fit to kneel down and undo the strap of his sandals. I have
baptised you with water, but he will baptise you with the Holy
Spirit."

It was at this time that Jesus came from Nazareth in Galilee and
was baptised in the Jordan by John. No sooner had he come up out
of the water than he saw the heavens torn apart and the Spirit, like a
dove, descending on him. And a voice came from heaven, "You are
my Son, the Beloved; my favour rests on you."

The Creed is said.

Prayer over the Offerings
Accept, O Lord, the offerings
we have brought to honour the revealing of your beloved Son,
so that the oblation of your faithful
may be transformed into the sacrifice of him
who willed in his compassion
to wash away the sins of the world.
Who lives and reigns for ever and ever.

Preface of the Baptism of the Lord, p. 95.

Communion Antiphon
Behold the One of whom John said:
I have seen and testified that this is the Son of God.   John 1:32. 34

Prayer after Communion
Nourished with these sacred gifts,
we humbly entreat your mercy, O Lord,
that, faithfully listening to your Only Begotten Son,
we may be your children in name and in truth.
Through Christ our Lord.

Ordinary Time now begins and continues until the Season of Lent.
For the Sundays of Ordinary Time, Year B, turn to p. 698.

THE BAPTISM OF THE LORD – C

You are my Son, the Beloved.
The Holy Spirit came down upon Jesus, the beloved Son of God, at his
baptism in the River Jordan. The same Holy Spirit comes down on each one
of us and helps us to live our lives so that we are faithful to our baptismal
calling.

Entrance Antiphon
After the Lord was baptised, the heavens were opened,
and the Spirit descended upon him like a dove,
and the voice of the Father thundered:
This is my beloved Son, with whom I am well pleased.

cf. Matthew 3:16-17

The Gloria is said or sung.

Collect
Almighty ever-living God,
who, when Christ had been baptised in the River Jordan
and as the Holy Spirit descended upon him,
solemnly declared him your beloved Son,
grant that your children by adoption,
reborn of water and the Holy Spirit,
may always be well pleasing to you.
Through our Lord Jesus Christ, your Son,
who lives and reigns with you in the unity of the Holy Spirit,
one God, for ever and ever.

or

O God, whose Only Begotten Son
has appeared in our very flesh,
grant, we pray, that we may be inwardly transformed
through him whom we recognise as outwardly like ourselves.
Who lives and reigns with you in the unity of the Holy Spirit,
one God, for ever and ever.

The first and second readings for Year A (see pp. 93-94) may be used as an alternative.

First Reading   Isaiah 40:1-5. 9-11
The glory of the Lord shall be revealed and all mankind shall see it.
"Console my people, console them"
says your God.
"Speak to the heart of Jerusalem
and call to her
that her time of service is ended,
that her sin is atoned for,
that she has received from the hand of the Lord
double punishment for all her crimes."

A voice cries, "Prepare in the wilderness
a way for the Lord.
Make a straight highway for our God
across the desert.
Let every valley be filled in,
every mountain and hill be laid low,
let every cliff become a plain,
and the ridges a valley;
then the glory of the Lord shall be revealed
and all mankind shall see it;
for the mouth of the Lord has spoken."

Go up on a high mountain,
joyful messenger to Zion.
Shout with a loud voice,
joyful messenger to Jerusalem.
Shout without fear,
say to the towns of Judah,
"Here is your God."

Here is the Lord God coming with power,
his arm subduing all things to him.
The prize of his victory is with him,
his trophies all go before him.

He is like a shepherd feeding his flock,
gathering lambs in his arms,
holding them against his breast
and leading to their rest the mother ewes.

Psalm   Psalm 103

R. **Bless the Lord, my soul!**
    Lord God, how great you are!

1. Lord God, how great you are,
   clothed in majesty and glory,
   wrapped in light as in a robe!
   You stretch out the heavens like a tent. R.

2. Above the rains you build your dwelling.
   You make the clouds your chariot,
   you walk on the wings of the wind,
   you make the winds your messengers
   and flashing fire your servants. R.

3. How many are your works, O Lord!
   In wisdom you have made them all.
   The earth is full of your riches.
   There is the sea, vast and wide,
   with its moving swarms past counting,
   living things great and small. R.

4. All of these look to you
   to give them their food in due season.
   You give it, they gather it up:
   you open your hand, they have their fill. R.

5. You take back your spirit, they die,
   returning to the dust from which they came.
   You send forth your spirit, they are created;
   and you renew the face of the earth. R.

Second Reading   Titus 2:11-14; 3:4-7

He saved us by means of the cleansing water of rebirth, and by renewing us with the Holy Spirit.

God's grace has been revealed, and it has made salvation possible for the whole human race and taught us that what we have to do is to give up everything that does not lead to God, and all our worldly ambitions; we must be self-restrained and live good and religious lives here in this present world, while we are waiting in hope for the blessing which will come with the Appearing of the glory of our great God and saviour Christ Jesus. He sacrificed himself for us in order to set us free from all wickedness and to purify a people so that it could be his very own and would have no ambition except to do good.

When the kindness and love of God our saviour for mankind were revealed, it was not because he was concerned with any righteous actions we might have done ourselves; it was for no reason except his own compassion that he saved us, by means of the cleansing water of rebirth and by renewing us with the Holy Spirit which he has so generously poured over us through Jesus Christ our saviour. He did this so that we should be justified by his grace, to become heirs looking forward to inheriting eternal life.

Gospel Acclamation

Alleluia, alleluia!

Someone is coming, said John, someone greater than I.

He will baptise you with the Holy Spirit and with fire.

Alleluia!   cf. Luke 3:16

Gospel   Luke 3:15-16. 21-22

While Jesus after his own baptism was at prayer, heaven opened.

A feeling of expectancy had grown among the people, who were beginning to think that John might be the Christ, so John declared before them all, "I baptise you with water, but someone is coming, someone who is more powerful that I am and I am not fit to undo the strap of his sandals; he will baptise you with the Holy Spirit and fire." Now when all the people had been baptised and while Jesus after his own baptism was at prayer, heaven opened and the Holy Spirit

descended on him in bodily shape, like a dove. And a voice came
from heaven, "You are my Son, the Beloved; my favour rests on you."

The Creed is said.

Prayer over the Offerings
Accept, O Lord, the offerings
we have brought to honour the revealing of your beloved Son,
so that the oblation of your faithful
may be transformed into the sacrifice of him
who willed in his compassion
to wash away the sins of the world.
Who lives and reigns for ever and ever.

Preface of the Baptism of the Lord, p. 95.

Communion Antiphon
Behold the One of whom John said:
I have seen and testified that this is the Son of God.

John 1:32. 34

Prayer after Communion
Nourished with these sacred gifts,
we humbly entreat your mercy, O Lord,
that, faithfully listening to your Only Begotten Son,
we may be your children in name and in truth.
Through Christ our Lord.

Ordinary Time now begins and continues until the Season of Lent.
For the Sundays of Ordinary Time, Year C, turn to p. 831.

ASH WEDNESDAY – ABC

Turn away from sin and be faithful to the Gospel.
The season of Lent reminds us of Christ's call to us to change the direction
of our lives, to turn away from sin and walk in the path of the Gospel.
Repentance means constantly taking stock of our lives so that we avoid
becoming complacent. Even though we have been baptised, we are still inclined
to sin. During the season of Lent we are called to have a change of heart and
to put Christ's message at the forefront of our lives.

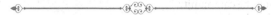

Entrance Antiphon
You are merciful to all, O Lord,
and despise nothing that you have made.
You overlook people's sins, to bring them to repentance,
and you spare them, for you are the Lord our God.

Wisdom 11:24. 25. 27

The Penitential Act is omitted, and the Distribution of Ashes takes
its place. The Gloria is not said or sung.

Collect
Grant, O Lord, that we may begin with holy fasting
this campaign of Christian service,
so that, as we take up battle against spiritual evils,
we may be armed with weapons of self-restraint.
Through our Lord Jesus Christ, your Son,
who lives and reigns with you in the unity of the Holy Spirit,
one God, for ever and ever.

First Reading   Joel 2:12-18
Let your hearts be broken, not your garments torn.
"Now, now – it is the Lord who speaks –
come back to me with all your heart,
fasting, weeping, mourning."
Let your hearts be broken not your garments torn,
turn to the Lord your God again,
for he is all tenderness and compassion,

slow to anger, rich in graciousness,
and ready to relent.
Who knows if he will not turn again, will not relent,
will not leave a blessing as he passes,
oblation and libation
for the Lord your God?
Sound the trumpet in Zion!
Order a fast,
proclaim a solemn assembly,
call the people together,
summon the community,
assemble the elders,
gather the children,
even the infants at the breast.
Let the bridegroom leave his bedroom
and the bride her alcove.
Between vestibule and altar let the priests,
the ministers of the Lord, lament.
Let them say,
"Spare your people, Lord!
Do not make your heritage a thing of shame,
a byword for the nations.
Why should it be said among the nations,
'Where is their God?'"
Then the Lord, jealous on behalf of his land,
took pity on his people.

Psalm   Psalm 50

R. **Have mercy on us, O Lord, for we have sinned.**

1. Have mercy on me, God, in your kindness.
    In your compassion blot out my offence,
    O wash me more and more from my guilt
    and cleanse me from my sin. R.

2. My offences truly I know them;
    my sin is always before me.
    Against you, you alone, have I sinned:
    what is evil in your sight I have done. R.

3. A pure heart create for me, O God,
   put a steadfast spirit within me.
   Do not cast me away from your presence,
   nor deprive me of your holy spirit. R.

4. Give me again the joy of your help;
   with a spirit of fervour sustain me,
   O Lord, open my lips
   and my mouth shall declare your praise. R.

Second Reading   2 Corinthians 5:20 – 6:2
Be reconciled to God... now is the favourable time.

We are ambassadors for Christ; it is as though God were appealing
through us, and the appeal that we make in Christ's name is: be
reconciled to God. For our sake God made the sinless one into sin,
so that in him we might become the goodness of God. As his fellow
workers, we beg you once again not to neglect the grace of God
that you have received. For he says: At the favourable time, I have
listened to you; on the day of salvation I came to your help. Well,
now is the favourable time; this is the day of salvation.

Gospel Acclamation

Praise to you, O Christ, king of eternal glory!
A pure heart create for me, O God,
and give me again the joy of your help.
Praise to you, O Christ, king of eternal glory!   Psalm 50:12. 14

or

Praise to you, O Christ, king of eternal glory!
Harden not your hearts today,
but listen to the voice of the Lord.
Praise to you, O Christ, king of eternal glory!   cf. Psalm 94:8

Gospel   Matthew 6:1-6. 16-18
Your Father, who sees all that is done in secret, will reward you.

Jesus said to his disciples:

"Be careful not to parade your good deeds before men to attract
their notice; by doing this you will lose all reward from your Father
in heaven. So when you give alms, do not have it trumpeted before
you; this is what the hypocrites do in the synagogues and in the

streets to win men's admiration. I tell you solemnly, they have had their reward. But when you give alms, your left hand must not know what your right is doing; your almsgiving must be secret, and your Father who sees all that is done in secret will reward you.

"And when you pray, do not imitate the hypocrites: they love to say their prayers standing up in the synagogues and at the street corners for people to see them. I tell you solemnly, they have had their reward. But when you pray, go to your private room and, when you have shut your door, pray to your Father who is in that secret place, and your Father who sees all that is done in secret will reward you.

"When you fast do not put on a gloomy look as the hypocrites do: they pull long faces to let men know they are fasting. I tell you solemnly, they have had their reward. But when you fast, put oil on your head and wash your face, so that no one will know you are fasting except your Father who sees all that is done in secret; and your Father who sees all that is done in secret will reward you."

Blessing and Distribution of Ashes

After the homily, the priest, standing with hands joined, says:

Dear brethren (brothers and sisters),
let us humbly ask God our Father
that he be pleased to bless with the abundance of his grace
these ashes, which we will put on our heads in penitence.

All pray in silence for a few moments. Then the priest says:

O God, who are moved by acts of humility
and respond with forgiveness to works of penance,
lend your merciful ear to our prayers
and in your kindness pour out the grace of your ✠ blessing
on your servants who are marked with these ashes,
that, as they follow the Lenten observances,
they may be worthy to come with minds made pure
to celebrate the Paschal Mystery of your Son.
Through Christ our Lord.
or

O God, who desire not the death of sinners,
but their conversion,
mercifully hear our prayers
and in your kindness be pleased to bless ✠ these ashes,
which we intend to receive upon our heads,
that we, who acknowledge we are but ashes
and shall return to dust,
may, through a steadfast observance of Lent,
gain pardon for sins and newness of life
after the likeness of your Risen Son.
Who lives and reigns for ever and ever.

The priest sprinkles the ashes with holy water. Then he places ashes
on the head of all those who come forward, saying to each:
Repent, and believe in the Gospel.

or

Remember that you are dust, and to dust you shall return.

Meanwhile, some of the following or other appropriate songs are sung.

Antiphon 1
Let us change our garments to sackcloth and ashes,
let us fast and weep before the Lord,
that our God, rich in mercy, might forgive us our sins.

Antiphon 2
Let the priests, the ministers of the Lord,
stand between the porch and the altar and weep and cry out:
Spare, O Lord, spare your people;
do not close the mouths of those who sing your praise, O Lord.

cf. Joel 2:17; Esther 4:17

Antiphon 3
Blot out my transgressions, O Lord.   Psalm 50:3
This antiphon may be repeated after each verse of Psalm 50, see
pp. 108-109.

Responsory
Let us correct our faults which we have committed in ignorance, let
us not be taken unawares by the day of our death, looking in vain
for leisure to repent.

Hear us, O Lord, and show us your mercy,
for we have sinned against you.
Help us, O God our Saviour; for the sake of your name,
O Lord, set us free.
Hear us, O Lord, and show us your mercy,
for we have sinned against you.   cf. Baruch 3:2; Psalm 78:9

After the distribution of ashes, the priest washes his hands; then
follows the Prayer of the Faithful.

The Creed is not said.

Prayer over the Offerings
As we solemnly offer
the annual sacrifice for the beginning of Lent,
we entreat you, O Lord,
that, through works of penance and charity,
we may turn away from harmful pleasures
and, cleansed from our sins, may become worthy
to celebrate devoutly the Passion of your Son.
Who lives and reigns for ever and ever.

Preface III or IV of Lent, pp. 494-495.

Communion Antiphon
He who ponders the law of the Lord day and night
will yield fruit in due season.   cf. Psalm 1:2-3

Prayer after Communion
May the Sacrament we have received sustain us, O Lord,
that our Lenten fast may be pleasing to you
and be for us a healing remedy.
Through Christ our Lord.

Prayer over the People
Pour out a spirit of compunction, O God,
on those who bow before your majesty,
and by your mercy may they merit the rewards you promise
to those who do penance.
Through Christ our Lord.

FIRST SUNDAY OF LENT – A

Christ conquers sin and temptation.
God created the human race free from sin, but our first parents yielded to the
temptation of evil. In them each one of us has sinned; but in Christ we are
given the power to overcome the temptations of the world just as he did.

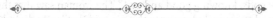

Entrance Antiphon
When he calls on me, I will answer him;
I will deliver him and give him glory,
I will grant him length of days.   cf. Psalm 90:15-16

The Gloria is not said or sung.

Collect
Grant, almighty God,
through the yearly observances of holy Lent,
that we may grow in understanding
of the riches hidden in Christ
and by worthy conduct pursue their effects.
Through our Lord Jesus Christ, your Son,
who lives and reigns with you in the unity of the Holy Spirit,
one God, for ever and ever.

First Reading   Genesis 2:7-9; 3:1-7
The creation and sin of our first parents.
The Lord God fashioned man of dust from the soil. Then he
breathed into his nostrils a breath of life, and thus man became a
living being.

The Lord God planted a garden in Eden which is in the east, and
there he put the man he had fashioned. The Lord God caused to
spring up from the soil every kind of tree, enticing to look at and
good to eat, with the tree of life and the tree of the knowledge of
good and evil in the middle of the garden.

The serpent was the most subtle of all the wild beasts that the

Lord God had made. It asked the woman, "Did God really say you were not to eat from any of the trees in the garden?" The woman answered the serpent, "We may eat the fruit of the trees in the garden. But of the fruit of the tree in the middle of the garden God said, 'You must not eat it, nor touch it, under pain of death'." Then the serpent said to the woman, "No! You will not die! God knows in fact that on the day you eat it your eyes will be opened and you will be like gods, knowing good and evil." The woman saw that the tree was good to eat and pleasing to the eye, and that it was desirable for the knowledge that it could give. So she took some of its fruit and ate it. She gave some also to her husband who was with her, and he ate it. Then the eyes of both of them were opened and they realised that they were naked. So they sewed fig-leaves together to make themselves loin-cloths.

Psalm   Psalm 50

R. **Have mercy on us, O Lord,
for we have sinned.**

1. Have mercy on me, God, in your kindness.
    In your compassion blot out my offence.
    O wash me more and more from my guilt
    and cleanse me from my sin. R.

2. My offences truly I know them;
    my sin is always before me.
    Against you, you alone, have I sinned;
    what is evil in your sight I have done. R.

3. A pure heart create for me, O God,
    put a steadfast spirit within me.
    Do not cast me away from your presence,
    nor deprive me of your holy spirit. R.

4. Give me again the joy of your help;
    with a spirit of fervour sustain me.
    O Lord, open my lips
    and my mouth shall declare your praise. R.

Second Reading   Romans 5:12-19

However great the number of sins committed, grace was even greater.

> Sin entered the world through one man, and through sin death, and thus death has spread through the whole human race because everyone has sinned.

Sin existed in the world long before the Law was given. There was no law and so no one could be accused of the sin of "law-breaking", yet death reigned over all from Adam to Moses, even though their sin, unlike that of Adam, was not a matter of breaking a law.

Adam prefigured the One to come, but the gift itself considerably outweighed the fall. If it is certain that through one man's fall so many died, it is even more certain that divine grace, coming through the one man, Jesus Christ, came to so many as an abundant free gift. The results of the gift also outweigh the results of one man's sin: for after one single fall came judgement with a verdict of condemnation, now after many falls comes grace with its verdict of acquittal.

> If it is certain that death reigned over everyone as the consequence of one man's fall, it is even more certain that one man, Jesus Christ, will cause everyone to reign in life who receives the free gift that he does not deserve, of being made righteous. Again, as one man's fall brought condemnation on everyone, so the good act of one man brings everyone life and makes them justified. As by one man's disobedience many were made sinners, so by one man's obedience many will be made righteous.

Gospel Acclamation

Praise to you, O Christ, king of eternal glory!
Man does not live on bread alone,
but on every word that comes from the mouth of God.
Praise to you, O Christ, king of eternal glory!   Matthew 4:4

Gospel   Matthew 4:1-11

Jesus fasts for forty days and is tempted.

Jesus was led by the Spirit out into the wilderness to be tempted by the devil. He fasted for forty days and forty nights, after which he was very hungry, and the tempter came and said to him, "If you are the Son of God, tell these stones to turn into loaves." But he replied, "Scripture says:

> Man does not live on bread alone
> but on every word that comes from the mouth of God."

The devil then took him to the holy city and made him stand on the parapet of the Temple. "If you are the Son of God," he said, "throw yourself down; for scripture says:

> He will put you in his angels' charge,
> and they will support you on their hands
> in case you hurt your foot against a stone."

Jesus said to him, "Scripture also says:

> You must not put the Lord your God to the test."

Next, taking him to a very high mountain, the devil showed him all the kingdoms of the world and their splendour. "I will give you all these", he said, "if you fall at my feet and worship me." Then Jesus replied, "Be off, Satan! For scripture says:

> You must worship the Lord your God,
> and serve him alone."

Then the devil left him, and angels appeared and looked after him.

The Creed is said.

Prayer over the Offerings
Give us the right dispositions, O Lord, we pray,
to make these offerings,
for with them we celebrate the beginning
of this venerable and sacred time.
Through Christ our Lord.

Preface
It is truly right and just, our duty and our salvation,
always and everywhere to give you thanks,
Lord, holy Father, almighty and eternal God,
through Christ our Lord.

By abstaining forty long days from earthly food,
he consecrated through his fast

the pattern of our Lenten observance
and, by overturning all the snares of the ancient serpent,
taught us to cast out the leaven of malice,
so that, celebrating worthily the Paschal Mystery,
we might pass over at last to the eternal paschal feast.

And so, with the company of Angels and Saints,
we sing the hymn of your praise,
as without end we acclaim:
Holy, Holy, Holy Lord God of hosts…

Communion Antiphon
One does not live by bread alone,
but by every word that comes forth from the mouth of God.

Matthew 4:4

or

The Lord will conceal you with his pinions,
and under his wings you will trust.   cf. Psalm 90:4

Prayer after Communion
Renewed now with heavenly bread,
by which faith is nourished, hope increased,
and charity strengthened,
we pray, O Lord,
that we may learn to hunger for Christ,
the true and living Bread,
and strive to live by every word
which proceeds from your mouth.
Through Christ our Lord.

Prayer over the People
May bountiful blessing, O Lord, we pray,
come down upon your people,
that hope may grow in tribulation,
virtue be strengthened in temptation,
and eternal redemption be assured.
Through Christ our Lord.

SECOND SUNDAY OF LENT – A

Jesus is transfigured in glory.
On the mountain Jesus is transfigured in the presence of his apostles. His
message to them, "Do not be afraid", reminds us that God calls us to bear the
hardships of this life in the knowledge that Christ is everything. He calls us to
be prepared to leave behind all things in order to proclaim his Gospel.

Entrance Antiphon
Of you my heart has spoken: Seek his face.
It is your face, O Lord, that I seek;
hide not your face from me.   cf. Psalm 26:8-9

or

Remember your compassion, O Lord,
and your merciful love, for they are from of old.
Let not our enemies exult over us.
Redeem us, O God of Israel, from all our distress.
                                              cf. Psalm 24:6. 2. 22

The Gloria is not said or sung.

Collect
O God, who have commanded us
to listen to your beloved Son,
be pleased, we pray,
to nourish us inwardly by your word,
that, with spiritual sight made pure,
we may rejoice to behold your glory.
Through our Lord Jesus Christ, your Son,
who lives and reigns with you in the unity of the Holy Spirit,
one God, for ever and ever.

First Reading   Genesis 12:1-4
The call of Abraham, father of the People of God.
The Lord said to Abram, "Leave your country, your family and your
father's house, for the land I will show you. I will make you a great

nation; I will bless you and make your name so famous that it will be used as a blessing.

"I will bless those who bless you:
I will curse those who slight you.
All the tribes of the earth
shall bless themselves by you."

So Abram went as the Lord told him.

Psalm   Psalm 32

R. **May your love be upon us, O Lord,**
   as we place all our hope in you.

1. The word of the Lord is faithful
   and all his works to be trusted.
   The Lord loves justice and right
   and fills the earth with his love. R.

2. The Lord looks on those who revere him,
   on those who hope in his love,
   to rescue their souls from death,
   to keep them alive in famine. R.

3. Our soul is waiting for the Lord.
   The Lord is our help and our shield.
   May your love be upon us, O Lord,
   as we place all our hope in you. R.

Second Reading   2 Timothy 1:8-10
God calls and enlightens us.

With me, bear the hardships for the sake of the Good News, relying on the power of God who has saved us and called us to be holy – not because of anything we ourselves have done but for his own purpose and by his own grace. This grace had already been granted to us, in Christ Jesus, before the beginning of time, but it has only been revealed by the Appearing of our saviour Christ Jesus. He abolished death, and he has proclaimed life and immortality through the Good News.

Gospel Acclamation

Glory and praise to you, O Christ!
From the bright cloud the Father's voice was heard:
"This is my Son, the Beloved. Listen to him."
Glory and praise to you, O Christ!   Matthew 17:5

Gospel   Matthew 17:1-9

His face shone like the sun.

Jesus took with him Peter and James and his brother John and led them up a high mountain where they could be alone. There in their presence he was transfigured; his face shone like the sun and his clothes became as white as the light. Suddenly Moses and Elijah appeared to them; they were talking with him. Then Peter spoke to Jesus. "Lord," he said "it is wonderful for us to be here; if you wish, I will make three tents here, one for you, one for Moses and one for Elijah." He was still speaking when suddenly a bright cloud covered them with shadow, and from the cloud there came a voice which said, "This is my Son, the Beloved; he enjoys my favour. Listen to him." When they heard this, the disciples fell on their faces, overcome with fear. But Jesus came up and touched them. "Stand up," he said "do not be afraid." And when they raised their eyes they saw no one but only Jesus.

As they came down from the mountain Jesus gave them this order. "Tell no one about the vision until the Son of Man has risen from the dead."

The Creed is said.

Prayer over the Offerings

May this sacrifice, O Lord, we pray,
cleanse us of our faults
and sanctify your faithful in body and mind
for the celebration of the paschal festivities.
Through Christ our Lord.

Preface

It is truly right and just, our duty and our salvation,
always and everywhere to give you thanks,
Lord, holy Father, almighty and eternal God,
through Christ our Lord.

For after he had told the disciples of his coming Death,
on the holy mountain he manifested to them his glory,
to show, even by the testimony of the law and the prophets,
that the Passion leads to the glory of the Resurrection.

And so, with the Powers of heaven,
we worship you constantly on earth,
and before your majesty
without end we acclaim:
Holy, Holy, Holy Lord God of hosts…

Communion Antiphon

This is my beloved Son, with whom I am well pleased;
listen to him.   Matthew 17:5

Prayer after Communion

As we receive these glorious mysteries,
we make thanksgiving to you, O Lord,
for allowing us while still on earth
to be partakers even now of the things of heaven.
Through Christ our Lord.

Prayer over the People

Bless your faithful, we pray, O Lord,
with a blessing that endures for ever,
and keep them faithful
to the Gospel of your Only Begotten Son,
so that they may always desire and at last attain
that glory whose beauty he showed in his own Body,
to the amazement of his Apostles.
Through Christ our Lord.

THIRD SUNDAY OF LENT – A

Christ, the spring of life.

Through baptism Christ becomes within us a source of the living waters of grace. Through the Holy Spirit the love of God is poured into our hearts and our spiritual thirst is quenched. We come alive. We become in our turn the wells of God's goodness at which people will drink.

Entrance Antiphon
My eyes are always on the Lord,
for he rescues my feet from the snare.
Turn to me and have mercy on me,
for I am alone and poor.   cf. Psalm 24:15-16

or

When I prove my holiness among you,
I will gather you from all the foreign lands;
and I will pour clean water upon you
and cleanse you from all your impurities,
and I will give you a new spirit, says the Lord.   cf. Ezekiel 36:23-26

The Gloria is not said or sung.

Collect
O God, author of every mercy and of all goodness,
who in fasting, prayer and almsgiving
have shown us a remedy for sin,
look graciously on this confession of our lowliness,
that we, who are bowed down by our conscience,
may always be lifted up by your mercy.
Through our Lord Jesus Christ, your Son,
who lives and reigns with you in the unity of the Holy Spirit,
one God, for ever and ever.

First Reading   Exodus 17:3-7

Give us water to drink.

Tormented by thirst, the people complained against Moses. "Why did you bring us out of Egypt?" they said. "Was it so that I should die of thirst, my children too, and my cattle?" Moses appealed to the Lord. "How am I to deal with this people?" he said. "A little more and they will stone me!" The Lord said to Moses, "Take with you some of the elders of Israel and move on to the forefront of the people; take in your hand the staff with which you struck the river, and go. I shall be standing before you there on the rock, at Horeb. You must strike the rock, and water will flow from it for the people to drink." This is what Moses did, in the sight of the elders of Israel. The place was named Massah and Meribah because of the grumbling of the sons of Israel and because they put the Lord to the test by saying, "Is the Lord with us, or not?"

Psalm   Psalm 94

R.   **O that today you would listen to his voice:**
      "Harden not your hearts."

1. Come, ring out our joy to the Lord;
    hail the rock who saves us.
    Let us come before him, giving thanks,
    with songs let us hail the Lord. R.

2. Come in; let us bow and bend low;
    let us kneel before the God who made us
    for he is our God and we
    the people who belong to his pasture,
    the flock that is led by his hand. R.

3. O that today you would listen to his voice!
    "Harden not your hearts as at Meribah,
    as on that day at Massah in the desert
    when your fathers put me to the test;
    when they tried me, though they saw my work." R.

Second Reading   Romans 5:1-2. 5-8

The love of God has been poured into our hearts by the Holy Spirit
which has been given us.

Through our Lord Jesus Christ by faith we are judged righteous
and at peace with God, since it is by faith and through Jesus that we
have entered this state of grace in which we can boast about looking
forward to God's glory. This hope is not deceptive, because the love
of God has been poured into our hearts by the Holy Spirit which
has been given us. We were still helpless when at his appointed
moment Christ died for sinful men. It is not easy to die even for
a good man – though of course for someone really worthy, a man
might be prepared to die – but what proves that God loves us is that
Christ died for us while we were still sinners.

Gospel Acclamation

Glory to you, O Christ, you are the Word of God!
Lord, you are really the saviour of the world;
give me the living water, so that I may never get thirsty.
Glory to you, O Christ, you are the Word of God!   cf. John 4:42. 15

Gospel   John 4:5-42

A spring of water welling up to eternal life.

Jesus came to the Samaritan town called Sychar, near the land that
Jacob gave to his son Joseph. Jacob's well is there and Jesus, tired
by the journey, sat straight down by the well. It was about the sixth
hour. When a Samaritan woman came to draw water, Jesus said to
her, "Give me a drink." His disciples had gone into the town to buy
food. The Samaritan woman said to him, "What? You are a Jew
and you ask me, a Samaritan, for a drink?" – Jews, in fact, do not
associate with Samaritans. Jesus replied:

"If you only knew what God is offering
and who it is that is saying to you:
Give me a drink,
you would have been the one to ask,
and he would have given you living water."

"You have no bucket, sir," she answered "and the well is deep: how
could you get this living water? Are you a greater man than our
father Jacob who gave us this well and drank from it himself with
his sons and his cattle?" Jesus replied:

> "Whoever drinks this water
> will get thirsty again;
> but anyone who drinks the water that I shall give
> will never be thirsty again:
> the water that I shall give
> will turn into a spring inside him, welling up to eternal life."

"Sir," said the woman "give me some of that water, so that I may never get thirsty and never have to come here again to draw water."

"Go and call your husband", said Jesus to her, "and come back here." The woman answered, "I have no husband." He said to her, "You are right to say, 'I have no husband'; for although you have had five, the one you have now is not your husband. You spoke the truth there."

"I see you are a prophet, sir", said the woman. "Our fathers worshipped on this mountain, while you say that Jerusalem is the place where one ought to worship." Jesus said:

> "Believe me, woman, the hour is coming
> when you will worship the Father
> neither on this mountain nor in Jerusalem.
> You worship what you do not know;
> we worship what we do know;
> for salvation comes from the Jews.
> But the hour will come – in fact it is here already –
> when true worshippers will worship the Father in spirit and
>   truth:
> that is the kind of worshipper
> the Father wants.
> God is spirit,
> and those who worship
> must worship in spirit and truth."

The woman said to him, "I know that Messiah – that is, Christ – is coming; and when he comes he will tell us everything." "I who am speaking to you," said Jesus, "I am he."

At this point his disciples returned, and were surprised to find him speaking to a woman, though none of them asked, "What do you want from her?" or, "Why are you talking to her?" The woman put down her water jar and hurried back to the town to tell the people, "Come and see a man who has told me everything I ever did;

I wonder if he is the Christ?" This brought people out of the town and they started walking towards him.

Meanwhile, the disciples were urging him, "Rabbi, do have something to eat." But he said, "I have food to eat that you do not know about." So the disciples asked one another, "Has someone been bringing him food?" But Jesus said:

> "My food
> is to do the will of the one who sent me,
> and to complete his work.
> Have you not got a saying:
> Four months and then the harvest?
> Well, I tell you:
> Look around you, look at the fields;
> already they are white, ready for harvest!
> Already the reaper is being paid his wages,
> already he is bringing in the grain for eternal life,
> and thus sower and reaper rejoice together.
> for here the proverb holds good:
> one sows, another reaps;
> I sent you to reap
> a harvest you had not worked for.
> Others worked for it;
> and you have come into the rewards of their trouble."

Many Samaritans of that town had believed in him on the strength of the woman's testimony when she said, "He told me all I have ever done," so, when the Samaritans came up to him, they begged him to stay with them. He stayed for two days, and when he spoke to them many more came to believe; and they said to the woman, "Now we no longer believe because of what you told us; we have heard him ourselves and we know that he really is the saviour of the world."

The Creed is said.

Prayer over the Offerings
Be pleased, O Lord, with these sacrificial offerings,
and grant that we who beseech pardon for our own sins,
may take care to forgive our neighbour.
Through Christ our Lord.

Preface

It is truly right and just, our duty and our salvation,
always and everywhere to give you thanks,
Lord, holy Father, almighty and eternal God,
through Christ our Lord.

For when he asked the Samaritan woman for water to drink,
he had already created the gift of faith within her
and so ardently did he thirst for her faith,
that he kindled in her the fire of divine love.

And so we, too, give you thanks
and with the Angels
praise your mighty deeds, as we acclaim:
Holy, Holy, Holy Lord God of hosts…

Communion Antiphon

For anyone who drinks it, says the Lord,
the water I shall give will become in him
a spring welling up to eternal life.

John 4:13-14

Prayer after Communion

As we receive the pledge
of things yet hidden in heaven
and are nourished while still on earth
with the Bread that comes from on high,
we humbly entreat you, O Lord,
that what is being brought about in us in mystery
may come to true completion.
Through Christ our Lord.

Prayer over the People

Direct, O Lord, we pray, the hearts of your faithful,
and in your kindness grant your servants this grace:
that, abiding in the love of you and their neighbour,
they may fulfil the whole of your commands.
Through Christ our Lord.

FOURTH SUNDAY OF LENT – A

Christ our shepherd and king.
Jesus Christ is descended from the line of David, a shepherd who was anointed
king by the prophet Samuel. Christ is our king who guides us with the tender
care of a shepherd. With him by our side we shall want for nothing, even
though we walk in the valley of darkness.

Entrance Antiphon
Rejoice, Jerusalem, and all who love her.
Be joyful, all who were in mourning;
exult and be satisfied at her consoling breast.   cf. Isaiah 66:10-11

The Gloria is not said or sung.

Collect
O God, who through your Word
reconcile the human race to yourself in a wonderful way,
grant, we pray,
that with prompt devotion and eager faith
the Christian people may hasten
toward the solemn celebrations to come.
Through our Lord Jesus Christ, your Son,
who lives and reigns with you in the unity of the Holy Spirit,
one God, for ever and ever.

First Reading   1 Samuel 16:1. 6-7. 10-13
David is anointed king of Israel.
The Lord said to Samuel, "Fill your horn with oil and go. I am
sending you to Jesse of Bethlehem, for I have chosen myself a king
among his sons." When Samuel arrived, he caught sight of Eliab and
thought, "Surely the Lord's anointed one stands there before him,"
but the Lord said to Samuel, "Take no notice of his appearance or
his height for I have rejected him; God does not see as man sees;
man looks at appearances but the Lord looks at the heart." Jesse

presented his seven sons to Samuel, but Samuel said to Jesse, "The Lord has not chosen these." He then asked Jesse, "Are these all the sons you have?" He answered, "There is still one left, the youngest; he is out looking after the sheep." Then Samuel said to Jesse, "Send for him; we will not sit down to eat until he comes." Jesse had him sent for, a boy of fresh complexion, with fine eyes and pleasant bearing. The Lord said, "Come, anoint him, for this is the one." At this, Samuel took the horn of oil and anointed him where he stood with his brothers; and the spirit of the Lord seized on David and stayed with him from that day on.

Psalm   Psalm 22

R. **The Lord is my shepherd;**
    there is nothing I shall want.

1. The Lord is my shepherd;
   there is nothing I shall want.
   Fresh and green are the pastures
   where he gives me repose.
   Near restful waters he leads me,
   to revive my drooping spirit. R.

2. He guides me along the right path;
   he is true to his name.
   If I should walk in the valley of darkness
   no evil would I fear.
   You are there with your crook and your staff;
   with these you give me comfort. R.

3. You have prepared a banquet for me
   in the sight of my foes.
   My head you have anointed with oil;
   my cup is overflowing. R.

4. Surely goodness and kindness shall follow me
   all the days of my life.
   In the Lord's own house shall I dwell
   for ever and ever. R.

Second Reading   Ephesians 5:8-14

Rise from the dead, and Christ will shine on you.

You were darkness once, but now you are light in the Lord; be like children of light, for the effects of the light are seen in complete goodness and right living and truth. Try to discover what the Lord wants of you, having nothing to do with the futile works of darkness but exposing them by contrast. The things which are done in secret are things that people are ashamed even to speak of; but anything exposed by the light will be illuminated and anything illuminated turns into light. That is why it is said:

> Wake up from your sleep,
> rise from the dead,
> and Christ will shine on you.

Gospel Acclamation

Glory to you, O Christ, you are the Word of God!
I am the light of the world, says the Lord;
anyone who follows me will have the light of life.
Glory to you, O Christ, you are the Word of God!   John 8:12

Gospel   John 9:1-41

He went off and washed himself, and came away with his sight restored.

As Jesus went along, he saw a man who had been blind from birth.

His disciples asked him, "Rabbi, who sinned, this man or his parents, for him to have been born blind?" "Neither he nor his parents sinned," Jesus answered "he was born blind so that the works of God might be displayed in him.

> "As long as the day lasts
> I must carry out the work of the one who sent me;
> the night will soon be here when no one can work.
> As long as I am in the world
> I am the light of the world."

Having said this,

he spat on the ground, made a paste with the spittle, put this over the eyes of the blind man and said to him, "Go and wash in the Pool of Siloam" (a name that means "sent"). So the blind man went off and washed himself, and came away with his sight restored.

His neighbours and people who earlier had seen him begging said, "Isn't this the man who used to sit and beg?" Some said, "Yes, it is the same one." Others said, "No, he only looks like him." The man himself said, "I am the man."

So they said to him, "Then how do your eyes come to be open?" "The man called Jesus", he answered, "made a paste, daubed my eyes with it and said to me, 'Go and wash at Siloam'; so I went, and when I washed I could see." They asked, "Where is he?" "I don't know," he answered.

They brought the man who had been blind to the Pharisees. It had been a sabbath day when Jesus made the paste and opened the man's eyes, so when the Pharisees asked him how he had come to see, he said, "He put a paste on my eyes, and I washed, and I can see." Then some of the Pharisees said, "This man cannot be from God: he does not keep the sabbath." Others said, "How could a sinner produce signs like this?" And there was disagreement among them. So they spoke to the blind man again, "What have you to say about him yourself, now that he has opened your eyes?" "He is a prophet" replied the man.

However, the Jews would not believe that the man had been blind and had gained his sight, without first sending for his parents and asking them, "Is this man really your son who you say was born blind? If so, how is it that he is now able to see?" His parents answered, "We know he is our son and we know he was born blind, but we don't know how it is that he can see now, or who opened his eyes. He is old enough: let him speak for himself." His parents spoke like this out of fear of the Jews, who had already agreed to expel from the synagogue anyone who should acknowledge Jesus as the Christ. This was why his parents said, "He is old enough; ask him."

So the Jews again sent for the man and said to him, "Give glory to God! For our part, we know that this man is a sinner." The man answered, "I don't know if he is a sinner; I only know that I was

blind and now I can see." They said to him, "What did he do to
you? How did he open your eyes?" He replied, "I have told you once
and you wouldn't listen. Why do you want to hear it all again? Do
you want to become his disciples too?" At this they hurled abuse at
him: "You can be his disciple," they said, "we are disciples of Moses:
we know that God spoke to Moses, but as for this man, we don't
know where he comes from." The man replied, "Now here is an
astonishing thing! He has opened my eyes, and you don't know
where he comes from! We know that God doesn't listen to sinners,
but God does listen to men who are devout and do his will. Ever
since the world began it is unheard of for anyone to open the eyes
of a man who was born blind; if this man were not from God, he
couldn't do a thing."

"Are you trying to teach us," they replied "and you a sinner
through and through, since you were born!" And they drove him
away.

Jesus heard they had driven him away, and when he found him
he said to him, "Do you believe in the Son of Man?" "Sir," the man
replied "tell me who he is so that I may believe in him." Jesus said,
"You are looking at him; he is speaking to you." The man said,
"Lord, I believe," and worshipped him.

Jesus said:

"It is for judgement
that I have come into this world,
so that those without sight may see
and those with sight turn blind."

Hearing this, some Pharisees who were present said to him, "We are
not blind, surely?" Jesus replied:

"Blind? If you were,
you would not be guilty,
but since you say, 'We see,'
your guilt remains."

The Creed is said.

Prayer over the Offerings

We place before you with joy these offerings,
which bring eternal remedy, O Lord,
praying that we may both faithfully revere them
and present them to you, as is fitting,
for the salvation of all the world.
Through Christ our Lord.

Preface

It is truly right and just, our duty and our salvation,
always and everywhere to give you thanks,
Lord, holy Father, almighty and eternal God,
through Christ our Lord.

By the mystery of the Incarnation,
he has led the human race that walked in darkness
into the radiance of the faith
and has brought those born in slavery to ancient sin
through the waters of regeneration
to make them your adopted children.

Therefore, all creatures of heaven and earth
sing a new song in adoration,
and we, with all the host of Angels,
cry out, and without end acclaim:
Holy, Holy, Holy Lord God of hosts…

Communion Antiphon

The Lord anointed my eyes: I went, I washed,
I saw and I believed in God.   cf. John 9:11. 38

Prayer after Communion

O God, who enlighten everyone who comes into this world,
illuminate our hearts, we pray,
with the splendour of your grace,
that we may always ponder
what is worthy and pleasing to your majesty
and love you in all sincerity.
Through Christ our Lord.

Prayer over the People
Look upon those who call to you, O Lord,
and sustain the weak;
give life by your unfailing light
to those who walk in the shadow of death,
and bring those rescued by your mercy from every evil
to reach the highest good.
Through Christ our Lord.

FIFTH SUNDAY OF LENT – A

Christ our resurrection and our life.
When we are dead through sin, Christ brings us his Spirit so that we may
truly live the new life of grace. We are brothers and sisters of Christ through
God's Spirit who raised Jesus from the dead.

Entrance Antiphon

Give me justice, O God,
and plead my cause against a nation that is faithless.
From the deceitful and cunning rescue me,
for you, O God, are my strength.   cf. Psalm 42:1-2

The Gloria is not said or sung.

Collect

By your help, we beseech you, Lord our God,
may we walk eagerly in that same charity
with which, out of love for the world,
your Son handed himself over to death.
Through our Lord Jesus Christ, your Son,
who lives and reigns with you in the unity of the Holy Spirit,
one God, for ever and ever.

First Reading   Ezekiel 37:12-14

I shall put my spirit in you, and you will live.

The Lord says this: I am now going to open your graves; I mean to
raise you from your graves, my people, and lead you back to the soil
of Israel. And you will know that I am the Lord, when I open your
graves and raise you from your graves, my people. And I shall put
my spirit in you, and you will live, and I shall resettle you on your
own soil; and you will know that I, the Lord, have said and done
this – it is the Lord who speaks.

Psalm　　　　　　　　　　　　　　　　　　Psalm 129

R.　**With the Lord there is mercy
　　and fullness of redemption.**

1. Out of the depths I cry to you, O Lord,
   Lord, hear my voice!
   O let your ears be attentive
   to the voice of my pleading. R.

2. If you, O Lord, should mark our guilt,
   Lord, who would survive?
   But with you is found forgiveness:
   for this we revere you. R.

3. My soul is waiting for the Lord,
   I count on his word.
   My soul is longing for the Lord
   more than watchman for daybreak.
   (Let the watchman count on daybreak
   and Israel on the Lord.) R.

4. Because with the Lord there is mercy
   and fullness of redemption,
   Israel indeed he will redeem
   from all its iniquity. R.

Second Reading　　　　　　　　　　　　Romans 8:8-11
The Spirit of him who raised Jesus from the dead is living in you.
People who are interested only in unspiritual things can never be
pleasing to God. Your interests, however, are not in the unspiritual,
but in the spiritual, since the Spirit of God has made his home in
you. In fact, unless you possessed the Spirit of Christ you would not
belong to him. Though your body may be dead it is because of sin,
but if Christ is in you then your spirit is life itself because you have
been justified; and if the Spirit of him who raised Jesus from the
dead is living in you, then he who raised Jesus from the dead will
give life to your own mortal bodies through his Spirit living in you.

Gospel Acclamation
Glory and praise to you, O Christ!
I am the resurrection and the life, says the Lord;
who ever believes in me will never die.
Glory and praise to you, O Christ!   John 11:25. 26

Gospel   John 11:1-45
I am the resurrection and the life.

There was a man named Lazarus who lived in the village of Bethany with the two sisters, Mary and Martha, and he was ill. It was the same Mary, the sister of the sick man Lazarus, who anointed the Lord with ointment and wiped his feet with her hair.

The sisters sent this message to Jesus, "Lord, the man you love is ill." On receiving the message, Jesus said, "This sickness will not end in death but in God's glory, and through it the Son of God will be glorified."

Jesus loved Martha and her sister and Lazarus, yet when he learned that Lazarus was ill he stayed where he was for two more days before saying to the disciples, "Let us go to Judaea."

The disciples said, "Rabbi, it is not long since the Jews wanted to stone you; are you going back again?" Jesus replied:

"Are there not twelve hours in the day?
A man can walk in the daytime without stumbling
because he has the light of this world to see by;
but if he walks at night he stumbles,
because there is no light to guide him."

He said that and then added, "Our friend Lazarus is resting, I am going to wake him." The disciples said to him "Lord, if he is able to rest he is sure to get better." The phrase Jesus used referred to the death of Lazarus, but they thought that by "rest" he meant "sleep", so Jesus put it plainly, "Lazarus is dead; and for your sake I am glad I was not there because now you will believe. But let us go to him." Then Thomas – known as the Twin – said to the other disciples, "Let us go too, and die with him."

On arriving, Jesus found that Lazarus had been in the tomb for four days already. Bethany is only about two miles from

Jerusalem, and many Jews had come to Martha and Mary to sympathise with them over their brother. When Martha heard that Jesus had come she went to meet him. Mary remained sitting in the house. Martha said to Jesus, "If you had been here, my brother would not have died, but I know that even now, whatever you ask of God, he will grant you." "Your brother", said Jesus to her, "will rise again." Martha said, "I know he will rise again at the resurrection on the last day." Jesus said:

"I am the resurrection and the life.
If anyone believes in me, even though he dies he will live,
and whoever lives and believes in me
will never die.
Do you believe this?"

"Yes Lord," she said, "I believe that you are the Christ, the Son of God, the one who was to come into this world."

When she had said this, she went and called her sister Mary, saying in a low voice, "The Master is here and he wants to see you." Hearing this, Mary got up quickly and went to him. Jesus had not yet come into the village; he was still at the place where Martha had met him. When the Jews who were in the house sympathising with Mary saw her get up so quickly and go out, they followed her, thinking that she was going to the tomb to weep there.

Mary went to Jesus, and as soon as she saw him she threw herself at his feet, saying, "Lord, if you had been here, my brother would not have died." At the sight of her tears, and those of the Jews who followed her,

Jesus said in great distress, with a sigh that came straight from the heart, "Where have you put him?" They said, "Lord, come and see." Jesus wept; and the Jews said, "See how much he loved him!" But there were some who remarked, "He opened the eyes of the blind man, could he not have prevented this man's death?" Still sighing, Jesus reached the tomb: it was a cave with a stone to close the opening. Jesus said, "Take the stone away." Martha said to him "Lord, by now he will smell; this is the fourth day." Jesus replied, "Have I not told you that if you believe you will see the glory of God?" So they took away the stone. Then Jesus lifted up his eyes and said:

"Father, I thank you for hearing my prayer.
I knew indeed that you always hear me,
but I speak
for the sake of all these who stand round me,
so that they may believe it was you who sent me."

When he had said this, he cried out in a loud voice, "Lazarus, here! Come out!" The dead man came out, his feet and hands bound with bands of stuff and a cloth round his face. Jesus said to them, "Unbind him, let him go free."

Many of the Jews who had come to visit Mary and had seen what he did believed in him.

The Creed is said.

Prayer over the Offerings
Hear us, almighty God,
and, having instilled in your servants
the teachings of the Christian faith,
graciously purify them
by the working of this sacrifice.
Through Christ our Lord.

Preface
It is truly right and just, our duty and our salvation,
always and everywhere to give you thanks,
Lord, holy Father, almighty and eternal God,
through Christ our Lord.

For as true man he wept for Lazarus his friend
and as eternal God raised him from the tomb,
just as, taking pity on the human race,
he leads us by sacred mysteries to new life.

Through him the host of Angels adores your majesty
and rejoices in your presence for ever.
May our voices, we pray, join with theirs
in one chorus of exultant praise, as we acclaim:
Holy, Holy, Holy Lord God of hosts…

Communion Antiphon
Everyone who lives and believes in me
will not die for ever, says the Lord.   cf. John 11:26

Prayer after Communion
We pray, almighty God,
that we may always be counted among the members of Christ,
in whose Body and Blood we have communion.
Who lives and reigns for ever and ever.

Prayer over the People
Bless, O Lord, your people,
who long for the gift of your mercy,
and grant that what, at your prompting, they desire
they may receive by your generous gift.
Through Christ our Lord.

The liturgies of Holy Week begin on p. 186.

FIRST SUNDAY OF LENT – B

Alive through the waters of Baptism.
We die to the world and live to God through the waters of Baptism. We will
still be tempted, as Christ was in the wilderness, but if we repent and believe
the Gospel we have nothing to fear. The Lord is faithful to those who keep their
promises to him.

Entrance Antiphon
When he calls on me, I will answer him;
I will deliver him and give him glory,
I will grant him length of days.   cf. Psalm 90:15-16

The Gloria is not said or sung.

Collect
Grant, almighty God,
through the yearly observances of holy Lent,
that we may grow in understanding
of the riches hidden in Christ
and by worthy conduct pursue their effects.
Through our Lord Jesus Christ, your Son,
who lives and reigns with you in the unity of the Holy Spirit,
one God, for ever and ever.

First Reading   **Genesis 9:8-15**
God's covenant with Noah after he had saved him from the waters
of the flood.
God spoke to Noah and his sons, "See, I establish my Covenant
with you, and with your descendants after you; also with every
living creature to be found with you, birds, cattle and every wild
beast with you: everything that came out of the ark, everything that
lives on the earth. I establish my Covenant with you: no thing of
flesh shall be swept away again by the waters of the flood. There
shall be no flood to destroy the earth again."

God said, "Here is the sign of the Covenant I make between myself and you and every living creature with you for all generations: I set my bow in the clouds and it shall be a sign of the Covenant between me and the earth. When I gather the clouds over the earth and the bow appears in the clouds, I will recall the Covenant between myself and you and every living creature of every kind. And so the waters shall never again become a flood to destroy all things of flesh."

Psalm   Psalm 24

R.   **Your ways, Lord, are faithfulness and love**
      for those who keep your covenant.

1. Lord, make me know your ways.
    Lord, teach me your paths.
    Make me walk in your truth, and teach me:
    for you are God my saviour. R.

2. Remember your mercy, Lord,
    and the love you have shown from of old.
    In your love remember me,
    because of your goodness, O Lord. R.

3. The Lord is good and upright.
    He shows the path to those who stray,
    he guides the humble in the right path;
    he teaches his way to the poor. R.

Second Reading   1 Peter 3:18-22
That water is a type of the baptism which saves you now.
Christ himself, innocent though he was, died once for sins, died for the guilty, to lead us to God. In the body he was put to death, in the spirit he was raised to life, and, in the spirit, he went to preach to the spirits in prison. Now it was long ago, when Noah was still building that ark which saved only a small group of eight people "by water", and when God was still waiting patiently, that these spirits refused to believe. That water is a type of the baptism which saves you now,

and which is not the washing off of physical dirt but a pledge made to God from a good conscience, through the resurrection of Jesus Christ, who has entered heaven and is at God's right hand, now that he has made the angels of the Dominations and Powers his subjects.

Gospel Acclamation
Praise to you, O Christ, king of eternal glory!
Man does not live on bread alone,
but on every word that comes from the mouth of God.
Praise to you, O Christ, king of eternal glory!   Matthew 4:4

Gospel   Mark 1:12-15
Jesus was tempted by Satan, and the angels looked after him.
The Spirit drove Jesus out into the wilderness and he remained there for forty days, and was tempted by Satan. He was with the wild beasts, and the angels looked after him.

After John had been arrested, Jesus went into Galilee. There he proclaimed the Good News from God. "The time has come" he said "and the kingdom of God is close at hand. Repent, and believe the Good News."

The Creed is said.

Prayer over the Offerings
Give us the right dispositions, O Lord, we pray,
to make these offerings,
for with them we celebrate the beginning
of this venerable and sacred time.
Through Christ our Lord.

Preface of the First Sunday of Lent, pp. 116-117.

Communion Antiphon
One does not live by bread alone,
but by every word that comes forth from the mouth of God.
Matthew 4:4

or

The Lord will conceal you with his pinions,
and under his wings you will trust.   cf. Psalm 90:4

Prayer after Communion
Renewed now with heavenly bread,
by which faith is nourished, hope increased,
and charity strengthened,
we pray, O Lord,
that we may learn to hunger for Christ,
the true and living Bread,
and strive to live by every word
which proceeds from your mouth.
Through Christ our Lord.

Prayer over the People
May bountiful blessing, O Lord, we pray,
come down upon your people,
that hope may grow in tribulation,
virtue be strengthened in temptation,
and eternal redemption be assured.
Through Christ our Lord.

SECOND SUNDAY OF LENT – B

God did not spare his own Son.
Christ did not come to explain away suffering; he came to fulfil it. Like
Abraham we are called to be prepared to sacrifice everything to God, and thus
we find fulfilment. God will refuse us nothing now that Christ, risen from the
dead, pleads our cause in heaven.

Entrance Antiphon
Of you my heart has spoken: Seek his face.
It is your face, O Lord, that I seek;
hide not your face from me.   cf. Psalm 26:8-9

or

Remember your compassion, O Lord,
and your merciful love, for they are from of old.
Let not our enemies exult over us.
Redeem us, O God of Israel, from all our distress.
                                                    cf. Psalm 24:6. 2. 22

The Gloria is not said or sung.

Collect
O God, who have commanded us
to listen to your beloved Son,
be pleased, we pray,
to nourish us inwardly by your word,
that, with spiritual sight made pure,
we may rejoice to behold your glory.
Through our Lord Jesus Christ, your Son,
who lives and reigns with you in the unity of the Holy Spirit,
one God, for ever and ever.

First Reading   Genesis 22:1-2. 9-13. 15-18
The sacrifice of Abraham, our father in faith.
God put Abraham to the test. "Abraham, Abraham" he called. "Here
I am" he replied. "Take your son," God said "your only child Isaac,

whom you love, and go to the land of Moriah. There you shall offer him as a burnt offering, on a mountain I will point out to you."

When they arrived at the place God had pointed out to him, Abraham built an altar there and arranged the wood. Then he stretched out his hand and seized the knife to kill his son.

But the angel of the Lord called to him from heaven. "Abraham, Abraham" he said. "I am here" he replied. "Do not raise your hand against the boy" the angel said. "Do not harm him, for now I know you fear God. You have not refused me your son, your only son." Then looking up, Abraham saw a ram caught by its horns in a bush. Abraham took the ram and offered it as a burnt-offering in place of his son.

The angel of the Lord called Abraham a second time from heaven. "I swear by my own self – it is the Lord who speaks – because you have done this, because you have not refused me your son, your only son, I will shower blessings on you, I will make your descendants as many as the stars of heaven and the grains of sand on the seashore. Your descendants shall gain possession of the gates of their enemies. All the nations of the earth shall bless themselves by your descendants, as a reward for your obedience."

Psalm   Psalm 115

R. **I will walk in the presence of the Lord**
    in the land of the living.

1. I trusted, even when I said:
   "I am sorely afflicted."
   O precious in the eyes of the Lord
   is the death of his faithful. R.

2. Your servant, Lord, your servant am I;
   you have loosened my bonds.
   A thanksgiving sacrifice I make:
   I will call on the Lord's name. R.

3. My vows to the Lord I will fulfil
   before all his people,
   in the courts of the house of the Lord,
   in your midst, O Jerusalem. R.

Second Reading   Romans 8:31-34

God did not spare his own Son.

With God on our side who can be against us? Since God did not spare his own Son, but gave him up to benefit us all, we may be certain, after such a gift, that he will not refuse anything he can give. Could anyone accuse those that God has chosen? When God acquits, could anyone condemn? Could Christ Jesus? No! He not only died for us – he rose from the dead, and there at God's right hand he stands and pleads for us.

Gospel Acclamation

Glory and praise to you, O Christ!

From the bright cloud the Father's voice was heard:

"This is my Son, the Beloved. Listen to him!"

Glory and praise to you, O Christ!   Matthew 17:5

Gospel   Mark 9:2-10

This is my Son, the Beloved.

Jesus took with him Peter and James and John and led them up a high mountain where they could be alone by themselves. There in their presence he was transfigured: his clothes became dazzlingly white, whiter than any earthly bleacher could make them. Elijah appeared to them with Moses; and they were talking with Jesus. Then Peter spoke to Jesus. "Rabbi", he said "it is wonderful for us to be here; so let us make three tents, one for you, one for Moses and one for Elijah." He did not know what to say; they were so frightened. And a cloud came, covering them in shadow; and there came a voice from the cloud, "This is my Son, the Beloved. Listen to him." Then suddenly, when they looked round, they saw no one with them any more but only Jesus.

As they came down the mountain he warned them to tell no one what they had seen, until after the Son of Man had risen from the dead. They observed the warning faithfully, though among themselves they discussed what "rising from the dead" could mean.

The Creed is said.

Prayer over the Offerings

May this sacrifice, O Lord, we pray,
cleanse us of our faults
and sanctify your faithful in body and mind
for the celebration of the paschal festivities.
Through Christ our Lord.

Preface of the Second Sunday of Lent, p. 121.

Communion Antiphon

This is my beloved Son, with whom I am well pleased;
listen to him.   Matthew 17:5

Prayer after Communion

As we receive these glorious mysteries,
we make thanksgiving to you, O Lord,
for allowing us while still on earth
to be partakers even now of the things of heaven.
Through Christ our Lord.

Prayer over the People

Bless your faithful, we pray, O Lord,
with a blessing that endures for ever,
and keep them faithful
to the Gospel of your Only Begotten Son,
so that they may always desire and at last attain
that glory whose beauty he showed in his own Body,
to the amazement of his Apostles.
Through Christ our Lord.

THIRD SUNDAY OF LENT – B

We preach a crucified Christ.
Christ gave his life in love to his Father; in a way beyond human
understanding, his death shows the wisdom of God. Christ rose again from the
dead; the message of eternal life is contained in Christ's death and resurrection.

Entrance Antiphon
My eyes are always on the Lord,
for he rescues my feet from the snare.
Turn to me and have mercy on me,
for I am alone and poor.   cf. Psalm 24:15-16

or

When I prove my holiness among you,
I will gather you from all the foreign lands;
and I will pour clean water upon you
and cleanse you from all your impurities,
and I will give you a new spirit, says the Lord.   cf. Ezekiel 36:23-26

The Gloria is not said or sung.

Collect
O God, author of every mercy and of all goodness,
who in fasting, prayer and almsgiving
have shown us a remedy for sin,
look graciously on this confession of our lowliness,
that we, who are bowed down by our conscience,
may always be lifted up by your mercy.
Through our Lord Jesus Christ, your Son,
who lives and reigns with you in the unity of the Holy Spirit,
one God, for ever and ever.

The readings for Year A may be used as an alternative. If this is
done, the Preface and Communion Antiphon for Year A are also
used. See pp. 123-127.

First Reading   Exodus 20:1-17

The Law was given through Moses.

God spoke all these words. He said, "I am the Lord your God who brought you out of the land of Egypt, out of the house of slavery.

"You shall have no gods except me.

"You shall not make yourself a carved image or any likeness of anything in heaven or on earth beneath or in the waters under the earth; you shall not bow down to them or serve them. For I, the Lord your God, am a jealous God and I punish the father's fault in the sons, the grandsons, and the great-grandsons of those who hate me; but I show kindness to thousands of those who love me and keep my commandments.

"You shall not utter the name of the Lord your God to misuse it, for the Lord will not leave unpunished the man who utters his name to misuse it.

"Remember the sabbath day and keep it holy.

For six days you shall labour and do all your work, but the seventh day is a sabbath for the Lord your God. You shall do no work that day, neither you nor your son nor your daughter nor your servants, men or women, nor your animals nor the stranger who lives with you. For in six days the Lord made the heavens and the earth and the sea and all that these hold, but on the seventh day he rested; that is why the Lord has blessed the sabbath and made it sacred.

"Honour your father and your mother so that you may have a long life in the land that the Lord your God has given to you.

"You shall not kill.

"You shall not commit adultery.

"You shall not steal.

"You shall not bear false witness against your neighbour.

"You shall not covet your neighbour's house. You shall not covet your neighbour's wife, or his servant, man or woman, or his ox, or his donkey, or anything that is his."

Psalm   Psalm 18

R.   **You, Lord, have the message of eternal life.**

1. The law of the Lord is perfect,
   it revives the soul.
   The rule of the Lord is to be trusted,
   it gives wisdom to the simple. R.

2. The precepts of the Lord are right,
   they gladden the heart.
   The command of the Lord is clear,
   it gives light to the eyes. R.

3. The fear of the Lord is holy,
   abiding for ever.
   The decrees of the Lord are truth
   and all of them just. R.

4. They are more to be desired than gold,
   than the purest of gold
   and sweeter are they than honey,
   than honey from the comb. R.

Second Reading   1 Corinthians 1:22-25
Here we are preaching a crucified Christ, an obstacle to men, but to
those who are called, the wisdom of God.
While the Jews demand miracles and the Greeks look for wisdom,
here are we preaching a crucified Christ; to the Jews an obstacle
that they cannot get over, to the pagans madness, but to those who
have been called, whether they are Jews or Greeks, a Christ who is
the power and the wisdom of God. For God's foolishness is wiser
than human wisdom, and God's weakness is stronger than human
strength.

Gospel Acclamation
Praise to you, O Christ, king of eternal glory!
I am the resurrection and the life, says the Lord,
whoever believes in me will never die.
Praise to you, O Christ, king of eternal glory!   John 11:25. 26

or

Praise to you, O Christ, king of eternal glory!
God loved the world so much that he gave his only Son;
everyone who believes in him has eternal life.
Praise to you, O Christ, king of eternal glory!   John 3:16

Gospel   John 2:13-25
Destroy this sanctuary, and in three days I will raise it up.
Just before the Jewish Passover Jesus went up to Jerusalem, and in
the Temple he found people selling cattle and sheep and pigeons,
and the money changers sitting at their counters there. Making a
whip out of some cord, he drove them all out of the Temple, cattle
and sheep as well, scattered the money changers' coins, knocked
their tables over and said to the pigeon-sellers, "Take all this out of
here and stop turning my Father's house into a market." Then his
disciples remembered the words of scripture: Zeal for your house
will devour me. The Jews intervened and said, "What sign can you
show us to justify what you have done?" Jesus answered, "Destroy
this sanctuary, and in three days I will raise it up." The Jews replied,
"It has taken forty-six years to build this sanctuary: are you going
to raise it up in three days?" But he was speaking of the sanctuary
that was his body, and when Jesus rose from the dead, his disciples
remembered that he had said this, and they believed the scripture
and the words he had said.

During his stay in Jerusalem for the Passover many believed in
his name when they saw the signs that he gave, but Jesus knew them
all and did not trust himself to them; he never needed evidence
about any man; he could tell what a man had in him.

The Creed is said.

Prayer over the Offerings
Be pleased, O Lord, with these sacrificial offerings,
and grant that we who beseech pardon for our own sins,
may take care to forgive our neighbour.
Through Christ our Lord.

Preface I or II of Lent, pp. 493-494.

Communion Antiphon
The sparrow finds a home,
and the swallow a nest for her young:
by your altars, O Lord of hosts, my King and my God.
Blessed are they who dwell in your house,
for ever singing your praise.   cf. Psalm 83:4-5

Prayer after Communion
As we receive the pledge
of things yet hidden in heaven
and are nourished while still on earth
with the Bread that comes from on high,
we humbly entreat you, O Lord,
that what is being brought about in us in mystery
may come to true completion.
Through Christ our Lord.

Prayer over the People
Direct, O Lord, we pray, the hearts of your faithful,
and in your kindness grant your servants this grace:
that, abiding in the love of you and their neighbour,
they may fulfil the whole of your commands.
Through Christ our Lord.

FOURTH SUNDAY OF LENT – B

The Lord is generous with his mercy.
Jesus Christ is given to the world by God the Father so that those who believe
in his name may be saved. He brings us new life because previously we were
dead through sin but now we are saved through grace. We are God's work of
art, created in Jesus Christ.

Entrance Antiphon
Rejoice, Jerusalem, and all who love her.
Be joyful, all who were in mourning;
exult and be satisfied at her consoling breast.   cf. Isaiah 66:10-11

The Gloria is not said or sung.

Collect
O God, who through your Word
reconcile the human race to yourself in a wonderful way,
grant, we pray,
that with prompt devotion and eager faith
the Christian people may hasten
toward the solemn celebrations to come.
Through our Lord Jesus Christ, your Son,
who lives and reigns with you in the unity of the Holy Spirit,
one God, for ever and ever.

The readings for Year A may be used as an alternative. If this is
done, the Preface and Communion Antiphon for Year A are also
used. See pp. 128-133.

First Reading   **2 Chronicles 36:14-16. 19-23**
The wrath and mercy of God are revealed in the exile and in the
release of his people.
All the heads of the priesthood, and the people too, added infidelity
to infidelity, copying all the shameful practices of the nations and

defiling the Temple that the Lord had consecrated for himself in Jerusalem. The Lord, the God of their ancestors, tirelessly sent them messenger after messenger, since he wished to spare his people and his house. But they ridiculed the messengers of God, they despised his words, they laughed at his prophets, until at last the wrath of the Lord rose so high against his people that there was no further remedy.

Their enemies burned down the Temple of God, demolished the walls of Jerusalem, set fire to all its palaces, and destroyed everything of value in it. The survivors were deported by Nebuchadnezzar to Babylon; they were to serve him and his sons until the kingdom of Persia came to power. This is how the word of the Lord was fulfilled that he spoke through Jeremiah, "Until this land has enjoyed its sabbath rest, until seventy years have gone by, it will keep sabbath throughout the days of its desolation."

And in the first year of Cyrus king of Persia, to fulfil the word of the Lord that was spoken through Jeremiah, the Lord roused the spirit of Cyrus king of Persia to issue a proclamation and to have it publicly displayed throughout his kingdom: "Thus speaks Cyrus king of Persia, 'The Lord, the God of heaven, has given me all the kingdoms of the earth; he has ordered me to build him a Temple in Jerusalem, in Judah. Whoever there is among you of all his people, may his God be with him! Let him go up.' "

Psalm   Psalm 136

R. **O let my tongue
    cleave to my mouth
    if I remember you not!**

1. By the rivers of Babylon
    there we sat and wept,
    remembering Zion;
    on the poplars that grew there
    we hung up our harps. R.

2. For it was there that they asked us,
    our captors, for songs,
    our oppressors, for joy.
    "Sing to us," they said,
    "one of Zion's songs." R.

3. O how could we sing
    the song of the Lord
    on alien soil?
    If I forget you, Jerusalem,
    let my right hand wither! R.

4. O let my tongue
    cleave to my mouth
    if I remember you not,
    if I prize not Jerusalem
    above all my joys! R.

Second Reading   Ephesians 2:4-10

You who were dead through your sins have been saved through grace.

God loved us with so much love that he was generous with his mercy: when we were dead through our sins, he brought us to life with Christ – it is through grace that you have been saved – and raised us up with him and gave us a place with him in heaven, in Christ Jesus.

This was to show for all ages to come, through his goodness towards us in Christ Jesus, how infinitely rich he is in grace. Because it is by his grace that you have been saved, through faith; not by anything of your own, but by a gift from God; not by anything that you have done, so that nobody can claim the credit. We are God's work of art, created in Christ Jesus to live the good life as from the beginning he had meant us to live it.

Gospel Acclamation

Glory and praise to you, O Christ!
God loved the world so much that he gave his only Son;
everyone who believes in him has eternal life.
Glory and praise to you, O Christ!   John 3:16

Gospel   John 3:14-21

God sent his Son so that through him the world might be saved.

Jesus said to Nicodemus:

"The Son of Man must be lifted up
as Moses lifted up the serpent in the desert,

so that everyone who believes may have eternal life in him.
Yes, God loved the world so much
that he gave his only Son,
so that everyone who believes in him may not be lost
but may have eternal life.
For God sent his Son into the world
not to condemn the world,
but so that through him the world might be saved.
No one who believes in him will be condemned;
but whoever refuses to believe is condemned already,
because he has refused to believe
in the name of God's only Son.
On these grounds is sentence pronounced:
that though the light has come into the world
men have shown they prefer darkness to the light
because their deeds were evil.
And indeed, everybody who does wrong
hates the light and avoids it,
for fear his actions should be exposed;
but the man who lives by the truth
comes out into the light,
so that it may be plainly seen that what he does is done in God."

The Creed is said.

Prayer over the Offerings
We place before you with joy these offerings,
which bring eternal remedy, O Lord,
praying that we may both faithfully revere them
and present them to you, as is fitting,
for the salvation of all the world.
Through Christ our Lord.

Preface I or II of Lent, pp. 493-494.

Communion Antiphon
Jerusalem is built as a city bonded as one together.
It is there that the tribes go up, the tribes of the Lord,
to praise the name of the Lord.   cf. Psalm 121:3-4

Prayer after Communion
O God, who enlighten everyone who comes into this world,
illuminate our hearts, we pray,
with the splendour of your grace,
that we may always ponder
what is worthy and pleasing to your majesty
and love you in all sincerity.
Through Christ our Lord.

Prayer over the People
Look upon those who call to you, O Lord,
and sustain the weak;
give life by your unfailing light
to those who walk in the shadow of death,
and bring those rescued by your mercy from every evil
to reach the highest good.
Through Christ our Lord.

FIFTH SUNDAY OF LENT – B

I will write my law on their hearts.
Christ, like a grain of wheat that dies in order to produce new life, dies for us.
Following his example, we are called to realise that if we want eternal life we
have to be prepared to give our lives to God. The Lord writes his law in our
hearts and we submit humbly to his will, even in times of pain and suffering.
There is no greater school in which to grow in holiness.

Entrance Antiphon

Give me justice, O God,
and plead my cause against a nation that is faithless.
From the deceitful and cunning rescue me,
for you, O God, are my strength.   cf. Psalm 42:1-2

The Gloria is not said or sung.

Collect

By your help, we beseech you, Lord our God,
may we walk eagerly in that same charity
with which, out of love for the world,
your Son handed himself over to death.
Through our Lord Jesus Christ, your Son,
who lives and reigns with you in the unity of the Holy Spirit,
one God, for ever and ever.

The readings for Year A may be used as an alternative. If this is
done, the Preface and Communion Antiphon for Year A are also
used. See pp. 135-140.

First Reading   Jeremiah 31:31-34

I will make a new covenant and never call their sin to mind.

See, the days are coming – it is the Lord who speaks – when I will
make a new covenant with the House of Israel and the House of
Judah, but not a covenant like the one I made with their ancestors
on the day I took them by the hand to bring them out of the land

of Egypt. They broke that covenant of mine, so I had to show them who was master. It is the Lord who speaks. No, this is the covenant I will make with the House of Israel when those days arrive – it is the Lord who speaks. Deep within them I will plant my Law, writing it on their hearts. Then I will be their God and they shall be my people. There will be no further need for neighbour to try to teach neighbour, or brother to say to brother, "Learn to know the Lord!" No, they will all know me, the least no less than the greatest – it is the Lord who speaks – since I will forgive their iniquity and never call their sin to mind.

Psalm   Psalm 50

R.   **A pure heart create for me, O God.**

1. Have mercy on me, God, in your kindness.
    In your compassion blot out my offence.
    O wash me more and more from my guilt
    and cleanse me from my sin. R.

2. A pure heart create for me, O God,
    put a steadfast spirit within me.
    Do not cast me away from your presence,
    nor deprive me of your holy spirit. R.

3. Give me again the joy of your help;
    with a spirit of fervour sustain me,
    that I may teach transgressors your ways
    and sinners may return to you. R.

Second Reading   Hebrews 5:7-9

He learnt to obey and became the source of eternal salvation.

During his life on earth, Christ offered up prayer and entreaty, aloud and in silent tears, to the one who had the power to save him out of death, and he submitted so humbly that his prayer was heard. Although he was Son, he learnt to obey through suffering; but having been made perfect, he became for all who obey him the source of eternal salvation.

Gospel Acclamation

Glory, to you, O Christ, you are the Word of God!
If a man serves me, says the Lord, he must follow me;
wherever I am, my servant will be there too.
Glory to you, O Christ, you are the Word of God!   John 12:26

Gospel   John 12:20-33

If a grain of wheat falls on the ground and dies, it yields a rich harvest.
Among those who went up to worship at the festival were some
Greeks. These approached Philip, who came from Bethsaida in
Galilee, and put this request to him, "Sir, we should like to see
Jesus." Philip went to tell Andrew, and Andrew and Philip together
went to tell Jesus. Jesus replied to them:

"Now the hour has come
for the Son of Man to be glorified.
I tell you, most solemnly,
unless a wheat grain falls on the ground and dies,
it remains only a single grain;
but if it dies,
it yields a rich harvest.
Anyone who loves his life loses it;
anyone who hates his life in this world
will keep it for the eternal life.
If a man serves me, he must follow me,
wherever I am, my servant will be there too.
If anyone serves me, my Father will honour him.
Now my soul is troubled.
What shall I say:
Father, save me from this hour?
But it was for this very reason that I have come to this hour.
Father, glorify your name!"

A voice came from heaven, "I have glorified it, and I will glorify it
again."

People standing by, who heard this, said it was a clap of thunder;
others said, "It was an angel speaking to him." Jesus answered, "It
was not for my sake that this voice came, but for yours.

"Now sentence is being passed on this world;

now the prince of this world is to be overthrown.
And when I am lifted up from the earth,
I shall draw all men to myself."

By these words he indicated the kind of death he would die.

The Creed is said.

Prayer over the Offerings
Hear us, almighty God,
and, having instilled in your servants
the teachings of the Christian faith,
graciously purify them
by the working of this sacrifice.
Through Christ our Lord.

Preface I or II of Lent, pp. 493-494.

Communion Antiphon
Amen, Amen I say to you: Unless a grain of wheat
falls to the ground and dies, it remains a single grain.
But if it dies, it bears much fruit.   John 12:24

Prayer after Communion
We pray, almighty God,
that we may always be counted among the members of Christ,
in whose Body and Blood we have communion.
Who lives and reigns for ever and ever.

Prayer over the People
Bless, O Lord, your people,
who long for the gift of your mercy,
and grant that what, at your prompting, they desire
they may receive by your generous gift.
Through Christ our Lord.

The liturgies of Holy Week begin on p. 186.

FIRST SUNDAY OF LENT – C

The Lord hears our voice.
In the midst of all our troubles the Lord hears us and will lead us into a
promised land of peace if only we are prepared to follow him. There is no
temptation that cannot be overcome if we are open to the Spirit who tells us
that Jesus is Lord, raised from the dead by God. Through the risen Jesus, God
is always with us, just as in the Old Testament the Lord rescued the Jews from
slavery in Egypt.

Entrance Antiphon
When he calls on me, I will answer him;
I will deliver him and give him glory,
I will grant him length of days.

cf. Psalm 90:15-16

The Gloria is not said or sung.

Collect
Grant, almighty God,
through the yearly observances of holy Lent,
that we may grow in understanding
of the riches hidden in Christ
and by worthy conduct pursue their effects.
Through our Lord Jesus Christ, your Son,
who lives and reigns with you in the unity of the Holy Spirit,
one God, for ever and ever.

First Reading   Deuteronomy 26:4-10
The creed of the chosen people.
Moses said to the people: "The priest shall take the pannier from
your hand and lay it before the altar of the Lord your God. Then, in
the sight of the Lord your God, you must make this pronouncement:
'My father was a wandering Aramaean. He went down into Egypt
to find refuge there, few in numbers; but there he became a nation,
great, mighty, and strong. The Egyptians ill-treated us, they gave
us no peace and inflicted harsh slavery on us. But we called on the
Lord, the God of our fathers. The Lord heard our voice and saw our

misery, our toil and our oppression; and the Lord brought us out of Egypt with mighty hand and outstretched arm, with great terror, and with signs and wonders. He brought us here and gave us this land, a land where milk and honey flow. Here then I bring the first-fruits of the produce of the soil that you, Lord, have given me.' You must then lay them before the Lord your God, and bow down in the sight of the Lord your God."

Psalm   Psalm 90

R.   **Be with me, O Lord, in my distress.**

1. He who dwells in the shelter of the Most High
   and abides in the shade of the Almighty
   says to the Lord: "My refuge,
   my stronghold, my God in whom I trust!" R.

2. Upon you no evil shall fall,
   no plague approach where you dwell.
   For you has he commanded his angels,
   to keep you in all your ways. R.

3. They shall bear you upon their hands
   lest you strike your foot against a stone.
   On the lion and the viper you will tread
   and trample the young lion and the dragon. R.

4. His love he set on me, so I will rescue him;
   protect him for he knows my name.
   When he calls I shall answer: "I am with you."
   I will save him in distress and give him glory. R.

Second Reading   Romans 10:8-13
The creed of the Christian.
Scripture says: The word, that is the faith we proclaim, is very near to you, it is on your lips and in your heart. If your lips confess that Jesus is Lord and if you believe in your heart that God raised him from the dead, then you will be saved. By believing from the heart you are made righteous; by confessing with your lips you are saved. When scripture says: those who believe in him will have no cause

for shame, it makes no distinction between Jew and Greek: all belong to the same Lord who is rich enough, however many ask for his help, for everyone who calls on the name of the Lord will be saved.

Gospel Acclamation
Praise to you, O Christ, king of eternal glory!
Man does not live on bread alone,
but on every word that comes from the mouth of God.
Praise to you, O Christ, king of eternal glory!   Matthew 4:4

Gospel   Luke 4:1-13
Jesus was led by the Spirit through the wilderness and was tempted there.

Filled with the Holy Spirit, Jesus left the Jordan and was led by the Spirit through the wilderness, being tempted there by the devil for forty days. During that time he ate nothing and at the end he was hungry. Then the devil said to him, "If you are the Son of God, tell this stone to turn into a loaf." But Jesus replied, "Scripture says: Man does not live on bread alone."

Then leading him to a height, the devil showed him in a moment of time all the kingdoms of the world and said to him, "I will give you all this power and the glory of these kingdoms, for it has been committed to me and I give it to anyone I choose. Worship me, then, and it shall all be yours." But Jesus answered him. "Scripture says:

You must worship the Lord your God,
and serve him alone."

Then he led him to Jerusalem and made him stand on the parapet of the Temple. "If you are the Son of God," he said to him "throw yourself down from here, for scripture says:

He will put his angels in charge of you
to guard you,

and again:

They will hold you up on their hands
in case you hurt your foot against a stone."

But Jesus answered him, "It has been said:

You must not put the Lord your God to the test."

Having exhausted all these ways of tempting him, the devil left him, to return at the appointed time.

The Creed is said.

Prayer over the Offerings
Give us the right dispositions, O Lord, we pray,
to make these offerings,
for with them we celebrate the beginning
of this venerable and sacred time.
Through Christ our Lord.

Preface of the First Sunday of Lent, pp. 116-117.

Communion Antiphon
One does not live by bread alone,
but by every word that comes forth from the mouth of God.

Matthew 4:4

or

The Lord will conceal you with his pinions,
and under his wings you will trust.

cf. Psalm 90:4

Prayer after Communion
Renewed now with heavenly bread,
by which faith is nourished, hope increased,
and charity strengthened,
we pray, O Lord,
that we may learn to hunger for Christ,
the true and living Bread,
and strive to live by every word
which proceeds from your mouth.
Through Christ our Lord.

Prayer over the People
May bountiful blessing, O Lord, we pray,
come down upon your people,
that hope may grow in tribulation,
virtue be strengthened in temptation,
and eternal redemption be assured.
Through Christ our Lord.

SECOND SUNDAY OF LENT – C

The Lord will transfigure us.
Jesus was transfigured in the presence of his apostles, and they realised how
wonderful it is to be with him. Jesus is always with us, ready to transform our
lives if through faith we believe in his power. He is as faithful to us as the Lord
was to Abraham, who put his faith in him.

Entrance Antiphon

Of you my heart has spoken: Seek his face.
It is your face, O Lord, that I seek;
hide not your face from me.

cf. Psalm 26:8-9

or

Remember your compassion, O Lord,
and your merciful love, for they are from of old.
Let not our enemies exult over us.
Redeem us, O God of Israel, from all our distress.

cf. Psalm 24:6. 2. 22

The Gloria is not said or sung.

Collect

O God, who have commanded us
to listen to your beloved Son,
be pleased, we pray,
to nourish us inwardly by your word,
that, with spiritual sight made pure,
we may rejoice to behold your glory.
Through our Lord Jesus Christ, your Son,
who lives and reigns with you in the unity of the Holy Spirit,
one God, for ever and ever.

First Reading   Genesis 15:5-12. 17-18

God enters into a Covenant with Abraham, the man of faith.
Taking Abram outside the Lord said, "Look up to heaven and count
the stars if you can. Such will be your descendants" he told him. Abram
put his faith in the Lord, who counted this as making him justified.

"I am the Lord" he said to him "who brought you out of Ur of the Chaldaeans to make you heir to this land." "My Lord, the Lord" Abram replied "how am I to know that I shall inherit it?" He said to him, "Get me a three-year-old heifer, a three-year-old goat, a three-year-old ram, a turtledove and a young pigeon." He brought him all these, cut them in half and put half on one side and half facing it on the other; but the birds he did not cut in half. Birds of prey came down on the carcasses but Abram drove them off.

Now as the sun was setting Abram fell into a deep sleep, and terror seized him. When the sun had set and darkness had fallen, there appeared a smoking furnace and a firebrand that went between the halves. That day the Lord made a Covenant with Abram in these terms:

> "To your descendants I give this land,
> from the wadi of Egypt to the Great River."

Psalm   Psalm 26

R. **The Lord is my light and my help.**

1. The Lord is my light and my help;
   whom shall I fear?
   The Lord is the stronghold of my life;
   before whom shall I shrink? R.

2. O Lord, hear my voice when I call;
   have mercy and answer.
   Of you my heart has spoken:
   "Seek his face." R.

3. It is your face, O Lord, that I seek;
   hide not your face.
   Dismiss not your servant in anger;
   you have been my help. R.

4. I am sure I shall see the Lord's goodness
   in the land of the living.
   Hope in him, hold firm and take heart.
   Hope in the Lord! R.

Second Reading   **Philippians 3:17 – 4:1**
Christ will transfigure our bodies into copies of his glorious body.

My brothers, be united in following my rule of life. Take as your models everybody who is already doing this and study them as you used to study us. I have told you often, and I repeat it today with tears, there are many who are behaving as the enemies of the cross of Christ. They are destined to be lost. They make foods into their god and they are proudest of something they ought to think shameful; the things they think important are earthly things.

For us, our homeland is in heaven, and from heaven comes the saviour we are waiting for, the Lord Jesus Christ, and he will transfigure these wretched bodies of ours into copies of his glorious body. He will do that by the same power with which he can subdue the whole universe.

So then, my brothers and dear friends, do not give way but remain faithful in the Lord. I miss you very much, dear friends; you are my joy and my crown.

Gospel Acclamation
Glory and praise to you, O Christ!
From the bright cloud the Father's voice was heard:
"This is my Son, the Beloved. Listen to him!"
Glory and praise to you, O Christ!   Matthew 17:5

Gospel   **Luke 9:28-36**
As Jesus prayed, the aspect of his face was changed.

Jesus took with him Peter and John and James and went up the mountain to pray. As he prayed, the aspect of his face was changed and his clothing became brilliant as lightning. Suddenly there were two men there talking to him; they were Moses and Elijah appearing in glory, and they were speaking of his passing which he was to accomplish in Jerusalem. Peter and his companions were heavy with sleep, but they kept awake and saw his glory and the two men standing with him. As these were leaving him, Peter said to Jesus, "Master, it is wonderful for us to be here; so let us make three tents, one for you, one for Moses and one for Elijah." He did not know what he was saying. As he spoke, a cloud came and covered them with shadow; and when they went into the cloud the disciples were afraid. And a voice came from the cloud saying, "This is my Son, the Chosen One. Listen to him." And after the voice had spoken, Jesus was found alone. The disciples kept silence and, at that time, told no one what they had seen.

The Creed is said.

Prayer over the Offerings
May this sacrifice, O Lord, we pray,
cleanse us of our faults
and sanctify your faithful in body and mind
for the celebration of the paschal festivities.
Through Christ our Lord.

Preface of the Second Sunday of Lent, p. 121.

Communion Antiphon
This is my beloved Son, with whom I am well pleased;
listen to him.   Matthew 17:5

Prayer after Communion
As we receive these glorious mysteries,
we make thanksgiving to you, O Lord,
for allowing us while still on earth
to be partakers even now of the things of heaven.
Through Christ our Lord.

Prayer over the People
Bless your faithful, we pray, O Lord,
with a blessing that endures for ever,
and keep them faithful
to the Gospel of your Only Begotten Son,
so that they may always desire and at last attain
that glory whose beauty he showed in his own Body,
to the amazement of his Apostles.
Through Christ our Lord.

THIRD SUNDAY OF LENT – C

God said: "I am who I am."
God the creator of all things is faithful to his word. God is the one who acts in
our lives. Despite God's goodness to the Hebrew people in the desert, many of
them fell away from their belief. The events that happened to them in the Old
Testament can teach us not to make the same mistakes.

Entrance Antiphon
My eyes are always on the Lord,
for he rescues my feet from the snare.
Turn to me and have mercy on me,
for I am alone and poor.   cf. Psalm 24:15-16

or

When I prove my holiness among you,
I will gather you from all the foreign lands;
and I will pour clean water upon you
and cleanse you from all your impurities,
and I will give you a new spirit, says the Lord.   cf. Ezekiel 36:23-26

The Gloria is not said or sung.

Collect
O God, author of every mercy and of all goodness,
who in fasting, prayer and almsgiving
have shown us a remedy for sin,
look graciously on this confession of our lowliness,
that we, who are bowed down by our conscience,
may always be lifted up by your mercy.
Through our Lord Jesus Christ, your Son,
who lives and reigns with you in the unity of the Holy Spirit,
one God, for ever and ever.

The readings for Year A may be used as an alternative. If this is
done, the Preface and Communion Antiphon for Year A are also
used. See pp. 123-127.

First Reading   Exodus 3:1-8. 13-15

I Am has sent me to you.

Moses was looking after the flock of Jethro, his father-in-law, priest of Midian. He led his flock to the far side of the wilderness and came to Horeb, the mountain of God. There the angel of the Lord appeared to him in the shape of a flame of fire, coming from the middle of a bush. Moses looked; there was the bush blazing but it was not being burnt up. "I must go and look at this strange sight," Moses said "and see why the bush is not burnt." Now the Lord saw him go forward to look, and God called to him from the middle of the bush. "Moses, Moses!" he said. "Here I am" he answered. "Come no nearer" he said. "Take off your shoes, for the place on which you stand is holy ground. I am the God of your father," he said, "the God of Abraham, the God of Isaac and the God of Jacob." At this Moses covered his face, afraid to look at God.

And the Lord said, "I have seen the miserable state of my people in Egypt. I have heard their appeal to be free of their slave-drivers. Yes, I am well aware of their sufferings. I mean to deliver them out of the hands of the Egyptians and bring them up out of that land to a land rich and broad, a land where milk and honey flow."

Then Moses said to God, "I am to go, then, to the sons of Israel and say to them, 'The God of your fathers has sent me to you.' But if they ask me what his name is, what am I to tell them?" And God said to Moses, "I Am who I Am. This" he added "is what you must say to the sons of Israel: 'The Lord, the God of your fathers, the God of Abraham, the God of Isaac, and the God of Jacob, has sent me to you.' This is my name for all time; by this name I shall be invoked for all generations to come."

Psalm   Psalm 102

R.   **The Lord is compassion and love.**

1. My soul, give thanks to the Lord,
   all my being, bless his holy name.
   My soul give thanks to the Lord
   and never forget all his blessings. R.

2. It is he who forgives all your guilt,
   who heals every one of your ills,
   who redeems your life from the grave,
   who crowns you with love and compassion. R.

3. The Lord does deeds of justice,
   gives judgement for all who are oppressed.
   He made known his ways to Moses
   and his deeds to Israel's sons. R.

4. The Lord is compassion and love,
   slow to anger and rich in mercy.
   For as the heavens are high above the earth
   so strong is his love for those who fear him. R.

Second Reading   1 Corinthians 10:1-6. 10-12
The life of the people under Moses in the desert was written down
to be a lesson for us.

I want to remind you, brothers, how our fathers were all
guided by a cloud above them and how they all passed through the
sea. They were all baptised into Moses in this cloud and in this sea;
all ate the same spiritual food and all drank the same spiritual drink,
since they all drank from the spiritual rock that followed them as
they went, and that rock was Christ. In spite of this, most of them
failed to please God and their corpses littered the desert.

These things all happened as warnings for us, not to have the
wicked lusts for forbidden things that they had. You must never
complain: some of them did, and they were killed by the Destroyer.

All this happened to them as a warning, and it was written down
to be a lesson for us who are living at the end of the age. The man
who thinks he is safe must be careful that he does not fall.

Gospel Acclamation
Glory to you, O Christ, you are the Word of God!
Repent, says the Lord,
for the kingdom of heaven is close at hand.
Glory to you, O Christ, you are the Word of God!   Matthew 4:17

Gospel   Luke 13:1-9
Unless you repent you will all perish as they did.

Some people arrived and told Jesus about the Galileans whose blood Pilate had mingled with that of their sacrifices. At this he said to them, "Do you suppose these Galileans who suffered like that were greater sinners than any other Galileans? They were not, I tell you. No; but unless you repent you will all perish as they did. Or those eighteen on whom the tower at Siloam fell and killed them? Do you suppose that they were more guilty than all the other people living in Jerusalem? They were not, I tell you. No; but unless you repent you will all perish as they did."

He told this parable: "A man had a fig tree planted in his vineyard, and he came looking for fruit on it but found none. He said to the man who looked after the vineyard, 'Look here, for three years now I have been coming to look for fruit on this fig tree and finding none. Cut it down: why should it be taking up the ground?' 'Sir,' the man replied 'leave it one more year and give me time to dig round it and manure it: it may bear fruit next year; if not, then you can cut it down.'"

The Creed is said.

Prayer over the Offerings
Be pleased, O Lord, with these sacrificial offerings,
and grant that we who beseech pardon for our own sins,
may take care to forgive our neighbour.
Through Christ our Lord.

Preface I or II of Lent, pp. 493-494.

Communion Antiphon
The sparrow finds a home,
and the swallow a nest for her young:
by your altars, O Lord of hosts, my King and my God.
Blessed are they who dwell in your house,
for ever singing your praise.   cf. Psalm 83:4-5

Prayer after Communion
As we receive the pledge
of things yet hidden in heaven
and are nourished while still on earth
with the Bread that comes from on high,
we humbly entreat you, O Lord,
that what is being brought about in us in mystery
may come to true completion.
Through Christ our Lord.

Prayer over the People
Direct, O Lord, we pray, the hearts of your faithful,
and in your kindness grant your servants this grace:
that, abiding in the love of you and their neighbour,
they may fulfil the whole of your commands.
Through Christ our Lord.

FOURTH SUNDAY OF LENT – C

God our Father reconciles us to himself in Christ.
Christ is our new creation. In him we are reborn. When we were dead
through sin Christ came to reconcile us to the Father. Now we are ambassadors
for Christ and are privileged to proclaim the Good News. Christ takes away
our shame if only we will return to the Father's house as prodigal sons and
daughters confessing our weakness and waywardness.

Entrance Antiphon
Rejoice, Jerusalem, and all who love her.
Be joyful, all who were in mourning;
exult and be satisfied at her consoling breast.   cf. Isaiah 66:10-11

The Gloria is not said or sung.

Collect
O God, who through your Word
reconcile the human race to yourself in a wonderful way,
grant, we pray,
that with prompt devotion and eager faith
the Christian people may hasten
toward the solemn celebrations to come.
Through our Lord Jesus Christ, your Son,
who lives and reigns with you in the unity of the Holy Spirit,
one God, for ever and ever.

The readings for Year A may be used as an alternative. If this is
done, the Preface and Communion Antiphon for Year A are also
used. See pp. 128-133.

First Reading   Joshua 5:9-12

The People of God keep the Passover on their entry into the
promised land.

The Lord said to Joshua, "Today I have taken the shame of Egypt
away from you."

  The Israelites pitched their camp at Gilgal and kept the Passover
there on the fourteenth day of the month, at evening in the plain
of Jericho. On the morrow of the Passover they tasted the produce
of that country, unleavened bread and roasted ears of corn, that
same day. From that time, from their first eating of the produce
of that country, the manna stopped falling. And having manna no
longer, the Israelites fed from that year onwards on what the land
of Canaan yielded.

Psalm   Psalm 33

R. **Taste and see that the Lord is good.**

1. I will bless the Lord at all times,
      his praise always on my lips;
      in the Lord my soul shall make its boast.
      The humble shall hear and be glad. R.

2. Glorify the Lord with me.
      Together let us praise his name.
      I sought the Lord and he answered me;
      from all my terrors he set me free. R.

3. Look towards him and be radiant;
      let your faces not be abashed.
      This poor man called; the Lord heard him
      and rescued him from all his distress. R.

Second Reading   2 Corinthians 5:17-21

God reconciled us to himself through Christ.

For anyone who is in Christ, there is a new creation; the old
creation has gone, and now the new one is here. It is all God's work.
It was God who reconciled us to himself through Christ and gave

us the work of handing on this reconciliation. In other words, God in Christ was reconciling the world to himself, not holding men's faults against them, and he has entrusted to us the news that they are reconciled. So we are ambassadors for Christ; it is as though God were appearing through us, and the appeal that we make in Christ's name is: be reconciled to God. For our sake God made the sinless one into sin, so that in him we might become the goodness of God.

Gospel Acclamation

Praise and honour to you, Lord Jesus!
I will leave this place and go to my father and say:
"Father, I have sinned against heaven and against you."
Praise and honour to you, Lord Jesus!   Luke 15:18

Gospel   Luke 15:1-3. 11-32

Your brother here was dead and has come to life.

The tax collectors and the sinners were all seeking the company of Jesus to hear what he had to say, and the Pharisees and the scribes complained. "This man" they said "welcomes sinners and eats with them." So he spoke this parable to them:

"A man had two sons. The younger said to his father, 'Father, let me have the share of the estate that would come to me.' So the father divided the property between them. A few days later, the younger son got together everything he had and left for a distant country where he squandered his money on a life of debauchery.

"When he had spent it all, that country experienced a severe famine, and now he began to feel the pinch, so he hired himself out to one of the local inhabitants who put him on his farm to feed the pigs. And he would willingly have filled his belly with the husks the pigs were eating but no one offered him anything. Then he came to his senses and said, 'How many of my father's paid servants have more food than they want, and here am I dying of hunger! I will leave this place and go to my father and say: Father, I have sinned against heaven and against you; I no longer deserve to be called your son; treat as one of your paid servants.' So he left the place and went back to his father.

"While he was still a long way off, his father saw him and was moved with pity. He ran to the boy, clasped him in his arms and kissed him tenderly. Then his son said, 'Father, I have sinned against heaven and against you. I no longer deserve to be called your son.' But the father said to his servants, 'Quick! Bring out the best robe and put it on him; put a ring on his finger and sandals on his feet. Bring the calf we have been fattening, and kill it; we are going to have a feast, a celebration, because this son of mine was dead and has come back to life; he was lost and is found.' And they began to celebrate.

"Now the elder son was out in the fields, and on his way back, as he drew near the house, he could hear music and dancing. Calling one of the servants he asked what it was all about. 'Your brother has come' replied the servant 'and your father has killed the calf we had fattened because he has got him back safe and sound.' He was angry then and refused to go in, and his father came out to plead with him; but he answered his father, 'Look, all these years I have slaved for you and never once disobeyed your orders, yet you never offered me so much as a kid for me to celebrate with my friends. But for this son of yours, when he comes back after swallowing up your property – he and his women – you kill the calf we had been fattening.'

"The father said, 'My son, you are with me always and all I have is yours. But it is only right we should celebrate and rejoice, because your brother here was dead and has come to life; he was lost and is found.'"

The Creed is said.

Prayer over the Offerings
We place before you with joy these offerings,
which bring eternal remedy, O Lord,
praying that we may both faithfully revere them
and present them to you, as is fitting,
for the salvation of all the world.
Through Christ our Lord.

Preface I or II of Lent, pp. 493-494.

Communion Antiphon
You must rejoice, my son,
for your brother was dead and has come to life;
he was lost and is found.   Luke 15:32

Prayer after Communion
O God, who enlighten everyone who comes into this world,
illuminate our hearts, we pray,
with the splendour of your grace,
that we may always ponder
what is worthy and pleasing to your majesty
and love you in all sincerity.
Through Christ our Lord.

Prayer over the People
Look upon those who call to you, O Lord,
and sustain the weak;
give life by your unfailing light
to those who walk in the shadow of death,
and bring those rescued by your mercy from every evil
to reach the highest good.
Through Christ our Lord.

FIFTH SUNDAY OF LENT – C

The Lord who forgives.
Christ came to show compassion and forgiveness for sinners. He condemned sin but let the woman guilty of adultery go free with the reminder that she was to sin no more. None of us is perfect; we can only hope that we will be saved. We suffer in this life but can accept the loss of everything as so much rubbish if we can only have Christ and be given a share in his resurrection. In this way God, through Christ, is doing something new and is calling us from sinfulness to a life of service.

Entrance Antiphon
Give me justice, O God,
and plead my cause against a nation that is faithless.
From the deceitful and cunning rescue me,
for you, O God, are my strength.

cf. Psalm 42:1-2

The Gloria is not said or sung.

Collect
By your help, we beseech you, Lord our God,
may we walk eagerly in that same charity
with which, out of love for the world,
your Son handed himself over to death.
Through our Lord Jesus Christ, your Son,
who lives and reigns with you in the unity of the Holy Spirit,
one God, for ever and ever.

The readings for Year A may be used as an alternative. If this is done, the Preface and Communion Antiphon for Year A are also used. See pp. 135-140.

First Reading   Isaiah 43:16-21
See, I am doing a new deed, and I will give my chosen people drink.
Thus says the Lord,
who made a way through the sea,
a path in the great waters;

who put chariots and horse in the field
and a powerful army,
which lay there never to rise again,
snuffed out, put out like a wick:

No need to recall the past,
no need to think about what was done before.
See, I am doing a new deed,
even now it comes to light; can you not see it?
Yes, I am making a road in the wilderness,
paths in the wilds.

The wild beasts will honour me,
jackals and ostriches,
because I am putting water in the wilderness
(rivers in the wild)
to give my chosen people drink.
The people I have formed for myself
will sing my praises.

Psalm   Psalm 125

R. **What marvels the Lord worked for us!**
    Indeed we were glad.

1. When the Lord delivered Zion from bondage,
   it seemed like a dream.
   Then was our mouth filled with laughter,
   on our lips there were songs. R.

2. The heathens themselves said: "What marvels
   the Lord worked for them!"
   What marvels the Lord worked for us!
   Indeed we were glad. R.

3. Deliver us, O Lord, from our bondage
   as streams in dry land.
   Those who are sowing in tears
   will sing when they reap. R.

4. They go out, they go out, full of tears,
   carrying seed for the sowing:
   they come back, they come back, full of song,
   carrying their sheaves. R.

Second Reading   Philippians 3:8-14

Reproducing the pattern of his death, I have accepted the loss of everything for Christ.

I believe nothing can happen that will outweigh the supreme advantage of knowing Christ Jesus my Lord. For him I have accepted the loss of everything, and I look on everything as so much rubbish if only I can have Christ and be given a place in him. I am no longer trying for perfection by my own efforts, the perfection that comes from the Law, but I want only the perfection that comes through faith in Christ, and is from God and based on faith. All I want is to know Christ and the power of his resurrection and to share his sufferings by reproducing the pattern of his death. That is the way I can hope to take my place in the resurrection of the dead. Not that I have become perfect yet: I have not yet won, but I am still running, trying to capture the prize for which Christ Jesus captured me. I can assure you my brothers, I am far from thinking that I have already won. All I can say is that I forget the past and I strain ahead for what is still to come; I am racing for the finish, for the prize to which God calls us upwards to receive in Christ Jesus.

Gospel Acclamation

Praise to you, O Christ, king of eternal glory!
Seek good and not evil so that you may live,
and that the Lord God of hosts may really be with you.
Praise to you, O Christ, king of eternal glory!   cf. Amos 5:14

or

Praise to you, O Christ, king of eternal glory!
Now, now – it is the Lord who speaks –
come back to me with all your heart,
for I am all tenderness and compassion.
Praise to you, O Christ, king of eternal glory!   Joel 2:12-13

Gospel   John 8:1-11

If there is one of you who has not sinned, let him be the first to throw a stone at her.

Jesus went to the Mount of Olives. At daybreak he appeared in the Temple again; and as all the people came to him, he sat down and began to teach them.

The scribes and Pharisees brought a woman along who had been caught committing adultery; and making her stand there in full view of everybody, they said to Jesus, "Master, this woman was caught in the very act of committing adultery, and Moses has ordered us in the Law to condemn women like this to death by stoning. What have you to say?" They asked him this as a test, looking for something to use against him. But Jesus bent down and started writing on the ground with his finger. As they persisted with their question, he looked up and said, "If there is one of you who has not sinned, let him be the first to throw a stone at her." Then he bent down and wrote on the ground again. When they heard this they went away one by one, beginning with the eldest, until Jesus was left alone with the woman, who remained standing there. He looked up and said, "Woman, where are they? Has no one condemned you?" "No one, sir," she replied. "Neither do I condemn you," said Jesus "go away, and don't sin any more."

The Creed is said.

Prayer over the Offerings
Hear us, almighty God,
and, having instilled in your servants
the teachings of the Christian faith,
graciously purify them
by the working of this sacrifice.
Through Christ our Lord.

Preface I or II of Lent, pp. 493-494.

Communion Antiphon

Has no one condemned you, woman? No one, Lord.
Neither shall I condemn you. From now on, sin no more.

John 8:10-11

Prayer after Communion

We pray, almighty God,
that we may always be counted among the members of Christ,
in whose Body and Blood we have communion.
Who lives and reigns for ever and ever.

Prayer over the People

Bless, O Lord, your people,
who long for the gift of your mercy,
and grant that what, at your prompting, they desire
they may receive by your generous gift.
Through Christ our Lord.

The liturgies for Holy Week begin on p. 186.

PALM SUNDAY OF THE PASSION OF THE LORD – ABC

Jesus is king!
The triumphal entry of Jesus into Jerusalem gives way to his Passion and Death. Yet within a few days Jesus will rise triumphant from the dead. He is the firm ground of our hope that all sufferings in this life are overcome in the power of his Resurrection.

THE COMMEMORATION OF THE LORD'S ENTRANCE INTO JERUSALEM

First Form: The Procession

The people, holding palm branches, gather in a place distinct from the church to which the procession will move. The following antiphon, or another suitable song, is sung:

Hosanna to the Son of David;
blessed is he who comes in the name of the Lord,
the King of Israel.
Hosanna in the highest.

Matthew 21:9

The priest then makes the Sign of the Cross, greets the people in the usual way and gives a brief introduction, inviting them to take a full part in the celebration of this day, in these or similar words:

Dear brethren (brothers and sisters),
since the beginning of Lent until now
we have prepared our hearts by penance and charitable works.
Today we gather together to herald with the whole Church
the beginning of the celebration
of our Lord's Paschal Mystery,
that is to say, of his Passion and Resurrection.
For it was to accomplish this mystery
that he entered his own city of Jerusalem.
Therefore, with all faith and devotion,
let us commemorate

the Lord's entry into the city for our salvation,
following in his footsteps,
so that, being made by his grace partakers of the Cross,
we may have a share also in his Resurrection and in his life.

Then the priest says one of the following prayers:

Let us pray.

Almighty ever-living God,
sanctify ✠ these branches with your blessing,
that we, who follow Christ the King in exultation,
may reach the eternal Jerusalem through him.
Who lives and reigns for ever and ever. **Amen.**

or

Increase the faith of those who place their hope in you, O God,
and graciously hear the prayers of those who call on you,
that we, who today hold high these branches
to hail Christ in his triumph,
may bear fruit for you by good works accomplished in him.
Who lives and reigns for ever and ever. **Amen.**

The priest sprinkles the branches with holy water.

Then the Gospel concerning the Lord's entrance is proclaimed,
according to the cycle for the year:

A

Gospel   Matthew 21:1-11

Blessings on him who comes in the name of the Lord!

When they were near Jerusalem and had come in sight of Bethphage
on the Mount of Olives, Jesus sent two disciples, saying to them,
"Go to the village facing you, and you will immediately find a
tethered donkey and a colt with her. Untie them and bring them
to me. If anyone says anything to you, you are to say, 'The Master
needs them and will send them back directly.'" This took place to
fulfil the prophecy:

Say to the daughter of Zion:
Look, your king comes to you;
he is humble, he rides on a donkey
and on a colt, the foal of a beast of burden.

So the disciples went out and did as Jesus had told them. They brought the donkey and the colt, then laid their cloaks on their backs and he sat on them. Great crowds of people spread their cloaks on the road, while others were cutting branches from the trees and spreading them in this path. The crowds who went in front of him and those who followed were all shouting:

"Hosanna to the Son of David!
Blessings on him who comes in the name of the Lord!
Hosanna in the highest heavens!"

And when he entered Jerusalem, the whole city was in turmoil. "Who is this?" people asked, and the crowds answered, "This is the prophet Jesus from Nazareth in Galilee."

B

Gospel   Mark 11:1-10
Blessings on him who comes in the name of the Lord!

When they were approaching Jerusalem, in sight of Bethphage and Bethany, close by the Mount of Olives, Jesus sent two of his disciples and said to them, "Go off to the village facing you, and as soon as you enter it you will find a tethered colt that no one has yet ridden. Untie it and bring it here. If anyone says to you, 'What are you doing?' say, 'The Master needs it and will send it back here directly.'" They went off and found a colt tethered near a door in the open street. As they untied it, some men standing there said, "What are you doing, untying that colt?" They gave the answer Jesus had told them, and the men let them go. Then they took the colt to Jesus and threw their cloaks on its back, and he sat on it. Many people spread their cloaks on the road, others greenery which they had cut in the fields. And those who went in front and those who followed were all shouting, "Hosanna! Blessings on the coming kingdom of our father David! Hosanna in the highest heavens!"

or

B

Gospel   John 12:12-16
Blessings on him who comes in the name of the Lord!

The crowds who had come up for the festival heard that Jesus was on his way to Jerusalem. They took branches of palm and went out to meet him, shouting, "Hosanna! Blessings on the King of Israel, who comes in the name of the Lord." Jesus found a young donkey and mounted it – as scripture says: Do not be afraid, daughter of Zion; see, your king is coming, mounted on the colt of a donkey. At the time his disciples did not understand this, but later, after Jesus had been glorified, they remembered that this had been written about him and that this was in fact how they had received him.

C

Gospel   Luke 19:28-40

Blessings on him who comes in the name of the Lord!

Jesus went on ahead, going up to Jerusalem. Now when he was near Bethphage and Bethany, close by the Mount of Olives as it is called, he sent two of the disciples, telling them, "Go off to the village opposite, and as you enter it you will find a tethered colt that no one has yet ridden. Untie it and bring it here. If anyone asks you, 'Why are you untying it?' you are to say this, 'The Master needs it.' " The messengers went off and found everything just as he had told them. As they were untying the colt, its owner said, "Why are you untying that colt?" and they answered, "The Master needs it."

So they took the colt to Jesus, and throwing their garments over its back they helped Jesus on to it. As he moved off, people spread their cloaks in the road, and now, as he was approaching the downward slope of the Mount of Olives, the whole group of disciples joyfully began to praise God at the top of their voices for all the miracles they had seen. They cried out:

"Blessings on the King who comes,
   in the name of the Lord!
Peace in heaven
   and glory in the highest heavens!"

Some Pharisees in the crowd said to him, "Master, check your disciples," but he answered, "I tell you, if these keep silence the stones will cry out."

After the Gospel, a brief homily may be given. Then, before the procession, an invitation may be given by the priest or another minister, in these or similar words:

Dear brethren (brothers and sisters),
like the crowds who acclaimed Jesus in Jerusalem,
let us go forth in peace.

or

Let us go forth in peace.
In the name of Christ. Amen.

The procession to the church where Mass will be celebrated then begins. During the procession, the choir and people may sing the following or other appropriate songs in honour of Christ the King.

Antiphon 1
**The children of the Hebrews, carrying olive branches,
went to meet the Lord, crying out and saying:
Hosanna in the highest.**

This antiphon may be repeated between the verses of the following Psalm:

Psalm 23
The Lord's is the earth and its fullness,
the world, and those who dwell in it.
It is he who set it on the seas;
on the rivers he made it firm. (Antiphon)

Who shall climb the mountain of the Lord?
The clean of hands and pure of heart,
whose soul is not set on vain things,
who has not sworn deceitful words. (Antiphon)

Blessings from the Lord shall he receive,
and right reward from the God who saves him.
Such are the people who seek him,
who seek the face of the God of Jacob. (Antiphon)

O gates, lift high your heads,
grow higher, ancient doors.
Let him enter, the king of glory!

Who is this king of glory?
The Lord, the mighty, the valiant;
the Lord, the valiant in war. (Antiphon)

O gates, lift high your heads;
grow higher, ancient doors.
Let him enter, the king of glory!
Who is this king of glory?
He, the Lord of hosts,
he is the king of glory. (Antiphon)

Antiphon 2

**The children of the Hebrews spread their garments on the road,
crying out and saying: Hosanna to the Son of David;
blessed is he who comes in the name of the Lord.**

This antiphon may be repeated between the verses of the following
Psalm:

Psalm 46

All peoples, clap your hands.
Cry to God with shouts of joy!
For the Lord, the Most High, is awesome,
the great king over all the earth. (Antiphon)

He humbles peoples under us
and nations under our feet.
Our heritage he chose for us,
the pride of Jacob whom he loves.
God goes up with shouts of joy.
The Lord goes up with trumpet blast. (Antiphon)

Sing praise for God; sing praise!
Sing praise to our king; sing praise!
God is king of all earth.
Sing praise with all your skill. (Antiphon)

God reigns over the nations.
God sits upon his holy throne.
The princes of the peoples are assembled

with the people of the God of Abraham.
The rulers of the earth belong to God,
who is greatly exalted. (Antiphon)

Hymn to Christ the King

R. **Glory and honour and praise be to you, Christ,
    King and Redeemer,
    to whom young children cried out loving Hosannas with joy.**

Israel's King are you, King David's magnificent offspring;
you are the ruler who come blest in the name of the Lord. R.

Heavenly hosts on high unite in singing your praises;
men and women on earth and all creation join in. R.

Bearing branches of palm, Hebrews came crowding to greet you;
see how with prayers and hymns we come to pay you our vows. R.

They offered gifts of praise to you, so near to your Passion;
see how we sing this song now to you reigning on high. R.

Those you were pleased to accept; now accept our gifts of devotion,
good and merciful King, lover of all that is good. R.

As the procession enters the church, the following responsory or
another song that refers to the Lord's entrance is sung.

As the Lord entered the holy city, the children of the Hebrews
proclaimed the resurrection of life. Waving their branches of palm,
they cried: Hosanna in the Highest.

When the people heard that Jesus was coming to Jerusalem, they
went out to meet him. Waving their branches of palm, they cried:
Hosanna in the Highest.

Then the Mass continues with the Collect, p. 194.

Second Form: The Solemn Entrance

If the procession outside the church cannot take place, the entrance
of the Lord is celebrated inside the church before the principal Mass.

The people, holding palm branches, gather either outside, in front
of the church door, or inside the church. The priest and ministers
and a representative group of the faithful go to a suitable place in the

church outside the sanctuary, so that most of the people can see the rite.

While the priest approaches the appointed place, the antiphon **Hosanna** (p. 186) or another appropriate song is sung. Then the blessing of branches and the proclamation of the Gospel of the Lord's entrance into Jerusalem take place as above (pp. 187-189). After the Gospel, the priest processes solemnly with the ministers and the representative group of the faithful through the church to the sanctuary, while the responsory **As the Lord entered** (p. 192) or another appropriate song is sung.

Then the Mass begins with the Collect, p. 194.

Third Form: The Simple Entrance

At all other Masses of this Sunday, if the Solemn Entrance is not held, the commemoration of the Lord's entrance into Jerusalem takes place by means of a Simple Entrance.

While the priest proceeds to the altar, the Entrance Antiphon (see below) or another song with the same theme is sung, and the Mass continues in the usual way.

At other Masses, in which singing at the entrance cannot take place, the priest, as soon as he has arrived at the altar and venerated it, greets the people, reads the Entrance Antiphon, and continues the Mass in the usual way.

THE MASS

Entrance Antiphon
Six days before the Passover,
when the Lord came into the city of Jerusalem,
the children ran to meet him;
in their hands they carried palm branches
and with a loud voice cried out:

Hosanna in the highest!
Blessed are you, who have come in your abundant mercy!

O gates, lift high your heads;
grow higher, ancient doors.
Let him enter, the king of glory!

Who is this king of glory?
He, the Lord of hosts, he is the king of glory.

Hosanna in the highest!
Blessed are you, who have come in your abundant mercy!

cf. John 12:1. 12-13; Psalm 23:9-10

Collect

Almighty ever-living God,
who as an example of humility for the human race to follow
caused our Saviour to take flesh and submit to the Cross,
graciously grant that we may heed his lesson of patient suffering
and so merit a share in his Resurrection.
Who lives and reigns with you in the unity of the Holy Spirit,
one God, for ever and ever.

First Reading   Isaiah 50:4-7

I did not cover my face against insult – I know I shall not be shamed.

The Lord has given me
a disciple's tongue.
So that I may know how to reply to the wearied
he provides me with speech.
Each morning he wakes me to hear,
to listen like a disciple.
The Lord has opened my ear.
For my part, I made no resistance,
neither did I turn away.
I offered my back to those who struck me,
my cheeks to those who tore at my beard;
I did not cover my face
against insult and spittle.
The Lord comes to my help,
so that I am untouched by the insults.
So, too, I set my face like flint;
I know I shall not be shamed.

Psalm   Psalm 21

R. **My God, my God, why have you forsaken me?**

1. All who see me deride me.
   They curl their lips, they toss their heads.

"He trusted in the Lord, let him save him;
let him release him if this is his friend." R.

2. Many dogs have surrounded me,
    a band of the wicked beset me.
    They tear holes in my hands and my feet.
    I can count every one of my bones. R.

3. They divide my clothing among them.
    They cast lots for my robe.
    O Lord, do not leave me alone,
    my strength, make haste to help me! R.

4. I will tell of your name to my brethren
    and praise you where they are assembled.
    "You who fear the Lord give him praise;
    all sons of Jacob, give him glory.
    Revere him, Israel's sons." R.

Second Reading   Philippians 2:6-11
He humbled himself, but God raised him high.
His state was divine,
yet Christ Jesus did not cling
to his equality with God
but emptied himself
to assume the condition of a slave,
and became as men are;
and being as all men are,
he was humbler yet,
even to accepting death,
death on a cross.
But God raised him high
and gave him the name
which is above all other names
so that all beings
in the heavens, on earth and in the underworld,
should bend the knee at the name of Jesus
and that every tongue should acclaim
Jesus Christ as Lord,
to the glory of God the Father.

Gospel Acclamation
Praise to you, O Christ, king of eternal glory:
Christ was humbler yet,
even to accepting death, death on a cross.
But God raised him high
and gave him the name which is above all names.
Praise to you, O Christ, king of eternal glory.   Philippians 2:8-9

The Passion of Year A, B or C is read according to the cycle for the year.
The Passion may be read by three people. One reads the narrative:
this part is marked **N.**; if possible the priest reads the words of Jesus
(**J.**); and a third person reads the words of other speakers (**O.**). The
usual greeting and conclusion to the Gospel reading are omitted.

A

Gospel   Matthew 26:14 – 27:66
The passion of our Lord Jesus Christ according to Matthew.
N. One of the Twelve, the man called Judas Iscariot, went to the
chief priests and said, O. "What are you prepared to give me if I
hand him over to you?" N. They paid him thirty silver pieces, and
from that moment he looked for an opportunity to betray him.

Now on the first day of Unleavened Bread the disciples came to
Jesus to say, O. "Where do you want us to make the preparations
for you to eat the Passover?" N. He replied: J. "Go to so-and-so in
the city and say to him, 'The Master says: My time is near. It is at
your house that I am keeping Passover with my disciples.' N. The
disciples did what Jesus told them and prepared the Passover.

When the evening came he was at table with the twelve disciples.
And while they were eating he said: J. "I tell you solemnly, one of you
is about to betray me." N. They were greatly distressed and started
asking him in turn, O. "Not I, Lord, surely?" N. He answered: J.
"Someone who has dipped his hand into the dish with me, will
betray me. The Son of Man is going to his fate, as the scriptures say
he will, but alas for that man by whom the Son of Man is betrayed!
Better for that man if he had never been born!" N. Judas, who was
to betray him, asked in his turn, O. "Not I, Rabbi surely?" N. Jesus
answered, J. "They are your own words." N. Now as they were

eating, Jesus took some bread, and when he had said the blessing he broke it and gave it to the disciples and said: J. "Take it and eat; this is my body." N. Then he took a cup, and when he had returned thanks he gave it to them saying J. "Drink all of you from this, for this is my blood, the blood of the covenant, which is to be poured out for many for the forgiveness of sins. From now on, I tell you, I shall not drink wine until the day I drink the new wine with you in the kingdom of my Father." N. After psalms had been sung they left for the Mount of Olives. Then Jesus said to them, J. "You will all lose faith in me this night, for the scripture says: I shall strike the shepherd and the sheep of the flock will be scattered. But after my resurrection I shall go before you to Galilee." N. At this, Peter said: O. "Though all lose faith in you, I will never lose faith." N. Jesus answered him, J. "I tell you solemnly, this very night, before the cock crows, you will have disowned me three times." N. Peter said to him, O. "Even if I have to die with you, I will never disown you." N. And all the disciples said the same.

Then Jesus came with them to a small estate called Gethsemane; and he said to his disciples, J. "Stay here while I go over there to pray." N. He took Peter and the two sons of Zebedee with him. And sadness came over him, and great distress. Then he said them: J. "My soul is sorrowful to the point of death. Wait here and keep awake with me." N. And going on a little further he fell on his face and prayed: J. "My Father, if it is possible let this cup pass me by. Nevertheless, let it be as you, not I, would have it." N. He came back to the disciples and found them sleeping, and he said to Peter: J. "So you had not the strength to keep awake with me one hour? You should be awake, and praying not to be put to the test. The Spirit is willing, but the flesh is weak." N. Again, a second time, he went away and prayed: J. "My Father, if this cup cannot pass by without my drinking it, your will be done!" N. And he came again back and found them sleeping, their eyes were so heavy. Leaving them there, he went away again and prayed for the third time, repeating the same words. Then he came back to the disciples and said to them, J. "You can sleep on now and take your rest. Now the hour has come when the Son of Man is to be betrayed into the hands of sinners. Get up! Let us go! My betrayer is already close at hand." N. He was still speaking when Judas, one of the Twelve, appeared, and with him a large number of men armed with swords and clubs, sent by the chief priests and elders of the people. Now the traitor had arranged a sign with them. He had said, O. "The one I kiss, he is the man. Take him in charge." N. So he went straight up to Jesus and said, O. "Greetings, Rabbi," N. and kissed him. Jesus said to him, J. "My friend, do what you are here for." N. Then they came forward, seized Jesus and took him in charge. At that, one of the followers of Jesus grasped his sword and drew it; he struck out at the high priest's servant, and cut off his ear. Jesus then said: J. "Put your sword back, for all who draw the sword will die by the sword. Or do you think that I cannot appeal to my Father who would promptly send more than twelve legions of angels to my defence? But then, how would the scriptures be fulfilled that say this is the way it must be?" N. It was at this time that Jesus said to the crowds: J. "Am I a brigand, that you had to set out to capture me with swords and clubs? I sat teaching in the Temple day after day and you never laid hands on me." N. Now all this happened to fulfil the prophecies in scripture. Then all the disciples deserted him and ran away.

The men who had arrested Jesus led him off to Caiaphas the high priest, where the scribes and the elders were assembled. Peter followed him at a distance, and when he reached the high priest's palace, he went in and sat down with the attendants to see what the end would be.

The chief priests and the whole Sanhedrin were looking for evidence against Jesus, however false, on which they might pass the death-sentence. But they could not find any, though several lying witnesses came forward. Eventually two stepped forward and made a statement, O. "This man said: 'I have power to destroy the Temple of God and in three days build it up.'" N. The high priest then stood up and said to him: O. "Have you no answer to that? What is this evidence these men are bringing against you?" N. But Jesus was silent. And the high priest said to him: O. "I put you on oath by the living God to tell us if you are the Christ, the Son of God." N. Jesus answered: J. "The words are your own. Moreover, I tell you that from this time onward you will see the Son of Man seated at the right hand of the Power and coming on the clouds of heaven." N. At this, the high priest tore his clothes and said: O. "He has blasphemed. What need of witnesses have we now? There! You have just heard the blasphemy. What is your opinion?" N. They answered, O. "He deserves to die". N. Then they spat in his face and hit him with their fists; others said as they struck him: O. "Play the prophet, Christ! Who hit you then?" N. Meanwhile Peter was sitting outside in the courtyard, and a servant-girl came up to him and said: O. "You too were with Jesus the Galilean". N. But he denied it in front of them all, saying: O. "I do not know what you are talking about." N. When he went out to the gateway another servant-girl saw him and said to the people there: O. "This man was with Jesus the Nazarene." N. And again, with an oath, he denied it, O. "I do not know the man." N. A little later the bystanders came up and said to Peter: O. "You are one of them for sure! Why, your accent gives you away." N. Then he started calling down curses on himself and swearing: O. "I do not know the man." N. At that moment the cock crew, and Peter remembered what Jesus had said, "Before the cock crows you will have disowned me three times." And he went outside and wept bitterly.

When morning came, all the chief priests and the elders of the people met in council to bring about the death of Jesus. They had him bound, and led him away to hand him over to Pilate, the governor. When he found that Jesus had been condemned, Judas his betrayer was filled with remorse and took the thirty pieces of silver back to the chief priests and elders, saying O. "I have sinned. I have betrayed innocent blood." N. They replied: O. "What is that to us? That is your concern." N. And flinging down the silver pieces in the sanctuary he made off, and went and hanged himself. The chief priests picked up the silver pieces and said: O. "It is against the Law to put this into the treasury; it is blood money." N. So they discussed the matter and bought the potter's field with it as a graveyard for foreigners, and this is why the field is called the Field of Blood today. The words of the prophet Jeremiah were then fulfilled: And they took the thirty silver pieces, the sum at which the precious One was priced by children of Israel, and they gave them for the potter's field, just as the Lord directed me.

Jesus, then, was brought before the governor, and the governor put to him this question: O. "Are you the king of the Jews?" N. Jesus replied: J. "It is you who say it." N. But when he was accused by the chief priests and the elders he refused to answer at all. Pilate then said to him: O. "Do you not hear how many charges they have brought against you?" N. But to the governor's complete amazement, he offered no reply to any of the charges.

At festival time it was the governor's practice to release a prisoner for the people, anyone they chose. Now there was at that time a notorious prisoner whose name was Barabbas. So when the crowd gathered, Pilate said to them, O. "Which do you want me to release for you: Barabbas or Jesus who is called Christ?" N. For Pilate knew it was out of jealousy that they had handed him over. Now as he was seated in the chair of judgement, his wife sent him a message, O. "Have nothing to do with that man; I have been upset all day by a dream I had about him." N. The chief priests and the elders, however, had persuaded the crowd to demand the release of Barabbas and the execution of Jesus. So when the governor spoke and asked them: O. "Which of the two do you want me to release for you?" N. they said: O. "Barabbas." N. Pilate said to them: O. "What am I to do with Jesus who is called Christ?" N. They all said: O. "Let him be crucified!" N. Pilate asked: O. "Why? What harm has he done?" N. But they shouted all the louder, O. "Let him be crucified!" N. Then Pilate saw that he was making no impression, that in fact a riot was imminent. So he took some water, washed his hands in front of the crowd and said: O. "I am innocent of this man's blood. It is your concern." N. And the people, to a man, shouted back: O. "His blood be on us and on our children!" N. Then he released Barabbas for them. He ordered Jesus to be first scourged and then handed over to be crucified.

The governor's soldiers took Jesus with them into the Praetorium and collected the whole cohort round him. Then they stripped him and made him wear a scarlet cloak, and having twisted some thorns into a crown they put this on his head and placed a reed in his right hand. To make fun of him they knelt to him saying: O. "Hail, king of the Jews!" N. And they spat on him and took the reed and struck him on the head with it. And when they had finished making fun of him, they took off the cloak and dressed him in his own clothes and led him away to crucify him.

On their way out, they came across a man from Cyrene, Simon by name, and enlisted him to carry his cross. When they had reached a place called Golgotha, that is, the place of the skull, they gave him wine to drink mixed with gall, which he tasted but refused to drink. When they had finished crucifying him they shared out his clothing by casting lots, and then sat down and stayed there keeping guard over him. Above his head was placed the charge against him; it read: "This is Jesus, the King of the Jews." At the same time two robbers were crucified with him, one on the right and one on the left.

The passers-by jeered at him; they shook their heads and said: O. "So you would destroy the Temple and rebuild it in three days! Then save yourself! If you are God's son, come down from the cross!" N. The chief priests with the scribes and elders mocked him in the same way, saying, O. "He saved others; he cannot save himself. He is the King of Israel; let him come down from the cross now, and we will believe in him. He put his trust in God; now let God rescue him if he wants him. For he did say, 'I am the son of God.'" N. Even the robbers who were crucified with him taunted him in the same way.

From the sixth hour there was darkness over all the land until the ninth hour. And about the ninth hour, Jesus cried out in a loud voice: J. "Eli, Eli, lama sabachthani?" N. That is: "My God, my God, why have you deserted me?" When some of those who stood there heard this, they said: O. "The man is calling on Elijah," N. and one of them quickly ran to get a sponge which he dipped in vinegar and, putting it on a reed, gave it him to drink. The rest of them said: O. "Wait! See if Elijah will come to save him." N. But Jesus, again crying out in a loud voice, yielded up his spirit.

All kneel and pause for a moment.

N. At that, the veil of the Temple was torn in two from top to bottom; the earth quaked; the rocks were split; the tombs opened and the bodies of many holy men rose from the dead, and these, after his resurrection, came out of the tombs, entered the Holy City and appeared to a number of people.

Meanwhile the centurion, together with the others guarding Jesus, had seen the earthquake and all that was taking place, and they were terrified and said: O. "In truth this was a son of God." N. And many women were there, watching from a distance, the same women who had followed Jesus from Galilee and looked after him. Among them were Mary of Magdala, Mary the mother of James and Joseph, and the mother of Zebedee's sons.

When it was evening, there came a rich man of Arimathaea, called Joseph, who had himself become a disciple of Jesus. This man went to Pilate and asked for the body of Jesus. Pilate thereupon ordered it to be handed over. So Joseph took the body, wrapped it in a clean shroud and put it in his own new tomb which he had hewn out of the rock. He then rolled a large stone across the entrance of the tomb and went away. Now Mary of Magdala and the other Mary were there, sitting opposite the sepulchre.

Next day, that is, when Preparation Day was over, the chief priests and the Pharisees went in a body to Pilate and said to him, O. "Your Excellency, we recall that this impostor said, while he was still alive, 'After three days I shall rise again.' Therefore give the order to have the sepulchre kept secure until the third day, for fear his disciples come and steal him away and tell the people, 'He has risen from the dead.' This last piece of fraud would be worse than what went before." N. Pilate said to them: O. "You may have your guards. Go and make all as secure as you know how." N. So they went and made the sepulchre secure, putting seals on the stone and mounting a guard.

This shorter alternative may be read instead:

Gospel   Matthew 27:11-54

The passion of our Lord Jesus Christ according to Matthew.

Jesus was brought before Pontius Pilate, the governor, and the governor put to him this question, "Are you the king of the Jews?" Jesus replied, "It is you who say it." But when he was accused by the chief priests and the elders he refused to answer at all. Pilate then said to him, "Do you not hear how many charges they have brought against you?" But to the governor's complete amazement, he offered no reply to any of the charges.

At festival time it was the governor's practice to release a prisoner for the people, anyone they chose. Now there was at that time a notorious prisoner whose name was Barabbas. So when the crowd gathered, Pilate said to them, "Which do you want me to release for you: Barabbas or Jesus who is called Christ?" For Pilate knew it was out of jealousy that they had handed him over.

Now as he was seated in the chair of judgement, his wife sent him a message, "Have nothing to do with that man; I have been upset all day by a dream I had about him."

The chief priests and the elders, however, had persuaded the crowd to demand the release of Barabbas and the execution of Jesus. So when the governor spoke and asked them: "Which of the two do you want me to release for you?" they said, "Barabbas." "But in that case," Pilate said to them, "what am I to do with Jesus who is called Christ?" They all said, "Let him be crucified!" "Why?" he asked, "What harm has he done?" But they shouted all the louder, "Let him be crucified!" Then Pilate saw that he was making no impression, that in fact a riot was imminent. So he took some water, washed his hands in front of the crowd and said, "I am innocent of this man's blood. It is your concern." And the people, to a man, shouted back, "His blood be on us and on our children!" Then he released Barabbas for them. He ordered Jesus to be first scourged and then handed over to be crucified.

The governor's soldiers took Jesus with them into the Praetorium and collected the whole cohort round him. Then they stripped him and made him wear a scarlet cloak, and having twisted some thorns into a crown they put this on his head and placed a reed in his right hand. To make fun of him they knelt to him saying: "Hail, king of the Jews!" And they spat on him and took the reed and struck him on the head with it. And when they had finished making fun of him, they took off the cloak and dressed him in his own clothes and led him away to crucify him.

On their way out, they came across a man from Cyrene, Simon by name, and enlisted him to carry his cross. When they had reached a place called Golgotha, that is, the place of the skull, they gave him wine to drink mixed with gall, which he tasted but refused to drink. When they had finished crucifying him they shared out his clothing by casting lots, and then sat down and stayed there keeping guard over him.

Above his head was placed the charge against him; it read: "This is Jesus, the King of the Jews." At the same time two robbers were crucified with him, one on the right and one on the left.

The passers-by jeered at him; they shook their heads and said, "So you would destroy the Temple and rebuild it in three days! Then save yourself! If you are God's son, come down from the cross!" The chief priests with the scribes and elders mocked him in the same way. "He saved others," they said, "he cannot save himself. He is the King of Israel; let him come down from the cross now, and we will believe in him. He put his trust in God; now let God rescue him if he wants him. For he did say, 'I am the son of God.'" Even the robbers who were crucified with him taunted him in the same way.

From the sixth hour there was darkness over all the land until the ninth hour. And about the ninth hour, Jesus cried out in a loud voice: "Eli, Eli, lama sabachthani?" that is: "My God, my God, why have you deserted me?" When some of those who stood there heard this, they said: "The man is calling on Elijah," and one of them quickly ran to get a sponge which he dipped in vinegar and, putting it on a reed, gave it him to drink. "Wait!" said the rest of them, "and see if Elijah will come to save him." But Jesus, again crying out in a loud voice, yielded up his spirit.

All kneel and pause for a moment.

At that, the veil of the Temple was torn in two from top to bottom; the earth quaked; the rocks were split; the tombs opened and the bodies of many holy men rose from the dead, and these, after his resurrection, came out of the tombs, entered the Holy City and appeared to a number of people.

Meanwhile the centurion, together with the others guarding Jesus, had seen the earthquake and all that was taking place, and they were terrified and said: "In truth this was a son of God."

B

Gospel   Mark 14:1 – 15:47

The passion of our Lord Jesus Christ according to Mark.

N. It was two days before the Passover and the feast of Unleavened Bread, and the chief priests and scribes were looking for a way to arrest Jesus by some trick and have him put to death. For they said, O. "It must not be during the festivities, or there will be a disturbance among the people." N. Jesus was at Bethany in the house of Simon the leper; he was at dinner when a woman came in with an alabaster jar of very costly ointment, pure nard. She broke the jar and poured the ointment on his head. Some who were there said to one another indignantly, O. "Why this waste of ointment? Ointment like this could have been sold for over three hundred denarii and the money given to the poor," N. and they were angry with her. But Jesus said, J. "Leave her alone. Why are you upsetting her? What she has done for me is one of the good works. You have the poor with you always, and you can be kind to them whenever you wish, but you will not always have me. She has done what was in her power to do; she has anointed my body beforehand for its burial. I tell you solemnly, wherever throughout all the world the Good News is proclaimed, what she has done will be told also, in remembrance of her." N. Judas Iscariot, one of the Twelve, approached the chief priests with an offer to hand Jesus over to them. They were delighted to hear it, and promised to give him money; and he looked for a way of betraying him when the opportunity should occur.

On the first day of Unleavened Bread, when the Passover lamb was sacrificed, his disciples said to him, O. "Where do you want us to go and make the preparations for you to eat the Passover?" N. So he sent two of his disciples, saying to them, J. "Go into the city and you will meet a man carrying a pitcher of water. Follow him, and say to the owner of the house which he enters, 'The Master says: Where is my dining room in which I can eat the Passover with my disciples?' He will show you a large upper room furnished with couches, all prepared. Make the preparations for us there." N. The disciples set out and went to the city and found everything as he had told them, and prepared the Passover.

When evening came he arrived with the Twelve. And while they were at table eating, Jesus said, J. "I tell you solemnly, one of you is about to betray me, one of you eating with me." N. They were distressed and asked him, one after another, O. "Not I, surely?" N. He said to them, J. "It is one of the Twelve, one who is dipping into the same dish with me. Yes, the Son of Man is going to his fate, as the scriptures say he will, but alas for that man by whom the Son of Man is betrayed! Better for that man if he had never been born!" N. And as they were eating he took some bread, and when he had said the blessing he broke it and gave it to them, saying, J. "Take it; this is my body." N. Then he took a cup, and when he had returned thanks he gave it to them, and all drank from it, and he said to them, J. "This is my blood, the blood of the covenant, which is to be poured out for many. I tell you solemnly, I shall not drink any more wine until the day I drink the new wine in the kingdom of God." N. After psalms had been sung they left for the Mount of Olives. And Jesus said to them, J. "You will all lose faith, for the scripture says, 'I shall strike the shepherd and the sheep will be scattered'. However after my resurrection I shall go before you to Galilee." N. Peter said, O. "Even if all lose faith, I will not." N. And Jesus said to him, J. "I tell you solemnly, this day, this very night, before the cock crows twice, you will have disowned me three times." N. But he repeated still more earnestly, O. "If I have to die with you, I will never disown you." N. And they all said the same.

They came to a small estate called Gethsemane, and Jesus said to his disciples, J. "Stay here while I pray." N. Then he took Peter and James and John with him. And a sudden fear came over him, and great distress. And he said to them, J. "My soul is sorrowful to the point of death. Wait here, and keep awake." N. And going on a little further he threw himself on the ground and prayed that, if it were possible, this hour might pass him by. He said, J. "Abba (Father)! Everything is possible for you. Take this cup away from me. But let it be as you, not I, would have it." N. He came back and found them sleeping, and he said to Peter, J. "Simon, are you asleep? Had you not the strength to keep awake one hour? You should be awake, and praying not to be put to the test. The spirit is willing but the flesh is weak." N. Again he went away and prayed, saying the same words. And once more he came back and found them sleeping, their eyes were so heavy; and they could find no answer for him. He came back a third time and said to them, J. "You can sleep on now and take your rest. It is all over. The hour has come. Now the Son of Man is to be betrayed into the hands of sinners. Get up! Let us go! My betrayer is close at hand already." N. Even while he was still speaking, Judas, one of the Twelve, came up with a number of men armed with swords and clubs, sent by the chief priests and the scribes and the elders. Now the traitor had arranged a signal with them. He had said, O. "The one I kiss, he is the man. Take him in charge, and see he is well guarded when you lead him away." N. So when the traitor came, he went straight up to Jesus and said, O. "Rabbi!" N. and kissed him. The others seized him and took him in charge. Then one of the bystanders drew his sword and struck out at the high priest's servant, and cut off his ear.

Then Jesus spoke, J. "Am I a brigand that you had to set out to capture me with swords and clubs? I was among you teaching in the Temple day after day and you never laid hands on me. But this is to fulfil the scriptures." N. And they all deserted him and ran away. A young man who followed him had nothing on but a linen cloth. They caught hold of him, but he left the cloth in their hands and ran away naked.

They led Jesus off to the high priest; and all the chief priests and the elders and the scribes assembled there. Peter had followed him at a distance, right into the high priest's palace, and was sitting with the attendants warming himself at the fire.

The chief priests and the whole Sanhedrin were looking for evidence against Jesus on which they might pass the death-sentence. But they could not find any. Several, indeed, brought false evidence against him, but their evidence was conflicting. Some stood up and submitted this false evidence against him, O. "We heard him say, 'I am going to destroy this Temple made by human hands, and in three days build another, not made by human hands.'" N. But even on this point their evidence was conflicting. The high priest then stood up before the whole assembly and put this question to Jesus, O. "Have you no answer to that? What is this evidence these men are bringing against you?" N. But he was silent and made no answer at all. The high priest put a second question to him, O. "Are you the Christ, the Son of the Blessed One?" N. Jesus said, J. "I am, and you will see the Son of Man seated at the right hand of the Power and coming with the clouds of heaven." N. The high priest tore his robes, and said, O. "What need of witnesses have we now? You heard the blasphemy. What is your finding?" N. And they all gave their verdict: he deserved to die. Some of them started spitting at him and, blindfolding him, began hitting him with their fists and shouting, O. "Play the prophet!" N. And the attendants rained blows on him.

While Peter was down below in the courtyard, one of the high-priest's servant-girls came up. She saw Peter warming himself there, stared at him and said, O. "You too were with Jesus, the man from Nazareth." N. But he denied it, saying O. "I do not know, I do not understand what you are talking about." N. And he went out into the forecourt. The servant-girl saw him and again started telling the bystanders, O. "This fellow is one of them." N. But he again denied it. A little later the bystanders themselves said to Peter, O. "You are one of them for sure! Why, you are a Galilean." N. But he started calling curses on himself and swearing, O. "I do not know the man you speak of." N. At that moment the cock crew for the second time, and Peter recalled how Jesus had said to him, "Before the cock crows twice, you will have disowned me three times." And he burst into tears.

First thing in the morning, the chief priest together with the elders and scribes, in short the whole Sanhedrin, had their plan ready. They had Jesus bound and took him away and handed him over to Pilate.

Pilate questioned him, O. "Are you the king of the Jews?" N. He answered, J. "It is you who say it." N. And the chief priests brought many accusations against him. Pilate questioned him again, O. "Have you no reply at all? See how many accusations they are bringing against you!" N. But to Pilate's amazement, Jesus made no further reply.

At festival time Pilate used to release a prisoner for them, anyone they asked for. Now a man called Barabbas was then in prison with the rioters who had committed murder during the uprising. When the crowd went up and began to ask Pilate the customary favour, Pilate answered them, O. "Do you want me to release for you the king of the Jews?" N. For he realised it was out of jealousy that the chief priests had handed Jesus over. The chief priests, however, had incited the crowd to demand that he should release Barabbas for them instead. Then Pilate spoke again. O. "But in that case, what am I to do with the man you call king of the Jews?" N. They shouted back. O. "Crucify him!" N. Pilate asked them, O. "Why? What harm has he done?" N. But they shouted all the louder, O. "Crucify him!" N. So Pilate, anxious to placate the crowd, released Barabbas for them and, having ordered Jesus to be scourged, handed him over to be crucified.

The soldiers led him away to the inner part of the palace, that is, the Praetorium, and called the whole cohort together. They dressed him up in purple, twisted some thorns into a crown and put it on him. And they began saluting him, O. "Hail, king of the Jews!" N. They struck his head with a reed and spat on him; and they went down on their knees to do him homage. And when they had finished making fun of him, they took off the purple and dressed him in his own clothes.

They led him out to crucify him. They enlisted a passer-by, Simon of Cyrene, father of Alexander and Rufus, who was coming in from the country, to carry his cross. They brought Jesus to the place called Golgotha, which means the place of the skull.

They offered him wine mixed with myrrh, but he refused it. Then they crucified him, and shared out his clothing, casting lots to decide what each should get. It was the third hour when they crucified him. The inscription giving the charge against him read: "The King of the Jews." And they crucified two robbers with him, one on his right and one on his left.

The passers-by jeered at him; they shook their heads and said, O. "Aha! So you would destroy the Temple and rebuild it in three days! Then save yourself: come down from the cross!" N. The chief priests and the scribes mocked him among themselves in the same way. They said, O. "He saved others, he cannot save himself. Let the Christ, the king of Israel, come down from the cross now, for us to see it and believe." N. Even those who were crucified with him taunted him.

When the sixth hour came there was darkness over the whole land until the ninth hour. And at the ninth hour Jesus cried out in a loud voice, J. "Eloi, Eloi, lama sabachthani?" N. This means "My God, my God, why have you deserted me?" When some of those who stood by heard this, they said, O. "Listen, he is calling on Elijah." N. Someone ran and soaked a sponge in vinegar and, putting it on a reed, gave it him to drink, saying, O. "Wait and see if Elijah will come to take him down." N. But Jesus gave a loud cry and breathed his last.

All kneel and pause for a moment.

N. And the veil of the Temple was torn in two from top to bottom. The centurion, who was standing in front of him, had seen how he had died, and he said, O. "In truth this man was a son of God."

N. There were some women watching from a distance. Among them were Mary of Magdala, Mary who was the mother of James the younger and Joset, and Salome. These used to follow him and look after him when he was in Galilee. And there were many other women there who had come up to Jerusalem with him.

It was now evening, and since it was Preparation Day (that is, the vigil of the sabbath), there came Joseph of Arimathaea, a prominent member of the Council, who himself lived in the hope of seeing the kingdom of God, and he boldly went to Pilate and asked for the body of Jesus. Pilate, astonished that he should have died so soon, summoned the centurion and enquired if he was already dead. Having been assured of this by the centurion, he granted the corpse to Joseph who brought a shroud, took Jesus down from the cross, wrapped him in the shroud and laid him in a tomb which had been hewn out of the rock. He then rolled a stone against the entrance of the tomb. Mary of Magdala and Mary the mother of Joset were watching and took note of where he was laid.

This shorter alternative may be read instead:

Gospel   Mark 15:1-39

The passion of our Lord Jesus Christ according to Mark.

First thing in the morning, the chief priest together with the elders and scribes, in short the whole Sanhedrin, had their plan ready. They had Jesus bound and took him away and handed him over to Pilate.

Pilate questioned him, "Are you the king of the Jews?" "It is you who say it" he answered. And the chief priests brought many accusations against him. Pilate questioned him again, "Have you no reply at all? See how many accusations they are bringing against you!" But to Pilate's amazement, Jesus made no further reply.

At festival time Pilate used to release a prisoner for them, anyone they asked for. Now a man called Barabbas was then in prison with the rioters who had committed murder during the uprising. When the crowd went up and began to ask Pilate the customary favour, Pilate answered them, "Do you want me to release for you the king of the Jews?" For he realised it was out of jealousy that the chief priests had handed Jesus over. The chief priests, however, had incited the crowd to demand that he should release Barabbas for them instead. Then Pilate spoke again. "But in that case," he said to them, "what am I to do with the man you call king of the Jews?" They shouted back. "Crucify him!" "Why?" Pilate asked them "What harm has he done?" But they shouted all the louder, "Crucify him!" So Pilate, anxious to placate the crowd, released Barabbas for them and, having ordered Jesus to be scourged, handed him over to be crucified.

The soldiers led him away to the inner part of the palace, that is, the Praetorium, and called the whole cohort together. They dressed him up in purple, twisted some thorns into a crown and put it on him. And they began saluting him, "Hail, king of the Jews!" They struck his head with a reed and spat on him; and they went down on their knees to do him homage. And when they had finished making fun of him, they took off the purple and dressed him in his own clothes.

They led him out to crucify him. They enlisted a passer-by, Simon of Cyrene, father of Alexander and Rufus, who was coming in from the country, to carry his cross. They brought Jesus to the place called Golgotha, which means the place of the skull.

They offered him wine mixed with myrrh, but he refused it. Then they crucified him, and shared out his clothing, casting lots to decide what each should get. It was the third hour when they crucified him. The inscription giving the charge against him read: "The King of the Jews." And they crucified two robbers with him, one on his right and one on his left.

The passers-by jeered at him; they shook their heads and said, "Aha! So you would destroy the Temple and rebuild it in three days! Then save yourself: come down from the cross!" The chief priests and the scribes mocked him among themselves in the same way. "He saved others," they said "he cannot save himself. Let the Christ, the king of Israel, come down from the cross now, for us to see it and believe." Even those who were crucified with him taunted him.

When the sixth hour came there was darkness over the whole land until the ninth hour. And at the ninth hour Jesus cried out in a loud voice, "Eloi, Eloi, lama sabachthani?" which means, "My God, my God, why have you deserted me?" When some of those who stood by heard this, they said, "Listen, he is calling on Elijah." Someone ran and soaked a sponge in vinegar and, putting it on a reed, gave it him to drink, saying, "Wait and see if Elijah will come to take him down." But Jesus gave a loud cry and breathed his last.

All kneel and pause for a moment.

And the veil of the Temple was torn in two from top to bottom. The centurion, who was standing in front of him, had seen how he had died, and he said, "In truth this man was a son of God."

C
Gospel   Luke 22:14 – 23:56
The passion of our Lord Jesus Christ according to Luke.

N. When the hour came Jesus took his place at table, and the apostles with him. And he said to them, J. "I have longed to eat this Passover with you before I suffer; because, I tell you, I shall not eat it again until it is fulfilled in the kingdom of God." N. Then, taking a cup, he gave thanks and said, J. "Take this and share it among you, because from now on, I tell you, I shall not drink wine until the kingdom of God comes." N. Then he took some bread, and when he had given thanks, broke it and gave it to them saying, J. "This is my body which will be given for you; do this as a memorial of me." N. He did the same with the cup after supper, and said, J. "This cup is the new covenant in my blood which will be poured out for you.

"And yet, here with me on the table is the hand of the man who betrays me. The Son of Man does indeed go to his fate even as it has been decreed, but alas for that man by whom he is betrayed!" N. And they began to ask one another which of them it could be who was to do this thing.

A dispute arose also between them about which should be reckoned the greatest, but he said to them, J. "Among pagans it is the kings who lord it over them, and those who have authority over them are given the title Benefactor. This must not happen with you. No; the greatest among you must behave as if he were the youngest, the leader as if he were the one who serves. For who is the greater: the one at table or the one who serves? The one at table, surely? Yet here am I among you as one who serves!

"You are the men who have stood by me faithfully in my trials; and now I confer a kingdom on you, just as my Father conferred one on me: you will eat and drink at my table in my kingdom, and you will sit on thrones to judge the twelve tribes of Israel.

"Simon, Simon! Satan, you must know, has got his wish to sift you all like wheat; but I have prayed for you, Simon, that your faith may not fail, and once you have recovered, you in your turn must strengthen your brothers." N. He answered, O. "Lord, I would be ready to go to prison with you, and to death." N. Jesus replied, J. "I tell you, Peter, by the time the cock crows today you will have denied three times that you know me."

N. He said to them, J. "When I sent you out without purse or haversack or sandals, were you short of anything?" N. They answered, O. "No." N. He said to them J. "But now if you have a purse, take it: if you have a haversack, do the same; if you have no sword, sell your cloak and buy one, because I tell you these words of scripture have to be fulfilled in me: He let himself be taken for a criminal. Yes, what scripture says about me is even now reaching its fulfilment."

N. They said, O. "Lord, there are two swords here now." N. He said to them, J. "That is enough!" N. He then left the upper room to make his way as usual to the Mount of Olives, with the disciples following. When they reached the place he said to them, J. "Pray not to be put to the test." N. Then he withdrew from them, about a stone's throw away, and knelt down and prayed, saying, J. "Father, if you are willing, take this cup away from me. Nevertheless, let your will be done, not mine." N. Then an angel appeared to him, coming from heaven to give him strength. In his anguish he prayed even more earnestly, and his sweat fell to the ground like great drops of blood.

When he rose from prayer he went to the disciples and found them sleeping for sheer grief. He said to them, J. "Why are you asleep? Get up and pray not to be put to the test." N. He was still speaking when a number of men appeared, and at the head of them the man called Judas, one of the Twelve, who went up to Jesus to kiss him. Jesus said, J. "Judas, are you betraying the Son of Man with a kiss?" N. His followers, seeing what was happening, said, O. "Lord, shall we use our swords?" N. And one of them struck out at the high priest's servant, and cut off his right ear. But at this Jesus spoke, J. "Leave off! That will do!" N. And touching the man's ear he healed him.

Then Jesus spoke to the chief priests and captains of the Temple guard and elders who had come for him. He said, J. "Am I a brigand that you had to set out with swords and clubs? When I was among you in the Temple day after day you never moved to lay hands on me. But this is your hour; this is the reign of darkness." N. They seized him then and led him away, and they took him to the high priest's house. Peter followed at a distance. They had lit a fire in the middle of the courtyard and Peter sat down among them, and as he was sitting there by the blaze a servant-girl saw him, peered at him and said, O. "This person was with him too." N. But he denied it, saying, O. "Woman, I do not know him." N. Shortly afterwards, someone else saw him and said, O. "You are another of them." N. But Peter replied, O. "I am not, my friend." N. About an hour later, another man insisted saying, O. "This fellow was certainly with him. Why, he is a Galilean." N. Peter said, O. "My friend, I do not know what you are talking about." N. At that instant, while he was still speaking, the cock crew, and the Lord turned and looked straight at Peter, and Peter remembered what the Lord had said to him, "Before the cock crows today, you will have disowned me three times." And he went outside and wept bitterly.

Meanwhile the men who guarded Jesus were mocking and beating him. They blindfolded him and questioned him, saying, O. "Play the prophet. Who hit you then?" N. And they continued heaping insults on him.

When day broke there was a meeting of the elders of the people, attended by the chief priests and scribes. He was brought before their council, and they said to him, O. "If you are the Christ, tell us." N. He replied, J. "If I tell you, you will not believe me, and if I question you, you will not answer. But from now on, the Son of Man will be seated at the right hand of the Power of God." N. Then they all said, O. "So you are the Son of God then?" N. He answered, J. "It is you who say I am." N. They said, O. "What need of witnesses have we now? We have heard it for ourselves from his own lips." N. The whole assembly then rose, and they brought him before Pilate.

They began their accusation by saying, O. "We found this man inciting our people to revolt, opposing payment of tribute to Caesar, and claiming to be Christ, a king." N. Pilate put to him this question, O. "Are you the king of the Jews?" N. He replied, J. "It is you who say it." N. Pilate then said to the chief priests and the crowd, O. "I find no case against this man." N. But they persisted, O. "He is inflaming the people with his teaching all over Judaea; it has come all the way from Galilee, where he started, down to here." N. When Pilate heard this, he asked if the man were a Galilean; and finding that he came under Herod's jurisdiction he passed him over to Herod who was also in Jerusalem at that time.

Herod was delighted to see Jesus; he had heard about him and had been wanting for a long time to set eyes on him; moreover, he was hoping to see some miracle worked by him. So he questioned him at some length; but without getting any reply. Meanwhile the chief priests and the scribes were there, violently pressing their accusations. Then Herod, together with his guards, treated him with contempt and made fun of him; he put a rich cloak on him and sent him back to Pilate. And though Herod and Pilate had been enemies before, they were reconciled that same day.

Pilate then summoned the chief priests and the leading men and the people. He said, O. "You brought this man before me as a political agitator. Now I have gone into the matter myself in your presence and found no case against him. Nor has Herod either, since he has sent him back to us. As you can see, the man has done nothing that deserves death, so I shall have him flogged and then let him go." N. But as one man they howled, O. "Away with him! Give us Barabbas!" N. This man had been thrown into prison for causing a riot in the city and for murder.

Pilate was anxious to set Jesus free and addressed them again, but they shouted back. O. "Crucify him! Crucify him!" N. And for the third time he spoke to them, O. "Why? What harm has this man done? I have found no case against him that deserves death, so I shall have him punished and then let him go." N. But they kept on shouting at the top of their voices, demanding that he should be crucified, and their shouts were growing louder.

Pilate then gave his verdict: their demand was to be granted. He released the man they asked for, who had been imprisoned for rioting and murder, and handed Jesus over to them to deal with as they pleased.

As they were leading him away they seized on a man, Simon from Cyrene, who was coming in from the country, and made him shoulder the cross and carry it behind Jesus. Large numbers of people followed him, and of women too, who mourned and lamented for him. But Jesus turned to them and said, J. "Daughters of Jerusalem, do not weep for me; weep rather for yourselves and for your children. For the days will surely come when people will say, 'Happy are those who are barren, the wombs that have never borne, the breasts that have never suckled!' Then they will begin to say to the mountains, 'Fall on us!'; to the hills, 'Cover us!' For if men use the green wood like this, what will happen when it is dry?" N. Now with him they were also leading out two other criminals to be executed.

When they reached the place called The Skull, they crucified him there and the two criminals also, one on the right, the other on the left. Jesus said, J. "Father, forgive them; they do not know what they are doing." N. Then they cast lots to share out his clothing. The people stayed there watching him. As for the leaders, they jeered at him, saying, O. "He saved others; let him save himself if he is the Christ of God, the Chosen One." N. The soldiers mocked him too, and when they approached to offer him vinegar they said, O. "If you are the king of the Jews, save yourself." N. Above him there was an inscription: "This is the King of the Jews."

One of the criminals hanging there abused him, saying, O. "Are you not the Christ? Save yourself and us as well." N. But the other spoke up and rebuked him. O. "Have you no fear of God at all? You got the same sentence as he did, but in our case we deserved it: we are paying for what we did. But this man has done nothing wrong. Jesus, remember me when you come into your kingdom." N. He replied J. "Indeed, I promise you, today you will be with me in paradise." N. It was now about the sixth hour and, with the sun eclipsed, a darkness came over the whole land until the ninth hour. The veil of the Temple was torn right down the middle; and when Jesus had cried out in a loud voice, he said, J. "Father, into your hands I commit my spirit." N. With these words he breathed his last.

All kneel and pause for a moment.

When the centurion saw what had taken place, he gave praise to God and said, O. "This was a great and good man." N. And when all the people who had gathered for the spectacle saw what had happened, they went home beating their breasts.

All his friends stood at a distance; so also did the women who had accompanied him from Galilee, and they saw all this happen.

Then a member of the council arrived, an upright and virtuous man named Joseph. He had not consented to what the others had planned and carried out. He came from Arimathaea, a Jewish town, and he lived in the hope of seeing the kingdom of God. This man went to Pilate and asked for the body of Jesus. He then took it down, wrapped it in a shroud and put him in a tomb which was hewn in stone in which no one had yet been laid. It was Preparation Day and the Sabbath was imminent.

Meanwhile the women who had come from Galilee with Jesus were following behind. They took note of the tomb and of the position of the body.

Then they returned and prepared spices and ointments. And on the sabbath day they rested, as the law required.

This shorter alternative may be read instead:

Gospel   **Luke 23:1-49**
The passion of our Lord Jesus Christ according to Luke.
The elders of the people and the chief priests and scribes rose, and they brought Jesus before Pilate.

They began their accusation by saying, "We found this man inciting our people to revolt, opposing payment of tribute to Caesar, and claiming to be Christ, a king." Pilate put to him this question, "Are you the king of the Jews?" "It is you who say it" he replied. Pilate then said to the chief priests and the crowd, "I find no case against this man." But they persisted, "He is inflaming the people with his teaching all over Judaea; it has come all the way from Galilee, where he started, down to here." When Pilate heard this, he asked if the man were a Galilean; and finding that he came under Herod's jurisdiction he passed him over to Herod who was also in Jerusalem at that time.

Herod was delighted to see Jesus; he had heard about him and had been wanting for a long time to set eyes on him; moreover, he was hoping to see some miracle worked by him. So he questioned him at some length; but without getting any reply. Meanwhile the chief priests and the scribes were there, violently pressing their accusations. Then Herod, together with his guards, treated him with contempt and made fun of him; he put a rich cloak on him and sent him back to Pilate. And though Herod and Pilate had been enemies before, they were reconciled that same day.

Pilate then summoned the chief priests and the leading men and the people. "You brought this man before me", he said, "as a political agitator. Now I have gone into the matter myself in your presence and found no case against the man in respect of all the charges you bring against him. Nor has Herod either, since he has sent him back to us. As you can see, the man has done nothing that deserves death, so I shall have him flogged and then let him go." But as one man they howled, "Away with him! Give us Barabbas!" (This man had been thrown into prison for causing a riot in the city and for murder.)

Pilate was anxious to set Jesus free and addressed them again, but they shouted back, "Crucify him! Crucify him!" And for the third time he spoke to them, "Why? What harm has this man done? I have found no case against him that deserves death, so I shall have him punished and then let him go. But they kept on shouting at the top of their voices, demanding that he should be crucified, and their shouts were growing louder.

Pilate then gave his verdict: their demand was to be granted. He released the man they asked for, who had been imprisoned for rioting and murder, and handed Jesus over to them to deal with as they pleased.

As they were leading him away they seized on a man, Simon from Cyrene, who was coming in from the country, and made him shoulder the cross and carry it behind Jesus. Large numbers of people followed him, and of women too, who mourned and lamented for him. But Jesus turned to them and said, "Daughters of Jerusalem, do not weep for me; weep rather for yourselves and for your children. For the days will surely come when people will say, "Happy are those who are barren, the wombs that have never borne, the breasts that have never suckled!" Then they will begin to say to the mountains, "Fall on us!"; to the hills, "Cover us!" For if men use the green wood like this, what will happen when it is dry?" Now with him they were also leading out two other criminals to be executed.

When they reached the place called The Skull, they crucified him there and the two criminals also, one on the right, the other on the left. Jesus said, "Father, forgive them; they do not know what they are doing." Then they cast lots to share out his clothing.

The people stayed there watching him. As for the leaders, they jeered at him, saying, "He saved others," they said, "let him save himself if he is the Christ of God, the Chosen One." The soldiers mocked him too and when they approached to offer him vinegar they said, "If you are the king of the Jews, save yourself." Above him there was an inscription: "This is the King of the Jews."

One of the criminals hanging there abused him. "Are you not the Christ?" he said. "Save yourself and us as well." But the other spoke up and rebuked him. "Have you no fear of God at all?" he said. "You got the same sentence as he did, but in our case we deserved it: we are paying for what we did. But this man has done nothing wrong. Jesus," he said, "remember me when you come into your kingdom." "Indeed, I promise you," he replied, "today you will be with me in paradise."

It was now about the sixth hour and, with the sun eclipsed, a darkness came over the whole land until the ninth hour. The veil of the Temple was torn right down the middle; and when Jesus had cried out in a loud voice, he said, "Father, into your hands I commit my spirit." With these words he breathed his last.

All kneel and pause for a moment.

When the centurion saw what had taken place, he gave praise to God and said, "This was a great and good man." And when all the people who had gathered for the spectacle saw what had happened, they went home beating their breasts.

All his friends stood at a distance; so also did the women who had accompanied him from Galilee, and they saw all this happen.

The Creed is said.

Prayer over the Offerings

Through the Passion of your Only Begotten Son, O Lord,
may our reconciliation with you be near at hand,
so that, though we do not merit it by our own deeds,
yet by this sacrifice made once for all,
we may feel already the effects of your mercy.
Through Christ our Lord.

Preface

It is truly right and just, our duty and our salvation,
always and everywhere to give you thanks,
Lord, holy Father, almighty and eternal God,
through Christ our Lord.

For though innocent he suffered willingly for sinners
and accepted unjust condemnation to save the guilty.
His Death has washed away our sins,
and his Resurrection has purchased our justification.

And so, with all the Angels,
we praise you, as in joyful celebration we acclaim:
Holy, Holy, Holy Lord God of hosts…

Communion Antiphon

Father, if this chalice cannot pass without my drinking it,
your will be done.

Matthew 26:42

Prayer after Communion

Nourished with these sacred gifts,
we humbly beseech you, O Lord,
that, just as through the death of your Son
you have brought us to hope for what we believe,
so by his Resurrection
you may lead us to where you call.
Through Christ our Lord.

The Solemn Blessing for the Passion of the Lord (pp. 510-511) or
the Prayer over the People (below) may be used.

Look, we pray, O Lord, on this your family,
for whom our Lord Jesus Christ
did not hesitate to be delivered into the hands of the wicked
and submit to the agony of the Cross.
Who lives and reigns for ever and ever.

MAUNDY THURSDAY – ABC
Evening Mass of the Lord's Supper

Christ celebrated the Passover with his disciples.
He gave them a new commandment, that they love one another as he loved
them. This love is shown in service. During the Last Supper, Christ washed
the feet of his disciples. He instituted the Sacrament of the Eucharist. The
Mass makes effectively present the events that took place on that night and is
the source from which all the other sacraments flow and towards which they all
lead. On this evening the old Jewish rite gives way to the new sacrifice given to
the Church by Jesus Christ.

Entrance Antiphon
We should glory in the Cross of our Lord Jesus Christ,
in whom is our salvation, life and resurrection,
through whom we are saved and delivered.   cf. Galatians 6:14

The Gloria is said or sung. While it is being sung, the church bells
are rung, and then they remain silent until the Gloria of the Easter
Vigil.

Collect
O God, who have called us to participate
in this most sacred Supper,
in which your Only Begotten Son,
when about to hand himself over to death,
entrusted to the Church a sacrifice new for all eternity,
the banquet of his love,
grant, we pray,
that we may draw from so great a mystery,
the fullness of charity and of life.
Through our Lord Jesus Christ, your Son,
who lives and reigns with you in the unity of the Holy Spirit,
one God, for ever and ever.

First Reading   Exodus 12:1-8. 11-14

Instructions concerning the Passover meal.

The Lord said to Moses and Aaron in the land of Egypt, "This month is to be the first of all the others for you, the first month of your year. Speak to the whole community of Israel and say, 'On the tenth day of this month each man must take an animal from the flock, one for each family: one animal for each household. If the household is too small to eat the animal, a man must join with his neighbour, the nearest to his house, as the number of persons requires. You must take into account what each can eat in deciding the number for the animal. It must be an animal without blemish, a male one year old; you may take it from either sheep or goats. You must keep it till the fourteenth day of the month when the whole assembly of the community of Israel shall slaughter it between two evenings. Some of the blood must be taken and put on the two doorposts and the lintel of the houses where it is eaten. That night, the flesh is to be eaten, roasted over the fire; it must be eaten with unleavened bread and bitter herbs. You shall eat it like this: with a girdle round your waist, sandals on your feet, a staff in your hand. You shall eat it hastily: it is a passover in honour of the Lord. That night, I will go through the land of Egypt and strike down all the first-born in the land of Egypt, man and beast alike, and I shall deal out punishment to all the gods of Egypt, I am the Lord. The blood shall serve to mark the houses that you live in. When I see the blood I will pass over you and you shall escape the destroying plague when I strike the land of Egypt. This day is to be a day of remembrance for you, and you must celebrate it as a feast in the Lord's honour. For all generations you are to declare it a day of festival, for ever.'"

Psalm   Psalm 115

R. **The blessing-cup that we bless
     is a communion with the blood of Christ.**

1. How can I repay the Lord
    for his goodness to me?
    The cup of salvation I will raise;
    I will call on the Lord's name. R.

2. O precious in the eyes of the Lord
   is the death of his faithful.
   Your servant, Lord, your servant am I;
   you have loosened my bonds. R.

3. A thanksgiving sacrifice I make:
   I will call on the Lord's name.
   My vows to the Lord I will fulfil
   before all his people. R.

Second Reading   1 Corinthians 11:23-26
Every time you eat this bread and drink this cup, you are proclaiming the death of the Lord.

This is what I received from the Lord, and in turn passed on to you: that on the same night that he was betrayed, the Lord Jesus took some bread, and thanked God for it and broke it, and he said, "This is my body, which is for you; do this as a memorial of me". In the same way he took the cup after supper, and said, "This cup is the new covenant in my blood. Whenever you drink it, do this as a memorial of me". Until the Lord comes, therefore, every time you eat this bread and drink this cup, you are proclaiming his death.

Gospel Acclamation
Praise and honour to you, Lord Jesus!
I give you a new commandment:
love one another just as I have loved you, says the Lord.
Praise and honour to you, Lord Jesus!   John 13:34

Gospel   John 13:1-15
Now he showed how perfect his love was.

It was before the festival of the Passover, and Jesus knew that the hour had come for him to pass from this world to the father. He had always loved those which were his in the world, but now he showed how perfect his love was.

They were at supper, and the devil had already put it into the mind of Judas Iscariot son of Simon, to betray him. Jesus knew that the Father had put everything into his hands, and that he had come from God and was returning to God, and he got up from table, removed his outer garment and, taking a towel, wrapped it round his waist; he then poured water into a basin and began to wash the disciples' feet and to wipe them with the towel he was wearing.

He came to Simon Peter, who said to him, "Lord, are you going to wash my feet?" Jesus answered, "At the moment you do not know what I am doing, but later you will understand." "Never!" said Peter, "You shall never wash my feet." Jesus replied, "If I do not wash you, you can have nothing in common with me." "Then, Lord," said Simon Peter, "not only my feet, but my hands and my head as well!" Jesus said, "No one who has taken a bath needs washing, he is clean all over. You too are clean, though not all of you are." He knew who was going to betray him, that was why he said, "though not all of you are."

When he had washed their feet and put on his clothes again he went back to the table. "Do you understand", he said, "what I have done to you? You call me Master and Lord, and rightly; so I am. If I, then, the Lord and Master, have washed your feet, you should wash each other's feet. I have given you an example so that you may copy what I have done to you."

The Washing of Feet

The washing of feet may follow the homily. Those who have been chosen are led by the ministers to seats prepared in a suitable place. Then the priest (removing his chasuble if necessary) goes to each one, and, with the help of the ministers, pours water over each one's feet and then dries them.

Meanwhile some of the following antiphons or other appropriate songs are sung.

Antiphon 1

After the Lord had risen from supper,
he poured water into a basin
and began to wash the feet of his disciples:
he left them this example.

cf. John 13:4. 5. 15

Antiphon 2

The Lord Jesus, after eating supper with his disciples,
washed their feet and said to them:
Do you know what I, your Lord and Master, have done for you?
I have given you an example, that you should do likewise.

cf. John 13:12. 13. 15

Antiphon 3

Lord, are you to wash my feet? Jesus said to him in answer:
If I do not wash your feet, you will have no share with me.

V. So he came to Simon Peter and Peter said to him:
    Lord, are you to wash my feet...

V. What I am doing, you do not know for now,
    but later you will come to know.
    Lord, are you to wash my feet...   John 13:6. 7. 8

Antiphon 4

If I, your Lord and Master, have washed your feet,
how much more should you wash each other's feet?   cf. John 13:14

Antiphon 5

This is how all will know that you are my disciples:
if you have love for one another.

V. Jesus said to his disciples:
    This is how all will know that you are my disciples:
    if you have love for one another.   John 13:35

Antiphon 6

I give you a new commandment,
that you love one another
as I have loved you, says the Lord.   John 13:34

Antiphon 7

Let faith, hope and charity, these three, remain among you,
but the greatest of these is charity.

V. Now faith, hope and charity, these three, remain;
    but the greatest of these is charity.
    Let faith, hope and charity, these three, remain among you,
    but the greatest of these is charity.   1 Corinthians 13:13

The Creed is not said. The Mass continues with the Prayer of the
Faithful.

The Liturgy of the Eucharist

At the beginning of the Liturgy of the Eucharist, there may be a procession of the faithful in which gifts for those who are poor may be presented with the bread and wine.

Meanwhile the following, or another appropriate song, is sung.

Antiphon
Where true charity is dwelling, God is present there.

V. By the love of Christ we have been brought together:
V. let us find in him our gladness and our pleasure;
V. may we love him and revere him, God the living,
V. and in love respect each other with sincere hearts.

Where true charity is dwelling, God is present there.

V. So when we as one are gathered all together,
V. let us strive to keep our minds free of division;
V. may there be an end to malice, strife and quarrels,
V. and let Christ our God be dwelling here among us.

Where true charity is dwelling, God is present there.

V. May your face thus be our vision, bright in glory,
V. Christ our God, with all the blessed Saints in heaven:
V. such delight is pure and faultless, joy unbounded,
V. which endures through countless ages world without end.
    Amen.

Prayer over the Offerings
Grant us, O Lord, we pray,
that we may participate worthily in these mysteries,
for whenever the memorial of this sacrifice is celebrated
the work of our redemption is accomplished.
Through Christ our Lord.

Preface I of the Most Holy Eucharist, p. 503.

Communion Antiphon
This is the Body that will be given up for you;
this is the Chalice of the new covenant in my Blood, says the Lord;
do this, whenever you receive it, in memory of me.

1 Corinthians 11:24-25

Prayer after Communion
Grant, almighty God,
that, just as we are renewed
by the Supper of your Son in this present age,
so we may enjoy his banquet for all eternity.
Who lives and reigns for ever and ever.

THE TRANSFER OF THE MOST BLESSED SACRAMENT

After the Prayer after Communion, the priest, accompanied by the ministers, carries the Blessed Sacrament in procession through the church to a place of repose. During the procession, the hymn **Pange, lingua** or another suitable hymn is sung.

When the procession reaches the place of repose, the singing is concluded with **Tantum ergo** or another suitable hymn.

After a period of silent adoration, the priest and ministers genuflect and return to the sacristy.

At an appropriate time, the altar is stripped and, if possible, the crosses are removed from the church or covered.

The people are invited to continue adoration before the Blessed Sacrament for a suitable length of time, according to local circumstances, but if it continues after midnight the adoration should take place without solemnity.

GOOD FRIDAY – ABC
The Celebration of the Passion of the Lord

It is accomplished.
We celebrate the Passion and Death of the Lord Jesus Christ. Christ died that
we might live, and by his wounds we are healed. He transforms the Cross of
shame into a symbol of triumph. We join in his sufferings through the giving of
our lives to him, knowing that if we die with him we will also rise with him.

The priest and ministers go to the altar in silence and prostrate
themselves or kneel and pray in silence. All others kneel.

All stand as the priest goes to the chair and faces the people. Then
the priest says one of the following:

Prayer
Remember your mercies, O Lord,
and with your eternal protection sanctify your servants,
for whom Christ your Son,
by the shedding of his Blood,
established the Paschal Mystery.
Who lives and reigns for ever and ever.

or

O God, who by the Passion of Christ your Son, our Lord,
abolished the death inherited from ancient sin
by every succeeding generation,
grant that just as, being conformed to him,
we have borne by the law of nature
the image of the man of earth,
so by the sanctification of grace
we may bear the image of the Man of heaven.
Through Christ our Lord.

First Part:
The Liturgy of the Word

First Reading   Isaiah 52:13 – 53:12

He was pierced through for our faults.

See, my servant will prosper,
he shall be lifted up, exalted, rise to great heights.

As the crowds were appalled on seeing him
– so disfigured did he look
that he seemed no longer human –
so will the crowds be astonished at him,
and kings stand speechless before him;
for they shall see something never told
and witness something never heard before:
"Who could believe what we have heard,
and to whom has the power of the Lord been revealed?"

Like a sapling he grew up in front of us,
like a root in arid ground.
Without beauty, without majesty (we saw him),
no looks to attract our eyes;
a thing despised and rejected by men,
a man of sorrows and familiar with suffering,
a man to make people screen their faces;
he was despised and we took no account of him.

And yet ours were the sufferings he bore,
ours the sorrows he carried.
But we, we thought of him as someone punished,
struck by God, and brought low.
Yet he was pierced for our faults,
crushed for our sins.
On him lies a punishment that brings us peace,
and through his wounds we are healed.

We had all gone astray like sheep,
each taking his own way,
and the Lord burdened him
with the sins of all of us.

Harshly dealt with, he bore it humbly,
he never opened his mouth,
like a lamb that is led to the slaughter-house,
like a sheep that is dumb before its shearers
never opening its mouth.

By force and by law he was taken;
would anyone plead his cause?
Yes, he was torn away from the land of the living;
for our faults struck down in death.
They gave him a grave with the wicked,
a tomb with the rich,
though he had done no wrong
and there had been no perjury in his mouth.
The Lord has been pleased to crush him with suffering.
If he offers his life in atonement,
he shall see his heirs, he shall have a long life
and through him what the Lord wishes will be done.

His soul's anguish over
he shall see the light and be content.
By his sufferings shall my servant justify many,
taking their faults on himself.

Hence I will grant whole hordes for his tribute,
he shall divide the spoil with the mighty,
for surrendering himself to death
and letting himself be taken for a sinner,
while he was bearing the faults of many
and praying all the time for sinners.

Psalm   Psalm 30

R. **Father, into your hands I commend my spirit.**

1. In you, O Lord, I take refuge.
   Let me never be put to shame.
   In your justice, set me free.
   Into your hands I commend my spirit.
   It is you who will redeem me, Lord. R.

2. In the face of all my foes
   I am a reproach,
   an object of scorn to my neighbours
   and of fear to my friends. R.

3. Those who see me in the street
   run far away from me.
   I am like a dead man, forgotten in men's hearts,
   like a thing thrown away. R.

4. But as for me, I trust in you, Lord,
   I say: "You are my God."
   My life is in your hands, deliver me
   from the hands of those who hate me. R.

5. Let your face shine on your servant.
   Save me in your love.
   Be strong, let your heart take courage,
   all who hope in the Lord. R.

Second Reading   Hebrews 4:14-16; 5:7-9

He learnt to obey through suffering and became for all who obey
him the source of eternal salvation.

Since in Jesus, the Son of God, we have the supreme high priest who
has gone through to the highest heaven, we must never let go of the
faith that we have professed. For it is not as if we had a high priest
who was incapable of feeling our weaknesses with us; but we have
one who has been tempted in every way that we are, though he is
without sin. Let us be confident, then, in approaching the throne of
grace, that we shall have mercy from him and find grace when we
are in need of help.

   During his life on earth, he offered up prayer and entreaty, aloud
and in silent tears, to the one who had the power to save him out
of death, and he submitted so humbly that his prayer was heard.
Although he was a Son, he learnt to obey through suffering; but
having been made perfect, he became for all who obey him the
source of eternal salvation.

Gospel Acclamation
Glory and praise to you, O Christ!
Christ was humbler yet,
even to accepting death, death on a cross.
But God raised him high
and gave him the name which is above all names.
Glory and praise to you, O Christ!   **Philippians 2:8-9**

The Passion may be read by three people. One reads the narrative: this part is marked N.; if possible the priest reads the words of Jesus (J.); and a third person reads the words of other speakers (O.). The usual greeting and conclusion to the Gospel reading are omitted.

Gospel   **John 18:1 – 19:42**
The passion of our Lord Jesus Christ according to John.
N. Jesus left with his disciples and crossed the Kedron valley. There was a garden there, and he went into it with his disciples. Judas the traitor knew the place well, since Jesus had often met his disciples there, and he brought the cohort to this place together with a detachment of guards sent by the chief priests and the Pharisees, all with lanterns and torches and weapons. Knowing everything that was going to happen to him, Jesus then came forward and said, J. "Who are you looking for?" N. They answered, O. "Jesus the Nazarene." N. He said, J. "I am he." N. Now Judas the traitor was standing among them. When Jesus said, "I am he", they moved back and fell to the ground. He asked them a second time, J. "Who are you looking for?" N. They said, O. "Jesus the Nazarene." N. Jesus replied, J. "I have told you that I am he. If I am the one you are looking for, let these others go". N. This was to fulfil the words he had spoken: "Not one of those you gave me have I lost."

Simon Peter, who carried a sword, drew it and wounded the high priest's servant, cutting off his right ear. The servant's name was Malchus. Jesus said to Peter, J. "Put your sword back in its scabbard; am I not to drink the cup that the Father has given me?" N. The cohort and its captain and the Jewish guards seized Jesus and bound him. They took him first to Annas, because Annas was the father-in-law of Caiaphas, who was high priest that year. It was Caiaphas who had suggested to the Jews, "It is better for one man to die for the people."

Simon Peter, with another disciple, followed Jesus. This disciple, who was known to the high priest, went with Jesus into the high priest's palace, but Peter stayed outside the door. So the other disciple, the one known to the high priest, went out, spoke to the woman who was keeping the door and brought Peter in. The maid on duty at the door said to Peter, O. "Aren't you another of that man's disciples?" N. He answered, O. "I am not." N. Now it was cold, and the servants and guards had lit a charcoal fire and were standing there warming themselves; so Peter stood there too, warming himself with the others.

The high priest questioned Jesus about his disciples and his teaching. Jesus answered, J. "I have spoken openly for all the world to hear; I have always taught in the synagogue and in the Temple where all the Jews meet together: I have said nothing in secret. But why ask me? Ask my hearers what I taught: they know what I said." N. At these words, one of the guards standing by gave Jesus a slap in the face, saying, O. "Is that the way to answer the high priest?" N. Jesus replied, J. "If there is something wrong in what I said, point it out; but if there is no offence in it, why did you strike me?" N. Then Annas sent him, still bound, to Caiaphas, the high priest.

As Simon Peter stood there warming himself, someone said to him, O. "Aren't you another of his disciples?" N. He denied it saying, O. "I am not." N. One of the high priest's servants, a relation of the man whose ear Peter had cut off, said, O. "Didn't I see you in the garden with him?" N. Again Peter denied it; and at once a cock crew.

They then led Jesus from the house of Caiaphas to the Praetorium. It was now morning. They did not go into the Praetorium themselves or they would be defiled and unable to eat the Passover. So Pilate came outside to them and said, O. "What charge do you bring against this man?" N. They replied, O. "If he were not a criminal, we should not be handing him over to you." N. Pilate said, O. "Take him yourselves, and try him by your own Law." N. The Jews answered, O. "We are not allowed to put a man to death." N. This was to fulfil the words Jesus had spoken indicating the way he was going to die.

So Pilate went back into the Praetorium and called Jesus to him, and asked, O. "Are you the king of the Jews?" N. Jesus replied, J. "Do you ask this of your own accord, or have others spoken to you about me? N. Pilate answered, O. "Am I a Jew? It is your own people and the chief priests who have handed you over to me: what have you done?" N. Jesus replied, J. "Mine is not a kingdom of this world; if my kingdom were of this world, my men would have fought to prevent me being surrendered to the Jews. But my kingdom is not of this kind." N. Pilate said, O. "So you are a king then?" N. Jesus answered, J. "It is you who say it. Yes, I am a king. I was born for this, I came into the world for this; to bear witness to the truth, and all who are on the side of truth listen to my voice." N. Pilate said, O. "Truth? What is that?" N. And with that he went out again to the Jews and said, O. "I find no case against him. But according to a custom of yours I should release one prisoner at the Passover; would you like me, then, to release the king of the Jews?" N. At this they shouted: O. "Not this man, but Barabbas". N. Barabbas was a brigand.

Pilate then had Jesus taken away and scourged; and after this, the soldiers twisted some thorns into a crown and put it on his head, and dressed him in a purple robe. They kept coming up to him and saying, O. "Hail, king of the Jews!" N. and they slapped him in the face.

Pilate came outside and said to them, O. "Look, I am going to bring him out to you to let you see that I find no case." N. Jesus then came out wearing the crown of thorns and the purple robe. Pilate said, O. "Here is the man." N. When they saw him the chief priests and the guards shouted, O. "Crucify him! Crucify him!" N. Pilate said, O. "Take him yourselves and crucify him: I can find no case against him." N. The Jews replied, O. "We have a Law, and according to the Law he ought to die, because he has claimed to be the Son of God." N. When Pilate heard them say this his fears increased. Re-entering the Praetorium, he said to Jesus, O. "Where do you come from?" N. But Jesus made no answer. Pilate then said to him, O. "Are you refusing to speak to me? Surely you know I have power to release you and I have power to crucify you?" N. Jesus replied, J. "You would have no power over me if it had not been given you from above; that is why the one who handed me over to you has the greater guilt."

N. From that moment Pilate was anxious to set him free, but the Jews shouted, O. "If you set him free you are no friend of Caesar's; anyone who makes himself king is defying Caesar." N. Hearing these words, Pilate had Jesus brought out, and seated himself on the chair of judgement at a place called the Pavement, in Hebrew Gabbatha. It was Passover Preparation Day, about the sixth hour. Pilate said to the Jews, O. "Here is your king." N. They said, O. "Take him away, take him away. Crucify him!" N. Pilate said, O. "Do you want me to crucify your king?" N. The chief priests answered, O. "We have no king except Caesar." N. So in the end Pilate handed him over to them to be crucified.

They then took charge of Jesus, and carrying his own cross he went out of the city to the place of the skull or, as it was called in Hebrew, Golgotha, where they crucified him with two others, one on either side with Jesus in the middle. Pilate wrote out a notice and had it fixed to the cross; it ran: "Jesus the Nazarene, King of the Jews." This notice was read by many of the Jews, because the place where Jesus was crucified was not far from the city, and the writing was in Hebrew, Latin and Greek. So the Jewish chief priests said to Pilate, O. "You should not write 'King of the Jews', but 'This man said: "I am King of the Jews."'" N. Pilate answered, O. "What I have written, I have written." N. When the soldiers had finished crucifying Jesus they took his clothing and divided it into four shares, one for each soldier. His undergarment was seamless, woven in one piece from neck to hem; so they said to one another, O. "Instead of tearing it, let's throw dice to decide who is to have it." N. In this way the words of scripture were fulfilled:

They shared out my clothing among them.
They cast lots for my clothes.

This is exactly what the soldiers did.

Near the cross of Jesus stood his mother and his mother's sister, Mary the wife of Clopas, and Mary of Magdala. Seeing his mother and the disciple he loved standing near her, Jesus said to his mother, J. "Woman, this is your son." N. Then to the disciple he said, J. "This is your mother." N. And from that moment the disciple made a place for her in his home.

After this, Jesus knew that everything had now been completed, and to fulfil the scripture perfectly he said: J. "I am thirsty." N. A jar full of vinegar stood there, so putting a sponge soaked in vinegar on a hyssop stick they held it up to his mouth. After Jesus had taken the vinegar he said, J. "It is accomplished", N. and bowing his head he gave up the spirit.

All kneel and pause for a moment.

N. It was Preparation Day, and to prevent the bodies remaining on the cross during the sabbath – since that sabbath was a day of special solemnity – the Jews asked Pilate to have the legs broken and the bodies taken away. Consequently the soldiers came and broke the legs of the first man who had been crucified with him and then of the other. When they came to Jesus, they found that he was already dead, and so instead of breaking his legs one of the soldiers pierced his side with a lance; and immediately there came out blood and water. This is the evidence of one who saw it – trustworthy evidence, and he knows he speaks the truth – and he gives it so that you may believe as well. Because all this happened to fulfil the words of scripture:

Not one bone of his body will be broken,

and again, in another place scripture says:

They will look upon the one whom they have pierced.

After this, Joseph of Arimathea, who was a disciple of Jesus – though a secret one because he was afraid of the Jews – asked Pilate to let him remove the body of Jesus. Pilate gave permission, so they came and took it away. Nicodemus came as well – the same one who had first come to Jesus at night-time – and he brought a mixture of myrrh and aloes, weighing about a hundred pounds. They took the body of Jesus and wrapped it with the spices in linen cloths, following the Jewish burial custom. At the place where he had been crucified there was a garden, and in the garden a new tomb in which no one had yet been buried. Since it was the Jewish Day of Preparation and the tomb was near at hand, they laid Jesus there.

After the reading of the Lord's Passion, the priest gives a brief homily and then the people may be invited to spend a short time in prayer.

The Solemn Intercessions

The Liturgy of the Word concludes with the Solemn Intercessions. The deacon or another minister sings or says the invitation in which the intention is expressed. All pray in silence for a while, and then the priest sings or says the prayer.

The people may remain either kneeling or standing throughout the entire period of the prayers.

I. For holy Church

Let us pray, dearly beloved, for the holy Church of God,
that our God and Lord be pleased to give her peace,
to guard her and to unite her throughout the whole world
and grant that, leading our life in tranquillity and quiet,
we may glorify God the Father almighty.

Silent prayer. Then the priest says or sings:

Almighty ever-living God,
who in Christ revealed your glory to all the nations,
watch over the works of your mercy,
that your Church, spread throughout all the world,
may persevere with steadfast faith in confessing your name.
Through Christ our Lord.
Amen.

II. For the Pope

Let us pray also for our most Holy Father Pope N.,
that our God and Lord,
who chose him for the Order of Bishops,
may keep him safe and unharmed for the Lord's holy Church,
to govern the holy People of God.

Silent prayer. Then the priest says or sings:

Almighty ever-living God,
by whose decree all things are founded,
look with favour on our prayers
and in your kindness protect the Pope chosen for us,
that, under him, the Christian people,

governed by you their maker,
may grow in merit by reason of their faith.
Through Christ our Lord.
Amen.

III. For all orders and degrees of the faithful
Let us pray also for our Bishop N.,
for all Bishops, Priests, and Deacons of the Church
and for the whole of the faithful people.

Silent prayer. Then the priest says or sings:

Almighty ever-living God,
by whose Spirit the whole body of the Church
is sanctified and governed,
hear our humble prayer for your ministers,
that, by the gift of your grace,
all may serve you faithfully.
Through Christ our Lord.
Amen.

IV. For catechumens
Let us pray also for (our) catechumens,
that our God and Lord
may open wide the ears of their inmost hearts
and unlock the gates of his mercy,
that, having received forgiveness of all their sins
through the waters of rebirth,
they, too, may be one with Christ Jesus our Lord.

Silent prayer. Then the priest says or sings:

Almighty ever-living God,
who make your Church ever fruitful with new offspring,
increase the faith and understanding of (our) catechumens,
that, reborn in the font of Baptism,
they may be added to the number of your adopted children.
Through Christ our Lord.
Amen.

V. For the unity of Christians
Let us pray also for all our brothers and sisters who believe in Christ,
that our God and Lord may be pleased,
as they live the truth,
to gather them together and keep them in his one Church.

Silent prayer. Then the priest says or sings:

Almighty ever-living God,
who gather what is scattered
and keep together what you have gathered,
look kindly on the flock of your Son,
that those whom one Baptism has consecrated
may be joined together by integrity of faith
and united in the bond of charity.
Through Christ our Lord.
Amen.

VI. For the Jewish people
Let us pray also for the Jewish people,
to whom the Lord our God spoke first,
that he may grant them to advance in love of his name
and in faithfulness to his covenant.

Silent prayer. Then the priest says or sings:

Almighty ever-living God,
who bestowed your promises on Abraham and his descendants,
graciously hear the prayers of your Church,
that the people you first made your own
may attain the fullness of redemption.
Through Christ our Lord.
Amen.

VII. For those who do not believe in Christ
Let us pray also for those who do not believe in Christ,
that, enlightened by the Holy Spirit,
they, too, may enter on the way of salvation.

Silent prayer. Then the priest says or sings:

Almighty ever-living God,
grant to those who do not confess Christ
that, by walking before you with a sincere heart,
they may find the truth
and that we ourselves, being constant in mutual love
and striving to understand more fully the mystery of your life,
may be made more perfect witnesses to your love in the world.
Through Christ our Lord.
Amen.

VIII. For those who do not believe in God
Let us pray also for those who do not acknowledge God,
that, following what is right in sincerity of heart,
they may find the way to God himself.

Silent prayer. Then the priest says or sings:

Almighty ever-living God,
who created all people
to seek you always by desiring you
and, by finding you, come to rest,
grant, we pray,
that, despite every harmful obstacle,
all may recognise the signs of your fatherly love
and the witness of the good works
done by those who believe in you,
and so in gladness confess you,
the one true God and Father of our human race.
Through Christ our Lord.
Amen.

IX. For those in public office
Let us pray also for those in public office,
that our God and Lord
may direct their minds and hearts according to his will
for the true peace and freedom of all.

Silent prayer. Then the priest says or sings:

Almighty ever-living God,
in whose hand lies every human heart
and the rights of peoples,
look with favour, we pray,
on those who govern with authority over us,
that throughout the whole world,
the prosperity of peoples,
the assurance of peace,
and freedom of religion
may through your gift be made secure.
Through Christ our Lord.
Amen.

X. For those in tribulation
Let us pray, dearly beloved,
to God the Father almighty,
that he may cleanse the world of all errors,
banish disease, drive out hunger,
unlock prisons, loosen fetters,
granting to travellers safety, to pilgrims return,
health to the sick, and salvation to the dying.

Silent prayer. Then the priest says or sings:

Almighty ever-living God,
comfort of mourners, strength of all who toil,
may the prayers of those who cry out in any tribulation
come before you,
that all may rejoice,
because in their hour of need
your mercy was at hand.
Through Christ our Lord.
Amen.

Second Part:
The Adoration of the Holy Cross

The Showing of the Holy Cross

The Cross is shown to the people three times, either from before the altar, while it is unveiled, or as it is carried in procession through the church to the sanctuary. Each time the priest says or sings:

Behold the wood of the Cross,
on which hung the salvation of the world.
Come, let us adore.

The Adoration of the Holy Cross

The priest, clergy, ministers and people approach to venerate the Cross, as if in procession. They show reverence to the Cross by a simple genuflection or by some other appropriate sign according to local custom, for example, kissing the Cross.

While the adoration of the Holy Cross is taking place, the following or other suitable songs may be sung.

Antiphon

We adore your Cross, O Lord,
we praise and glorify your holy Resurrection,
for behold, because of the wood of a tree
joy has come to the whole world.

May God have mercy on us and bless us;
may he let his face shed its light upon us
and have mercy on us.   cf. Psalm 66:2

We adore your Cross, O Lord,
we praise and glorify your holy Resurrection,
for behold, because of the wood of a tree
joy has come to the whole world.

The Reproaches

Parts assigned to one of the two choirs separately are indicated by the numbers 1 (first choir) and 2 (second choir); parts sung by both choirs together are marked 1 and 2.

I

1 and 2: My people, what have I done to you?
Or how have I grieved you? Answer me!

1:    Because I led you out of the land of Egypt,
      you have prepared a Cross for your Saviour.

1:    Hagios o Theos,
2:    Holy is God,
1:    Hagios Ischyros,
2:    Holy and Mighty,
1:    Hagios Athanatos, eleison himas.
2:    Holy and Immortal One, have mercy on us.

1 and 2: Because I led you out through the desert forty years
and fed you with manna and brought you into a land of plenty,
you have prepared a Cross for your Saviour.

1:    Hagios o Theos,
2:    Holy is God,
1:    Hagios Ischyros,
2:    Holy and Mighty,
1:    Hagios Athanatos, eleison himas.
2:    Holy and Immortal One, have mercy on us.

1 and 2: What more should I have done for you and have not done?
Indeed, I planted you as my most beautiful chosen vine
and you have turned very bitter for me,
for in my thirst you gave me vinegar to drink
and with a lance you pierced your Saviour's side.

1:    Hagios o Theos,
2:    Holy is God,
1:    Hagios Ischyros,
2:    Holy and Mighty,
1:    Hagios Athanatos, eleison himas.
2:    Holy and Immortal One, have mercy on us.

II

Cantors:

I scourged Egypt for your sake with its firstborn sons,
and you scourged me and handed me over.

1 and 2:

My people, what have I done to you?
Or how have I grieved you? Answer me!

Cantors:

I led you out from Egypt as Pharaoh lay sunk in the Red Sea,
and you handed me over to the chief priests.

1 and 2:

My people...

Cantors:

I opened up the sea before you,
and you opened my side with a lance.

1 and 2:

My people...

Cantors:

I went before you in a pillar of cloud,
and you led me into Pilate's palace.

1 and 2:

My people...

Cantors:

I fed you with manna in the desert,
and on me you rained blows and lashes.

1 and 2:

My people...

Cantors:

I gave you saving water from the rock to drink,
and for drink you gave me gall and vinegar.

1 and 2:
My people…

Cantors:
I struck down for you the kings of the Canaanites,
and you struck my head with a reed.

1 and 2:
My people…

Cantors:
I put in your hand a royal sceptre,
and you put on my head a crown of thorns.

1 and 2:
My people…

Cantors:
I exalted you with great power,
and you hung me on the scaffold of the Cross.

1 and 2:
My people…

Hymn
All:
Faithful Cross the Saints rely on,
Noble tree beyond compare!
Never was there such a scion,
Never leaf or flower so rare.
Sweet the timber, sweet the iron,
Sweet the burden that they bear!

Cantors:
Sing, my tongue, in exultation
Of our banner and device!
Make a solemn proclamation
Of a triumph and its price:
How the Saviour of creation
Conquered by his sacrifice!

All:

Faithful Cross the Saints rely on,
Noble tree beyond compare!
Never was there such a scion,
Never leaf or flower so rare.

Cantors:

For, when Adam first offended,
Eating that forbidden fruit,
Not all hopes of glory ended
With the serpent at the root:
Broken nature would be mended
By a second tree and shoot.

All:

Sweet the timber, sweet the iron,
Sweet the burden that they bear!

Cantors:

Thus the tempter was outwitted
By a wisdom deeper still:
Remedy and ailment fitted,
Means to cure and means to kill;
That the world might be acquitted,
Christ would do his Father's will.

All:

Faithful Cross the Saints rely on,
Noble tree beyond compare!
Never was there such a scion,
Never leaf or flower so rare.

Cantors:

So the Father, out of pity
For our self-inflicted doom,
Sent him from the heavenly city
When the holy time had come:
He, the Son and the Almighty,
Took our flesh in Mary's womb.

All:

Sweet the timber, sweet the iron,
Sweet the burden that they bear!

Cantors:

Hear a tiny baby crying,
Founder of the seas and strands;
See his virgin Mother tying
Cloth around his feet and hands;
Find him in a manger lying
Tightly wrapped in swaddling-bands!

All:

Faithful Cross the Saints rely on,
Noble tree beyond compare!
Never was there such a scion,
Never leaf or flower so rare.

Cantors:

So he came, the long-expected,
Not in glory, not to reign;
Only born to be rejected,
Choosing hunger, toil and pain,
Till the scaffold was erected
And the Paschal Lamb was slain.

All:

Sweet the timber, sweet the iron,
Sweet the burden that they bear!

Cantors:

No disgrace was too abhorrent:
Nailed and mocked and parched he died;
Blood and water, double warrant,
Issue from his wounded side,
Washing in a mighty torrent
Earth and stars and oceantide.

All:

Faithful Cross the Saints rely on,
Noble tree beyond compare!

Never was there such a scion,
Never leaf or flower so rare.

Cantors:
Lofty timber, smooth your roughness,
Flex your boughs for blossoming;
Let your fibres lose their toughness,
Gently let your tendrils cling;
Lay aside your native gruffness,
Clasp the body of your King!

All:
Sweet the timber, sweet the iron,
Sweet the burden that they bear!

Cantors:
Noblest tree of all created,
Richly jewelled and embossed:
Post by Lamb's blood consecrated;
Spar that saves the tempest-tossed;
Scaffold-beam which, elevated,
Carries what the world has cost!

All:
Faithful Cross the Saints rely on,
Noble tree beyond compare!
Never was there such a scion,
Never leaf or flower so rare.

The following conclusion is never to be omitted.

All:
Wisdom, power, and adoration
To the blessèd Trinity
For redemption and salvation
Through the Paschal Mystery,
Now, in every generation,
And for all eternity. Amen.

Third Part:
Holy Communion

The altar is prepared and the deacon or the priest brings the Blessed Sacrament from the place of repose to the altar, while all stand in silence. Then the priest introduces the Lord's Prayer:

At the Saviour's command
and formed by divine teaching,
we dare to say:

**Our Father, who art in heaven,
hallowed be thy name;
thy kingdom come,
thy will be done
on earth as it is in heaven.
Give us this day our daily bread,
and forgive us our trespasses,
as we forgive those who trespass against us;
and lead us not into temptation,
but deliver us from evil.**

Deliver us, Lord, we pray, from every evil,
graciously grant peace in our days,
that, by the help of your mercy,
we may be always free from sin
and safe from all distress,
as we await the blessed hope
and the coming of our Saviour, Jesus Christ.

**For the kingdom,
the power and the glory are yours
now and for ever.**

After his private prayer of preparation the priest genuflects, takes the host, and, holding it slightly raised over the ciborium, facing the people, says aloud:

Behold the Lamb of God,
behold him who takes away the sins of the world.
Blessed are those called to the supper of the Lamb.

Lord, I am not worthy
that you should enter under my roof,
but only say the word
and my soul shall be healed.

After the priest has reverently consumed the Body of Christ, Communion is distributed to the faithful in the usual way.

Prayer after Communion
Almighty ever-living God,
who have restored us to life
by the blessed Death and Resurrection of your Christ,
preserve in us the work of your mercy,
that, by partaking of this mystery,
we may have a life unceasingly devoted to you.
Through Christ our Lord.

Prayer over the People
May abundant blessing, O Lord, we pray,
descend upon your people,
who have honoured the Death of your Son
in the hope of their resurrection:
may pardon come,
comfort be given,
holy faith increase,
and everlasting redemption be made secure.
Through Christ our Lord.

After genuflecting to the Cross, all depart in silence.

Easter Sunday of the Resurrection of the Lord.

THE EASTER VIGIL IN
THE HOLY NIGHT – ABC

Most blessed of all nights!
The night of the Passover when Christ passed from death to life is the most
important moment in the Christian year. We celebrate our passing over,
through Baptism, from the death of sin to the life of grace. From the earliest
times, Christians devoted this night to watching and waiting. We, too, keep our
vigil, knowing that the Lord will rise triumphant from the tomb to establish
his Church among us. The grain of seed has died and now the Church is born,
and will give shelter to countless numbers of people till the end of time.

By most ancient tradition, this is the night of keeping vigil for the Lord (Exodus 12:42). The Gospel reminds us to have our lamps burning ready, to be like those waiting for the Lord's return, so that when he arrives he may find us awake and invite us to sit at his table (Luke 12:35-37).

The Vigil is arranged in four parts:
- The first part is the Lucernarium, or service of light.
- In the second part, the Liturgy of the Word, we meditate on the history of salvation, remembering the wonderful things that the Lord has done for his people since the very beginning.
- The third part is the Liturgy of Baptism, in which new members of the Church are reborn and we renew our promises as the day of Resurrection approaches.
- The final part is the Liturgy of the Eucharist, when the whole Church is called to the table the Lord has prepared for his people, the memorial of his Death and Resurrection until he comes again.

The entire celebration must take place during the night, so that it begins after nightfall and ends before daybreak on the Sunday.

Anyone who participates in the Mass of the night may receive Communion again at Mass during the day.

First Part:
The Solemn Beginning of the Vigil or Lucernarium

The Blessing of the Fire and Preparation of the Candle

A fire is prepared outside the church and everyone gathers around it. If for any reason a fire cannot be lit outside the church, the rite is adapted to the circumstances.

The priest makes the Sign of the Cross, greets the people in the usual way and briefly instructs them about the vigil in these or similar words:

Dear brethren (brothers and sisters),
on this most sacred night,
in which our Lord Jesus Christ
passed over from death to life,
the Church calls upon her sons and daughters,
scattered throughout the world,
to come together to watch and pray.
If we keep the memorial
of the Lord's paschal solemnity in this way,
listening to his word and celebrating his mysteries,
then we shall have the sure hope
of sharing his triumph over death
and living with him in God.

Then the priest blesses the fire, saying:

Let us pray.

O God, who through your Son
bestowed upon the faithful the fire of your glory,
sanctify ✠ this new fire, we pray,
and grant that,
by these paschal celebrations,
we may be so inflamed with heavenly desires,
that with minds made pure
we may attain festivities of unending splendour.
Through Christ our Lord.
Amen.

Then one of the ministers brings the paschal candle to the priest, who cuts a cross into the candle with a stylus. Then he traces the Greek letter Alpha above the cross, the letter Omega below, and the four numerals of the current year between the arms of the cross. Meanwhile he says:

Christ yesterday and today;
the Beginning and the End;
the Alpha;
and the Omega.
All time belongs to him;
and all the ages.
To him be glory and power;
through every age and for ever. Amen.

When the cutting of the cross and of the other signs has been completed, the priest may insert five grains of incense into the candle in the form of a cross, meanwhile saying:

By his holy
and glorious wounds,
may Christ the Lord
guard us
and protect us. Amen.

The priest lights the paschal candle from the new fire, saying:

May the light of Christ rising in glory
dispel the darkness of our hearts and minds.

Procession
All enter the church, carrying unlit candles, led by the deacon or the priest carrying the lighted paschal candle.

At the door of the church the deacon or priest raises up the candle and sings:

The Light of Christ.
Thanks be to God.

Then the deacon or priest moves forward to the middle of the church and, raising up the candle, sings a second time:

The Light of Christ.
Thanks be to God.

All light their candles from the flame of the paschal candle and continue in procession.

When the deacon or priest arrives before the altar, he stands facing the people, raises up the candle and sings a third time:

The Light of Christ.
Thanks be to God.

Then the deacon or priest places the paschal candle on a stand next to the ambo or in the middle of the sanctuary.

The lights are lit throughout the church, except for the altar candles.

The Easter Proclamation (Exsultet)
The Easter Proclamation is sung, in the longer or shorter form, with all standing and holding lighted candles in their hands.

Longer Form
Exult, let them exult, the hosts of heaven,
exult, let Angel ministers of God exult,
let the trumpet of salvation
sound aloud our mighty King's triumph!
Be glad, let earth be glad, as glory floods her,
ablaze with light from her eternal King,
let all corners of the earth be glad,
knowing an end to gloom and darkness.
Rejoice, let Mother Church also rejoice,
arrayed with the lightning of his glory,
let this holy building shake with joy,
filled with the mighty voices of the peoples.

(Therefore, dearest friends,
standing in the awesome glory of this holy light,
invoke with me, I ask you,
the mercy of God almighty,
that he, who has been pleased to number me,
though unworthy, among the Levites,
may pour into me his light unshadowed,
that I may sing this candle's perfect praises.

The Lord be with you.
And with your spirit.)

Lift up your hearts.
We lift them up to the Lord.

Let us give thanks to the Lord our God.
It is right and just.

It is truly right and just,
with ardent love of mind and heart
and with devoted service of our voice,
to acclaim our God invisible, the almighty Father,
and Jesus Christ, our Lord, his Son, his Only Begotten.

Who for our sake paid Adam's debt to the eternal Father,
and, pouring out his own dear Blood,
wiped clean the record of our ancient sinfulness.

These then are the feasts of Passover,
in which is slain the Lamb, the one true Lamb,
whose Blood anoints the doorposts of believers.

This is the night,
when once you led our forebears, Israel's children,
from slavery in Egypt
and made them pass dry-shod through the Red Sea.

This is the night
that with a pillar of fire
banished the darkness of sin.

This is the night
that even now, throughout the world,
sets Christian believers apart from worldly vices
and from the gloom of sin,
leading them to grace
and joining them to his holy ones.

This is the night,
when Christ broke the prison-bars of death
and rose victorious from the underworld.

Our birth would have been no gain,
had we not been redeemed.

O wonder of your humble care for us!
O love, O charity beyond all telling,
to ransom a slave you gave away your Son!

O truly necessary sin of Adam,
destroyed completely by the Death of Christ!

O happy fault
that earned so great, so glorious a Redeemer!

O truly blessed night,
worthy alone to know the time and hour
when Christ rose from the underworld!

This is the night
of which it is written:
The night shall be as bright as day,
dazzling is the night for me,
and full of gladness.

The sanctifying power of this night
dispels wickedness, washes faults away,
restores innocence to the fallen, and joy to mourners,
drives out hatred, fosters concord, and brings down the mighty.

On this, your night of grace, O holy Father,
accept this candle, a solemn offering,
the work of bees and of your servants' hands,

an evening sacrifice of praise,
this gift from your most holy Church.

But now we know the praises of this pillar,
which glowing fire ignites for God's honour,
a fire into many flames divided,
yet never dimmed by sharing of its light,
for it is fed by melting wax,
drawn out by mother bees
to build a torch so precious.

O truly blessed night,
when things of heaven are wed to those of earth,
and divine to the human.

Therefore, O Lord,
we pray you that this candle,
hallowed to the honour of your name,
may persevere undimmed,
to overcome the darkness of this night.

Receive it as a pleasing fragrance,
and let it mingle with the lights of heaven.
May this flame be found still burning
by the Morning Star:
the one Morning Star who never sets,
Christ your Son,
who, coming back from death's domain,
has shed his peaceful light on humanity,
and lives and reigns for ever and ever.
Amen.

Shorter Form
Exult, let them exult, the hosts of heaven,
exult, let Angel ministers of God exult,
let the trumpet of salvation
sound aloud our mighty King's triumph!
Be glad, let earth be glad, as glory floods her,
ablaze with light from her eternal King,

let all corners of the earth be glad,
knowing an end to gloom and darkness.
Rejoice, let Mother Church also rejoice,
arrayed with the lightning of his glory,
let this holy building shake with joy,
filled with the mighty voices of the peoples.

(The Lord be with you.
And with your spirit.)

Lift up your hearts.
We lift them up to the Lord.

Let us give thanks to the Lord our God.
It is right and just.

It is truly right and just,
with ardent love of mind and heart
and with devoted service of our voice,
to acclaim our God invisible, the almighty Father,
and Jesus Christ, our Lord, his Son, his Only Begotten.

Who for our sake paid Adam's debt to the eternal Father,
and, pouring out his own dear Blood,
wiped clean the record of our ancient sinfulness.

These then are the feasts of Passover,
in which is slain the Lamb, the one true Lamb,
whose Blood anoints the doorposts of believers.

This is the night,
when once you led our forebears, Israel's children,
from slavery in Egypt
and made them pass dry-shod through the Red Sea.

This is the night
that with a pillar of fire
banished the darkness of sin.

This is the night
that even now, throughout the world,
sets Christian believers apart from worldly vices
and from the gloom of sin,
leading them to grace
and joining them to his holy ones.

This is the night,
when Christ broke the prison-bars of death
and rose victorious from the underworld.

O wonder of your humble care for us!
O love, O charity beyond all telling,
to ransom a slave you gave away your Son!

O truly necessary sin of Adam,
destroyed completely by the Death of Christ!

O happy fault
that earned so great, so glorious a Redeemer!
The sanctifying power of this night
dispels wickedness, washes faults away,
restores innocence to the fallen, and joy to mourners.

O truly blessed night,
when things of heaven are wed to those of earth
and divine to the human.

On this, your night of grace, O holy Father,
accept this candle, a solemn offering,
the work of bees and of your servants' hands,
an evening sacrifice of praise,
this gift from your most holy Church.

Therefore, O Lord,
we pray you that this candle,
hallowed to the honour of your name,
may persevere undimmed,
to overcome the darkness of this night.

Receive it as a pleasing fragrance,
and let it mingle with the lights of heaven.
May this flame be found still burning
by the Morning Star:
the one Morning Star who never sets,
Christ your Son,
who, coming back from death's domain,
has shed his peaceful light on humanity,
and lives and reigns for ever and ever.
Amen.

Second Part:
The Liturgy of the Word

In this vigil, the mother of all vigils, nine readings are provided: seven from the Old Testament and two from the New Testament (the Letter and Gospel), all of which should be read whenever this can be done.

For pastoral reasons, the number of readings from the Old Testament may, on occasion, be reduced. At least three readings should be read from the Old Testament, and the reading of chapter 14 of Exodus with its canticle must never be omitted.

All set aside their candles and sit. Before the readings begin, the priest addresses the people in these or similar words:
Dear brethren (brothers and sisters),
now that we have begun our solemn Vigil,
let us listen with quiet hearts to the Word of God.
Let us meditate on how God in times past saved his people
and in these, the last days, has sent us his Son as our Redeemer.
Let us pray that our God may complete this
    paschal work of salvation
by the fullness of redemption.

First Reading　　　　　　　　　　　　　　　　　**Genesis 1:1 – 2:2**

God saw all he had made, and indeed it was very good.

| In the beginning God created the heavens and the earth.

Now the earth was a formless void, there was darkness over the deep, and God's spirit hovered over the water.

God said, "Let there be light," and there was light. God saw that light was good, and God divided light from darkness. God called light "day", and darkness he called "night". Evening came and morning came: the first day.

God said, "Let there be a vault in the waters to divide the waters in two." And so it was. God made the vault, and it divided the waters above the vault from the waters under the vault. God called the vault "heaven". Evening came and morning came: the second day.

God said, "Let the waters under heaven come together into a single mass, and let dry land appear." And so it was. God called the dry land "earth" and the mass of water "seas", and God saw that it was good.

God said, "Let the earth produce vegetation: seed-bearing plants, and fruit trees bearing fruit with their seed inside, on the earth." And so it was. The earth produced vegetation: plants bearing seed in their several kinds and trees bearing fruit with their seed inside in their several kinds, God saw that it was good. Evening came and morning came; the third day.

God said, "Let there be lights in the vault of heaven to divide day from night, and let them indicate festivals, days and years. Let them be lights in the vault of heaven to shine on the earth." And so it was. God made the two great lights: the greater light to govern the day, the smaller light to govern the night, and the stars. God set them in the vault of heaven to shine on the earth, to govern the day and the night and to divide light from darkness. God saw that it was good. Evening came and morning came: the fourth day.

God said, "Let the waters teem with living creatures, and let birds fly above the earth within the vault of heaven." And so it was. God created great sea-serpents and every kind of living creature with which the waters teem, and every kind of winged creature. God saw that it was good. God blessed them, saying "Be fruitful, multiply, and fill the waters of the seas; and let the birds multiply upon the earth." Evening came and morning came: the fifth day.

God said, "Let the earth produce every kind of living creature: cattle, reptiles, and every kind of wild beast." And so it was. God made every kind of wild beast, every kind of cattle, and every kind of land reptile. God saw that it was good.

God said, "Let us make man in our own image, in the likeness of ourselves, and let them be masters of the fish of the sea, the birds of heaven, the cattle, all the wild beasts and all the reptiles that crawl upon the earth."

God created man in the image of himself,
in the image of God he created him,
male and female he created them.

God blessed them, saying to them, "Be fruitful, multiply, fill the earth and conquer it. Be masters of the fish of the sea, the birds of heaven and all living animals on the earth." God said, "See, I give you all the seed-bearing fruit; this shall be your food. To all wild beasts, all birds of heaven and all living reptiles on the earth I give all the foliage of plants for food." And so it was. God saw all he had made, and indeed it was very good.

Evening came and morning came: the sixth day.

Thus heaven and earth were completed with all their array. On the seventh day God completed the work he had been doing. He rested on the seventh day after all the work he had been doing.

The Psalm or a period of silence follows.

Psalm   Psalm 103

R. **Send forth your spirit, O Lord,**
    and renew the face of the earth.

1. Bless the Lord, my soul!
   Lord God, how great you are,
   clothed in majesty and glory,
   wrapped in light as in a robe! R.

2. You founded the earth on its base,
   to stand firm from age to age.
   You wrapped it with the ocean like a cloak:
   the waters stood higher than the mountains. R.

3. You make springs gush forth in the valleys:
   they flow in between the hills.
   On their banks dwell the birds of heaven;
   from the branches they sing their song. R.

4. From your dwelling you water the hills;
   earth drinks its fill of your gift.
   You make the grass grow for the cattle
   and the plants to serve man's needs. R.

5. How many are your works, O Lord!
   In wisdom you have made them all.
   The earth is full of your riches.
   Bless the Lord, my soul! R.

or

Psalm   Psalm 32

R. **The Lord fills the earth with his love.**

1. The word of the Lord is faithful
   and all his works to be trusted.
   The Lord loves justice and right
   and fills the earth with his love. R.

2. By his word the heavens were made,
   by the breath of his mouth all the stars.
   He collects the waves of the ocean;
   he stores up the depths of the sea. R.

3. They are happy, whose God is the Lord,
   the people he has chosen as his own.
   From the heavens the Lord looks forth,
   he sees all the children of men. R.

4. Our soul is waiting for the Lord.
   The Lord is jour help and our shield.
   May your love be upon us, O Lord,
   as we place all our hope in you. R.

All stand.

Prayer
Let us pray.

Almighty ever-living God,
who are wonderful in the ordering of all your works,
may those you have redeemed understand
that there exists nothing more marvellous
than the world's creation in the beginning
except that, at the end of the ages,
Christ our Passover has been sacrificed.
Who lives and reigns for ever and ever.

or

O God, who wonderfully created human nature
and still more wonderfully redeemed it,
grant us, we pray,
to set our minds against the enticements of sin,
that we may merit to attain eternal joys.
Through Christ our Lord.

All sit.

Second Reading   Genesis 22:1-18
The sacrifice of Abraham, our father in faith.

God put Abraham to the test. "Abraham, Abraham", he called.
"Here I am", he replied. "Take your son," God said, "your only
child Isaac, whom you love, and go to the land of Moriah. There
you shall offer him as a burnt offering, on a mountain I will point
out to you."

Rising early next morning Abraham saddled his ass and took
with him two of his servants and his son Isaac. He chopped wood
for the burnt offering and started on his journey to the place God
had pointed out to him. On the third day Abraham looked up and
saw the place in the distance. Then Abraham said to his servants,
"Stay here with the donkey. The boy and I will go over there, we will
worship and come back to you."

Abraham took the wood for the burnt offering, loaded it on Isaac, and carried in his own hands the fire and the knife. Then the two of them set out together. Isaac spoke to his father Abraham, "Father", he said. "Yes, my son", he replied. "Look," he said, "here are the fire and the wood, but where is the lamb for the burnt offering?" Abraham answered, "My son, God himself will provide the lamb for the burnt offering." Then the two of them went on together.

When they arrived at the place God had pointed out to him, Abraham built an altar there, and arranged the wood. Then he bound his son Isaac and put him on the altar on top of the wood. Abraham stretched out his hand and seized the knife to kill his son.

But the angel of the Lord called to him from heaven, "Abraham, Abraham", he said. "I am here", he replied. "Do not raise your hand against the boy," the angel said. "Do not harm him, for now I know you fear God. You have not refused me your son, your only son." Then looking up, Abraham saw a ram caught by its horns in a bush. Abraham took the ram and offered it as a burnt-offering in place of his son.

Abraham called this place "The Lord provides", and hence the saying today: On the mountain the Lord provides.

The angel of the Lord called Abraham a second time from heaven. "I swear by my own self – it is the Lord who speaks – because you have done this, because you have not refused me your son, your only son, I will shower blessings on you, I will make your descendants as many as the stars of heaven and the grains of sand on the seashore. Your descendants shall gain possession of the gates of their enemies. All the nations of the earth shall bless themselves by your descendants, as a reward for your obedience."

The Psalm or a period of silence follows.

Psalm   Psalm 15

R. **Preserve me, God, I take refuge in you.**

1. O Lord, it is you who are my portion and cup;
   it is you yourself who are my prize.
   I keep the Lord ever in my sight:
   since he is at my right hand, I shall stand firm. R.

2. And so my heart rejoices, my soul is glad;
   even my body shall rest in safety.
   For you will not leave my soul among the dead,
   nor let your beloved know decay. R.

3. You will show me the path of life,
   the fullness of joy in your presence,
   at your right hand happiness for ever. R.

All stand.

Prayer
Let us pray.

O God, supreme Father of the faithful,
who increase the children of your promise
by pouring out the grace of adoption
throughout the whole world
and who through the Paschal Mystery
make your servant Abraham father of nations,
as once you swore,
grant, we pray,
that your peoples may enter worthily
into the grace to which you call them.
Through Christ our Lord.

All sit.

Third Reading   Exodus 14:15 – 15:1
The sons of Israel went on dry ground right into the sea.

The Lord said to Moses, "Why do you cry to me so? Tell the sons of
Israel to march on. For yourself, raise your staff and stretch out your
hand over the sea and part it for the sons of Israel to walk through the
sea on dry ground. I for my part will make the heart of the Egyptians
so stubborn that they will follow them. So shall I win myself glory at
the expense of Pharaoh, of all his army, his chariots, his horsemen.
And when I have won glory for myself, at the expense of Pharaoh and
his chariots and his army, the Egyptians will learn that I am the Lord."

   Then the angel of the Lord, who marched at the front of the army
of Israel, changed station and moved to their rear. The pillar of cloud
changed station from the front to the rear of them, and remained

there. It came between the camp of the Egyptians and the camp of Israel. The cloud was dark, and the night passed without the armies drawing any closer the whole night long. Moses stretched out his hand over the sea. The Lord drove back the sea with a strong easterly wind all night, and he made dry land of the sea. The waters parted and the sons of Israel went on dry ground right into the sea, walls of water to right and to left of them. The Egyptians gave chase: after them they went, right into the sea, all Pharaoh's horses, his chariots, and his horsemen. In the morning watch, the Lord looked down on the army of the Egyptians from the pillar of fire and cloud, and threw the army into confusion. He so clogged their chariot wheels that they could scarcely make headway. "Let us flee from the Israelites," the Egyptians cried, "the Lord is fighting for them against the Egyptians!" "Stretch out your hand over the sea," the Lord said to Moses, "that the waters may flow back on the Egyptians and their chariots and their horsemen." Moses stretched out his hand over the sea and, as day broke, the sea returned to its bed. The fleeing Egyptians marched right into it, and the Lord overthrew the Egyptians in the very middle of the sea. The returning waters overwhelmed the chariots and the horsemen of Pharaoh's whole army, which had followed the Israelites into the sea; not a single one of them was left. But the sons of Israel had marched through the sea on dry ground, walls of water to right and to left of them. That day, the Lord rescued Israel from the Egyptians, and Israel saw the Egyptians lying dead on the shore. Israel witnessed the great act that the Lord had performed against the Egyptians, and the people venerated the Lord; they put their faith in the Lord and in Moses, his servant.

It was then that Moses and the sons of Israel sang this song in honour of the Lord:

The following Psalm is taken up immediately.

Psalm   Exodus 15

R. **I will sing to the Lord, glorious his triumph!**

1. I will sing to the Lord, glorious his triumph!
   Horse and rider he has thrown into the sea!
   The Lord is my strength, my song, my salvation.

This is my God and I extol him,
my father's God and I gave him praise. R.

2. The Lord is a warrior! The Lord is his name.
   The chariots of Pharaoh he hurled into the sea,
   the flower of his army is drowned in the sea.
   The deeps hide them; they sank like a stone. R.

3. Your right hand, Lord, glorious in its power,
   your right hand, Lord, has shattered the enemy.
   In the greatness of your glory you crushed the foe. R.

4. You will lead them and plant them on your mountain,
   the place, O Lord, where you have made your home,
   the sanctuary, Lord, which your hands have made.
   The Lord will reign for ever and ever. R.

All stand.

Prayer
Let us pray.

O God, whose ancient wonders
remain undimmed in splendour even in our day,
for what you once bestowed on a single people,
freeing them from Pharaoh's persecution
by the power of your right hand
now you bring about as the salvation of the nations
through the waters of rebirth,
grant, we pray, that the whole world
may become children of Abraham
and inherit the dignity of Israel's birthright.
Through Christ our Lord.

or

O God, who by the light of the New Testament
have unlocked the meaning
of wonders worked in former times,
so that the Red Sea prefigures the sacred font
and the nation delivered from slavery
foreshadows the Christian people,

grant, we pray, that all nations,
obtaining the privilege of Israel by merit of faith,
may be reborn by partaking of your Spirit.
Through Christ our Lord.

All sit.

Fourth Reading   Isaiah 54:5-14

With everlasting love the Lord your redeemer has taken pity on you.

Now your creator will be your husband,
his name, the Lord of hosts;
your redeemer will be the Holy One of Israel,
he is called the God of the whole earth.
Yes, like a forsaken wife, distressed in spirit,
the Lord calls you back.
Does a man cast off the wife of his youth?
says your God.

I did forsake you for a brief moment,
but with great love will I take you back.
In excess of anger, for a moment
I hid my face from you.
But with everlasting love I have taken pity on you,
says the Lord, your redeemer.

I am now as I was in the days of Noah
when I swore that Noah's waters
should never flood the world again.
So now I swear concerning my anger with you
and the threats I made against you;

for the mountains may depart,
the hills be shaken,
but my love for you will never leave you
and my covenant of peace with you will never be shaken,
says the Lord who takes pity on you.

Unhappy creature, storm-tossed, disconsolate,
see, I will set your stones on carbuncles
and your foundations on sapphires.

I will make rubies your battlements,
your gates crystal,
and your entire wall precious stones.
Your sons will all be taught by the Lord.
The prosperity of your sons will be great.
You will be founded on integrity;
remote from oppression, you will have nothing to fear;
remote from terror, it will not approach you.

The Psalm or a period of silence follows.

Psalm   Psalm 29

R.   **I will praise you, Lord, you have rescued me.**

1. I will praise you, Lord, you have rescued me
   and have not let my enemies rejoice over me.
   O Lord, you have raised my soul from the dead,
   restored me to life from those who sink into the grave. R.

2. Sing psalms to the Lord, you who love him,
   give thanks to his holy name.
   His anger lasts but a moment; his favour through life.
   At night there are tears, but joy comes with dawn. R.

3. The Lord listened and had pity.
   The Lord came to my help.
   For me you have changed my mourning into dancing,
   O Lord my God, I will thank you for ever. R.

All stand.

Prayer
Let us pray.

Almighty ever-living God,
surpass, for the honour of your name,
what you pledged to the Patriarchs by reason of their faith,
and through sacred adoption increase the children of your promise,
so that what the Saints of old never doubted would come to pass
your Church may now see in great part fulfilled.
Through Christ our Lord.

Alternative prayers may be used from among those which follow any readings that may have been omitted.

All sit.

Fifth Reading   Isaiah 55:1-11

Come to me and your soul will live, and I will make an everlasting covenant with you.

Thus says the Lord:

Oh, come to the water all you who are thirsty;
though you have no money, come!
Buy corn without money, and eat,
and, at no cost, wine and milk.
Why spend money on what is not bread,
your wages on what fails to satisfy?
Listen, listen to me, and you will have good things to eat
and rich food to enjoy.
Pay attention, come to me;
listen, and your soul will live.

With you I will make an everlasting covenant
out of the favours promised to David.
See, I have made of you a witness to the peoples,
a leader and a master of the nations.
See, you will summon a nation you never knew,
those unknown will come hurrying to you,
for the sake of the Lord your God,
of the Holy One of Israel who will glorify you.

Seek the Lord while he is still to be found,
call to him while he is still near.
Let the wicked man abandon his way,
the evil man his thoughts.
Let him turn back to the Lord who will take pity on him,
to our God who is rich in forgiving;
for my thoughts are not your thoughts,
my ways are not your ways – it is the Lord who speaks.
Yes, the heavens are as high above earth
as my ways are above your ways,
my thoughts above your thoughts.

Yes, as the rain and the snow come down from the heavens and do not return without watering the earth, making it yield and giving growth to provide seed for the sower and bread for the eating, so the word that goes from my mouth does not return to me empty, without carrying out my will and succeeding in what it was sent to do.

The Psalm or a period of silence follows.

Psalm   Isaiah 12

R. **With joy you will draw water from the wells of salvation.**

1. Truly God is my salvation,
   I trust, I shall not fear.
   For the Lord is my strength, my song,
   he became my saviour.
   With joy you will draw water
   from the wells of salvation. R.

2. Give thanks to the Lord, give praise to his name!
   Make his mighty deeds known to the peoples,
   declare the greatness of his name. R.

3. Sing a psalm to the Lord
   for he has done glorious deeds,
   make them known to all the earth!
   People of Zion, sing and shout for joy
   for great in your midst is the Holy One of Israel. R.

All stand.

Prayer
Let us pray.

Almighty ever-living God,
sole hope of the world,
who by the preaching of your Prophets
unveiled the mysteries of this present age,
graciously increase the longing of your people,
for only at the prompting of your grace
do the faithful progress in any kind of virtue.
Through Christ our Lord.

All sit.

Sixth Reading   Baruch 3:9-15. 32 – 4:4

In the radiance of the Lord make your way to light.

Listen, Israel, to commands that bring life;
hear, and learn what knowledge means.
Why, Israel, why are you in the country of your enemies,
growing older and older in an alien land,
sharing defilement with the dead,
reckoned with those who go to Sheol?
Because you have forsaken the fountain of wisdom.
Had you walked in the way of God,
you would have lived in peace for ever.
Learn where knowledge is, where strength,
where understanding, and so learn
where length of days is, where life,
where the light of the eyes and where peace.
But who has found out where she lives,
who has entered her treasure house?

But the One who knows all knows her,
he has grasped her with his own intellect,
he has set the earth firm for ever
and filled it with four-footed beasts,
he sends the light – and it goes,
he recalls it – and trembling it obeys;
the stars shine joyfully at their set times:
when he calls them, they answer, "Here we are";
they gladly shine for their creator.
It is he who is our God,
no other can compare with him.
He has grasped the whole way of knowledge,
and confided it to his servant Jacob,
to Israel his well-beloved;
so causing her to appear on earth
and move among men.

This is the book of the commandments of God,
the Law that stands for ever;

those who keep her live,
those who desert her die.
Turn back, Jacob, seize her,
on her radiance make your way to light:
do not yield your glory to another,
your privilege to a people not your own.
Israel, blessed are we:
what pleases God has been revealed to us.

The Psalm or a period of silence follows.

Psalm   Psalm 18

R. **You have the message of eternal life, O Lord.**

1. The law of the Lord is perfect,
    it revives the soul.
    The rule of the Lord is to be trusted,
    it gives wisdom to the simple. R.

2. The precepts of the Lord are right,
    they gladden the heart.
    They command of the Lord is clear,
    it gives light to the eyes. R.

3. The fear of the Lord is holy,
    abiding for ever.
    The decrees of the Lord are truth
    and all of them just. R.

4. They are more to be desired than gold,
    than the purest of gold
    and sweeter are they than honey,
    than honey from the comb. R.

All stand.

Prayer

Let us pray.

O God, who constantly increase your Church
by your call to the nations,
graciously grant
to those you wash clean in the waters of Baptism
the assurance of your unfailing protection.
Through Christ our Lord.

All sit.

Seventh Reading   Ezekiel 36:16-17a. 18-28

I shall pour clean water over you, and I shall give you a new heart.

The word of the Lord was addressed to me as follows: "Son of man,
the members of the House of Israel used to live in their own land,
but they defiled it by their conduct and actions. I then discharged
my fury at them because of the blood they shed in their land and the
idols with which they defiled it. I scattered them among the nations
and dispersed them in foreign countries. I sentenced them as their
conduct and actions deserved. And now they have profaned my
holy name among the nations where they have gone, so that people
say of them, 'These are the people of the Lord; they have been exiled
from his land.' But I have been concerned about my holy name,
which the House of Israel has profaned among the nations where
they have gone. And so, say to the House of Israel, 'The Lord says
this: I am not doing this for your sake, House of Israel, but for the
sake of my holy name, which you have profaned among the nations
where you have gone. I mean to display the holiness of my great
name, which has been profaned among the nations, which you have
profaned among them. And the nations will learn that I am the Lord
– it is the Lord who speaks – when I display my holiness for your
sake before their eyes. Then I am going to take you from among the
nations and gather you together from all the foreign countries, and
bring you home to your own land. I shall pour clean water over you
and you will be cleansed; I shall cleanse you of all your defilement
and all your idols. I shall give you a new heart, and put a new spirit
in you; I shall remove the heart of stone from your bodies and give
you a heart of flesh instead. I shall put my spirit in you, and make

you keep my laws and sincerely respect my observances. You will live in the land which I gave your ancestors. You shall be my people and I will be your God.' "

The Psalm or a period of silence follows.

Psalm   Psalms 41 and 42

R. **Like the deer that yearns for running streams,
     so my soul is yearning for you, my God.**

1. My soul is thirsting for God.
    the God of my life:
    when can I enter and see
    the face of God? R.

2. These things will I remember
    as I pour out my soul:
    how I would lead the rejoicing crowd
    into the house of God,
    amid cries of gladness and thanksgiving,
    the throng wild with joy. R.

3. O send forth your light and your truth;
    let these be my guide.
    Let them bring me to your holy mountain
    to the place where you dwell. R.

4. And I will come to the altar of God,
    the God of my joy.
    My redeemer, I will thank you on the harp,
    O God, my God. R.

If a Baptism takes place, the Psalm which follows the fifth reading (p. 273) is used, or Psalm 50 as follows:

Psalm   Psalm 50

R. **A pure heart create for me, O God.**

1. A pure heart create for me, O God.
    put a steadfast spirit within me.

Do not cast me away from your presence,
nor deprive me of your holy spirit. R.

2. Give me again the joy of your help;
with a spirit of fervour sustain me,
that I may teach transgressors your ways
and sinners may return to you. R.

3. For in sacrifice you take no delight,
burnt offering from me you would refuse,
my sacrifice, a contrite spirit.
A humbled, contrite heart you will not spurn. R.

All stand.

Prayer
Let us pray.

O God of unchanging power and eternal light,
look with favour on the wondrous mystery of the whole Church
and serenely accomplish the work of human salvation,
which you planned from all eternity;
may the whole world know and see
that what was cast down is raised up,
what had become old is made new,
and all things are restored to integrity through Christ,
just as by him they came into being.
Who lives and reigns for ever and ever.

or

O God, who by the pages of both Testaments
instruct and prepare us to celebrate the Paschal Mystery,
grant that we may comprehend your mercy,
so that the gifts we receive from you this night
may confirm our hope of the gifts to come.
Through Christ our Lord.

After the last reading from the Old Testament with its Psalm and
prayer, the altar candles are lit, and the priest intones the Gloria,
which is taken up by all, while the church bells are rung, according
to local custom.

After the Gloria, the priest says the Collect.

Collect

O God, who make this most sacred night radiant
with the glory of the Lord's Resurrection,
stir up in your Church a spirit of adoption,
so that, renewed in body and mind,
we may render you undivided service.
Through our Lord Jesus Christ, your Son,
who lives and reigns with you in the unity of the Holy Spirit,
one God, for ever and ever.

All sit.

New Testament Reading   Romans 6:3-11

Christ, having been raised from the dead, will never die again.

When we were baptised in Christ Jesus we were baptised in his
death: in other words, when we were baptised we went into the
tomb with him and joined him in death, so that as Christ was raised
from the dead by the Father's glory, we too might live a new life.

If in union with Christ we have imitated his death, we shall also
imitate him in his resurrection. We must realise that our former
selves have been crucified with him to destroy this sinful body and
to free us from the slavery of sin. When a man dies, of course, he
has finished with sin.

But we believe that having died with Christ we shall return to life
with him: Christ, as we know, having been raised from the dead will
never die again. Death has no power over him any more. When he
died, he died, once for all, to sin, so his life now is life with God; and
in that way, you too must consider yourselves to be dead to sin but
alive for God in Christ Jesus.

All stand, then the priest intones the Alleluia three times with all
repeating it.

Psalm   Psalm 117

R. **Alleluia, alleluia, alleluia!**

1. Give thanks to the Lord for he is good,
   for his love has no end.

Let the sons of Israel say;
"His love has no end." R.

2. The Lord's right hand has triumphed;
his right hand raised me up.
I shall not die, I shall live
and recount his deeds. R.

3. The stone which the builders rejected
has become the corner stone.
This is the work of the Lord,
a marvel in our eyes. R.

The Gospel for either Year A, B or C is read, according to the cycle for the year.

A

Gospel   Matthew 28:1-10

He has risen from the dead and now he is going before you into Galilee.

After the sabbath, and towards dawn on the first day of the week, Mary of Magdala and the other Mary went to visit the sepulchre. And all at once there was a violent earthquake, for the angel of the Lord, descended from heaven, came and rolled away the stone and sat on it. His face was like lightning, his robe white as snow. The guards were so shaken, so frightened of him, that they were like dead men. But the angel spoke; and he said to the women, "There is no need for you to be afraid. I know you are looking for Jesus, who was crucified. He is not here, for he has risen, as he said he would. Come and see the place where he lay then go quickly and tell his disciples, 'He has risen from the dead and now he is going before you to Galilee; it is there you will see him.' Now I have told you." Filled with awe and great joy the women came quickly away from the tomb and ran to tell the disciples.

    And there, coming to meet them, was Jesus. "Greetings", he said. And the women came up to him and, falling down before him, clasped his feet. Then Jesus said to them, "Do not be afraid; go and tell my brothers that they must leave for Galilee; they will see me there."

B

Gospel   Mark 16:1-7

Jesus of Nazareth, who was crucified, has risen.

When the sabbath was over, Mary of Magdala, Mary the mother
of James, and Salome, brought spices with which to go and anoint
him. And very early in the morning on the first day of the week they
went to the tomb, just as the sun was rising.

They had been saying to one another, "Who will roll away the
stone for us from the entrance to the tomb?" But when they looked
they could see that the stone – which was very big – had already
been rolled back. On entering the tomb they saw a young man in a
white robe seated on the right-hand side, and they were struck with
amazement. But he said to them, "There is no need for alarm. You
are looking for Jesus of Nazareth, who was crucified: he has risen,
he is not here. See, here is the place where they laid him. But you
must go and tell his disciples and Peter, 'He is going before you to
Galilee; it is there you will see him, just as he told you.'"

C

Gospel   Luke 24:1-12

Why look among the dead for someone who is alive?

On the first day of the week, at the first sign of dawn, the women
went to the tomb with the spices they had prepared. They found
that the stone had been rolled away from the tomb, but on entering
discovered that the body of the Lord Jesus was not there. As they
stood there not knowing what to think, two men in brilliant clothes
suddenly appeared at their side. Terrified, the women lowered their
eyes. But the two men said to them, "Why look among the dead for
someone who is alive? He is not here; he has risen. Remember what
he told you when he was still in Galilee: that the Son of Man had to
be handed over into the power of sinful men and be crucified, and
rise again on the third day?" And they remembered his words.

When the women returned from the tomb they told all this to the
Eleven and to all the others. The women were Mary of Magdala,
Joanna, and Mary the mother of James. The other women with
them also told the apostles, but this story of theirs seemed pure
nonsense, and they did not believe them.

Peter, however, went running to the tomb. He bent down and saw the binding cloths, but nothing else; he then went back home, amazed at what had happened.

Third Part:
The Liturgy of Baptism

The priest goes with the ministers to the baptismal font, if this can be seen by the people. Otherwise a vessel with water is placed in the sanctuary.

Catechumens, if there are any, are called forward and presented by their godparents. If they are children, their parents and godparents bring them forward.

Then the priest addresses the people in the following or similar words.

If there are candidates to be baptised:
Dearly beloved,
with one heart and one soul, let us by our prayers
come to the aid of these our brothers and sisters in their blessed hope,
so that, as they approach the font of rebirth,
the almighty Father may bestow on them
all his merciful help.

If the font is to be blessed, but no one is to be baptised:
Dearly beloved,
let us humbly invoke upon this font
the grace of God the almighty Father,
that those who from it are born anew
may be numbered among the children of adoption in Christ.

If no one is to be baptised and the font is not to be blessed, the Blessing of Water follows (pp. 286-287).

Litany of Saints
Lord, have mercy.   **Lord, have mercy.**
Christ, have mercy.   **Christ, have mercy.**
Lord, have mercy.   **Lord, have mercy.**

Holy Mary, Mother of God,	**pray for us.**
Saint Michael,	**pray for us.**
Holy Angels of God,	**pray for us.**
Saint John the Baptist,	**pray for us.**
Saint Joseph,	**pray for us.**
Saint Peter and Saint Paul,	**pray for us.**
Saint Andrew,	**pray for us.**
Saint John,	**pray for us.**
Saint Mary Magdalene,	**pray for us.**
Saint Stephen,	**pray for us.**
Saint Ignatius of Antioch,	**pray for us.**
Saint Lawrence,	**pray for us.**
Saint Perpetua and Saint Felicity,	**pray for us.**
Saint Agnes,	**pray for us.**
Saint Gregory,	**pray for us.**
Saint Augustine,	**pray for us.**
Saint Athanasius,	**pray for us.**
Saint Basil,	**pray for us.**
Saint Martin,	**pray for us.**
Saint Benedict,	**pray for us.**
Saint Francis and Saint Dominic,	**pray for us.**
Saint Francis Xavier,	**pray for us.**
Saint John Vianney,	**pray for us.**
Saint Catherine of Siena,	**pray for us.**
Saint Teresa of Jesus,	**pray for us.**
All holy men and women, Saints of God,	**pray for us.**
Lord, be merciful,	**Lord, deliver us, we pray.**
From all evil,	**Lord, deliver us, we pray.**
From every sin,	**Lord, deliver us, we pray.**
From everlasting death,	**Lord, deliver us, we pray.**
By your Incarnation,	**Lord, deliver us, we pray.**
By your Death and Resurrection,	**Lord, deliver us, we pray.**
By the outpouring of the Holy Spirit,	**Lord, deliver us, we pray.**
Be merciful to us sinners,	**Lord, we ask you, hear our prayer.**

If there are candidates to be baptised:
Bring these chosen ones to new birth through the grace of baptism.
Lord, we ask you, hear our prayer.

If there is no one to be baptised:
Make this font holy by your grace for the new birth of your children,
Lord, we ask you, hear our prayer.

Jesus, Son of the living God,
Lord, we ask you, hear our prayer.

Christ, hear us.
Christ, hear us.

Christ, graciously hear us.
Christ, graciously hear us.

If there are candidates to be baptised, the priest says the following
prayer:
Almighty ever-living God,
be present by the mysteries of your great love
and send forth the spirit of adoption
to create the new peoples
brought to birth for you in the font of Baptism,
so that what is to be carried out by our humble service
may be brought to fulfilment by your mighty power.
Through Christ our Lord.

Blessing of Baptismal Water
The priest then blesses the baptismal water, saying the following
prayer:
O God, who by invisible power
accomplish a wondrous effect
through sacramental signs
and who in many ways have prepared water, your creation,
to show forth the grace of Baptism;

O God, whose Spirit
in the first moments of the world's creation
hovered over the waters,

so that the very substance of water
would even then take to itself the power to sanctify;

O God, who by the outpouring of the flood
foreshadowed regeneration,
so that from the mystery of one and the same element of water
would come an end to vice and a beginning of virtue;

O God, who caused the children of Abraham
to pass dry-shod through the Red Sea,
so that the chosen people,
set free from slavery to Pharaoh,
would prefigure the people of the baptised;

O God, whose Son,
baptised by John in the waters of the Jordan,
was anointed with the Holy Spirit,
and, as he hung upon the Cross,
gave forth water from his side along with blood,
and after his Resurrection, commanded his disciples:
"Go forth, teach all nations, baptising them
in the name of the Father and of the Son and of the Holy Spirit",
look now, we pray, upon the face of your Church
and graciously unseal for her the fountain of Baptism.

May this water receive by the Holy Spirit
the grace of your Only Begotten Son,
so that human nature, created in your image
and washed clean through the Sacrament of Baptism
from all the squalor of the life of old,
may be found worthy to rise to the life of newborn children
through water and the Holy Spirit.

The priest may lower the paschal candle into the water either once
or three times, as he continues:
May the power of the Holy Spirit,
O Lord, we pray,
come down through your Son
into the fullness of this font,

Holding the candle in the water, he continues:
so that all who have been buried with Christ
by Baptism into death
may rise again to life with him.
Who lives and reigns with you in the unity of the Holy Spirit,
one God, for ever and ever.
Amen.

Then the candle is lifted out of the water, as the people acclaim:
Springs of water, bless the Lord;
praise and exalt him above all for ever.

If there are candidates to be baptised, the rite of Baptism (and,
if appropriate, Confirmation) takes place now. After the rite of
Baptism, turn to the Renewal of Baptismal Promises on pp. 287-288.
If no one is to be baptised, and the font is not to be blessed, the
priest blesses the water in the following way.

The Blessing of Water
The priest says:
Dear brothers and sisters,
let us humbly beseech the Lord our God
to bless this water he has created,
which will be sprinkled upon us
as a memorial of our Baptism.
May he graciously renew us,
that we may remain faithful to the Spirit
whom we have received.

All pray silently for a brief while. Then the priest continues:

Lord our God,
in your mercy be present to your people
who keep vigil on this most sacred night,
and, for us who recall the wondrous work of our creation
and the still greater work of our redemption,
graciously bless this water.
For you created water to make the fields fruitful
and to refresh and cleanse our bodies.
You also made water the instrument of your mercy:

for through water you freed your people from slavery
and quenched their thirst in the desert;
through water the Prophets proclaimed the new covenant
you were to enter upon with the human race;
and last of all,
through water, which Christ made holy in the Jordan,
you have renewed our corrupted nature
in the bath of regeneration.
Therefore, may this water be for us
a memorial of the Baptism we have received,
and grant that we may share
in the gladness of our brothers and sisters,
who at Easter have received their Baptism.
Through Christ our Lord.
Amen.

The Renewal of Baptismal Promises

All stand, holding lighted candles, and renew their baptismal profession of faith, unless this has already been done together with those to be baptised. The priest addresses the people in these or similar words:

Dear brethren (brothers and sisters), through the Paschal Mystery
we have been buried with Christ in Baptism,
so that we may walk with him in newness of life.
And so, now that our Lenten observance is concluded,
let us renew the promises of Holy Baptism,
by which we once renounced Satan and his works
and promised to serve God in the holy Catholic Church.
And so I ask you:

Do you renounce Satan?
I do.

And all his works?
I do.

And all his empty show?
I do.

or

Do you renounce sin,
so as to live in the freedom of the children of God?
I do.

Do you renounce the lure of evil,
so that sin may have no mastery over you?
I do.

Do you renounce Satan,
the author and prince of sin?
I do.

Then the priest continues:
Do you believe in God,
the Father almighty,
Creator of heaven and earth?
I do.

Do you believe in Jesus Christ, his only Son, our Lord,
who was born of the Virgin Mary,
suffered death and was buried,
rose again from the dead
and is seated at the right hand of the Father?
I do.

Do you believe in the Holy Spirit,
the holy Catholic Church,
the communion of saints,
the forgiveness of sins,
the resurrection of the body,
and life everlasting?
I do.

The priest concludes:
And may almighty God, the Father of our Lord Jesus Christ,
who has given us new birth by water and the Holy Spirit
and bestowed on us forgiveness of our sins,
keep us by his grace,
in Christ Jesus our Lord,
for eternal life.
Amen.

The priest sprinkles the people with the blessed water, while all sing the following antiphon, or another song that is baptismal in character.

Antiphon
I saw water flowing from the Temple,
from its right-hand side, alleluia;
and all to whom this water came were saved
and shall say: Alleluia, alleluia.

Meanwhile the newly baptised are led to their place among the faithful.

If the blessing of baptismal water has not taken place in the baptistery, the ministers reverently carry the vessel of water to the font.

If the blessing of the font has not occurred, the blessed water is put aside in an appropriate place.

After the sprinkling, the priest returns to the chair.

The Creed is not said, and the priest directs the Prayer of the Faithful, in which the newly baptised participate for the first time.

Fourth Part:
The Liturgy of the Eucharist

The priest goes to the altar and begins the Liturgy of the Eucharist in the usual way. (Turn to p. 460 for the Order of Mass.)

It is fitting that the bread and wine be brought forward by the newly baptised or, if they are small children, by their parents or godparents.

Prayer over the Offerings
Accept, we ask, O Lord,
the prayers of your people
with the sacrificial offerings,
that what has begun in the paschal mysteries
may, by the working of your power,
bring us to the healing of eternity.
Through Christ our Lord.

Preface I of Easter, p. 495.

Before saying "Behold the Lamb of God..." the priest may briefly address those newly baptised about receiving their first Communion, and about the Eucharist as the centre of the Christian life.

Communion Antiphon
Christ our Passover has been sacrificed;
therefore let as keep the feast
with the unleavened bread of purity and truth, alleluia.

1 Corinthians 5:7-8

Prayer after Communion
Pour out on us, O Lord, the Spirit of your love,
and in your kindness make those you have nourished
by this paschal Sacrament
one in mind and heart.
Through Christ our Lord.

Solemn Blessing
May almighty God bless you
through today's Easter Solemnity
and, in his compassion,
defend you from every assault of sin. **Amen.**

And may he, who restores you to eternal life
in the Resurrection of his Only Begotten,
endow you with the prize of immortality. **Amen.**

Now that the days of the Lord's Passion have drawn to a close,
may you who celebrate the gladness of the Paschal Feast
come with Christ's help, and exulting in spirit,
to those feasts that are celebrated in eternal joy. **Amen.**

And may the blessing of almighty God,
the Father, and the Son, ✠ and the Holy Spirit,
come down on you and remain with you for ever. **Amen.**

Dismissal
Go forth, the Mass is ended, alleluia, alleluia.
or
Go in peace, alleluia, alleluia.
Thanks be to God, alleluia, alleluia.

EASTER SUNDAY – ABC

Christ our hope is risen!
Christ dies to rise again so that his Father will be glorified. We too are brought
back to true life in Christ. If we die with him, we will rise with him, and be
living witnesses to the power of the Resurrection.

Entrance Antiphon
I have risen, and I am with you still, alleluia.
You have laid your hand upon me, alleluia.
Too wonderful for me, this knowledge, alleluia, alleluia.
cf. Psalm 138:18. 5-6

or

The Lord is truly risen, alleluia.
To him be glory and power
for all the ages of eternity, alleluia, alleluia.
Luke 24:34; cf. Apocalypse 1:6

The Gloria is sung or said.

Collect
O God, who on this day,
through your Only Begotten Son,
have conquered death
and unlocked for us the path to eternity,
grant, we pray, that we who keep
the solemnity of the Lord's Resurrection
may, through the renewal brought by your Spirit,
rise up in the light of life.
Through our Lord Jesus Christ, your Son,
who lives and reigns with you in the unity of the Holy Spirit,
one God, for ever and ever.

First Reading   Acts 10:34. 37-43
We have eaten and drunk with him after his resurrection.
Peter addressed Cornelius and his household: "You must have heard
about the recent happenings in Judaea; about Jesus of Nazareth and
how he began in Galilee, after John had been preaching baptism.

God had anointed him with the Holy Spirit and with power, and because God was with him, Jesus went about doing good and curing all who had fallen into the power of the devil. Now I, and those with me, can witness to everything he did throughout the countryside of Judaea and in Jerusalem itself: and also to the fact that they killed him by hanging him on a tree, yet three days afterwards God raised him to life and allowed him to be seen, not by the whole people but only by certain witnesses God had chosen beforehand. Now we are those witnesses – we have eaten and drunk with him after his resurrection from the dead – and he has ordered us to proclaim this to his people and to tell them that God has appointed him to judge everyone, alive or dead. It is to him that all the prophets bear this witness: that all who believe in Jesus will have their sins forgiven through his name."

Psalm   **Psalm 117**

R. **This day was made by the Lord;**
    we rejoice and are glad.

or

R. **Alleluia, alleluia, alleluia!**

1. Give thanks to the Lord for he is good,
    for his love has no end.
    Let the sons of Israel say:
    "His love has no end." R.

2. The Lord's right hand has triumphed;
    his right hand raised me up.
    I shall not die, I shall live
    and recount his deeds. R.

3. The stone which the builders rejected
    has become the corner stone.
    This is the work of the Lord,
    a marvel in our eyes. R.

Second Reading
Colossians 3:1-4

You must look for the things that are in heaven, where Christ is.

Since you have been brought back to true life with Christ, you must look for the things that are in heaven, where Christ is, sitting at God's right hand. Let your thoughts be on heavenly things, not on the things that are on the earth, because you have died, and now the life you have is hidden with Christ in God. But when Christ is revealed – and he is your life – you too will be revealed in all your glory with him.

or

Second Reading
1 Corinthians 5:6-8

Get rid of all the old yeast, make yourselves into a completely new batch of bread.

You must know how even a small amount of yeast is enough to leaven all the dough, so get rid of all the old yeast, and make yourselves into a completely new batch of bread, unleavened as you are meant to be. Christ, our passover, has been sacrificed; let us celebrate the feast, by getting rid of all the old yeast of evil and wickedness, having only the unleavened bread of sincerity and truth.

Sequence

Christians, to the Paschal Victim offer sacrifice and praise.
The sheep are ransomed by the Lamb;
and Christ, the undefiled,
hath sinners to his Father reconciled.
Death with life contended: combat strangely ended!
Life's own Champion, slain, yet lives to reign.
Tell us, Mary: say what thou didst see upon the way.
The tomb the Living did enclose;
I saw Christ's glory as he rose!
The angels there attesting;
shroud with grave-clothes resting.
Christ, my hope, has risen: he goes before you into Galilee.
That Christ is truly risen from the dead we know.
Victorious king, thy mercy show!

Gospel Acclamation
Alleluia, alleluia!
Christ, our passover, has been sacrificed;
let us celebrate the feast then, in the Lord.
Alleluia!   1 Corinthians 5:7-8

Gospel   John 20:1-9
He must rise from the dead.

It was very early on the first day of the week and still dark, when Mary of Magdala came to the tomb. She saw that the stone had been moved away from the tomb and came running to Simon Peter and the other disciple, the one Jesus loved. "They have taken the Lord out of the tomb", she said, "and we don't know where they have put him."

So Peter set out with the other disciple to go to the tomb. They ran together, but the other disciple, running faster than Peter, reached the tomb first; he bent down and saw the linen cloths lying on the ground, but did not go in. Simon Peter who was following now came up, went right into the tomb, saw the linen cloths on the ground, and also the cloth that had been over his head; this was not with the linen cloths but rolled up in a place by itself. Then the other disciple who had reached the tomb first also went in; he saw and he believed. Till this moment they had failed to understand the teaching of scripture, that he must rise from the dead.

The Gospel of the Mass of Easter Night may be read instead, pp. 280-282.

At an evening Mass, the Gospel of the 3rd Sunday of Easter, Year A, may be read instead, pp. 303-304.

The Creed is said.

The rite of the Renewal of Baptismal Promises may take place after the homily, according to the text used at the Easter Vigil, pp. 287-288. In that case the Creed is omitted.

Prayer over the Offerings
Exultant with paschal gladness, O Lord,
we offer the sacrifice
by which your Church
is wondrously reborn and nourished.
Through Christ our Lord

Preface I of Easter, p. 495.

Communion Antiphon
Christ our Passover has been sacrificed, alleluia;
therefore let us keep the feast with the unleavened bread
of purity and truth, alleluia, alleluia.   1 Corinthians 5:7-8

Prayer after Communion
Look upon your Church, O God,
with unfailing love and favour,
so that, renewed by the paschal mysteries,
she may come to the glory of the resurrection.
Through Christ our Lord.

The Solemn Blessing for the Mass of the Easter Vigil may be used,
p. 290.

Dismissal
Go forth, the Mass is ended, alleluia, alleluia.

or

Go in peace, alleluia, alleluia.

Thanks be to God, alleluia, alleluia.

SECOND SUNDAY OF EASTER – A
(or of Divine Mercy)

We do not see, yet we believe!
God our Father has created a new human family through raising Jesus Christ
from the dead. It is our belief in the Resurrection of Christ that becomes the
source of Christ's life within us. Our faith overcomes our doubts and we
acknowledge the power of the risen Christ.

Entrance Antiphon
Like newborn infants, you must long for the pure, spiritual milk,
that in him you may grow to salvation, alleluia. 1 Peter 2:2

or

Receive the joy of your glory, giving thanks to God,
who has called you into the heavenly kingdom, alleluia.

4 Esdras 2:36-37

The Gloria is said or sung.

Collect
God of everlasting mercy,
who, in the very recurrence of the paschal feast
kindle the faith of the people you have made your own,
increase, we pray, the grace you have bestowed,
that all may grasp and rightly understand
in what font they have been washed,
by whose Spirit they have been reborn,
by whose Blood they have been redeemed.
Through our Lord Jesus Christ, your Son,
who lives and reigns with you in the unity of the Holy Spirit,
one God, for ever and ever.

First Reading Acts 2:42-47
The faithful all lived together and owned everything in common.
The whole community remained faithful to the teaching of the
apostles, to the brotherhood, to the breaking of bread and to the
prayers.

The many miracles and signs worked through the apostles made a deep impression on everyone.

The faithful all lived together, and owned everything in common; they sold their goods and possessions and shared out the proceeds among themselves according to what each one needed.

They went as a body to the Temple every day but met in their houses for the breaking of bread; they shared their food gladly and generously; they praised God and were looked up to by everyone. Day by day the Lord added to their community those destined to be saved.

Psalm   **Psalm 117**

R. **Give thanks to the Lord for he is good,**
    for his love has no end.

or **Alleluia, alleluia, alleluia!**

1. Let the sons of Israel say:
   "His love has no end."
   Let the sons of Aaron say:
   "His love has no end."
   Let those who fear the Lord say:
   "His love has no end." R.

2. I was thrust, thrust down and falling
   but the Lord was my helper.
   The Lord is my strength and my song;
   he was my saviour.
   There are shouts of joy and victory
   in the tents of the just. R.

3. The stone which the builders rejected
   has become the corner stone.
   This is the work of the Lord,
   a marvel in our eyes.
   This day was made by the Lord;
   we rejoice and are glad. R.

Second Reading   **1 Peter 1:3-9**

In his great mercy he has given us a new birth as his sons by raising Jesus from the dead.

Blessed be God the Father of our Lord Jesus Christ, who in his great mercy has given us a new birth as his sons, by raising Jesus Christ from the dead, so that we have a sure hope and the promise of an inheritance that can never be spoilt or soiled and never fade away, because it is being kept for you in the heavens. Through your faith God's power will guard you until the salvation which has been prepared is revealed at the end of time. This is a cause of great joy for you, even though you may for a short time have to bear being plagued by all sorts of trials; so that, when Jesus Christ is revealed, your faith will have been tested and proved like gold – only it is more precious than gold, which is corruptible even though it bears testing by fire – and then you will have praise and glory and honour. You did not see him, yet you love him; and still without seeing him, you are already filled with a joy so glorious that it cannot be described, because you believe; and you are sure of the end to which your faith looks forward, that is, the salvation of your souls.

Gospel Acclamation
Alleluia, alleluia!
Jesus said: "You believe because you can see me.
Happy are those who have not seen and yet believe."
Alleluia!   John 20:29

Gospel   John 20:19-31

Eight days later, Jesus came.

In the evening of that same day, the first day of the week, the doors were closed in the room where the disciples were, for fear of the Jews. Jesus came and stood among them. He said to them, "Peace be with you," and showed them his hands and his side. The disciples were filled with joy when they saw the Lord, and he said to them again, "Peace be with you.

"As the Father sent me,
    so am I sending you."

After saying this he breathed on them and said:

"Receive the Holy Spirit.
For those whose sins you forgive,
they are forgiven;
for those whose sins you retain,
they are retained."

Thomas, called the Twin, who was one of the Twelve, was not with them when Jesus came. When the disciples said, "We have seen the Lord," he answered, "Unless I see the holes that the nails made in his hands and can put my finger into the holes they made, and unless I can put my hand into his side, I refuse to believe." Eight days later the disciples were in the house again and Thomas was with them. The doors were closed, but Jesus came in and stood among them. "Peace be with you," he said. Then he spoke to Thomas, "Put your finger here; look, here are my hands. Give me your hand; put it into my side. Doubt no longer but believe." Thomas replied, "My Lord and my God!"

Jesus said to him:

"You believe because you can see me.
Happy are those who have not seen and yet believe."

There were many other signs that Jesus worked and the disciples saw, but they are not recorded in this book. These are recorded so that you may believe that Jesus is the Christ, the Son of God, and that believing this you may have life through his name.

The Creed is said.

Prayer over the Offerings
Accept, O Lord, we pray,
the oblations of your people
(and of those you have brought to new birth),
that, renewed by confession of your name and by Baptism,
they may attain unending happiness.
Through Christ our Lord.

Preface I of Easter, p. 495.

Communion Antiphon
Bring your hand and feel the place of the nails,
and do not be unbelieving but believing, alleluia.   cf. John 20:27

Prayer after Communion
Grant, we pray, almighty God,
that our reception of this paschal Sacrament
may have a continuing effect
in our minds and hearts.
Through Christ our Lord.

The Solemn Blessing for the Mass of the Easter Vigil (p. 290) or for
Easter Time (p. 511) may be used.

Dismissal
Go forth, the Mass is ended, alleluia, alleluia.

or

Go in peace, alleluia, alleluia.

Thanks be to God, alleluia, alleluia.

THIRD SUNDAY OF EASTER – A

Christ feeds us.
Like the disciples on the road to Emmaus, we meet Christ as pilgrims and
strangers, and come to recognise him in the breaking of the bread. He fulfils
the message of the prophets. Through him, and through his Resurrection, we can
have faith and hope in God.

Entrance Antiphon
Cry out with joy to God, all the earth;
O sing to the glory of his name.
O render him glorious praise, alleluia.   cf. Psalm 65:1-2

The Gloria is said or sung.

Collect
May your people exult for ever, O God,
in renewed youthfulness of spirit,
so that, rejoicing now in the restored glory of our adoption,
we may look forward in confident hope
to the rejoicing of the day of resurrection.
Through our Lord Jesus Christ, your Son,
who lives and reigns with you in the unity of the Holy Spirit,
one God, for ever and ever.

First Reading   Acts 2:14. 22-33
It was impossible for him to be held in the power of Hades.
On the day of Pentecost Peter stood up with the Eleven and
addressed the crowd in a loud voice: "Men of Israel, listen to what
I am going to say: Jesus the Nazarene was a man commended
to you by God by the miracles and portents and signs that God
worked through him when he was among you, as you all know. This
man, who was put into your power by the deliberate intention and
foreknowledge of God, you took and had crucified by men outside
the Law. You killed him, but God raised him to life, freeing him

from the pangs of Hades; for it was impossible for him to be held in its power since, as David says of him:

I saw the Lord before me always,
for with him at my right hand nothing can shake me.
So my heart was glad
and my tongue cried out with joy:
my body, too, will rest in the hope
that you will not abandon my soul to Hades
nor allow your holy one to experience corruption.
You have made known the way of life to me,
you will fill me with gladness through your presence."

"Brothers, no one can deny that the patriarch David himself is dead and buried: his tomb is still with us. But since he was a prophet, and knew that God had sworn him an oath to make one of his descendants succeed him on the throne, what he foresaw and spoke about was the resurrection of the Christ: he is the one who was not abandoned to Hades, and whose body did not experience corruption. God raised this man Jesus to life, and all of us are witnesses to that. Now raised to the heights by God's right hand, he has received from the Father the Holy Spirit, who was promised, and what you see and hear is the outpouring of that Spirit."

Psalm   Psalm 15

R. **Show us, Lord, the path of life.**

or **Alleluia!**

1. Preserve me, God, I take refuge in you.
   I say to the Lord: "You are my God.
   O Lord, it is you who are my portion and cup;
   it is you yourself who are my prize." R.

2. I will bless the Lord who gives me counsel,
   who even at night directs my heart.
   I keep the Lord ever in my sight:
   since he is at my right hand, I shall stand firm. R.

3. And so my heart rejoices, my soul is glad;
   even my body shall rest in safety.
   For you will not leave my soul among the dead,
   nor let your beloved know decay. R.

4. You will show me the path of life,
   the fullness of joy in your presence,
   at your right hand happiness for ever. R.

Second Reading   1 Peter 1:17-21
Your ransom was paid in the precious blood of a lamb without spot
or stain, namely, Christ.

If you are acknowledging as your Father one who has no favourites
and judges everyone according to what he has done, you must be
scrupulously careful as long as you are living away from your home.
Remember, the ransom that was paid to free you from the useless
way of life your ancestors handed down was not paid in anything
corruptible, neither in silver nor gold, but in the precious blood of
a lamb without spot or stain, namely Christ; who, though known
since before the world was made, has been revealed only in our
time, the end of the ages, for your sake. Through him you now have
faith in God, who raised him from the dead and gave him glory for
that very reason – so that you would have faith and hope in God.

Gospel Acclamation
Alleluia, alleluia!
Lord Jesus, explain the scriptures to us.
Make our hearts burn within us as you talk to us.
Alleluia!   cf. Luke 24:32

Gospel   Luke 24:13-35
They recognised him at the breaking of bread.

Two of the disciples of Jesus were on their way to a village called
Emmaus, seven miles from Jerusalem, and they were talking
together about all that had happened. Now as they talked this over,
Jesus himself came up and walked by their side; but something
prevented them from recognising him. He said to them, "What

matters are you discussing as you walk along?" They stopped short, their faces downcast.

Then one of them, called Cleopas, answered him, "You must be the only person staying in Jerusalem who does not know the things that have been happening there these last few days." "What things?" he asked. "All about Jesus of Nazareth," they answered, "who proved he was a great prophet by the things he said and did in the sight of God and of the whole people; and how our chief priests and our leaders handed him over to be sentenced to death, and had him crucified. Our own hope had been that he would be the one to set Israel free. And this is not all: two whole days have gone by since it all happened; and some women from our group have astounded us: they went to the tomb in the early morning, and when they did not find the body, they came back to tell us they had seen a vision of angels who declared he was alive. Some of our friends went to the tomb and found everything exactly as the women had reported, but of him they saw nothing."

Then he said to them, "You foolish men! So slow to believe the full message of the prophets! Was it not ordained that the Christ should suffer and so enter into his glory?" Then, starting with Moses and going through all the prophets, he explained to them the passages throughout the scriptures that were about himself.

When they drew near to the village to which they were going, he made as if to go on; but they pressed him to stay with them. "It is nearly evening," they said, "and the day is almost over." So he went in to stay with them. Now while he was with them at the table, he took the bread and said the blessing; then he broke it and handed it to them. And their eyes were opened and they recognised him; but he had vanished from their sight. Then they said to each other, "Did not our hearts burn within us as he talked to us on the road and explained the scriptures to us?"

They set out that instant and returned to Jerusalem. There they found the Eleven assembled together with their companions, who said to them, "Yes, it is true. The Lord has risen and has appeared to Simon." Then they told their story of what had happened on the road and how they had recognised him at the breaking of bread.

The Creed is said.

Prayer over the Offerings
Receive, O Lord, we pray,
these offerings of your exultant Church,
and, as you have given her cause for such great gladness,
grant also that the gifts we bring
may bear fruit in perpetual happiness.
Through Christ our Lord.

Preface I-V of Easter, pp. 495-497.

Communion Antiphon
The disciples recognised the Lord Jesus
in the breaking of the bread, alleluia.   Luke 24:35

Prayer after Communion
Look with kindness upon your people, O Lord,
and grant, we pray,
that those you were pleased to renew by eternal mysteries
may attain in their flesh
the incorruptible glory of the resurrection.
Through Christ our Lord.

The Solemn Blessing for Easter Time may be used, p. 511.

FOURTH SUNDAY OF EASTER – A

Christ the Good Shepherd brings us life.
God has appointed Christ as the Shepherd of the whole human race. He has
become our gateway to eternal life because he has laid down his life for us.
Even though we have gone astray through sin, still by his wounds we are healed
and given a new direction in our lives.

Entrance Antiphon
The merciful love of the Lord fills the earth;
by the word of the Lord the heavens were made, alleluia.

cf. Psalm 32:5-6

The Gloria is said or sung.

Collect
Almighty ever-living God,
lead us to a share in the joys of heaven,
so that the humble flock may reach
where the brave Shepherd has gone before.
Who lives and reigns with you in the unity of the Holy Spirit,
one God, for ever and ever.

First Reading Acts 2:14. 36-41
God has made him both Lord and Christ.
On the day of Pentecost Peter stood up with the Eleven and
addressed the crowd with a loud voice: "The whole House of Israel
can be certain that God has made this Jesus whom you crucified
both Lord and Christ."

Hearing this, they were cut to the heart and said to Peter and the
apostles, "What must we do, brothers?" "You must repent," Peter
answered, "and every one of you must be baptised in the name of
Jesus Christ for the forgiveness of your sins, and you will receive
the gift of the Holy Spirit. The promise that was made is for you
and your children, and for all those who are far away, for all those
whom the Lord our God will call to himself." He spoke to them

for a long time using many arguments, and he urged them, "Save yourselves from this perverse generation." They were convinced by his arguments, and they accepted what he said and were baptised. That very day about three thousand were added to their number.

Psalm   Psalm 22

R. **The Lord is my shepherd;**
     there is nothing I shall want.

or **Alleluia!**

1. The Lord is my shepherd;
     there is nothing I shall want.
     Fresh and green are the pastures
     where he gives me repose.
     Near restful waters he leads me,
     to revive my drooping spirit. R.

2. He guides me along the right path;
     he is true to his name.
     If I should walk in the valley of darkness
     no evil would I fear.
     You are there with your crook and your staff;
     with these you give me comfort. R.

3. You have prepared a banquet for me
     in the sight of my foes.
     My head you have anointed with oil;
     my cup is overflowing. R.

4. Surely goodness and kindness shall follow me
     all the days of my life.
     In the Lord's own house shall I dwell
     for ever and ever. R.

Second Reading   1 Peter 2:20-25
You have come back to the shepherd of your souls.
The merit, in the sight of God, is in bearing punishment patiently
when you are punished after doing your duty.

This, in fact, is what you were called to do, because Christ
suffered for you and left an example for you to follow the way he
took. He had not done anything wrong, and there had been no
perjury in his mouth. He was insulted and did not retaliate with
insults; when he was tortured he made no threats but he put his
trust in the righteous judge. He was bearing our faults in his own
body on the cross, so that we might die to our faults and live for
holiness; through his wounds you have been healed. You had gone
astray like sheep but now you have come back to the shepherd and
guardian of your souls.

Gospel Acclamation
Alleluia, alleluia!
I am the good shepherd, says the Lord;
I know my own sheep and my own know me.
Alleluia!   John 10:14

Gospel   John 10:1-10
I am the gate of the sheepfold.
Jesus said: "I tell you most solemnly, anyone who does not enter the
sheepfold through the gate, but gets in some other way is a thief and
a brigand. The one who enters through the gate is the shepherd of
the flock; the gatekeeper lets him in, the sheep hear his voice, one
by one he calls his own sheep and leads them out. When he has
brought out his flock, he goes ahead of them, and the sheep follow
because they know his voice. They never follow a stranger but run
away from him: they do not recognise the voice of strangers."

Jesus told them this parable but they failed to understand what he
meant by telling it to them.

So Jesus spoke to them again:

"I tell you most solemnly,
I am the gate of the sheepfold.
All others who have come

are thieves and brigands;
but the sheep took no notice of them.
I am the gate.
Anyone who enters through me will be safe:
he will go freely in and out
and be sure of finding pasture.
The thief comes
only to steal and kill and destroy.
I have come
so that they may have life
and have it to the full."

The Creed is said.

Prayer over the Offerings
Grant, we pray, O Lord,
that we may always find delight in these paschal mysteries,
so that the renewal constantly at work within us
may be the cause of our unending joy.
Through Christ our Lord.

Preface I-V of Easter, pp. 495-497.

Communion Antiphon
The Good Shepherd has risen,
who laid down his life for his sheep
and willingly died for his flock, alleluia.

Prayer after Communion
Look upon your flock, kind Shepherd,
and be pleased to settle in eternal pastures
the sheep you have redeemed
by the Precious Blood of your Son.
Who lives and reigns for ever and ever.

The Solemn Blessing for Easter Time may be used, p. 511.

FIFTH SUNDAY OF EASTER – A

Christ is the Way, the Truth and the Life.
We are a chosen race, a royal priesthood, a consecrated nation, a people set apart
to sing the praises of God. God has poured out all these gifts on us through the
Holy Spirit. We are called to proclaim God's word revealed to us in Christ,
and to trust that Christ always has a special love and care for us.

Entrance Antiphon
O sing a new song to the Lord,
for he has worked wonders;
in the sight of the nations
he has shown his deliverance, alleluia.   cf. Psalm 97:1-2

The Gloria is said or sung.

Collect
Almighty ever-living God,
constantly accomplish the Paschal Mystery within us,
that those you were pleased to make new in Holy Baptism
may, under your protective care, bear much fruit
and come to the joys of life eternal.
Through our Lord Jesus Christ, your Son,
who lives and reigns with you in the unity of the Holy Spirit,
one God, for ever and ever.

First Reading   Acts 6:1-7
They elected seven men full of the Holy Spirit.
About this time, when the number of disciples was increasing,
the Hellenists made a complaint against the Hebrews: in the daily
distribution their own widows were being overlooked. So the
Twelve called a full meeting of the disciples and addressed them, "It
would not be right for us to neglect the word of God so as to give
out food; you, brothers, must select from among yourselves seven
men of good reputation, filled with the Spirit and with wisdom; we
will hand over this duty to them, and continue to devote ourselves

to prayer and to the service of the word." The whole assembly approved of this proposal and elected Stephen, a man full of faith and of the Holy Spirit, together with Philip, Prochorus, Nicanor, Timon, Parmenas, and Nicolaus of Antioch, a convert to Judaism. They presented these to the apostles, who prayed and laid their hands on them.

The word of the Lord continued to spread: the number of disciples in Jerusalem was greatly increased, and a large group of priests made their submission to the faith.

Psalm   Psalm 32

R. **May your love be upon us, O Lord,**
     as we place all our hope in you.

or **Alleluia!**

1. Ring out your joy to the Lord, O you just;
     for praise is fitting for loyal hearts.
     Give thanks to the Lord upon the harp,
     with a ten-stringed lute sing him songs. R.

2. For the word of the Lord is faithful
     and all his works to be trusted.
     The Lord loves justice and right
     and fills the earth with his love. R.

3. The Lord looks on those who revere him,
     on those who hope in his love,
     to rescue their souls from death,
     to keep them alive in famine. R.

Second Reading   1 Peter 2:4-9
But you are a chosen race, a royal priesthood.
The Lord is the living stone, rejected by men but chosen by God and precious to him; set yourselves close to him so that you too, the holy priesthood that offers the spiritual sacrifices which Jesus Christ has made acceptable to God, may be living stones making a spiritual house. As scripture says: See how I lay in Zion a precious cornerstone that I have chosen and the man who rests his trust on it will not be disappointed. That means that for you who are believers,

it is precious; but for unbelievers, the stone rejected by the builders has proved to be the keystone, a stone to stumble over, a rock to bring men down. They stumble over it because they do not believe in the word; it was the fate in store for them.

But you are a chosen race, a royal priesthood, a consecrated nation, a people set apart to sing the praises of God who called you out of the darkness into his wonderful light.

Gospel Acclamation
Alleluia, alleluia!
Jesus said: "I am the Way, the Truth and the Life.
No one can come to the Father except through me."
Alleluia!

John 14:6

Gospel
John 14:1-12

I am the Way, the Truth and the Life.

Jesus said to his disciples:

"Do not let your hearts be troubled.
Trust in God still, and trust in me.
There are many rooms in my Father's house;
if there were not, I should have told you.
I am now going to prepare a place for you,
and after I have gone and prepared you a place,
I shall return to take you with me;
so that where I am
you may be too.
You know the way to the place where I am going."

Thomas said, "Lord, we do not know where you are going, so how can we know the way?" Jesus said:

"I am the Way, the Truth and the Life.
No one can come to the Father except through me.
If you know me, you know my Father too.
From this moment you know him and have seen him."

Philip said, "Lord, let us see the Father and then we shall be satisfied." "Have I been with you all this time, Philip," said Jesus to him, "and you still do not know me?"

"To have seen me is to have seen the Father,
so how can you say, 'Let us see the Father'?
Do you not believe
that I am in the Father and the Father is in me?
The words I say to you I do not speak as from myself:
it is the Father, living in me, who is doing this work.
You must believe me when I say
that I am in the Father and the Father is in me;
believe it on the evidence of this work, if for no other reason.
I tell you most solemnly,
whoever believes in me
will perform the same works as I do myself,
he will perform even greater works,
because I am going to the Father."

The Creed is said.

Prayer over the Offerings
O God, who by the wonderful exchange effected in this sacrifice
have made us partakers of the one supreme Godhead,
grant, we pray,
that, as we have come to know your truth,
we may make it ours by a worthy way of life.
Through Christ our Lord.

Preface I-V of Easter, pp. 495-497.

Communion Antiphon
I am the true vine and you are the branches, says the Lord.
Whoever remains in me, and I in him, bears fruit in plenty,
    alleluia.   cf. John 15:1. 5

Prayer after Communion
Graciously be present to your people, we pray, O Lord,
and lead those you have imbued with heavenly mysteries
to pass from former ways to newness of life.
Through Christ our Lord.

The Solemn Blessing for Easter Time may be used, p. 511.

SIXTH SUNDAY OF EASTER – A

The Holy Spirit restores us to life.
Christ promised that he would send the Holy Spirit on his Church after his Resurrection. This is the source of our hope. Through the Spirit we can do great things in the Lord's name. In the Spirit we are healed and called to take part in the healing mission of the Church.

Entrance Antiphon
Proclaim a joyful sound and let it be heard;
proclaim to the ends of the earth:
The Lord has freed his people, alleluia.   cf. Isaiah 48:20

The Gloria is said or sung.

Collect
Grant, almighty God,
that we may celebrate with heartfelt devotion these days of joy,
which we keep in honour of the risen Lord,
and that what we relive in remembrance
we may always hold to in what we do.
Through our Lord Jesus Christ, your Son,
who lives and reigns with you in the unity of the Holy Spirit,
one God, for ever and ever.

First Reading   **Acts 8:5-8. 14-17**
They laid hands on them, and they received the Holy Spirit.
Philip went to a Samaritan town and proclaimed the Christ to them.
The people united in welcoming the message Philip preached,
either because they had heard of the miracles he worked or because
they saw them for themselves. There were, for example, unclean
spirits that came shrieking out of many who were possessed, and
several paralytics and cripples were cured. As a result there was
great rejoicing in that town.
    When the apostles in Jerusalem heard that Samaria had accepted

the word of God, they sent Peter and John to them, and they went down there, and prayed for the Samaritans to receive the Holy Spirit, for as yet he had not come down on any of them: they had only been baptised in the name of the Lord Jesus. Then they laid hands on them, and they received the Holy Spirit.

Psalm   Psalm 65

R. **Cry out with joy to God all the earth.**

or **Alleluia!**

1. Cry out with joy to God all the earth,
   O sing to the glory of his name.
   O render him glorious praise.
   Say to God: "How tremendous your deeds!" R.

2. "Before you all the earth shall bow;
   shall sing to you, sing to your name!"
   Come and see the works of God,
   tremendous his deeds among men. R.

3. He turned the sea into dry land,
   they passed through the river dry-shod.
   Let our joy then be in him;
   he rules for ever by his might. R.

4. Come and hear, all who fear God.
   I will tell what he did for my soul:
   Blessed be God who did not reject my prayer
   nor withhold his love from me. R.

Second Reading   1 Peter 3:15-18
In the body he was put to death, in the spirit he was raised to life.
Reverence the Lord Christ in your hearts, and always have your answer ready for people who ask you the reason for the hope that you all have. But give it with courtesy and respect and with a clear conscience, so that those who slander you when you are living a

good life in Christ may be proved wrong in the accusations that they bring. And if it is the will of God that you should suffer, it is better to suffer for doing right than for doing wrong.

Why, Christ himself, innocent though he was, had died once for sins, died for the guilty, to lead us to God. In the body he was put to death, in the spirit he was raised to life.

Gospel Acclamation

Alleluia, alleluia!
Jesus said: "If anyone loves me he will keep my word,
and my Father will love him, and we shall come to him."
Alleluia!   John 14:23

Gospel   John 14:15-21

I shall ask the Father, and he will give you another Advocate.
Jesus said to his disciples:

"If you love me you will keep my commandments.
I shall ask the Father,
and he will give you another Advocate
to be with you for ever,
that Spirit of truth
whom the world can never receive
since it neither sees nor knows him;
but you know him,
because he is with you, he is in you.
I will not leave you orphans;
I will come back to you.
In a short time the world will no longer see me;
but you will see me,
because I live and you will live.
On that day
you will understand that I am in my Father
and you in me and I in you.
Anybody who receives my commandments and keeps them
will be one who loves me;
and anybody who loves me will be loved by my Father,
and I shall love him and show myself to him."

The Creed is said.

Prayer over the Offerings
May our prayers rise up to you, O Lord,
together with the sacrificial offerings,
so that, purified by your graciousness,
we may be conformed to the mysteries of your mighty love.
Through Christ our Lord.

Preface I-V of Easter, pp. 495-497.

Communion Antiphon
If you love me, keep my commandments, says the Lord,
and I will ask the Father and he will send you another Paraclete,
to abide with you for ever, alleluia.   John 14:15-16

Prayer after Communion
Almighty ever-living God,
who restore us to eternal life in the Resurrection of Christ,
increase in us, we pray, the fruits of this paschal Sacrament
and pour into our hearts the strength of this saving food.
Through Christ our Lord.

The Solemn Blessing for Easter Time may be used, p. 511.

THE ASCENSION OF THE LORD – A

Christ ascends to his Father.
The Ascension of Jesus Christ is our guarantee that one day we will be with
him in heaven to praise the glory of God our Father. The Ascension is our hope
of the great inheritance that awaits those who believe in the power of the risen
Christ. Now we can know that he is with us to the end of time.

Entrance Antiphon
Men of Galilee, why gaze in wonder at the heavens?
This Jesus whom you saw ascending into heaven
will return as you saw him go, alleluia. Acts 1:11

The Gloria is said or sung.

Collect
Gladden us with holy joys, almighty God,
and make us rejoice with devout thanksgiving,
for the Ascension of Christ your Son
is our exaltation,
and, where the Head has gone before in glory,
the Body is called to follow in hope.
Through our Lord Jesus Christ, your Son,
who lives and reigns with you in the unity of the Holy Spirit,
one God, for ever and ever.

or

Grant, we pray, almighty God,
that we, who believe that your Only Begotten Son, our Redeemer,
ascended this day to the heavens,
may in spirit dwell already in heavenly realms.
Who lives and reigns with you in the unity of the Holy Spirit,
one God, for ever and ever.

First Reading   Acts 1:1-11

He was lifted up while they looked on.

In my earlier work, Theophilus, I dealt with everything Jesus had done and taught from the beginning until the day he gave his instructions to the apostles he had chosen through the Holy Spirit, and was taken up to heaven. He had shown himself alive to them after his Passion by many demonstrations: for forty days he had continued to appear to them and tell them about the kingdom of God. When he had been at table with them, he had told them not to leave Jerusalem, but to wait there for what the Father had promised. "It is", he had said, "what you have heard me speak about: John baptised with water but you, not many days from now, will be baptised with the Holy Spirit."

Now having met together, they asked him, "Lord, has the time come? Are you going to restore the kingdom to Israel?" He replied, "It is not for you to know times or dates that the Father has decided by his own authority, but you will receive power when the Holy Spirit comes on you, and then you will be my witnesses not only in Jerusalem but throughout Judaea and Samaria, and indeed to the ends of the earth."

As he said this he was lifted up while they looked on, and a cloud took him from their sight. They were still staring into the sky when suddenly two men in white were standing near them and they said, "Why are you men from Galilee standing here looking into the sky? Jesus who has been taken up from you into heaven, this same Jesus will come back in the same way as you have seen him go there."

Psalm   Psalm 46

R. **God goes up with shouts of joy;**
   the Lord goes up with trumpet blast.

or **Alleluia!**

1. All peoples, clap your hands,
   cry to God with shouts of joy!
   For the Lord, the Most High, we must fear,
   great king over all the earth. R.

2. God goes up with shouts of joy;
   the Lord goes up with trumpet blast.
   Sing praise for God, sing praise,
   sing praise to our king, sing praise. R.

3. God is king of all the earth.
   Sing praise with all your skill.
   God is king over the nations;
   God reigns on his holy throne. R.

Second Reading   Ephesians 1:17-23
He made him sit at his right hand in heaven.

May the God of our Lord Jesus Christ, the Father of glory, give
you a spirit of wisdom and perception of what is revealed, to bring
you to full knowledge of him. May he enlighten the eyes of your
mind so that you can see what hope his call holds for you, what rich
glories he has promised the saints will inherit and how infinitely
great is the power that he has exercised for us believers. This you
can tell from the strength of his power at work in Christ, when he
used it to raise him from the dead and to make him sit at his right
hand, in heaven, far above every Sovereignty, Authority, Power, or
Domination, or any other name that can be named, not only in this
age, but also in the age to come. He has put all things under his feet,
and made him as the ruler of everything, the head of the Church;
which is his body, the fullness of him who fills the whole creation.

Gospel Acclamation
Alleluia, alleluia!
Go, make disciples of all the nations;
I am with you always; yes, to the end of time.
Alleluia!   Matthew 28:19-20

Gospel   Matthew 28:16-20
All authority in heaven and on earth has been given to me.

The eleven disciples set out for Galilee, to the mountain where Jesus
had arranged to meet them. When they saw him they fell down
before him, though some hesitated. Jesus came up and spoke to

them. He said, "All authority in heaven and on earth has been given to me. Go, therefore, make disciples of all the nations; baptise them in the name of the Father and of the Son and of the Holy Spirit, and teach them to observe all the commands I gave you. And know that I am with you always; yes, to the end of time."

The Creed is said.

Prayer over the Offerings
We offer sacrifice now in supplication, O Lord,
to honour the wondrous Ascension of your Son:
grant, we pray,
that through this most holy exchange
we, too, may rise up to the heavenly realms.
Through Christ our Lord.

Preface I or II of the Ascension of the Lord, p. 498.

Communion Antiphon
Behold, I am with you always,
even to the end of the age, alleluia.   Matthew 28:20

Prayer after Communion
Almighty ever-living God,
who allow those on earth to celebrate divine mysteries,
grant, we pray,
that Christian hope may draw us onward
to where our nature is united with you.
Through Christ our Lord.

The Solemn Blessing for the Ascension of the Lord may be used, pp. 511-512.

SEVENTH SUNDAY OF EASTER – A

Christ our model of prayer and suffering.
Prayer is the birthright of every Christian. It is as natural to us as the air we
breathe. The early Christians were people of deep prayer and suffered for their
faith. Prayer and suffering are two sides of the same coin by which Christ
gives glory to God in us.

Entrance Antiphon
O Lord, hear my voice, for I have called to you;
of you my heart has spoken: Seek his face;
hide not your face from me, alleluia.   cf. Psalm 26:7-9

The Gloria is said or sung.

Collect
Graciously hear our supplications, O Lord,
so that we, who believe that the Saviour of the human race
is with you in your glory,
may experience, as he promised,
until the end of the world,
his abiding presence among us.
Who lives and reigns with you in the unity of the Holy Spirit,
one God, for ever and ever.

First Reading   Acts 1:12-14
All joined in continuous prayer.
After Jesus was taken up into heaven, the apostles went back from the
Mount of Olives, as it is called, to Jerusalem, a short distance away,
no more than a sabbath walk; and when they reached the city they
went to the upper room where they were staying; there were Peter
and John, James and Andrew, Philip and Thomas, Bartholomew and
Matthew, James son of Alphaeus and Simon the Zealot, and Jude son
of James. All these joined in continuous prayer, together with several
women, including Mary the mother of Jesus, and with his brothers.

Psalm   Psalm 26

R. **I am sure I shall see the Lord's goodness
     in the land of the living.**

or **Alleluia!**

1. The Lord is my light and my help;
    whom shall I fear?
    The Lord is the stronghold of my life;
    before whom shall I shrink? R.

2. There is one thing I ask of the Lord,
    for this I long,
    to live in the house of the Lord,
    all the days of my life,
    to savour the sweetness of the Lord,
    to behold his temple. R.

3. O Lord, hear my voice when I call;
    have mercy and answer.
    Of you my heart has spoken:
    "Seek his face." R.

Second Reading   1 Peter 4:13-16

It is a blessing for you when they insult you for bearing the name
of Christ.

If you can have some share in the sufferings of Christ, be glad,
because you will enjoy a much greater gladness when his glory is
revealed. It is a blessing for you when they insult you for bearing the
name of Christ, because it means that you have the Spirit of glory,
the Spirit of God resting on you. None of you should ever deserve to
suffer for being a murderer, a thief, a criminal or an informer; but if
anyone of you should suffer for being a Christian, then he is not to
be ashamed of it; he should thank God that he has been called one.

Gospel Acclamation
Alleluia, alleluia!
I will not leave you orphans, says the Lord;
I will come back to you, and your hearts will be full of joy.
Alleluia!   cf. John 14:18

Gospel   John 17:1-11
Father, glorify your Son.
Jesus raised his eyes to heaven and said:

"Father, the hour has come:
glorify your Son
so that your Son may glorify you;
and, through the power over all mankind that you have given
    him,
let him give eternal life to all those you have entrusted to him.
And eternal life is this:
to know you,
the only true God,
and Jesus Christ whom you have sent.
I have glorified you on earth
and finished the work
that you gave me to do.
Now, Father, it is time for you to glorify me
with that glory I had with you
before ever the world was.
I have made your name known
to the men you took from the world to give me.
They were yours and you gave them to me,
and they have kept your word.
Now at last they know
that all you have given me comes indeed from you;
for I have given them
the teaching you gave to me,
and they have truly accepted this, that I came from you,
and have believed that it was you who sent me.
I pray for them;
I am not praying for the world

but for those you have given me,
because they belong to you:
all I have is yours
and all you have is mine,
and in them I am glorified.
I am not in the world any longer,
but they are in the world,
and I am coming to you."

The Creed is said.

Prayer over the Offerings
Accept, O Lord, the prayers of your faithful
with the sacrificial offerings,
that through these acts of devotedness
we may pass over to the glory of heaven.
Through Christ our Lord.

Preface I-V of Easter, or I-II of the Ascension, pp. 495-498.

Communion Antiphon
Father, I pray that they may be one
as we also are one, alleluia.   John 17:22

Prayer after Communion
Hear us, O God our Saviour,
and grant us confidence,
that through these sacred mysteries
there will be accomplished in the body of the whole Church
what has already come to pass in Christ her Head.
Who lives and reigns for ever and ever.

The Solemn Blessing for Easter Time may be used, p. 511.

PENTECOST SUNDAY – A

The coming of the Holy Spirit upon the Church.
The message "Jesus is Lord" is to be preached to every corner of the earth. We
cannot do this unless we receive the Holy Spirit. Today we pray that we may
be open to the power of the Spirit, and that the Spirit will come and fill the
hearts of the faithful.

Entrance Antiphon
The Spirit of the Lord has filled the whole world
and that which contains all things
understands what is said, alleluia.

Wisdom 1:7

or

The love of God has been poured into our hearts
through the Spirit of God dwelling within us, alleluia.

Romans 5:5; cf. 8:11

The Gloria is said or sung.

Collect
O God, who by the mystery of today's great feast
sanctify your whole Church in every people and nation,
pour out, we pray, the gifts of the Holy Spirit
across the face of the earth
and, with the divine grace that was at work
when the Gospel was first proclaimed,
fill now once more the hearts of believers.
Through our Lord Jesus Christ, your Son,
who lives and reigns with you in the unity of the Holy Spirit,
one God, for ever and ever.

First Reading   Acts 2:1-11
They were all filled with the Holy Spirit and began to speak.
When Pentecost day came round, the apostles had all met in one
room, when suddenly they heard what sounded like a powerful
wind from heaven, the noise of which filled the entire house in

which they were sitting; and something appeared to them that seemed like tongues of fire; these separated and came to rest on the head of each of them. They were filled with the Holy Spirit, and began to speak foreign languages as the Spirit gave them the gift of speech.

Now there were devout men living in Jerusalem from every nation under heaven, and at this sound they all assembled, each one bewildered to hear these men speaking his own language. They were amazed and astonished. "Surely", they said, "all these men speaking are Galileans? How does it happen that each of us hears them in his own native language? Parthians, Medes and Elamites; people from Mesopotamia, Judaea and Cappadocia, Pontus and Asia, Phrygia and Pamphylia, Egypt and the parts of Libya round Cyrene; as well as visitors from Rome – Jews and proselytes alike – Cretans and Arabs; we hear them preaching in our own language about the marvels of God."

Psalm   Psalm 103

R. **Send forth your Spirit, O Lord,**
     and renew the face of the earth.

or **Alleluia.**

1. Bless the Lord, my soul!
   Lord God, how great you are.
   How many are your works, O Lord!
   The earth is full of your riches. R.

2. You take back your spirit, they die,
   returning to the dust from which they came.
   You send forth your spirit, they are created;
   and you renew the face of the earth. R.

3. May the glory of the Lord last for ever!
   May the Lord rejoice in his works!
   May my thoughts be pleasing to him.
   I find my joy in the Lord. R.

Second Reading   1 Corinthians 12:3-7. 12-13

In the one Spirit we were all baptised.

No one can say, "Jesus is Lord" unless he is under the influence of the Holy Spirit.

There is a variety of gifts but always the same Spirit; there are all sorts of service to be done, but always to the same Lord; working in all sorts of different ways in different people, it is the same God who is working in all of them. The particular way in which the Spirit is given to each person is for a good purpose.

Just as a human body, though it is made up of many parts, is a single unit because all these parts, though many, make one body, so it is with Christ. In the one Spirit we were all baptised, Jews as well as Greeks, slaves as well as citizens, and one Spirit was given to us all to drink.

Sequence

Holy Spirit, Lord of light,
From the clear celestial height
Thy pure beaming radiance give.

Come, thou Father of the poor,
Come with treasures which endure;
Come, thou light of all that live!

Thou, of all consolers best,
Thou, the soul's delightful guest,
Dost refreshing peace bestow;

Thou in toil art comfort sweet;
Pleasant coolness in the heat;
Solace in the midst of woe.

Light immortal, light divine,
Visit thou these hearts of thine,
And our inmost being fill:

If thou take thy grace away,
Nothing pure in man will stay;
All his good is turned to ill.

Heal our wounds, our strength renew;
On our dryness pour thy dew;
Wash the stains of guilt away:

Bend the stubborn heart and will;
Melt the frozen, warm the chill;
Guide the steps that go astray.

Thou, on us who evermore
Thee confess and thee adore,
With thy sevenfold gifts descend:

Give us comfort when we die;
Give us life with thee on high;
Give us joys that never end.

Gospel Acclamation
Alleluia, alleluia!
Come, Holy Spirit, fill the hearts of your faithful
and kindle in them the fire of your love.
Alleluia!

Gospel   John 20:19-23
As the Father sent me, so am I sending you: receive the Holy Spirit.
In the evening of the first day of the week, the doors were closed in
the room where the disciples were, for fear of the Jews. Jesus came
and stood among them. He said to them, "Peace be with you," and
showed them his hands and his side. The disciples were filled with
joy when they saw the Lord, and he said to them again, "Peace be
with you.

"As the Father sent me,
so am I sending you."

After saying this he breathed on them and said:

"Receive the Holy Spirit.
For those whose sins you forgive,
they are forgiven;
for those whose sins you retain,
they are retained."

The Creed is said.

Prayer over the Offerings
Grant, we pray, O Lord,
that, as promised by your Son,
the Holy Spirit may reveal to us more abundantly
the hidden mystery of this sacrifice
and graciously lead us into all truth.
Through Christ our Lord.

Preface
It is truly right and just, our duty and our salvation,
always and everywhere to give you thanks,
Lord, holy Father, almighty and eternal God.

For, bringing your Paschal Mystery to completion,
you bestowed the Holy Spirit today
on those you made your adopted children
by uniting them to your Only Begotten Son.
This same Spirit, as the Church came to birth,
opened to all peoples the knowledge of God
and brought together the many languages of the earth
in profession of the one faith.

Therefore, overcome with paschal joy,
every land, every people exults in your praise
and even the heavenly Powers, with the angelic hosts,
sing together the unending hymn of your glory,
as they acclaim:
Holy, Holy, Holy Lord God of hosts…

Communion Antiphon
They were all filled with the Holy Spirit
and spoke of the marvels of God, alleluia.   Acts 2:4. 11

Prayer after Communion
O God, who bestow heavenly gifts upon your Church,
safeguard, we pray, the grace you have given,
that the gift of the Holy Spirit poured out upon her
may retain all its force
and that this spiritual food
may gain her abundance of eternal redemption.
Through Christ our Lord.

The Solemn Blessing for the Holy Spirit may be used, p.512.

Dismissal
Go forth, the Mass is ended, alleluia, alleluia.

or

Go in peace, alleluia, alleluia.

Thanks be to God, alleluia, alleluia.

Easter Time is now concluded. For the Solemnity of the Most Holy Trinity, turn to p. 403.

SECOND SUNDAY OF EASTER – B
(or of Divine Mercy)

Our faith is the victory over the world.
We believe that Jesus Christ rose from the dead. It is this faith that Jesus is the
Son of God which helps us to overcome the world's temptations and doubts.
We have not seen, yet we believe. Like Thomas, we acclaim Christ as our Lord
and our God.

Entrance Antiphon
Like newborn infants, you must long for the pure, spiritual milk,
that in him you may grow to salvation, alleluia. 1 Peter 2:2

or

Receive the joy of your glory, giving thanks to God,
who has called you into the heavenly kingdom, alleluia.
4 Esdras 2:36-37

The Gloria is said or sung.

Collect
God of everlasting mercy,
who, in the very recurrence of the paschal feast
kindle the faith of the people you have made your own,
increase, we pray, the grace you have bestowed,
that all may grasp and rightly understand
in what font they have been washed,
by whose Spirit they have been reborn,
by whose Blood they have been redeemed.
Through our Lord Jesus Christ, your Son,
who lives and reigns with you in the unity of the Holy Spirit,
one God, for ever and ever.

First Reading Acts 4:32-35
United, heart and soul.
The whole group of believers was united, heart and soul; no one
claimed for his own use anything that he had, as everything they

owned was held in common.

The apostles continued to testify to the resurrection of the Lord Jesus with great power, and they were all given great respect.

None of their members was ever in want, as all those who owned land or houses would sell them, and bring the money from them, to present it to the apostles; it was then distributed to any members who might be in need.

Psalm   Psalm 117

R. **Give thanks to the Lord for he is good,**
   for his love has no end.

or **Alleluia, alleluia, alleluia!**

1. Let the sons of Israel say:
   "His love has no end."
   Let the sons of Aaron say:
   "His love has no end."
   Let those who fear the Lord say:
   "His love has no end." R.

2. The Lord's right hand has triumphed;
   his right hand raised me up.
   I shall not die, I shall live
   and recount his deeds.
   I was punished, I was punished by the Lord,
   but not doomed to die. R.

3. The stone which the builders rejected
   has become the corner stone.
   This is the work of the Lord,
   a marvel in our eyes.
   This day was made by the Lord;
   we rejoice and are glad. R.

Second Reading
1 John 5:1-6

Anyone who has been begotten by God has already overcome the world.

Whoever believes that Jesus is the Christ
has been begotten by God;
and whoever loves the Father that begot him
loves the child whom he begets.
We can be sure that we love God's children
if we love God himself and do what he has commanded us;
this is what loving God is –
keeping his commandments;
and his commandments are not difficult,
because anyone who has been begotten by God
has already overcome the world;
this is the victory over the world –
our faith.
Who can overcome the world?
Only the man who believes that Jesus is the Son of God;
Jesus Christ who came by water and blood,
not with water only,
but with water and blood;
with the Spirit as another witness –
since the Spirit is the truth.

Gospel Acclamation

Alleluia, alleluia!
Jesus said: "You believe because you can see me.
Happy are those who have not seen and yet believe."
Alleluia!

John 20:29

Gospel
John 20:19-31

Eight days later, Jesus came.

In the evening of that same day, the first day of the week, the doors were closed in the room where the disciples were, for fear of the Jews. Jesus came and stood among them. He said to them, "Peace be with you," and showed them his hands and his side. The disciples were filled with joy when they saw the Lord, and he said to them again, "Peace be with you.

As the Father sent me,
so am I sending you."

After saying this he breathed on them and said:

"Receive the Holy Spirit.
For those whose sins you forgive,
they are forgiven;
for those whose sins you retain,
they are retained."

Thomas, called the Twin, who was one of the Twelve, was not with them when Jesus came. When the disciples said, "We have seen the Lord," he answered, "Unless I see the holes that the nails made in his hands and can put my finger into the holes they made, and unless I can put my hand into his side, I refuse to believe." Eight days later the disciples were in the house again and Thomas was with them. The doors were closed, but Jesus came in and stood among them. "Peace be with you," he said. Then he spoke to Thomas, "Put your finger here; look, here are my hands. Give me your hand; put it into my side. Doubt no longer but believe." Thomas replied, "My Lord and my God!" Jesus said to him:

"You believe because you can see me.
Happy are those who have not seen and yet believe."

There were many other signs that Jesus worked and the disciples saw, but they are not recorded in this book. These are recorded so that you may believe that Jesus is the Christ, the Son of God, and that believing this you may have life through his name.

The Creed is said.

Prayer over the Offerings
Accept, O Lord, we pray,
the oblations of your people
(and of those you have brought to new birth),
that, renewed by confession of your name and by Baptism,
they may attain unending happiness.
Through Christ our Lord.

Preface I of Easter, p. 495.

Communion Antiphon

Bring your hand and feel the place of the nails,
and do not be unbelieving but believing, alleluia.   cf. John 20:27

Prayer after Communion

Grant, we pray, almighty God,
that our reception of this paschal Sacrament
may have a continuing effect
in our minds and hearts.
Through Christ our Lord.

The Solemn Blessing for the Mass of the Easter Vigil (p. 290) or for
Easter Time (p. 511) may be used.

Dismissal

Go forth, the Mass is ended, alleluia, alleluia.

or

Go in peace, alleluia, alleluia.

Thanks be to God, alleluia, alleluia.

THIRD SUNDAY OF EASTER – B

Christ is the sacrifice that takes our sins away.
Jesus Christ died for the sins of the world. God the Father raised him to life,
and in his Resurrection we too find life. In the light of Easter we can turn
away from sin and discover the peace of Christ. We are witnesses to God's
saving power in our everyday lives.

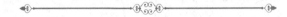

Entrance Antiphon
Cry out with joy to God, all the earth;
O sing to the glory of his name.
O render him glorious praise, alleluia. cf. Psalm 65:1-2

The Gloria is said or sung.

Collect
May your people exult for ever, O God,
in renewed youthfulness of spirit,
so that, rejoicing now in the restored glory of our adoption,
we may look forward in confident hope
to the rejoicing of the day of resurrection.
Through our Lord Jesus Christ, your Son,
who lives and reigns with you in the unity of the Holy Spirit,
one God, for ever and ever.

First Reading Acts 3:13-15. 17-19
You killed the prince of life. God, however, raised him from the
dead.
Peter said to the people: "You are Israelites, and it is the God of
Abraham, Isaac and Jacob, the God of our ancestors, who has
glorified his servant Jesus, the same Jesus you handed over and
then disowned in the presence of Pilate, after Pilate had decided
to release him. It was you who accused the Holy One, the Just One,
you who demanded the reprieve of a murderer while you killed the
prince of life. God, however, raised him from the dead, and to that
fact we are the witnesses.

"Now I know, brothers, that neither you nor your leaders had any idea what you were really doing; this was the way God carried out what he had foretold, when he said through all his prophets that his Christ would suffer. Now you must repent and turn to God, so that your sins may be wiped out."

Psalm   Psalm 4

R. **Lift up the light of your face on us, O Lord.**

or **Alleluia!**

1. When I call, answer me, O God of justice;
    from anguish you released me, have mercy and hear me! R.

2. It is the Lord who grants favours to those whom he loves;
    the Lord hears me whenever I call him. R.

3. "What can bring us happiness?" many say.
    Lift up the light of your face on us, O Lord. R.

4. I will lie down in peace and sleep comes at once,
    for you alone, Lord, make me dwell in safety. R.

Second Reading   1 John 2:1-5
He is the sacrifice that takes our sins away, and not only ours, but the whole world's.

I am writing this, my children,
to stop you sinning;
but if anyone should sin
we have our advocate with the Father,
Jesus Christ, who is just;
he is the sacrifice that takes our sins away,
and not only ours,
but the whole world's.
We can be sure that we know God
only by keeping his commandments.
Anyone who says, "I know him,"

and does not keep his commandments,
is a liar,
refusing to admit the truth.
But when anyone does obey what he has said,
God's love comes to perfection in him.

Gospel Acclamation
Alleluia, alleluia!
Lord Jesus, explain the scriptures to us.
Make our hearts burn within us as you talk to us.
Alleluia!   cf. Luke 24:32

Gospel   Luke 24:35-48
So you see how it is written that the Christ would suffer and on the
third day rise from the dead.
The disciples told their story of what had happened on the road and
how they had recognised Jesus at the breaking of bread.

They were still talking about this when Jesus himself stood
among them and said to them, "Peace be with you!" In a state of
alarm and fright, they thought they were seeing a ghost. But he said,
"Why are you so agitated, and why are these doubts rising in your
hearts? Look at my hands and feet; yes, it is I indeed. Touch me
and see for yourselves; a ghost has no flesh and bones as you can
see I have." And as he said this he showed them his hands and feet.
Their joy was so great that they could not believe it, and they stood
dumbfounded; so he said to them, "Have you anything here to eat?"
And they offered him a piece of grilled fish, which he took and ate
before their eyes.

Then he told them, "This is what I meant when I said, while I
was still with you, that everything written about me in the Law of
Moses, in the Prophets and in the Psalms, has to be fulfilled." He
then opened their minds to understand the scriptures, and he said
to them, "So you see how it is written that the Christ would suffer
and on the third day rise from the dead, and that, in his name,
repentance for the forgiveness of sins would be preached to all the
nations, beginning from Jerusalem. You are witnesses to this."

The Creed is said.

Prayer over the Offerings
Receive, O Lord, we pray,
these offerings of your exultant Church,
and, as you have given her cause for such great gladness,
grant also that the gifts we bring
may bear fruit in perpetual happiness.
Through Christ our Lord.

Preface I-V of Easter, pp. 495-497.

Communion Antiphon
The Christ had to suffer and on the third day rise from the dead;
in his name repentance and remission of sins
must be preached to all the nations, alleluia.   Luke 24:46-47

Prayer after Communion
Look with kindness upon your people, O Lord,
and grant, we pray,
that those you were pleased to renew by eternal mysteries
may attain in their flesh
the incorruptible glory of the resurrection.
Through Christ our Lord.

The Solemn Blessing for Easter Time may be used, p. 511.

FOURTH SUNDAY OF EASTER – B

Jesus Christ the Good Shepherd.
Christ the Good Shepherd lays down his life for us. This gives us some idea
of how lavish God our Father's love is, allowing us to be called his children.
Through the name of the Lord Jesus we can be sure that one day we shall see
God as he really is.

Entrance Antiphon
The merciful love of the Lord fills the earth;
by the word of the Lord the heavens were made, alleluia.

cf. Psalm 32:5-6

The Gloria is said or sung.

Collect
Almighty ever-living God,
lead us to a share in the joys of heaven,
so that the humble flock may reach
where the brave Shepherd has gone before.
Who lives and reigns with you in the unity of the Holy Spirit,
one God, for ever and ever.

First Reading Acts 4:8-12
This is the only name by which we can be saved.

Filled with the Holy Spirit, Peter said: "Rulers of the people, and elders! If you are questioning us today about an act of kindness to a cripple, and asking us how he was healed, then I am glad to tell you all, and would indeed be glad to tell the whole people of Israel, that it was by the name of Jesus Christ the Nazarene, the one you crucified, whom God raised from the dead, by this name and by no other that this man is able to stand up perfectly healthy, here in your presence today. This is the stone rejected by you the builders, but which has proved to be the keystone. For of all the names in the world given to men, this is the only one by which we can be saved."

Psalm   Psalm 117

R. **The stone which the builders rejected
has become the corner stone.**

or **Alleluia!**

1. Give thanks to the Lord for he is good,
   for his love has no end.
   It is better to take refuge in the Lord
   than to trust in men:
   it is better to take refuge in the Lord
   than to trust in princes. R.

2. I will thank you for you have given answer
   and you are my saviour.
   The stone which the builders rejected
   has become the corner stone.
   This is the work of the Lord,
   a marvel in our eyes. R.

3. Blessed in the name of the Lord
   is he who comes.
   We bless you from the house of the Lord;
   I will thank you for you have given answer
   and you are my saviour.
   Give thanks to the Lord for he is good;
   for his love has no end. R.

Second Reading   1 John 3:1-2
We shall see God as he really is.
Think of the love that the Father has lavished on us,
by letting us be called God's children;
and that is what we are.
Because the world refused to acknowledge him,
therefore it does not acknowledge us.
My dear people, we are already the children of God
but what we are to be in the future has not yet been revealed;

all we know is, that when it is revealed
we shall be like him
because we shall see him as he really is.

Gospel Acclamation
Alleluia, alleluia!
I am the good shepherd, says the Lord;
I know my own sheep and my own know me.
Alleluia!   John 10:14

Gospel   John 10:11-18
The good shepherd is one who lays down his life for his sheep.
Jesus said:

"I am the good shepherd:
the good shepherd is one who lays down his life for his sheep.
The hired man, since he is not the shepherd
and the sheep do not belong to him,
abandons the sheep and runs away
as soon as he sees a wolf coming,
and then the wolf attacks and scatters the sheep;
this is because he is only a hired man
and has no concern for the sheep.
I am the good shepherd;
I know my own
and my own know me,
just as the Father knows me
and I know the Father;
and I lay down my life for my sheep.
And there are other sheep I have
that are not of this fold,
and these I have to lead as well.
They too will listen to my voice,
and there will be only one flock,
and one shepherd.
The Father loves me,
because I lay down my life
in order to take it up again.

No one takes it from me;
I lay it down of my own free will,
and as it is in my power to lay it down,
so it is in my power to take it up again;
and this is the command I have been given by my Father."

The Creed is said.

Prayer over the Offerings
Grant, we pray, O Lord,
that we may always find delight in these paschal mysteries,
so that the renewal constantly at work within us
may be the cause of our unending joy.
Through Christ our Lord.

Preface I-V of Easter, pp. 495-497.

Communion Antiphon
The Good Shepherd has risen,
who laid down his life for his sheep
and willingly died for his flock, alleluia.

Prayer after Communion
Look upon your flock, kind Shepherd,
and be pleased to settle in eternal pastures
the sheep you have redeemed
by the Precious Blood of your Son.
Who lives and reigns for ever and ever.

The Solemn Blessing for Easter Time may be used, p. 511.

FIFTH SUNDAY OF EASTER – B

Jesus is the true vine.
We are called to share the life of God through grace. It is like the sap in the
branches that comes to them from the vine. If we really love God, then we
will allow Christ to come into our lives and to remain in us. If we keep the
commandment of love, God will live in us, and we will live in God.

Entrance Antiphon
O sing a new song to the Lord,
for he has worked wonders;
in the sight of the nations
he has shown his deliverance, alleluia.   cf. Psalm 97:1-2

The Gloria is said or sung.

Collect
Almighty ever-living God,
constantly accomplish the Paschal Mystery within us,
that those you were pleased to make new in Holy Baptism
may, under your protective care, bear much fruit
and come to the joys of life eternal.
Through our Lord Jesus Christ, your Son,
who lives and reigns with you in the unity of the Holy Spirit,
one God, for ever and ever.

First Reading   Acts 9:26-31
Barnabas explained how the Lord had appeared to Saul on his
journey.
When Saul got to Jerusalem he tried to join the disciples, but
they were all afraid of him: they could not believe he was really a
disciple. Barnabas, however, took charge of him, introduced him to
the apostles, and explained how the Lord had appeared to Saul and
spoken to him on his journey, and how he had preached boldly at
Damascus in the name of Jesus. Saul now started to go round with
them in Jerusalem, preaching fearlessly in the name of the Lord. But

after he had spoken to the Hellenists, and argued with them, they became determined to kill him. When the brothers knew, they took him to Caesarea, and sent him off from there to Tarsus.

The churches throughout Judaea, Galilee and Samaria were now left in peace, building themselves up, living in the fear of the Lord, and filled with the consolation of the Holy Spirit.

Psalm   Psalm 21

R. **You, Lord, are my praise in the great assembly.**

or **Alleluia!**

1. My vows I will pay before those who fear him.
   The poor shall eat and shall have their fill.
   They shall praise the Lord, those who seek him.
   May their hearts live for ever and ever! R.

2. All the earth shall remember and return to the Lord,
   all families of the nations worship before him.
   They shall worship him, all the mighty of the earth;
   before him shall bow all who go down to the dust. R.

3. And my soul shall live for him, my children serve him.
   They shall tell of the Lord to generations yet to come,
   declare his faithfulness to peoples yet unborn:
   "These things the Lord has done." R.

Second Reading   1 John 3:18-24
His commandments are these: that we believe in his Son and that we love one another.
My children,
our love is not to be just words or mere talk,
but something real and active;
only by this can we be certain
that we are the children of the truth
and be able to quieten our conscience in his presence,
whatever accusations it may raise against us,
because God is greater than our conscience and he knows
    everything.

My dear people,
if we cannot be condemned by our own conscience,
we need not be afraid in God's presence,
and whatever we ask him,
we shall receive,
because we keep his commandments
and live the kind of life that he wants.
His commandments are these:
that we believe in the name of his Son Jesus Christ
and that we love one another
as he told us to.
Whoever keeps his commandments
lives in God and God lives in him.
We know that he lives in us
by the Spirit that he has given us.

Gospel Acclamation
Alleluia, alleluia!
Make your home in me, as I make mine in you.
Whoever remains in me bears fruit in plenty.
Alleluia!   John 15:4-5

Gospel   John 15:1-8
Whoever remains in me, with me in him, bears fruit in plenty.
Jesus said to his disciples:

"I am the true vine,
and my Father is the vinedresser.
Every branch in me that bears no fruit
he cuts away,
and every branch that does bear fruit he prunes
to make it bear even more.
You are pruned already,
by means of the word that I have spoken to you.
Make your home in me, as I make mine in you.
As a branch cannot bear fruit all by itself,
but must remain part of the vine,
neither can you unless you remain in me.
I am the vine,

you are the branches.
Whoever remains in me, with me in him,
bears fruit in plenty;
for cut off from me you can do nothing.
Anyone who does not remain in me
is like a branch that has been thrown away
– he withers;
these branches are collected and thrown on the fire,
and they are burnt.
If you remain in me
and my words remain in you,
you may ask what you will
and you shall get it.
It is to the glory of my Father that you should bear much fruit,
and then you will be my disciples."

The Creed is said.

Prayer over the Offerings

O God, who by the wonderful exchange effected in this sacrifice
have made us partakers of the one supreme Godhead,
grant, we pray,
that, as we have come to know your truth,
we may make it ours by a worthy way of life.
Through Christ our Lord.

Preface I-V of Easter, pp. 495-497.

Communion Antiphon

I am the true vine and you are the branches, says the Lord.
Whoever remains in me, and I in him, bears fruit in plenty,
    alleluia.   cf. John 15:1. 5

Prayer after Communion

Graciously be present to your people, we pray, O Lord,
and lead those you have imbued with heavenly mysteries
to pass from former ways to newness of life.
Through Christ our Lord.

The Solemn Blessing for Easter Time may be used, p. 511.

SIXTH SUNDAY OF EASTER – B

God is love.
True love is from God. The Holy Spirit lives not only in us but in many
people who may seem to be outside the community of faith that is the Church.
We show we are Christians by the generous love we show to one another and
to all people, irrespective of race, colour or creed.

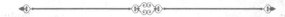

Entrance Antiphon
Proclaim a joyful sound and let it be heard;
proclaim to the ends of the earth:
The Lord has freed his people, alleluia.   cf. Isaiah 48:20

The Gloria is said or sung.

Collect
Grant, almighty God,
that we may celebrate with heartfelt devotion these days of joy,
which we keep in honour of the risen Lord,
and that what we relive in remembrance
we may always hold to in what we do.
Through our Lord Jesus Christ, your Son,
who lives and reigns with you in the unity of the Holy Spirit,
one God, for ever and ever.

First Reading   Acts 10:25-26. 34-35. 44-48
The Holy Spirit has been poured out on the pagans too.
As Peter reached the house Cornelius went out to meet him, knelt
at his feet and prostrated himself. But Peter helped him up. "Stand
up," he said, "I am only a man after all!"

Then Peter addressed them: "The truth I have now come to
realise", he said, "is that God does not have favourites, but that
anybody of any nationality who fears God and does what is right is
acceptable to him."

While Peter was still speaking the Holy Spirit came down on all the listeners. Jewish believers who had accompanied Peter were all astonished that the gift of the Holy Spirit should be poured out on the pagans too, since they could hear them speaking strange languages and proclaiming the greatness of God. Peter himself then said, "Could anyone refuse the water of baptism to these people, now they have received the Holy Spirit just as much as we have?" He then gave orders for them to be baptised in the name of Jesus Christ. Afterwards they begged him to stay on for some days.

Psalm   Psalm 97

R. **The Lord has shown his salvation to the nations.**

or **Alleluia!**

1. Sing a new song to the Lord
    for he has worked wonders.
    His right hand and his holy arm
    have brought salvation. R.

2. The Lord has made known his salvation;
    has shown his justice to the nations.
    He has remembered his truth and love
    for the house of Israel. R.

3. All the ends of the earth have seen
    the salvation of our God.
    Shout to the Lord all the earth,
    ring out your joy. R.

Second Reading   1 John 4:7-10
God is love.
My dear people,
let us love one another
since love comes from God
and everyone who loves is begotten by God and knows God.
Anyone who fails to love can never have known God,
because God is love.
God's love for us was revealed
when God sent into the world his only Son

so that we could have life through him;
this is the love I mean:
not our love for God,
but God's love for us when he sent his Son
to be the sacrifice that takes our sins away.

Gospel Acclamation
Alleluia, alleluia!
Jesus said: "If anyone loves me he will keep my word,
and my Father will love him, and we shall come to him."
Alleluia!   John 14:23

Gospel   John 15:9-17
A man can have no greater love than to lay down his life for his
friends.
Jesus said to his disciples:

"As the Father has loved me,
so I have loved you.
Remain in my love.
If you keep my commandments
you will remain in my love,
just as I have kept my Father's commandments
and remain in his love.
I have told you this
so that my own joy may be in you
and your joy be complete.
This is my commandment:
love one another,
as I have loved you.
A man can have no greater love
than to lay down his life for his friends.
You are my friends,
if you do what I command you.
I shall not call you servants any more,
because a servant does not know
his master's business;
I call you friends,

because I have made known to you
everything I have learnt from my Father.
You did not choose me,
no, I chose you;
and I commissioned you
to go out and to bear fruit,
fruit that will last;
and then the Father will give you
anything you ask him in my name.
What I command you
is to love one another."

The Creed is said.

Prayer over the Offerings
May our prayers rise up to you, O Lord,
together with the sacrificial offerings,
so that, purified by your graciousness,
we may be conformed to the mysteries of your mighty love.
Through Christ our Lord.

Preface I-V of Easter, pp. 495-497.

Communion Antiphon
If you love me, keep my commandments, says the Lord,
and I will ask the Father and he will send you another Paraclete,
to abide with you for ever, alleluia.   John 14:15-16

Prayer after Communion
Almighty ever-living God,
who restore us to eternal life in the Resurrection of Christ,
increase in us, we pray, the fruits of this paschal Sacrament
and pour into our hearts the strength of this saving food.
Through Christ our Lord.

The Solemn Blessing for Easter Time may be used, p. 511.

THE ASCENSION OF THE LORD – B

Christ ascends to his Father.

Jesus Christ's Ascension fills us with the hope that we will follow him, and one day be with him in heaven to praise the glory of God our Father. The Ascension is our hope of the great inheritance that awaits those who believe in the power of the risen Christ. He calls us to proclaim the Good News to all creation, and through his Spirit gives us many gifts to enable us to do so.

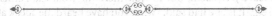

Entrance Antiphon
Men of Galilee, why gaze in wonder at the heavens?
This Jesus whom you saw ascending into heaven
will return as you saw him go, alleluia.   Acts 1:11

The Gloria is said or sung.

Collect
Gladden us with holy joys, almighty God,
and make us rejoice with devout thanksgiving,
for the Ascension of Christ your Son
is our exaltation,
and, where the Head has gone before in glory,
the Body is called to follow in hope.
Through our Lord Jesus Christ, your Son,
who lives and reigns with you in the unity of the Holy Spirit,
one God, for ever and ever.

or

Grant, we pray, almighty God,
that we, who believe that your Only Begotten Son, our Redeemer,
ascended this day to the heavens,
may in spirit dwell already in heavenly realms.
Who lives and reigns with you in the unity of the Holy Spirit,
one God, for ever and ever.

First Reading   Acts 1:1-11

He was lifted up while they looked on.

In my earlier work, Theophilus, I dealt with everything Jesus had done and taught from the beginning until the day he gave his instructions to the apostles he had chosen through the Holy Spirit, and was taken up to heaven. He had shown himself alive to them after his Passion by many demonstrations: for forty days he had continued to appear to them and tell them about the kingdom of God. When he had been at table with them, he had told them not to leave Jerusalem, but to wait there for what the Father had promised. "It is", he had said, "what you have heard me speak about: John baptised with water but you, not many days from now, will be baptised with the Holy Spirit."

Now having met together, they asked him, "Lord, has the time come? Are you going to restore the kingdom to Israel?" He replied, "It is not for you to know times or dates that the Father has decided by his own authority, but you will receive power when the Holy Spirit comes on you, and then you will be my witnesses not only in Jerusalem but throughout Judaea and Samaria, and indeed to the ends of the earth."

As he said this he was lifted up while they looked on, and a cloud took him from their sight. They were still staring into the sky when suddenly two men in white were standing near them and they said, "Why are you men from Galilee standing here looking into the sky? Jesus who has been taken from you into heaven, this same Jesus will come back in the same way as you have seen him go there."

Psalm   Psalm 46

R. **God goes up with shouts of joy;**
   the Lord goes up with trumpet blast.

or **Alleluia!**

1. All peoples, clap your hands,
   cry to God with shouts of joy!
   For the Lord, the Most High, we must fear,
   great king over all the earth. R.

2. God goes up with shouts of joy;
   the Lord goes up with trumpet blast.
   Sing praise for God, sing praise,
   sing praise to our king, sing praise. R.

3. God is king of all the earth.
   Sing praise with all your skill.
   God is king over the nations;
   God reigns on his holy throne. R.

Second Reading   Ephesians 1:17-23

He made him sit at his right hand in heaven.

May the God of our Lord Jesus Christ, the Father of glory, give
you a spirit of wisdom and perception of what is revealed, to bring
you to full knowledge of him. May he enlighten the eyes of your
mind so that you can see what hope his call holds for you, what rich
glories he has promised the saints will inherit and how infinitely
great is the power that he has exercised for us believers. This you
can tell from the strength of his power at work in Christ, when he
used it to raise him from the dead and to make him sit at his right
hand, in heaven, far above every Sovereignty, Authority, Power, or
Domination, or any other name that can be named, not only in this
age, but also in the age to come. He has put all things under his feet,
and made him as the ruler of everything, the head of the Church;
which is his body, the fullness of him who fills the whole creation.

or

Second Reading   Ephesians 4:1-13

Fully mature with the fullness of Christ.

I, the prisoner in the Lord, implore you to lead a life worthy of
your vocation. Bear with one another charitably, in complete
selflessness, gentleness and patience. Do all you can to preserve
the unity of the Spirit by the peace that binds you together. There
is one Body, one Spirit, just as you were all called into one and the
same hope when you were called. There is one Lord, one faith,
one baptism, and one God who is Father of all, over all, through
all and within all.

Each one of us, however, has been given his own share of grace, given as Christ allotted it.

It was said that he would:

When he ascended to the height, he captured prisoners,
he gave gifts to men.

When it says, "he ascended", what can it mean if not that he descended right down to the lower regions of the earth?

The one who rose higher than all the heavens to fill all things is none other than the one who descended. And to some, his gift was that they should be apostles; to some, prophets; to some, evangelists; to some, pastors and teachers; so that the saints together make a unity in the work of service, building up the body of Christ. In this way we are all to come to unity in our faith and in our knowledge of the Son of God, until we become the perfect Man, fully mature with the fullness of Christ himself.

Gospel Acclamation
Alleluia, alleluia!
Go, make disciples of all the nations;
I am with you always; yes, to the end of time.
Alleluia!   Matthew 28:19-20

Gospel   **Mark 16:15-20**
He was taken up into heaven: there at the right hand of God he took his place.

Jesus showed himself to the Eleven, and said to them, "Go out to the whole world; proclaim the Good News to all creation. He who believes and is baptised will be saved; he who does not believe will be condemned. These are the signs that will be associated with believers: in my name they will cast out devils; they will have the gift of tongues; they will pick up snakes in their hands, and be unharmed should they drink deadly poison; they will lay their hands on the sick, who will recover."

And so the Lord Jesus, after he had spoken to them, was taken up into heaven: there at the right hand of God he took his place, while they, going out, preached everywhere, the Lord working with them and confirming the word by the signs that accompanied it.

The Creed is said.

Prayer over the Offerings
We offer sacrifice now in supplication, O Lord,
to honour the wondrous Ascension of your Son:
grant, we pray,
that through this most holy exchange
we, too, may rise up to the heavenly realms.
Through Christ our Lord.

Preface I or II of the Ascension of the Lord, p. 498.

Communion Antiphon
Behold, I am with you always,
even to the end of the age, alleluia.   Matthew 28:20

Prayer after Communion
Almighty ever-living God,
who allow those on earth to celebrate divine mysteries,
grant, we pray,
that Christian hope may draw us onward
to where our nature is united with you.
Through Christ our Lord.

The Solemn Blessing for the Ascension of the Lord may be used,
pp. 511-512.

SEVENTH SUNDAY OF EASTER – B

In love we are united.
God is love, and if we are to live in God then this comes about through love,
God's gift to us in the Holy Spirit. Christ is always with us and constantly
prays for us to his Father. He prays that we may be united, just as he is one
with the Father and the Holy Spirit. In this way we will witness to his truth.
Anyone who lives in love lives in God.

Entrance Antiphon
O Lord, hear my voice, for I have called to you;
of you my heart has spoken: Seek his face;
hide not your face from me, alleluia.   cf. Psalm 26:7-9

The Gloria is said or sung.

Collect
Graciously hear our supplications, O Lord,
so that we, who believe that the Saviour of the human race
is with you in your glory,
may experience, as he promised,
until the end of the world,
his abiding presence among us.
Who lives and reigns with you in the unity of the Holy Spirit,
one God, for ever and ever.

First Reading   Acts 1:15-17. 20-26
We must choose one of these to be a witness to his resurrection
with us.
One day Peter stood up to speak to the brothers – there were about
a hundred and twenty persons in the congregation: "Brothers, the
passage of scripture had to be fulfilled in which the Holy Spirit,
speaking through David, foretells the fate of Judas, who offered
himself as a guide to the men who arrested Jesus – after having
been one of our number and actually sharing this ministry of ours.

"In the Book of Psalms it says:

Let someone else take his office.

"We must therefore choose someone who has been with us the whole time that the Lord Jesus was travelling round with us, someone who was with us right from the time when John was baptising until the day when he was taken up from us – and he can act with us as a witness to his resurrection."

Having nominated two candidates, Joseph known as Barsabbas, whose surname was Justus, and Matthias, they prayed, "Lord, you can read everyone's heart; show us therefore which of these two you have chosen to take over this ministry and apostolate, which Judas abandoned to go to his proper place." They then drew lots for them, and as the lot fell to Matthias, he was listed as one of the twelve apostles.

Psalm   Psalm 102

R. **The Lord has set his sway in heaven.**

or **Alleluia!**

1. My soul, give thanks to the Lord,
   all my being, bless his holy name.
   My soul, give thanks to the Lord
   and never forget all his blessings. R.

2. For as the heavens are high above the earth
   so strong is his love for those who fear him.
   As far as the east is from the west
   so far does he remove our sins. R.

3. The Lord has set his sway in heaven
   and his kingdom is ruling over all.
   Give thanks to the Lord, all his angels,
   mighty in power, fulfilling his word. R.

Second Reading   1 John 4:11-16
Anyone who lives in love lives in God, and God lives in him.
My dear people,
since God has loved us so much,
we too should love one another.
No one has ever seen God;
but as long as we love one another

God will live in us
and his love will be complete in us.
We can know that we are living in him
and he is living in us
because he lets us share his Spirit.
We ourselves saw and we testify
that the Father sent his Son
as saviour of the world.
If anyone acknowledges that Jesus is the Son of God,
God lives in him, and he in God.
We ourselves have known and put our faith in
God's love towards ourselves.
God is love
and anyone who lives in love lives in God,
and God lives in him.

Gospel Acclamation

Alleluia, alleluia!
I will not leave you orphans, says the Lord;
I will come back to you, and your hearts will be full of joy.
Alleluia!   cf. John 14:18

Gospel   John 17:11-19

That they may be one like us!

Jesus raised his eyes to heaven and said:
    "Holy Father,
    keep those you have given me true to your name,
    so that they may be one like us.
    While I was with them,
    I kept those you had given me true to your name.
    I have watched over them and not one is lost
    except the one who chose to be lost,
    and this was to fulfil the scriptures.
    But now I am coming to you
    and while still in the world I say these things
    to share my joy with them to the full.
    I passed your word on to them,
    and the world hated them,

because they belong to the world
no more than I belong to the world.
I am not asking you to remove them from the world,
but to protect them from the evil one.
They do not belong to the world
any more than I belong to the world.
Consecrate them in the truth;
your word is truth.
As you sent me into the world,
I have sent them into the world,
and for their sake I consecrate myself
so that they too may be consecrated in truth."

The Creed is said.

Prayer over the Offerings
Accept, O Lord, the prayers of your faithful
with the sacrificial offerings,
that through these acts of devotedness
we may pass over to the glory of heaven.
Through Christ our Lord.

Preface I-V of Easter, or I-II of the Ascension, pp. 495-498.

Communion Antiphon
Father, I pray that they may be one
as we also are one, alleluia.   John 17:22

Prayer after Communion
Hear us, O God our Saviour,
and grant us confidence,
that through these sacred mysteries
there will be accomplished in the body of the whole Church
what has already come to pass in Christ her Head.
Who lives and reigns for ever and ever.

The Solemn Blessing for Easter Time may be used, p. 511.

PENTECOST SUNDAY – B

The coming of the Holy Spirit upon the Church.
Christ promised his disciples that he would send to them the Spirit of truth,
to teach them and to guide them. Today we celebrate the coming of that Holy
Spirit, who brings us many good gifts. We pray that we may be open to the
power of the Spirit, and that the Spirit will come anew and fill the hearts of
the faithful.

Entrance Antiphon
The Spirit of the Lord has filled the whole world
and that which contains all things
understands what is said, alleluia.   Wisdom 1:7

or

The love of God has been poured into our hearts
through the Spirit of God dwelling within us, alleluia.
                                       Romans 5:5; cf. 8:11

The Gloria is said or sung.

Collect
O God, who by the mystery of today's great feast
sanctify your whole Church in every people and nation,
pour out, we pray, the gifts of the Holy Spirit
across the face of the earth
and, with the divine grace that was at work
when the Gospel was first proclaimed,
fill now once more the hearts of believers.
Through our Lord Jesus Christ, your Son,
who lives and reigns with you in the unity of the Holy Spirit,
one God, for ever and ever.

First Reading   Acts 2:1-11
They were all filled with the Holy Spirit and began to speak.

When Pentecost day came round, the apostles had all met in one room, when suddenly they heard what sounded like a powerful wind from heaven, the noise of which filled the entire house in which they were sitting; and something appeared to them that seemed like tongues of fire; these separated and came to rest on the head of each of them. They were filled with the Holy Spirit, and began to speak foreign languages as the Spirit gave them the gift of speech.

Now there were devout men living in Jerusalem from every nation under heaven, and at this sound they all assembled, each one bewildered to hear these men speaking his own language. They were amazed and astonished. "Surely", they said, "all these men speaking are Galileans? How does it happen that each of us hears them in his own native language? Parthians, Medes and Elamites; people from Mesopotamia, Judaea and Cappadocia, Pontus and Asia, Phrygia and Pamphylia, Egypt and the parts of Libya round Cyrene; as well as visitors from Rome – Jews and proselytes alike – Cretans and Arabs; we hear them preaching in our own language about the marvels of God."

Psalm   Psalm 103

R. **Send forth your Spirit, O Lord,**
    and renew the face of the earth.

or **Alleluia.**

1. Bless the Lord, my soul!
    Lord God, how great you are.
    How many are your works, O Lord!
    The earth is full of your riches. R.

2. You take back your spirit, they die,
    returning to the dust from which they came.
    You send forth your spirit, they are created;
    and you renew the face of the earth. R.

3. May the glory of the Lord last for ever!
   May the Lord rejoice in his works!
   May my thoughts be pleasing to him.
   I find my joy in the Lord. R.

The Second Reading and Gospel for Year A may be used as an alternative in any year. See pp. 328-329.

Second Reading   Galatians 5:16-25
The fruit of the Spirit.

If you are guided by the Spirit you will be in no danger of yielding to self-indulgence, since self-indulgence is the opposite of the Spirit, the Spirit is totally against such a thing, and it is precisely because the two are so opposed that you do not always carry out your good intentions. If you are led by the Spirit, no law can touch you. When self-indulgence is at work the results are obvious: fornication, gross indecency and sexual irresponsibility; idolatry and sorcery; feuds and wrangling, jealousy, bad temper and quarrels; disagreements, factions, envy; drunkenness, orgies and similar things. I warn you now, as I warned you before: those who behave like this will not inherit the kingdom of God. What the Spirit brings is very different: love, joy, peace, patience, kindness, goodness, trustfulness, gentleness and self-control. There can be no law against things like that, of course. You cannot belong to Christ Jesus unless you crucify all self-indulgent passions and desire.

Since the Spirit is our life, let us be directed by the Spirit.

The Sequence may be said or sung. See pp. 328-329.

Gospel Acclamation
Alleluia, alleluia!
Come, Holy Spirit, fill the hearts of your faithful
and kindle in them the fire of your love.
Alleluia!

Gospel   John 15:26-27; 16:12-15
The Spirit of truth will lead you to the complete truth.
Jesus said to his disciples:

"When the Advocate comes,
whom I shall send to you from the Father,
the Spirit of truth who issues from the Father,
he will be my witness.
And you too will be witnesses,
because you have been with me from the outset.

"I still have many things to say to you
but they would be too much for you now.
But when the Spirit of truth comes
he will lead you to the complete truth,
since he will not be speaking as from himself
but will say only what he has learnt;
and he will tell you of the things to come.
He will glorify me,
since all he tells you
will be taken from what is mine.
Everything the Father has is mine;
that is why I said:
All he tells you
will be taken from what is mine."

The Creed is said.

Prayer over the Offerings
Grant, we pray, O Lord,
that, as promised by your Son,
the Holy Spirit may reveal to us more abundantly
the hidden mystery of this sacrifice
and graciously lead us into all truth.
Through Christ our Lord.

Preface of Pentecost, p. 330.

Communion Antiphon
They were all filled with the Holy Spirit
and spoke of the marvels of God, alleluia.   Acts 2:4. 11

Prayer after Communion
O God, who bestow heavenly gifts upon your Church,
safeguard, we pray, the grace you have given,
that the gift of the Holy Spirit poured out upon her
may retain all its force
and that this spiritual food
may gain her abundance of eternal redemption.
Through Christ our Lord.

The Solemn Blessing for the Holy Spirit may be used, p. 512.

Dismissal
Go forth, the Mass is ended, alleluia, alleluia.

or

Go in peace, alleluia, alleluia.

Thanks be to God, alleluia, alleluia.

Easter Time is now concluded. For the Solemnity of the Most Holy
Trinity, turn to p. 418.

SECOND SUNDAY OF EASTER – C
(or of Divine Mercy)

Receive the Holy Spirit.
Jesus, our risen Lord, bestows his Spirit on us. We believe, even though we have
not seen, that he is our Lord and God. We are apostles of his Resurrection and
we live the life of the Spirit. As the Father sent Christ, so now we are sent to
preach the Good News to all people. The Spirit will help us on our mission.

Entrance Antiphon
Like newborn infants, you must long for the pure, spiritual milk,
that in him you may grow to salvation, alleluia. 1 Peter 2:2

or

Receive the joy of your glory, giving thanks to God,
who has called you into the heavenly kingdom, alleluia.
4 Esdras 2:36-37

The Gloria is said or sung.

Collect
God of everlasting mercy,
who, in the very recurrence of the paschal feast
kindle the faith of the people you have made your own,
increase, we pray, the grace you have bestowed,
that all may grasp and rightly understand
in what font they have been washed,
by whose Spirit they have been reborn,
by whose Blood they have been redeemed.
Through our Lord Jesus Christ, your Son,
who lives and reigns with you in the unity of the Holy Spirit,
one God, for ever and ever.

First Reading   Acts 5:12-16

The numbers of men and women who came to believe in the Lord increased steadily.

The faithful all used to meet by common consent in the Portico of Solomon. No one else ever dared to join them, but the people were loud in their praise and the numbers of men and women who came to believe in the Lord increased steadily. So many signs and wonders were worked among the people at the hands of the apostles that the sick were even taken out into the streets and laid on beds and sleeping-mats in the hope that at least the shadow of Peter might fall across some of them as he went past. People even came crowding in from the towns round about Jerusalem, bringing with them their sick and those tormented by unclean spirits, and all of them were cured.

Psalm   Psalm 117

R.   **Give thanks to the Lord for he is good,**
     for his love has no end.

or   **Alleluia, alleluia, alleluia!**

1. Let the sons of Israel say:
   "His love has no end."
   Let the sons of Aaron say:
   "His love has no end."
   Let those who fear the Lord say:
   "His love has no end." R.

2. The stone which the builders rejected
   has become the corner stone.
   This is the work of the Lord,
   a marvel in our eyes.
   This day was made by the Lord;
   we rejoice and are glad. R.

3. O Lord, grant us salvation;
   O Lord, grant success.
   Blessed in the name of the Lord

is he who comes.
We bless you from the house of the Lord;
the Lord God is our light. R.

Second Reading   Apocalypse 1:9-13. 17-19
I was dead and now I am to live for ever and ever.

My name is John, and through our union in Jesus I am your brother
and share your sufferings, your kingdom, and all you endure. I
was on the island of Patmos for having preached God's word and
witnessed for Jesus; it was the Lord's day and the Spirit possessed
me, and I heard a voice behind me, shouting like a trumpet, "Write
down all that you see in a book." I turned round to see who had
spoken to me, and when I turned I saw seven golden lamp-stands
and, surrounded by them, a figure like a Son of man, dressed in a
long robe tied at the waist with a golden girdle.

When I saw him, I fell in a dead faint at his feet, but he touched me
with his right hand and said, "Do not be afraid; it is I, the First and
the Last; I am the Living One. I was dead and now I am to live for
ever and ever, and I hold the keys of death and of the underworld.
Now write down all that you see of present happenings and things
that are still to come."

Gospel Acclamation
Alleluia, alleluia!
Jesus said: "You believe because you can see me.
Happy are those who have not seen and yet believe."
Alleluia!   John 20:29

Gospel   John 20:19-31
Eight days later, Jesus came.

In the evening of that same day, the first day of the week, the doors
were closed in the room where the disciples were, for fear of the
Jews. Jesus came and stood among them. He said to them, "Peace
be with you," and showed them his hands and his side. The disciples
were filled with joy when they saw the Lord, and he said to them
again,

"Peace be with you.

"As the Father sent me,
so am I sending you."

After saying this he breathed on them and said:

"Receive the Holy Spirit.
For those whose sins you forgive,
they are forgiven;
for those whose sins you retain,
they are retained."

Thomas, called the Twin, who was one of the Twelve, was not with them when Jesus came. When the disciples said, "We have seen the Lord," he answered, "Unless I see the holes that the nails made in his hands and can put my finger into the holes they made, and unless I can put my hand into his side, I refuse to believe." Eight days later the disciples were in the house again and Thomas was with them. The doors were closed, but Jesus came in and stood among them. "Peace be with you," he said. Then he spoke to Thomas, "Put your finger here; look, here are my hands. Give me your hand; put it into my side. Doubt no longer but believe." Thomas replied, "My Lord and my God!" Jesus said to him:

"You believe because you can see me.
Happy are those who have not seen and yet believe."

There were many other signs that Jesus worked and the disciples saw, but they are not recorded in this book. These are recorded so that you may believe that Jesus is the Christ, the Son of God, and that believing this you may have life through his name.

The Creed is said.

Prayer over the Offerings
Accept, O Lord, we pray,
the oblations of your people
(and of those you have brought to new birth),
that, renewed by confession of your name and by Baptism,
they may attain unending happiness.
Through Christ our Lord.

Preface I of Easter, p. 495.

Communion Antiphon

Bring your hand and feel the place of the nails,
and do not be unbelieving but believing, alleluia.   cf. John 20:27

Prayer after Communion

Grant, we pray, almighty God,
that our reception of this paschal Sacrament
may have a continuing effect
in our minds and hearts.
Through Christ our Lord.

The Solemn Blessing for the Mass of the Easter Vigil (p. 290) or for
Easter Time (p. 511) may be used.

Dismissal

Go forth, the Mass is ended, alleluia, alleluia.

or

Go in peace, alleluia, alleluia.

Thanks be to God, alleluia, alleluia.

THIRD SUNDAY OF EASTER – C

We are witnesses to the Resurrection.
The Holy Spirit gives us the courage to witness to the power of Christ's
Resurrection. Jesus is the Lamb of God to whom all praise, honour, glory
and power must be given for ever and ever. We will suffer opposition and
misunderstanding because of our belief, but Christ promises
he will always be with us.

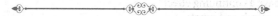

Entrance Antiphon
Cry out with joy to God, all the earth;
O sing to the glory of his name.
O render him glorious praise, alleluia.   cf. Psalm 65:1-2

The Gloria is said or sung.

Collect
May your people exult for ever, O God,
in renewed youthfulness of spirit,
so that, rejoicing now in the restored glory of our adoption,
we may look forward in confident hope
to the rejoicing of the day of resurrection.
Through our Lord Jesus Christ, your Son,
who lives and reigns with you in the unity of the Holy Spirit,
one God, for ever and ever.

First Reading   Acts 5:27-32. 40-41
We are witnesses of all this, we and the Holy Spirit.
The high priest demanded an explanation of the apostles. "We gave
you a formal warning", he said, "not to preach in this name, and
what have you done? You have filled Jerusalem with your teaching,
and seem determined to fix the guilt of this man's death on us." In
reply Peter and the apostles said, "Obedience to God comes before
obedience to men; it was the God of our ancestors who raised up
Jesus, but it was you who had him executed by hanging on a tree.

By his own right hand God has now raised him up to be leader and saviour, to give repentance and forgiveness of sins through him to Israel. We are witnesses to all this, we and the Holy Spirit whom God has given to those who obey him." They warned the apostles not to speak in the name of Jesus and released them. And so they left the presence of the Sanhedrin glad to have had the honour of suffering humiliation for the sake of the name.

Psalm   Psalm 29

R. **I will praise you, Lord,
    you have rescued me.**

or **Alleluia!**

1. I will praise you, Lord, you have rescued me
    and have not let my enemies rejoice over me.
    O Lord, you have raised my soul from the dead,
    restored me to life from those who sink into the grave. R.

2. Sing psalms to the Lord, you who love him,
    give thanks to his holy name.
    His anger lasts but a moment; his favour through life.
    At night there are tears, but joy comes with dawn. R.

3. The Lord listened and had pity.
    The Lord came to my help.
    For me you have changed my mourning into dancing,
    O Lord my God, I will thank you for ever. R.

Second Reading   Apocalypse 5:11-14
The Lamb that was sacrificed is worthy to be given riches and power.

In my vision, I, John, heard the sound of an immense number of angels gathered round the throne and the animals and the elders; there were ten thousand times ten thousand of them and thousands upon thousands, shouting, "The Lamb that was sacrificed is worthy to be given power, riches, wisdom, strength, honour, glory and blessing." Then I heard all the living things in creation – everything that lives in the air, and on the ground, and under the ground, and in the sea, crying, "To the One who is sitting on the throne and to the Lamb, be all praise, honour, glory and power, for ever and ever." And the four animals said, "Amen"; and the elders prostrated themselves to worship.

Gospel Acclamation
Alleluia, alleluia!
Lord Jesus, explain the scriptures to us.
Make our hearts burn within us as you talk to us.
Alleluia!

cf. Luke 24:32

or

Alleluia, alleluia!
Christ has risen: he who created all things,
and has granted his mercy to men.
Alleluia!

Gospel   John 21:1-19
Jesus stepped forward, took the bread and gave it to them, and the same with the fish.

Jesus showed himself again to the disciples. It was by the Sea of Tiberias, and it happened like this: Simon Peter, Thomas called the Twin, Nathanael from Cana in Galilee, the sons of Zebedee and two more of his disciples were together. Simon Peter said, "I'm going fishing." They replied, "We'll come with you." They went out and got into the boat but caught nothing that night.

It was light by now and there stood Jesus on the shore, though the disciples did not realise that it was Jesus. Jesus called out, "Have you caught anything, friends?" And when they answered, "No," he said, "Throw the net out to starboard and you'll find something." So they dropped the net, and there were so many fish that they could not haul it in. The disciple Jesus loved said to Peter, "It is the Lord." At these words "It is the Lord," Simon Peter, who had practically nothing on, wrapped his cloak round him and jumped into the water. The other disciples came on in the boat, towing the net and the fish; they were only about a hundred yards from land.

As soon as they came ashore they saw that there was some bread there, and a charcoal fire with fish cooking on it. Jesus said, "Bring some of the fish you have just caught." Simon Peter went aboard and dragged the net to the shore, full of big fish, one hundred and fifty-three of them; and in spite of there being so many the net was not broken. Jesus said to them, "Come and have breakfast." None of the disciples was bold enough to ask, "Who are you?"; they knew quite well it was the Lord. Jesus then stepped forward, took the bread and gave it to them, and the same with the fish. This was the third time that Jesus showed himself to the disciples after rising from the dead.

After the meal Jesus said to Simon Peter, "Simon son of John, do you love me more than these others do?" He answered, "Yes Lord, you know I love you." Jesus said to him, "Feed my lambs." A second time he said to him, "Simon son of John, do you love me?" He replied, "Yes, Lord, you know I love you." Jesus said to him, "Look after my sheep." Then he said to him a third time, "Simon son of John, do you love me?" Peter was upset that he asked him the third time, "Do you love me?" and said, "Lord, you know everything; you know I love you." Jesus said to him, "Feed my sheep.

"I tell you most solemnly,
when you were young
you put on your own belt
and walked where you liked;
but when you grow old
you will stretch out your hands,
and somebody else will put a belt round you
and take you where you would rather not go."

In these words he indicated the kind of death by which Peter would give glory to God. After this he said, "Follow me."

The Creed is said.

Prayer over the Offerings
Receive, O Lord, we pray,
these offerings of your exultant Church,
and, as you have given her cause for such great gladness,
grant also that the gifts we bring
may bear fruit in perpetual happiness.
Through Christ our Lord.

Preface I-V of Easter, pp. 495-497.

Communion Antiphon
Jesus said to his disciples: Come and eat.
And he took bread and gave it to them, alleluia.   cf. John 21:12-13

Prayer after Communion
Look with kindness upon your people, O Lord,
and grant, we pray,
that those you were pleased to renew by eternal mysteries
may attain in their flesh
the incorruptible glory of the resurrection.
Through Christ our Lord.

The Solemn Blessing for Easter Time may be used, p. 511.

FOURTH SUNDAY OF EASTER – C

Christ gives eternal life to all who listen to his voice.
Jesus Christ is the Good Shepherd who will lead us to springs of living water,
where God will wipe away all tears from our eyes. We are a light for the
nations so that the salvation of Christ may be preached to the ends of the earth.
We have a mission to everyone, even though at times people may turn against
us because of our belief. But the Holy Spirit can fill us with joy.

Entrance Antiphon
The merciful love of the Lord fills the earth;
by the word of the Lord the heavens were made, alleluia.

cf. Psalm 32:5-6

The Gloria is said or sung.

Collect
Almighty ever-living God,
lead us to a share in the joys of heaven,
so that the humble flock may reach
where the brave Shepherd has gone before.
Who lives and reigns with you in the unity of the Holy Spirit,
one God, for ever and ever.

First Reading   Acts 13:14. 43-52
We must turn to the pagans.
Paul and Barnabas carried on from Perga till they reached Antioch
in Pisidia. Here they went to synagogue on the sabbath and took
their seats.

When the meeting broke up, many Jews and devout converts joined
Paul and Barnabas, and in their talks with them Paul and Barnabas
urged them to remain faithful to the grace God had given them.

The next sabbath almost the whole town assembled to hear the
word of God. When they saw the crowds, the Jews, prompted by
jealousy, used blasphemies and contradicted everything Paul said.

Then Paul and Barnabas spoke out boldly. "We had to proclaim the word of God to you first, but since you have rejected it, since you do not think yourselves worthy of eternal life, we must turn to the pagans. For this is what the Lord commanded us to do when he said:

I have made you a light for the nations,
so that my salvation may reach the ends of the earth."

It made the pagans very happy to hear this and they thanked the Lord for his message; all who were destined for eternal life became believers. Thus the word of the Lord spread through the whole countryside.

But the Jews worked upon some of the devout women of the upper classes and the leading men of the city and persuaded them to turn against Paul and Barnabas and expel them from their territory. So they shook the dust from their feet in defiance and went off to Iconium; but the disciples were filled with joy and the Holy Spirit.

Psalm   Psalm 99

R. **We are his people, the sheep of his flock.**

or **Alleluia!**

1. Cry out with joy to the Lord, all the earth.
   Serve the Lord with gladness.
   Come before him, singing for joy. R.

2. Know that he, the Lord, is God.
   He made us, we belong to him,
   we are his people, the sheep of his flock. R.

3. Indeed, how good is the Lord,
   eternal his merciful love.
   He is faithful from age to age. R.

Second Reading   Apocalypse 7:9. 14-17
The Lamb will be their shepherd and will lead them to springs of living water.
I, John, saw a huge number, impossible to count, of people from every nation, race, tribe and language; they were standing in front

of the throne and in front of the Lamb, dressed in white robes and holding palms in their hands. One of the elders said to me, "These are the people who have been through the great persecution, and because they have washed their robes white again in the blood of the Lamb, they now stand in front of God's throne and serve him day and night in his sanctuary; and the One who sits on the throne will spread his tent over them. They will never hunger or thirst again; neither the sun nor scorching wind will ever plague them, because the Lamb who is at the throne will be their shepherd and will lead them to springs of living water, and God will wipe away all tears from their eyes."

Gospel Acclamation
Alleluia, alleluia!
I am the good shepherd, says the Lord;
I know my own sheep and my own know me.
Alleluia!

John 10:14

Gospel   John 10:27-30
I give eternal life to the sheep that belong to me.
Jesus said:

"The sheep that belong to me listen to my voice;
I know them and they follow me.
I give them eternal life;
they will never be lost
and no one will ever steal them from me.
The Father who gave them to me is greater than anyone,
and no one can steal from the Father.
The Father and I are one."

The Creed is said.

Prayer over the Offerings
Grant, we pray, O Lord,
that we may always find delight in these paschal mysteries,
so that the renewal constantly at work within us
may be the cause of our unending joy.
Through Christ our Lord.

Preface I-V of Easter, pp. 495-497.

Communion Antiphon
The Good Shepherd has risen,
who laid down his life for his sheep
and willingly died for his flock, alleluia.

Prayer after Communion
Look upon your flock, kind Shepherd,
and be pleased to settle in eternal pastures
the sheep you have redeemed
by the Precious Blood of your Son.
Who lives and reigns for ever and ever.

The Solemn Blessing for Easter Time may be used, p.511.

FIFTH SUNDAY OF EASTER – C

Love one another.
Jesus tells us that we will be known as his disciples by the love that we show
for one another. He teaches us to love one another as he has loved us. In this
way we will open the door of faith to all people, and give them the opportunity
to praise God who makes all things new.

Entrance Antiphon
O sing a new song to the Lord,
for he has worked wonders;
in the sight of the nations
he has shown his deliverance, alleluia. cf. Psalm 97:1-2

The Gloria is said or sung.

Collect
Almighty ever-living God,
constantly accomplish the Paschal Mystery within us,
that those you were pleased to make new in Holy Baptism
may, under your protective care, bear much fruit
and come to the joys of life eternal.
Through our Lord Jesus Christ, your Son,
who lives and reigns with you in the unity of the Holy Spirit,
one God, for ever and ever.

First Reading Acts 14:21-27
They gave an account to the church of all that God had done with
them.
Paul and Barnabas went back through Lystra and Iconium to
Antioch. They put fresh heart into the disciples, encouraging them
to persevere in the faith. "We all have to experience many hardships",
they said, "before we enter the kingdom of God." In each of these
churches they appointed elders, and with prayer and fasting they
commended them to the Lord in whom they had come to believe.

They passed through Pisidia and reached Pamphylia. Then after proclaiming the word at Perga they went down to Attalia and from there sailed for Antioch, where they had originally been commended to the grace of God for the work they had now completed.

On their arrival they assembled the church and gave an account of all that God had done with them, and how he had opened the door of faith to the pagans.

Psalm   Psalm 144

R. **I will bless your name for ever, O God my King.**

or **Alleluia!**

1. The Lord is kind and full of compassion,
    slow to anger, abounding in love.
    How good is the Lord to all,
    compassionate to all his creatures. R.

2. All your creatures shall thank you, O Lord,
    and your friends shall repeat their blessing.
    They shall speak of the glory of your reign
    and declare your might, O God,
    to make known to men your mighty deeds
    and the glorious splendour of your reign. R.

3. Yours is an everlasting kingdom;
    your rule lasts from age to age. R.

Second Reading   Apocalypse 21:1-5

God will wipe away all tears from their eyes.

I, John, saw a new heaven and a new earth; the first heaven and the first earth had disappeared now, and there was no longer any sea. I saw the holy city, and the new Jerusalem, coming down from God out of heaven, as beautiful as a bride all dressed for her husband. Then I heard a loud voice call from the throne, "You see this city? Here God lives among men. He will make his home among them; they shall be his people, and he will be their God; his name is God-with-them. He will wipe away all tears from their eyes; there will be no more death, and no more mourning or sadness. The world of the past has gone."

Then the One sitting on the throne spoke: "Now I am making the whole of creation new."

Gospel Acclamation
Alleluia, alleluia!
Jesus said: "I give you a new commandment:
love one another, just as I have loved you."
Alleluia!   John 13:34

Gospel   John 13:31-35
I give you a new commandment: love one another.
When Judas had gone Jesus said:

"Now has the Son of Man been glorified,
and in him God has been glorified.
If God has been glorified in him,
God will in turn glorify him in himself,
and will glorify him very soon.
My little children,
I shall not be with you much longer.
I give you a new commandment:
love one another;
just as I have loved you,
you also must love one another.
By this love you have for one another,
everyone will know that you are my disciples."

The Creed is said.

Prayer over the Offerings
O God, who by the wonderful exchange effected in this sacrifice
have made us partakers of the one supreme Godhead,
grant, we pray,
that, as we have come to know your truth,
we may make it ours by a worthy way of life.
Through Christ our Lord.

Preface I-V of Easter, pp. 495-497.

Communion Antiphon
I am the true vine and you are the branches, says the Lord.
Whoever remains in me, and I in him, bears fruit in plenty,
   alleluia.   cf. John 15:1. 5

Prayer after Communion
Graciously be present to your people, we pray, O Lord,
and lead those you have imbued with heavenly mysteries
to pass from former ways to newness of life.
Through Christ our Lord.

The Solemn Blessing for Easter Time may be used, p.511.

SIXTH SUNDAY OF EASTER – C

Peace I give to you.
The Holy Spirit is sent by the Father in the name of Christ to inspire a new
life in us. What is important is not external rules and regulations but keeping
God's law through a real conversion of heart. Then the peace of Christ, which
the world cannot give, will come to us as Christ's gift.

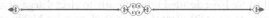

Entrance Antiphon

Proclaim a joyful sound and let it be heard;
proclaim to the ends of the earth:
The Lord has freed his people, alleluia.   cf. Isaiah 48:20

The Gloria is said or sung.

Collect

Grant, almighty God,
that we may celebrate with heartfelt devotion these days of joy,
which we keep in honour of the risen Lord,
and that what we relive in remembrance
we may always hold to in what we do.
Through our Lord Jesus Christ, your Son,
who lives and reigns with you in the unity of the Holy Spirit,
one God, for ever and ever.

First Reading   Acts 15:1-2. 22-29

It has been decided by the Holy Spirit and by ourselves not to saddle
you with any burden beyond these essentials.

Some men came down from Judaea and taught the brothers,
"Unless you have yourselves circumcised in the tradition of Moses
you cannot be saved." This led to disagreement, and after Paul and
Barnabas had had a long argument with these men it was arranged
that Paul and Barnabas and others of the church should go up to
Jerusalem and discuss the problem with the apostles and elders.

Then the apostles and elders decided to choose delegates to send to Antioch with Paul and Barnabas; the whole church concurred with this. They chose Judas known as Barsabbas and Silas, both leading men in the brotherhood, and gave them this letter to take with them:

"The apostles and elders, your brothers, send greetings to the brothers of pagan birth in Antioch, Syria and Cilicia. We hear that some of our members have disturbed you with their demands and have unsettled your minds. They acted without any authority from us, and so we have decided unanimously to elect delegates and to send them to you with Barnabas and Paul, men we highly respect who have dedicated their lives to the name of our Lord Jesus Christ. Accordingly we are sending you Judas and Silas, who will confirm by word of mouth what we have written in this letter. It has been decided by the Holy Spirit and by ourselves not to saddle you with any burden beyond these essentials: you are to abstain from food sacrificed to idols, from blood, from the meat of strangled animals and from fornication. Avoid these, and you will do what is right. Farewell."

Psalm   Psalm 66

R. **Let the peoples praise you, O God;**
   let all the peoples praise you.

or **Alleluia!**

1. O God, be gracious and bless us
   and let your face shed its light upon us.
   So will your ways be known upon earth
   and all nations learn your saving help. R.

2. Let the nations be glad and exult
   for you rule the world with justice.
   With fairness you rule the peoples,
   you guide the nations on earth. R.

3. Let the peoples praise you, O God;
   let all the peoples praise you.
   May God still give us his blessing
   till the ends of the earth revere him. R.

Second Reading   Apocalypse 21:10-14. 22-23

He showed me the holy city coming down out of heaven.

In the spirit, the angel took me to the top of an enormous high mountain and showed me Jerusalem, the holy city, coming down from God out of heaven. It had all the radiant glory of God and glittered like some precious jewel of crystal-clear diamond. The walls of it were of a great height, and had twelve gates; at each of the twelve gates there was an angel, and over the gates were written the names of the twelve tribes of Israel; on the east there were three gates, on the north three gates, on the south three gates, and on the west three gates. The city walls stood on twelve foundation stones, each one of which bore the name of one of the twelve apostles of the Lamb.

I saw that there was no temple in the city since the Lord God Almighty and the Lamb were themselves the temple, and the city did not need the sun or the moon for light, since it was lit by the radiant glory of God and the Lamb was a lighted torch for it.

Gospel Acclamation

Alleluia, alleluia!

Jesus said: "If anyone loves me he will keep my word,
and my Father will love him, and we shall come to him."

Alleluia!   John 14:23

Gospel   John 14:23-29

The Holy Spirit will remind you of all I have said to you.

Jesus said to his disciples:

"If anyone loves me he will keep my word,
    and my Father will love him,
    and we shall come to him
    and make our home with him.
Those who do not love me do not keep my words.
And my word is not my own:
    it is the word of the one who sent me.
I have said these things to you
    while still with you;
but the Advocate, the Holy Spirit,

whom the Father will send in my name,
will teach you everything
and remind you of all I have said to you.
Peace I bequeath to you,
my own peace I give you,
a peace the world cannot give, this is my gift to you.
Do not let your hearts be troubled or afraid.
You heard me say:
I am going away, and shall return.
If you loved me you would have been glad to know that I am
  going to the Father,
for the Father is greater than I.
I have told you this now before it happens,
so that when it does happen you may believe."

The Creed is said.

Prayer over the Offerings
May our prayers rise up to you, O Lord,
together with the sacrificial offerings,
so that, purified by your graciousness,
we may be conformed to the mysteries of your mighty love.
Through Christ our Lord.

Preface I-V of Easter, pp. 495-497.

Communion Antiphon
If you love me, keep my commandments, says the Lord,
and I will ask the Father and he will send you another Paraclete,
to abide with you for ever, alleluia.   John 14:15-16

Prayer after Communion
Almighty ever-living God,
who restore us to eternal life in the Resurrection of Christ,
increase in us, we pray, the fruits of this paschal Sacrament
and pour into our hearts the strength of this saving food.
Through Christ our Lord.

The Solemn Blessing for Easter Time may be used, p. 511.

THE ASCENSION OF THE LORD – C

Christ ascends to his Father.

Through his Ascension, Christ promises that one day we will be with him in heaven to praise the glory of God our Father. The Ascension is our hope of the great inheritance that awaits those who believe in the power of the risen Christ. He calls us to be witnesses to all that he has done. We profess our hope in him, our great high priest.

Entrance Antiphon

Men of Galilee, why gaze in wonder at the heavens?
This Jesus whom you saw ascending into heaven
will return as you saw him go, alleluia.   Acts 1:11

The Gloria is said or sung.

Collect

Gladden us with holy joys, almighty God,
and make us rejoice with devout thanksgiving,
for the Ascension of Christ your Son
is our exaltation,
and, where the Head has gone before in glory,
the Body is called to follow in hope.
Through our Lord Jesus Christ, your Son,
who lives and reigns with you in the unity of the Holy Spirit,
one God, for ever and ever.

or

Grant, we pray, almighty God,
that we, who believe that your Only Begotten Son, our Redeemer,
ascended this day to the heavens,
may in spirit dwell already in heavenly realms.
Who lives and reigns with you in the unity of the Holy Spirit,
one God, for ever and ever.

First Reading   Acts 1:1-11

He was lifted up while they looked on.

In my earlier work, Theophilus, I dealt with everything Jesus had done and taught from the beginning until the day he gave his instructions to the apostles he had chosen through the Holy Spirit, and was taken up to heaven. He had shown himself alive to them after his Passion by many demonstrations: for forty days he had continued to appear to them and tell them about the kingdom of God. When he had been at table with them, he had told them not to leave Jerusalem, but to wait there for what the Father had promised. "It is", he had said, "what you have heard me speak about: John baptised with water but you, not many days from now, will be baptised with the Holy Spirit."

Now having met together, they asked him, "Lord, has the time come? Are you going to restore the kingdom to Israel?" He replied, "It is not for you to know times or dates that the Father has decided by his own authority, but you will receive power when the Holy Spirit comes on you, and then you will be my witnesses not only in Jerusalem but throughout Judaea and Samaria, and indeed to the ends of the earth."

As he said this he was lifted up while they looked on, and a cloud took him from their sight. They were still staring into the sky when suddenly two men in white were standing near them and they said, "Why are you men from Galilee standing here looking into the sky? Jesus who has been taken from you into heaven, this same Jesus will come back in the same way as you have seen him go there."

Psalm   Psalm 46

R. **God goes up with shouts of joy;**
     the Lord goes up with trumpet blast.

or **Alleluia!**

1. All peoples, clap your hands,
     cry to God with shouts of joy!
     For the Lord, the Most High, we must fear,
     great king over all the earth. R.

2. God goes up with shouts of joy;
   the Lord goes up with trumpet blast.
   Sing praise for God, sing praise,
   sing praise to our king, sing praise. R.

3. God is king of all the earth.
   Sing praise with all your skill.
   God is king over the nations;
   God reigns on his holy throne. R.

Second Reading   Ephesians 1:17-23
He made him sit at his right hand in heaven.

May the God of our Lord Jesus Christ, the Father of glory, give
you a spirit of wisdom and perception of what is revealed, to bring
you to full knowledge of him. May he enlighten the eyes of your
mind so that you can see what hope his call holds for you, what rich
glories he has promised the saints will inherit and how infinitely
great is the power that he has exercised for us believers. This you
can tell from the strength of his power at work in Christ, when he
used it to raise him from the dead and to make him sit at his right
hand, in heaven, far above every Sovereignty, Authority, Power, or
Domination, or any other name that can be named, not only in this
age, but also in the age to come. He has put all things under his feet,
and made him, as the ruler of everything, the head of the Church;
which is his body, the fullness of him who fills the whole creation.

or

Second Reading   Hebrews 9:24-28; 10:19-23
Christ has entered heaven itself.

It is not as though Christ had entered a man-made sanctuary which
was only modelled on the real one; but it was heaven itself, so that
he could appear in the actual presence of God on our behalf. And
he does not have to offer himself again and again, like the high
priest going into the sanctuary year after year with the blood that is
not his own, or else he would have had to suffer over and over again
since the world began. Instead of that, he has made his appearance

once and for all, now at the end of the last age, to do away with sin by sacrificing himself. Since men only die once, and after that comes judgement, so Christ, too, offers himself only once to take the faults of many on himself, and when he appears a second time, it will not be to deal with sin but to reward with salvation those who are waiting for him.

In other words, brothers, through the blood of Jesus we have the right to enter the sanctuary, by a new way which he has opened for us, a living opening through the curtain, that is to say, his body. And we have the supreme high priest over all the house of God. So as we go in, let us be sincere in heart and filled with faith, our minds sprinkled and free from any trace of bad conscience and our bodies washed with pure water. Let us keep firm in the hope we profess, because the one who made the promise is faithful.

Gospel Acclamation
Alleluia, alleluia!
Go, make disciples of all the nations;
I am with you always; yes, to the end of time.
Alleluia!   Matthew 28:19-20

Gospel   Luke 24:46-53
As he blessed them he was carried up to heaven.
Jesus said to his disciples: "You see how it is written that the Christ would suffer and on the third day rise from the dead, and that, in his name, repentance for the forgiveness of sins would be preached to all the nations, beginning from Jerusalem. You are witnesses to this.

"And now I am sending down to you what the Father has promised. Stay in the city then, until you are clothed with the power from on high." Then he took them out as far as the outskirts of Bethany, and lifting up his hands he blessed them. Now as he blessed them, he withdrew from them and was carried up to heaven. They worshipped him and then went back to Jerusalem full of joy; and they were continually in the Temple praising God.

The Creed is said.

Prayer over the Offerings
We offer sacrifice now in supplication, O Lord,
to honour the wondrous Ascension of your Son:
grant, we pray,
that through this most holy exchange
we, too, may rise up to the heavenly realms.
Through Christ our Lord.

Preface I or II of the Ascension of the Lord, p. 498.

Communion Antiphon
Behold, I am with you always,
even to the end of the age, alleluia.   Matthew 28:20

Prayer after Communion
Almighty ever-living God,
who allow those on earth to celebrate divine mysteries,
grant, we pray,
that Christian hope may draw us onward
to where our nature is united with you.
Through Christ our Lord.

The Solemn Blessing for the Ascension of the Lord may be used,
pp. 511-512.

SEVENTH SUNDAY OF EASTER – C

Come, Lord Jesus!

Jesus Christ is ascended into heaven. We await his second coming and, like Stephen, in faith we see him standing at the right hand of God, where he is constantly praying for us. We join him in our prayers that soon we may be with him.

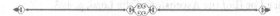

Entrance Antiphon

O Lord, hear my voice, for I have called to you;
of you my heart has spoken: Seek his face;
hide not your face from me, alleluia.   cf. Psalm 26:7-9

The Gloria is said or sung.

Collect

Graciously hear our supplications, O Lord,
so that we, who believe that the Saviour of the human race
is with you in your glory,
may experience, as he promised,
until the end of the world,
his abiding presence among us.
Who lives and reigns with you in the unity of the Holy Spirit,
one God, for ever and ever.

First Reading   Acts 7:55-60

I can see the Son of Man standing at the right hand of God.

Stephen, filled with the Holy Spirit, gazed into heaven and saw the glory of God, and Jesus standing at God's right hand. "I can see heaven thrown open," he said, "and the Son of Man standing at the right hand of God." At this all the members of the council shouted out and stopped their ears with their hands; then they all rushed at him, sent him out of the city and stoned him. The witnesses put down their clothes at the feet of a young man called Saul. As they were stoning him, Stephen said in invocation, "Lord Jesus, receive my spirit." Then he knelt down and said aloud, "Lord, do not hold this sin against them"; and with these words he fell asleep.

Psalm   **Psalm 96**

R. **The Lord is king, most high above all the earth.**

or **Alleluia!**

1. The Lord is king, let earth rejoice,
   the many coastlands be glad.
   His throne is justice and right. R.

2. The skies proclaim his justice;
   all peoples see his glory.
   All you spirits, worship him. R.

3. For you indeed are the Lord
   most high above all the earth
   exalted far above all spirits. R.

Second Reading   **Apocalypse 22:12-14. 16-17. 20**
Come, Lord Jesus!

I, John, heard a voice speaking to me: "Very soon now, I shall be with you again, bringing the reward to be given to every man according to what he deserves. I am the Alpha and the Omega, the First and the Last, the Beginning and the End. Happy are those who will have washed their robes clean, so that they will have the right to feed on the tree of life and can come through the gates into the city."

I, Jesus, have sent my angel to make these revelations to you for the sake of the churches. I am of David's line, the root of David and the bright star of the morning.

The Spirit and the Bride say, "Come." Let everyone who listens answer, "Come." Then let all who are thirsty come; all who want it may have the water of life, and have it free.

The one who guarantees these revelations repeats his promise: I shall indeed be with you. Amen; come, Lord Jesus.

Gospel Acclamation
Alleluia, alleluia!
I will not leave you orphans, says the Lord;
I will come back to you, and your hearts will be full of joy.
Alleluia!   cf. John 14:18

Gospel   John 17:20-26
May they be completely one.
Jesus raised his eyes to heaven and said:

"Holy Father,
I pray not only for these,
but for those also
who through their words will believe in me.
May they all be one.
Father, may they be one in us,
as you are in me and I am in you,
so that the world may believe it was you who sent me.
I have given them the glory you gave to me,
that they may be one as we are one.
With me in them and you in me,
may they be so completely one
that the world will realise that it was you who sent me
and that I have loved them as much as you love me.
Father,
I want those you have given me
to be with me where I am,
so that they may always see the glory
you have given me
because you loved me
before the foundation of the world.
Father, Righteous One,
the world has not known you,
but I have known you,
and these have known
that you have sent me.
I have made your name known to them
and will continue to make it known,

so that the love with which you loved me may be in them,
and so that I may be in them."

The Creed is said.

Prayer over the Offerings
Accept, O Lord, the prayers of your faithful
with the sacrificial offerings,
that through these acts of devotedness
we may pass over to the glory of heaven.
Through Christ our Lord.

Preface I-V of Easter, or I-II of the Ascension, pp. 495-498.

Communion Antiphon
Father, I pray that they may be one
as we also are one, alleluia.   John 17:22

Prayer after Communion
Hear us, O God our Saviour,
and grant us confidence,
that through these sacred mysteries
there will be accomplished in the body of the whole Church
what has already come to pass in Christ her Head.
Who lives and reigns for ever and ever.

The Solemn Blessing for Easter Time may be used, p. 511.

PENTECOST SUNDAY – C

The coming of the Holy Spirit upon the Church.
Christ promised that the Advocate, the Holy Spirit, would come to be with his disciples, and today we celebrate the fulfilment of that promise. The Spirit lives within us, bearing witness that we are indeed children of God our Father. We pray that we may be open to the power of the Spirit living in us, and that the Spirit will come anew and fill the hearts of the faithful, kindling in us all the fire of love.

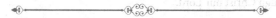

Entrance Antiphon
The Spirit of the Lord has filled the whole world
and that which contains all things
understands what is said, alleluia.

Wisdom 1:7

or

The love of God has been poured into our hearts
through the Spirit of God dwelling within us, alleluia.

Romans 5:5; cf. 8:11

The Gloria is said or sung.

Collect
O God, who by the mystery of today's great feast
sanctify your whole Church in every people and nation,
pour out, we pray, the gifts of the Holy Spirit
across the face of the earth
and, with the divine grace that was at work
when the Gospel was first proclaimed,
fill now once more the hearts of believers.
Through our Lord Jesus Christ, your Son,
who lives and reigns with you in the unity of the Holy Spirit,
one God, for ever and ever.

First Reading   Acts 2:1-11

They were all filled with the Holy Spirit and began to speak.

When Pentecost day came round, the apostles had all met in one room, when suddenly they heard what sounded like a powerful wind from heaven, the noise of which filled the entire house in which they were sitting; and something appeared to them that seemed like tongues of fire; these separated and came to rest on the head of each of them. They were filled with the Holy Spirit, and began to speak foreign languages as the Spirit gave them the gift of speech.

Now there were devout men living in Jerusalem from every nation under heaven, and at this sound they all assembled, each one bewildered to hear these men speaking his own language. They were amazed and astonished. "Surely", they said, "all these men speaking are Galileans? How does it happen that each of us hears them in his own native language? Parthians, Medes and Elamites; people from Mesopotamia, Judaea and Cappadocia, Pontus and Asia, Phrygia and Pamphylia, Egypt and the parts of Libya round Cyrene; as well as visitors from Rome – Jews and proselytes alike – Cretans and Arabs; we hear them preaching in our own language about the marvels of God."

Psalm   Psalm 103

R. **Send forth your Spirit, O Lord,**
    and renew the face of the earth.

or **Alleluia.**

1. Bless the Lord, my soul!
    Lord God, how great you are.
    How many are your works, O Lord!
    The earth is full of your riches. R.

2. You take back your spirit, they die,
    returning to the dust from which they came.
    You send forth your spirit, they are created;
    and you renew the face of the earth. R.

3. May the glory of the Lord last for ever!
   May the Lord rejoice in his works!
   May my thoughts be pleasing to him.
   I find my joy in the Lord. R.

The Second Reading and Gospel for Year A may be used as an alternative in any year. See pp. 328-329.

Second Reading   Romans 8:8-17
Everyone moved by the Spirit is a son of God.

People who are interested only in unspiritual things can never be pleasing to God. Your interests, however, are not in the unspiritual, but in the spiritual, since the Spirit of God has made his home in you. In fact, unless you possessed the Spirit of Christ you would not belong to him. Though your body may be dead it is because of sin, but if Christ is in you then your spirit is life itself because you have been justified; and if the Spirit of him who raised Jesus from the dead is living in you, then he who raised Jesus from the dead will give life to your own mortal bodies through his Spirit living in you.

So then, my brothers, there is no necessity for us to obey our unspiritual selves or to live unspiritual lives. If you do live in that way, you are doomed to die; but if by the Spirit you put an end to the misdeeds of the body you will live.

Everyone moved by the Spirit is a son of God. The spirit you received is not the spirit of slaves bringing fear into your lives again; it is the spirit of sons, and it makes us cry out, "Abba Father!" The Spirit himself and our spirit bear united witness that we are children of God. And if we are children we are heirs as well: heirs of God and coheirs with Christ, sharing his sufferings so as to share his glory.

The Sequence may be said or sung. See pp. 328-329.

Gospel Acclamation
Alleluia, alleluia!
Come, Holy Spirit, fill the hearts of your faithful
and kindle in them the fire of your love.
Alleluia!

Gospel   **John 14:15-16. 23-26**

The Holy Spirit will teach you everything.

Jesus said to his disciples

"If you love me you will keep my commandments.
I shall ask the Father
and he will give you another Advocate
to be with you for ever.

"If anyone loves me he will keep my word,
and my Father will love him,
and we shall come to him
and make our home with him.
Those who do not love me do not keep my words.
And my word is not my own;
it is the word of the one who sent me.
I have said these things to you
while still with you;
but the Advocate, the Holy Spirit,
whom the Father will send in my name,
will teach you everything
and remind you of all I have said to you."

The Creed is said.

Prayer over the Offerings
Grant, we pray, O Lord,
that, as promised by your Son,
the Holy Spirit may reveal to us more abundantly
the hidden mystery of this sacrifice
and graciously lead us into all truth.
Through Christ our Lord.

Preface of Pentecost, p. 330.

Communion Antiphon
They were all filled with the Holy Spirit
and spoke of the marvels of God, alleluia.   Acts 2:4. 11

Prayer after Communion
O God, who bestow heavenly gifts upon your Church,
safeguard, we pray, the grace you have given,
that the gift of the Holy Spirit poured out upon her
may retain all its force
and that this spiritual food
may gain her abundance of eternal redemption.
Through Christ our Lord.

The Solemn Blessing for the Holy Spirit may be used, p. 512.

Dismissal
Go forth, the Mass is ended, alleluia, alleluia.

or

Go in peace, alleluia, alleluia.

Thanks be to God, alleluia, alleluia.

Easter Time is now concluded. For the Solemnity of the Most Holy Trinity, turn to p. 431.

THE MOST HOLY TRINITY – A

Father, Son and Holy Spirit.
Through our life in Christ we live the life of the Trinity. God is a perfect
community and if we model our lives on the Trinity, then the God of love and
peace will be with us.

Entrance Antiphon
Blest be God the Father,
and the Only Begotten Son of God,
and also the Holy Spirit,
for he has shown us his merciful love.

The Gloria is said or sung.

Collect
God our Father, who by sending into the world
the Word of truth and the Spirit of sanctification
made known to the human race your wondrous mystery,
grant us, we pray, that in professing the true faith,
we may acknowledge the Trinity of eternal glory
and adore your Unity, powerful in majesty.
Through our Lord Jesus Christ, your Son,
who lives and reigns with you in the unity of the Holy Spirit,
one God, for ever and ever.

First Reading   Exodus 34:4-6. 8-9
Lord, Lord, a God of tenderness and compassion.

With the two tablets of stone in his hands, Moses went up the
mountain of Sinai in the early morning as the Lord had commanded
him. And the Lord descended in the form of a cloud, and Moses
stood with him there.

   He called on the name of the Lord. The Lord passed before him
and proclaimed, "Lord, Lord, a God of tenderness and compassion,
slow to anger, rich in kindness and faithfulness." And Moses bowed
down to the ground at once and worshipped. "If I have indeed won

your favour, Lord," he said, "let my Lord come down with us, I beg. True, they are a headstrong people, but forgive us our faults and our sins, and adopt us as your heritage."

Psalm   Daniel 3

1. You are blest, Lord God of our fathers.
    R. **To you glory and praise for evermore.**
    Blest your glorious holy name.
    R. **To you glory and praise for evermore.**

2. You are blest in the temple of your glory.
    R. **To you glory and praise for evermore.**
    You are blest on the throne of your kingdom.
    R. **To you glory and praise for evermore.**

3. You are blest who gaze into the depths.
    R. **To you glory and praise for evermore.**
    You are blest in the firmament of heaven.
    R. **To you glory and praise for evermore.**

Second Reading   2 Corinthians 13:11-13
The grace of Jesus Christ, the love of God, and the fellowship of the Holy Spirit.

Brothers, we wish you happiness; try to grow perfect; help one another. Be united; live in peace, and the God of love and peace will be with you.

Greet one another with the holy kiss. All the saints send you greetings.

The grace of the Lord Jesus Christ, the love of God and the fellowship of the Holy Spirit be with you all.

Gospel Acclamation
Alleluia, alleluia!
Glory be to the Father, and to the Son, and to the Holy Spirit,
the God who is, who was, and who is to come.
Alleluia!   cf. Apocalypse 1:8

Gospel   John 3:16-18

God sent his Son so that through him the world might be saved.

Jesus said to Nicodemus,

"God loved the world so much
that he gave his only Son,
so that everyone who believes in him may not be lost
but may have eternal life.
For God sent his Son into the world
not to condemn the world,
but so that through him the world might be saved.
No one who believes in him will be condemned;
but whoever refuses to believe is condemned already,
because he has refused to believe
in the name of God's only Son."

The Creed is said.

Prayer over the Offerings

Sanctify by the invocation of your name,
we pray, O Lord our God,
this oblation of our service,
and by it make of us an eternal offering to you.
Through Christ our Lord.

Preface

It is truly right and just, our duty and our salvation,
always and everywhere to give you thanks,
Lord, holy Father, almighty and eternal God.

For with your Only Begotten Son and the Holy Spirit
you are one God, one Lord:
not in the unity of a single person,
but in a Trinity of one substance.

For what you have revealed to us of your glory
we believe equally of your Son
and of the Holy Spirit,
so that, in the confessing of the true and eternal Godhead,
you might be adored in what is proper to each Person,

their unity in substance,
and their equality in majesty.

For this is praised by Angels and Archangels,
Cherubim, too, and Seraphim,
who never cease to cry out each day,
as with one voice they acclaim:
Holy, Holy, Holy Lord God of hosts…

Communion Antiphon
Since you are children of God,
God has sent into your hearts the Spirit of his Son,
the Spirit who cries out: Abba, Father.   Galatians 4:6

Prayer after Communion
May receiving this Sacrament, O Lord our God,
bring us health of body and soul,
as we confess your eternal holy Trinity and undivided Unity.
Through Christ our Lord.

THE MOST HOLY BODY
AND BLOOD OF CHRIST – A
(CORPUS CHRISTI)

Christ our food and drink.
Just as in our physical lives we need food and drink to sustain us, so also
we need Christ to sustain our spiritual lives. He feeds us with himself, just
as God fed the Jewish people with manna in the wilderness. Our sharing of
the Body and Blood of Christ means that we share with each other Christ's
eternal life.

Entrance Antiphon
He fed them with the finest wheat
and satisfied them with honey from the rock.   cf. Psalm 80:17

The Gloria is said or sung.

Collect
O God, who in this wonderful Sacrament
have left us a memorial of your Passion,
grant us, we pray,
so to revere the sacred mysteries of your Body and Blood
that we may always experience in ourselves
the fruits of your redemption.
Who live and reign with God the Father
in the unity of the Holy Spirit,
one God, for ever and ever.

First Reading   Deuteronomy 8:2-3. 14-16
He fed you with manna which neither you nor your fathers had
known.
Moses said to the people: "Remember how the Lord your God
led you for forty years in the wilderness, to humble you, to test
you and know your inmost heart – whether you would keep his
commandments or not. He humbled you, he made you feel hunger,

he fed you with manna which neither you nor your fathers had known, to make you understand that man does not live on bread alone but that man lives on everything that comes from the mouth of the Lord.

"Do not then forget the Lord your God who brought you out of the land of Egypt, out of the house of slavery; who guided you through this vast and dreadful wilderness, a land of fiery serpents, scorpions, thirst; who in this waterless place brought you water from the hardest rock; who in this wilderness fed you with manna that your fathers had not known."

Psalm   Psalm 147

R. **O praise the Lord, Jerusalem!**

or **Alleluia!**

1. O praise the Lord, Jerusalem!
   Zion, praise your God!
   He has strengthened the bars of your gates,
   he has blessed the children within you. R.

2. He established peace on your borders,
   he feeds you with finest wheat.
   He sends out his word to the earth
   and swiftly runs his command. R.

3. He makes his word known to Jacob,
   to Israel his laws and decrees.
   He has not dealt thus with other nations;
   He has not taught them his decrees. R.

Second Reading   1 Corinthians 10:16-17

That there is only one loaf means that, though there are many of us, we form a single body.

The blessing-cup that we bless is a communion with the blood of Christ, and the bread that we break is a communion with the body of Christ. The fact that there is only one loaf means that, though there are many of us, we form a single body because we all have a share in this one loaf.

Sequence

The optional Sequence may be said or sung in full, or using the shorter form indicated by the asterisked verses.

Sing forth, O Zion, sweetly sing
The praises of thy Shepherd-King,
    In hymns and canticles divine;
Dare all thou canst, thou hast no song
Worthy his praises to prolong,
    So far surpassing powers like thine.

Today no theme of common praise
Forms the sweet burden of thy lays –
    The living, life-dispensing food –
That food which at the sacred board
Unto the brethren twelve our Lord
    His parting legacy bestowed.

Then be the anthem clear and strong,
Thy fullest note, thy sweetest song,
    The very music of the breast:
For now shines forth the day sublime
That brings remembrance of the time
    When Jesus first his table blessed.

Within our new King's banquet-hall
They meet to keep the festival
    That closed the ancient paschal rite:
The old is by the new replaced;
The substance hath the shadow chased;
    And rising day dispels the night.

Christ willed what he himself had done
Should be renewed while time should run,
    In memory of his parting hour:
Thus, tutored in his school divine,
We consecrate the bread and wine;
    And lo – a Host of saving power.

This faith to Christian men is given –
Bread is made flesh by words from heaven:
   Into his blood the wine is turned:
What though it baffles nature's powers
Of sense and sight? This faith of ours
   Proves more than nature e'er discerned.

Concealed beneath the two-fold sign,
Meet symbols of the gifts divine,
   There lie the mysteries adored:
The living body is our food;
Our drink the ever-precious blood;
   In each, one undivided Lord.

Not he that eateth it divides
The sacred food, which whole abides
   Unbroken still, nor knows decay;
Be one, or be a thousand fed,
They eat alike that living bread
   Which, still received, ne'er wastes away.

The good, the guilty share therein,
With sure increase of grace or sin,
   The ghostly life, or ghostly death:
Death to the guilty; to the good
Immortal life. See how one food
   Man's joy or woe accomplisheth.

We break the Sacrament; but bold
And firm thy faith shall keep its hold;
Deem not the whole doth more enfold
   Than in the fractured part resides:
Deem not that Christ doth broken lie;
'Tis but the sign that meets the eye;
The hidden deep reality
   In all its fullness still abides.

*Behold the bread of angels, sent
For pilgrims in their banishment,
The bread for God's true children meant,

That may not unto dogs be given:
Oft in the olden types foreshadowed;
In Isaac on the altar bowed,
And in the ancient paschal food,
   And in the manna sent from heaven.

*Come then, good shepherd, bread divine,
Still show to us thy mercy sign;
Oh, feed us still, still keep us thine;
So we may see thy glories shine;
   In fields of immortality;

*O thou, the wisest, mightiest best,
Our present food, our future rest,
Come, make us each thy chosen guest,
Co-heirs of thine, and comrades blest
   With saints whose dwelling is with thee.

Gospel Acclamation

Alleluia, alleluia!
I am the living bread which has come down from heaven,
says the Lord.
Anyone who eats this bread will live for ever.
Alleluia!
                               John 6:51-52

Gospel
                                      John 6:51-58

My flesh is real food and my blood is real drink.

Jesus said to the Jews:

"I am the living bread which has come down from heaven.
Anyone who eats this bread will live for ever;
and the bread that I shall give
is my flesh, for the life of the world."

Then the Jews started arguing with one another. "How can this
man give us his flesh to eat?" they said. Jesus replied:

"I tell you most solemnly,
if you do not eat the flesh of the Son of Man
and drink his blood,

you will not have life in you.
Anyone who does eat my flesh and drink my blood
has eternal life,
and I shall raise him up on the last day.
For my flesh is real food
and my blood is real drink.
He who eats my flesh and drinks my blood
lives in me
and I live in him.
As I, who am sent by the living Father,
myself draw life from the Father,
so whoever eats me will draw life from me.
This is the bread come down from heaven;
not like the bread our ancestors ate:
they are dead,
but anyone who eats this bread will live for ever."

The Creed is said.

Prayer over the Offerings
Grant your Church, O Lord, we pray,
the gifts of unity and peace,
whose signs are to be seen in mystery
in the offerings we here present.
Through Christ our Lord.

Preface I or II of the Most Holy Eucharist, pp. 503-504.

Communion Antiphon
Whoever eats my flesh and drinks my blood
remains in me and I in him, says the Lord.   John 6:57

Prayer after Communion
Grant, O Lord, we pray,
that we may delight for all eternity
in that share in your divine life,
which is foreshadowed in the present age
by our reception of your precious Body and Blood.
Who live and reign for ever and ever.

THE MOST SACRED HEART OF JESUS – A

The Lord set his heart on you.
God loves us because it is God's very nature to love. We show ourselves to
be God's people if we have love for each other. We can do this by modelling
ourselves on Jesus Christ, who is gentle and humble of heart.

Entrance Antiphon
The designs of his Heart are from age to age,
to rescue their souls from death,
and to keep them alive in famine.　　　　　　　*Psalm 32:11. 19*

The Gloria is said or sung.

Collect
Grant, we pray, almighty God,
that we, who glory in the Heart of your beloved Son
and recall the wonders of his love for us,
may be made worthy to receive
an overflowing measure of grace
from that fount of heavenly gifts.
Through our Lord Jesus Christ, your Son,
who lives and reigns with you in the unity of the Holy Spirit,
one God, for ever and ever.

or

O God, who in the Heart of your Son,
wounded by our sins,
bestow on us in mercy
the boundless treasures of your love,
grant, we pray,
that, in paying him the homage of our devotion,
we may also offer worthy reparation.
Through our Lord Jesus Christ, your Son,
who lives and reigns with you in the unity of the Holy Spirit,
one God, for ever and ever.

First Reading   Deuteronomy 7:6-11

The Lord set his heart on you and chose you.

Moses said to the people: "You are a people consecrated to the Lord your God; it is you that the Lord our God has chosen to be his very own people out of all the peoples on the earth.

"If the Lord set his heart on you and chose you, it was not because you outnumbered other peoples: you were the least of all peoples. It was for love of you and to keep the oath he swore to your fathers that the Lord brought you out with his mighty hand and redeemed you from the house of slavery, from the power of Pharaoh king of Egypt. Know then that the Lord your God is God indeed, the faithful God who is true to his covenant and his graciousness for a thousand generations towards those who love him and keep his commandments, but who punishes in their own persons those that hate him. He makes him work out his punishment in person. You are therefore to keep and observe the commandments and statutes and ordinances that I lay down for you today."

Psalm   Psalm 102

R. **The love of the Lord is everlasting**
    upon those who hold him in fear.

1. My soul, give thanks to the Lord.
   all my being, bless his holy name.
   My soul, give thanks to the Lord
   and never forget all his blessings. R.

2. It is he who forgives all your guilt,
   who heals every one of your ills,
   who redeems your life from the grave,
   who crowns you with love and compassion. R.

3. The Lord does deeds of justice,
   gives judgement for all who are oppressed.
   He made known his ways to Moses
   and his deeds to Israel's sons. R.

4. The Lord is compassion and love,
    slow to anger and rich in mercy.
    He does not treat us according to our sins
    nor repay us according to our faults. R.

Second Reading   1 John 4:7-16

Love comes from God.

My dear people,
let us love one another
since love comes from God
and everyone who loves is begotten by God and knows God.
Anyone who fails to love can never have known God,
because God is love.
God's love for us was revealed
when God sent into the world his only Son
so that we could have life through him;
this is the love I mean:
not our love for God,
but God's love for us when he sent his Son
to be the sacrifice that takes our sins away.
My dear people,
since God has loved us so much,
we too should love one another.
No one has ever seen God;
but as long as we love one another
God will live in us
and his love will be complete in us.
We can know that we are living in him
and he is living in us
because he lets us share his Spirit.
We ourselves saw and we testify
that the Father sent his Son
as saviour of the world.
If anyone acknowledges that Jesus is the Son of God,
God lives in him, and he in God.
We ourselves have known and put our faith in
God's love towards ourselves.

God is love
and anyone who lives in love lives in God,
and God lives in him.

Gospel Acclamation
Alleluia, alleluia!
Shoulder my yoke and learn from me,
for I am gentle and humble in heart.
Alleluia.   Matthew 11:29

Gospel   Matthew 11:25-30
I am gentle and humble in heart.
Jesus exclaimed, "I bless you, Father, Lord of heaven and of earth, for hiding these things from the learned and the clever and revealing them to mere children. Yes, Father, for this is what it pleased you to do. Everything has been entrusted to me by my Father; and no one knows the Son except the Father, just as no one knows the Father except the Son and those to whom the Son chooses to reveal him.

"Come to me, all you who labour and are overburdened, and I will give you rest. Shoulder my yoke and learn from me, for I am gentle and humble in heart, and you will find rest for your souls. Yes, my yoke is easy and my burden light."

The Creed is said.

Prayer over the Offerings
Look, O Lord, we pray, on the surpassing charity
in the Heart of your beloved Son,
that what we offer may be a gift acceptable to you
and an expiation of our offences.
Through Christ our Lord.

Preface
It is truly right and just, our duty and our salvation,
always and everywhere to give you thanks,
Lord, holy Father, almighty and eternal God,
through Christ our Lord.

For raised up high on the Cross,
he gave himself up for us with a wonderful love
and poured out blood and water from his pierced side,
the wellspring of the Church's Sacraments,
so that, won over to the open heart of the Saviour,
all might draw water joyfully from the springs of salvation.

And so, with all the Angels and Saints,
we praise you, as without end we acclaim:
Holy, Holy, Holy Lord God of hosts…

Communion Antiphon
Thus says the Lord:
Let whoever is thirsty come to me and drink.
Streams of living water will flow
from within the one who believes in me.   cf. John 7:37-38

or

One of the soldiers opened his side with a lance,
and at once there came forth blood and water.   John 19:34

Prayer after Communion
May this sacrament of charity, O Lord,
make us fervent with the fire of holy love,
so that, drawn always to your Son,
we may learn to see him in our neighbour.
Through Christ our Lord.

THE MOST HOLY TRINITY – B

Children of God.
We have received the Holy Spirit, who makes us aware that we are truly God's
children and not slaves. We have the freedom of those whom the Lord has chosen
as his own. Our spirit and God's Spirit are united as we call God,
"Abba, Father".

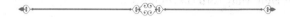

Entrance Antiphon
Blest be God the Father,
and the Only Begotten Son of God,
and also the Holy Spirit,
for he has shown us his merciful love.

The Gloria is said or sung.

Collect
God our Father, who by sending into the world
the Word of truth and the Spirit of sanctification
made known to the human race your wondrous mystery,
grant us, we pray, that in professing the true faith,
we may acknowledge the Trinity of eternal glory
and adore your Unity, powerful in majesty.
Through our Lord Jesus Christ, your Son,
who lives and reigns with you in the unity of the Holy Spirit,
one God, for ever and ever.

First Reading   Deuteronomy 4:32-34. 39-40
The Lord is God indeed, in heaven above as on earth beneath, he
and no other.

Moses said to the people: "Put this question to the ages that are past,
that went before you, from the time God created man on earth:
Was there ever a word so majestic, from one end of heaven to the
other? Was anything ever heard? Did ever a people hear the voice

of the living God speaking from the heart of the fire, as you heard it, and remain alive? Has any god ventured to take to himself one nation from the midst of another by ordeals, signs, wonders, war with mighty hand and outstretched arm, by fearsome terrors – all this that the Lord your God did for you before your eyes in Egypt?

"Understand this today, therefore, and take it to heart: The Lord is God indeed, in heaven above as on earth beneath, he and no other. Keep his laws and commandments as I give them to you today, so that you and your children may prosper and live long in the land that the Lord your God gives you for ever."

Psalm   Psalm 32

R. **Happy the people the Lord has chosen as his own.**

1. The word of the Lord is faithful
   and all his works to be trusted.
   The Lord loves justice and right
   and fills the earth with his love. R.

2. By his word the heavens were made,
   by the breath of his mouth all the stars.
   He spoke; and they came to be.
   He commanded; they sprang into being. R.

3. The Lord looks on those who revere him,
   on those who hope in his love,
   to rescue their souls from death,
   to keep them alive in famine. R.

4. Our soul is waiting for the Lord.
   The Lord is our help and our shield.
   May your love be upon us, O Lord,
   as we place all our hope in you. R.

Second Reading   Romans 8:14-17
You received the spirit of sons, and it makes us cry out, "Abba, Father!"

Everyone moved by the Spirit is a son of God. The spirit you received is not the spirit of slaves bringing fear into your lives again; it is the spirit of sons, and it makes us cry out, "Abba, Father!" The Spirit himself and our spirit bear united witness that we are children of God. And if we are children we are heirs as well: heirs of God and coheirs with Christ, sharing his sufferings so as to share his glory.

Gospel Acclamation
Alleluia, alleluia!
Glory be to the Father, and to the Son, and to the Holy Spirit,
the God who is, who was, and who is to come.
Alleluia!   cf. Apocalypse 1:8

Gospel   Matthew 28:16-20
Baptise them in the name of the Father and of the Son and of the Holy Spirit.

The eleven disciples set out for Galilee, to the mountain where Jesus had arranged to meet them. When they saw him they fell down before him, though some hesitated. Jesus came up and spoke to them. He said, "All authority in heaven and on earth has been given to me. Go, therefore, make disciples of all the nations; baptise them in the name of the Father and of the Son and of the Holy Spirit, and teach them to observe all the commands I gave you. And know that I am with you always; yes, to the end of time."

The Creed is said.

Prayer over the Offerings
Sanctify by the invocation of your name,
we pray, O Lord our God,
this oblation of our service,
and by it make of us an eternal offering to you.
Through Christ our Lord.

Preface of the Most Holy Trinity, pp. 405-406.

Communion Antiphon
Since you are children of God,
God has sent into your hearts the Spirit of his Son,
the Spirit who cries out: Abba, Father.   Galatians 4:6

Prayer after Communion
May receiving this Sacrament, O Lord our God,
bring us health of body and soul,
as we confess your eternal holy Trinity and undivided Unity.
Through Christ our Lord.

THE MOST HOLY BODY AND BLOOD OF CHRIST – B (CORPUS CHRISTI)

Christ our high priest.
Christ is our high priest who constantly makes intercession for us. He offers
himself to his Father as an atonement for our sins and establishes a new
covenant with God in his own Body and Blood. This is far greater than the old
Jewish sacrifice of goats and bull calves. It wins for us the eternal inheritance
that we have been promised.

Entrance Antiphon
He fed them with the finest wheat
and satisfied them with honey from the rock.   cf. Psalm 80:17

The Gloria is said or sung.

Collect
O God, who in this wonderful Sacrament
have left us a memorial of your Passion,
grant us, we pray,
so to revere the sacred mysteries of your Body and Blood
that we may always experience in ourselves
the fruits of your redemption.
Who live and reign with God the Father
in the unity of the Holy Spirit,
one God, for ever and ever.

First Reading   Exodus 24:3-8
This is the blood of the Covenant that the Lord has made with you.
Moses went and told the people all the commands of the Lord and
all the ordinances. In answer, all the people said with one voice, "We
will observe all the commands that the Lord has decreed." Moses put
all the commands of the Lord into writing, and early next morning

he built an altar at the foot of the mountain, with twelve standing-stones for the twelve tribes of Israel. Then he directed certain young Israelites to offer holocausts and to immolate bullocks to the Lord as communion sacrifices. Half of the blood Moses took up and put into basins, the other half he cast on the altar. And taking the Book of the Covenant he read it to the listening people, and they said, "We will observe all that the Lord has decreed; we will obey." Then Moses took the blood and cast it towards the people. "This", he said, "is the blood of the Covenant that the Lord has made with you, containing all these rules."

Psalm   Psalm 115

R. **The cup of salvation I will raise;**
    I will call on the Lord's name.

or **Alleluia!**

1. How can I repay the Lord
    for his goodness to me?
    The cup of salvation I will raise;
    I will call on the Lord's name. R.

2. O precious in the eyes of the Lord
    is the death of his faithful.
    Your servant, Lord, your servant am I;
    you have loosened my bonds. R.

3. A thanksgiving sacrifice I make:
    I will call on the Lord's name.
    My vows to the Lord I will fulfil
    before all his people. R.

Second Reading   Hebrews 9:11-15
The blood of Christ can purify our inner self from dead actions.
Now Christ has come, as the high priest of all the blessings which were to come. He has passed through the greater, the more perfect tent, which is better than one made by men's hands because it is not

of this created order; and he has entered the sanctuary once and for all, taking with him not the blood of goats and bull calves, but his own blood, having won an eternal redemption for us. The blood of goats and bulls and the ashes of a heifer are sprinkled on those who have incurred defilement and they restore the holiness of their outward lives; how much more effectively the blood of Christ, who offered himself as the perfect sacrifice to God through the eternal Spirit, can purify our inner self from dead actions so that we do our service to the living God.

He brings a new covenant, as the mediator, only so that the people who were called to an eternal inheritance may actually receive what was promised: his death took place to cancel the sins that infringed the earlier covenant.

The Sequence may be said or sung. See pp. 409-411.

Gospel Acclamation
Alleluia, alleluia!
I am the living bread which has come down from heaven,
says the Lord.
Anyone who eats this bread will live for ever.
Alleluia!   John 6:51-52

Gospel   Mark 14:12-16. 22-26
This is my body. This is my blood.
On the first day of Unleavened Bread, when the Passover lamb was sacrificed, his disciples said to Jesus, "Where do you want us to go and make the preparations for you to eat the passover?" So he sent two of his disciples, saying to them, "Go into the city and you will meet a man carrying a pitcher of water. Follow him, and say to the owner of the house which he enters, 'The Master says: Where is my dining room in which I can eat the passover with my disciples?' He will show you a large upper room furnished with couches, all prepared. Make the preparations for us there." The disciples set out and went to the city and found everything as he had told them, and prepared the Passover.

And as they were eating he took some bread, and when he had

said the blessing he broke it and gave it to them, "Take it," he said, "this is my body." Then he took a cup, and when he had returned thanks he gave it to them, and all drank from it, and he said to them, "This is my blood, the blood of the covenant, which is to be poured out for many. I tell you solemnly, I shall not drink any more wine until the day I drink the new wine in the kingdom of God."

After psalms had been sung they left for the Mount of Olives.

The Creed is said.

Prayer over the Offerings
Grant your Church, O Lord, we pray,
the gifts of unity and peace,
whose signs are to be seen in mystery
in the offerings we here present.
Through Christ our Lord.

Preface I or II of the Most Holy Eucharist, pp. 503-504.

Communion Antiphon
Whoever eats my flesh and drinks my blood
remains in me and I in him, says the Lord.   John 6:57

Prayer after Communion
Grant, O Lord, we pray,
that we may delight for all eternity
in that share in your divine life,
which is foreshadowed in the present age
by our reception of your precious Body and Blood.
Who live and reign for ever and ever.

THE MOST SACRED HEART OF JESUS – B

May Christ live in your hearts.
The love that Christ has for each one of us is beyond all human understanding.
No one can love us as he does. To prove this he gave his life for us. We pray to
be able to return that love so that we too will be filled with the
utter fullness of God.

Entrance Antiphon
The designs of his Heart are from age to age,
to rescue their souls from death,
and to keep them alive in famine.

Psalm 32:11. 19

The Gloria is said or sung.

Collect
Grant, we pray, almighty God,
that we, who glory in the Heart of your beloved Son
and recall the wonders of his love for us,
may be made worthy to receive
an overflowing measure of grace
from that fount of heavenly gifts.
Through our Lord Jesus Christ, your Son,
who lives and reigns with you in the unity of the Holy Spirit,
one God, for ever and ever.

or

O God, who in the Heart of your Son,
wounded by our sins,
bestow on us in mercy
the boundless treasures of your love,
grant, we pray,
that, in paying him the homage of our devotion,
we may also offer worthy reparation.

Through our Lord Jesus Christ, your Son,
who lives and reigns with you in the unity of the Holy Spirit,
one God, for ever and ever.

First Reading   Hosea 11:1. 3-4. 8-9
My heart recoils from it.
Listen to the word of the Lord:

> When Israel was a child I loved him,
> and I called my son out of Egypt.
> I myself taught Ephraim to walk,
> I took them in my arms;
> yet they have not understood that I was the one looking after
>   them.
> I led them with reins of kindness,
> with leading-strings of love.
> I was like someone who lifts an infant close against his cheek;
> stooping down to him I gave him his food.
> How could I treat you like Admah,
> or deal with you like Zeboiim?
> My heart recoils from it,
> my whole being trembles at the thought.
> I will not give rein to my fierce anger,
> I will not destroy Ephraim again,
> for I am God, not man:
> I am the Holy One in your midst
> and have no wish to destroy.

Psalm   Isaiah 12

R. **With joy you will draw water
    from the wells of the Saviour.**

1. Truly God is my salvation,
   I trust, I shall not fear.
   For the Lord is my strength, my song,
   he became my saviour.
   With joy you will draw water
   from the wells of salvation. R.

2. Give thanks to the Lord, give praise to his name!
   Make his mighty deeds known to the peoples!
   Declare the greatness of his name. R.

3. Sing a psalm to the Lord
   for he has done glorious deeds;
   make them known to all the earth!
   People of Zion, sing and shout for joy
   for great in your midst is the Holy One of Israel. R.

Second Reading   Ephesians 3:8-12. 14-19

The love of Christ is beyond all knowledge.

I, Paul, who am less than the least of all the saints, have been entrusted with this special grace, not only of proclaiming to the pagans the infinite treasure of Christ but also of explaining how the mystery is to be dispensed. Through all the ages, this has been kept hidden in God, the creator of everything. Why? So that the Sovereignties and Powers should learn only now, through the Church, how comprehensive God's wisdom really is, exactly according to the plan which he had had from all eternity in Christ Jesus our Lord. This is why we are bold enough to approach God in complete confidence, through our faith in him.

This, then, is what I pray, kneeling before the Father, from whom every family, whether spiritual or natural, takes its name:

Out of his infinite glory, may he give you the power through his Spirit for your hidden self to grow strong, so that Christ may live in your hearts through faith, and then, planted in love and built on love, you will with all the saints have strength to grasp the breadth and the length, the height and the depth; until, knowing the love of Christ, which is beyond all knowledge, you are filled with the utter fullness of God.

Gospel Acclamation
Alleluia, alleluia!
Shoulder my yoke and learn from me,
for I am gentle and humble in heart.
Alleluia!   Matthew 11:29

or

Alleluia, alleluia!
This is the love I mean:
God's love for us when he sent his Son
to be the sacrifice that takes our sins away.
Alleluia!

1 John 4:10

Gospel   John 19:31-37
One of the soldiers pierced his side and there came out blood and
water.

It was Preparation Day, and to prevent the bodies remaining on
the cross during the sabbath – since that sabbath was a day of
special solemnity –the Jews asked Pilate to have the legs broken
and the bodies taken away. Consequently the soldiers came and
broke the legs of the first man who had been crucified with him
and then of the other. When they came to Jesus, they found he was
already dead, and so instead of breaking his legs one of the soldiers
pierced his side with a lance; and immediately there came out blood
and water. This is the evidence of one who saw it – trustworthy
evidence, and he knows he speaks the truth – and he gives it so
that you may believe as well. Because all this happened to fulfil the
words of scripture:

Not one bone of his will be broken;

and again, in another place scripture says:

They will look on the one whom they have pierced.

The Creed is said.

Prayer over the Offerings
Look, O Lord, we pray, on the surpassing charity
in the Heart of your beloved Son,
that what we offer may be a gift acceptable to you
and an expiation of our offences.
Through Christ our Lord.

Preface of the Most Sacred Heart of Jesus, pp. 416-417.

Communion Antiphon
Thus says the Lord:
Let whoever is thirsty come to me and drink.
Streams of living water will flow
from within the one who believes in me.   cf. John 7:37-38

or

One of the soldiers opened his side with a lance,
and at once there came forth blood and water.   John 19:34

Prayer after Communion
May this sacrament of charity, O Lord,
make us fervent with the fire of holy love,
so that, drawn always to your Son,
we may learn to see him in our neighbour.
Through Christ our Lord.

THE MOST HOLY TRINITY – C

The Spirit of truth.
The Wisdom of God existed before the universe came into being. Jesus promises
us the Holy Spirit of God our Father, who will lead us into the fullness of
truth. The Spirit has poured the love of God into our hearts, and leads us into
a deeper understanding of what the Gospel of Christ really means.

Entrance Antiphon
Blest be God the Father,
and the Only Begotten Son of God,
and also the Holy Spirit,
for he has shown us his merciful love.

The Gloria is said or sung.

Collect
God our Father, who by sending into the world
the Word of truth and the Spirit of sanctification
made known to the human race your wondrous mystery,
grant us, we pray, that in professing the true faith,
we may acknowledge the Trinity of eternal glory
and adore your Unity, powerful in majesty.
Through our Lord Jesus Christ, your Son,
who lives and reigns with you in the unity of the Holy Spirit,
one God, for ever and ever.

First Reading   Proverbs 8:22-31
Before the earth came into being, Wisdom was born.
The Wisdom of God cries aloud:
    The Lord created me when his purpose first unfolded,
    before the oldest of his works.
    From everlasting I was firmly set,
    from the beginning, before earth came into being.
    The deep was not, when I was born,

there were no springs to gush with water.
Before the mountains were settled,
before the hills, I came to birth;
before he made the earth, the countryside,
or the first grains of the world's dust.
When he fixed the heavens firm, I was there,
when he drew a ring on the surface of the deep,
when he thickened the clouds above,
when he fixed fast the springs of the deep,
when he assigned the sea its boundaries
– and the waters will not invade the shore –
when he laid down the foundations of the earth,
I was by his side, a master craftsman,
delighting him day after day,
ever at play in his presence,
at play everywhere in his world,
delighting to be with the sons of men.

Psalm   Psalm 8

R. **How great is your name, O Lord our God,
    through all the earth!**

1. When I see the heavens, the work of your hands,
   the moon and the stars which you arranged,
   what is man that you should keep him in mind,
   mortal man that you care for him? R.

2. Yet you have made him little less than a god;
   with glory and honour you crowned him,
   gave him power over the works of your hand,
   put all things under his feet. R.

3. All of them, sheep and cattle,
   yes, even the savage beasts,
   birds of the air, and fish
   that make their way through the waters. R.

Second Reading   Romans 5:1-5

To God, through Christ, in the love poured out by the Spirit.

Through our Lord Jesus Christ, by faith we are judged righteous and at peace with God, since it is by faith and through Jesus that we have entered this state of grace in which we can boast about looking forward to God's glory. But that is not all we can boast about; we can boast about our sufferings. These sufferings bring patience, as we know, and patience brings perseverance, and perseverance brings hope, and this hope is not deceptive, because the love of God has been poured into our hearts by the Holy Spirit which has been given us.

Gospel Acclamation

Alleluia, alleluia!
Glory be to the Father, and to the Son, and to the Holy Spirit,
the God who is, who was, and who is to come.
Alleluia!   cf. Apocalypse 1:8

Gospel   John 16:12-15

Everything the Father has is mine; all the Spirit tells you will be taken from what is mine.

Jesus said to his disciples:

"I still have many things to say to you
but they would be too much for you now.
But when the Spirit of truth comes
he will lead you to the complete truth,
since he will not be speaking as from himself
but will say only what he has learnt;
and he will tell you of the things to come.
He will glorify me,
since all he tells you
will be taken from what is mine.
Everything the Father has is mine;
that is why I said:
All he tells you
will be taken from what is mine."

The Creed is said.

Prayer over the Offerings
Sanctify by the invocation of your name,
we pray, O Lord our God,
this oblation of our service,
and by it make of us an eternal offering to you.
Through Christ our Lord.

Preface of the Most Holy Trinity, pp. 405-406.

Communion Antiphon
Since you are children of God,
God has sent into your hearts the Spirit of his Son,
the Spirit who cries out: Abba, Father.   Galatians 4:6

Prayer after Communion
May receiving this Sacrament, O Lord our God,
bring us health of body and soul,
as we confess your eternal holy Trinity and undivided Unity.
Through Christ our Lord.

THE MOST HOLY BODY
AND BLOOD OF CHRIST – C
(CORPUS CHRISTI)

You are a priest for ever.
We share in the priesthood of Christ through the Holy Spirit. Every time we
eat his Body and drink his Blood we proclaim the power of his Death and
Resurrection until he comes again. The Eucharist is not just a memorial of a
past event, but something that effectively flows into our lives today.

Entrance Antiphon
He fed them with the finest wheat
and satisfied them with honey from the rock.   cf. Psalm 80:17

The Gloria is said or sung.

Collect
O God, who in this wonderful Sacrament
have left us a memorial of your Passion,
grant us, we pray,
so to revere the sacred mysteries of your Body and Blood
that we may always experience in ourselves
the fruits of your redemption.
Who live and reign with God the Father
in the unity of the Holy Spirit,
one God, for ever and ever.

First Reading   Genesis 14:18-20
He brought bread and wine.
Melchizedek king of Salem brought bread and wine; he was a priest
of God Most High. He pronounced this blessing:

> "Blessed be Abraham by God Most High, creator of heaven and
> earth,
> and blessed be God Most High for handing over your enemies to
> you."

And Abraham gave him a tithe of everything.

Psalm   Psalm 109

R.   **You are a priest for ever,**
     a priest like Melchizedek of old.

1. The Lord's revelation to my Master:
   "Sit on my right:
   I will put your foes beneath your feet." R.

2. The Lord will send from Zion
   your sceptre of power:
   rule in the midst of all your foes. R.

3. A prince from the day of your birth
   on the holy mountains;
   from the womb before the daybreak I begot you. R.

4. The Lord has sworn an oath he will not change.
   "You are a priest for ever,
   a priest like Melchizedek of old." R.

Second Reading   1 Corinthians 11:23-26
Every time you eat this bread and drink this cup, you are proclaiming
the Lord's death.
This is what I received from the Lord, and in turn passed on to
you: that on the same night that he was betrayed, the Lord Jesus
took some bread, and thanked God for it and broke it, and he said,
"This is my body, which is for you; do this as a memorial of me." In
the same way he took the cup after supper, and said, "This cup is
the new covenant in my blood. Whenever you drink it, do this as a
memorial of me." Until the Lord comes, therefore, every time you
eat this bread and drink this cup, you are proclaiming his death.

The Sequence may be said or sung. See pp. 409-411.

Gospel Acclamation
Alleluia, alleluia!
I am the living bread which has come down from heaven,
says the Lord.
Anyone who eats this bread will live for ever.
Alleluia!   John 6:51-52

Gospel   Luke 9:11-17

They all ate as much as they wanted.

Jesus made the crowds welcome and talked to them about the kingdom of God; and he cured those who were in need of healing.

It was late afternoon when the Twelve came to him and said, "Send the people away, and they can go to the villages and farms round about to find lodging and food; for we are in a lonely place here." He replied, "Give them something to eat yourselves." But they said, "We have no more than five loaves and two fish, unless we are to go ourselves and buy food for all these people." For there were about five thousand men. But he said to his disciples, "Get them to sit down in parties of about fifty." They did so and made them all sit down. Then he took the five loaves and the two fish, raised his eyes to heaven, and said the blessing over them; then he broke them and handed them to his disciples to distribute among the crowd. They all ate as much as they wanted, and when the scraps remaining were collected they filled twelve baskets.

The Creed is said.

Prayer over the Offerings

Grant your Church, O Lord, we pray,
the gifts of unity and peace,
whose signs are to be seen in mystery
in the offerings we here present.
Through Christ our Lord.

Preface I or II of the Most Holy Eucharist, pp. 503-504.

Communion Antiphon

Whoever eats my flesh and drinks my blood
remains in me and I in him, says the Lord.   John 6:57

Prayer after Communion

Grant, O Lord, we pray,
that we may delight for all eternity
in that share in your divine life,
which is foreshadowed in the present age
by our reception of your precious Body and Blood.
Who live and reign for ever and ever.

THE MOST SACRED HEART OF JESUS – C

Christ's love reconciles us to God.
Christ died for us while we were still sinners. He gave his life as our Shepherd
so that we, his sheep, might find new pastures. He will not abandon us but
constantly looks for the lost one, bandages the wounded and
makes the weak strong.

❧ ❧ ❧

Entrance Antiphon
The designs of his Heart are from age to age,
to rescue their souls from death,
and to keep them alive in famine. Psalm 32:11. 19

The Gloria is said or sung.

Collect
Grant, we pray, almighty God,
that we, who glory in the Heart of your beloved Son
and recall the wonders of his love for us,
may be made worthy to receive
an overflowing measure of grace
from that fount of heavenly gifts.
Through our Lord Jesus Christ, your Son,
who lives and reigns with you in the unity of the Holy Spirit,
one God, for ever and ever.

or

O God, who in the Heart of your Son,
wounded by our sins,
bestow on us in mercy
the boundless treasures of your love,
grant, we pray,
that, in paying him the homage of our devotion,
we may also offer worthy reparation.
Through our Lord Jesus Christ, your Son,
who lives and reigns with you in the unity of the Holy Spirit,
one God, for ever and ever.

First Reading   Ezekiel 34:11-16

I myself will pasture my sheep, I myself will show them where to rest.

The Lord God says this: I am going to look after my flock myself and keep all of it in view. As a shepherd keeps all his flock in view when he stands up in the middle of his scattered sheep, so shall I keep my sheep in view. I shall rescue them from wherever they have been scattered during the mist and darkness. I shall bring them out of the countries where they are; I shall gather them together from foreign countries and bring them back to their own land. I shall pasture them on the mountains of Israel, in the ravines and in every inhabited place in the land. I shall feed them in good pasturage; the high mountains of Israel will be their grazing ground. There they will rest in good grazing ground; they will browse in rich pastures on the mountains of Israel. I myself will pasture my sheep, I myself will show them where to rest – it is the Lord who speaks. I shall look for the lost one, bring back the stray, bandage the wounded and make the weak strong. I shall watch over the fat and healthy. I shall be a true shepherd to them.

Psalm   Psalm 22

R. **The Lord is my shepherd;**
     there is nothing I shall want.

1. The Lord is my shepherd;
     there is nothing I shall want.
     Fresh and green are the pastures
     where he gives me repose.
     Near restful waters he leads me,
     to revive my drooping spirit. R.

2. He guides me along the right path;
     he is true to his name.
     If I should walk in the valley of darkness
     no evil would I fear.
     You are there with your crook and your staff;
     with these you give me comfort. R.

3. You have prepared a banquet for me
   in the sight of my foes,
   My head you have anointed with oil;
   my cup is overflowing. R.

4. Surely goodness and kindness shall follow me
   all the days of my life.
   In the Lord's own house shall I dwell
   for ever and ever. R.

Second Reading   Romans 5:5-11
What proves that God loves us is that Christ died for us.
The love of God has been poured into our hearts by the Holy
Spirit which has been given us. We were still helpless when at his
appointed moment Christ died for sinful men. It is not easy to die
even for a good man – though of course for someone really worthy,
a man might be prepared to die – but what proved that God loves
us is that Christ died for us while we were still sinners. Having died
to make us righteous, is it likely that he would now fail to save us
from God's anger? When we were reconciled to God by the death
of his Son, we were still enemies; now that we have been reconciled,
surely we may count on being saved by the life of his Son? Not
merely because we have been reconciled but because we are filled
with joyful trust in God, through our Lord Jesus Christ, through
whom we have already gained our reconciliation.

Gospel Acclamation
Alleluia, alleluia!
Shoulder my yoke and learn from me,
for I am gentle and humble in heart.
Alleluia!
                                                   Matthew 11:29

or

Alleluia, alleluia!
I am the good shepherd, says the Lord;
I know my sheep and my own know me.
Alleluia!
                                                   John 10:14

Gospel   Luke 15:3-7

Rejoice with me, I have found my sheep that was lost.

Jesus spoke this parable to the scribes and Pharisees:

> "What man among you with a hundred sheep, losing one, would not leave the ninety-nine in the wilderness and go after the missing one till he found it? And when he found it, would he not joyfully take it on his shoulders and then, when he got home, call together his friends and neighbours? 'Rejoice with me,' he would say, 'I have found my sheep that was lost.' In the same way, I tell you, there will be more rejoicing in heaven over one repentant sinner than over ninety-nine virtuous men who have no need of repentance."

The Creed is said.

Prayer over the Offerings

Look, O Lord, we pray, on the surpassing charity
in the Heart of your beloved Son,
that what we offer may be a gift acceptable to you
and an expiation of our offences.
Through Christ our Lord.

Preface of the Most Sacred Heart of Jesus, pp. 416-417.

Communion Antiphon

Thus says the Lord:
Let whoever is thirsty come to me and drink.
Streams of living water will flow
from within the one who believes in me.   cf. John 7:37-38

or

One of the soldiers opened his side with a lance,
and at once there came forth blood and water.   John 19:34

Prayer after Communion

May this sacrament of charity, O Lord,
make us fervent with the fire of holy love,
so that, drawn always to your Son,
we may learn to see him in our neighbour.
Through Christ our Lord.

THE ORDER OF MASS

PRAYERS BEFORE MASS

A pilgrimage song
I rejoiced when I heard them say:
"Let us go to God's house."
And now our feet are standing
within your gates, O Jerusalem.

Jerusalem is built as a city
strongly compact.
It is there that the tribes go up,
the tribes of the Lord.

For Israel's law it is,
there to praise the Lord's name.
There were set the thrones of judgement
of the house of David.

For the peace of Jerusalem pray:
"Peace be to your homes!
May peace reign in your walls,
in your palaces, peace!"

For love of my brethren and friends
I say: "Peace upon you!"
For love of the house of the Lord
I will ask for your good.

Psalm 121

Prayer of Saint Thomas Aquinas

Almighty and ever-living God,
I approach the sacrament of your only-begotten Son, our Lord
    Jesus Christ.
I come sick to the doctor of life,
unclean to the fountain of mercy,
blind to the radiance of eternal light,
and poor and needy to the Lord of heaven and earth.
Lord, in your great generosity,
heal my sickness, wash away my defilement,
enlighten my blindness, enrich my poverty,
and clothe my nakedness.
May I receive the bread of angels,
the King of kings and Lord of lords,
with humble reverence,
with the purity and faith,
the repentance and love, and the determined purpose
that will help bring me to salvation.
May I receive the sacrament of the Lord's body and blood,
and its reality and power.
Kind God,
may I receive the body of your only-begotten Son, our Lord Jesus
    Christ,
born from the womb of the Virgin Mary,
and so be received into his mystical body,
and numbered among his members.
Loving Father,
as on my earthly pilgrimage
I now receive your beloved Son
under the veil of a sacrament,
may I one day see him face to face in glory,
who lives and reigns with you for ever. Amen.

Prayer of Saint Ambrose
Lord Jesus Christ,
I approach your banquet table
in fear and trembling,
for I am a sinner,
and dare not rely on my own worth,
but only on your goodness and mercy.
I am defiled by many sins in body and soul,
and by my unguarded thoughts and words.

Gracious God of majesty and awe,
I seek your protection,
I look for your healing.
Poor troubled sinner that I am,
I appeal to you, the fountain of all mercy.
I cannot bear your judgement,
but I trust in your salvation.
Lord, I show my wounds to you
and uncover my shame before you.
I know my sins are many and great,
and they fill me with fear,
but I hope in your mercies,
for they cannot be numbered.

Lord Jesus Christ, eternal king, divine and human,
crucified for humanity,
look upon me with mercy and hear my prayer,
for I trust in you.
Have mercy on me,
full of sorrow and sin,
for the depth of your compassion never ends.
Praise to you, saving sacrifice,
offered on the wood of the cross for me and for all.
Praise to the noble and precious blood,
flowing from the wounds of my crucified Lord Jesus Christ
and washing away the sins of the whole world.

Remember, Lord, your creature,
whom you have redeemed with your blood.
I repent my sins,
and I long to put right what I have done.

Merciful Father, take away all my offences and sins;
purify me in body and soul,
and make me worthy to taste the holy of holies.
May your body and blood,
which I intend to receive, although I am unworthy,
be for me the remission of my sins,
the washing away of my guilt,
the end of my evil thoughts,
and the rebirth of my better instincts.
May it spur me on to works pleasing to you
and profitable to my health in body and soul,
and be a firm defence
against the wiles of my enemies.
Amen.

Invitation to Praise God
Acclaim the Lord, all the earth,
serve the Lord gladly,
come into his presence with songs of joy!

Know that he, the Lord, is God,
he made us and we belong to him,
we are his people, the flock that he pastures.

Walk through his porticos giving thanks,
enter his courts praising him,
give thanks to him, bless his name!

Yes, the Lord is good,
his love is everlasting,
his faithfulness endures from age to age.

Psalm 100

A Loving Prayer

My God, I love thee: not because
I hope for heaven thereby,
nor yet because who love thee not
are lost eternally.

Thou, O my Jesus, thou didst me
upon the cross embrace;
for me didst bear the nails and spear
and manifold disgrace.

And griefs and torments numberless
and sweat of agony;
even death itself – and all for one
who was thine enemy.

Then why, O blessed Jesu Christ,
should I not love thee well;
not for the sake of winning heaven
or of escaping hell;

Not with the hope of gaining aught,
nor seeking a reward:
but as thyself has loved me,
O ever-loving Lord!

Even so I love thee, and will love
and in thy praise will sing,
solely because thou art my God,
and my eternal King.

attributed to Saint Francis Xavier

Disturb us, Lord

Disturb us, Lord, when we are too well pleased with ourselves,
when our dreams have come true because we dreamed too little;
when we arrive safely because we sailed too close to the shore.

Disturb us, Lord, when with abundance of things we possess,
we have lost our thirst for the waters of life;
having fallen in love with life,
we have ceased to dream of eternity,
and in our efforts to build a new earth,
we have allowed our vision of the new heaven to dim.

Disturb us, Lord, to dare more boldly,
to venture on wider seas,
where storms will show your mastery;
where losing sight of land, we shall find the stars.
We ask you to push back the horizons of our hopes,
and to guide us into the future in strength,
courage, hope and love.

Spirit of God, disturb, renew, encourage
and guide us day by day.
Amen.

Sir Francis Drake

Eucharistic Offering

O Lord, to whom belongs all that is in heaven and earth, I desire to
consecrate myself wholly to you and to be yours for evermore. This
day I offer myself to you, O Lord, in singleness of heart, to serve
and obey you always, and I offer you without ceasing a sacrifice of
praise and thanksgiving. Receive me, O my Saviour, in union with
the holy oblation of your precious blood which I offer to you this
day, in the presence of angels, that this sacrifice may avail unto my
salvation and that of the whole world.

The Imitation of Christ

Adoro Te Devote

Godhead here in hiding, whom I do adore
Masked by these bare shadows, shape and nothing more,
See, Lord, at thy service low lies here a heart
Lost, all lost in wonder at the God thou art.

Seeing, touching, tasting are in thee deceived;
How says trusty hearing? That shall be believed;
What God's Son has told me, take for truth I do;
Truth himself speaks truly or there's nothing true.

On the cross thy Godhead made no sign to men;
Here thy very manhood steals from human ken;
Both are my confession, both are my belief,
And I pray the prayer of the dying thief.

I am not like Thomas, wounds I cannot see,
But can plainly call thee Lord and God as he:
Let me to a deeper faith daily nearer move,
Daily make me harder hope and dearer love.

O thou our reminder of Christ crucified,
Living Bread, the life of us for whom he died,
Lend this life to me then: feed and feast my mind,
There be thou the sweetness man was meant to find.

Bring the tender tale true of the Pelican;
Bathe me, Jesu Lord, in what thy bosom ran –
Blood whereof a single drop has power to win
All the world forgiveness of its world of sin.

Jesu, whom I look at shrouded here below,
I beseech thee send me what I thirst for so,
Some day to gaze on thee face to face in light
And be blest for ever with thy glory's sight.
Amen.

Saint Thomas Aquinas, trans. Gerard Manley Hopkins

Shema Israel
Hear, O Israel
The Lord is our God, the Lord alone.
You shall love the Lord your God
with all your heart,
with all your soul,
with all your might.
Keep these words that I command you today
Always in your heart.

Recite them to your children
and talk about them when you are at home
and when you are away,
when you lie down and when you rise.

Deuteronomy 6:4-7

Prayer to the Holy Spirit
Come, Holy Spirit, fill the hearts of your faithful,
and enkindle in them the fire of your love.
Send forth your Spirit and they shall be created.
And you shall renew the face of the earth.
O God, who has taught the hearts of the faithful
by the light of the Holy Spirit,
grant that by the gift of the same Spirit
we may be always truly wise
and ever rejoice in his consolation.

The Introductory Rites

The purpose of the Introductory Rites is to help the assembled people to become a worshipping community and to prepare to listen to God's word and to celebrate the Eucharist.

These rites may be omitted on certain occasions.

All stand.
The priest comes to the altar while the Entrance Song is sung. If there is no singing, the Entrance Antiphon is said.

Sign of the Cross

After the Entrance Song, the priest and the people make the sign of the cross as the priest says or sings:

Priest: In the name of the Father, and of the Son,
and of the Holy Spirit.
People: **Amen.**

Greeting

The priest greets the people, extending his hands and saying one of the following:

The grace of our Lord Jesus Christ,
and the love of God,
and the communion of the Holy Spirit
be with you all.
And with your spirit.

or

Grace to you and peace from God our Father
and the Lord Jesus Christ.
And with your spirit.

or

The Lord be with you.
And with your spirit.

A Bishop, instead of **The Lord be with you**, says: **Peace be with you**.

The priest, or another minister, may briefly introduce the Mass of the day.

Penitential Act

There are three forms of the Penitential Act which may be chosen as appropriate. From time to time the blessing and sprinkling of water may take place instead. This can be found on pages 556-559.

The priest invites the people to penitence:

Brethren (brothers and sisters), let us acknowledge our sins, and so prepare ourselves to celebrate the sacred mysteries.

A brief pause for silence follows.

Then either:

I confess to almighty God
and to you, my brothers and sisters,
that I have greatly sinned,
in my thoughts and in my words,
in what I have done and in what I have failed to do,

(all strike their breast and say:)

through my fault, through my fault,
through my most grievous fault;

therefore I ask blessed Mary ever-Virgin,
all the Angels and Saints,
and you, my brothers and sisters,
to pray for me to the Lord our God.

---

or

Have mercy on us, O Lord.
For we have sinned against you.

Show us, O Lord, your mercy.
And grant us your salvation.

---

or (other similar words may be used for the invocations, but the people's response remains the same):

You were sent to heal the contrite of heart:

| Lord, have mercy. | or | Kyrie, eleison. |
| **Lord, have mercy.** | | **Kyrie, eleison.** |

You came to call sinners:

| Christ, have mercy. | or | Christe, eleison. |
| **Christ, have mercy.** | | **Christe, eleison.** |

You are seated at the right hand of the Father to intercede for us:

| Lord, have mercy. | or | Kyrie, eleison. |
| **Lord, have mercy.** | | **Kyrie, eleison.** |

The absolution by the priest follows:

May almighty God have mercy on us,
forgive us our sins,
and bring us to everlasting life.
Amen.

The Kyrie, eleison (Lord, have mercy) invocations follow, unless they have already occurred as part of the Penitential Act.

| Lord, have mercy. | or | Kyrie, eleison. |
| **Lord, have mercy.** | | **Kyrie, eleison.** |

| Christ, have mercy. | or | Christe, eleison. |
| **Christ, have mercy.** | | **Christe, eleison.** |

| Lord, have mercy. | or | Kyrie, eleison. |
| **Lord, have mercy.** | | **Kyrie, eleison.** |

Gloria

On Sundays (except in Advent and Lent) and other feast days, this hymn is either sung or said:

Glory to God in the highest,
and on earth peace to people of good will.

We praise you,
we bless you,
we adore you,
we glorify you,
we give you thanks for your great glory,
Lord God, heavenly King,
O God, almighty Father.

Lord Jesus Christ, Only Begotten Son,
Lord God, Lamb of God, Son of the Father,
you take away the sins of the world,
    have mercy on us;
you take away the sins of the world,
    receive our prayer;
you are seated at the right hand of the Father,
    have mercy on us.

For you alone are the Holy One,
you alone are the Lord,
you alone are the Most High,
Jesus Christ,
with the Holy Spirit,
in the glory of God the Father.
Amen.

Collect

Let us pray.

We spend a few moments praying in silence together.
Then the priest says the Collect, a special prayer expressing the character of today's celebration, at the end of which the people acclaim:
Amen.

The Liturgy of the Word

God speaks to us of redemption and salvation, and nourishes us with his Word. We are not just listening to past history. The God who speaks to Israel and the early Church speaks to us today and reveals the pattern of God's plan for our lives.

All sit.
Following each of the readings there may be a brief period of silence to enable us to take the Word of God to heart and begin prayerfully to respond to it.

First Reading

The reader proclaims the First Reading.

At the end of the reading, the reader acclaims:

The word of the Lord.
Thanks be to God.

Psalm

The reader or cantor sings or says the Psalm, and all make the response.

Second Reading

On Sundays and some other days there is a Second Reading, at the end of which the reader acclaims:

The word of the Lord.
Thanks be to God.

Gospel

All stand.
Christ is present among us through his saving word. We remain standing for the proclamation of the Good News.

The Gospel Acclamation may be sung or said.

The deacon or the priest says or sings:

The Lord be with you **And with your spi - rit**

A reading from the holy Gospel according to

Mat - thew.
Mark.
Luke.
John.

The deacon or the priest makes the Sign of the Cross on the book and, together with the people, on his forehead, lips and breast. The people acclaim:

Glory to you, O Lord.

At the end of the Gospel, the deacon or the priest acclaims:

The Gospel of the Lord. **Praise to you, Lord Je - sus Christ.**

Homily

All sit.

A homily is preached on all Sundays, holydays and other suitable occasions. After the homily there may be a brief period of silence for reflection.

Profession of Faith

All stand. The following Profession of Faith, or Creed, is said or sung on Sundays and certain other days. The Apostles' Creed (opposite page) may be used instead, especially during Lent and Easter Time.

I believe in one God,
the Father almighty,
maker of heaven and earth,
of all things visible and invisible.

I believe in one Lord Jesus Christ,
the Only Begotten Son of God,
born of the Father before all ages.
God from God, Light from Light,
true God from true God,
begotten, not made, consubstantial with the Father;
through him all things were made.
For us men and for our salvation
he came down from heaven,

(all bow during the next two lines)

and by the Holy Spirit was incarnate of the Virgin Mary,
and became man.

For our sake he was crucified under Pontius Pilate,
he suffered death and was buried,
and rose again on the third day
in accordance with the Scriptures.
He ascended into heaven
and is seated at the right hand of the Father.
He will come again in glory
to judge the living and the dead
and his kingdom will have no end.

I believe in the Holy Spirit, the Lord, the giver of life,
who proceeds from the Father and the Son,
who with the Father and the Son is adored and glorified,
who has spoken through the prophets.

I believe in one, holy, catholic and apostolic Church.
I confess one Baptism for the forgiveness of sins
and I look forward to the resurrection of the dead
and the life of the world to come. Amen.

The Apostles' Creed
I believe in God,
the Father almighty,
Creator of heaven and earth,
and in Jesus Christ, his only Son, our Lord,

(all bow during the next two lines)

who was conceived by the Holy Spirit,
born of the Virgin Mary,
suffered under Pontius Pilate,
was crucified, died and was buried;
he descended into hell;
on the third day he rose again from the dead;
he ascended into heaven,
and is seated at the right hand of God the Father almighty;
from there he will come to judge the living and the dead.

I believe in the Holy Spirit,
the holy catholic Church,
the communion of saints,
the forgiveness of sins,
the resurrection of the body,
and life everlasting. Amen.

Prayer of the Faithful (Bidding Prayers)

Through baptism we have been made one with Christ, our high priest, and we share in his intercessions before the Father for the needs of the Church, of the world and of all people.

After each intention there is a pause while all pray. This time of silent prayer may simply be followed by the next intention, or by a response such as:

Lord, in your mercy.
Hear our prayer.

The priest concludes the biddings with a prayer.

The Liturgy of the Eucharist

At the Last Supper Christ took bread and wine, gave thanks, broke the bread and gave these gifts to his disciples. In the Eucharist we bring our gifts to the altar and when the priest has given thanks to God, the bread is broken and we receive in Communion the Body and Blood of the Lord.

All sit.

The gifts of bread and wine, together with other offerings of the people, are taken to the altar. During the procession a hymn may be sung.

When he has received the bread and wine, the priest offers prayers of blessing at the altar, which may be said quietly or aloud. If the prayers are said aloud, the people make the acclamation at the end of each prayer.

Blessed are you, Lord God of all creation,
for through your goodness we have received
the bread we offer you:
fruit of the earth and work of human hands,
it will become for us the bread of life.

Blessed be God for ever.

Blessed are you, Lord God of all creation,
for through your goodness we have received
the wine we offer you:
fruit of the vine and work of human hands,
it will become our spiritual drink.

Blessed be God for ever.

The priest completes additional personal preparatory rites, then all stand as he says:

Pray, brethren (brothers and sisters),
that my sacrifice and yours
may be acceptable to God,
the almighty Father.

May the Lord accept the sacrifice at your hands
for the praise and glory of his name,
for our good
and the good of all his holy Church.

The priest says the Prayer over the Offerings, at the end of which the
people acclaim:

Amen.

THE EUCHARISTIC PRAYER

*The great prayer of praise and thanksgiving proclaims the wonderful
works of God. The priest offers it in the name of us all, and so through
our reflective attention we join ourselves with Christ in praise to the
Father.*

The Lord be with you. **And with your spir-it.**

Lift up your hearts. **We lift them up to the Lord.**

Let us give thanks to the Lord our God. **It is right and just.**

The priest continues with the Preface, giving praise and thanks to
God for the work of salvation. The Preface varies according to the
season and occasion, and will be selected from those found on pp.
490–507, or found in the Propers for the day. Then the priest and
people join together to sing or say:

Holy, Holy, Holy Lord God of hosts.
Heaven and earth are full of your glory.
Hosanna in the highest.
Blessed is he who comes in the name of the Lord.
Hosanna in the highest.

Ho - ly, Ho - ly, Ho - ly Lord God of hosts. Heav-en and earth are

full of your glo - ry. Ho-san-na in the high-est. Bless-ed is he

who comes in the name of the Lord. Ho- san - na in the high est.

Then the people kneel, and the priest continues with the Eucharistic Prayer.

Texts for the four principal Eucharistic Prayers follow.

The texts for the additional Eucharistic Prayers are provided on pp. 528-555.

Eucharistic Prayer I
(The Roman Canon)

To you, therefore, most merciful Father,
we make humble prayer and petition
through Jesus Christ, your Son, our Lord:
that you accept
and bless ✠ these gifts, these offerings,
these holy and unblemished sacrifices,
which we offer you firstly
for your holy catholic Church.
Be pleased to grant her peace,
to guard, unite and govern her
throughout the whole world,
together with your servant N. our Pope
and N. our Bishop,
and all those who, holding to the truth,
hand on the catholic and apostolic faith.

Commemoration of the Living

Remember, Lord, your servants N. and N.
and all gathered here,
whose faith and devotion are known to you.
For them, we offer you this sacrifice of praise
or they offer it for themselves
and all who are dear to them:
for the redemption of their souls,
in hope of health and well-being,
and paying their homage to you,
the eternal God, living and true.

Communicantes

In communion with those whose memory we venerate,
especially the glorious ever-Virgin Mary,
Mother of our God and Lord, Jesus Christ,
† and blessed Joseph, her Spouse,
your blessed Apostles and Martyrs,
Peter and Paul, Andrew,
(James, John,
Thomas, James, Philip,
Bartholomew, Matthew,
Simon and Jude;
Linus, Cletus, Clement, Sixtus,
Cornelius, Cyprian,
Lawrence, Chrysogonus,
John and Paul,
Cosmas and Damian)
and all your Saints;
we ask that through their merits and prayers,
in all things we may be defended
by your protecting help.
(Through Christ our Lord. Amen.)

PROPER FORMS OF THE COMMUNICANTES

On the Nativity of the Lord and throughout the Octave

Celebrating the most sacred night (day)
on which blessed Mary the immaculate Virgin
brought forth the Saviour for this world,
and in communion with those whose memory we venerate,
especially the glorious ever-Virgin Mary,
Mother of our God and Lord, Jesus Christ, †

On the Epiphany of the Lord

Celebrating the most sacred day
on which your Only Begotten Son,
eternal with you in your glory,

appeared in a human body, truly sharing our flesh,
and in communion with those whose memory we venerate,
especially the glorious ever-Virgin Mary,
Mother of our God and Lord, Jesus Christ, †

On the Thursday of Holy Week at the Evening Mass of the Lord's Supper

Celebrating the most sacred day
on which our Lord Jesus Christ
was handed over for our sake,
and in communion with those whose memory we venerate,
especially the glorious ever-Virgin Mary,
Mother of our God and Lord, Jesus Christ, †

From the Mass of the Easter Vigil until the Second Sunday of Easter

Celebrating the most sacred night (day)
of the Resurrection of our Lord Jesus Christ in the flesh,
and in communion with those whose memory we venerate,
especially the glorious ever-Virgin Mary,
Mother of our God and Lord, Jesus Christ, †

On the Ascension of the Lord

Celebrating the most sacred day
on which your Only Begotten Son, our Lord,
placed at the right hand of your glory
our weak human nature,
which he had united to himself,
and in communion with those whose memory we venerate,
especially the glorious ever-Virgin Mary,
Mother of our God and Lord, Jesus Christ, †

On Pentecost Sunday

Celebrating the most sacred day of Pentecost,
on which the Holy Spirit
appeared to the Apostles in tongues of fire,
and in communion with those whose memory we venerate,
especially the glorious ever-Virgin Mary,
Mother of our God and Lord, Jesus Christ, †

Hanc Igitur

Therefore, Lord, we pray:
graciously accept this oblation of our service,
that of your whole family;
order our days in your peace,
and command that we be delivered from eternal damnation
and counted among the flock of those you have chosen.
(Through Christ our Lord. Amen.)

PROPER FORMS OF THE HANC IGITUR

On the Thursday of Holy Week at the Evening Mass of the Lord's Supper

Therefore, Lord, we pray:
graciously accept this oblation of our service,
that of your whole family,
which we make to you
as we observe the day
on which our Lord Jesus Christ
handed on the mysteries of his Body and Blood
for his disciples to celebrate;
order our days in your peace,
and command that we be delivered from eternal damnation
and counted among the flock of those you have chosen.
(Through Christ our Lord. Amen.)

From the Mass of the Easter Vigil until the Second Sunday of Easter

Therefore, Lord, we pray:
graciously accept this oblation of our service,
that of your whole family,
which we make to you
also for those to whom you have been pleased to give
the new birth of water and the Holy Spirit,
granting them forgiveness of all their sins;
order our days in your peace,
and command that we be delivered from eternal damnation
and counted among the flock of those you have chosen.
(Through Christ our Lord. Amen.)

Be pleased, O God, we pray,
to bless, acknowledge,
and approve this offering in every respect;
make it spiritual and acceptable,
so that it may become for us
the Body and Blood of your most beloved Son,
our Lord Jesus Christ.

On the day before he was to suffer,
† he took bread in his holy and venerable hands,
and with eyes raised to heaven
to you, O God, his almighty Father,
giving you thanks, he said the blessing,
broke the bread
and gave it to his disciples, saying:

TAKE THIS, ALL OF YOU, AND EAT OF IT,
FOR THIS IS MY BODY,
WHICH WILL BE GIVEN UP FOR YOU.

In a similar way, when supper was ended,
he took this precious chalice
in his holy and venerable hands,
and once more giving you thanks, he said the blessing
and gave the chalice to his disciples, saying:

TAKE THIS, ALL OF YOU, AND DRINK FROM IT,
FOR THIS IS THE CHALICE OF MY BLOOD,
THE BLOOD OF THE NEW AND ETERNAL COVENANT,
WHICH WILL BE POURED OUT FOR YOU AND FOR MANY
FOR THE FORGIVENESS OF SINS.

DO THIS IN MEMORY OF ME.

On the Thursday of Holy Week at the Evening Mass of the Lord's Supper

On the day before he was to suffer
for our salvation and the salvation of all,
that is today, †

The mystery of faith.

The people acclaim:

We pro-claim your Death, O Lord, and pro-fess your Res-ur-rec- tion

un - til you come a- gain.

or

When we eat this Bread and drink this Cup, we pro-claim your

Death, O Lord, un- til you come a- gain.

or

Save us, Sav-iour of the world, for by your Cross and Res-ur- rec-tion

you have set us free.

Therefore, O Lord,
as we celebrate the memorial of the blessed Passion,
the Resurrection from the dead,
and the glorious Ascension into heaven
of Christ, your Son, our Lord,
we, your servants and your holy people,
offer to your glorious majesty
from the gifts that you have given us,

this pure victim,
this holy victim,
this spotless victim,
the holy Bread of eternal life
and the Chalice of everlasting salvation.

Be pleased to look upon these offerings
with a serene and kindly countenance,
and to accept them,
as once you were pleased to accept
the gifts of your servant Abel the just,
the sacrifice of Abraham, our father in faith,
and the offering of your high priest Melchizedek,
a holy sacrifice, a spotless victim.

In humble prayer we ask you, almighty God:
command that these gifts be borne
by the hands of your holy Angel
to your altar on high
in the sight of your divine majesty,
so that all of us, who through this participation at the altar
receive the most holy Body and Blood of your Son,
may be filled with every grace and heavenly blessing.
(Through Christ our Lord. Amen.)

Commemoration of the Dead

Remember also, Lord, your servants N. and N.,
who have gone before us with the sign of faith
and rest in the sleep of peace.
Grant them, O Lord, we pray,
and all who sleep in Christ,
a place of refreshment, light and peace.
(Through Christ our Lord. Amen.)

To us, also, your servants, who, though sinners,
hope in your abundant mercies,
graciously grant some share

and fellowship with your holy Apostles and Martyrs:
with John the Baptist, Stephen,
Matthias, Barnabas,
(Ignatius, Alexander,
Marcellinus, Peter,
Felicity, Perpetua,
Agatha, Lucy,
Agnes, Cecilia, Anastasia)
and all your Saints;
admit us, we beseech you,
into their company,
not weighing our merits,
but granting us your pardon,
through Christ our Lord.

Through whom
you continue to make all these good things, O Lord;
you sanctify them, fill them with life,
bless them, and bestow them upon us.

The priest takes the chalice and the paten with the host and, raising both, he sings or says:

Through him, and with him, and in him, O God, almighty Father,

in the unity of the Ho-ly Spir-it, all glo-ry and hon-our is yours,

for ev-er and ev-er. A-men.

Then follows the Communion Rite, p. 485.

EUCHARISTIC PRAYER II

This Eucharistic Prayer has its own Preface, but it may also be used with other Prefaces.

The Lord be with you.
And with your spirit.

Lift up your hearts.
We lift them up to the Lord.

Let us give thanks to the Lord our God.
It is right and just.

It is truly right and just, our duty and our salvation,
always and everywhere to give you thanks, Father most holy,
through your beloved Son, Jesus Christ,
your Word through whom you made all things,
whom you sent as our Saviour and Redeemer,
incarnate by the Holy Spirit and born of the Virgin.

Fulfilling your will and gaining for you a holy people,
he stretched out his hands as he endured his Passion,
so as to break the bonds of death and manifest the resurrection.

And so, with the Angels and all the Saints
we declare your glory,
as with one voice we acclaim:

Holy, Holy, Holy Lord God of hosts.
Heaven and earth are full of your glory.
Hosanna in the highest.
Blessed is he who comes in the name of the Lord.
Hosanna in the highest.

The people kneel.

You are indeed Holy, O Lord,
the fount of all holiness.

Make holy, therefore, these gifts, we pray,
by sending down your Spirit upon them like the dewfall,
so that they may become for us
the Body and ✠ Blood of our Lord, Jesus Christ.

At the time he was betrayed
and entered willingly into his Passion,
he took bread and, giving thanks, broke it,
and gave it to his disciples, saying:

TAKE THIS, ALL OF YOU, AND EAT OF IT,
FOR THIS IS MY BODY,
WHICH WILL BE GIVEN UP FOR YOU.

In a similar way, when supper was ended,
he took the chalice
and, once more giving thanks,
he gave it to his disciples, saying:

TAKE THIS, ALL OF YOU, AND DRINK FROM IT,
FOR THIS IS THE CHALICE OF MY BLOOD,
THE BLOOD OF THE NEW AND ETERNAL COVENANT,
WHICH WILL BE POURED OUT FOR YOU AND FOR MANY
FOR THE FORGIVENESS OF SINS.

DO THIS IN MEMORY OF ME.

The mystery of faith.

The people acclaim:

We pro-claim your Death, O Lord, and pro-fess your Res-ur-rec- tion

un - til you come a- gain.

or

When we eat this Bread and drink this Cup, we pro-claim your

Death, O Lord, un-til you come a-gain.

or

Save us, Sav-iour of the world, for by your Cross and Res-ur-rec-tion

you have set us free.

Therefore, as we celebrate
the memorial of his Death and Resurrection,
we offer you, Lord,
the Bread of life and the Chalice of salvation,
giving thanks that you have held us worthy
to be in your presence and minister to you.

Humbly we pray
that, partaking of the Body and Blood of Christ,
we may be gathered into one by the Holy Spirit.

Remember, Lord, your Church,
spread throughout the world,
and bring her to the fullness of charity,
together with N. our Pope and N. our Bishop
and all the clergy.

In Masses for the Dead, the following may be added:
Remember your servant N.,
whom you have called (today)
from this world to yourself.
Grant that he (she) who was united with your Son in a death like his,
may also be one with him in his Resurrection.

Remember also our brothers and sisters
who have fallen asleep in the hope of the resurrection,
and all who have died in your mercy:
welcome them into the light of your face.
Have mercy on us all, we pray,
that with the Blessed Virgin Mary, Mother of God,
with the blessed Apostles,
and all the Saints who have pleased you throughout the ages,
we may merit to be coheirs to eternal life,
and may praise and glorify you
through your Son, Jesus Christ.

The priest takes the chalice and the paten with the host and, raising both, he sings or says:

Through him, and with him, and in him, O God, almighty Father,
in the unity of the Holy Spirit, all glory and honour is yours,
for ever and ever. **A- men.**

Then follows the Communion Rite, p. 485.

Eucharistic Prayer III

You are indeed Holy, O Lord,
and all you have created
rightly gives you praise,
for through your Son our Lord Jesus Christ,
by the power and working of the Holy Spirit,
you give life to all things and make them holy,
and you never cease to gather a people to yourself,
so that from the rising of the sun to its setting
a pure sacrifice may be offered to your name.

Therefore, O Lord, we humbly implore you:
by the same Spirit graciously make holy
these gifts we have brought to you for consecration,
that they may become the Body and ✠ Blood
of your Son our Lord Jesus Christ,
at whose command we celebrate these mysteries.

For on the night he was betrayed
he himself took bread,
and giving you thanks, he said the blessing,
broke the bread and gave it to his disciples, saying:

Take this, all of you, and eat of it,
for this is my Body,
which will be given up for you.

In a similar way, when supper was ended,
he took the chalice,
and, giving you thanks, he said the blessing,
and gave the chalice to his disciples, saying:

Take this, all of you, and drink from it,
for this is the chalice of my Blood,
the Blood of the new and eternal covenant,
which will be poured out for you and for many
for the forgiveness of sins.

Do this in memory of me.

The mystery of faith.

The people acclaim:

We pro-claim your Death, O Lord, and pro-fess your Res-ur-rec- tion

un - til you come a - gain.

or

When we eat this Bread and drink this Cup, we pro-claim your

Death, O Lord, un - til you come a- gain.

or

Save us, Sav-iour of the world, for by your Cross and Res-ur- rec-tion

you have set us free.

Therefore, O Lord, as we celebrate the memorial
of the saving Passion of your Son,
his wondrous Resurrection
and Ascension into heaven,
and as we look forward to his second coming,
we offer you in thanksgiving
this holy and living sacrifice.

Look, we pray, upon the oblation of your Church
and, recognising the sacrificial Victim by whose death

you willed to reconcile us to yourself,
grant that we, who are nourished
by the Body and Blood of your Son
and filled with his Holy Spirit,
may become one body, one spirit in Christ.

May he make of us
an eternal offering to you,
so that we may obtain an inheritance with your elect,
especially with the most Blessed Virgin Mary, Mother of God,
with your blessed Apostles and glorious Martyrs
(with Saint N.: the Saint of the day or Patron Saint)
and with all the Saints,
on whose constant intercession in your presence
we rely for unfailing help.

May this Sacrifice of our reconciliation,
we pray, O Lord,
advance the peace and salvation of all the world.
Be pleased to confirm in faith and charity
your pilgrim Church on earth,
with your servant N. our Pope and N. our Bishop,
the Order of Bishops, all the clergy,
and the entire people you have gained for your own.

Listen graciously to the prayers of this family,
whom you have summoned before you:
in your compassion, O merciful Father,
gather to yourself all your children
scattered throughout the world.

† To our departed brothers and sisters
and to all who were pleasing to you
at their passing from this life,
give kind admittance to your kingdom.
There we hope to enjoy for ever the fullness of your glory
through Christ our Lord,
through whom you bestow on the world all that is good. †

The priest takes the chalice and the paten with the host and, raising both, he sings or says:

Through him, and with him, and in him, O God, almighty Father,

in the unity of the Ho - ly Spir - it, all glo - ry and hon-our is yours,

for ev - er and ev - er. A - men.

Then follows the Communion Rite, p. 485.

When this Eucharistic Prayer is used in Masses for the Dead, the following may be said:

† Remember your servant N.
whom you have called (today)
from this world to yourself.
Grant that he (she) who was united with your Son in a death like his,
may also be one with him in his Resurrection,
when from the earth
he will raise up in the flesh those who have died,
and transform our lowly body
after the pattern of his own glorious body.
To our departed brothers and sisters, too,
and to all who were pleasing to you
at their passing from this life,
give kind admittance to your kingdom.
There we hope to enjoy for ever the fullness of your glory,
when you will wipe away every tear from our eyes.
For seeing you, our God, as you are,
we shall be like you for all the ages
and praise you without end,
through Christ our Lord,
through whom you bestow on the world all that is good. †

EUCHARISTIC PRAYER IV

It is not permitted to change the Preface of this Eucharistic Prayer because of the structure of the Prayer itself, which presents a summary of the history of salvation.

The Lord be with you.
And with your spirit.

Lift up your hearts.
We lift them up to the Lord.

Let us give thanks to the Lord our God.
It is right and just.

It is truly right to give you thanks,
truly just to give you glory, Father most holy,
for you are the one God living and true,
existing before all ages and abiding for all eternity,
dwelling in unapproachable light;
yet you, who alone are good, the source of life,
have made all that is,
so that you might fill your creatures with blessings
and bring joy to many of them by the glory of your light.

And so, in your presence are countless hosts of Angels,
who serve you day and night
and, gazing upon the glory of your face,
glorify you without ceasing.

With them we, too, confess your name in exultation,
giving voice to every creature under heaven,
as we acclaim:

Holy, Holy, Holy Lord God of hosts.
Heaven and earth are full of your glory.
Hosanna in the highest.
Blessed is he who comes in the name of the Lord.
Hosanna in the highest.

The people kneel.

We give you praise, Father most holy,
for you are great
and you have fashioned all your works
in wisdom and in love.
You formed man in your own image
and entrusted the whole world to his care,
so that in serving you alone, the Creator,
he might have dominion over all creatures.
And when through disobedience he had lost your friendship,
you did not abandon him to the domain of death.
For you came in mercy to the aid of all,
so that those who seek might find you.
Time and again you offered them covenants
and through the prophets
taught them to look forward to salvation.

And you so loved the world, Father most holy,
that in the fullness of time
you sent your Only Begotten Son to be our Saviour.
Made incarnate by the Holy Spirit
and born of the Virgin Mary,
he shared our human nature
in all things but sin.
To the poor he proclaimed the good news of salvation,
to prisoners, freedom,
and to the sorrowful of heart, joy.
To accomplish your plan,
he gave himself up to death,
and, rising from the dead,
he destroyed death and restored life.

And that we might live no longer for ourselves
but for him who died and rose again for us,
he sent the Holy Spirit from you, Father,
as the first fruits for those who believe,
so that, bringing to perfection his work in the world,
he might sanctify creation to the full.

Therefore, O Lord, we pray:
may this same Holy Spirit
graciously sanctify these offerings,
that they may become
the Body and ✠ Blood of our Lord Jesus Christ
for the celebration of this great mystery,
which he himself left us
as an eternal covenant.

For when the hour had come
for him to be glorified by you, Father most holy,
having loved his own who were in the world,
he loved them to the end:
and while they were at supper,
he took bread, blessed and broke it,
and gave it to his disciples, saying:

TAKE THIS, ALL OF YOU, AND EAT OF IT,
FOR THIS IS MY BODY,
WHICH WILL BE GIVEN UP FOR YOU.

In a similar way,
taking the chalice filled with the fruit of the vine,
he gave thanks,
and gave the chalice to his disciples, saying:

TAKE THIS, ALL OF YOU, AND DRINK FROM IT,
FOR THIS IS THE CHALICE OF MY BLOOD,
THE BLOOD OF THE NEW AND ETERNAL COVENANT,
WHICH WILL BE POURED OUT FOR YOU AND FOR MANY
FOR THE FORGIVENESS OF SINS.

DO THIS IN MEMORY OF ME.

The mystery of faith.

The people acclaim:

We pro-claim your Death, O Lord, and pro-fess your Res-ur-rec-tion

un-til you come a-gain.

or

When we eat this Bread and drink this Cup, we pro-claim your

Death, O Lord, un-til you come a-gain.

or

Save us, Sav-iour of the world, for by your Cross and Res-ur-rec-tion

you have set us free.

Therefore, O Lord,
as we now celebrate the memorial of our redemption,
we remember Christ's Death
and his descent to the realm of the dead,
we proclaim his Resurrection
and his Ascension to your right hand,
and as we await his coming in glory,
we offer you his Body and Blood,
the sacrifice acceptable to you
which brings salvation to the whole world.

Look, O Lord, upon the Sacrifice
which you yourself have provided for your Church,
and grant in your loving kindness
to all who partake of this one Bread and one Chalice
that, gathered into one body by the Holy Spirit,
they may truly become a living sacrifice in Christ
to the praise of your glory.

Therefore, Lord, remember now
all for whom we offer this sacrifice:
especially your servant N. our Pope,
N. our Bishop, and the whole Order of Bishops,
all the clergy,
those who take part in this offering,
those gathered here before you,
your entire people,
and all who seek you with a sincere heart.

Remember also
those who have died in the peace of your Christ
and all the dead,
whose faith you alone have known.

To all of us, your children,
grant, O merciful Father,
that we may enter into a heavenly inheritance
with the Blessed Virgin Mary, Mother of God,
and with your Apostles and Saints in your kingdom.
There, with the whole of creation,
freed from the corruption of sin and death,
may we glorify you through Christ our Lord,
through whom you bestow on the world all that is good.

The priest takes the chalice and the paten with the host and, raising both, he sings or says:

Through him, and with him, and in him, O God, almighty Father,

in the unity of the Ho-ly Spir-it, all glo-ry and hon-our is yours,

for ev-er and ev-er. A-men.

The Communion Rite
The Lord's Prayer

All stand.

At the Saviour's command
and formed by divine teaching,
we dare to say:

**Our Father, who art in heaven,
hallowed be thy name;
thy kingdom come,
thy will be done
on earth as it is in heaven.
Give us this day our daily bread,
and forgive us our trespasses,
as we forgive those who trespass against us;
and lead us not into temptation,
but deliver us from evil.**

Deliver us, Lord, we pray, from every evil,
graciously grant peace in our days,
that, by the help of your mercy,
we may be always free from sin
and safe from all distress,
as we await the blessed hope
and the coming of our Saviour, Jesus Christ.

**For the kingdom,
the power and the glory are yours
now and for ever.**

The Peace

Lord Jesus Christ,
who said to your Apostles:
Peace I leave you, my peace I give you,
look not on our sins,
but on the faith of your Church,

and graciously grant her peace and unity
in accordance with your will.
Who live and reign for ever and ever.
Amen.

The peace of the Lord be with you always.
And with your spirit.

Then the deacon, or the priest, says:

Let us offer each other the sign of peace.

And all offer one another the customary sign of peace: an
expression of peace, communion and charity.

Breaking of the Bread

Then the priest takes the host, breaks it over the paten, and places a
small piece in the chalice.

Meanwhile all sing or say:

**Lamb of God, you take away the sins of the world,
     have mercy on us.
Lamb of God, you take away the sins of the world,
     have mercy on us.
Lamb of God, you take away the sins of the world,
     grant us peace.**

Invitation to Communion

All kneel.
After his private prayers of preparation the priest genuflects, takes
the host and, holding it slightly raised above the paten or above the
chalice, says aloud:

Behold the Lamb of God,
behold him who takes away the sins of the world.
Blessed are those called to the supper of the Lamb.

**Lord, I am not worthy
that you should enter under my roof,
but only say the word
and my soul shall be healed.**

Communion Procession

After the priest has consumed the Body and Blood of Christ, the people come forward in reverent procession to receive Communion. The Communion Antiphon may be said or sung, or a hymn or psalm may be sung. The priest or minister raises the host slightly and shows it to each of the communicants, saying:

The Body of Christ.
Amen.

When Communion is ministered under both kinds, the minister of the chalice offers it to each of the communicants, saying:

The Blood of Christ.
Amen.

After the distribution of Communion, if appropriate, a silence may be observed, or a psalm or other canticle of praise or a hymn may be sung.

Prayer after Communion

Then the priest says:

Let us pray.

All stand and pray in silence. Then the priest says the Prayer after Communion, at the end of which the people acclaim:
Amen.

The Concluding Rites

We are sent out to fulfil in our daily lives our mission to witness to Christ in the world.

Any brief announcements now follow.

Blessing

On certain days, another more solemn form of blessing may be used instead (see pages 508-518).

The Lord be with you.
And with your spirit.

May almighty God bless you,
the Father, and the Son, ✠ and the Holy Spirit.
Amen.

In a Pontifical Mass, the celebrant says:

The Lord be with you.
And with your spirit.

Blessed be the name of the Lord.
Now and for ever.

Our help is in the name of the Lord.
Who made heaven and earth.

May almighty God bless you,
the Father, ✠ and the Son, ✠ and the Holy ✠ Spirit.
Amen.

Dismissal

Then the deacon or the priest says or sings:

Go forth, the Mass is ended.

or

Go and announce the Gospel of the Lord.

or

Go in peace, glorifying the Lord by your life.

or

Go in peace.

Thanks be to God.

A hymn may be sung as the priest and ministers leave the altar.

Prefaces

PREFACE I OF ADVENT

From the First Sunday of Advent to 16 December.

It is truly right and just, our duty and our salvation,
always and everywhere to give you thanks,
Lord, holy Father, almighty and eternal God,
through Christ our Lord.

For he assumed at his first coming
the lowliness of human flesh,
and so fulfilled the design you formed long ago,
and opened for us the way to eternal salvation,
that, when he comes again in glory and majesty
and all is at last made manifest,
we who watch for that day
may inherit the great promise
in which now we dare to hope.

And so, with Angels and Archangels,
with Thrones and Dominions,
and with all the hosts and Powers of heaven,
we sing the hymn of your glory,
as without end we acclaim:

Holy, Holy, Holy Lord God of hosts…

PREFACE II OF ADVENT

From 17 December to 24 December.

It is truly right and just, our duty and our salvation,
always and everywhere to give you thanks,
Lord, holy Father, almighty and eternal God,
through Christ our Lord.

For all the oracles of the prophets foretold him,
the Virgin Mother longed for him
with love beyond all telling,
John the Baptist sang of his coming
and proclaimed his presence when he came.

It is by his gift that already we rejoice
at the mystery of his Nativity,
so that he may find us watchful in prayer
and exultant in his praise.

And so, with Angels and Archangels,
with Thrones and Dominions,
and with all the hosts and Powers of heaven,
we sing the hymn of your glory,
as without end we acclaim:

Holy, Holy, Holy Lord God of hosts…

PREFACE I OF THE NATIVITY OF THE LORD

It is truly right and just, our duty and our salvation,
always and everywhere to give you thanks,
Lord, holy Father, almighty and eternal God.

For in the mystery of the Word made flesh
a new light of your glory has shone upon the eyes of our mind,
so that, as we recognise in him God made visible,
we may be caught up through him in love of things invisible.

And so, with Angels and Archangels,
with Thrones and Dominions,
and with all the hosts and Powers of heaven,
we sing the hymn of your glory,
as without end we acclaim:

Holy, Holy, Holy Lord God of hosts…

PREFACE II OF THE NATIVITY OF THE LORD

It is truly right and just, our duty and our salvation,
always and everywhere to give you thanks,
Lord, holy Father, almighty and eternal God,
through Christ our Lord.

For on the feast of this awe-filled mystery,
though invisible in his own divine nature,
he has appeared visibly in ours;
and begotten before all ages,
he has begun to exist in time;
so that, raising up in himself all that was cast down,
he might restore unity to all creation
and call straying humanity back to the heavenly Kingdom.

And so, with all the Angels, we praise you,
as in joyful celebration we acclaim:

Holy, Holy, Holy Lord God of hosts…

PREFACE III OF THE NATIVITY OF THE LORD

It is truly right and just, our duty and our salvation,
always and everywhere to give you thanks,
Lord, holy Father, almighty and eternal God,
through Christ our Lord.

For through him the holy exchange that restores our life
has shone forth today in splendour:
when our frailty is assumed by your Word
not only does human mortality receive unending honour
but by this wondrous union we, too, are made eternal.

And so, in company with the choirs of Angels,
we praise you, and with joy we proclaim:

Holy, Holy, Holy Lord God of hosts…

PREFACE OF THE EPIPHANY OF THE LORD

It is truly right and just, our duty and our salvation,
always and everywhere to give you thanks,
Lord, holy Father, almighty and eternal God.

For today you have revealed the mystery
of our salvation in Christ
as a light for the nations,
and, when he appeared in our mortal nature,
you made us new by the glory of his immortal nature.

And so, with Angels and Archangels,
with Thrones and Dominions,
and with all the hosts and Powers of heaven,
we sing the hymn of your glory,
as without end we acclaim:

Holy, Holy, Holy Lord God of hosts...

PREFACE I OF LENT

It is truly right and just, our duty and our salvation,
always and everywhere to give you thanks,
Lord, holy Father, almighty and eternal God,
through Christ our Lord.

For by your gracious gift each year
your faithful await the sacred paschal feasts
with the joy of minds made pure,
so that, more eagerly intent on prayer
and on the works of charity,
and participating in the mysteries
by which they have been reborn,
they may be led to the fullness of grace
that you bestow on your sons and daughters.

And so, with Angels and Archangels,
with Thrones and Dominions,
and with all the hosts and Powers of heaven,
we sing the hymn of your glory,
as without end we acclaim:

Holy, Holy, Holy Lord God of hosts...

PREFACE II OF LENT

It is truly right and just, our duty and our salvation,
always and everywhere to give you thanks,
Lord, holy Father, almighty and eternal God.

For you have given your children a sacred time
for the renewing and purifying of their hearts,
that, freed from disordered affections,
they may so deal with the things of this passing world
as to hold rather to the things that eternally endure.

And so, with all the Angels and Saints,
we praise you, as without end we acclaim:

Holy, Holy, Holy Lord God of hosts…

PREFACE III OF LENT

It is truly right and just, our duty and our salvation,
always and everywhere to give you thanks,
Lord, holy Father, almighty and eternal God.

For you will that our self-denial should give you thanks,
humble our sinful pride,
contribute to the feeding of the poor,
and so help us imitate you in your kindness.

And so we glorify you with countless Angels,
as with one voice of praise we acclaim:

Holy, Holy, Holy Lord God of hosts…

PREFACE IV OF LENT

It is truly right and just, our duty and our salvation,
always and everywhere to give you thanks,
Lord, holy Father, almighty and eternal God.

For through bodily fasting you restrain our faults,
raise up our minds,

and bestow both virtue and its rewards,
through Christ our Lord.

Through him the Angels praise your majesty,
Dominions adore and Powers tremble before you.
Heaven and the Virtues of heaven and the blessed Seraphim
worship together with exultation.
May our voices, we pray, join with theirs
in humble praise, as we acclaim:

Holy, Holy, Holy Lord God of hosts…

PREFACE I OF EASTER

It is truly right and just, our duty and our salvation,
at all times to acclaim you, O Lord,
but (on this night / on this day / in this time) above all
to laud you yet more gloriously,
when Christ our Passover has been sacrificed.

For he is the true Lamb
who has taken away the sins of the world;
by dying he has destroyed our death,
and by rising, restored our life.

Therefore, overcome with paschal joy,
every land, every people exults in your praise
and even the heavenly Powers, with the angelic hosts,
sing together the unending hymn of your glory,
as they acclaim:

Holy, Holy, Holy Lord God of hosts…

PREFACE II OF EASTER

It is truly right and just, our duty and our salvation,
at all times to acclaim you, O Lord,
but in this time above all to laud you yet more gloriously,
when Christ our Passover has been sacrificed.

Through him the children of light rise to eternal life
and the halls of the heavenly Kingdom
are thrown open to the faithful;
for his Death is our ransom from death,
and in his rising the life of all has risen.

Therefore, overcome with paschal joy,
every land, every people exults in your praise
and even the heavenly Powers, with the angelic hosts,
sing together the unending hymn of your glory,
as they acclaim:

Holy, Holy, Holy Lord God of hosts...

PREFACE III OF EASTER

It is truly right and just, our duty and our salvation,
at all times to acclaim you, O Lord,
but in this time above all to laud you yet more gloriously,
when Christ our Passover has been sacrificed.

He never ceases to offer himself for us
but defends us and ever pleads our cause before you:
he is the sacrificial Victim who dies no more,
the Lamb, once slain, who lives for ever.

Therefore, overcome with paschal joy,
every land, every people exults in your praise
and even the heavenly Powers, with the angelic hosts,
sing together the unending hymn of your glory,
as they acclaim:

Holy, Holy, Holy Lord God of hosts...

PREFACE IV OF EASTER

It is truly right and just, our duty and our salvation,
at all times to acclaim you, O Lord,
but in this time above all to laud you yet more gloriously,
when Christ our Passover has been sacrificed.

For, with the old order destroyed,
a universe cast down is renewed,
and integrity of life is restored to us in Christ.

Therefore, overcome with paschal joy,
every land, every people exults in your praise
and even the heavenly Powers, with the angelic hosts,
sing together the unending hymn of your glory,
as they acclaim:

Holy, Holy, Holy Lord God of hosts…

PREFACE V OF EASTER

It is truly right and just, our duty and our salvation,
at all times to acclaim you, O Lord,
but in this time above all to laud you yet more gloriously,
when Christ our Passover has been sacrificed.

By the oblation of his Body,
he brought the sacrifices of old to fulfilment
in the reality of the Cross
and, by commending himself to you for our salvation,
showed himself the Priest, the Altar, and the Lamb of sacrifice.

Therefore, overcome with paschal joy,
every land, every people exults in your praise
and even the heavenly Powers, with the angelic hosts,
sing together the unending hymn of your glory,
as they acclaim:

Holy, Holy, Holy Lord God of hosts…

PREFACE I OF THE ASCENSION OF THE LORD

It is truly right and just, our duty and our salvation,
always and everywhere to give you thanks,
Lord, holy Father, almighty and eternal God.

For the Lord Jesus, the King of glory,
conqueror of sin and death,
ascended (today) to the highest heavens,
as the Angels gazed in wonder.

Mediator between God and man,
judge of the world and Lord of hosts,
he ascended, not to distance himself from our lowly state
but that we, his members, might be confident of following
where he, our Head and Founder, has gone before.

Therefore, overcome with paschal joy,
every land, every people exults in your praise
and even the heavenly Powers, with the angelic hosts,
sing together the unending hymn of your glory,
as they acclaim:

Holy, Holy, Holy Lord God of hosts…

PREFACE II OF THE ASCENSION OF THE LORD

It is truly right and just, our duty and our salvation,
always and everywhere to give you thanks,
Lord, holy Father, almighty and eternal God,
through Christ our Lord.

For after his Resurrection
he plainly appeared to all his disciples
and was taken up to heaven in their sight,
that he might make us sharers in his divinity.

Therefore, overcome with paschal joy,
every land, every people exults in your praise
and even the heavenly Powers, with the angelic hosts,
sing together the unending hymn of your glory,
as they acclaim:

Holy, Holy, Holy Lord God of hosts…

PREFACE I OF THE SUNDAYS IN ORDINARY TIME

It is truly right and just, our duty and our salvation,
always and everywhere to give you thanks,
Lord, holy Father, almighty and eternal God,
through Christ our Lord.

For through his Paschal Mystery,
he accomplished the marvellous deed,
by which he has freed us from the yoke of sin and death,
summoning us to the glory of being now called
a chosen race, a royal priesthood,
a holy nation, a people for your own possession,
to proclaim everywhere your mighty works,
for you have called us out of darkness
into your own wonderful light.

And so, with Angels and Archangels,
with Thrones and Dominions,
and with all the hosts and Powers of heaven,
we sing the hymn of your glory,
as without end we acclaim:

Holy, Holy, Holy Lord God of hosts…

PREFACE II OF THE SUNDAYS IN ORDINARY TIME

It is truly right and just, our duty and our salvation,
always and everywhere to give you thanks,
Lord, holy Father, almighty and eternal God,
through Christ our Lord.

For out of compassion for the waywardness that is ours,
he humbled himself and was born of the Virgin;
by the passion of the Cross he freed us from unending death,
and by rising from the dead he gave us life eternal.

And so, with Angels and Archangels,
with Thrones and Dominions,
and with all the hosts and Powers of heaven,
we sing the hymn of your glory,
as without end we acclaim:

Holy, Holy, Holy Lord God of hosts…

PREFACE III OF THE SUNDAYS IN ORDINARY TIME

It is truly right and just, our duty and our salvation,
always and everywhere to give you thanks,
Lord, holy Father, almighty and eternal God.

For we know it belongs to your boundless glory,
that you came to the aid of mortal beings with your divinity
and even fashioned for us a remedy out of mortality itself,
that the cause of our downfall
might become the means of our salvation,
through Christ our Lord.

Through him the host of Angels adores your majesty
and rejoices in your presence for ever.
May our voices, we pray, join with theirs
in one chorus of exultant praise, as we acclaim:

Holy, Holy, Holy Lord God of hosts…

PREFACE IV OF THE SUNDAYS IN ORDINARY TIME

It is truly right and just, our duty and our salvation,
always and everywhere to give you thanks,
Lord, holy Father, almighty and eternal God,
through Christ our Lord.

For by his birth he brought renewal
to humanity's fallen state,
and by his suffering cancelled out our sins;
by his rising from the dead
he has opened the way to eternal life,
and by ascending to you, O Father,
he has unlocked the gates of heaven.

And so, with the company of Angels and Saints,
we sing the hymn of your praise,
as without end we acclaim:

Holy, Holy, Holy Lord God of hosts…

PREFACE V OF THE SUNDAYS IN ORDINARY TIME

It is truly right and just, our duty and our salvation,
always and everywhere to give you thanks,
Lord, holy Father, almighty and eternal God.

For you laid the foundations of the world
and have arranged the changing of times and seasons;
you formed man in your own image
and set humanity over the whole world in all its wonder,
to rule in your name over all you have made
and for ever praise you in your mighty works,
through Christ our Lord.

And so, with all the Angels, we praise you,
as in joyful celebration we acclaim:

Holy, Holy, Holy Lord God of hosts...

PREFACE VI OF THE SUNDAYS IN ORDINARY TIME

It is truly right and just, our duty and our salvation,
always and everywhere to give you thanks,
Lord, holy Father, almighty and eternal God.

For in you we live and move and have our being,
and while in this body
we not only experience the daily effects of your care,
but even now possess the pledge of life eternal.

For, having received the first fruits of the Spirit,
through whom you raised up Jesus from the dead,
we hope for an everlasting share in the Paschal Mystery.

And so, with all the Angels, we praise you,
as in joyful celebration we acclaim:

Holy, Holy, Holy Lord God of hosts...

PREFACE VII OF THE SUNDAYS IN ORDINARY TIME

It is truly right and just, our duty and our salvation,
always and everywhere to give you thanks,
Lord, holy Father, almighty and eternal God.

For you so loved the world
that in your mercy you sent us the Redeemer,
to live like us in all things but sin,
so that you might love in us what you loved in your Son,
by whose obedience we have been restored to those gifts of yours
that, by sinning, we had lost in disobedience.

And so, Lord, with all the Angels and Saints,
we, too, give you thanks, as in exultation we acclaim:

Holy, Holy, Holy Lord God of hosts...

PREFACE VIII OF THE SUNDAYS IN ORDINARY TIME

It is truly right and just, our duty and our salvation,
always and everywhere to give you thanks,
Lord, holy Father, almighty and eternal God.

For, when your children were scattered afar by sin,
through the Blood of your Son and the power of the Spirit,
you gathered them again to yourself,
that a people, formed as one by the unity of the Trinity,
made the body of Christ and the temple of the Holy Spirit,
might, to the praise of your manifold wisdom,
be manifest as the Church.

And so, in company with the choirs of Angels,
we praise you, and with joy we proclaim:

Holy, Holy, Holy Lord God of hosts...

PREFACE I OF THE MOST HOLY EUCHARIST

It is truly right and just, our duty and our salvation,
always and everywhere to give you thanks,
Lord, holy Father, almighty and eternal God,
through Christ our Lord.

For he is the true and eternal Priest,
who instituted the pattern of an everlasting sacrifice
and was the first to offer himself as the saving Victim,
commanding us to make this offering as his memorial.
As we eat his flesh that was sacrificed for us,
we are made strong,
and, as we drink his Blood that was poured out for us,
we are washed clean.

And so, with Angels and Archangels,
with Thrones and Dominions,
and with all the hosts and Powers of heaven,
we sing the hymn of your glory,
as without end we acclaim:

Holy, Holy, Holy Lord God of hosts…

PREFACE II OF THE MOST HOLY EUCHARIST

It is truly right and just, our duty and our salvation,
always and everywhere to give you thanks,
Lord, holy Father, almighty and eternal God,
through Christ our Lord.

For at the Last Supper with his Apostles,
establishing for the ages to come the saving memorial of the Cross,
he offered himself to you as the unblemished Lamb,
the acceptable gift of perfect praise.

Nourishing your faithful by this sacred mystery,
you make them holy, so that the human race,
bounded by one world,
may be enlightened by one faith
and united by one bond of charity.

And so, we approach the table of this wondrous Sacrament,
so that, bathed in the sweetness of your grace,
we may pass over to the heavenly realities here foreshadowed.

Therefore, all creatures of heaven and earth
sing a new song in adoration,
and we, with all the host of Angels,
cry out, and without end we acclaim:

Holy, Holy, Holy Lord God of hosts…

PREFACE I OF THE BLESSED VIRGIN MARY

It is truly right and just, our duty and our salvation,
always and everywhere to give you thanks,
Lord, holy Father, almighty and eternal God,
and to praise, bless, and glorify your name
(on the Solemnity of the Motherhood / on the feast day / on the
    Nativity / in veneration)
of the Blessed ever-Virgin Mary.

For by the overshadowing of the Holy Spirit
she conceived your Only Begotten Son,
and without losing the glory of virginity,
brought forth into the world the eternal Light,
Jesus Christ our Lord.

Through him the Angels praise your majesty,
Dominions adore and Powers tremble before you.
Heaven and the Virtues of heaven and the blessed Seraphim
worship together with exultation.
May our voices, we pray, join with theirs
in humble praise, as we acclaim:

Holy, Holy, Holy Lord God of hosts…

PREFACE I FOR THE DEAD

It is truly right and just, our duty and our salvation,
always and everywhere to give you thanks,
Lord, holy Father, almighty and eternal God,
through Christ our Lord.

In him the hope of blessed resurrection has dawned,
that those saddened by the certainty of dying
might be consoled by the promise of immortality to come.
Indeed for your faithful, Lord,
life is changed not ended,
and, when this earthly dwelling turns to dust,
an eternal dwelling is made ready for them in heaven.

And so, with Angels and Archangels,
with Thrones and Dominions,
and with all the hosts and Powers of heaven,
we sing the hymn of your glory,
as without end we acclaim:

Holy, Holy, Holy Lord God of hosts…

PREFACE II FOR THE DEAD

It is truly right and just, our duty and our salvation,
always and everywhere to give you thanks,
Lord, holy Father, almighty and eternal God,
through Christ our Lord.

For as one alone he accepted death,
so that we might all escape from dying;
as one man he chose to die,
so that in your sight we all might live for ever.

And so, in company with the choirs of Angels,
we praise you, and with joy we proclaim:

Holy, Holy, Holy Lord God of hosts…

PREFACE III FOR THE DEAD

It is truly right and just, our duty and our salvation,
always and everywhere to give you thanks,
Lord, holy Father, almighty and eternal God,
through Christ our Lord.

For he is the salvation of the world,
the life of the human race,
the resurrection of the dead.

Through him the host of Angels adores your majesty
and rejoices in your presence for ever.
May our voices, we pray, join with theirs
in one chorus of exultant praise, as we acclaim:

Holy, Holy, Holy Lord God of hosts…

PREFACE IV FOR THE DEAD

It is truly right and just, our duty and our salvation,
always and everywhere to give you thanks,
Lord, holy Father, almighty and eternal God.

For it is at your summons that we come to birth,
by your will that we are governed,
and at your command that we return,
on account of sin,
to the earth from which we came.

And when you give the sign,
we who have been redeemed by the Death of your Son,
shall be raised up to the glory of his Resurrection.

And so, with the company of Angels and Saints,
we sing the hymn of your praise,
as without end we acclaim:

Holy, Holy, Holy Lord God of hosts…

PREFACE V FOR THE DEAD

It is truly right and just, our duty and our salvation,
always and everywhere to give you thanks,
Lord, holy Father, almighty and eternal God.

For even though by our own fault we perish,
yet by your compassion and your grace,
when seized by death according to our sins,
we are redeemed through Christ's great victory,
and with him called back into life.

And so, with the Powers of heaven,
we worship you constantly on earth,
and before your majesty
without end we acclaim:

Holy, Holy, Holy Lord God of hosts…

Solemn Blessings at the End of Mass

Advent
May the almighty and merciful God,
by whose grace you have placed your faith
in the First Coming of his Only Begotten Son
and yearn for his coming again
sanctify you by the radiance of Christ's Advent
and enrich you with his blessing.
Amen.

As you run the race of this present life,
may he make you firm in faith,
joyful in hope and active in charity.
Amen.

So that, rejoicing now with devotion
at the Redeemer's coming in the flesh,
you may be endowed with the rich reward of eternal life
when he comes again in majesty.
Amen.

And may the blessing of almighty God,
the Father, and the Son, ✠ and the Holy Spirit,
come down on you and remain with you for ever.
Amen.

The Nativity of the Lord
May the God of infinite goodness,
who by the Incarnation of his Son has driven darkness from the
    world
and by that glorious Birth has illumined this most holy night (day),
drive far from you the darkness of vice
and illumine your hearts with the light of virtue.
Amen.

May God, who willed that the great joy
of his Son's saving Birth
be announced to shepherds by the Angel,
fill your minds with the gladness he gives
and make you heralds of his Gospel.
Amen.

And may God, who by the Incarnation
brought together the earthly and heavenly realm,
fill you with the gift of his peace and favour
and make you sharers with the Church in heaven.
Amen.

And may the blessing of almighty God,
the Father, and the Son, ✠ and the Holy Spirit,
come down on you and remain with you for ever.
Amen.

The Beginning of the Year
May God, the source and origin of all blessing,
grant you grace,
pour out his blessing in abundance,
and keep you safe from harm throughout the year.
Amen.

May he give you integrity in the faith,
endurance in hope,
and perseverance in charity
with holy patience to the end.
Amen.

May he order your days and your deeds in his peace,
grant your prayers in this and in every place,
and lead you happily to eternal life.
Amen.

And may the blessing of almighty God,
the Father, and the Son, ✠ and the Holy Spirit,
come down on you and remain with you for ever.
Amen.

The Epiphany of the Lord
May God, who has called you
out of darkness into his wonderful light,
pour out in kindness his blessing upon you
and make your hearts firm
in faith, hope and charity.
Amen.

And since in all confidence you follow Christ,
who today appeared in the world
as a light shining in darkness,
may God make you, too,
a light for your brothers and sisters.
Amen.

And so when your pilgrimage is ended,
may you come to him
whom the Magi sought as they followed the star
and whom they found with great joy, the Light from Light,
who is Christ the Lord.
Amen.

And may the blessing of almighty God,
the Father, and the Son, ✠ and the Holy Spirit,
come down on you and remain with you for ever.
Amen.

The Passion of the Lord
May God, the Father of mercies,
who has given you an example of love
in the Passion of his Only Begotten Son,
grant that, by serving God and your neighbour,
you may lay hold of the wondrous gift of his blessing.
Amen.

So that you may receive the reward of everlasting life from him,
through whose earthly Death
you believe that you escape eternal death.
Amen.

And by following the example of his self-abasement,
may you possess a share in his Resurrection.
Amen.

And may the blessing of almighty God,
the Father, and the Son, ✠ and the Holy Spirit,
come down on you and remain with you for ever.
Amen.

Easter Time
May God, who by the Resurrection of his Only Begotten Son
was pleased to confer on you
the gift of redemption and of adoption,
give you gladness by his blessing.
Amen.

May he, by whose redeeming work
you have received the gift of everlasting freedom,
make you heirs to an eternal inheritance.
Amen.

And may you, who have already risen with Christ
in Baptism through faith,
by living in a right manner on this earth,
be united with him in the homeland of heaven.
Amen.

And may the blessing of almighty God,
the Father, and the Son, ✠ and the Holy Spirit,
come down on you and remain with you for ever.
Amen.

The Ascension of the Lord
May almighty God bless you,
for on this very day his Only Begotten Son
pierced the heights of heaven
and unlocked for you the way
to ascend to where he is.
Amen.

May he grant that,
as Christ after his Resurrection
was seen plainly by his disciples,
so when he comes as Judge
he may show himself merciful to you for all eternity.
Amen.

And may you, who believe he is seated
with the Father in his majesty,
know with joy the fulfilment of his promise
to stay with you until the end of time.
Amen.

And may the blessing of almighty God,
the Father, and the Son, ✠ and the Holy Spirit,
come down on you and remain with you for ever.
Amen.

The Holy Spirit

May God, the Father of lights,
who was pleased to enlighten the disciples' minds
by the outpouring of the Spirit, the Paraclete,
grant you gladness by his blessing
and make you always abound with the gifts of the same Spirit.
Amen.

May the wondrous flame that appeared above the disciples,
powerfully cleanse your hearts from every evil
and pervade them with its purifying light.
Amen.

And may God, who has been pleased to unite many tongues
in the profession of one faith,
give you perseverance in that same faith
and, by believing, may you journey from hope to clear vision.
Amen.

And may the blessing of almighty God,
the Father, and the Son, ✠ and the Holy Spirit,
come down on you and remain with you for ever.
Amen.

Ordinary Time I

May the Lord bless you and keep you.
Amen.

May he let his face shine upon you
and show you his mercy.
Amen.

May he turn his countenance towards you
and give you his peace.
Amen.

And may the blessing of almighty God,
the Father, and the Son, ✠ and the Holy Spirit,
come down on you and remain with you for ever.
Amen.

Ordinary Time II

May the peace of God,
which surpasses all understanding,
keep your hearts and minds
in the knowledge and love of God,
and of his Son, our Lord Jesus Christ.
Amen.

And may the blessing of almighty God,
the Father, and the Son, ✠ and the Holy Spirit,
come down on you and remain with you for ever.
Amen.

Ordinary Time III

May almighty God bless you in his kindness
and pour out saving wisdom upon you.
Amen.

May he nourish you always with the teachings of the faith
and make you persevere in holy deeds.
Amen.

May he turn your steps towards himself
and show you the path of charity and peace.
Amen.

And may the blessing of almighty God,
the Father, and the Son, ✠ and the Holy Spirit,
come down on you and remain with you for ever.
Amen.

Ordinary Time IV
May the God of all consolation order your days in his peace
and grant you the gifts of his blessing.
Amen.

May he free you always from every distress
and confirm your hearts in his love.
Amen.

So that on this life's journey
you may be effective in good works,
rich in the gifts of hope, faith and charity,
and may come happily to eternal life.
Amen.

And may the blessing of almighty God,
the Father, and the Son, ✠ and the Holy Spirit,
come down on you and remain with you for ever.
Amen.

Ordinary Time V
May almighty God always keep every adversity far from you
and in his kindness pour out upon you the gifts of his blessing.
Amen.

May God keep your hearts attentive to his words,
that they may be filled with everlasting gladness.
Amen.

And so, may you always understand what is good and right,
and be found ever hastening along
in the path of God's commands,
made coheirs with the citizens of heaven.
Amen.

And may the blessing of almighty God,
the Father, and the Son, ✠ and the Holy Spirit,
come down on you and remain with you for ever.
Amen.

Ordinary Time VI
May God bless you with every heavenly blessing,
make you always holy and pure in his sight,
pour out in abundance upon you the riches of his glory,
and teach you with the words of truth;
may he instruct you in the Gospel of salvation,
and ever endow you with fraternal charity.
Through Christ our Lord.
Amen.

And may the blessing of almighty God,
the Father, and the Son, ✠ and the Holy Spirit,
come down on you and remain with you for ever.
Amen.

The Blessed Virgin Mary
May God, who through the childbearing of the Blessed Virgin Mary
willed in his great kindness to redeem the human race,
be pleased to enrich you with his blessing.
Amen.

May you know always and everywhere
the protection of her,
through whom you have been found worthy to receive
the author of life.
Amen.

May you, who have devoutly gathered on this day,
carry away with you the gifts of spiritual joys and heavenly rewards.
Amen.

And may the blessing of almighty God,
the Father, and the Son, ✠ and the Holy Spirit,
come down on you and remain with you for ever.
Amen.

Saints Peter and Paul, Apostles
May almighty God bless you,
for he has made you steadfast in Saint Peter's saving confession
and through it has set you on the solid rock of the Church's faith.
Amen.

And having instructed you
by the tireless preaching of Saint Paul,
may God teach you constantly by his example
to win brothers and sisters for Christ.
Amen.

So that by the keys of Saint Peter and the words of Saint Paul,
and by the support of their intercession,
God may bring us happily to that homeland
that Peter attained on a cross
and Paul by the blade of a sword.
Amen.

And may the blessing of almighty God,
the Father, and the Son, ✠ and the Holy Spirit,
come down on you and remain with you for ever.
Amen.

The Apostles
May God, who has granted you
to stand firm on apostolic foundations,
graciously bless you through the glorious merits
of the holy Apostles N. and N. (the holy Apostle N.).
Amen.

And may he who endowed you
with the teaching and example of the Apostles,
make you, under their protection,
witnesses to the truth before all.
Amen.

So that through the intercession of the Apostles,
you may inherit the eternal homeland,
for by their teaching you possess firmness of faith.
Amen.

And may the blessing of almighty God,
the Father, and the Son, ✠ and the Holy Spirit,
come down on you and remain with you for ever.
Amen.

All Saints
May God, the glory and joy of the Saints,
who has caused you to be strengthened
by means of their outstanding prayers,
bless you with unending blessings
Amen.

Freed through their intercession from present ills
and formed by the example of their holy way of life,
may you be ever devoted
to serving God and your neighbour.
Amen.

So that, together with all,
you may possess the joys of the homeland,
where Holy Church rejoices
that her children are admitted in perpetual peace
to the company of the citizens of heaven.
Amen.

And may the blessing of almighty God,
the Father, and the Son, ✠ and the Holy Spirit,
come down on you and remain with you for ever.
Amen.

For the Dedication of a Church
May God, the Lord of heaven and earth,
who has gathered you today for the dedication of this church,
make you abound in heavenly blessings.
Amen.

And may he who has willed that all his scattered children
should be gathered together in his Son,
grant that you may become his temple
and the dwelling place of the Holy Spirit.
Amen.

And so, when you are thoroughly cleansed,
may God dwell within you
and grant you to possess with all the Saints
the inheritance of eternal happiness.
Amen.

And may the blessing of almighty God,
the Father, and the Son, ✠ and the Holy Spirit,
come down on you and remain with you for ever.
Amen.

In Celebrations for the Dead
May the God of all consolation bless you,
for in his unfathomable goodness he created the human race,
and in the Resurrection of his Only Begotten Son
he has given believers the hope of rising again.
Amen.

To us who are alive, may God grant pardon for our sins,
and to all the dead, a place of light and peace.
Amen.

So may we all live happily for ever with Christ,
whom we believe truly rose from the dead.
Amen.

And may the blessing of almighty God,
the Father, and the Son, ✠ and the Holy Spirit,
come down on you and remain with you for ever.
Amen.

THANKSGIVING AFTER MASS

Prayer of Thanksgiving to God the Father
We thank you, holy Father,
for your holy name
which you have made dwell in our hearts,
and for the knowledge, faith and immortality
which you have made known to us through your servant Jesus.
Glory be to you for ever.

You, almighty Lord,
created all things for your glory,
and you give food and drink to humankind
that they may enjoy it and give thanks to you.
But to us you give spiritual food and drink
and life eternal through your servant.
Above all we thank you for your power.
Glory be to you for ever.

Be mindful of your Church, Lord,
deliver her from all evil,
perfect her in your love,
gather her, your holy Church, from the four winds
into the kingdom you have prepared for her.
For yours is the power and the glory
for ever and ever.
Let grace come, and this world pass away!
Hosanna to the God of David!
If anyone is holy, let him draw near;
if anyone is not holy, let him repent.
Come, Lord! Amen!

The Didache, **first or second century**

Litany of Thanksgiving
Alleluia!

Give thanks to the Lord, for he is good,
   his love is everlasting!
Give thanks to the God of gods,
   his love is everlasting!
Give thanks to the Lord of lords,
   his love is everlasting!

He alone performs great marvels,
   his love is everlasting!
His wisdom made the heavens,
   his love is everlasting!
He set the earth on the waters,
   his love is everlasting!

He made the great lights,
   his love is everlasting!
The sun to govern the day,
   his love is everlasting!
Moon and stars to govern the night,
   his love is everlasting!

He struck down the first-born of Egypt,
   his love is everlasting!
And brought Israel out,
   his love is everlasting!
With mighty hand and outstretched arm,
   his love is everlasting!

He split the Sea of Reeds,
   his love is everlasting!
Led Israel through the middle,
   his love is everlasting!
Drowned Pharaoh and his army,
   his love is everlasting!

He led his people through the wilderness,
    his love is everlasting!
He remembered us when we were down,
    his love is everlasting!
And snatched us from our oppressors,
    his love is everlasting!

He provides for all living creatures,
    his love is everlasting!
Give thanks to the God of Heaven,
    his love is everlasting!

Psalm 136:1-16. 23-26

Magnificat
My soul proclaims the greatness of the Lord
and my spirit exults in God my saviour;
because he has looked upon his lowly handmaid.
Yes, from this day forward all generations will call me blessed,
for the Almighty has done great things for me.
Holy is his name,
and his mercy reaches from age to age for those who fear him.
He has shown the power of his arm,
he has routed the proud of heart.
He has pulled down princes from their thrones and exalted the
    lowly.
The hungry he has filled with good things, the rich sent empty
    away.
He has come to the help of Israel his servant, mindful of his mercy
– according to the promise he made to our ancestors –
of his mercy to Abraham and to his descendants for ever.

Luke 1:46-55

Prayer to Jesus Christ Crucified
My good and dear Jesus,
I kneel before you,
asking you most earnestly
to engrave upon my heart
a deep and lively faith, hope and charity,
with true repentance for my sins,
and a firm resolve to make amends.
As I reflect upon your five wounds,
and dwell upon them with deep compassion and grief,
I recall, good Jesus, the words the prophet David spoke
long ago concerning yourself:
they have pierced my hands and my feet,
they have counted all my bones!

Prayer to our Redeemer
Soul of Christ, make me holy.
Body of Christ, be my salvation.
Blood of Christ, let me drink your wine.
Water flowing from the side of Christ, wash me clean.
Passion of Christ, strengthen me.
Kind Jesus, hear my prayer;
hide me within your wounds
and keep me close to you.
Defend me from the evil enemy.
Call me at my death
to the fellowship of your saints,
that I may sing your praise with them
through all eternity. Amen.

Prayer of Self-dedication to Jesus Christ
Lord Jesus Christ,
take all my freedom,
my memory, my understanding, and my will.
All that I have and cherish
you have given me.
I surrender it all to be guided by your will.
Your grace and your love
are wealth enough for me.
Give me these, Lord Jesus,
and I ask for nothing more.

Prayer to the Virgin Mary
Mary, holy virgin mother,
I have received your Son, Jesus Christ.
With love you became his mother,
gave birth to him, nursed him,
and helped him grow to manhood.
With love I return him to you,
to hold once more,
to love with all your heart,
and to offer to the Holy Trinity
as our supreme act of worship
for your honour and for the good
of all your pilgrim brothers and sisters.

Mother, ask God to forgive my sins
and to help me serve him more faithfully.
Keep me true to Christ until death,
and let me come to praise him with you
for ever and ever. Amen.

The Universal Prayer
Lord, I believe in you: increase my faith.
I trust in you: strengthen my trust.
I love you: let me love you more and more.
I am sorry for my sins: deepen my sorrow.

I worship you as my first beginning,
I long for you as my last end,
I praise you as my constant helper,
and call on you as my loving protector.

Guide me by your wisdom,
correct me with your justice,
comfort me with your mercy,
protect me with your power.

I offer you, Lord, my thoughts: to be fixed on you;
my words: to have you for their theme;
my actions: to reflect my love for you;
my sufferings: to be endured for your greater glory.

I want to do what you ask of me:
in the way you ask,
for as long as you ask,
because you ask it.

Lord, enlighten my understanding,
strengthen my will,
purify my heart,
and make me holy.

Help me to repent of my past sins
and to resist temptation in the future.
Help me to rise above my human weaknesses
and to grow stronger as a Christian.

Let me love you, my Lord and my God,
and see myself as I really am:
a pilgrim in this world,
a Christian called to respect and love
all those whose lives I touch,
those in authority over me
or those under my authority,
my friends and my enemies.

Help me to conquer anger with gentleness,
greed by generosity,
apathy by fervour.
Help me to forget myself
and reach out to others.

Make me prudent in planning,
courageous in taking risks.
Make me patient in suffering, unassuming in prosperity.

Keep me, Lord, attentive at prayer,
temperate in food and drink,
diligent in my work,
firm in my intentions.

Let my conscience be clear,
my conduct without fault,
my speech blameless,
my life well-ordered.

Put me on my guard against my human weaknesses.
Let me cherish your love for me,
keep your law,
and come at last to your salvation.

Teach me to realise that this world is passing,
that my true future is the happiness of heaven,
that life on earth is short,
and the life to come eternal.

Help me to prepare for death
with a proper fear of judgement,
but a greater trust in your goodness.
Lead me safely through death
to the endless joy of heaven.

Grant this through Christ our Lord. Amen.

attributed to Pope Clement XI

Prayer for Good Humour
Grant me, O Lord, good digestion,
and also something to digest.
Grant me a healthy body, and
the necessary good humour to maintain it.
Grant me a simple soul that knows
to treasure all that is good and that
doesn't frighten easily at the sight of evil,
but rather finds the means to put things
back in their place.
Give me a soul that knows not boredom,
grumblings, sigh and laments,
nor success of stress, because of that
obstructing thing called "I".
Grant me, O Lord, a sense of good humour.
Allow me the grace to be able to take a joke
to discover in life a bit of joy,
and to be able to share it with others.

Saint Thomas More

Appendix to the Order of Mass

Eucharistic Prayers
for Reconciliation

Although these Eucharistic Prayers have been provided with a
proper Preface, they may also be used with other Prefaces that refer
to penance and conversion.

I

The Lord be with you.
And with your spirit.

Lift up your hearts.
We lift them up to the Lord.

Let us give thanks to the Lord our God.
It is right and just.

It is truly right and just
that we should always give you thanks,
Lord, holy Father, almighty and eternal God.

For you do not cease to spur us on
to possess a more abundant life
and, being rich in mercy,
you constantly offer pardon
and call on sinners
to trust in your forgiveness alone.

Never did you turn away from us,
and, though time and again we have broken your covenant,
you have bound the human family to yourself
through Jesus your Son, our Redeemer,
with a new bond of love so tight
that it can never be undone.

Even now you set before your people
a time of grace and reconciliation,
and, as they turn back to you in spirit,
you grant them hope in Christ Jesus
and a desire to be of service to all,
while they entrust themselves
more fully to the Holy Spirit.

And so, filled with wonder,
we extol the power of your love,
and, proclaiming our joy
at the salvation that comes from you,
we join in the heavenly hymn of countless hosts,
as without end we acclaim:

Holy, Holy, Holy Lord God of hosts.
Heaven and earth are full of your glory.
Hosanna in the highest.
Blessed is he who comes in the name of the Lord.
Hosanna in the highest.

The people kneel.

You are indeed Holy, O Lord,
and from the world's beginning
are ceaselessly at work,
so that the human race may become holy,
just as you yourself are holy.

Look, we pray, upon your people's offerings
and pour out on them the power of your Spirit,
that they may become the Body and ✠ Blood
of your beloved Son, Jesus Christ,
in whom we, too, are your sons and daughters.

Indeed, though we once were lost
and could not approach you,
you loved us with the greatest love:
for your Son, who alone is just,
handed himself over to death,

and did not disdain to be nailed for our sake
to the wood of the Cross.

But before his arms were outstretched between heaven and earth,
to become the lasting sign of your covenant,
he desired to celebrate the Passover with his disciples.

As he ate with them,
he took bread
and, giving you thanks, he said the blessing,
broke the bread and gave it to them, saying:

Take this, all of you, and eat of it,
for this is my Body,
which will be given up for you.

In a similar way, when supper was ended,
knowing that he was about to reconcile all things in himself
through his Blood to be shed on the Cross,
he took the chalice, filled with the fruit of the vine,
and once more giving you thanks,
handed the chalice to his disciples, saying:

Take this, all of you, and drink from it,
for this is the chalice of my Blood,
the Blood of the new and eternal covenant,
which will be poured out for you and for many
for the forgiveness of sins.

Do this in memory of me.

The mystery of faith.

The people acclaim:

**We proclaim your Death, O Lord,
and profess your Resurrection
until you come again.**

or

When we eat this Bread and drink this Cup,
we proclaim your Death, O Lord,
until you come again.

or

Save us, Saviour of the world,
for by your Cross and Resurrection
you have set us free.

Therefore, as we celebrate
the memorial of your Son Jesus Christ,
who is our Passover and our surest peace,
we celebrate his Death and Resurrection from the dead,
and looking forward to his blessed Coming,
we offer you, who are our faithful and merciful God,
this sacrificial Victim
who reconciles to you the human race.

Look kindly, most compassionate Father,
on those you unite to yourself
by the Sacrifice of your Son,
and grant that, by the power of the Holy Spirit,
as they partake of this one Bread and one Chalice,
they may be gathered into one Body in Christ,
who heals every division.

Be pleased to keep us always
in communion of mind and heart,
together with N. our Pope and N. our Bishop.
Help us to work together
for the coming of your Kingdom,
until the hour when we stand before you,
Saints among the Saints in the halls of heaven,
with the Blessed Virgin Mary, Mother of God,
the blessed Apostles and all the Saints,
and with our deceased brothers and sisters,
whom we humbly commend to your mercy.

Then, freed at last from the wound of corruption
and made fully into a new creation,
we shall sing to you with gladness
the thanksgiving of Christ,
who lives for all eternity.

The priest takes the chalice and the paten with the host and, raising
both, he sings or says:

Through him, and with him, and in him,
O God, almighty Father,
in the unity of the Holy Spirit,
all glory and honour is yours,
for ever and ever.
Amen.

Then follows the Communion Rite, p. 485.

II

The Lord be with you.
And with your spirit.

Lift up your hearts.
We lift them up to the Lord.

Let us give thanks to the Lord our God.
It is right and just.

It is truly right and just
that we should give you thanks and praise,
O God, almighty Father,
for all you do in this world,
through our Lord Jesus Christ.

For though the human race
is divided by dissension and discord,
yet we know that by testing us
you change our hearts
to prepare them for reconciliation.

Even more, by your Spirit you move human hearts
that enemies may speak to each other again,
adversaries join hands,
and peoples seek to meet together.

By the working of your power
it comes about, O Lord,
that hatred is overcome by love,
revenge gives way to forgiveness,
and discord is changed to mutual respect.

Therefore, as we give you ceaseless thanks
with the choirs of heaven,
we cry out to your majesty on earth,
and without end we acclaim:

Holy, Holy, Holy Lord God of hosts.
Heaven and earth are full of your glory.
Hosanna in the highest.
Blessed is he who comes in the name of the Lord.
Hosanna in the highest.

The people kneel.

You, therefore, almighty Father,
we bless through Jesus Christ your Son,
who comes in your name.
He himself is the Word that brings salvation,
the hand you extend to sinners,
the way by which your peace is offered to us.
When we ourselves had turned away from you
on account of our sins,
you brought us back to be reconciled, O Lord,
so that, converted at last to you,
we might love one another
through your Son,
whom for our sake you handed over to death.

And now, celebrating the reconciliation
Christ has brought us,
we entreat you:
sanctify these gifts by the outpouring of your Spirit,
that they may become the Body and ✠ Blood of your Son,
whose command we fulfil
when we celebrate these mysteries.

For when about to give his life to set us free,
as he reclined at supper,
he himself took bread into his hands,
and, giving you thanks, he said the blessing,
broke the bread and gave it to his disciples, saying:

TAKE THIS, ALL OF YOU, AND EAT OF IT,
FOR THIS IS MY BODY,
WHICH WILL BE GIVEN UP FOR YOU.

In a similar way, on that same evening,
he took the chalice of blessing in his hands,
confessing your mercy,
and gave the chalice to his disciples, saying:

Take this, all of you, and drink from it,
for this is the chalice of my Blood,
the Blood of the new and eternal covenant,
which will be poured out for you and for many
for the forgiveness of sins.

Do this in memory of me.

The mystery of faith.

The people acclaim:

**We proclaim your Death, O Lord,
and profess your Resurrection
until you come again.**

or

**When we eat this Bread and drink this Cup,
we proclaim your Death, O Lord,
until you come again.**

or

**Save us, Saviour of the world,
for by your Cross and Resurrection
you have set us free.**

Celebrating, therefore, the memorial
of the Death and Resurrection of your Son,
who left us this pledge of his love,
we offer you what you have bestowed on us,
the Sacrifice of perfect reconciliation.

Holy Father, we humbly beseech you
to accept us also, together with your Son,
and in this saving banquet
graciously to endow us with his very Spirit,
who takes away everything
that estranges us from one another.

May he make your Church a sign of unity
and an instrument of your peace among all people
and may he keep us in communion
with N. our Pope and N. our Bishop
and all the Bishops
and your entire people.

Just as you have gathered us now at the table of your Son,
so also bring us together,
with the glorious Virgin Mary, Mother of God,
with your blessed Apostles and all the Saints,
with our brothers and sisters
and those of every race and tongue
who have died in your friendship.
Bring us to share with them the unending banquet of unity
in a new heaven and a new earth,
where the fullness of your peace will shine forth
in Christ Jesus our Lord.

*The priest takes the chalice and the paten with the host and, raising
both, he sings or says:*

Through him, and with him, and in him,
O God, almighty Father,
in the unity of the Holy Spirit,
all glory and honour is yours,
for ever and ever.
Amen.

Then follows the Communion Rite, p. 485.

Eucharistic Prayers for Use in Masses for Various Needs

I

The Church on the Path of Unity

The Lord be with you.
And with your spirit.

Lift up your hearts.
We lift them up to the Lord.

Let us give thanks to the Lord our God.
It is right and just.

It is truly right and just to give you thanks
and raise to you a hymn of glory and praise,
O Lord, Father of infinite goodness.

For by the word of your Son's Gospel
you have brought together one Church
from every people, tongue, and nation,
and, having filled her with life by the power of your Spirit,
you never cease through her
to gather the whole human race into one.

Manifesting the covenant of your love,
she dispenses without ceasing
the blessed hope of your Kingdom
and shines bright as the sign of your faithfulness,
which in Christ Jesus our Lord
you promised would last for eternity.

And so, with all the Powers of heaven,
we worship you constantly on earth,
while, with all the Church,
as one voice we acclaim:

Holy, Holy, Holy Lord God of hosts.
Heaven and earth are full of your glory.
Hosanna in the highest.
Blessed is he who comes in the name of the Lord.
Hosanna in the highest.

The people kneel.

You are indeed Holy and to be glorified, O God,
who love the human race
and who always walk with us on the journey of life.
Blessed indeed is your Son,
present in our midst
when we are gathered by his love,
and when, as once for the disciples, so now for us,
he opens the Scriptures and breaks the bread.

Therefore, Father most merciful,
we ask that you send forth your Holy Spirit
to sanctify these gifts of bread and wine,
that they may become for us
the Body and ✠ Blood
of our Lord Jesus Christ.

On the day before he was to suffer,
on the night of the Last Supper,
he took bread and said the blessing,
broke the bread and gave it to his disciples, saying:

TAKE THIS, ALL OF YOU, AND EAT OF IT,
FOR THIS IS MY BODY,
WHICH WILL BE GIVEN UP FOR YOU.

In a similar way, when supper was ended,
he took the chalice, gave you thanks
and gave the chalice to his disciples, saying:

TAKE THIS, ALL OF YOU, AND DRINK FROM IT,
FOR THIS IS THE CHALICE OF MY BLOOD,
THE BLOOD OF THE NEW AND ETERNAL COVENANT,
WHICH WILL BE POURED OUT FOR YOU AND FOR MANY
FOR THE FORGIVENESS OF SINS.

DO THIS IN MEMORY OF ME.

The mystery of faith.

The people acclaim:

**We proclaim your Death, O Lord,
and profess your Resurrection
until you come again.**

or

**When we eat this Bread and drink this Cup,
we proclaim your Death, O Lord,
until you come again.**

or

**Save us, Saviour of the world,
for by your Cross and Resurrection
you have set us free.**

Therefore, holy Father,
as we celebrate the memorial of Christ your Son, our Saviour,
whom you led through his Passion and Death on the Cross
to the glory of the Resurrection,
and whom you have seated at your right hand,
we proclaim the work of your love until he comes again
and we offer you the Bread of life
and the Chalice of blessing.

Look with favour on the oblation of your Church,
in which we show forth
the paschal Sacrifice of Christ that has been handed on to us,
and grant that, by the power of the Spirit of your love,
we may be counted now and until the day of eternity
among the members of your Son,
in whose Body and Blood we have communion.

Lord, renew your Church (which is in N.)
by the light of the Gospel.
Strengthen the bond of unity
between the faithful and the pastors of your people,
together with N. our Pope, N. our Bishop,
and the whole Order of Bishops,
that in a world torn by strife
your people may shine forth
as a prophetic sign of unity and concord.

Remember our brothers and sisters (N. and N.),
who have fallen asleep in the peace of your Christ,
and all the dead, whose faith you alone have known.
Admit them to rejoice in the light of your face,
and in the resurrection give them the fullness of life.

Grant also to us,
when our earthly pilgrimage is done,
that we may come to an eternal dwelling place
and live with you for ever;
there, in communion with the Blessed Virgin Mary,
Mother of God,
with the Apostles and Martyrs,
(with Saint N.: the Saint of the day or Patron)
and with all the Saints,
we shall praise and exalt you
through Jesus Christ, your Son.

The priest takes the chalice and the paten with the host and, raising both, he sings or says:

Through him, and with him, and in him,
O God, almighty Father,
in the unity of the Holy Spirit,
all glory and honour is yours,
for ever and ever.
Amen.

Then follows the Communion Rite, p. 485.

II

God Guides his Church along the Way of Salvation

The Lord be with you.
And with your spirit.

Lift up your hearts.
We lift them up to the Lord.

Let us give thanks to the Lord our God.
It is right and just.

It is truly right and just, our duty and our salvation,
always and everywhere to give you thanks,
Lord, holy Father,
creator of the world and source of all life.

For you never forsake the works of your wisdom,
but by your providence are even now at work in our midst.
With mighty hand and outstretched arm
you led your people Israel through the desert.
Now, as your Church makes her pilgrim journey in the world,
you always accompany her
by the power of the Holy Spirit
and lead her along the paths of time
to the eternal joy of your Kingdom,
through Christ our Lord.

And so, with the Angels and Saints,
we, too, sing the hymn of your glory,
as without end we acclaim:

Holy, Holy, Holy Lord God of hosts.
Heaven and earth are full of your glory.
Hosanna in the highest.
Blessed is he who comes in the name of the Lord.
Hosanna in the highest.

The people kneel.

You are indeed Holy and to be glorified, O God,
who love the human race
and who always walk with us on the journey of life.
Blessed indeed is your Son,
present in our midst
when we are gathered by his love
and when, as once for the disciples, so now for us,
he opens the Scriptures and breaks the bread.

Therefore, Father most merciful,
we ask that you send forth your Holy Spirit
to sanctify these gifts of bread and wine,
that they may become for us
the Body and ✠ Blood
of our Lord Jesus Christ.

On the day before he was to suffer,
on the night of the Last Supper,
he took bread and said the blessing,
broke the bread and gave it to his disciples, saying:

Take this, all of you, and eat of it,
for this is my Body,
which will be given up for you.

In a similar way, when supper was ended,
he took the chalice, gave you thanks
and gave the chalice to his disciples, saying:

Take this, all of you, and drink from it,
for this is the chalice of my Blood,
the Blood of the new and eternal covenant,
which will be poured out for you and for many
for the forgiveness of sins.

Do this in memory of me.

The mystery of faith.

The people acclaim:

**We proclaim your Death, O Lord,
and profess your Resurrection
until you come again.**

or

**When we eat this Bread and drink this Cup,
we proclaim your Death, O Lord,
until you come again.**

or

**Save us, Saviour of the world,
for by your Cross and Resurrection
you have set us free.**

Therefore, holy Father,
as we celebrate the memorial of Christ your Son, our Saviour,
whom you led through his Passion and Death on the Cross
to the glory of the Resurrection,
and whom you have seated at your right hand,
we proclaim the work of your love until he comes again
and we offer you the Bread of life
and the Chalice of blessing.

Look with favour on the oblation of your Church,
in which we show forth
the paschal Sacrifice of Christ that has been handed on to us,
and grant that, by the power of the Spirit of your love,
we may be counted now and until the day of eternity
among the members of your Son,
in whose Body and Blood we have communion.

And so, having called us to your table, Lord,
confirm us in unity,
so that, together with N. our Pope and N. our Bishop,
with all Bishops, Priests and Deacons,
and your entire people,
as we walk your ways with faith and hope,
we may strive to bring joy and trust into the world.

Remember our brothers and sisters (N. and N.),
who have fallen asleep in the peace of your Christ,
and all the dead, whose faith you alone have known.
Admit them to rejoice in the light of your face,
and in the resurrection give them the fullness of life.

Grant also to us,
when our earthly pilgrimage is done,
that we may come to an eternal dwelling place
and live with you for ever;
there, in communion with the Blessed Virgin Mary,
Mother of God,
with the Apostles and Martyrs,
(with Saint N.: the Saint of the day or Patron)
and with all the Saints,
we shall praise and exalt you
through Jesus Christ, your Son.

The priest takes the chalice and the paten with the host and, raising
both, he sings or says:

Through him, and with him, and in him,
O God, almighty Father,
in the unity of the Holy Spirit,
all glory and honour is yours,
for ever and ever.
Amen.

Then follows the Communion Rite, p. 485.

III

Jesus, the Way to the Father

The Lord be with you.
And with your spirit.

Lift up your hearts.
We lift them up to the Lord.

Let us give thanks to the Lord our God.
It is right and just.

It is truly right and just, our duty and our salvation,
always and everywhere to give you thanks,
holy Father, Lord of heaven and earth,
through Christ our Lord.

For by your Word you created the world
and you govern all things in harmony.
You gave us the same Word made flesh as Mediator,
and he has spoken your words to us
and called us to follow him.
He is the way that leads us to you,
the truth that sets us free,
the life that fills us with gladness.

Through your Son
you gather men and women,
whom you made for the glory of your name,
into one family,
redeemed by the Blood of his Cross
and signed with the seal of the Spirit.

Therefore now and for ages unending,
with all the Angels,
we proclaim your glory,
as in joyful celebration we acclaim:

Holy, Holy, Holy Lord God of hosts.
Heaven and earth are full of your glory.
Hosanna in the highest.
Blessed is he who comes in the name of the Lord.
Hosanna in the highest.

The people kneel.

You are indeed Holy and to be glorified, O God,
who love the human race
and who always walk with us on the journey of life.
Blessed indeed is your Son,
present in our midst
when we are gathered by his love
and when, as once for the disciples, so now for us,
he opens the Scriptures and breaks the bread.

Therefore, Father most merciful,
we ask that you send forth your Holy Spirit
to sanctify these gifts of bread and wine,
that they may become for us
the Body and ✠ Blood
of our Lord Jesus Christ.

On the day before he was to suffer,
on the night of the Last Supper,
he took bread and said the blessing,
broke the bread and gave it to his disciples, saying:

Take this, all of you, and eat of it,
for this is my Body,
which will be given up for you.

In a similar way, when supper was ended,
he took the chalice, gave you thanks
and gave the chalice to his disciples, saying:

Take this, all of you, and drink from it,
for this is the chalice of my Blood,
the Blood of the new and eternal covenant,

WHICH WILL BE POURED OUT FOR YOU AND FOR MANY
FOR THE FORGIVENESS OF SINS.

DO THIS IN MEMORY OF ME.

The mystery of faith.

The people acclaim:

**We proclaim your Death, O Lord,
and profess your Resurrection
until you come again.**

or

**When we eat this Bread and drink this Cup,
we proclaim your Death, O Lord,
until you come again.**

or

**Save us, Saviour of the world,
for by your Cross and Resurrection
you have set us free.**

Therefore, holy Father,
as we celebrate the memorial of Christ your Son, our Saviour,
whom you led through his Passion and Death on the Cross
to the glory of the Resurrection,
and whom you have seated at your right hand,
we proclaim the work of your love until he comes again
and we offer you the Bread of life
and the Chalice of blessing.

Look with favour on the oblation of your Church,
in which we show forth
the paschal Sacrifice of Christ that has been handed on to us,
and grant that, by the power of the Spirit of your love,
we may be counted now and until the day of eternity
among the members of your Son,
in whose Body and Blood we have communion.

By our partaking of this mystery, almighty Father,
give us life through your Spirit,
grant that we may be conformed to the image of your Son,
and confirm us in the bond of communion,
together with N. our Pope and N. our Bishop,
with all other Bishops,
with Priests and Deacons,
and with your entire people.

Grant that all the faithful of the Church,
looking into the signs of the times by the light of faith,
may constantly devote themselves
to the service of the Gospel.
Keep us attentive to the needs of all
that, sharing their grief and pain,
their joy and hope,
we may faithfully bring them the good news of salvation
and go forward with them
along the way of your Kingdom.

Remember our brothers and sisters (N. and N.),
who have fallen asleep in the peace of your Christ,
and all the dead, whose faith you alone have known.
Admit them to rejoice in the light of your face,
and in the resurrection give them the fullness of life.

Grant also to us,
when our earthly pilgrimage is done,
that we may come to an eternal dwelling place
and live with you for ever;
there, in communion with the Blessed Virgin Mary, Mother of God,
with the Apostles and Martyrs,
(with Saint N.: the Saint of the day or Patron)
and with all the Saints,
we shall praise and exalt you
through Jesus Christ, your Son.

The priest takes the chalice and the paten with the host and, raising
both, he sings or says:

Through him, and with him, and in him,
O God, almighty Father,
in the unity of the Holy Spirit,
all glory and honour is yours,
for ever and ever.
Amen.

Then follows the Communion Rite, p. 485.

IV

Jesus, who Went About Doing Good

The Lord be with you.
And with your spirit.

Lift up your hearts.
We lift them up to the Lord.

Let us give thanks to the Lord our God.
It is right and just.

It is truly right and just, our duty and our salvation,
always and everywhere to give you thanks,
Father of mercies and faithful God.

For you have given us Jesus Christ, your Son,
as our Lord and Redeemer.

He always showed compassion
for children and for the poor,
for the sick and for sinners,
and he became a neighbour
to the oppressed and the afflicted.

By word and deed he announced to the world
that you are our Father
and that you care for all your sons and daughters.

And so, with all the Angels and Saints,
we exalt and bless your name
and sing the hymn of your glory,
as without end we acclaim:

Holy, Holy, Holy Lord God of hosts.
Heaven and earth are full of your glory.
Hosanna in the highest.
Blessed is he who comes in the name of the Lord.
Hosanna in the highest.

The people kneel.

You are indeed Holy and to be glorified, O God,
who love the human race
and who always walk with us on the journey of life.
Blessed indeed is your Son,
present in our midst
when we are gathered by his love
and when, as once for the disciples, so now for us,
he opens the Scriptures and breaks the bread.

Therefore, Father most merciful,
we ask that you send forth your Holy Spirit
to sanctify these gifts of bread and wine,
that they may become for us
the Body and ✠ Blood
of our Lord Jesus Christ.

On the day before he was to suffer,
on the night of the Last Supper,
he took bread and said the blessing,
broke the bread and gave it to his disciples, saying:

TAKE THIS, ALL OF YOU, AND EAT OF IT,
FOR THIS IS MY BODY,
WHICH WILL BE GIVEN UP FOR YOU.

In a similar way, when supper was ended,
he took the chalice, gave you thanks
and gave the chalice to his disciples, saying:

TAKE THIS, ALL OF YOU, AND DRINK FROM IT,
FOR THIS IS THE CHALICE OF MY BLOOD,
THE BLOOD OF THE NEW AND ETERNAL COVENANT,
WHICH WILL BE POURED OUT FOR YOU AND FOR MANY
FOR THE FORGIVENESS OF SINS.

DO THIS IN MEMORY OF ME.

The mystery of faith.

The people acclaim:

We proclaim your Death, O Lord,
and profess your Resurrection
until you come again.

or

When we eat this Bread and drink this Cup,
we proclaim your Death, O Lord,
until you come again.

or

Save us, Saviour of the world,
for by your Cross and Resurrection
you have set us free.

Therefore, holy Father,
as we celebrate the memorial of Christ your Son, our Saviour,
whom you led through his Passion and Death on the Cross
to the glory of the Resurrection,
and whom you have seated at your right hand,
we proclaim the work of your love until he comes again
and we offer you the Bread of life
and the Chalice of blessing.

Look with favour on the oblation of your Church,
in which we show forth
the paschal Sacrifice of Christ that has been handed on to us,
and grant that, by the power of the Spirit of your love,
we may be counted now and until the day of eternity
among the members of your Son,
in whose Body and Blood we have communion.

Bring your Church, O Lord,
to perfect faith and charity,
together with N. our Pope and N. our Bishop,
with all Bishops, Priests and Deacons,
and the entire people you have made your own.

Open our eyes
to the needs of our brothers and sisters;
inspire in us words and actions
to comfort those who labour and are burdened.
Make us serve them truly,
after the example of Christ and at his command.
And may your Church stand as a living witness
to truth and freedom,
to peace and justice,
that all people may be raised up to a new hope.

Remember our brothers and sisters (N. and N.),
who have fallen asleep in the peace of your Christ,
and all the dead, whose faith you alone have known.
Admit them to rejoice in the light of your face,
and in the resurrection give them the fullness of life.

Grant also to us,
when our earthly pilgrimage is done,
that we may come to an eternal dwelling place
and live with you for ever;
there, in communion with the Blessed Virgin Mary,
Mother of God,
with the Apostles and Martyrs,
(with Saint N.: the Saint of the day or Patron)
and with all the Saints,
we shall praise and exalt you
through Jesus Christ, your Son.

The priest takes the chalice and the paten with the host and, raising both, he sings or says:

Through him, and with him, and in him,
O God, almighty Father,
in the unity of the Holy Spirit,
all glory and honour is yours,
for ever and ever.
Amen.

Then follows the Communion Rite, p. 485.

Rite for the Blessing
and Sprinkling of Water

After the greeting, the priest, with a vessel containing the water to be blessed, calls upon the people to pray in these or similar words:

Dear brethren (brothers and sisters),
let us humbly beseech the Lord our God
to bless this water he has created,
which will be sprinkled on us
as a memorial of our Baptism.
May he help us by his grace
to remain faithful to the Spirit we have received.

And after a brief pause for silence, he continues:

Almighty ever-living God,
who willed that through water,
the fountain of life and the source of purification,
even souls should be cleansed
and receive the gift of eternal life;
be pleased, we pray, to ✠ bless this water,
by which we seek protection on this your day, O Lord.
Renew the living spring of your grace within us
and grant that by this water we may be defended
from all ills of spirit and body,
and so approach you with hearts made clean
and worthily receive your salvation.
Through Christ our Lord.
Amen.

or

Almighty Lord and God,
who are the source and origin of all life,
whether of body or soul,
we ask you to ✠ bless this water,
which we use in confidence
to implore forgiveness for our sins
and to obtain the protection of your grace

against all illness and every snare of the enemy.
Grant, O Lord, in your mercy,
that living waters may always spring up for our salvation,
and so may we approach you with a pure heart
and avoid all danger to body and soul.
Through Christ our Lord.
Amen.

or, during Easter Time:

Lord our God,
in your mercy be present to your people's prayers,
and, for us who recall the wondrous work of our creation
and the still greater work of our redemption,
graciously ✠ bless this water.
For you created water to make the fields fruitful
and to refresh and cleanse our bodies.
You also made water the instrument of your mercy:
for through water you freed your people from slavery
and quenched their thirst in the desert;
through water the Prophets proclaimed the new covenant
you were to enter upon with the human race;
and last of all,
through water, which Christ made holy in the Jordan,
you have renewed our corrupted nature
in the bath of regeneration.
Therefore, may this water be for us
a memorial of the Baptism we have received,
and grant that we may share
in the gladness of our brothers and sisters
who at Easter have received their Baptism.
Through Christ our Lord.
Amen.

Where it is appropriate, salt may be mixed with the holy water. The
priest blesses the salt, saying:

We humbly ask you, almighty God:
be pleased in your faithful love to bless ✠ this salt

you have created,
for it was you who commanded the prophet Elisha
to cast salt into water,
that impure water might be purified.
Grant, O Lord, we pray,
that, wherever this mixture of salt and water is sprinkled,
every attack of the enemy may be repulsed
and your Holy Spirit may be present
to keep us safe at all times.
Through Christ our Lord.
Amen.

Then he pours the salt into the water.
Afterwards, the priest sprinkles himself and the people, moving
through the church, if appropriate.
Meanwhile, one of the following chants, or another appropriate
chant is sung.

Outside Easter Time

Antiphon 1
Sprinkle me with hyssop, O Lord, and I shall be cleansed;
wash me and I shall be whiter than snow.   Psalm 50:9

Antiphon 2
I will pour clean water upon you,
and you will be made clean of all your impurities,
and I shall give you a new spirit, says the Lord.   Ezekiel 36:25-26

Hymn
Blessed be the God and Father of our Lord Jesus Christ,
who in his great mercy has given us new birth into a living hope
through the Resurrection of Jesus Christ from the dead,
into an inheritance that will not perish,
preserved for us in heaven
for the salvation to be revealed in the last time!   cf. 1 Peter 1:3-5

During Easter Time

Antiphon 1

I saw water flowing from the Temple,
from its right-hand side, alleluia:
and all to whom this water came
were saved and shall say: alleluia, alleluia.   cf. Ezekiel 47:1-2. 9

Antiphon 2

On the day of my resurrection, says the Lord, alleluia,
I will gather the nations and assemble the kingdoms
and I will pour clean water upon you, alleluia.

cf. Wisdom 3:8; Ezekiel 36:25

Antiphon 3

You springs and all that moves in the waters,
sing a hymn to God, alleluia.   cf. Daniel 3:77. 79

Antiphon 4

O chosen race, royal priesthood, holy nation,
proclaim the mighty works of him
who called you out of darkness into his wonderful light, alleluia.

1 Peter 2:9

Antiphon 5

From your side, O Christ,
bursts forth a spring of water,
by which the squalor of the world is washed away
and life is made new again, alleluia.

The priest concludes the rite by saying:
May almighty God cleanse us of our sins,
and through the celebration of this Eucharist
make us worthy to share at the table of his Kingdom.
Amen.

SECOND SUNDAY IN ORDINARY TIME – A

Christ the light of the nations.

The Holy Spirit rested on Jesus Christ when he was baptised by John the Baptist. Through the coming of the Spirit John recognised Christ as the Lamb of God who takes away the sin of the world. Through the gift of the Spirit, we too are called to take our place among the saints and become the light of the world, proclaiming salvation to the ends of the earth.

Entrance Antiphon

All the earth shall bow down before you, O God,
and shall sing to you,
shall sing to your name, O Most High!   Psalm 65:4

The Gloria is said or sung.

Collect

Almighty ever-living God,
who govern all things,
both in heaven and on earth,
mercifully hear the pleading of your people
and bestow your peace on our times.
Through our Lord Jesus Christ, your Son,
who lives and reigns with you in the unity of the Holy Spirit,
one God, for ever and ever.

First Reading   Isaiah 49:3. 5-6

I will make you the light of the nations so that my salvation may
reach to the ends of the earth.

The Lord said to me, "You are my servant, Israel,
in whom I shall be glorified";
I was honoured in the eyes of the Lord,
my God was my strength.

And now the Lord has spoken,
he who formed me in the womb to be his servant,
to bring Jacob back to him,
to gather Israel to him:

"It is not enough for you to be my servant,
to restore the tribes of Jacob and bring back the survivors of
Israel;
I will make you the light of the nations
so that my salvation may reach to the ends of the earth."

Psalm   Psalm 39

R. **Here I am, Lord!**
     I come to do your will.

1. I waited, I waited for the Lord
     and he stooped down to me;
     he heard my cry.
     He put a new song into my mouth,
     praise of our God. R.

2. You do not ask for sacrifice and offerings,
     but an open ear.
     You do not ask for holocaust and victim.
     Instead, here am I. R.

3. In the scroll of the book it stands written
     that I should do your will.
     My God, I delight in your law
     in the depth of my heart. R.

4. Your justice I have proclaimed
     in the great assembly.
     My lips I have not sealed;
     you know it, O Lord. R.

Second Reading   1 Corinthians 1:1-3

May God our Father and the Lord Jesus Christ send you grace and peace.

I, Paul, appointed by God to be an apostle, together with brother Sosthenes, send greetings to the church of God in Corinth, to the holy people of Jesus Christ, who are called to take their place among all the saints everywhere who pray to our Lord Jesus Christ; for he is their Lord no less than ours. May God our Father and the Lord Jesus Christ send you grace and peace.

Gospel Acclamation

Alleluia, alleluia!

Blessings on the King who comes,

in the name of the Lord!

Peace in heaven

and glory in the highest heavens!

Alleluia!   Luke 19:38

or

Alleluia, alleluia!

The Word was made flesh and lived among us;

to all who did accept him

he gave power to become children of God.

Alleluia!   John 1:14. 12

Gospel   John 1:29-34

Look, there is the lamb of God that takes away the sin of the world.

Seeing Jesus coming towards him, John said, "Look, there is the lamb of God that takes away the sin of the world. This is the one I spoke of when I said: A man is coming after me who ranks before me because he existed before me. I did not know him myself, and yet it was to reveal him to Israel that I came baptising with water." John also declared, "I saw the Spirit coming down on him from heaven like a dove and resting on him. I did not know him myself, but he who sent me to baptise with water had said to me, 'The man on whom you see the Spirit come down and rest is the one who is going to baptise with the Holy Spirit.' Yes, I have seen and I am the witness that he is the Chosen One of God."

The Creed is said.

Prayer over the Offerings
Grant us, O Lord, we pray,
that we may participate worthily in these mysteries,
for whenever the memorial of this sacrifice is celebrated
the work of our redemption is accomplished.
Through Christ our Lord.

Preface I-VIII of the Sundays in Ordinary Time, pp. 499-502.

Communion Antiphon
You have prepared a table before me,
and how precious is the chalice that quenches my thirst.

cf. Psalm 22:5

or

We have come to know and to believe
in the love that God has for us.

1 John 4:16

Prayer after Communion
Pour on us, O Lord, the Spirit of your love,
and in your kindness
make those you have nourished
by this one heavenly Bread
one in mind and heart.
Through Christ our Lord.

THIRD SUNDAY IN
ORDINARY TIME – A

Christ our light and our help.
Jesus Christ lightens our darkness, and helps us to see the real meaning of life
and to put aside our differences. Christ calls us to follow him, to enable his
light to shine in us and so to proclaim the Good News of the kingdom.

Entrance Antiphon
O sing a new song to the Lord;
sing to the Lord, all the earth.
In his presence are majesty and splendour,
strength and honour in his holy place.   cf. Psalm 95:1. 6

The Gloria is said or sung.

Collect
Almighty ever-living God,
direct our actions according to your good pleasure,
that in the name of your beloved Son
we may abound in good works.
Through our Lord Jesus Christ, your Son,
who lives and reigns with you in the unity of the Holy Spirit,
one God, for ever and ever.

First Reading   Isaiah 8:23 – 9:3
In Galilee of the nations the people has seen a great light.
In days past the Lord humbled the land of Zebulun and the land of
Naphtali, but in days to come he will confer glory on the Way of the
Sea on the far side of Jordan, province of the nations.

The people that walked in darkness
has seen a great light;
on those who live in a land of deep shadow
a light has shone.
You have made their gladness greater,

you have made their joy increase;
they rejoice in your presence
as men rejoice at harvest time,
as men are happy when they are dividing the spoils.

For the yoke that was weighing on him,
the bar across his shoulders,
the rod of his oppressor,
these you break as on the day of Midian.

Psalm   Psalm 26

R. **The Lord is my light and my help.**

1. The Lord is my light and my help;
   whom shall I fear?
   The Lord is the stronghold of my life;
   before whom shall I shrink? R.

2. There is one thing I ask of the Lord,
     for this I long,
   to live in the house of the Lord,
   all the days of my life,
   to savour the sweetness of the Lord,
   to behold his temple. R.

3. I am sure I shall see the Lord's goodness
   in the land of the living.
   Hope in him, hold firm and take heart.
   Hope in the Lord! R.

Second Reading   1 Corinthians 1:10-13. 17
Make up the differences between you instead of disagreeing among
yourselves.
I appeal to you, brothers, for the sake of our Lord Jesus Christ, to
make up the differences between you, and instead of disagreeing
among yourselves, to be united again in your belief and practice.
From what Chloe's people have been telling me, my dear brothers,

it is clear that there are serious differences among you. What I mean are all these slogans that you have, like: "I am for Paul", "I am for Apollos", "I am for Cephas", "I am for Christ." Has Christ been parcelled out? Was it Paul that was crucified for you? Were you baptised in the name of Paul?

For Christ did not send me to baptise, but to preach the Good News, and not to preach that in the terms of philosophy in which the crucifixion of Christ cannot be expressed.

Gospel Acclamation
Alleluia, alleluia!
Jesus proclaimed the Good News of the kingdom,
and cured all kinds of sickness among the people.
Alleluia!

Matthew 4:23

Gospel   Matthew 4:12-23
He went and settled in Capernaum: in this way the prophecy of Isaiah was to be fulfilled.

Hearing that John had been arrested Jesus went back to Galilee, and leaving Nazareth he went and settled in Capernaum, a lakeside town on the borders of Zebulun and Naphtali. In this way the prophecy of Isaiah was to be fulfilled:

Land of Zebulun! Land of Naphtali!
Way of the sea on the far side of Jordan,
Galilee of the nations!
The people that lived in darkness
has seen a great light;
on those who dwell in the land and shadow of death
a light has dawned.

From that moment Jesus began his preaching with the message, "Repent, for the kingdom of heaven is close at hand."

As he was walking by the Sea of Galilee he saw two brothers, Simon, who was called Peter, and his brother Andrew; they were making a cast in the lake with their net, for they were fishermen. And he said to them, "Follow me and I will make you fishers of men." And they left their nets at once and followed him.

Going on from there he saw another pair of brothers, James son of Zebedee and his brother John; they were in their boat with their father Zebedee, mending their nets, and he called them. At once, leaving the boat and their father, they followed him.

He went round the whole of Galilee teaching in their synagogues, proclaiming the Good News of the kingdom and curing all kinds of diseases and sickness among the people.

The Creed is said.

Prayer over the Offerings
Accept our offerings, O Lord, we pray,
and in sanctifying them
grant that they may profit us for salvation.
Through Christ our Lord.

Preface I-VIII of the Sundays in Ordinary Time, pp. 499-502.

Communion Antiphon
Look toward the Lord and be radiant;
let your faces not be abashed.   cf. Psalm 33:6

or

I am the light of the world, says the Lord;
whoever follows me will not walk in darkness,
but will have the light of life.   John 8:12

Prayer after Communion
Grant, we pray, almighty God,
that, receiving the grace
by which you bring us to new life,
we may always glory in your gift.
Through Christ our Lord.

FOURTH SUNDAY IN ORDINARY TIME – A

Blessed are the poor in spirit!

In the Beatitudes Jesus tells us how happy and blessed we are if we are poor in spirit, because then the kingdom of heaven will be ours. Poverty of spirit means having a standard of values in which we put Christ first. We are rich in Christ when we recognise that everything of lasting worth comes from him.

Entrance Antiphon

Save us, O Lord our God!
And gather us from the nations,
to give thanks to your holy name,
and make it our glory to praise you.

Psalm 105:47

The Gloria is said or sung.

Collect

Grant us, Lord our God,
that we may honour you with all our mind,
and love everyone in truth of heart.
Through our Lord Jesus Christ, your Son,
who lives and reigns with you in the unity of the Holy Spirit,
one God, for ever and ever.

First Reading   Zephaniah 2:3; 3:12-13

In your midst I will leave a humble and lowly people.

Seek the Lord
all you, the humble of the earth,
who obey his commands.
Seek integrity,
seek humility:
you may perhaps find shelter
on the day of the anger of the Lord.
In your midst I will leave

a humble and lowly people,
and those who are left in Israel will seek refuge in the name of the
   Lord.
They will do no wrong,
will tell no lies;
and the perjured tongue will no longer
be found in their mouths.
But they will be able to graze and rest
with no one to disturb them.

Psalm   Psalm 145

R. **How happy are the poor in spirit;**
      theirs is the kingdom of heaven.

or **Alleluia!**

1. It is the Lord who keeps faith for ever,
      who is just to those who are oppressed.
      It is he who gives bread to the hungry,
      the Lord, who sets prisoners free. R.

2. It is the Lord who gives sight to the blind,
      who raises up those who are bowed down,
      the Lord, who protects the stranger
      and upholds the widow and orphan. R.

3. It is the Lord who loves the just
      but thwarts the path of the wicked.
      The Lord will reign for ever,
      Zion's God, from age to age. R.

Second Reading   1 Corinthians 1:26-31
God chose what is foolish by human reckoning.
Take yourselves, brothers, at the time when you were called: how
many of you were wise in the ordinary sense of the word, how many
were influential people, or came from noble families? No, it was to

shame the wise that God chose what is foolish by human reckoning, and to shame what is strong that he chose what is weak by human reckoning; those whom the world thinks common and contemptible are the ones that God has chosen – those who are nothing at all to show up those who are everything. The human race has nothing to boast about to God, but you, God has made members of Christ Jesus and by God's doing he has become our wisdom, and our virtue, and our holiness, and our freedom. As scripture says: if anyone wants to boast, let him boast about the Lord.

Gospel Acclamation
Alleluia, alleluia!
Blessed are you, Father,
Lord of heaven and earth,
for revealing the mysteries of the kingdom
to mere children.
Alleluia!   cf. Matthew 11:25

or

Alleluia, alleluia!
Rejoice and be glad:
your reward will be great in heaven.
Alleluia!   Matthew 5:12

Gospel   Matthew 5:1-12
How happy are the poor in spirit.
Seeing the crowds, Jesus went up the hill. There he sat down and was joined by his disciples. Then he began to speak. This is what he taught them:

"How happy are the poor in spirit;
theirs is the kingdom of heaven.
Happy the gentle:
they shall have the earth for their heritage.
Happy those who mourn:
they shall be comforted.
Happy those who hunger and thirst for what is right:
they shall be satisfied.
Happy the merciful:

they shall have mercy shown them.
Happy the pure in heart:
they shall see God.
Happy the peacemakers:
they shall be called sons of God.
Happy those who are persecuted in the cause of right:
theirs is the kingdom of heaven.

"Happy are you when people abuse you and persecute you and speak all kinds of calumny against you on my account. Rejoice and be glad, for your reward will be great in heaven."

The Creed is said.

Prayer over the Offerings
O Lord, we bring to your altar
these offerings of our service:
be pleased to receive them, we pray,
and transform them
into the Sacrament of our redemption.
Through Christ our Lord.

Preface I-VIII of the Sundays in Ordinary Time, pp. 499-502.

Communion Antiphon
Let your face shine on your servant.
Save me in your merciful love.
O Lord, let me never be put to shame, for I call on you.
cf. Psalm 30:17-18

or

Blessed are the poor in spirit,
for theirs is the Kingdom of Heaven.
Blessed are the meek, for they shall possess the land.   Matthew 5:3-4

Prayer after Communion
Nourished by these redeeming gifts,
we pray, O Lord,
that through this help to eternal salvation
true faith may ever increase.
Through Christ our Lord.

FIFTH SUNDAY IN ORDINARY TIME – A

Salt of the earth and light of the world.
Jesus calls us to be the salt of the earth, and gives us the example to follow in
his own life and death. We are also called to be, through our good works, a light
shining in the darkness so that others may be guided on their journey to God.

Entrance Antiphon
O come, let us worship God
and bow low before the God who made us,
for he is the Lord our God.

Psalm 94:6-7

The Gloria is said or sung.

Collect
Keep your family safe, O Lord, with unfailing care,
that, relying solely on the hope of heavenly grace,
they may be defended always by your protection.
Through our Lord Jesus Christ, your Son,
who lives and reigns with you in the unity of the Holy Spirit,
one God, for ever and ever.

First Reading   Isaiah 58:7-10
Then will your light shine like the dawn.
Thus says the Lord:

Share your bread with the hungry,
and shelter the homeless poor,

clothe the man you see to be naked
and turn not from your own kin.
Then will your light shine like the dawn
and your wound be quickly healed over.

Your integrity will go before you
and the glory of the Lord behind you.

Cry, and the Lord will answer;
call, and he will say, "I am here."

If you do away with the yoke,
the clenched fist, the wicked word,
if you give your bread to the hungry,
and relief to the oppressed,
your light will rise in the darkness,
and your shadows become like noon.

Psalm   Psalm 111

R. **The good man is a light in the darkness for the upright.**

or **Alleluia!**

1. He is a light in the darkness for the upright:
    he is generous, merciful and just.
    The good man takes pity and lends,
    he conducts his affairs with honour. R.

2. The just man will never waver:
    he will be remembered for ever.
    He has no fear of evil news;
    with a firm heart he trusts in the Lord. R.

3. With a steadfast heart he will not fear;
    open-handed, he gives to the poor;
    his justice stands firm for ever.
    His head will be raised in glory. R.

Second Reading   1 Corinthians 2:1-5
During my stay with you, the only knowledge I claimed to have was
about Jesus as the crucified Christ.

When I came to you, brothers, it was not with any show of oratory
or philosophy, but simply to tell you what God had guaranteed.
During my stay with you, the only knowledge I claimed to have
was about Jesus, and only about him as the crucified Christ. Far

from relying on any power of my own, I came among you in great "fear and trembling" and in my speeches and the sermons that I gave, there were none of the arguments that belong to philosophy; only a demonstration of the power of the Spirit. And I did this so that your faith should not depend on human philosophy but on the power of God.

Gospel Acclamation
Alleluia, alleluia!
I am the light of the world, says the Lord,
anyone who follows me
will have the light of life.
Alleluia!

John 8:12

Gospel   Matthew 5:13-16
You are the light of the world.
Jesus said to his disciples: "You are the salt of the earth. But if salt becomes tasteless, what can make it salty again? It is good for nothing, and can only be thrown out to be trampled underfoot by men.

"You are the light of the world. A city built on a hill-top cannot be hidden. No one lights a lamp to put it under a tub; they put it on the lamp-stand where it shines for everyone in the house. In the same way your light must shine in the sight of men, so that, seeing your good works, they may give the praise to your Father in heaven."

The Creed is said.

Prayer over the Offerings
O Lord, our God,
who once established these created things
to sustain us in our frailty,
grant, we pray,
that they may become for us now
the Sacrament of eternal life.
Through Christ our Lord.

Preface I-VIII of the Sundays in Ordinary Time, pp. 499-502.

Communion Antiphon
Let them thank the Lord for his mercy,
his wonders for the children of men,
for he satisfies the thirsty soul,
and the hungry he fills with good things.   cf. Psalm 106:8-9

or

Blessed are those who mourn, for they shall be consoled.
Blessed are those who hunger and thirst for righteousness,
for they shall have their fill.   Matthew 5:5-6

Prayer after Communion
O God, who have willed that we be partakers
in the one Bread and the one Chalice,
grant us, we pray, so to live
that, made one in Christ,
we may joyfully bear fruit
for the salvation of the world.
Through Christ our Lord.

SIXTH SUNDAY IN
ORDINARY TIME – A

The Law of God is for human fulfilment and happiness.
God's ways are other than ours. When we try to penetrate deeper into the
meaning of the Law we realise that it is only God's Spirit that can help us to
plumb the depths of God's commandments. Jesus is the fulfilment of the Law.
If we follow him, we will keep God's word.

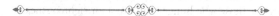

Entrance Antiphon
Be my protector, O God,
a mighty stronghold to save me.
For you are my rock, my stronghold!
Lead me, guide me, for the sake of your name.   cf. Psalm 30:3-4

The Gloria is said or sung.

Collect
O God, who teach us that you abide
in hearts that are just and true,
grant that we may be so fashioned by your grace
as to become a dwelling pleasing to you.
Through our Lord Jesus Christ, your Son,
who lives and reigns with you in the unity of the Holy Spirit,
one God, for ever and ever.

First Reading   Ecclesiasticus 15:15-20
He never commanded anyone to be godless.
If you wish, you can keep the commandments,
to behave faithfully is within your power.
He has set fire and water before you;
put out your hand to whichever you prefer.
Man has life and death before him,
whichever a man likes better will be given him.
For vast is the wisdom of the Lord;

he is almighty and all-seeing.
His eyes are on those who fear him,
he notes every action of man.
He never commanded anyone to be godless,
he has given no one permission to sin.

Psalm   Psalm 118

R. **They are happy who follow God's law!**

1. They are happy whose life is blameless,
   who follow God's law!
   They are happy those who do his will,
   seeking him with all their hearts. R.

2. You have laid down your precepts
   to be obeyed with care.
   May my footsteps be firm
   to obey your statutes. R.

3. Bless your servant and I shall live
   and obey your word.
   Open my eyes that I may consider
   the wonders of your law. R.

4. Teach me the demands of your statutes
   and I will keep them to the end.
   Train me to observe your law,
   to keep it with my heart. R.

Second Reading   1 Corinthians 2:6-10
God predestined wisdom to be for our glory before the ages began.
We have a wisdom to offer those who have reached maturity: not a
philosophy of our age, it is true, still less of the masters of our age,
which are coming to their end. The hidden wisdom of God which
we teach in our mysteries is the wisdom that God predestined to
be for our glory before the ages began. It is a wisdom that none of
the masters of this age have ever known, or they would not have

crucified the Lord of Glory; we teach what scripture calls: the things that no eye has seen and no ear has heard, things beyond the mind of man, all that God has prepared for those who love him.

These are the very things that God has revealed to us through the Spirit, for the Spirit reaches the depths of everything, even the depths of God.

Gospel Acclamation
Alleluia, alleluia!
Speak, Lord, your servant is listening:
you have the message of eternal life.
Alleluia!   1 Samuel 3:9; John 6:68

or

Alleluia, alleluia!
Blessed are you, Father,
Lord of heaven and earth,
for revealing the mysteries of the kingdom
to mere children.
Alleluia!   cf. Matthew 11:25

Gospel   Matthew 5:17-37
You have learnt how it was said to our ancestors; but I say this to you.

| Jesus said to his disciples:

"Do not imagine that I have come to abolish the Law or the Prophets. I have come not to abolish them but to complete them. I tell you solemnly, till heaven and earth disappear, not one dot, not one little stroke, shall disappear from the Law until its purpose is achieved. Therefore, the man who infringes even one of the least of these commandments and teaches others to do the same will be considered the least in the kingdom of heaven; but the man who keeps them and teaches them will be considered great in the kingdom of heaven.

"(For) I tell you, if your virtue goes no deeper than that of the scribes and Pharisees, you will never get into the kingdom of heaven.

"You have learnt how it was said to our ancestors: You must not kill; and if anyone does kill he must answer for it before the court. But I say this to you: anyone who is angry with his brother will answer for it before the court;

if a man calls his brother 'Fool' he will answer for it before the Sanhedrin; and if a man calls him 'Renegade' he will answer for it in hell fire. So then, if you are bringing your offering to the altar and there remember that your brother has something against you, leave your offering there before the altar, go and be reconciled with your brother first, and then come back and present your offering. Come to terms with your opponent in good time while you are still on the way to the court with him, or he may hand you over to the judge and the judge to the officer, and you will be thrown into prison. I tell you solemnly, you will not get out till you have paid the last penny.

"You have learnt how it was said: You must not commit adultery. But I say this to you: if a man looks at a woman lustfully, he has already committed adultery with her in his heart.

If your right eye should cause you to sin, tear it out and throw it away; for it will do you less harm to lose one part of you than to have your whole body thrown into hell. And if your right hand should cause you to sin, cut if off and throw it away; for it will do you less harm to lose one part of you than to have your whole body go to hell.

"It has also been said: Anyone who divorces his wife must give her a writ of dismissal. But I say this to you: everyone who divorces his wife, except for the case of fornication, makes her an adulteress; and anyone who marries a divorced woman commits adultery.

"Again, you have learnt how it was said to our ancestors: You must not break your oath, but must fulfil your oaths to the Lord. But I say this to you: do not swear at all,

either by heaven, since that is God's throne; or by the earth, since that is his footstool; or by Jerusalem, since that is the city of the great king. Do not swear by your own head either, since you cannot turn a single hair white or black.

All you need say is 'Yes' if you mean yes, 'No' if you mean no; anything more than this comes from the evil one."

The Creed is said.

Prayer over the Offerings
May this oblation, O Lord, we pray,
cleanse and renew us
and may it become for those who do your will
the source of eternal reward.
Through Christ our Lord.

Preface I-VIII of the Sundays in Ordinary Time, pp. 499-502.

Communion Antiphon
They ate and had their fill,
and what they craved the Lord gave them;
they were not disappointed in what they craved.   cf. Psalm 77:29-30

or

God so loved the world
that he gave his Only Begotten Son,
so that all who believe in him may not perish,
but may have eternal life.   John 3:16

Prayer after Communion
Having fed upon these heavenly delights,
we pray, O Lord,
that we may always long
for that food by which we truly live.
Through Christ our Lord.

SEVENTH SUNDAY IN ORDINARY TIME – A

Love your enemies.
Every human being is made in the image and likeness of God. Jesus teaches us
to look upon our neighbours as friends and not enemies. We are all brothers
and sisters in Christ. In this way we will become holy as God wants us to be.

Entrance Antiphon

O Lord, I trust in your merciful love.
My heart will rejoice in your salvation.
I will sing to the Lord who has been bountiful with me.   Psalm 12:6

The Gloria is said or sung.

Collect

Grant, we pray, almighty God,
that, always pondering spiritual things,
we may carry out in both word and deed
that which is pleasing to you.
Through our Lord Jesus Christ, your Son,
who lives and reigns with you in the unity of the Holy Spirit,
one God, for ever and ever.

First Reading   Leviticus 19:1-2. 17-18

You must love your neighbour as yourself.

The Lord spoke to Moses; he said: "Speak to the whole community
of the sons of Israel and say to them: 'Be holy, for I, the Lord your
God, am holy.

'You must not bear hatred for your brother in your heart. You
must openly tell him, your neighbour, of his offence; this way you
will not take a sin upon yourself. You must not exact vengeance, nor
must you bear a grudge against the children of your people. You
must love your neighbour as yourself. I am the Lord.' "

Psalm   Psalm 102

R. **The Lord is compassion and love.**

1. My soul, give thanks to the Lord,
   all my being, bless his holy name.
   My soul, give thanks to the Lord
   and never forget all his blessings. R.

2. It is he who forgives all your guilt,
   who heals every one of your ills,
   who redeems your life from the grave,
   who crowns you with love and compassion. R.

3. The Lord is compassion and love,
   slow to anger and rich in mercy.
   He does not treat us according to our sins,
   Nor repay us according to our faults. R.

4. As far as the east is from the west
   so far does he remove our sins.
   As a father has compassion on his sons,
   the Lord has pity on those who fear him. R.

Second Reading   1 Corinthians 3:16-23
All are your servants, but you belong to Christ and Christ belongs
to God.
Didn't you realise that you were God's temple and that the Spirit of
God was living among you? If anybody should destroy the temple
of God, God will destroy him, because the temple of God is sacred;
and you are that temple.

Make no mistake about it: if any one of you thinks of himself as
wise, in the ordinary sense of the word, then he must learn to be a
fool before he really can be wise. Why? Because the wisdom of this
world is foolishness to God. As scripture says: The Lord knows wise
men's thoughts: he knows how useless they are; or again: God is
not convinced by the arguments of the wise. So there is nothing to
boast about in anything human: Paul, Apollos, Cephas, the world,

life and death, the present and the future, are all your servants; but you belong to Christ and Christ belongs to God.

Gospel Acclamation
Alleluia, alleluia!
If anyone loves me he will keep my word,
and my Father will love him,
and we shall come to him.
Alleluia!   John 14:23

or

Alleluia, alleluia!
When anyone obeys what Christ has said,
God's love comes to perfection in him.
Alleluia!   1 John 2:5

Gospel   Matthew 5:38-48
Love your enemies.
Jesus said to his disciples: "You have learnt how it was said: Eye for eye and tooth for tooth. But I say this to you: offer the wicked man no resistance. On the contrary, if anyone hits you on the right cheek, offer him the other as well; if a man takes you to law and would have your tunic, let him have your cloak as well. And if anyone orders you to go one mile, go two miles with him. Give to anyone who asks, and if anyone wants to borrow, do not turn away.

"You have learnt how it was said: You must love your neighbour and hate your enemy. But I say this to you: love your enemies and pray for those who persecute you; in this way you will be sons of your Father in heaven, for he causes his sun to rise on bad men as well as good, and his rain to fall on honest and dishonest men alike. For if you love those who love you, what right have you to claim any credit? Even the tax collectors do as much, do they not? And if you save your greetings for your brothers, are you doing anything exceptional? Even the pagans do as much, do they not? You must therefore be perfect just as your heavenly Father is perfect."

The Creed is said.

Prayer over the Offerings
As we celebrate your mysteries, O Lord,
with the observance that is your due,
we humbly ask you,
that what we offer to the honour of your majesty
may profit us for salvation.
Through Christ our Lord.

Preface I-VIII of the Sundays in Ordinary Time, pp. 499-502.

Communion Antiphon
I will recount all your wonders,
I will rejoice in you and be glad,
and sing psalms to your name, O Most High.   Psalm 9:2-3

or

Lord, I have come to believe that you are the Christ,
the Son of the living God, who is coming into this world.
                                                             John 11:27

Prayer after Communion
Grant, we pray, almighty God,
that we may experience the effects of the salvation
which is pledged to us by these mysteries.
Through Christ our Lord.

EIGHTH SUNDAY IN ORDINARY TIME – A

Do not worry about tomorrow.
The teaching of Jesus penetrates to the nerve centre of all our fears and worries.
The past is behind us and the future yet to come. Jesus teaches us to live every
moment to the full, since we have only today. God never abandons us, and
knows the deepest desires and intentions of our hearts.

Entrance Antiphon

The Lord became my protector.
He brought me out to a place of freedom;
he saved me because he delighted in me.   cf. Psalm 17:19-20

The Gloria is said or sung.

Collect

Grant us, O Lord, we pray,
that the course of our world
may be directed by your peaceful rule
and that your Church may rejoice,
untroubled in her devotion.
Through our Lord Jesus Christ, your Son,
who lives and reigns with you in the unity of the Holy Spirit,
one God, for ever and ever.

First Reading   Isaiah 49:14-15

I will never forget you.
Zion was saying, "The Lord has abandoned me,
the Lord has forgotten me."
Does a woman forget her baby at the breast,
or fail to cherish the son of her womb?
Yet even if these forget,
I will never forget you.

Psalm   Psalm 61

R. **In God alone is my soul at rest.**

1. In God alone is my soul at rest;
    my help comes from him.
    He alone is my rock, my stronghold,
    my fortress: I stand firm. R.

2. In God alone be at rest, my soul;
    for my hope comes from him.
    He alone is my rock, my stronghold,
    my fortress: I stand firm. R.

3. In God is my safety and glory,
    the rock of my strength.
    Take refuge in God all you people.
    Trust him at all times.
    Pour out your hearts before him. R.

Second Reading   1 Corinthians 4:1-5
The Lord will reveal the secret intentions of men's hearts.
People must think of us as Christ's servants, stewards entrusted with
the mysteries of God. What is expected of stewards is that each one
should be found worthy of his trust. Not that it makes the slightest
difference to me whether you, or indeed any human tribunal, find
me worthy or not. I will not even pass judgement on myself. True,
my conscience does not reproach me at all, but that does not prove
that I am acquitted: the Lord alone is my judge. There must be no
passing of premature judgement. Leave that until the Lord comes:
he will light up all that is hidden in the dark and reveal the secret
intentions of men's hearts. Then will be the time for each one to
have whatever praise he deserves, from God.

Gospel Acclamation
Alleluia, alleluia!
Your word is truth, O Lord,
consecrate us in the truth.
Alleluia!   John 17:17

or

Alleluia, alleluia!
The word of God is something alive and active;
it can judge secret emotions and thoughts.
Alleluia!

Hebrews 4:12

Gospel   Mathew 6:24-34

Do not worry about tomorrow.

Jesus said to his disciples: "No one can be the slave of two masters: he will either hate the first and love the second, or treat the first with respect and the second with scorn. You cannot be the slave both of God and of money.

"That is why I am telling you not to worry about your life and what you are to eat, nor about your body and how you are to clothe it. Surely life means more than food, and the body more than clothing! Look at the birds in the sky. They do not sow or reap or gather into barns; yet your heavenly Father feeds them. Are you not worth much more than they are? Can any of you, for all his worrying, add one single cubit to his span of life? And why worry about clothing? Think of the flowers growing in the fields; they never have to work or spin; yet I assure you that not even Solomon in all his regalia was robed like one of these. Now if that is how God clothes the grass in the field which is there today and thrown into the furnace tomorrow, will he not much more look after you, you men of little faith? So do not worry; do not say, 'What are we to eat? What are we to drink? How are we to be clothed?' It is the pagans who set their hearts on all these things. Your heavenly Father knows you need them all. Set your hearts on his kingdom first, and on his righteousness, and all these other things will be given you as well. So do not worry about tomorrow: tomorrow will take care of itself. Each day has enough trouble of its own."

The Creed is said.

Prayer over the Offerings
O God, who provide gifts to be offered to your name
and count our oblations as signs
of our desire to serve you with devotion,
we ask of your mercy
that what you grant as the source of merit
may also help us to attain merit's reward.
Through Christ our Lord.

Preface I-VIII of the Sundays in Ordinary Time, pp. 499-502.

Communion Antiphon
I will sing to the Lord who has been bountiful with me,
sing psalms to the name of the Lord Most High.   cf. Psalm 12:6

or

Behold, I am with you always,
even to the end of the age, says the Lord.   Matthew 28:20

Prayer after Communion
Nourished by your saving gifts,
we beseech your mercy, Lord,
that by this same Sacrament
with which you feed us in the present age,
you may make us partakers of life eternal.
Through Christ our Lord.

NINTH SUNDAY IN
ORDINARY TIME – A

Faith as strong as a rock.
Faith is God's gift to us and we are called to let it penetrate into our hearts
and souls. Jesus teaches us to let all our actions spring from the deep well of
faith rather than from the external observance of law. In times of trouble and
temptation our faith will stand firm like a house built on a rock.

Entrance Antiphon

Turn to me and have mercy on me, O Lord,
for I am alone and poor.
See my lowliness and suffering
and take away all my sins, my God.   cf. Psalm 24:16. 18

The Gloria is said or sung.

Collect

O God, whose providence never fails in its design,
keep from us, we humbly beseech you,
all that might harm us
and grant all that works for our good.
Through our Lord Jesus Christ, your Son,
who lives and reigns with you in the unity of the Holy Spirit,
one God, for ever and ever.

First Reading   Deuteronomy 11:18. 26-28. 32

See, I set before you today a blessing and a curse.

Moses said to the people: "Let these words of mine remain in your
heart and in your soul; fasten them on your hand as a sign and on
your forehead as a circlet.

"See, I set before you today a blessing and a curse: a blessing, if
you obey the commandments of the Lord our God that I enjoin on
you today; a curse, if you disobey the commandments of the Lord
your God and leave the way I have marked out for you today, by
going after other gods you have not known. You must keep and
observe all the laws and customs that I set before you today."

Psalm   Psalm 30

R. **Be a rock of refuge for me, O Lord.**

1. In you, O Lord, I take refuge.
    Let me never be put to shame.
    In your justice, set me free,
    hear me and speedily rescue me. R.

2. Be a rock of refuge to me,
    a mighty stronghold to save me,
    for you are my rock, my stronghold.
    For your name's sake, lead me and guide me. R.

3. Let your face shine on your servant.
    Save me in your love.
    Be strong, let your heart take courage,
    all who hope in the Lord. R.

Second Reading   Romans 3:21-25. 28

*A man is justified by faith and not by doing something the Law tells
him to do.*

God's justice that was made known through the Law and the
Prophets has now been revealed outside the Law, since it is the same
justice of God that comes through faith to everyone, Jew and pagan
alike, who believes in Jesus Christ. Both Jew and pagan sinned and
forfeited God's glory, and both are justified through the free gift
of his grace by being redeemed in Christ Jesus who was appointed
by God to sacrifice his life so as to win reconciliation through
faith since, as we see it, a man is justified by faith and not by doing
something the Law tells him to do.

Gospel Acclamation
Alleluia, alleluia!
If anyone loves me he will keep my word,
and my Father will love him,
and we shall come to him.
Alleluia!

                                                            John 14:23

or

Alleluia, alleluia!
I am the vine, you are the branches,
says the Lord.
Whoever remains in me, with me in him,
bears fruit in plenty.
Alleluia!   John 15:5

Gospel   Matthew 7:21-27
The house built on rock and the house built on sand.

Jesus said to his disciples: "It is not those who say to me, 'Lord, Lord', who will enter the kingdom of heaven, but the person who does the will of my Father in heaven. When the day comes many will say to me, 'Lord, Lord, did we not prophesy in your name, cast out demons in your name, work many miracles in your name?' Then I shall tell them to their faces: I have never known you; away from me, you evil men!

"Therefore, everyone who listens to these words of mine and acts on them will be like a sensible man who built his house on rock. Rain came down, floods rose, gales blew and hurled themselves against that house, and it did not fall: it was founded on rock. But everyone who listens to these words of mine and does not act on them will be like a stupid man who built his house on sand. Rain came down, floods rose, gales blew and struck that house, and it fell; and what a fall it had!"

The Creed is said.

Prayer over the Offerings
Trusting in your compassion, O Lord,
we come eagerly with our offerings to your sacred altar,
that, through the purifying action of your grace,
we may be cleansed by the very mysteries we serve.
Through Christ our Lord.

Preface I-VIII of the Sundays in Ordinary Time, pp. 499-502.

Communion Antiphon

To you I call, for you will surely heed me, O God;
turn your ear to me; hear my words.   cf. Psalm 16:6

or

Amen, I say to you: Whatever you ask for in prayer,
believe you will receive it,
and it will be yours, says the Lord.   Mark 11:23. 24

Prayer after Communion

Govern by your Spirit, we pray, O Lord,
those you feed with the Body and Blood of your Son,
that, professing you not just in word or in speech,
but also in works and in truth,
we may merit to enter the Kingdom of Heaven.
Through Christ our Lord.

TENTH SUNDAY IN ORDINARY TIME – A

What God wants is mercy, not sacrifice.
The Lord tells us that love must be sincere and flow from a deep faith in
him. God does not want the mere externals of sacrifice. Faith and love show
themselves in action. We are called to be merciful like Christ towards sinners,
because it is those who are sick who have need of a doctor.

Entrance Antiphon

The Lord is my light and my salvation; whom shall I fear?
The Lord is the stronghold of my life; whom should I dread?
When those who do evil draw near, they stumble and fall.

cf. Psalm 26:1-2

The Gloria is said or sung.

Collect

O God, from whom all good things come,
grant that we, who call on you in our need,
may at your prompting discern what is right,
and by your guidance do it.
Through our Lord Jesus Christ, your Son,
who lives and reigns with you in the unity of the Holy Spirit,
one God, for ever and ever.

First Reading   Hosea 6:3-6

What I want is love, not sacrifice.

Let us set ourselves to know the Lord;
that he will come is as certain as the dawn
his judgement will rise like the light,
he will come to us as showers come,
like spring rains watering the earth.

What am I to do with you, Ephraim?
What am I to do with you, Judah?

This love of yours is like a morning cloud,
like the dew that quickly disappears.
This is why I have torn them to pieces by the prophets,
why I slaughtered them with the words from my mouth,
since what I want is love, not sacrifice;
knowledge of God, not holocausts.

Psalm   Psalm 49

R. **I will show God's salvation to the upright.**

1. The God of gods, the Lord,
    has spoken and summoned the earth,
    from the rising of the sun to its setting.
    "I find no fault with your sacrifices,
    your offerings are always before me. R.

2. "Were I hungry, I would not tell you,
    for I own the world and all it holds.
    Do you think I eat the flesh of bulls,
    or drink the blood of goats? R.

3. "Pay your sacrifice of thanksgiving to God
    and render him your votive offerings.
    Call on me in the day of distress.
    I will free you and you shall honour me." R.

Second Reading   Romans 4:18-25
Abraham drew strength from faith and gave glory to God.
Though it seemed Abraham's hope could not be fulfilled, he hoped
and he believed, and through doing so he did become the father of
many nations exactly as he had been promised: Your descendants
will be as many as the stars. Even the thought that his body was
past fatherhood – he was about a hundred years old – and Sarah
too old to become a mother, did not shake his belief. Since God had
promised it, Abraham refused either to deny it or even to doubt
it, but drew strength from faith and gave glory to God, convinced

that God had power to do what he had promised. This is the faith that was "considered as justifying him". Scripture however does not refer only to him but to us as well when it says that his faith was thus "considered"; our faith too will be "considered" if we believe in him who raised Jesus our Lord from the dead, Jesus who was put to death for our sins and raised to life to justify us.

Gospel Acclamation
Alleluia, alleluia!
Open our heart, O Lord,
to accept the words of your Son.
Alleluia!   cf. Acts 16:14

or

Alleluia, alleluia!
The Lord has sent me to bring the good news to the poor,
to proclaim liberty to captives.
Alleluia!   Luke 4:18

Gospel   Matthew 9:9-13
I did not come to call the virtuous, but sinners.
As Jesus was walking on he saw a man named Matthew sitting by the customs house, and he said to him, "Follow me." And he got up and followed him.

While he was at dinner in the house it happened that a number of tax collectors and sinners came to sit at the table with Jesus and his disciples. When the Pharisees saw this, they said to his disciples, "Why does your master eat with tax collectors and sinners?" When he heard this he replied, "It is not the healthy who need the doctor, but the sick. Go and learn the meaning of the words: What I want is mercy, not sacrifice. And indeed I did not come to call the virtuous, but sinners."

The Creed is said.

Prayer over the Offerings
Look kindly upon our service, O Lord, we pray,
that what we offer
may be an acceptable oblation to you
and lead us to grow in charity.
Through Christ our Lord.

Preface I-VIII of the Sundays in Ordinary Time, pp. 499-502.

Communion Antiphon
The Lord is my rock, my fortress, and my deliverer;
my God is my saving strength.   Psalm 17:3

or

God is love, and whoever abides in love
abides in God, and God in him.   1 John 4:16

Prayer after Communion
May your healing work, O Lord,
free us, we pray, from doing evil
and lead us to what is right.
Through Christ our Lord.

ELEVENTH SUNDAY IN ORDINARY TIME – A

Christ our reconciliation.
We are reconciled to God our Father by the death of his Son, and we trust
that God will give us new life through Christ's Resurrection. We share in his
Gospel and proclaim to everyone that the kingdom of heaven is close at hand.
This is the mission that we share with all the followers of Christ.

Entrance Antiphon

O Lord, hear my voice, for I have called to you; be my help.
Do not abandon or forsake me, O God, my Saviour!

cf. Psalm 26:7. 9

The Gloria is said or sung.

Collect

O God, strength of those who hope in you,
graciously hear our pleas,
and, since without you mortal frailty can do nothing,
grant us always the help of your grace,
that in following your commands
we may please you by our resolve and our deeds.
Through our Lord Jesus Christ, your Son,
who lives and reigns with you in the unity of the Holy Spirit,
one God, for ever and ever.

First Reading   Exodus 19:2-6

I will count you a kingdom of priests, a consecrated nation.

From Rephidim the Israelites set out again; and when they reached
the wilderness of Sinai, there in the wilderness they pitched their
camp; there facing the mountain Israel pitched camp.

Moses then went up to God, and the Lord called to him from
the mountain, saying, "Say this to the House of Jacob, declare this
to the sons of Israel, 'You yourselves have seen what I did with the

Egyptians, how I carried you on eagle's wings and brought you to myself. From this you know that now, if you obey my voice and hold fast to my covenant, you of all the nations shall be my very own, for all the earth is mine. I will count you a kingdom of priests, a consecrated nation.'"

Psalm   Psalm 99

R. **We are his people:**
    the sheep of his flock.

1. Cry out with joy to the Lord, all the earth.
    Serve the Lord with gladness.
    Come before him, singing for joy. R.

2. Know that he, the Lord, is God.
    He made us, we belong to him,
    we are his people, the sheep of his flock. R.

3. Indeed, how good is the Lord,
    eternal his merciful love.
    He is faithful from age to age. R.

Second Reading   Romans 5:6-11
Now that we have been reconciled by the death of his Son, surely we may count on being saved by the life of his Son.

We were still helpless when at his appointed moment Christ died for sinful men. It is not easy to die even for a good man – though of course for someone really worthy, a man might be prepared to die – but what proves that God loves us is that Christ died for us while we were still sinners. Having died to make us righteous, is it likely that he would now fail to save us from God's anger? When we were reconciled to God by the death of his Son, we were still enemies; now that we have been reconciled, surely we may count on being saved by the life of his Son? Not merely because we have been reconciled but because we are filled with joyful trust in God through our Lord Jesus Christ, through whom we have already gained our reconciliation.

Gospel Acclamation

Alleluia, alleluia!
The sheep that belong to me listen to my voice,
says the Lord,
I know them and they follow me.
Alleluia!   John 10:27

or

Alleluia, alleluia!
The kingdom of God is close at hand.
Repent, and believe the good news.
Alleluia!   Mark 1:15

Gospel   Matthew 9:36 – 10:8

He summoned his twelve disciples, and sent them out.

When Jesus saw the crowds he felt sorry for them because they were harassed and dejected, like sheep without a shepherd. Then he said to his disciples, "The harvest is rich but the labourers are few, so ask the Lord of the harvest to send labourers to his harvest."

He summoned his twelve disciples, and gave them authority over unclean spirits with power to cast them out and to cure all kinds of diseases and sickness.

These are the names of the twelve apostles: first, Simon who is called Peter, and his brother Andrew; James the son of Zebedee, and his brother John; Philip and Bartholomew; Thomas, and Matthew the tax collector; James the son of Alphaeus, and Thaddaeus; Simon the Zealot and Judas Iscariot, the one who was to betray him. These twelve Jesus sent out, instructing them as follows:

"Do not turn your steps to pagan territory, and do not enter any Samaritan town; go rather to the lost sheep of the House of Israel. And as you go, proclaim that the kingdom of heaven is close at hand. Cure the sick, raise the dead, cleanse the lepers, cast out devils. You received without charge, give without charge."

The Creed is said.

Prayer over the Offerings
O God, who in the offerings presented here
provide for the twofold needs of human nature,
nourishing us with food
and renewing us with your Sacrament,
grant, we pray,
that the sustenance they provide
may not fail us in body or in spirit.
Through Christ our Lord.

Preface I-VIII of the Sundays in Ordinary Time, pp. 499-502.

Communion Antiphon
There is one thing I ask of the Lord, only this do I seek:
to live in the house of the Lord all the days of my life.   Psalm 26:4

or

Holy Father, keep in your name those you have given me,
that they may be one as we are one, says the Lord.   John 17:11

Prayer after Communion
As this reception of your Holy Communion, O Lord,
foreshadows the union of the faithful in you,
so may it bring about unity in your Church.
Through Christ our Lord.

TWELFTH SUNDAY IN ORDINARY TIME – A

Do not be afraid.
We have no need to be afraid since God is always at our side supporting and
strengthening us in times of weakness and temptation. The evil effects of sin
are swallowed up in the victory of Christ. He gives life to our souls and with
him we have no cause for fear.

Entrance Antiphon
The Lord is the strength of his people,
a saving refuge for the one he has anointed.
Save your people, Lord, and bless your heritage,
and govern them for ever.   cf. Psalm 27:8-9

The Gloria is said or sung.

Collect
Grant, O Lord,
that we may always revere and love your holy name,
for you never deprive of your guidance
those you set firm on the foundation of your love.
Through our Lord Jesus Christ, your Son,
who lives and reigns with you in the unity of the Holy Spirit,
one God, for ever and ever.

First Reading   Jeremiah 20:10-13
He has delivered the soul of the needy from the hands of evil men.
Jeremiah said:

> I hear so many disparaging me,
> " 'Terror from every side!'
> Denounce him! Let us denounce him!"
> All those who used to be my friends
> watched for my downfall,
> "Perhaps he will be seduced into error.
> Then we will master him

and take our revenge!"
But the Lord is at my side, a mighty hero;
my opponents will stumble, mastered,
confounded by their failure;
everlasting, unforgettable disgrace will be theirs.
But you, Lord of Hosts, you who probe with justice,
who scrutinise the loins and heart,
let me see the vengeance you will take on them,
for I have committed my cause to you.
Sing to the Lord,
praise the Lord,
for he has delivered the soul of the needy
from the hands of evil men.

Psalm   Psalm 68

R. **In your great love, answer me, O God.**

1. It is for you that I suffer taunts,
   that shame covers my face,
   that I have become a stranger to my brothers,
   an alien to my own mother's sons.
   I burn with zeal for your house
   and taunts against you fall on me. R.

2. This is my prayer to you,
   my prayer for your favour.
   In your great love, answer me, O God,
   with your help that never fails:
   Lord, answer, for your love is kind;
   in your compassion, turn towards me. R.

3. The poor when they see it will be glad
   and God-seeking hearts will revive;
   for the Lord listens to the needy
   and does not spurn his servants in their chains.
   Let the heavens and the earth give him praise,
   the sea and all its living creatures. R.

Second Reading   **Romans 5:12-15**

The gift considerably outweighed the fall.

Sin entered the world through one man, and through sin death, and thus death has spread through the whole human race because everyone has sinned. Sin existed in the world long before the Law was given. There was no law and so no one could be accused of the sin of "law-breaking", yet death reigned over all from Adam to Moses, even though their sin, unlike that of Adam, was not a matter of breaking a law.

   Adam prefigured the One to come, but the gift itself considerably outweighed the fall. If it is certain that through one man's fall so many died, it is even more certain that divine grace, coming through the one man, Jesus Christ, came to so many as an abundant free gift.

Gospel Acclamation

Alleluia, alleluia!
The Word was made flesh and lived among us;
to all who did accept him
he gave power to become children of God.
Alleluia!   John 1:14. 12

or

Alleluia, alleluia!
The Spirit of truth will be my witness;
and you too will be my witnesses.
Alleluia!   John 15:26. 27

Gospel   **Matthew 10:26-33**

Do not be afraid of those who kill the body.

Jesus instructed the Twelve as follows: "Do not be afraid. For everything that is now covered will be uncovered, and everything now hidden will be made clear. What I say to you in the dark, tell in the daylight; what you hear in whispers, proclaim from the house-tops.

   "Do not be afraid of those who kill the body but cannot kill the soul; fear him rather who can destroy both body and soul in hell. Can you not buy two sparrows for a penny? And yet not one falls to the ground without your Father knowing. Why, every hair on your head has been counted. So there is no need to be afraid; you are worth more than hundreds of sparrows.

"So if anyone declares himself for me in the presence of men, I will declare myself for him in the presence of my Father in heaven. But the one who disowns me in the presence of men, I will disown in the presence of my Father in heaven."

The Creed is said.

Prayer over the Offerings
Receive, O Lord, the sacrifice of conciliation and praise
and grant that, cleansed by its action,
we may make offering of a heart pleasing to you.
Through Christ our Lord.

Preface I-VIII of the Sundays in Ordinary Time, pp. 499-502.

Communion Antiphon
The eyes of all look to you, Lord,
and you give them their food in due season.   Psalm 144:15

or

I am the Good Shepherd,
and I lay down my life for my sheep, says the Lord.   John 10:11. 15

Prayer after Communion
Renewed and nourished
by the Sacred Body and Precious Blood of your Son,
we ask of your mercy, O Lord,
that what we celebrate with constant devotion
may be our sure pledge of redemption.
Through Christ our Lord.

THIRTEENTH SUNDAY IN ORDINARY TIME – A

If we die with Christ we shall live with him.
In our daily lives we are called to take up our cross and follow Christ,
knowing that by joining him in his suffering we will be joining him in eternal
life. We are dead to sin and alive to God. There is within us a new creation as
we welcome Christ daily within us as our new life.

Entrance Antiphon
All peoples, clap your hands.
Cry to God with shouts of joy!

Psalm 46:2

The Gloria is said or sung.

Collect
O God, who through the grace of adoption
chose us to be children of light,
grant, we pray,
that we may not be wrapped in the darkness of error
but always be seen to stand in the bright light of truth.
Through our Lord Jesus Christ, your Son,
who lives and reigns with you in the unity of the Holy Spirit,
one God, for ever and ever.

First Reading 2 Kings 4:8-11. 14-16
This is a holy man of God, let him rest there.

One day as Elisha was on his way to Shunem, a woman of rank who lived there pressed him to stay and eat there. After this he always broke his journey for a meal when he passed that way. She said to her husband, "Look, I am sure the man who is constantly passing our way must be a holy man of God. Let us build him a small room on the roof, and put him a bed in it, and a table and chair and lamp; whenever he comes to us he can rest there."

One day when he came, he retired to the upper room and lay

down. "What can be done for her?" he asked. Gehazi, his servant, answered, "Well, she has no son and her husband is old." Elisha said, "Call her." The servant called her and she stood at the door. "This time next year," Elisha said "you will hold a son in your arms."

Psalm   Psalm 88

R. **I will sing for ever of your love, O Lord.**

1. I will sing for ever of your love, O Lord;
    through all ages my mouth will proclaim your truth.
    Of this I am sure, that your love lasts for ever,
    that your truth is firmly established as the heavens. R.

2. Happy the people who acclaim such a king,
    who walk, O Lord, in the light of your face,
    who find their joy every day in your name,
    who make your justice the source of their bliss. R.

3. For it is you, O Lord, who are the glory of their strength;
    it is by your favour that our might is exalted:
    for our ruler is in the keeping of the Lord;
    our king in the keeping of the Holy One of Israel. R.

Second Reading   Romans 6:3-4. 8-11
When we were baptised we went into the tomb with Christ, so that we too might live a new life.

When we were baptised in Christ Jesus we were baptised in his death; in other words, when we were baptised we went into the tomb with him and joined him in death, so that as Christ was raised from the dead by the Father's glory, we too might live a new life.

But we believe that having died with Christ we shall return to life with him: Christ, as we know, having been raised from the dead will never die again. Death has no power over him any more. When he died, he died, once for all, to sin, so his life now is life with God; and in that way, you too must consider yourselves to be dead to sin but alive for God in Christ Jesus.

Gospel Acclamation
Alleluia, alleluia!
Open our heart, O Lord,
to accept the words of your Son.
Alleluia!   cf. Acts 16:14

or

Alleluia, alleluia!
You are a chosen race, a royal priesthood, a people set apart
to sing the praises of God
who called you out of darkness into his wonderful light.
Alleluia!   1 Peter 2:9

Gospel   Matthew 10:37-42
Anyone who does not take his cross is not worthy of me. Anyone
who welcomes you welcomes me.
Jesus instructed the Twelve as follows: "Anyone who prefers father
or mother to me is not worthy of me. Anyone who prefers son or
daughter to me is not worthy of me. Anyone who does not take his
cross and follow in my footsteps is not worthy of me. Anyone who
finds his life will lose it; anyone who loses his life for my sake will
find it.

"Anyone who welcomes you welcomes me; and those who
welcome me welcome the one who sent me.

"Anyone who welcomes a prophet because he is a prophet will
have a prophet's reward; and anyone who welcomes a holy man
because he is a holy man will have a holy man's reward.

"If anyone gives so much as a cup of cold water to one of these
little ones because he is a disciple, then I tell you solemnly, he will
most certainly not lose his reward."

The Creed is said.

Prayer over the Offerings

O God, who graciously accomplish
the effects of your mysteries,
grant, we pray,
that the deeds by which we serve you
may be worthy of these sacred gifts.
Through Christ our Lord.

Preface I-VIII of the Sundays in Ordinary Time, pp. 499-502.

Communion Antiphon

Bless the Lord, O my soul,
and all within me, his holy name.   cf. Psalm 102:1

or

O Father, I pray for them, that they may be one in us,
that the world may believe that you have sent me, says the Lord.
                                                            John 17:20-21

Prayer after Communion

May this divine sacrifice we have offered and received
fill us with life, O Lord, we pray,
so that, bound to you in lasting charity,
we may bear fruit that lasts for ever.
Through Christ our Lord.

FOURTEENTH SUNDAY IN ORDINARY TIME – A

Christ's yoke is easy and his burden light.
Christ, even though he is the Son of God, humbles himself and comes among
us in human form. He embraces our condition and knows at first hand our
worries and anxieties. Through the Holy Spirit Christ lives in us, so that we
may find rest for our souls.

Entrance Antiphon
Your merciful love, O God,
we have received in the midst of your temple.
Your praise, O God, like your name,
reaches the ends of the earth;
your right hand is filled with saving justice.   cf. Psalm 47:10-11

The Gloria is said or sung.

Collect
O God, who in the abasement of your Son
have raised up a fallen world,
fill your faithful with holy joy,
for on those you have rescued from slavery to sin
you bestow eternal gladness.
Through our Lord Jesus Christ, your Son,
who lives and reigns with you in the unity of the Holy Spirit,
one God, for ever and ever.

First Reading   Zechariah 9:9-10
See now, your king comes humbly to you
The Lord says this:

"Rejoice heart and soul, daughter of Zion!
Shout with gladness, daughter of Jerusalem!
See now, your king comes to you;
he is victorious, he is triumphant,

humble and riding on a donkey,
on a colt, the foal of a donkey.
He will banish chariots from Ephraim
and horses from Jerusalem;
the bow of war will be banished.
He will proclaim peace for the nations.
His empire shall stretch from sea to sea,
from the River to the ends of the earth."

Psalm   Psalm 144

R. **I will bless your name for ever,
      O God my King.**

or **Alleluia!**

1. I will give you glory, O God my King,
   I will bless your name for ever.
   I will bless you day after day
   and praise your name for ever. R.

2. The Lord is kind and full of compassion,
   slow to anger, abounding in love.
   How good is the Lord to all,
   compassionate to all his creatures. R.

3. All your creatures shall thank you, O Lord,
   and your friends shall repeat their blessing.
   They shall speak of the glory of your reign
   and declare your might, O God. R.

4. The Lord is faithful in all his words
   and loving in all his deeds.
   The Lord supports all who fall
   and raises all who are bowed down. R.

Second Reading   Romans 8:9. 11-13

If by the Spirit you put an end to the misdeeds of the body, you will live.

Your interests are not in the unspiritual, but in the spiritual, since the Spirit of God has made his home in you. In fact, unless you possessed the Spirit of Christ you would not belong to him, and if the Spirit of him who raised Jesus from the dead is living in you, then he who raised Jesus from the dead will give life to your own mortal bodies through his Spirit living in you.

So then, my brothers, there is no necessity for us to obey our unspiritual selves or to live unspiritual lives. If you do live in that way, you are doomed to die; but if by the Spirit you put an end to the misdeeds of the body you will live.

Gospel Acclamation

Alleluia, alleluia!
Blessed are you, Father, Lord of heaven and earth,
for revealing the mysteries of the kingdom to mere children.
Alleluia!   cf. Matthew 11:25

Gospel   Matthew 11:25-30

I am gentle and humble of heart.

Jesus exclaimed, "I bless you, Father, Lord of heaven and of earth, for hiding these things from the learned and the clever and revealing them to mere children. Yes, Father, for that is what it pleased you to do. Everything has been entrusted to me by my Father; and no one knows the Son except the Father, just as no one knows the Father except the Son and those to whom the Son chooses to reveal him.

"Come to me, all you who labour and are overburdened, and I will give you rest. Shoulder my yoke and learn from me, for I am gentle and humble in heart, and you will find rest for your souls. Yes, my yoke is easy and my burden light."

The Creed is said.

Prayer over the Offerings
May this oblation dedicated to your name
purify us, O Lord,
and day by day bring our conduct
closer to the life of heaven.
Through Christ our Lord.

Preface I-VIII of the Sundays in Ordinary Time, pp. 499-502.

Communion Antiphon
Taste and see that the Lord is good;
blessed the man who seeks refuge in him.   Psalm 33:9

or

Come to me, all who labour and are burdened,
and I will refresh you, says the Lord.   Matthew 11:28

Prayer after Communion
Grant, we pray, O Lord,
that, having been replenished by such great gifts,
we may gain the prize of salvation
and never cease to praise you.
Through Christ our Lord.

FIFTEENTH SUNDAY IN ORDINARY TIME – A

The seed of faith.
God does nothing in vain. All our suffering has a meaning, and through it we are deepened in our spiritual lives so that we yield a rich harvest. The world longs for the Spirit of Christ to come and set us free from clinging to the things of this world.

Entrance Antiphon

As for me, in justice I shall behold your face;
I shall be filled with the vision of your glory.   cf. Psalm 16:15

The Gloria is said or sung.

Collect

O God, who show the light of your truth
to those who go astray,
so that they may return to the right path,
give all who for the faith they profess
are accounted Christians
the grace to reject whatever is contrary to the name of Christ
and to strive after all that does it honour.
Through our Lord Jesus Christ, your Son,
who lives and reigns with you in the unity of the Holy Spirit,
one God, for ever and ever.

First Reading   Isaiah 55:10-11

The rain makes the earth give growth.

Thus says the Lord: "As the rain and the snow come down from the heavens and do not return without watering the earth, making it yield and giving growth to provide seed for the sower and bread for the eating, so the word that goes from my mouth does not return to me empty, without carrying out my will and succeeding in what it was sent to do."

Psalm   Psalm 64

R. **Some seed fell into rich soil
and produced its crop.**

1. You care for the earth, give it water,
   you fill it with riches.
   Your river in heaven brims over
   to provide its grain. R.

2. And thus you provide for the earth;
   you drench its furrows,
   you level it, soften it with showers,
   you bless its growth. R.

3. You crown the year with your goodness.
   Abundance flows in your steps,
   in the pastures of the wilderness it flows. R.

4. The hills are girded with joy,
   the meadows covered with flocks,
   the valleys are decked with wheat.
   They shout for joy, yes, they sing. R.

Second Reading   Romans 8:18-23
The whole creation is eagerly waiting for God to reveal his sons.
I think that what we suffer in this life can never be compared to the
glory, as yet unrevealed, which is waiting for us. The whole creation
is eagerly waiting for God to reveal his sons. It was not for any fault
on the part of creation that it was made unable to attain its purpose,
it was made so by God; but creation still retains the hope of being
freed, like us, from its slavery to decadence, to enjoy the same
freedom and glory as the children of God. From the beginning till
now the entire creation, as we know, has been groaning in one great
act of giving birth; and not only creation, but all of us who possess
the first-fruits of the Spirit, we too groan inwardly as we wait for
our bodies to be set free.

Gospel Acclamation
Alleluia, alleluia!
Speak, Lord, your servant is listening;
you have the message of eternal life.
Alleluia!   1 Samuel 3:9; John 6:68

or

Alleluia, alleluia!
The seed is the word of God, Christ the sower;
whoever finds this seed will remain for ever.
Alleluia!

Gospel   Matthew 13:1-23

A sower went out to sow.

Jesus left the house and sat by the lakeside, but such crowds gathered round him that he got into a boat and sat there. The people all stood on the beach, and he told them many things in parables.

He said, "Imagine a sower going out to sow. As he sowed, some seeds fell on the edge of the path, and the birds came and ate them up. Others fell on patches of rock where they found little soil and sprang up straight away, because there was no depth of earth; but as soon as the sun came up they were scorched and, not having any roots, they withered away. Others fell among thorns, and the thorns grew up and choked them. Others fell on rich soil and produced their crop, some a hundredfold, some sixty, some thirty. Listen, anyone who has ears!"

Then the disciples went up to him and asked, "Why do you talk to them in parables?" "Because" he replied "the mysteries of the kingdom of heaven are revealed to you, but they are not revealed to them. For anyone who has will be given more, and he will have more than enough; but from anyone who has not, even what he has will be taken away. The reason I talk to them in parables is that they look without seeing and listen without hearing or understanding. So in their case this prophecy of Isaiah is being fulfilled:

You will listen and listen again, but not understand,
see and see again, but not perceive.
For the heart of this nation has grown coarse,
their ears are dull of hearing, and they have shut their eyes,
for fear they should see with their eyes,
hear with their ears,
understand with their heart,
and be converted
and be healed by me.

"But happy are your eyes because they see, your ears because they hear! I tell you solemnly, many prophets and holy men longed to see what you see, and never saw it; to hear what you hear, and never heard it.

"You, therefore, are to hear the parable of the sower. When anyone hears the word of the kingdom without understanding, the evil one comes and carries off what was sown in his heart: this is the man who received the seed on the edge of the path. The one who received it on patches of rock is the man who hears the word and welcomes it at once with joy. But he has no root in him, he does not last; let some trial come, or some persecution on account of the word, and he falls away at once. The one who received the seed in thorns is the man who hears the word, but the worries of this world and the lure of riches choke the word and so he produces nothing. And the one who received the seed in rich soil is the man who hears the word and understands it; he is the one who yields a harvest and produces now a hundredfold, now sixty, now thirty."

The Creed is said.

Prayer over the Offerings
Look upon the offerings of the Church, O Lord,
as she makes her prayer to you,
and grant that, when consumed by those who believe,
they may bring ever greater holiness.
Through Christ our Lord.

Preface I-VIII of the Sundays in Ordinary Time, pp. 499-502.

Communion Antiphon
The sparrow finds a home,
and the swallow a nest for her young:
by your altars, O Lord of hosts, my King and my God.
Blessed are they who dwell in your house,
for ever singing your praise.   cf. Psalm 83:4-5

or

Whoever eats my flesh and drinks my blood
remains in me and I in him, says the Lord.   John 6:57

Prayer after Communion
Having consumed these gifts, we pray, O Lord,
that, by our participation in this mystery,
its saving effects upon us may grow.
Through Christ our Lord.

SIXTEENTH SUNDAY IN ORDINARY TIME – A

The Spirit is our help.
We are a people full of weakness through our sin. We cannot pray for
repentance unless the Spirit comes to help us in our weakness. Our God is
mild in judgement, and we pray that God's mercy will be with us, so that like
wheat we will be gathered into God's barn.

Entrance Antiphon
See, I have God for my help.
The Lord sustains my soul.
I will sacrifice to you with willing heart,
and praise your name, O Lord, for it is good.   Psalm 53:6. 8

The Gloria is said or sung.

Collect
Show favour, O Lord, to your servants
and mercifully increase the gifts of your grace,
that, made fervent in hope, faith and charity,
they may be ever watchful in keeping your commands.
Through our Lord Jesus Christ, your Son,
who lives and reigns with you in the unity of the Holy Spirit,
one God, for ever and ever.

First Reading   Wisdom 12:13. 16-19
After sin you will grant repentance.
There is no god, other than you, who cares for everything,
to whom you might have to prove that you never judged unjustly.
Your justice has its source in strength,
your sovereignty over all makes you lenient to all.
You show your strength when your sovereign power is questioned
and you expose the insolence of those who know it;
but, disposing of such strength, you are mild in judgement,

you govern us with great lenience,
for you have only to will, and your power is there.
By acting thus you have taught a lesson to your people
how the virtuous man must be kindly to his fellow men,
and you have given your sons the good hope
that after sin you will grant repentance.

Psalm   Psalm 85

R. **O Lord, you are good and forgiving.**

1. O Lord, you are good and forgiving,
   full of love to all who call.
   Give heed, O Lord, to my prayer
   and attend to the sound of my voice. R.

2. All the nations shall come to adore you
   and glorify your name, O Lord:
   for you are great and do marvellous deeds,
   you who alone are God. R.

3. But you, God of mercy and compassion,
   slow to anger, O Lord,
   abounding in love and truth,
   turn and take pity on me. R.

Second Reading   Romans 8:26-27
The Spirit expresses our plea in a way that could never be put into
words.
The Spirit comes to help us in our weakness. For when we cannot
choose words in order to pray properly, the Spirit himself expresses
our plea in a way that could never be put into words, and God
who knows everything in our hearts knows perfectly well what he
means, and that the pleas of the saints expressed by the Spirit are
according to the mind of God.

Gospel Acclamation
Alleluia, alleluia!
May the Father of our Lord Jesus Christ
enlighten the eyes of our mind,
so that we can see what hope his call holds for us.
Alleluia!   cf. Ephesians 1:17. 18

or

Alleluia, alleluia!
Blessed are you, Father,
Lord of heaven and earth,
for revealing the mysteries of the kingdom
to mere children. Alleluia!   cf. Matthew 11:25

Gospel   Matthew 13:24-43
Let them both grow till the harvest.

Jesus put a parable before the crowds, "The kingdom of heaven
may be compared to a man who sowed good seed in his field.
While everybody was asleep his enemy came, sowed darnel all
among the wheat, and made off. When the new wheat sprouted
and ripened, the darnel appeared as well. The owner's servants
went to him and said, 'Sir, was it not good seed that you sowed in
your field? If so, where does the darnel come from?' 'Some enemy
has done this,' he answered. And the servants said, 'Do you want
us to go and weed it out?' But he said, 'No, because when you
weed out the darnel you might pull up the wheat with it. Let them
both grow till the harvest; and at harvest time I shall say to the
reapers: First collect the darnel and tie it in bundles to be burnt,
then gather the wheat into my barn.' "

He put another parable before them, "The kingdom of heaven is
like a mustard seed which a man took and sowed in his field. It is
the smallest of all the seeds, but when it has grown it is the biggest
shrub of all and becomes a tree so that the birds of the air come and
shelter in its branches."

He told them another parable, "The kingdom of heaven is like the yeast a woman took and mixed in with three measures of flour till it was leavened all through."

In all this Jesus spoke to the crowds in parables; indeed, he would never speak to them except in parables. This was to fulfil the prophecy:

I will speak to you in parables
and expound things hidden since the foundation of the world.

Then, leaving the crowds, he went to the house; and his disciples came to him and said, "Explain the parable about the darnel in the field to us." He said in reply, "The sower of the good seed is the Son of Man. The field is the world; the good seed is the subjects of the kingdom; the darnel, the subjects of the evil one; the enemy who sowed them, the devil; the harvest is the end of the world; the reapers are the angels. Well then, just as the darnel is gathered up and burnt in the fire, so it will be at the end of time. The Son of Man will send his angels and they will gather out of his kingdom all things that provoke offences and all who do evil, and throw them into the blazing furnace, where there will be weeping and grinding of teeth. Then the virtuous will shine like the sun in the kingdom of their Father. Listen, anyone who has ears!"

The Creed is said.

Prayer over the Offerings
O God, who in the one perfect sacrifice
brought to completion varied offerings of the law,
accept, we pray, this sacrifice from your faithful servants
and make it holy, as you blessed the gifts of Abel,
so that what each has offered to the honour of your majesty
may benefit the salvation of all.
Through Christ our Lord.

Preface I-VIII of the Sundays in Ordinary Time, pp. 499-502.

Communion Antiphon

The Lord, the gracious, the merciful,
has made a memorial of his wonders;
he gives food to those who fear him.   Psalm 110:4-5

or

Behold, I stand at the door and knock, says the Lord.
If anyone hears my voice and opens the door to me,
I will enter his house and dine with him, and he with me.

Apocalypse 3:20

Prayer after Communion

Graciously be present to your people, we pray, O Lord,
and lead those you have imbued with heavenly mysteries
to pass from former ways to newness of life.
Through Christ our Lord.

SEVENTEENTH SUNDAY IN ORDINARY TIME – A

Faith is a priceless treasure.
God turns everything to our good. God gives us a wisdom by which we can
discern true values in the world around us. Our greatest gift is faith, which
gives us a deeper wisdom even than that of Solomon.

Entrance Antiphon
God is in his holy place,
God who unites those who dwell in his house;
he himself gives might and strength to his people.

cf. Psalm 67:6-7. 36

The Gloria is said or sung.

Collect
O God, protector of those who hope in you,
without whom nothing has firm foundation, nothing is holy,
bestow in abundance your mercy upon us
and grant that, with you as our ruler and guide,
we may use the good things that pass
in such a way as to hold fast even now
to those that ever endure.
Through our Lord Jesus Christ, your Son,
who lives and reigns with you in the unity of the Holy Spirit,
one God, for ever and ever.

First Reading
1 Kings 3:5. 7-12

You have asked for a discerning judgement for yourself.

The Lord appeared to Solomon in a dream and said, "Ask what you
would like me to give you." Solomon replied, "Lord, my God, you
have made your servant king in succession to David my father. But
I am a very young man, unskilled in leadership. Your servant finds
himself in the midst of this people of yours that you have chosen, a

people so many its numbers cannot be counted or reckoned. Give your servant a heart to understand how to discern between good and evil, for who could govern this people of yours that is so great?" It pleased the Lord that Solomon should have asked for this. "Since you have asked for this" the Lord said "and not asked for long life for yourself or riches or the lives of your enemies, but have asked for a discerning judgement for yourself, here and now I do what you ask. I give you a heart wise and shrewd as none before you has had and none will have after you."

Psalm   Psalm 118

R. **Lord, how I love your law!**

1. My part, I have resolved, O Lord,
   is to obey your word.
   The law from your mouth means more to me
   than silver and gold. R.

2. Let your love be ready to console me
   by your promise to your servant.
   Let your love come to me and I shall live
   for your law is my delight. R.

3. That is why I love your commands
   more than finest gold.
   That is why I rule my life by your precepts:
   I hate false ways. R.

4. Your will is wonderful indeed;
   therefore I obey it.
   The unfolding of your word gives light
   and teaches the simple. R.

Second Reading   **Romans 8:28-30**

God intended us to become true images of his Son.

We know that by turning everything to their good God co-operates
with all those who love him, with all those that he has called
according to his purpose. They are the ones he chose specially long
ago and intended to become true images of his Son, so that his Son
might be the eldest of many brothers. He called those he intended
for this; those he called he justified, and with those he justified he
shared his glory.

Gospel Acclamation

Alleluia, alleluia!
I call you friends, says the Lord,
because I have made known to you
everything I have learnt from my Father.
Alleluia!   John 15:15

or

Alleluia, alleluia!
Blessed are you, Father,
Lord of heaven and earth,
for revealing the mysteries of the kingdom
to mere children.
Alleluia!   cf. Matthew 11:25

Gospel   **Matthew 13:44-52**

He sells everything he owns and buys the field.

Jesus said to the crowds, "The kingdom of heaven is like treasure
hidden in a field which someone has found; he hides it again,
goes off happy, sells everything he owns and buys the field.

"Again, the kingdom of heaven is like a merchant looking for
fine pearls; when he finds one of great value he goes and sells
everything he owns and buys it.

"Again, the kingdom of heaven is like a dragnet cast into the sea
that brings in a haul of all kinds. When it is full, the fishermen haul
it ashore; then, sitting down, they collect the good ones in a basket
and throw away those that are no use. This is how it will be at the

end of time: the angels will appear and separate the wicked from the just to throw them into the blazing furnace where there will be weeping and grinding of teeth.

"Have you understood all this?" They said, "Yes." And he said to them, "Well then, every scribe who becomes a disciple of the kingdom of heaven is like a householder who brings out from his storeroom things both new and old."

The Creed is said.

Prayer over the Offerings
Accept, O Lord, we pray, the offerings
which we bring from the abundance of your gifts,
that through the powerful working of your grace
these most sacred mysteries may sanctify our present way of life
and lead us to eternal gladness.
Through Christ our Lord.

Preface I-VIII of the Sundays in Ordinary Time, pp. 499-502.

Communion Antiphon
Bless the Lord, O my soul,
and never forget all his benefits.   Psalm 102:2

or

Blessed are the merciful, for they shall receive mercy.
Blessed are the clean of heart, for they shall see God.
                                                        Matthew 5:7-8

Prayer after Communion
We have consumed, O Lord, this divine Sacrament,
the perpetual memorial of the Passion of your Son;
grant, we pray, that this gift,
which he himself gave us with love beyond all telling,
may profit us for salvation.
Through Christ our Lord.

EIGHTEENTH SUNDAY IN ORDINARY TIME – A

Christ gives us food to eat.
The Lord freely gives us our spiritual food and drink. He gives us his own
Son in the Eucharist so that nothing can come between us and the love of God
made visible in Christ. Christ takes pity on us; he knows our needs, which he
will always satisfy if only we turn to him.

Entrance Antiphon
O God, come to my assistance;
O Lord, make haste to help me!
You are my rescuer, my help;
O Lord, do not delay.   Psalm 69:2. 6

The Gloria is said or sung.

Collect
Draw near to your servants, O Lord,
and answer their prayers with unceasing kindness,
that, for those who glory in you as their Creator and guide,
you may restore what you have created
and keep safe what you have restored.
Through our Lord Jesus Christ, your Son,
who lives and reigns with you in the unity of the Holy Spirit,
one God, for ever and ever.

First Reading   Isaiah 55:1-3
Come and eat.
Thus says the Lord:

Oh, come to the water all you who are thirsty;
though you have no money, come!
Buy corn without money, and eat,
and, at no cost, wine and milk.
Why spend money on what is not bread,

your wages on what fails to satisfy?
Listen, listen to me and you will have good things to eat
and rich food to enjoy.
Pay attention, come to me;
listen, and your soul will live.
With you I will make an everlasting covenant
out of the favours promised to David.

Psalm   Psalm 144

R. **You open wide your hand, O Lord,
     you grant our desires.**

1. The Lord is kind and full of compassion,
    slow to anger, abounding in love.
    How good is the Lord to all,
    compassionate to all his creatures. R.

2. The eyes of all creatures look to you
    and you give them their food in due time.
    You open wide your hand,
    grant the desires of all who live. R.

3. The Lord is just in all his ways
    and loving in all his deeds.
    He is close to all who call him,
    call on him from their hearts. R.

Second Reading   Romans 8:35. 37-39
No created thing can ever come between us and the love of God
made visible in Christ.

Nothing can come between us and the love of Christ, even if we
are troubled or worried, or being persecuted, or lacking food or
clothes, or being threatened or even attacked. These are the trials
through which we triumph, by the power of him who loved us.

For I am certain of this: neither death nor life, no angel, no prince,
nothing that exists, nothing still to come, not any power, or height
or depth, nor any created thing, can ever come between us and the
love of God made visible in Christ Jesus our Lord.

Gospel Acclamation

Alleluia, alleluia!
Blessings on the King who comes,
in the name of the Lord!
Peace in heaven
and glory in the highest heavens!
Alleluia!   Luke 19:38; 2:14

or

Alleluia, alleluia!
Man does not live on bread alone,
but on every word that comes from the mouth of God.
Alleluia!   Matthew 4:4

Gospel   Matthew 14:13-21

They all ate as much as they wanted.

When Jesus received the news of John the Baptist's death he withdrew
by boat to a lonely place where they could be by themselves. But the
people heard of this and, leaving the towns, went after him on foot.
So as he stepped ashore he saw a large crowd; and he took pity on
them and healed their sick.

When evening came, the disciples went to him and said, "This
is a lonely place, and the time has slipped by; so send the people
away, and they can go to the villages to buy themselves some
food." Jesus replied, "There is no need for them to go: give them
something to eat yourselves." But they answered, "All we have with
us is five loaves and two fish." "Bring them here to me," he said.
He gave orders that the people were to sit down on the grass; then
he took the five loaves and the two fish, raised his eyes to heaven
and said the blessing. And breaking the loaves he handed them to
his disciples who gave them to the crowds. They all ate as much
as they wanted, and they collected the scraps remaining, twelve
baskets full. Those who ate numbered about five thousand men, to
say nothing of women and children.

The Creed is said.

Prayer over the Offerings

Graciously sanctify these gifts, O Lord, we pray,
and, accepting the oblation of this spiritual sacrifice,
make of us an eternal offering to you.
Through Christ our Lord.

Preface I-VIII of the Sundays in Ordinary Time, pp. 499-502.

Communion Antiphon

You have given us, O Lord, bread from heaven,
endowed with all delights and sweetness in every taste.

Wisdom 16:20

or

I am the bread of life, says the Lord;
whoever comes to me will not hunger
and whoever believes in me will not thirst.

John 6:35

Prayer after Communion

Accompany with constant protection, O Lord,
those you renew with these heavenly gifts
and, in your never-failing care for them,
make them worthy of eternal redemption.
Through Christ our Lord.

NINETEENTH SUNDAY IN ORDINARY TIME – A

God speaks in a gentle breeze.
Jesus spoke to the storm and there followed a great calm. God spoke to Elijah in
the whisper of a gentle breeze. In every aspect of our lives, especially in moments
of trial, God speaks to us in Christ if only we will listen to his voice.

Entrance Antiphon

Look to your covenant, O Lord,
and forget not the life of your poor ones for ever.
Arise, O God, and defend your cause,
and forget not the cries of those who seek you.

cf. Psalm 73:20. 19. 22. 23

The Gloria is said or sung.

Collect

Almighty ever-living God,
whom, taught by the Holy Spirit,
we dare to call our Father,
bring, we pray, to perfection in our hearts
the spirit of adoption as your sons and daughters,
that we may merit to enter into the inheritance
which you have promised.
Through our Lord Jesus Christ, your Son,
who lives and reigns with you in the unity of the Holy Spirit,
one God, for ever and ever.

First Reading   1 Kings 19:9. 11-13

Stand on the mountain before the Lord.

When Elijah reached Horeb, the mountain of God, he went into the
cave and spent the night in it. Then he was told, "Go out and stand
on the mountain before the Lord." Then the Lord himself went by.
There came a mighty wind, so strong it tore the mountains and

shattered the rocks before the Lord. But the Lord was not in the wind. After the wind came an earthquake. But the Lord was not in the earthquake. After the earthquake came a fire. But the Lord was not in the fire. And after the fire there came the sound of a gentle breeze. And when Elijah heard this, he covered his face with his cloak and went out and stood at the entrance of the cave.

Psalm   Psalm 84

R. **Let us see, O Lord, your mercy
    and give us your saving help.**

1. I will hear what the Lord God has to say,
    a voice that speaks of peace.
    His help is near for those who fear him
    and his glory will dwell in our land. R.

2. Mercy and faithfulness have met;
    justice and peace have embraced.
    Faithfulness shall spring from the earth
    and justice look down from heaven. R.

3. The Lord will make us prosper
    and our earth shall yield its fruit.
    Justice shall march before him
    and peace shall follow his steps. R.

Second Reading   Romans 9:1-5
I would willingly be condemned if it could help my brothers.
What I want to say is no pretence; I say it in union with Christ – it is the truth – my conscience in union with the Holy Spirit assures me of it too. What I want to say is this: my sorrow is so great, my mental anguish so endless, I would willingly be condemned and be cut off from Christ if it could help my brothers of Israel, my own flesh and blood. They were adopted as sons, they were given the glory and the covenants; the Law and the ritual were drawn up for them, and the promises were made to them. They are descended from the patriarchs and from their flesh and blood came Christ who is above all, God for ever blessed! Amen.

Gospel Acclamation
Alleluia, alleluia!
Blessings on the King who comes, in the name of the Lord!
Peace in heaven and glory in the highest heavens!
Alleluia!   Luke 19:38

or

Alleluia, alleluia!
My soul is waiting for the Lord,
I count on his word.
Alleluia!   Psalm 129:5

Gospel   Matthew 14:22-33
Tell me to come to you across the water.

Jesus made the disciples get into the boat and go on ahead to the
other side while he would send the crowds away. After sending the
crowds away he went up into the hills by himself to pray. When
evening came, he was there alone, while the boat, by now far out on
the lake, was battling with a heavy sea, for there was a headwind.
In the fourth watch of the night he went towards them, walking on
the lake, and when the disciples saw him walking on the lake they
were terrified. "It is a ghost," they said, and cried out in fear. But
at once Jesus called out to them, saying, "Courage! It is I! Do not
be afraid." It was Peter who answered. "Lord," he said, "if it is you,
tell me to come to you across the water." "Come," said Jesus. Then
Peter got out of the boat and started walking towards Jesus across
the water, but as soon as he felt the force of the wind, he took fright
and began to sink. "Lord! Save me!" he cried. Jesus put out his hand
at once and held him. "Man of little faith," he said "why did you
doubt?" And as they got into the boat the wind dropped. The men
in the boat bowed down before him and said, "Truly, you are the
Son of God."

The Creed is said.

Prayer over the Offerings
Be pleased, O Lord, to accept the offerings of your Church,
for in your mercy you have given them to be offered
and by your power you transform them
into the mystery of our salvation.
Through Christ our Lord.

Preface I-VIII of the Sundays in Ordinary Time, pp. 499-502.

Communion Antiphon
O Jerusalem, glorify the Lord,
who gives you your fill of finest wheat.   Psalm 147:12. 14

or

The bread that I will give, says the Lord,
is my flesh for the life of the world.   cf. John 6:51

Prayer after Communion
May the communion in your Sacrament
that we have consumed, save us, O Lord,
and confirm us in the light of your truth.
Through Christ our Lord.

TWENTIETH SUNDAY IN ORDINARY TIME – A

God shows mercy to all.

The Lord named the Jews as his chosen race but many failed to recognise Jesus Christ. In his own lifetime Jesus acknowledged that he discovered great faith in many who were outside the fold of God's chosen people. Many people in the world around us seem to have a deeper faith than we have as Christians. This can make us more aware of God's generosity to all, and give us a greater appreciation of the gift of faith.

Entrance Antiphon
Turn your eyes, O God, our shield;
and look on the face of your anointed one;
one day within your courts
is better than a thousand elsewhere.   Psalm 83:10-11

The Gloria is said or sung.

Collect
O God, who have prepared for those who love you
good things which no eye can see,
fill our hearts, we pray, with the warmth of your love,
so that, loving you in all things and above all things,
we may attain your promises,
which surpass every human desire.
Through our Lord Jesus Christ, your Son,
who lives and reigns with you in the unity of the Holy Spirit,
one God, for ever and ever.

First Reading   Isaiah 56:1. 6-7
I will bring foreigners to my holy mountain.
Thus says the Lord: Have a care for justice, act with integrity, for soon my salvation will come and my integrity be manifest.

Foreigners who have attached themselves to the Lord to serve him and to love his name and be his servants – all who observe the sabbath, not profaning it, and cling to my covenant – these I will bring to my holy mountain. I will make them joyful in my house of prayer. Their holocausts and their sacrifices will be accepted on my altar, for my house will be called a house of prayer for all the peoples.

Psalm   Psalm 66

R. **Let the peoples praise you, O God;**
     let all the peoples praise you.

1. O God, be gracious and bless us
    and let your face shed its light upon us.
    So will your ways be known upon earth
    and all nations learn your saving help. R.

2. Let the nations be glad and exult
    for you rule the world with justice.
    With fairness you rule the peoples,
    you guide the nations on earth. R.

3. Let the peoples praise you, O God;
    let all the peoples praise you.
    May God still give us his blessing
    till the ends of the earth revere him. R.

Second Reading   Romans 11:13-15. 29-32
With Israel, God never takes back his gifts or revokes his choice.
Let me tell you pagans this: I have been sent to the pagans as their apostle, and I am proud of being sent, but the purpose of it is to make my own people envious of you, and in this way save some of them. Since their rejection meant the reconciliation of the world, do you know what their admission will mean? Nothing less than a resurrection from the dead! God never takes back his gifts or revokes his choice.

Just as you changed from being disobedient to God, and now enjoy mercy because of their disobedience, so those who are disobedient now – and only because of the mercy shown to you – will also enjoy mercy eventually. God has imprisoned all men in their own disobedience only to show mercy to all mankind.

Gospel Acclamation
Alleluia, alleluia!
The sheep that belong to me listen to my voice,
says the Lord,
I know them and they follow me.
Alleluia!   John 10:27

or

Alleluia, alleluia!
Jesus proclaimed the Good News of the kingdom,
and cured all kinds of sickness among the people.
Alleluia!   cf. Matthew 4:23

Gospel   Matthew 15:21-28
Woman, you have great faith.

Jesus left Gennesaret and withdrew to the region of Tyre and Sidon. Then out came a Canaanite woman from that district and started shouting, "Sir, Son of David, take pity on me. My daughter is tormented by a devil." But he answered her not a word. And his disciples went and pleaded with him. "Give her what she wants," they said "because she is shouting after us." He said in reply, "I was sent only to the lost sheep of the House of Israel." But the woman had come up and was kneeling at his feet. "Lord," she said "help me." He replied, "It is not fair to take the children's food and throw it to the house-dogs." She retorted, "Ah yes, sir; but even house-dogs can eat the scraps that fall from their master's table." Then Jesus answered her, "Woman, you have great faith. Let your wish be granted." And from that moment her daughter was well again.

The Creed is said.

Prayer over the Offerings

Receive our oblation, O Lord,
by which is brought about a glorious exchange,
that, by offering what you have given,
we may merit to receive your very self.
Through Christ our Lord.

Preface I-VIII of the Sundays in Ordinary Time, pp. 499-502.

Communion Antiphon

With the Lord there is mercy;
in him is plentiful redemption.   Psalm 129:7

or

I am the living bread that came down from heaven, says the Lord.
Whoever eats of this bread will live for ever.   John 6:51-52

Prayer after Communion

Made partakers of Christ through these Sacraments,
we humbly implore your mercy, Lord,
that, conformed to his image on earth,
we may merit also to be his coheirs in heaven.
Who lives and reigns for ever and ever.

TWENTY-FIRST SUNDAY IN ORDINARY TIME – A

The keys of the kingdom.
Jesus Christ chose Peter as the rock on which he would build his Church.
Peter was a man of faith and it is upon faith that Christ always builds.
When we proclaim: "You are the Christ", we also ask for
a deepening of our faith. Through faith we fix our eyes on God
who is infinite wisdom, and it is for God's good purposes that we were chosen
to be members of Christ's Church on earth.

Entrance Antiphon
Turn your ear, O Lord, and answer me;
save the servant who trusts in you, my God.
Have mercy on me, O Lord, for I cry to you all the day long.

cf. Psalm 85:1-3

The Gloria is said or sung.

Collect
O God, who cause the minds of the faithful
to unite in a single purpose,
grant your people to love what you command
and to desire what you promise,
that, amid the uncertainties of this world,
our hearts may be fixed on that place
where true gladness is found.
Through our Lord Jesus Christ, your Son,
who lives and reigns with you in the unity of the Holy Spirit,
one God, for ever and ever.

First Reading   Isaiah 22:19-23
I place the key of the House of David upon his shoulder.
Thus says the Lord of hosts to Shebna, the master of the palace:
    I dismiss you from your office,

I remove you from your post,
and the same day I call on my servant
Eliakim son of Hilkiah.
I invest him with your robe,
gird him with your sash,
entrust him with your authority;
and he shall be a father
to the inhabitants of Jerusalem
and to the House of Judah.
I place the key of the House of David
on his shoulder;
should he open, no one shall close,
should he close, no one shall open.
I drive him like a peg
into a firm place;
he will become a throne of glory
for his father's house.

Psalm   Psalm 137

R. **Your love, O Lord, is eternal,**
   discard not the work of your hands.

1. I thank you, Lord, with all my heart,
   you have heard the words of my mouth.
   Before the angels I will bless you.
   I will adore before your holy temple. R.

2. I thank you for your faithfulness and love
   which excel all we ever knew of you.
   On the day I called, you answered;
   you increased the strength of my soul. R.

3. The Lord is high yet he looks on the lowly
   and the haughty he knows from afar.
   Your love, O Lord, is eternal,
   discard not the work of your hands. R.

Second Reading   Romans 11:33-36

All that exists comes from him; all is by him and for him.

How rich are the depths of God – how deep his wisdom and
knowledge – and how impossible to penetrate his motives or
understand his methods! Who could ever know the mind of the
Lord? Who could ever be his counsellor? Who could ever give him
anything or lend him anything? All that exists comes from him; all
is by him and for him. To him be glory for ever! Amen.

Gospel Acclamation
Alleluia, alleluia!
God in Christ was reconciling the world to himself,
and he has entrusted to us the news that they are reconciled.
Alleluia!   2 Corinthians 5:19

or

Alleluia, alleluia!
You are Peter
and on this rock I will build my Church.
And the gates of the underworld can never hold out against it.
Alleluia!   Matthew 16:18

Gospel   Matthew 16:13-20

You are Peter, and I will give you the keys of the kingdom of heaven.

When Jesus came to the region of Caesarea Philippi he put this
question to his disciples, "Who do people say the Son of Man is?"
And they said, "Some say he is John the Baptist, some Elijah, and
others Jeremiah or one of the prophets." "But you," he said, "who do
you say I am?" Then Simon Peter spoke up, "You are the Christ,"
he said, "the Son of the living God." Jesus replied, "Simon son of
Jonah, you are a happy man! Because it was not flesh and blood that
revealed this to you but my Father in heaven. So I now say to you:
You are Peter and on this rock I will build my Church. And the gates
of the underworld can never hold out against it. I will give you the
keys of the kingdom of heaven: whatever you bind on earth shall
be considered bound in heaven; whatever you loose on earth shall
be considered loosed in heaven." Then he gave the disciples strict
orders not to tell anyone that he was the Christ.

The Creed is said.

Prayer over the Offerings
O Lord, who gained for yourself a people by adoption
through the one sacrifice offered once for all,
bestow graciously on us, we pray,
the gifts of unity and peace in your Church.
Through Christ our Lord.

Preface I-VIII of the Sundays in Ordinary Time, pp. 499-502.

Communion Antiphon
The earth is replete with the fruits of your work, O Lord;
you bring forth bread from the earth
and wine to cheer the heart.   cf. Psalm 103:13-15

or

Whoever eats my flesh and drinks my blood
has eternal life, says the Lord,
and I will raise him up on the last day.   cf. John 6:54

Prayer after Communion
Complete within us, O Lord, we pray,
the healing work of your mercy
and graciously perfect and sustain us,
so that in all things we may please you.
Through Christ our Lord.

TWENTY-SECOND SUNDAY IN ORDINARY TIME – A

Take up your cross.
Christ tells us to take up our cross daily and follow him. It is in apparently losing our lives that we will find them in a newer, deeper way, and then we shall be rewarded according to our behaviour. This will never be easy, but it is the only path to real holiness and happiness.

Entrance Antiphon

Have mercy on me, O Lord, for I cry to you all the day long.
O Lord, you are good and forgiving,
full of mercy to all who call to you.   cf. Psalm 85:3. 5

The Gloria is said or sung.

Collect

God of might, giver of every good gift,
put into our hearts the love of your name,
so that, by deepening our sense of reverence,
you may nurture in us what is good
and, by your watchful care,
keep safe what you have nurtured.
Through our Lord Jesus Christ, your Son,
who lives and reigns with you in the unity of the Holy Spirit,
one God, for ever and ever.

First Reading   Jeremiah 20:7-9

The word of the Lord has meant insult for me.
You have seduced me, Lord, and I have let myself be seduced;
you have overpowered me: you were the stronger.
I am a daily laughing-stock,
everybody's butt.
Each time I speak the word, I have to howl
and proclaim: "Violence and ruin!"

The word of the Lord has meant for me
insult, derision, all day long.
I used to say, "I will not think about him,
I will not speak in his name any more."
Then there seemed to be a fire burning in my heart,
imprisoned in my bones.
The effort to restrain it wearied me,
I could not bear it.

Psalm   Psalm 62

R.   **For you my soul is thirsting,**
     O Lord my God.

1. O God, you are my God, for you I long;
    for you my soul is thirsting.
    My body pines for you
    like a dry, weary land without water. R.

2. So I gaze on you in the sanctuary
    to see your strength and your glory.
    For your love is better than life,
    my lips will speak your praise. R.

3. So I will bless you all my life,
    in your name I will lift up my hands.
    My soul shall be filled as with a banquet,
    my mouth shall praise you with joy. R.

4. For you have been my help;
    in the shadow of your wings I rejoice.
    My soul clings to you;
    your right hand holds me fast. R.

Second Reading   Romans 12:1-2
Offer your bodies as a living sacrifice.
Think of God's mercy, my brothers, and worship him, I beg you,
in a way that is worthy of thinking beings, by offering your living

bodies as a holy sacrifice, truly pleasing to God. Do not model yourselves on the behaviour of the world around you, but let your behaviour change, modelled by your new mind. This is the only way to discover the will of God and know what is good, what it is that God wants, what is the perfect thing to do.

Gospel Acclamation

Alleluia, alleluia!
May the Father of our Lord Jesus Christ
enlighten the eyes of our mind,
so that we can see
what hope his call holds for us.
Alleluia!   cf. Ephesians 1:17. 18

Gospel   Matthew 16:21-27

If anyone wants to be a follower of mine, let him renounce himself.

Jesus began to make it clear to his disciples that he was destined to go to Jerusalem and suffer grievously at the hands of the elders and chief priests and scribes, to be put to death and to be raised up on the third day. Then, taking him aside, Peter started to remonstrate with him. "Heaven preserve you, Lord," he said. "This must not happen to you." But he turned and said to Peter, "Get behind me, Satan! You are an obstacle in my path, because the way you think is not God's way but man's."

Then Jesus said to his disciples, "If anyone wants to be a follower of mine, let him renounce himself and take up his cross and follow me. For anyone who wants to save his life will lose it; but anyone who loses his life for my sake will find it. What, then, will a man gain if he wins the whole world and ruins his life? Or what has a man to offer in exchange for his life?

"For the Son of Man is going to come in the glory of his Father with his angels, and, when he does, he will reward each one according to his behaviour."

The Creed is said.

Prayer over the Offerings
May this sacred offering, O Lord,
confer on us always the blessing of salvation,
that what it celebrates in mystery
it may accomplish in power.
Through Christ our Lord.

Preface I-VIII of the Sundays in Ordinary Time, pp. 499-502.

Communion Antiphon
How great is the goodness, Lord,
that you keep for those who fear you.   Psalm 30:20

or

Blessed are the peacemakers,
for they shall be called children of God.
Blessed are they who are persecuted for the sake of righteousness,
for theirs is the Kingdom of Heaven.   Matthew 5:9-10

Prayer after Communion
Renewed by this bread from the heavenly table,
we beseech you, Lord,
that, being the food of charity,
it may confirm our hearts
and stir us to serve you in our neighbour.
Through Christ our Lord.

TWENTY-THIRD SUNDAY IN ORDINARY TIME – A

Correct one another in charity.
We live together in society and we are called to be prepared to
correct and encourage each other. No one is an island.
If Christ is among us, then we will encourage and help each other.
Love is the one thing that cannot hurt your neighbour.

Entrance Antiphon
You are just, O Lord, and your judgement is right;
treat your servant in accord with your merciful love.

Psalm 118:137. 124

The Gloria is said or sung.

Collect
O God, by whom we are redeemed and receive adoption,
look graciously upon your beloved sons and daughters,
that those who believe in Christ
may receive true freedom
and an everlasting inheritance.
Through our Lord Jesus Christ, your Son,
who lives and reigns with you in the unity of the Holy Spirit,
one God, for ever and ever.

First Reading   Ezekiel 33:7-9
If you do not speak to the wicked man, I will hold you responsible
for his death.
The word of the Lord was addressed to me as follows, "Son of man, I
have appointed you as sentry to the House of Israel. When you hear
a word from my mouth, warn them in my name. If I say to a wicked
man: Wicked wretch, you are to die, and you do not speak to warn
the wicked man to renounce his ways, then he shall die for his sin,
but I will hold you responsible for his death. If, however, you do

warn a wicked man to renounce his ways and repent, and he does not repent, then he shall die for his sin, but you yourself will have saved your life."

Psalm   Psalm 94

R. **O that today you would listen to his voice!**
     Harden not your hearts.

1. Come, ring out our joy to the Lord;
   hail the rock who saves us.
   Let us come before him, giving thanks,
   with songs let us hail the Lord. R.

2. Come in; let us bow and bend low;
   let us kneel before the God who made us
   for he is our God and we
   the people who belong to his pasture,
   the flock that is led by his hand. R.

3. O that today you would listen to his voice!
   "Harden not your hearts as at Meribah,
   as on that day at Massah in the desert
   when your fathers put me to the test;
   when they tried me, though they saw my work." R.

Second Reading   Romans 13:8-10
Love is the answer to every one of the commandments.
Avoid getting into debt, except the debt of mutual love. If you love your fellow men you have carried out your obligations. All the commandments: You shall not commit adultery, you shall not kill, you shall not steal, you shall not covet, and so on, are summed up in this single command: You must love your neighbour as yourself. Love is the one thing that cannot hurt your neighbour; that is why it is the answer to every one of the commandments.

Gospel Acclamation
Alleluia, alleluia!
Your word is truth, O Lord,
consecrate us in the truth.
Alleluia!   John 17:17

or

Alleluia, alleluia!
God in Christ was reconciling the world to himself,
and he has entrusted to us the news that they are reconciled.
Alleluia!   2 Corinthians 5:19

Gospel   Matthew 18:15-20
If he listens to you, you have won back your brother.
Jesus said to his disciples: "If your brother does something wrong,
go and have it out with him alone, between your two selves. If he
listens to you, you have won back your brother. If he does not listen,
take one or two others along with you: the evidence of two or three
witnesses is required to sustain any charge. But if he refuses to listen
to these, report it to the community; and if he refuses to listen to the
community, treat him like a pagan or a tax collector.

"I tell you solemnly, whatever you bind on earth shall be
considered bound in heaven; whatever you loose on earth shall be
considered loosed in heaven.

"I tell you solemnly once again, if two of you on earth agree to ask
anything at all, it will be granted to you by my Father in heaven. For
where two or three meet in my name, I shall be there with them."

The Creed is said.

Prayer over the Offerings
O God, who give us the gift of true prayer and of peace,
graciously grant that through this offering,
we may do fitting homage to your divine majesty
and, by partaking of the sacred mystery,
we may be faithfully united in mind and heart.
Through Christ our Lord.

Preface I-VIII of the Sundays in Ordinary Time, pp. 499-502.

Communion Antiphon
Like the deer that yearns for running streams,
so my soul is yearning for you, my God;
my soul is thirsting for God, the living God.   cf. Psalm 41:2-3

or

I am the light of the world, says the Lord;
whoever follows me will not walk in darkness,
but will have the light of life.   John 8:12

Prayer after Communion
Grant that your faithful, O Lord,
whom you nourish and endow with life
through the food of your Word and heavenly Sacrament,
may so benefit from your beloved Son's great gifts
that we may merit an eternal share in his life.
Who lives and reigns for ever and ever.

TWENTY-FOURTH SUNDAY IN ORDINARY TIME – A

Forgive from the heart.
Jesus Christ is the perfect example of forgiveness. He died for us when we were
still his enemies by sin. Through his death we are brought to life. Christ's life
and death have an influence on us all. We are to forgive each other as Christ
forgives us, since we ask God our Father to forgive our trespasses as we forgive
those who trespass against us.

Entrance Antiphon

Give peace, O Lord, to those who wait for you,
that your prophets be found true.
Hear the prayers of your servant,
and of your people Israel.   cf. Ecclesiasticus 36:18

The Gloria is said or sung.

Collect

Look upon us, O God,
Creator and ruler of all things,
and, that we may feel the working of your mercy,
grant that we may serve you with all our heart.
Through our Lord Jesus Christ, your Son,
who lives and reigns with you in the unity of the Holy Spirit,
one God, for ever and ever.

First Reading   Ecclesiasticus 27:30 – 28:7

Forgive your neighbour the hurt he does you, and when you pray,
your sins will be forgiven.
Resentment and anger, these are foul things,
and both are found with the sinner.
He who exacts vengeance will experience the vengeance of the Lord,
who keeps strict account of sin.
Forgive your neighbour the hurt he does you,
and when you pray, your sins will be forgiven.
If a man nurses anger against another,

can he then demand compassion from the Lord?
Showing no pity for a man like himself,
can he then plead for his own sins?
Mere creature of flesh, he cherishes resentment;
who will forgive him his sins?
Remember the last things, and stop hating,
remember dissolution and death, and live by the commandments.
Remember the commandments, and do not bear your neighbour
    ill-will;
remember the covenant of the Most High, and overlook the offence.

Psalm   Psalm 102

R. **The Lord is compassion and love,
      slow to anger and rich in mercy.**

1. My soul, give thanks to the Lord,
    all my being, bless his holy name.
    My soul, give thanks to the Lord
    and never forget all his blessings. R.

2. It is he who forgives all your guilt,
    who heals every one of your ills,
    who redeems your life from the grave,
    who crowns you with love and compassion. R.

3. His wrath will come to an end;
    he will not be angry for ever.
    He does not treat us according to our sins
    nor repay us according to our faults. R.

4. For as the heavens are high above the earth
    so strong is his love for those who fear him.
    As far as the east is from the west
    so far does he remove our sins. R.

Second Reading   Romans 14:7-9
Alive or dead we belong to the Lord.
The life and death of each of us has its influence on others; if we
live, we live for the Lord; and if we die, we die for the Lord, so that

alive or dead we belong to the Lord. This explains why Christ both died and came to life, it was so that he might be Lord both of the dead and of the living.

Gospel Acclamation

Alleluia, alleluia!
Speak, Lord, your servant is listening:
you have the message of eternal life.
Alleluia!   1 Samuel 3:9; John 6:68

or

Alleluia, alleluia!
I give you a new commandment:
love one another, just as I have loved you,
says the Lord.
Alleluia!   John 13:34

Gospel   Matthew 18:21-35

I do not tell you to forgive seven times, but seventy-seven times.

Peter went up to Jesus and said, "Lord, how often must I forgive my brother if he wrongs me? As often as seven times?" Jesus answered, "Not seven, I tell you, but seventy-seven times.

"And so the kingdom of heaven may be compared to a king who decided to settle his accounts with his servants. When the reckoning began, they brought him a man who owed ten thousand talents; but he had no means of paying, so his master gave orders that he should be sold, together with his wife and children and all his possessions, to meet the debt. At this, the servant threw himself down at his master's feet. 'Give me time', he said, 'and I will pay the whole sum.' And the servant's master felt so sorry for him that he let him go and cancelled the debt. Now as this servant went out, he happened to meet a fellow servant who owed him one hundred denarii; and he seized him by the throat and began to throttle him. 'Pay what you owe me', he said. His fellow servant fell at his feet and implored him, saying, 'Give me time and I will pay you.' But the other would not agree; on the contrary, he had him thrown into prison till he should pay the debt. His fellow servants were deeply distressed when they saw what had happened, and they went to their master and reported the whole affair to him. Then the master sent for him. 'You wicked servant,' he said, 'I cancelled all that debt of yours when you appealed to me. Were you not bound, then, to have pity on your fellow servant just as I had pity on you?' And in his anger the master handed him over to the torturers till he should pay all his debt. And that is how my heavenly Father will deal with you unless you each forgive your brother from your heart."

The Creed is said.

Prayer over the Offerings
Look with favour on our supplications, O Lord,
and in your kindness accept these, your servants' offerings,
that what each has offered to the honour of your name
may serve the salvation of all.
Through Christ our Lord.

Preface I-VIII of the Sundays in Ordinary Time, pp. 499-502.

Communion Antiphon
How precious is your mercy, O God!
The children of men seek shelter in the shadow of your wings.
cf. Psalm 35:8

or

The chalice of blessing that we bless
is a communion in the Blood of Christ;
and the bread that we break
is a sharing in the Body of the Lord.
cf. 1 Corinthians 10:16

Prayer after Communion
May the working of this heavenly gift, O Lord, we pray,
take possession of our minds and bodies,
so that its effects, and not our own desires,
may always prevail in us.
Through Christ our Lord.

TWENTY-FIFTH SUNDAY IN ORDINARY TIME – A

God's ways are not our ways.
We judge by human standards. If we want our judgements to be the right ones,
then we are to pray for guidance so that we may always judge generously. God
rewards everyone individually, according to God's judgement, not ours. We are
called to see people through God's eyes.

Entrance Antiphon

I am the salvation of the people, says the Lord.
Should they cry to me in any distress,
I will hear them, and I will be their Lord for ever.

The Gloria is said or sung.

Collect

O God, who founded all the commands of your sacred Law
upon love of you and of our neighbour,
grant that, by keeping your precepts,
we may merit to attain eternal life.
Through our Lord Jesus Christ, your Son,
who lives and reigns with you in the unity of the Holy Spirit,
one God, for ever and ever.

First Reading   Isaiah 55:6-9

My thoughts are not your thoughts.

Seek the Lord while he is still to be found,
call to him while he is still near.
Let the wicked man abandon his way,
the evil man his thoughts.
Let him turn back to the Lord who will take pity on him,
to our God who is rich in forgiving;
for my thoughts are not your thoughts,
my ways not your ways – it is the Lord who speaks.
Yes, the heavens are as high above earth
as my ways are above your ways,
my thoughts above your thoughts.

Psalm   Psalm 144

R. **The Lord is close to all who call him.**

1. I will bless you day after day
   and praise your name for ever.
   The Lord is great, highly to be praised,
   his greatness cannot be measured. R.

2. The Lord is kind and full of compassion,
   slow to anger, abounding in love.
   How good is the Lord to all,
   compassionate to all his creatures. R.

3. The Lord is just in all his ways
   and loving in all his deeds.
   He is close to all who call him,
   who call on him from their hearts. R.

Second Reading   Philippians 1:20-24. 27
Life to me is Christ.

Christ will be glorified in my body, whether by my life or by my
death. Life to me, of course, is Christ, but then death would bring
me something more; but then again, if living in this body means
doing work which is having good results – I do not know what I
should choose. I am caught in this dilemma: I want to be gone and
be with Christ, which would be very much the better, but for me to
stay alive in this body is a more urgent need for your sake.

Avoid anything in your everyday lives that would be unworthy of
the gospel of Christ.

Gospel Acclamation

Alleluia, alleluia!
Blessings on the King who comes,
in the name of the Lord!
Peace in heaven
and glory in the highest heavens!
Alleluia!   Luke 19:38

or

Alleluia, alleluia!
Open our heart, O Lord,
to accept the words of your Son.
Alleluia!

cf. Acts 16:14

Gospel   Matthew 20:1-16

Why be envious because I am generous?

Jesus said to his disciples: "The kingdom of heaven is like a landowner going out at daybreak to hire workers for his vineyard. He made an agreement with the workers for one denarius a day, and sent them to his vineyard. Going out at about the third hour he saw others standing idle in the market place and said to them, 'You go to my vineyard too and I will give you a fair wage.' So they went. At about the sixth hour and again at about the ninth hour, he went out and did the same. Then at about the eleventh hour he went out and found more men standing round, and he said to them, 'Why have you been standing here idle all day?' 'Because no one has hired us', they answered. He said to them, 'You go into my vineyard too.' In the evening, the owner of the vineyard said to his bailiff, 'Call the workers and pay them their wages, starting with the last arrivals and ending with the first.' So those who were hired at about the eleventh hour came forward and received one denarius each. When the first came, they expected to get more, but they too received one denarius each. They took it, but grumbled at the landowner. 'The men who came last', they said, 'have done only one hour, and you have treated them the same as us, though we have done a heavy day's work in all the heat.' He answered one of them and said, 'My friend, I am not being unjust to you; did we not agree on one denarius? Take your earnings and go. I choose to pay the last-comer as much as I pay you. Have I no right to do what I like with my own? Why be envious because I am generous?' Thus the last will be first, and the first, last."

The Creed is said.

Prayer over the Offerings
Receive with favour, O Lord, we pray,
the offerings of your people,
that what they profess with devotion and faith
may be theirs through these heavenly mysteries.
Through Christ our Lord.

Preface I-VIII of the Sundays in Ordinary Time, pp. 499-502.

Communion Antiphon
You have laid down your precepts to be carefully kept;
may my ways be firm in keeping your statutes.   Psalm 118:4-5

or

I am the Good Shepherd, says the Lord;
I know my sheep, and mine know me.   John 10:14

Prayer after Communion
Graciously raise up, O Lord,
those you renew with this Sacrament,
that we may come to possess your redemption
both in mystery and in the manner of our life.
Through Christ our Lord.

TWENTY-SIXTH SUNDAY IN ORDINARY TIME – A

Christ came to forgive sinners.
We are all in need of God's forgiveness and it was for this reason that Christ
came, humbling himself to accept death on the cross. When we renounce sin we
will truly live. We are all called to put the needs of others before our own, and
never to take our place in God's kingdom for granted.

Entrance Antiphon

All that you have done to us, O Lord,
you have done with true judgement,
for we have sinned against you
and not obeyed your commandments.
But give glory to your name
and deal with us according to the bounty of your mercy.

Daniel 3:31. 29. 30. 43. 42

The Gloria is said or sung.

Collect

O God, who manifest your almighty power
above all by pardoning and showing mercy,
bestow, we pray, your grace abundantly upon us
and make those hastening to attain your promises
heirs to the treasures of heaven.
Through our Lord Jesus Christ, your Son,
who lives and reigns with you in the unity of the Holy Spirit,
one God, for ever and ever.

First Reading   Ezekiel 18:25-28

When the sinner renounces sin, he shall certainly live.

The word of the Lord was addressed to me as follows: "You object, 'What the Lord does is unjust.' Listen, you House of Israel: is what I do unjust? Is it not what you do that is unjust? When the upright man renounces his integrity to commit sin and dies because of this, he dies because of the evil that he himself has committed. When the sinner renounces sin to become law-abiding and honest, he deserves to live. He has chosen to renounce all his previous sins; he shall certainly live; he shall not die."

Psalm   Psalm 24

R. **Remember your mercy, Lord.**

1. Lord, make me know your ways.
   Lord, teach me your paths.
   Make me walk in your truth, and teach me:
   for you are God my saviour. R.

2. Remember your mercy, Lord,
   and the love you have shown from of old.
   Do not remember the sins of my youth.
   In your love remember me,
   because of your goodness, O Lord. R.

3. The Lord is good and upright.
   He shows the path to those who stray,
   he guides the humble in the right path;
   he teaches his way to the poor. R.

Second Reading   Philippians 2:1-11
In your minds you must be the same as Christ Jesus.

If our life in Christ means anything to you, if love can persuade at all, or the Spirit that we have in common, or any tenderness and sympathy, then be united in your convictions and united in your love, with a common purpose and a common mind. That is the one thing which would make me completely happy. There must be no competition among you, no conceit; but everybody is to be self-effacing. Always consider the other person to be better than yourself, so that nobody thinks of his own interests first but everybody thinks of other people's interests instead. In your minds you must be the same as Christ Jesus:

His state was divine,
yet he did not cling
to his equality with God

but emptied himself
to assume the condition of a slave,
and became as men are;
and being as all men are,
he was humbler yet,
even to accepting death,
death on a cross.
But God raised him high
and gave him the name
which is above all other names
so that all beings
in the heavens, on earth and in the underworld,
should bend the knee at the name of Jesus
and that every tongue should acclaim
Jesus Christ as Lord,
to the glory of God the Father.

Gospel Acclamation
Alleluia, alleluia!
If anyone loves me he will keep my word,
and my Father will love him,
and we shall come to him.
Alleluia!   John 14:23

or

Alleluia, alleluia!
The sheep that belong to me listen to my voice,
says the Lord,
I know them and they follow me.
Alleluia!   John 10:27

Gospel   Matthew 21:28-32
He thought better of it and went. Tax collectors and prostitutes are
making their way into the kingdom of God before you.
Jesus said to the chief priests and the elders of the people, "What is
your opinion? A man had two sons. He went and said to the first,
'My boy, you go and work in the vineyard today.' He answered, 'I

will not go,' but afterwards thought better of it and went. The man then went and said the same thing to the second who answered, 'Certainly, sir,' but did not go. Which of the two did the father's will?" "The first," they said. Jesus said to them, "I tell you solemnly, tax collectors and prostitutes are making their way into the kingdom of God before you. For John came to you, a pattern of true righteousness, but you did not believe him, and yet the tax collectors and prostitutes did. Even after seeing that, you refused to think better of it and believe in him."

The Creed is said.

Prayer over the Offerings
Grant us, O merciful God,
that this our offering may find acceptance with you
and that through it the wellspring of all blessing
may be laid open before us.
Through Christ our Lord.

Preface I-VIII of the Sundays in Ordinary Time, pp. 499-502.

Communion Antiphon
Remember your word to your servant, O Lord,
by which you have given me hope.
This is my comfort when I am brought low.   cf. Psalm 118:49-50

or

By this we came to know the love of God:
that Christ laid down his life for us;
so we ought to lay down our lives for one another.   1 John 3:16

Prayer after Communion
May this heavenly mystery, O Lord,
restore us in mind and body,
that we may be coheirs in glory with Christ,
to whose suffering we are united
whenever we proclaim his Death.
Who lives and reigns for ever and ever.

TWENTY-SEVENTH SUNDAY IN ORDINARY TIME – A

The Lord of the vineyard.
God is master of all creation and giver of all gifts. Do we use the gifts
God has given us as God wants us to? If our lives are full of prayer and
thanksgiving, then the God of peace will always be with us.

Entrance Antiphon

Within your will, O Lord, all things are established,
and there is none that can resist your will.
For you have made all things, the heaven and the earth,
and all that is held within the circle of heaven;
you are the Lord of all.

cf. Esther 4:17

The Gloria is said or sung.

Collect

Almighty ever-living God,
who in the abundance of your kindness
surpass the merits and the desires of those who entreat you,
pour out your mercy upon us
to pardon what conscience dreads
and to give what prayer does not dare to ask.
Through our Lord Jesus Christ, your Son,
who lives and reigns with you in the unity of the Holy Spirit,
one God, for ever and ever.

First Reading

Isaiah 5:1-7

The vineyard of the Lord God of hosts is the House of Israel.

Let me sing to my friend
the song of his love for his vineyard.
My friend had a vineyard
on a fertile hillside.
He dug the soil, cleared it of stones,

and planted choice vines in it.
In the middle he built a tower,
he dug a press there too.
He expected it to yield grapes,
but sour grapes were all that it gave.

And now, inhabitants of Jerusalem
and men of Judah,
I ask you to judge
between my vineyard and me.
What could I have done for my vineyard
that I have not done?
I expected it to yield grapes.
Why did it yield sour grapes instead?

Very well, I will tell you
what I am going to do to my vineyard:
I will take away its hedge for it to be grazed on,
and knock down its wall for it to be trampled on.
I will lay it waste, unpruned, undug;
overgrown by the briar and the thorn.
I will command the clouds
to rain no rain on it.
Yes, the vineyard of the Lord of hosts
is the House of Israel,
and the men of Judah
that chosen plant.
He expected justice, but found bloodshed,
integrity, but only a cry of distress.

Psalm   Psalm 79

R. **The vineyard of the Lord**
   is the House of Israel.

1. You brought a vine out of Egypt;
   to plant it you drove out the nations.
   It stretched out its branches to the sea,
   to the Great River it stretched out its shoots. R.

2. Then why have you broken down its walls?
   It is plucked by all who pass by.
   It is ravaged by the boar of the forest,
   devoured by the beasts of the field. R.

3. God of hosts, turn again, we implore,
   look down from heaven and see.
   Visit this vine and protect it,
   the vine your right hand has planted. R.

4. And we shall never forsake you again:
   give us life that we may call upon your name.
   God of hosts, bring us back;
   let your face shine on us and we shall be saved. R.

Second Reading   Philippians 4:6-9
The God of peace will be with you.
There is no need to worry; but if there is anything you need, pray
for it, asking God for it with prayer and thanksgiving, and that
peace of God, which is so much greater than we can understand,
will guard your hearts and your thoughts, in Christ Jesus. Finally,
brothers, fill your minds with everything that is true, everything
that is noble, everything that is good and pure, everything that we
love and honour, and everything that can be thought virtuous or
worthy of praise. Keep doing all the things that you learnt from me
and have been taught by me and have heard or seen that I do. Then
the God of peace will be with you.

Gospel Acclamation
Alleluia, alleluia!
I call you friends, says the Lord,
because I have made known to you
everything I have learnt from my Father.
Alleluia!   John 15:15

or

Alleluia, alleluia!
I chose you from the world
to go out and bear fruit,
fruit that will last,
says the Lord.
Alelluia!   cf. John 15:16

Gospel   Matthew 21:33-43
He will lease the vineyard to other tenants.

Jesus said to the chief priests and the elders of the people, "Listen
to another parable. There was a man, a landowner, who planted a
vineyard; he fenced it round, dug a winepress in it and built a tower;
then he leased it to tenants and went abroad. When vintage time
drew near he sent his servants to the tenants to collect his produce.
But the tenants seized his servants, thrashed one, killed another and
stoned a third. Next he sent some more servants, this time a larger
number, and they dealt with them in the same way. Finally he sent
his son to them. 'They will respect my son,' he said. But when the
tenants saw the son, they said to each other, 'This is the heir. Come
on, let us kill him and take over his inheritance.' So they seized him
and threw him out of the vineyard and killed him. Now when the
owner of the vineyard comes, what will he do to those tenants?"
They answered, "He will bring those wretches to a wretched end
and lease the vineyard to other tenants who will deliver the produce
to him when the season arrives." Jesus said to them, "Have you
never read in the scriptures:

It was the stone rejected by the builders
that became the keystone.
This was the Lord's doing
and it is wonderful to see?

"I tell you, then, that the kingdom of God will be taken from you
and given to a people who will produce its fruit."

The Creed is said.

Prayer over the Offerings
Accept, O Lord, we pray,
the sacrifices instituted by your commands
and, through the sacred mysteries,
which we celebrate with dutiful service,
graciously complete the sanctifying work
by which you are pleased to redeem us.
Through Christ our Lord.

Preface I-VIII of the Sundays in Ordinary Time, pp. 499-502.

Communion Antiphon
The Lord is good to those who hope in him,
to the soul that seeks him.   Lamentations 3:25

or

Though many, we are one bread, one body,
for we all partake of the one Bread and one Chalice.
                                          cf. 1 Corinthians 10:17

Prayer after Communion
Grant us, almighty God,
that we may be refreshed and nourished
by the Sacrament which we have received,
so as to be transformed into what we consume.
Through Christ our Lord.

TWENTY-EIGHTH SUNDAY IN ORDINARY TIME – A

The Lord has prepared a banquet.
God the Father invites us all to share in the wedding feast of his Son. He knows our poverty and wants to share his riches with us. In this banquet we will be joyful and every tear will be wiped from our eyes.

Entrance Antiphon
If you, O Lord, should mark iniquities,
Lord, who could stand?
But with you is found forgiveness,
O God of Israel.

Psalm 129:3-4

The Gloria is said or sung.

Collect
May your grace, O Lord, we pray,
at all times go before us and follow after
and make us always determined
to carry out good works.
Through our Lord Jesus Christ, your Son,
who lives and reigns with you in the unity of the Holy Spirit,
one God, for ever and ever.

First Reading   Isaiah 25:6-10
The Lord will prepare a banquet, and will wipe away tears from every cheek.
On this mountain,
the Lord of hosts will prepare for all people
a banquet of rich food, a banquet of fine wines,
of food rich and juicy, of fine strained wines.
On this mountain he will remove
the mourning veil covering all peoples,
and the shroud enwrapping all nations,

he will destroy Death for ever.
The Lord will wipe away
the tears from every cheek;
he will take away his people's shame
everywhere on earth,
for the Lord has said so.
That day, it will be said: See, this is our God
in whom we hoped for salvation;
the Lord is the one in whom we hoped.
We exult and we rejoice
that he has saved us;
for the hand of the Lord
rests on this mountain.

Psalm   Psalm 22

R. **In the Lord's own house shall I dwell
for ever and ever.**

1. The Lord is my shepherd;
there is nothing I shall want.
Fresh and green are the pastures
where he gives me repose.
Near restful waters he leads me,
to revive my drooping spirit. R.

2. He guides me along the right path;
he is true to his name.
If I should walk in the valley of darkness
no evil would I fear.
You are there with your crook and your staff;
with these you give me comfort. R.

3. You have prepared a banquet for me
in the sight of my foes.
My head you have anointed with oil;
my cup is overflowing. R.

4. Surely goodness and kindness shall follow me
   all the days of my life.
   In the Lord's own house shall I dwell
   for ever and ever. R.

Second Reading   Philippians 4:12-14. 19-20

There is nothing I cannot master with the help of the One who gives me strength.

I know how to be poor and I know how to be rich too. I have been through my initiation and now I am ready for anything anywhere: full stomach or empty stomach, poverty or plenty. There is nothing I cannot master with the help of the One who gives me strength. All the same, it was good of you to share with me in my hardships. In return my God will fulfil all your needs, in Christ Jesus, as lavishly as only God can. Glory to God, our Father, for ever and ever. Amen.

Gospel Acclamation

Alleluia, alleluia!
The Word was made flesh and lived among us;
to all who did accept him
he gave power to become children of God.
Alleluia!   John 1:12. 14

or

Alleluia, alleluia!
May the Father of our Lord Jesus Christ
enlighten the eyes of our mind,
so that we can see what hope his call holds for us.
Alleluia!   cf. Ephesians 1:17. 18

Gospel   Matthew 22:1-14

Invite everyone you can find to the wedding.

Jesus said to the chief priests and elders of the people: "The kingdom of heaven may be compared to a king who gave a feast for his son's wedding. He sent his servants to call those who had been invited, but they would not come. Next he sent some more servants. 'Tell those who have been invited,' he said, 'that I have my banquet all prepared, my oxen and fattened cattle have been slaughtered, everything is ready. Come to the wedding.' But they were not interested: one went off to his farm, another to his business, and the rest seized his servants, maltreated them and killed them. The king was furious. He despatched his troops, destroyed those murderers and burnt their town. Then he said to his servants, 'The wedding is ready; but as those who were invited proved to be unworthy, go to the crossroads in the town and invite everyone you can find to the wedding.' So these servants went out on to the roads and collected together everyone they could find, bad and good alike; and the wedding hall was filled with guests.

When the king came in to look at the guests he noticed one man who was not wearing a wedding garment, and said to him, 'How did you get in here, my friend, without a wedding garment?' And the man was silent. Then the king said to the attendants, 'Bind him hand and foot and throw him out into the dark, where there will be weeping and grinding of teeth.' For many are called, but few are chosen."

The Creed is said.

Prayer over the Offerings
Accept, O Lord, the prayers of your faithful
with the sacrificial offerings,
that, through these acts of devotedness,
we may pass over to the glory of heaven.
Through Christ our Lord.

Preface I-VIII of the Sundays in Ordinary Time, pp. 499-502.

Communion Antiphon
The rich suffer want and go hungry,
but those who seek the Lord lack no blessing.   cf. Psalm 33:11

or

When the Lord appears, we shall be like him,
for we shall see him as he is.   1 John 3:2

Prayer after Communion
We entreat your majesty most humbly, O Lord,
that, as you feed us with the nourishment
which comes from the most holy Body and Blood of your Son,
so you may make us sharers of his divine nature.
Who lives and reigns for ever and ever.

TWENTY-NINTH SUNDAY IN ORDINARY TIME – A

Give the Lord glory and power!

The Lord alone is king, and to him we are to give the homage of our love and obedience. All earthly power is subordinate to God's rule over the universe. It is important to get our priorities right: God first; everything else only in relation to God.

Entrance Antiphon

To you I call; for you will surely heed me, O God;
turn your ear to me; hear my words.
Guard me as the apple of your eye;
in the shadow of your wings protect me. cf. Psalm 16:6. 8

The Gloria is said or sung.

Collect

Almighty ever-living God,
grant that we may always conform our will to yours
and serve your majesty in sincerity of heart.
Through our Lord Jesus Christ, your Son,
who lives and reigns with you in the unity of the Holy Spirit,
one God, for ever and ever.

First Reading Isaiah 45:1. 4-6

I have taken Cyrus by his right hand to subdue nations before him.

Thus says the Lord to his anointed, to Cyrus,
whom he has taken by his right hand
to subdue nations before him
and strip the loins of kings,
to force gateways before him
that their gates be closed no more:

It is for the sake of my servant Jacob,
of Israel my chosen one,

that I have called you by your name,
conferring a title though you do not know me.
I am the Lord, unrivalled;
there is no other God besides me.
Though you do not know me, I arm you
that men may know from the rising to the setting of the sun
that, apart from me, all is nothing.

Psalm   Psalm 95

R. **Give the Lord glory and power.**

1. O sing a new song to the Lord,
   sing to the Lord all the earth.
   Tell among the nations his glory
   and his wonders among all the peoples. R.

2. The Lord is great and worthy of praise,
   to be feared above all gods;
   the gods of the heathens are naught.
   It was the Lord who made the heavens. R.

3. Give the Lord, you families of peoples,
   give the Lord glory and power,
   give the Lord the glory of his name.
   Bring an offering and enter his courts. R.

4. Worship the Lord in his temple.
   O earth, tremble before him.
   Proclaim to the nations: "God is king."
   He will judge the peoples in fairness. R.

Second Reading   1 Thessalonians 1:1-5
We constantly remember your faith, your love and your hope.
From Paul, Silvanus and Timothy, to the Church in Thessalonika
which is in God the Father and the Lord Jesus Christ; wishing you
grace and peace from God the Father and the Lord Jesus Christ.

   We always mention you in our prayers and thank God for you

all, and constantly remember before God our Father how you have shown your faith in action, worked for love and persevered through hope, in our Lord Jesus Christ.

We know, brothers, that God loves you and that you have been chosen, because when we brought the Good News to you, it came to you not only as words, but as power and as the Holy Spirit and as utter conviction.

Gospel Acclamation
Alleluia, alleluia!
Your word is truth, O Lord,
consecrate us in the truth.
Alleluia!   John 17:17

or

Alleluia, alleluia!
You will shine in the world like bright stars
because you are offering it the word of life.
Alleluia!   Philippians 2:15-16

Gospel   Matthew 22:15-21
Give back to Caesar what belongs to Caesar – and to God what belongs to God.

The Pharisees went away to work out between them how to trap Jesus in what he said. And they sent their disciples to him, together with the Herodians, to say, "Master, we know that you are an honest man and teach the way of God in an honest way, and that you are not afraid of anyone, because a man's rank means nothing to you. Tell us your opinion, then. Is it permissible to pay taxes to Caesar or not?" But Jesus was aware of their malice and replied, "You hypocrites! Why do you set this trap for me? Let me see the money you pay the tax with." They handed him a denarius, and he said, "Whose head is this? Whose name?" "Caesar's," they replied. He then said to them, "Very well, give back to Caesar what belongs to Caesar – and to God what belongs to God."

The Creed is said.

Prayer over the Offerings
Grant us, Lord, we pray,
a sincere respect for your gifts,
that, through the purifying action of your grace,
we may be cleansed by the very mysteries we serve.
Through Christ our Lord.

Preface I-VIII of the Sundays in Ordinary Time, pp. 499-502.

Communion Antiphon
Behold, the eyes of the Lord
are on those who fear him,
who hope in his merciful love,
to rescue their souls from death,
to keep them alive in famine.   cf. Psalm 32:18-19

or

The Son of Man has come
to give his life as a ransom for many.   Mark 10:45

Prayer after Communion
Grant, O Lord, we pray,
that, benefiting from participation in heavenly things,
we may be helped by what you give in this present age
and prepared for the gifts that are eternal.
Through Christ our Lord.

THIRTIETH SUNDAY IN ORDINARY TIME – A

Love God and your neighbour.

We are made in the image of the God who is love. We are called to love God with all our heart, soul and mind; this is to mould the pattern of our lives. Jesus says that we are to love our neighbours too, knowing that God lives in them. The quality of our love is shown by how we treat our neighbours.

Entrance Antiphon

Let the hearts that seek the Lord rejoice;
turn to the Lord and his strength;
constantly seek his face.

cf. Psalm 104:3-4

The Gloria is said or sung.

Collect

Almighty ever-living God,
increase our faith, hope and charity,
and make us love what you command,
so that we may merit what you promise.
Through our Lord Jesus Christ, your Son,
who lives and reigns with you in the unity of the Holy Spirit,
one God, for ever and ever.

First Reading   Exodus 22:20-26

If you are harsh with the widow, the orphan, my anger will flare against you.

The Lord said to Moses, "Tell the sons of Israel this, 'You must not molest the stranger or oppress him, for you lived as strangers in the land of Egypt. You must not be harsh with the widow, or with the orphan; if you are harsh with them, they will surely cry out to me, and be sure I shall hear their cry; my anger will flare and I shall kill you with the sword, your own wives will be widows, your own children orphans.

'If you lend money to any of my people, to any poor man among you, you must not play the usurer with him: you must not demand interest from him.

'If you take another's cloak as a pledge, you must give it back to him before sunset. It is all the covering he has; it is the cloak he wraps his body in; what else would he sleep in? If he cries to me, I will listen, for I am full of pity.' ''

Psalm   Psalm 17

R. **I love you, Lord, my strength.**

1. I love you, Lord, my strength,
   my rock, my fortress, my saviour.
   My God is the rock where I take refuge;
   my shield, my mighty help, my stronghold.
   The Lord is worthy of all praise:
   when I call I am saved from my foes. R.

2. Long life to the Lord, my rock!
   Praised be the God who saves me.
   He has given great victories to his king
   and shown his love for his anointed. R.

Second Reading   1 Thessalonians 1:5-10
You broke with idolatry and became servants of God; you are now waiting for his Son.

You observed the sort of life we lived when we were with you, which was for your instruction, and you were led to become imitators of us, and of the Lord; and it was with the joy of the Holy Spirit that you took to the gospel, in spite of the great opposition all round you. This has made you the great example to all believers in Macedonia and Achaia since it was from you that the word of the Lord started to spread – and not only throughout Macedonia and Achaia, for the news of your faith in God has spread everywhere. We do not need to tell other people about it: other people tell us how we started the work among you, how you broke with idolatry when you were converted to God and became servants of the real, living God; and how you are now waiting for Jesus, his Son, whom he raised from the dead, to come from heaven to save us from the retribution which is coming.

Gospel Acclamation
Alleluia, alleluia!
Open our heart, O Lord,
to accept the words of your Son.
Alleluia!

cf. Acts 16:14

or

Alleluia, alleluia!
If anyone loves me he will keep my word,
and my Father will love him,
and we shall come to him.
Alleluia!

John 14:23

Gospel   Matthew 22:34-40
You must love the Lord your God and your neighbour as yourself.
When the Pharisees heard that Jesus had silenced the Sadducees they got together and, to disconcert him, one of them put a question, "Master, which is the greatest commandment of the Law?" Jesus said, "You must love the Lord your God with all your heart, with all your soul, and with all your mind. This is the greatest and the first commandment. The second resembles it: You must love your neighbour as yourself. On these two commandments hang the whole Law, and the Prophets also."

The Creed is said.

Prayer over the Offerings
Look, we pray, O Lord,
on the offerings we make to your majesty,
that whatever is done by us in your service
may be directed above all to your glory.
Through Christ our Lord.

Preface I-VIII of the Sundays in Ordinary Time, pp. 499-502.

Communion Antiphon
We will ring out our joy at your saving help
and exult in the name of our God.   cf. Psalm 19:6

or

Christ loved us and gave himself up for us,
as a fragrant offering to God.   Ephesians 5:2

Prayer after Communion
May your Sacraments, O Lord, we pray,
perfect in us what lies within them,
that what we now celebrate in signs
we may one day possess in truth.
Through Christ our Lord.

THIRTY-FIRST SUNDAY IN ORDINARY TIME – A

Practise what you preach.
The Pharisees were singled out by Jesus as being hypocrites. They were not prepared to ease the burdens of others and so became a stumbling block to the faith of many people. We proclaim the Good News not so much by what we say as by the way in which we live.

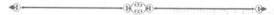

Entrance Antiphon

Forsake me not, O Lord, my God;
be not far from me!
Make haste and come to my help,
O Lord, my strong salvation!

cf. Psalm 37:22-23

The Gloria is said or sung.

Collect

Almighty and merciful God,
by whose gift your faithful offer you
right and praiseworthy service,
grant, we pray,
that we may hasten without stumbling
to receive the things you have promised.
Through our Lord Jesus Christ, your Son,
who lives and reigns with you in the unity of the Holy Spirit,
one God, for ever and ever.

First Reading

Malachi 1:14 – 2:2. 8-10

You have strayed from the way; you have caused many to stumble by your teaching.

I am a great king, says the Lord of hosts, and my name is feared throughout the nations. And now, priests, this warning is for you. If you do not listen, if you do not find it in your heart to glorify my name, says the Lord of hosts, I will send the curse on you and curse your very blessing. You have strayed from the way; you have caused many to stumble by your teaching. You have destroyed the covenant of Levi, says the Lord of hosts. And so I in my turn have made you contemptible and vile in the eyes of the whole people in repayment for the way you have not kept to my paths but have shown partiality in your administration.

Have we not all one Father? Did not one God create us? Why, then, do we break faith with one another, profaning the covenant of our ancestors?

Psalm	Psalm 130

R. **Keep my soul in peace before you, O Lord.**

1. O Lord, my heart is not proud
   nor haughty my eyes.
   I have not gone after things too great
   nor marvels beyond me. R.

2. Truly I have set my soul
   in silence and peace.
   A weaned child on its mother's breast,
   even so is my soul. R.

3. O Israel, hope in the Lord
   both now and for ever. R.

Second Reading	1 Thessalonians 2:7-9. 13

We were eager to hand over to you not only the Good News but our lives as well.

Like a mother feeding and looking after her own children, we felt so devoted and protective towards you, and had come to love you so much, that we were eager to hand over to you not only the Good News but our whole lives as well. Let me remind you, brothers, how hard we used to work, slaving night and day so as not to be a burden on any one of you while we were proclaiming God's Good News to you.

Another reason why we constantly thank God for you is that as soon as you heard the message that we brought you as God's message, you accepted it for what it really is, God's message and not some human thinking; and it is still a living power among you who believe it.

Gospel Acclamation

Alleluia, alleluia!
Speak, Lord, your servant is listening:
you have the message of eternal life.
Alleluia!

1 Samuel 3:9; John 6:68

or

Alleluia, alleluia!
You have only one Father, and he is in heaven;
you have only one Teacher, the Christ!
Alleluia!

Matthew 23:9. 10

Gospel

Matthew 23:1-12

They do not practise what they preach.

Addressing the people and his disciples Jesus said, "The scribes and the Pharisees occupy the chair of Moses. You must therefore do what they tell you and listen to what they say; but do not be guided by what they do: since they do not practise what they preach. They tie up heavy burdens and lay them on men's shoulders, but will they lift a finger to move them? Not they! Everything they do is done to attract attention, like wearing broader phylacteries and longer tassels, like wanting to take the place of honour at banquets and the front seats in the synagogues, being greeted obsequiously in the market squares and having people call them Rabbi.

"You, however, must not allow yourselves to be called Rabbi, since you have only one Master, and you are all brothers. You must call no one on earth your father, since you have only one Father, and he is in heaven. Nor must you allow yourselves to be called teachers, for you have only one Teacher, the Christ. The greatest among you must be your servant. Anyone who exalts himself will be humbled, and anyone who humbles himself will be exalted."

The Creed is said.

Prayer over the Offerings
May these sacrificial offerings, O Lord,
become for you a pure oblation,
and for us a holy outpouring of your mercy.
Through Christ our Lord.

Preface I-VIII of the Sundays in Ordinary Time, pp. 499-502.

Communion Antiphon
You will show me the path of life,
the fullness of joy in your presence, O Lord.   cf. Psalm 15:11

or

Just as the living Father sent me
and I have life because of the Father,
so whoever feeds on me
shall have life because of me, says the Lord.   John 6:58

Prayer after Communion
May the working of your power, O Lord,
increase in us, we pray,
so that, renewed by these heavenly Sacraments,
we may be prepared by your gift
for receiving what they promise.
Through Christ our Lord.

THIRTY-SECOND SUNDAY IN ORDINARY TIME – A

The bridegroom is here!

We await the second coming of Christ just as the ten bridesmaids waited for the bridegroom. We are called to be awake and patient at all times so that we will be ready when the shout goes up, "He is here!" We have no need to worry about those who have died before us, as they too will rise from the dead with Christ in glory.

Entrance Antiphon
Let my prayer come into your presence.
Incline your ear to my cry for help, O Lord. cf. Psalm 87:3

The Gloria is said or sung.

Collect
Almighty and merciful God,
graciously keep from us all adversity,
so that, unhindered in mind and body alike,
we may pursue in freedom of heart
the things that are yours.
Through our Lord Jesus Christ, your Son,
who lives and reigns with you in the unity of the Holy Spirit,
one God, for ever and ever.

First Reading Wisdom 6:12-16
Wisdom is found by those who look for her.
Wisdom is bright, and does not grow dim.
By those who love her she is readily seen,
and found by those who look for her.
Quick to anticipate those who desire her, she makes herself known
   to them.
Watch for her early and you will have no trouble;
you will find her sitting at your gates.

Even to think about her is understanding fully grown;
be on the alert for her and anxiety will quickly leave you.
She herself walks about looking for those who are worthy of her
and graciously shows herself to them as they go,
in every thought of theirs coming to meet them.

Psalm   Psalm 62

R. **For you my soul is thirsting, O God, my God.**

1. O God, you are my God, for you I long;
    for you my soul is thirsting.
    My body pines for you
    like a dry, weary land without water. R.

2. So I gaze on you in the sanctuary
    to see your strength and your glory.
    For your love is better than life,
    my lips will speak your praise. R.

3. So I will bless you all my life,
    in your name I will lift up my hands.
    My soul shall be filled as with a banquet,
    my mouth shall praise you with joy. R.

4. On my bed I remember you.
    On you I muse through the night
    for you have been my help;
    in the shadow of your wings I rejoice. R.

Second Reading   1 Thessalonians 4:13-18
God will bring with him those who have died in Jesus.

> We want you to be quite certain, brothers, about those who have
> died, to make sure that you do not grieve about them, like the
> other people who have no hope. We believe that Jesus died and
> rose again, and that it will be the same for those who have died in
> Jesus: God will bring them with him.

We can tell you this from the Lord's own teaching, that any of us who are left alive until the Lord's coming will not have any advantage over those who have died. At the trumpet of God, the voice of the archangel will call out the command and the Lord himself will come down from heaven; those who have died in Christ will be the first to rise, and then those of us who are still alive will be taken up in the clouds, together with them, to meet the Lord in the air. So we shall stay with the Lord for ever. With such thoughts as these you should comfort one another.

Gospel Acclamation
Alleluia, alleluia!
Stay awake and stand ready,
because you do not know the hour
when the Son of Man is coming.
Alleluia!

Matthew 24:42. 44

Gospel Matthew 25:1-13
The bridegroom is here! Go out and meet him.
Jesus told this parable to his disciples: "The kingdom of heaven will be like this: Ten bridesmaids took their lamps and went to meet the bridegroom. Five of them were foolish and five were sensible: the foolish ones did take their lamps, but they brought no oil, whereas the sensible ones took flasks of oil as well as their lamps. The bridegroom was late, and they all grew drowsy and fell asleep. But at midnight there was a cry, 'The bridegroom is here! Go out and meet him.' At this, all those bridesmaids woke up and trimmed their lamps, and the foolish ones said to the sensible ones, 'Give us some of your oil: our lamps are going out.' But they replied, 'There may not be enough for us and for you; you had better go to those who sell it and buy some for yourselves.' They had gone off to buy it when the bridegroom arrived. Those who were ready went in with him to the wedding hall and the door was closed. The other bridesmaids arrived later. 'Lord, Lord,' they said 'open the door for us.' But he replied, 'I tell you solemnly, I do not know you.' So stay awake, because you do not know either the day or the hour."

The Creed is said.

Prayer over the Offerings
Look with favour, we pray, O Lord,
upon the sacrificial gifts offered here,
that, celebrating in mystery the Passion of your Son,
we may honour it with loving devotion.
Through Christ our Lord.

Preface I-VIII of the Sundays in Ordinary Time, pp. 499-502.

Communion Antiphon
The Lord is my shepherd; there is nothing I shall want.
Fresh and green are the pastures where he gives me repose,
near restful waters he leads me.   cf. Psalm 22:1-2

or

The disciples recognised the Lord Jesus in the breaking of bread.
                                                    cf. Luke 24:35

Prayer after Communion
Nourished by this sacred gift, O Lord,
we give you thanks and beseech your mercy,
that, by the pouring forth of your Spirit,
the grace of integrity may endure
in those your heavenly power has entered.
Through Christ our Lord.

THIRTY-THIRD SUNDAY IN ORDINARY TIME – A

God-given talents.
The Lord gives talents to each one of us, and asks us to use them in his name.
We are not to relax our efforts; rather we are continually to do all in our
power to work as children of the light. We are all called to be a blessing in the
family of God.

Entrance Antiphon
The Lord said: I think thoughts of peace and not of affliction.
You will call upon me, and I will answer you,
and I will lead back your captives from every place.

Jeremiah 29:11. 12. 14

The Gloria is said or sung.

Collect
Grant us, we pray, O Lord our God,
the constant gladness of being devoted to you,
for it is full and lasting happiness
to serve with constancy
the author of all that is good.
Through our Lord Jesus Christ, your Son,
who lives and reigns with you in the unity of the Holy Spirit,
one God, for ever and ever.

First Reading   Proverbs 31:10-13. 19-20. 30-31
A perfect wife – who can find her?
A perfect wife – who can find her?
She is far beyond the price of pearls.
Her husband's heart has confidence in her,
from her he will derive no little profit.
Advantage and not hurt she brings him
all the days of her life.

She is always busy with wool and with flax,
she does her work with eager hands.
She sets her hands to the distaff,
her fingers grasp the spindle.
She holds out her hand to the poor,
she opens her arms to the needy.
Charm is deceitful, and beauty empty;
the woman who is wise is the one to praise.
Give her a share in what her hands have worked for,
and let her works tell her praises at the city gates.

Psalm   Psalm 127

R. **O blessed are those who fear the Lord.**

1. O blessed are those who fear the Lord
   and walk in his ways!
   By the labour of your hands you shall eat.
   You will be happy and prosper. R.

2. Your wife like a fruitful vine
   in the heart of your house;
   your children like shoots of the olive,
   around your table. R.

3. Indeed thus shall be blessed
   the man who fears the Lord.
   May the Lord bless you from Zion
   in a happy Jerusalem
   all the days of your life. R.

Second Reading   1 Thessalonians 5:1-6
Let not the Day of the Lord overtake you like a thief.
You will not be expecting us to write anything to you, brothers,
about "times and seasons", since you know well that the Day of the
Lord is going to come like a thief in the night. It is when people
are saying, "How quiet and peaceful it is" that the worst suddenly
happens, as suddenly as labour pains come on a pregnant woman;

and there will be no way for anybody to evade it.

But it is not as if you live in the dark, my brothers, for that Day to overtake you like a thief. No, you are all sons of light and sons of the day: we do not belong to the night or to darkness, so we should not go on sleeping, as everyone else does, but stay wide awake and sober.

Gospel Acclamation

Alleluia, alleluia!
Even if you have to die, says the Lord,
keep faithful, and I will give you
the crown of life.
Alleluia!

Apocalypse 2:10

or

Alleluia, alleluia!
Make your home in me, as I make mine in you,
says the Lord.
Whoever remains in me bears fruit in plenty.
Alleluia!

John 15:4. 5

Gospel

Matthew 25:14-30

You have been faithful in small things; come and join in your master's happiness.

Jesus spoke this parable to his disciples: "The kingdom of heaven is like a man on his way abroad who summoned his servants and entrusted his property to them. To one he gave five talents, to another two, to a third one; each in proportion to his ability. Then he set out. The man who had received the five talents promptly went and traded with them and made five more. The man who had received two made two more in the same way. But the man who had received one went off and dug a hole in the ground and hid his master's money. Now a long time after, the master of those servants came back and went through his accounts with them. The man who had received the five talents came forward bringing five more. 'Sir,' he said, 'you entrusted me with five talents; here are five more that I have made.' His master said to him, 'Well done, good and faithful servant; you have shown you can be faithful in small things, I will trust you with greater; come and join in your master's happiness.' Next the man with two talents came forward. 'Sir,' he said, 'you entrusted me with two talents; here are two more that I have made.' His master said to him, 'Well done, good and faithful servant; you have shown you can be faithful in small things, I will trust you with greater; come and join in your master's happiness.' Last came forward the man who had the one talent. 'Sir,' said he, 'I had heard you were a hard man, reaping where you have not sown and gathering where you have not scattered; so I was afraid, and I went off and hid your talent in the ground. Here it is; it was yours, you have it back.' But his master answered him, 'You wicked and lazy servant! So you knew that I reap where I have not sown and gather where I have not scattered? Well then, you should have deposited my money with the bankers, and on my return I would have recovered my capital with interest. So now, take the talent from him and give it to the man who has the five talents. For to everyone who has will be given more, and he will have more than enough; but from the man who has not, even what he has will be taken away. As for this good-for-nothing servant, throw him out into the dark, where there will be weeping and grinding of teeth.'"

The Creed is said.

Prayer over the Offerings
Grant, O Lord, we pray,
that what we offer in the sight of your majesty
may obtain for us the grace of being devoted to you
and gain us the prize of everlasting happiness.
Through Christ our Lord.

Preface I-VIII of the Sundays in Ordinary Time, pp. 499-502.

Communion Antiphon
To be near God is my happiness,
to place my hope in God the Lord.   Psalm 72:28

or

Amen, I say to you: Whatever you ask in prayer,
believe that you will receive,
and it shall be given to you, says the Lord. Mark 11:23-24

Prayer after Communion
We have partaken of the gifts of this sacred mystery,
humbly imploring, O Lord,
that what your Son commanded us to do
in memory of him
may bring us growth in charity.
Through Christ our Lord.

Last Sunday in Ordinary Time

OUR LORD JESUS CHRIST, KING OF THE UNIVERSE – A

Christ the King.
The Lord looks after his sheep through Jesus Christ, our Shepherd and King.
Christ is anointed King of the universe by his Father. We will be judged by
our actions in this life, and finally Christ will present us to his Father. If we
live our lives for Christ the King, and in service of his brothers and sisters, he
promises that we will enter with him into glory.

Entrance Antiphon
How worthy is the Lamb who was slain,
to receive power and divinity,
and wisdom and strength and honour.
To him belong glory and power for ever and ever.

Apocalypse 5:12; 1:6

The Gloria is said or sung.

Collect
Almighty ever-living God,
whose will is to restore all things
in your beloved Son, the King of the universe,
grant, we pray,
that the whole creation, set free from slavery,
may render your majesty service
and ceaselessly proclaim your praise.
Through our Lord Jesus Christ, your Son,
who lives and reigns with you in the unity of the Holy Spirit,
one God, for ever and ever.

First Reading   Ezekiel 34:11-12. 15-17

As for you, my sheep, I will judge between sheep and sheep.

The Lord says this: I am going to look after my flock myself and keep all of it in view. As a shepherd keeps all his flock in view when he stands up in the middle of his scattered sheep, so shall I keep my sheep in view. I shall rescue them from wherever they have been scattered during the mist and darkness. I myself will pasture my sheep, I myself will show them where to rest – it is the Lord who speaks. I shall look for the lost one, bring back the stray, bandage the wounded and make the weak strong. I shall watch over the fat and healthy. I shall be a true shepherd to them.

  As for you, my sheep, the Lord says this: I will judge between sheep and sheep, between rams and he-goats.

Psalm   Psalm 22

R. **The Lord is my shepherd;**
     there is nothing I shall want.

1. The Lord is my shepherd;
    there is nothing I shall want.
    Fresh and green are the pastures
    where he gives me repose. R.

2. Near restful waters he leads me,
    to revive my drooping spirit.
    He guides me along the right path;
    he is true to his name. R.

3. You have prepared a banquet for me
    in the sight of my foes.
    My head you have anointed with oil;
    my cup is overflowing. R.

4. Surely goodness and kindness shall follow me
    all the days of my life.
    In the Lord's own house shall I dwell
    for ever and ever. R.

Second Reading   1 Corinthians 15:20-26. 28

He will hand over the kingdom to God the Father, so that God may be all in all.

Christ has been raised from the dead, the first-fruits of all who have fallen asleep. Death came through one man and in the same way the resurrection of the dead has come through one man. Just as all men die in Adam, so all men will be brought to life in Christ; but all of them in their proper order: Christ as the first-fruits and then, after the coming of Christ, those who belong to him. After that will come the end, when he hands over the kingdom to God the Father, having done away with every sovereignty, authority and power. For he must be king until he has put all his enemies under his feet and the last of the enemies to be destroyed is death. And when everything is subjected to him, then the Son himself will be subject in his turn to the One who subjected all things to him, so that God may be all in all.

Gospel Acclamation
Alleluia, alleluia!
Blessings on him who comes in the name of the Lord!
Blessings on the coming kingdom of our father David!
Alleluia!   Mark 11:10

Gospel   Matthew 25:31-46

He will take his seat on his throne of glory, and he will separate men one from another.

Jesus said to his disciples: "When the Son of Man comes in his glory, escorted by all the angels, then he will take his seat on his throne of glory. All the nations will be assembled before him and he will separate men one from another as the shepherd separates sheep from goats. He will place the sheep on his right hand and the goats on his left. Then the King will say to those on his right hand, 'Come, you whom my Father has blessed, take for your heritage the kingdom prepared for you since the foundation of the world. For I was hungry and you gave me food; I was thirsty and you gave me drink; I was a stranger and you made me welcome; naked and you clothed me, sick and you visited me, in prison and you came to see me.' Then the virtuous will say to him in reply, 'Lord, when did we see you hungry and feed you; or thirsty and give you drink? When did we see you a stranger and make you welcome; naked and clothe you; sick or in prison and go to see you?' And the King will answer, 'I tell you solemnly, in so far as you did this to one of the least of these brothers of mine, you did it to me.' Next he will say to those on his left hand, 'Go away from me, with your curse upon you, to the eternal fire prepared for the devil and his angels. For I was hungry and you never gave me food; I was thirsty and you never gave me anything to drink; I was a stranger and you never made me welcome, naked and you never clothed me, sick and in prison and you never visited me.' Then it will be their turn to ask, 'Lord, when did we see you hungry or thirsty, a stranger or naked, sick or in prison, and did not come to your help?' Then he will answer, 'I tell you solemnly, in so far as you neglected to do this to one of the least of these, you neglected to do it to me.' And they will go away to eternal punishment, and the virtuous to eternal life."

The Creed is said.

Prayer over the Offerings
As we offer you, O Lord, the sacrifice
by which the human race is reconciled to you,
we humbly pray,
that your Son himself may bestow on all nations
the gifts of unity and peace.
Through Christ our Lord.

Preface
It is truly right and just, our duty and our salvation,
always and everywhere to give you thanks,
Lord, holy Father, almighty and eternal God.

For you anointed your Only Begotten Son,
our Lord Jesus Christ, with the oil of gladness
as eternal Priest and King of all creation,
so that, by offering himself on the altar of the Cross
as a spotless sacrifice to bring us peace,

he might accomplish the mysteries of human redemption
and, making all created things subject to his rule,
he might present to the immensity of your majesty
an eternal and universal kingdom,
a kingdom of truth and life,
a kingdom of holiness and grace,
a kingdom of justice, love and peace.

And so, with Angels and Archangels,
with Thrones and Dominions,
and with all the hosts and Powers of heaven,
we sing the hymn of your glory,
as without end we acclaim:
Holy, Holy, Holy Lord God of hosts…

Communion Antiphon
The Lord sits as King for ever.
The Lord will bless his people with peace.   Psalm 28:10-11

Prayer after Communion
Having received the food of immortality,
we ask, O Lord,
that, glorying in obedience
to the commands of Christ, the King of the universe,
we may live with him eternally in his heavenly Kingdom.
Who lives and reigns for ever and ever.

SECOND SUNDAY IN ORDINARY TIME – B

Here I am, Lord.

We are called by Christ to follow him. When we respond to his call, we become one with him in the Spirit and offer our lives to him as part of his Church. When he calls us, in whatever situation we find ourselves, we reply: "Here I am, since you called me."

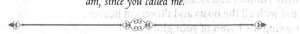

Entrance Antiphon

All the earth shall bow down before you, O God,
and shall sing to you,
shall sing to your name, O Most High!

Psalm 65:4

The Gloria is said or sung.

Collect

Almighty ever-living God,
who govern all things,
both in heaven and on earth,
mercifully hear the pleading of your people
and bestow your peace on our times.
Through our Lord Jesus Christ, your Son,
who lives and reigns with you in the unity of the Holy Spirit,
one God, for ever and ever.

First Reading   1 Samuel 3:3-10. 19

Speak, Lord, your servant is listening.

Samuel was lying in the sanctuary of the Lord where the ark of God was, when the Lord called, "Samuel! Samuel!" He answered, "Here I am." Then he ran to Eli and said, "Here I am, since you called me." Eli said, "I did not call. Go back and lie down." So he went and lay down. Once again the Lord called, "Samuel! Samuel!" Samuel got up and went to Eli and said, "Here I am, since you called me." He replied, "I did not call you, my son; go back and lie down." Samuel had as yet no knowledge of the Lord and the word of the Lord had not yet been revealed to him. Once again the Lord called, the third time. He got up and went to Eli and said, "Here I am, since you called me." Eli then understood that it was the Lord who was calling the boy, and he said to Samuel, "Go and lie down, and if someone calls say, 'Speak, Lord, your servant is listening.'" So Samuel went and lay down in his place.

The Lord then came and stood by, calling as he had done before, "Samuel! Samuel!" Samuel answered, "Speak, Lord, your servant is listening."

Samuel grew up and the Lord was with him and let no word of his fall to the ground.

Psalm   Psalm 39

R. **Here I am, Lord!**
    I come to do your will.

1. I waited, I waited for the Lord
   and he stooped down to me;
   he heard my cry.
   He put a new song into my mouth,
   praise of our God. R.

2. You do not ask for sacrifice and offerings,
   but an open ear.
   You do not ask for holocaust and victim.
   Instead, here am I. R.

3. In the scroll of the book it stands written
   that I should do your will.
   My God, I delight in your law
   in the depth of my heart. R.

4. Your justice I have proclaimed
   in the great assembly.
   My lips I have not sealed;
   you know it, O Lord. R.

Second Reading   1 Corinthians 6:13-15. 17-20
Your bodies are members making up the body of Christ.

The body is not meant for fornication; it is for the Lord, and the
Lord for the body. God who raised the Lord from the dead, will by
his power raise us up too.

You know, surely, that your bodies are members making up the
body of Christ; anyone who is joined to the Lord is one spirit with
him.

Keep away from fornication. All the other sins are committed
outside the body; but to fornicate is to sin against your own body.
Your body, you know, is the temple of the Holy Spirit, who is in you
since you received him from God. You are not your own property;
you have been bought and paid for. That is why you should use your
body for the glory of God.

Gospel Acclamation
Alleluia, alleluia!
Speak, Lord, your servant is listening:
you have the message of eternal life.
Alleluia!   1 Samuel 3:9; John 6:68

or

Alleluia, alleluia!
We have found the Messiah – which means Christ –
grace and truth have come through him.
Alleluia!   John 1:41. 17

Gospel   John 1:35-42
They saw where he lived, and stayed with him.

As John stood with two of his disciples, Jesus passed, and John
stared hard at him and said, "Look, there is the lamb of God."
Hearing this, the two disciples followed Jesus. Jesus turned round,
saw them following and said, "What do you want?" They answered,
"Rabbi" – which means Teacher – "where do you live?" "Come and
see," he replied; so they went and saw where he lived, and stayed
with him the rest of that day. It was about the tenth hour.

One of these two who became followers of Jesus after hearing

what John had said was Andrew, the brother of Simon Peter. Early
next morning, Andrew met his brother and said to him, "We have
found the Messiah" – which means the Christ – and he took Simon
to Jesus. Jesus looked hard at him and said, "You are Simon son of
John; you are to be called Cephas" – meaning Rock.

The Creed is said.

Prayer over the Offerings
Grant us, O Lord, we pray,
that we may participate worthily in these mysteries,
for whenever the memorial of this sacrifice is celebrated
the work of our redemption is accomplished.
Through Christ our Lord.

Preface I-VIII of the Sundays in Ordinary Time, pp. 499-502.

Communion Antiphon
You have prepared a table before me,
and how precious is the chalice that quenches my thirst.
cf. Psalm 22:5

or

We have come to know and to believe
in the love that God has for us.
1 John 4:16

Prayer after Communion
Pour on us, O Lord, the Spirit of your love,
and in your kindness
make those you have nourished
by this one heavenly Bread
one in mind and heart.
Through Christ our Lord.

THIRD SUNDAY IN ORDINARY TIME – B

Repent and believe the Good News.
Christ calls us constantly to review our lives in the light of the Gospel. This is
something we are to do throughout our daily lives, and we can ask the Lord to
show us his ways so that we can choose the right path. The world as we know
it is passing away, and it is important not to allow worldly cares to distract us
from the Lord's calling.

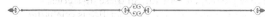

Entrance Antiphon
O sing a new song to the Lord;
sing to the Lord, all the earth.
In his presence are majesty and splendour,
strength and honour in his holy place.   cf. Psalm 95:1. 6

The Gloria is said or sung.

Collect
Almighty ever-living God,
direct our actions according to your good pleasure,
that in the name of your beloved Son
we may abound in good works.
Through our Lord Jesus Christ, your Son,
who lives and reigns with you in the unity of the Holy Spirit,
one God, for ever and ever.

First Reading   Jonah 3:1-5. 10
The people of Nineveh renounce their evil behaviour.
The word of the Lord was addressed to Jonah: "Up!" he said "Go to
Nineveh, the great city, and preach to them as I told you to." Jonah
set out and went to Nineveh in obedience to the word of the Lord.
Now Nineveh was a city great beyond compare: it took three days
to cross it. Jonah went on into the city, making a day's journey. He
preached in these words, "Only forty days more and Nineveh is going
to be destroyed." And the people of Nineveh believed in God; they
proclaimed a fast and put on sackcloth, from the greatest to the least.

God saw their efforts to renounce their evil behaviour. And God relented: he did not inflict on them the disaster which he had threatened.

Psalm   Psalm 24

R. **Lord, make me know your ways.**

1. Lord, make me know your ways.
   Lord, teach me your paths.
   Make me walk in your truth, and teach me:
   for you are God my saviour. R.

2. Remember your mercy, Lord,
   and the love you have shown from of old.
   In your love remember me,
   because of your goodness, O Lord. R.

3. The Lord is good and upright.
   He shows the path to those who stray,
   he guides the humble in the right path;
   he teaches his way to the poor. R.

Second Reading   1 Corinthians 7:29-31

The world as we know it is passing away.

Brothers: our time is growing short. Those who have wives should live as though they had none, and those who mourn should live as though they had nothing to mourn for; those who are enjoying life should live as though there were nothing to laugh about; those whose life is buying things should live as though they had nothing of their own; and those who have to deal with the world should not become engrossed in it. I say this because the world as we know it is passing away.

Gospel Acclamation
Alleluia, alleluia!
The kingdom of God is close at hand;
believe the Good News.
Alleluia!

                                                                Mark 1:15

Gospel   Mark 1:14-20

Repent, and believe the Good News.

After John had been arrested, Jesus went into Galilee. There he proclaimed the Good News from God. "The time has come," he said, "and the kingdom of God is close at hand. Repent, and believe the Good News."

As he was walking along by the Sea of Galilee he saw Simon and his brother Andrew casting a net in the lake – for they were fishermen. And Jesus said to them, "Follow me and I will make you into fishers of men." And at once they left their nets and followed him.

Going on a little further, he saw James son of Zebedee and his brother John; they too were in their boat, mending their nets. He called them at once and, leaving their father Zebedee in the boat with the men he employed, they went after him.

The Creed is said.

Prayer over the Offerings

Accept our offerings, O Lord, we pray,
and in sanctifying them
grant that they may profit us for salvation.
Through Christ our Lord.

Preface I-VIII of the Sundays in Ordinary Time, pp. 499-502.

Communion Antiphon

Look toward the Lord and be radiant;
let your faces not be abashed.   cf. Psalm 33:6

or

I am the light of the world, says the Lord;
whoever follows me will not walk in darkness,
but will have the light of life.   John 8:12

Prayer after Communion

Grant, we pray, almighty God,
that, receiving the grace
by which you bring us to new life,
we may always glory in your gift.
Through Christ our Lord.

FOURTH SUNDAY IN ORDINARY TIME – B

Christ teaches with authority.

Jesus Christ is the great prophet for all times. He speaks to us today with the same authority as he did in his own home town at Capernaum.

When we are set free from worrying about unnecessary things, we can more fully serve the Lord. If we allow the Lord to speak through our lives, we can become his prophets.

Entrance Antiphon

Save us, O Lord our God!
And gather us from the nations,
to give thanks to your holy name,
and make it our glory to praise you.   Psalm 105:47

The Gloria is said or sung.

Collect

Grant us, Lord our God,
that we may honour you with all our mind,
and love everyone in truth of heart.
Through our Lord Jesus Christ, your Son,
who lives and reigns with you in the unity of the Holy Spirit,
one God, for ever and ever.

First Reading   Deuteronomy 18:15-20

I will raise up a prophet and I will put my words into his mouth.

Moses said to the people: "Your God will raise up for you a prophet like myself, from among yourselves, from your own brothers; to him you must listen. This is what you yourselves asked of the Lord your God at Horeb on the day of the Assembly. 'Do not let me hear again', you said, 'the voice of the Lord my God, nor look any longer on this great fire, or I shall die'; and the Lord said to me, 'All they have spoken is well said. I will raise up a prophet like yourself for them from their own brothers; I will put my words into his mouth and he shall tell them all I command him. The man who does not listen to my words that he speaks in my name shall be held answerable to me for it. But the prophet who presumes to say in my name a thing I have not commanded him to say, or who speaks in the name of other gods, that prophet shall die'."

Psalm   Psalm 94

R. **O that today you would listen to his voice!**
    Harden not your hearts.

1. Come, ring out our joy to the Lord;
    hail the rock who saves us.
    Let us come before him, giving thanks,
    with songs let us hail the Lord. R.

2. Come in; let us kneel and bend low;
    let us kneel before the God who made us
    for he is our God and we
    the people who belong to his pasture,
    the flock that is led by his hand. R.

3. O that today you would listen to his voice!
    "Harden not your hearts as at Meribah,
    as on that day at Massah in the desert
    when your fathers put me to the test;
    when they tried me, though they saw my work." R.

Second Reading   1 Corinthians 7:32-35

An unmarried woman can devote herself to the Lord's affairs; all she need worry about is being holy.

I would like to see you free from all worry. An unmarried man can devote himself to the Lord's affairs, all he need worry about is pleasing the Lord; but a married man has to bother about the world's affairs and devote himself to pleasing his wife: he is torn two ways. In the same way an unmarried woman, like a young girl, can devote herself to the Lord's affairs; all she need worry about is being holy in body and spirit. The married woman, on the other hand, has to worry about the world's affairs and devote herself to pleasing her husband. I say this only to help you, not to put a halter round your necks, but simply to make sure that everything is as it should be, and that you give your undivided attention to the Lord.

Gospel Acclamation
Alleluia, alleluia!
Blessed are you, Father,
Lord of heaven and earth,
for revealing the mysteries of the kingdom
to mere children.
Alleluia!   cf. Matthew 11:25

or

Alleluia, alleluia!
The people that lived in darkness
has seen a great light;
on those who dwell in the land and shadow of death
a light has dawned.
Alleluia!   Matthew 4:16

Gospel   Mark 1:21-28
He taught them with authority.

Jesus and his followers went as far as Capernaum, and as soon as the sabbath came Jesus went to the synagogue and began to teach. And his teaching made a deep impression on them because, unlike the scribes, he taught them with authority.

  In their synagogue just then there was a man possessed by an unclean spirit, and it shouted, "What do you want with us, Jesus of Nazareth? Have you come to destroy us? I know who you are: the Holy One of God." But Jesus said sharply, "Be quiet! Come out of him!" And the unclean spirit threw the man into convulsions and with a loud cry went out of him. The people were so astonished that they started asking each other what it all meant. "Here is a teaching that is new", they said, "and with authority behind it: he gives orders even to unclean spirits and they obey him." And his reputation rapidly spread everywhere, through all the surrounding Galilean countryside.

The Creed is said.

Prayer over the Offerings

O Lord, we bring to your altar
these offerings of our service:
be pleased to receive them, we pray,
and transform them
into the Sacrament of our redemption.
Through Christ our Lord.

Preface I-VIII of the Sundays in Ordinary Time, pp. 499-502.

Communion Antiphon

Let your face shine on your servant.
Save me in your merciful love.
O Lord, let me never be put to shame, for I call on you.

cf. Psalm 30:17-18

or

Blessed are the poor in spirit,
for theirs is the Kingdom of Heaven.
Blessed are the meek, for they shall possess the land.

Matthew 5:3-4

Prayer after Communion

Nourished by these redeeming gifts,
we pray, O Lord,
that through this help to eternal salvation
true faith may ever increase.
Through Christ our Lord.

FIFTH SUNDAY IN ORDINARY TIME – B

Looking for Christ.

Jesus Christ gives meaning to our lives. Without him life can seem no better than hired drudgery, but with his Spirit in us, all our service of others is done for love. This is a service that brings perfect freedom. The world needs Christ, and it is our calling to bring him to everyone.

Entrance Antiphon
O come, let us worship God
and bow low before the God who made us,
for he is the Lord our God.

Psalm 94:6-7

The Gloria is said or sung.

Collect
Keep your family safe, O Lord, with unfailing care,
that, relying solely on the hope of heavenly grace,
they may be defended always by your protection.
Through our Lord Jesus Christ, your Son,
who lives and reigns with you in the unity of the Holy Spirit,
one God, for ever and ever.

First Reading   Job 7:1-4. 6-7
Restlessly I fret till twilight falls.
Job began to speak:

Is not man's life on earth nothing more than pressed service,
his time no better than hired drudgery?
Like the slave, sighing for the shade,
or the workman with no thought but his wages,
months of delusion I have assigned to me,
nothing for my own but nights of grief.
Lying in bed I wonder, "When will it be day?"
Risen I think, "How slowly evening comes!"

Restlessly I fret till twilight falls.
Swifter than a weaver's shuttle my days have passed,
and vanished, leaving no hope behind.
Remember that my life is but a breath,
and that my eyes will never again see joy.

Psalm   Psalm 146

R. **Praise the Lord who heals the broken-hearted.**

or **Alleluia!**

1. Praise the Lord for he is good;
   sing to our God for he is loving:
   to him our praise is due. R.

2. The Lord builds up Jerusalem
   and brings back Israel's exiles,
   he heals the broken-hearted,
   he binds up all their wounds.
   He fixes the number of the stars;
   he calls each one by its name. R.

3. Our Lord is great and almighty;
   his wisdom can never be measured.
   The Lord raises the lowly;
   he humbles the wicked to the dust. R.

Second Reading   1 Corinthians 9:16-19. 22-23
I should be punished if I did not preach the Gospel.
I do not boast of preaching the gospel, since it is a duty which has
been laid on me; I should be punished if I did not preach it! If I had
chosen this work myself, I might have been paid for it, but as I have
not, it is a responsibility which has been put into my hands. Do you
know what my reward is? It is this: in my preaching, to be able to
offer the Good News free, and not insist on the rights which the
gospel gives me.

So though I am not a slave of any man I have made myself the slave of everyone so as to win as many as I could. For the weak I made myself weak. I made myself all things to all men in order to save some at any cost; and I still do this, for the sake of the gospel, to have a share in its blessings.

Gospel Acclamation
Alleluia, alleluia!
I am the light of the world, says the Lord,
anyone who follows me
will have the light of life.
Alleluia!   John 8:12

or

Alleluia, alleluia!
He took our sicknesses away,
and carried our diseases for us.
Alleluia!   Matthew 8:17

Gospel   Mark 1:29-39
He cured many who suffered from diseases of one kind or another.
On leaving the synagogue, Jesus went with James and John straight to the house of Simon and Andrew. Now Simon's mother-in-law had gone to bed with fever, and they told him about her straightaway. He went to her, took her by the hand and helped her up. And the fever left her and she began to wait on them.

That evening, after sunset, they brought to him all who were sick and those who were possessed by devils. The whole town came crowding round the door, and he cured many who were suffering from diseases of one kind or another; he also cast out many devils, but he would not allow them to speak, because they knew who he was.

In the morning, long before dawn, he got up and left the house, and went off to a lonely place and prayed there. Simon and his companions set out in search of him, and when they found him they said, "Everybody is looking for you." He answered, "Let us go elsewhere, to the neighbouring country towns, so that I can preach there too, because that is why I came." And he went all through Galilee, preaching in their synagogues and casting out devils.

The Creed is said.

Prayer over the Offerings
O Lord, our God,
who once established these created things
to sustain us in our frailty,
grant, we pray,
that they may become for us now
the Sacrament of eternal life.
Through Christ our Lord.

Preface I-VIII of the Sundays in Ordinary Time, pp. 499-502.

Communion Antiphon
Let them thank the Lord for his mercy,
his wonders for the children of men,
for he satisfies the thirsty soul,
and the hungry he fills with good things.   cf. Psalm 106:8-9

or

Blessed are those who mourn, for they shall be consoled.
Blessed are those who hunger and thirst for righteousness,
for they shall have their fill.   Matthew 5:5-6

Prayer after Communion
O God, who have willed that we be partakers
in the one Bread and the one Chalice,
grant us, we pray, so to live
that, made one in Christ,
we may joyfully bear fruit
for the salvation of the world.
Through Christ our Lord.

SIXTH SUNDAY IN ORDINARY TIME – B

Be cured.

Like the leper, we cry out to Christ, who alone can cure us of all our troubles and weakness. He reaches out and touches us with his grace, telling us to be cured. We belong to Christ in the company of the saints, and are called to do everything for the glory of God. We are a people of joy because we know that Christ delivers us from our sins.

Entrance Antiphon

Be my protector, O God,
a mighty stronghold to save me.
For you are my rock, my stronghold!
Lead me, guide me, for the sake of your name.   cf. Psalm 30:3-4

The Gloria is said or sung.

Collect

O God, who teach us that you abide
in hearts that are just and true,
grant that we may be so fashioned by your grace
as to become a dwelling pleasing to you.
Through our Lord Jesus Christ, your Son,
who lives and reigns with you in the unity of the Holy Spirit,
one God, for ever and ever.

First Reading   Leviticus 13:1-2. 44-46

The leper must live apart: he must live outside the camp.

The Lord said to Moses and Aaron, "If a swelling or scab or shiny spot appears on a man's skin, a case of leprosy of the skin is to be suspected. The man must be taken to Aaron, the priest, or to one of the priests who are his sons.

"The man is leprous: he is unclean. The priest must declare him unclean; he is suffering from leprosy of the head. A man infected with leprosy must wear his clothing torn and his hair disordered; he must shield his upper lip and cry, 'Unclean, unclean.' As long as the disease lasts he must be unclean; and therefore he must live apart; he must live outside the camp."

Psalm   Psalm 31

R. **You are my refuge, O Lord;**
    you fill me with the joy of salvation.

1. Happy the man whose offence is forgiven,
   whose sin is remitted.
   O happy the man to whom the Lord
   imputes no guilt,
   in whose spirit is no guile. R.

2. But now I have acknowledged my sins;
   my guilt I did not hide.
   I said: "I will confess
   my offence to the Lord."
   And you, Lord, have forgiven
   the guilt of my sin. R.

3. Rejoice, rejoice in the Lord,
   exult, you just!
   O come, ring out your joy,
   all you upright of heart. R.

Second Reading   1 Corinthians 10:31 – 11:1
Take me for your model, as I take Christ.
Whatever you eat, whatever you drink, whatever you do at all, do it for the glory of God. Never do anything offensive to anyone – to Jews or Greeks or to the Church of God; just as I try to be helpful to everyone at all times, not anxious for my own advantage but for the advantage of everybody else, so that they may be saved.
     Take me for your model, as I take Christ.

Gospel Acclamation
Alleluia, alleluia!
May the Father of our Lord Jesus Christ
enlighten the eyes of our mind,
so that we can see what hope his call holds for us.
Alleluia!   cf. Ephesians 1:17. 18

or

Alleluia, alleluia!
A great prophet has appeared among us;
God has visited his people.
Alleluia!   Luke 7:16

Gospel   Mark 1:40-45
The leprosy left him at once and he was cured.

A leper came to Jesus and pleaded on his knees: "If you want to", he said, "you can cure me." Feeling sorry for him, Jesus stretched out his hand and touched him. "Of course I want to!" he said. "Be cured!" And the leprosy left him at once and he was cured. Jesus immediately sent him away and sternly ordered him, "Mind you say nothing to anyone, but go and show yourself to the priest, and make the offering for your healing prescribed by Moses as evidence of your recovery." The man went away, but then started talking about it freely and telling the story everywhere, so that Jesus could no longer go openly into any town, but had to stay outside in places where nobody lived. Even so, people from all around would come to him.

The Creed is said.

Prayer over the Offerings
May this oblation, O Lord, we pray,
cleanse and renew us
and may it become for those who do your will
the source of eternal reward.
Through Christ our Lord.

Preface I-VIII of the Sundays in Ordinary Time, pp. 499-502.

Communion Antiphon
They ate and had their fill,
and what they craved the Lord gave them;
they were not disappointed in what they craved.

cf. Psalm 77:29-30

or

God so loved the world
that he gave his Only Begotten Son,
so that all who believe in him may not perish,
but may have eternal life.

John 3:16

Prayer after Communion
Having fed upon these heavenly delights,
we pray, O Lord,
that we may always long
for that food by which we truly live.
Through Christ our Lord.

SEVENTH SUNDAY IN ORDINARY TIME – B

Your sins are forgiven.

Christ came to forgive sinners. His greatest miracles were a healing of the soul, not just the body. There is no need for us to worry about the past. We can bring everything to the Lord, who alone blots out our sins. He has given us the Spirit that we carry in our hearts.

Entrance Antiphon

O Lord, I trust in your merciful love.
My heart will rejoice in your salvation.
I will sing to the Lord who has been bountiful with me.

Psalm 12:6

The Gloria is said or sung.

Collect

Grant, we pray, almighty God,
that, always pondering spiritual things,
we may carry out in both word and deed
that which is pleasing to you.
Through our Lord Jesus Christ, your Son,
who lives and reigns with you in the unity of the Holy Spirit,
one God, for ever and ever.

First Reading   Isaiah 43:18-19. 21-22. 24-25

It is who must blot out everything.

Thus says the Lord:

No need to recall the past,
   no need to think about what was done before.
See, I am doing a new deed,
   even now it comes to light; can you not see it?
Yes, I am making a road in the wilderness,
   paths in the wilds.

The people I have formed for myself
will sing my praises.
Jacob, you have not invoked me,
you have not troubled yourself, Israel, on my behalf.
Instead you have burdened me with your sins,
troubled me with your iniquities.
I it is, I it is, who must blot out everything
and not remember your sins.

Psalm   Psalm 40

R. **Heal my soul for I have sinned against you.**

1. Happy the man who considers the poor and the weak.
   The Lord will save him in the day of evil,
   will guard him, give him life, make him happy in the land
   and will not give him up to the will of his foes. R.

2. The Lord will help him on his bed of pain,
   he will bring him back from sickness to health.
   As for me, I said: "Lord, have mercy on me,
   heal my soul for I have sinned against you." R.

3. If you uphold me I shall be unharmed
   and set in your presence for evermore.
   Blessed be the Lord, the God of Israel
   from age to age. Amen. Amen. R.

Second Reading   2 Corinthians 1:18-22
Jesus was never Yes and No: with him it was always Yes.

I swear by God's truth, there is no Yes and No about what we say to
you. The Son of God, the Christ Jesus that we proclaimed among
you – I mean Silvanus and Timothy and I – was never Yes and No:
with him it was always Yes, and however many the promises God
made, the Yes to them all is in him. That is why it is "through him"
that we answer Amen to the praise of God. Remember it is God
himself who assures us all, and you, of our standing in Christ, and
has anointed us, marking us with his seal and giving us the pledge,
the Spirit, that we carry in our hearts.

Gospel Acclamation
Alleluia, alleluia!
The Word was made flesh and lived among us;
to all who did accept him
he gave power to become children of God.
Alleluia!   John 1:12. 14

or

Alleluia, alleluia!
The Lord has sent me to bring the good news to the poor,
to proclaim liberty to captives.
Alleluia!   cf. Luke 4:18

Gospel   Mark 2:1-12
The Son of Man has authority on earth to forgive sins.
When Jesus returned to Capernaum, word went round that he
was back; and so many people collected that there was no room
left, even in front of the door. He was preaching the word to them
when some people came bringing him a paralytic carried by four
men, but as the crowds made it impossible to get the man to him,
they stripped the roof over the place where Jesus was; and when
they had made an opening they lowered the stretcher on which
the paralytic lay. Seeing their faith, Jesus said to the paralytic, "My
child, your sins are forgiven." Now some scribes were sitting there,
and they thought to themselves, "How can this man talk like that?
He is blaspheming. Who can forgive sins but God?" Jesus, inwardly
aware that this was what they were thinking, said to them, "Why do
you have these thoughts in your hearts? Which of these is easier: to
say to the paralytic, 'Your sins are forgiven' or to say, 'Get up, pick up
your stretcher and walk?' But to prove to you that the Son of Man
has authority on earth to forgive sins," – he said to the paralytic – "I
order you: get up, pick up your stretcher, and go off home." And
the man got up, picked up his stretcher at once and walked out in
front of everyone, so that they were all astounded and praised God
saying, "We have never seen anything like this."

The Creed is said.

Prayer over the Offerings
As we celebrate your mysteries, O Lord,
with the observance that is your due,
we humbly ask you,
that what we offer to the honour of your majesty
may profit us for salvation.
Through Christ our Lord.

Preface I-VIII of the Sundays in Ordinary Time, pp. 499-502.

Communion Antiphon
I will recount all your wonders,
I will rejoice in you and be glad,
and sing psalms to your name, O Most High.   Psalm 9:2-3

or

Lord, I have come to believe that you are the Christ,
the Son of the living God, who is coming into this world.

John 11:27

Prayer after Communion
Grant, we pray, almighty God,
that we may experience the effects of the salvation
which is pledged to us by these mysteries.
Through Christ our Lord.

EIGHTH SUNDAY IN ORDINARY TIME – B

Christ the bridegroom.
The Lord is compassion and love. God's tender love for us is shown in Jesus
Christ, and it is the Spirit who writes that love in our hearts. By the manner
in which we live as followers of Christ, we become an open letter of invitation
to others to see what true love really means. Such love brings life.

Entrance Antiphon
The Lord became my protector.
He brought me out to a place of freedom;
he saved me because he delighted in me.   cf. Psalm 17:19-20

The Gloria is said or sung.

Collect
Grant us, O Lord, we pray,
that the course of our world
may be directed by your peaceful rule
and that your Church may rejoice,
untroubled in her devotion.
Through our Lord Jesus Christ, your Son,
who lives and reigns with you in the unity of the Holy Spirit,
one God, for ever and ever.

First Reading   Hosea 2:16-17. 21-22
I will betroth you to myself for ever.
Thus says the Lord:

I am going to lure her
and lead her out into the wilderness
and speak to her heart.
There she will respond to me as she did when she was young,
as she did when she came out of the land of Egypt.
I will betroth you to myself for ever,

betroth you with integrity and justice,
with tenderness and love;
I will betroth you to myself with faithfulness,
and you will come to know the Lord.

Psalm   Psalm 102

R. **The Lord is compassion and love.**

1. My soul, give thanks to the Lord,
   all my being, bless his holy name.
   My soul, give thanks to the Lord
   and never forget all his blessings. R.

2. It is he who forgives all your guilt,
   who heals every one of your ills,
   who redeems your life from the grave,
   who crowns you with love and compassion. R.

3. The Lord is compassion and love,
   slow to anger and rich in mercy.
   He does not treat us according to our sins
   nor repay us according to our faults. R.

4. So far as the east is from the west
   so far does he remove our sins.
   As a father has compassion on his sons,
   the Lord has pity on those who fear him. R.

Second Reading   2 Corinthians 3:1-6
You are a letter from Christ drawn up by us.
Unlike other people, we need no letters of recommendation either
to you or from you, because you are yourselves our letter, written in
our hearts, that anybody can see and read, and it is plain that you
are a letter from Christ, drawn up by us, and written not with ink
but with the Spirit of the living God, not on stone tablets but on the
tablets of your living hearts.

Before God, we are confident of this through Christ: not that we are qualified in ourselves to claim anything as our own work: all our qualifications come from God. He is the one who has given us the qualifications to be the administrators of this new covenant, which is not a covenant of written letters but of the Spirit: the written letters bring death, but the Spirit gives life.

Gospel Acclamation

Alleluia, alleluia!
The sheep that belong to me listen to my voice,
says the Lord,
I know them and they follow me.
Alleluia!

John 10:27

or

Alleluia, alleluia!
By his own choice the Father made us his children
by the message of the truth,
so that we should be a sort of first-fruits
of all that he created.
Alleluia!

James 1:18

Gospel

Mark 2:18-22

The bridegroom is with them.

One day when John's disciples and the Pharisees were fasting, some people came and said to Jesus, "Why is it that John's disciples and the disciples of the Pharisees fast, but your disciples do not?" Jesus replied, "Surely the bridegroom's attendants would never think of fasting while the bridegroom is still with them? As long as they have the bridegroom with them, they could not think of fasting. But the time will come for the bridegroom to be taken away from them, and then, on that day, they will fast. No one sews a piece of unshrunken cloth on an old cloak; if he does, the patch pulls away from it, the new from the old, and the tear gets worse. And nobody puts new wine into old wineskins; if he does, the wine will burst the skins, and the wine is lost and the skins too. No! New wine, fresh skins!"

The Creed is said.

Prayer over the Offerings
O God, who provide gifts to be offered to your name
and count our oblations as signs
of our desire to serve you with devotion,
we ask of your mercy
that what you grant as the source of merit
may also help us to attain merit's reward.
Through Christ our Lord.

Preface I-VIII of the Sundays in Ordinary Time, pp. 499-502.

Communion Antiphon
I will sing to the Lord who has been bountiful with me,
sing psalms to the name of the Lord Most High.   cf. Psalm 12:6

or

Behold, I am with you always,
even to the end of the age, says the Lord.   Matthew 28:20

Prayer after Communion
Nourished by your saving gifts,
we beseech your mercy, Lord,
that by this same Sacrament
with which you feed us in the present age,
you may make us partakers of life eternal.
Through Christ our Lord.

NINTH SUNDAY IN ORDINARY TIME – B

Christ is master of the sabbath.

It is good to set aside times to worship God, yet we can worship God at all times and in all places. Christ has the message of eternal life, which transcends all human rules and barriers. We are fragile earthenware jars, but filled with the light of the knowledge of God's glory in Christ. We are called to let that light shine out, even in times of great difficulty and hardship.

Entrance Antiphon

Turn to me and have mercy on me, O Lord,
for I am alone and poor.
See my lowliness and suffering
and take away all my sins, my God.   cf. Psalm 24:16. 18

The Gloria is said or sung.

Collect

O God, whose providence never fails in its design,
keep from us, we humbly beseech you,
all that might harm us
and grant all that works for our good.
Through our Lord Jesus Christ, your Son,
who lives and reigns with you in the unity of the Holy Spirit,
one God, for ever and ever.

First Reading   Deuteronomy 5:12-15

Remember that you were a servant in the land of Egypt.

The Lord says this: "Observe the sabbath day and keep it holy, as the Lord your God has commanded you. For six days you shall labour and do all your work, but the seventh day is a sabbath for the Lord your God. You shall do no work that day, neither you nor your son nor your daughter nor your servants, men or women, nor your ox nor your donkey nor any of your animals, nor the stranger who lives with you. Thus your servant, man or woman, shall rest as you do. Remember that you were a servant in the land of Egypt, and that the Lord your God brought you out from there with mighty hand and outstretched arm; because of this, the Lord your God has commanded you to keep the sabbath day."

Psalm   Psalm 80

R. **Ring out your joy to God our strength.**

1. Raise a song and sound the timbrel,
   the sweet-sounding harp and the lute,
   blow the trumpet at the new moon,
   when the moon is full, on our feast. R.

2. For this is Israel's law,
   a command of the God of Jacob.
   He imposed it as a rule on Joseph,
   when he went out against the land of Egypt. R.

3. A voice I did not know said to me:
   "I freed your shoulder from the burden;
   your hands were freed from the load.
   You called in distress and I saved you. R.

4. "Let there be no foreign god among you,
   no worship of an alien god.
   I am the Lord your God,
   who brought you from the land of Egypt." R.

Second Reading   2 Corinthians 4:6-11
In our mortal flesh the life of Jesus is openly shown.
It is the same God that said, "Let there be light shining out of darkness," who has shone in our minds to radiate the light of the knowledge of God's glory, the glory on the face of Christ.

We are only the earthenware jars that hold this treasure, to make it clear that such an overwhelming power comes from God and not from us. We are in difficulties on all sides, but never cornered; we see no answer to our problems, but never despair; we have been persecuted, but never deserted; knocked down, but never killed; always, wherever we may be, we carry with us in our body the death of Jesus, so that the life of Jesus, too, may always be seen in our body. Indeed, while we are still alive, we are consigned to our death every day, for the sake of Jesus, so that in our mortal flesh the life of Jesus, too, may be openly shown.

Gospel Acclamation
Alleluia, alleluia!
Your words are spirit, Lord,
and they are life:
you have the message of eternal life.
Alleluia!   cf. John 6:63. 68

or

Alleluia, alleluia!
Your word is truth, O Lord,
consecrate us in the truth.
Alleluia!   cf. John 17:17

Gospel   **Mark 2:23 – 3:6**
The Son of Man is master even of the sabbath.

One sabbath day Jesus happened to be taking a walk through the cornfields, and his disciples began to pick ears of corn as they went along. And the Pharisees said to him, "Look, why are they doing something on the sabbath day that is forbidden?" And he replied, "Did you never read what David did in his time of need when he and his followers were hungry – how he went into the house of God when Abiathar was high priest, and ate the loaves of offering which only the priests are allowed to eat, and how he also gave some to the men with him?"

And he said to them, "The sabbath was made for man, not man for the sabbath; so the Son of Man is master even of the sabbath."

He went again into a synagogue, and there was a man there who had a withered hand. And they were watching him to see if he would cure him on the sabbath day, hoping for something to use against him. He said to the man with the withered hand, "Stand up out in the middle!" Then he said to them, "Is it against the law on the sabbath day to do good, or to do evil; to save life, or to kill?" But they said nothing. Then, grieved to find them so obstinate, he looked angrily round at them, and said to the man, "Stretch out your hand." He stretched it out and his hand was better. The Pharisees went out and at once began to plot with the Herodians against him, discussing how to destroy him.

The Creed is said.

Prayer over the Offerings
Trusting in your compassion, O Lord,
we come eagerly with our offerings to your sacred altar,
that, through the purifying action of your grace,
we may be cleansed by the very mysteries we serve.
Through Christ our Lord.

Preface I-VIII of the Sundays in Ordinary Time, pp. 499-502.

Communion Antiphon
To you I call, for you will surely heed me, O God;
turn your ear to me; hear my words.   cf. Psalm 16:6

or

Amen, I say to you: Whatever you ask for in prayer,
believe you will receive it,
and it will be yours, says the Lord.   Mark 11:23. 24

Prayer after Communion
Govern by your Spirit, we pray, O Lord,
those you feed with the Body and Blood of your Son,
that, professing you not just in word or in speech,
but also in works and in truth,
we may merit to enter the Kingdom of Heaven.
Through Christ our Lord.

TENTH SUNDAY IN
ORDINARY TIME – B

Mother of Christ.
We are constantly being tempted to put other people and things before God.
Our Lady gives us the example to follow, and encourages us not to weaken.
She is not only the physical mother of Jesus, but is also his mother because she
hears the will of God and keeps it.

Entrance Antiphon

The Lord is my light and my salvation; whom shall I fear?
The Lord is the stronghold of my life; whom should I dread?
When those who do evil draw near, they stumble and fall.

cf. Psalm 26:1-2

The Gloria is said or sung.

Collect

O God, from whom all good things come,
grant that we, who call on you in our need,
may at your prompting discern what is right,
and by your guidance do it.
Through our Lord Jesus Christ, your Son,
who lives and reigns with you in the unity of the Holy Spirit,
one God, for ever and ever.

First Reading   Genesis 3:9-15

I will make you enemies of each other: you and the woman, your
offspring and her offspring.

The Lord God called to the man after he had eaten of the tree.
"Where are you?" he asked. "I heard the sound of you in the garden,"
he replied. "I was afraid because I was naked, so I hid." Who told
you that you were naked?" he asked "Have you been eating of the
tree I forbade you to eat?" The man replied, "It was the woman
you put with me; she gave me the fruit, and I ate it." Then the Lord

God asked the woman, "What is this you have done?" The woman replied, "The serpent tempted me and I ate."

Then the Lord God said to the serpent, "Because you have done this,

"Be accursed beyond all cattle,
all wild beasts.
You shall crawl on your belly and eat dust
every day of your life.
I will make you enemies of each other:
you and the woman,
your offspring and her offspring.
It will crush your head
and you will strike its heel."

Psalm   Psalm 129

R. **With the Lord there is mercy
    and fullness of redemption.**

1. Out of the depths I cry to you, O Lord,
   Lord, hear my voice!
   O let your ears be attentive
   to the voice of my pleading. R.

2. If you, O Lord, should mark our guilt,
   Lord, who would survive?
   But with you is found forgiveness:
   for this we revere you. R.

3. My soul is waiting for the Lord,
   I count on his word.
   My soul is longing for the Lord
   more than watchman for daybreak. R.

4. Because with the Lord there is mercy
   and fullness of redemption,
   Israel indeed he will redeem
   from all its iniquity. R.

Second Reading   2 Corinthians 4:13 – 5:1

We believe, and therefore we speak.

As we have the same spirit of faith that is mentioned in scripture – I believed, and therefore I spoke – we too believe and therefore we too speak, knowing that he who raised the Lord Jesus to life will raise us with Jesus in our turn, and put us by his side and you with us. You see, all this is for your benefit, so that the more grace is multiplied among people, the more thanksgiving there will be, to the glory of God.

That is why there is no weakening on our part, and instead, though this outer man of ours may be falling into decay, the inner man is renewed day by day. Yes, the troubles which are soon over, though they weigh little, train us for the carrying of a weight of eternal glory which is out of all proportion to them. And so we have no eyes for things that are visible, but only for things that are invisible; for visible things last only for a time, and the invisible things are eternal.

For we know that when the tent that we live in on earth is folded up, there is a house built by God for us, an everlasting home not made by human hands, in the heavens.

Gospel Acclamation

Alleluia, alleluia!
If anyone loves me he will keep my word,
and my Father will love him,
and we shall come to him.   John 14:23

or

Alleluia, alleluia!
Now the prince of this world is to be overthrown,
says the Lord.
And when I am lifted up from the earth,
I shall draw all men to myself.
Alleluia!   John 12:31. 32

Gospel   Mark 3:20-35

It is the end of Satan.

Jesus went home with his disciples, and such a crowd collected that they could not even have a meal. When his relatives heard of this, they set out to take charge of him, convinced he was out of his mind.

The scribes who had come down from Jerusalem were saying, "Beelzebul is in him," and, "It is through the prince of devils that he casts devils out." So he called them to him and spoke to them in parables, "How can Satan cast out Satan? If a kingdom is divided against itself, that kingdom cannot last. And if a household is divided against itself, that household can never stand. Now if Satan has rebelled against himself and is divided, he cannot stand either – it is the end of him. But no one can make his way into a strong man's house and burgle his property unless he has tied up the strong man first. Only then can he burgle his house.

"I tell you solemnly, all men's sins will be forgiven, and all their blasphemies; but let anyone blaspheme against the Holy Spirit and he will never have forgiveness: he is guilty of an eternal sin." This was because they were saying, "An unclean spirit is in him."

His mother and brothers now arrived and, standing outside, sent in a message asking for him. A crowd was sitting round him by the time the message was passed to him, "Your mother and brothers and sisters are outside asking for you." He replied, "Who are my mother and my brothers?" And looking round at those sitting in a circle about him, he said, "Here are my mother and my brothers. Anyone who does the will of God, that person is my brother and sister and mother."

The Creed is said.

Prayer over the Offerings

Look kindly upon our service, O Lord, we pray,
that what we offer
may be an acceptable oblation to you
and lead us to grow in charity.
Through Christ our Lord.

Preface I-VIII of the Sundays in Ordinary Time, pp. 499-502.

Communion Antiphon

The Lord is my rock, my fortress, and my deliverer;
my God is my saving strength.   Psalm 17:3

or

God is love, and whoever abides in love
abides in God, and God in him.   1 John 4:16

Prayer after Communion

May your healing work, O Lord,
free us, we pray, from doing evil
and lead us to what is right.
Through Christ our Lord.

ELEVENTH SUNDAY IN ORDINARY TIME – B

The mustard seed.

The mustard seed is tiny, yet when it grows in good soil it becomes a large shrub, to which birds can come to find shelter to build their nests. The kingdom of God is like a tiny seed within us, yet if we allow it to grow by doing things that are pleasing to God, then people will see that we are truly witnesses to Christ. It is God who gives the increase, for which we give thanks.

Entrance Antiphon

O Lord, hear my voice, for I have called to you; be my help.
Do not abandon or forsake me, O God, my Saviour!

cf. Psalm 26:7. 9

The Gloria is said or sung.

Collect

O God, strength of those who hope in you,
graciously hear our pleas,
and, since without you mortal frailty can do nothing,
grant us always the help of your grace,
that in following your commands
we may please you by our resolve and our deeds.
Through our Lord Jesus Christ, your Son,
who lives and reigns with you in the unity of the Holy Spirit,
one God, for ever and ever.

First Reading — Ezekiel 17:22-24

I make low trees grow.
The Lord says this:

> "From the top of the cedar,
> from the highest branch I will take a shoot
> and plant it myself on a very high mountain.
> I will plant it on the high mountain of Israel.

It will sprout branches and bear fruit,
and become a noble cedar.
Every kind of bird will live beneath it,
every winged creature rest in the shade of its branches.
And every tree of the field will learn that I, the Lord, am the one
who stunts tall trees and makes the low ones grow,
who withers green trees and makes the withered green.
I, the Lord, have spoken, and I will do it."

Psalm   Psalm 91

R. **It is good to give you thanks, O Lord.**

1. It is good to give thanks to the Lord
    to make music to your name, O Most High,
    to proclaim your love in the morning
    and your truth in the watches of the night. R.

2. The just will flourish like the palm-tree
    and grow like a Lebanon cedar. R.

3. Planted in the house of the Lord
    they will flourish in the courts of our God,
    still bearing fruit when they are old,
    still full of sap, still green,
    to proclaim that the Lord is just.
    In him, my rock, there is no wrong. R.

Second Reading   2 Corinthians 5:6-10
Whether we are living in the body or exiled from it, we are intent
on pleasing the Lord.
We are always full of confidence when we remember that to live
in the body means to be exiled from the Lord, going as we do by
faith and not by sight – we are full of confidence, I say, and actually
want to be exiled from the body and make our home with the Lord.
Whether we are living in the body or exiled from it, we are intent
on pleasing him. For all the truth about us will be brought out in the
law court of Christ, and each of us will get what he deserves for the
things he did in the body, good or bad.

Gospel Acclamation
Alleluia, alleluia!
I call you friends, says the Lord,
because I have made known to you
everything I have learnt from my Father.
Alleluia!   John 15:15

or

Alleluia, alleluia!
The seed is the word of God, Christ the sower;
whoever finds the seed will remain for ever.
Alleluia!

Gospel   Mark 4:26-34
It is the smallest of all the seeds; yet it grows into the biggest shrub
of them all.

Jesus said to the crowds: "This is what the kingdom of God is like.
A man throws seed on the land. Night and day, while he sleeps,
when he is awake, the seed is sprouting and growing; how, he does
not know. Of its own accord the land produces first the shoot, then
the ear, then the full grain in the ear. And when the crop is ready,
he loses no time: he starts to reap because the harvest has come."

He also said, "What can we say the kingdom of God is like? What
parable can we find for it? It is like a mustard seed which at the time
of its sowing in the soil is the smallest of all the seeds on earth; yet
once it is sown it grows into the biggest shrub of them all and puts
out big branches so that the birds of the air can shelter in its shade."

Using many parables like these, he spoke the word to them, so
far as they were capable of understanding it. He would not speak to
them except in parables, but he explained everything to his disciples
when they were alone.

The Creed is said.

Prayer over the Offerings
O God, who in the offerings presented here
provide for the twofold needs of human nature,
nourishing us with food
and renewing us with your Sacrament,
grant, we pray,
that the sustenance they provide
may not fail us in body or in spirit.
Through Christ our Lord.

Preface I-VIII of the Sundays in Ordinary Time, pp. 499-502.

Communion Antiphon
There is one thing I ask of the Lord, only this do I seek:
to live in the house of the Lord all the days of my life.

Psalm 26:4

or

Holy Father, keep in your name those you have given me,
that they may be one as we are one, says the Lord.

John 17:11

Prayer after Communion
As this reception of your Holy Communion, O Lord,
foreshadows the union of the faithful in you,
so may it bring about unity in your Church.
Through Christ our Lord.

TWELFTH SUNDAY IN ORDINARY TIME – B

Why are you so frightened?
Fear plays too large a part in our lives. Love casts out fear, and God's love endures for ever. Fear may be due to a lack of faith that God really cares for us. Christ may seem to be asleep, but he is with us always, and has the power to calm even the stormiest troubles of our lives.

Entrance Antiphon
The Lord is the strength of his people,
a saving refuge for the one he has anointed.
Save your people, Lord, and bless your heritage,
and govern them for ever.   cf. Psalm 27:8-9

The Gloria is said or sung.

Collect
Grant, O Lord,
that we may always revere and love your holy name,
for you never deprive of your guidance
those you set firm on the foundation of your love.
Through our Lord Jesus Christ, your Son,
who lives and reigns with you in the unity of the Holy Spirit,
one God, for ever and ever.

First Reading   Job 38:1. 8-11
Here your proud waves shall break.
From the heart of the tempest the Lord gave Job his answer. He said:

Who pent up the sea behind closed doors
when it leapt tumultuous out of the womb,
when I wrapped it in a robe of mist
and made black clouds its swaddling bands;
when I marked the bounds it was not to cross
and made it fast with a bolted gate?
Come thus far, I said, and no farther:
here your proud waves shall break.

Psalm   Psalm 106

R. **O give thanks to the Lord,
    for his love endures for ever.**

or **Alleluia!**

1. Some sailed to the sea in ships
   to trade on the mighty waters.
   These men have seen the Lord's deeds,
   the wonders he does in the deep. R.

2. For he spoke; he summoned the gale,
   tossing the waves of the sea
   up to heaven and back into the deep;
   their soul melted away in their distress. R.

3. Then they cried to the Lord in their need
   and he rescued them from their distress.
   He stilled the storm to a whisper:
   all the waves of the sea were hushed. R.

4. They rejoiced because of the calm
   and he led them to the haven they desired.
   Let them thank the Lord for his love,
   the wonders he does for men. R.

Second Reading   2 Corinthians 5:14-17

Now the new creation is here.

The love of Christ overwhelms us when we reflect that if one man
has died for all, then all men should be dead; and the reason he died
for all was so that living men should live no longer for themselves,
but for him who died and was raised to life for them.

From now onwards, therefore, we do not judge anyone by the
standards of the flesh. Even if we did once know Christ in the flesh,
that is not how we know him now. And for anyone who is in Christ,
there is a new creation; the old creation has gone, and now the new
one is here.

Gospel Acclamation
Alleluia, alleluia!
May the Father of our Lord Jesus Christ
enlighten the eyes of our mind,
so that we can see what hope his call holds for us.
Alleluia! cf. Ephesians 1:17. 18

or

Alleluia, alleluia!
A great prophet has appeared among us;
God has visited his people.
Alleluia! Luke 7:16

Gospel Mark 4:35-41
Who can this be? Even the wind and the sea obey him.

With the coming of evening, Jesus said to his disciples, "Let us cross over to the other side." And leaving the crowd behind they took him, just as he was, in the boat; and there were other boats with him. Then it began to blow a gale and the waves were breaking into the boat so that it was almost swamped. But he was in the stern, his head on the cushion, asleep. They woke him and said to him, "Master, do you not care? We are going down!" And he woke up and rebuked the wind and said to the sea, "Quiet now! Be calm!" And the wind dropped, and all was calm again. Then he said to them, "Why are you so frightened? How is it that you have no faith?" They were filled with awe and said to one another, "Who can this be? Even the wind and the sea obey him."

The Creed is said.

Prayer over the Offerings
Receive, O Lord, the sacrifice of conciliation and praise
and grant that, cleansed by its action,
we may make offering of a heart pleasing to you.
Through Christ our Lord.

Preface I-VIII of the Sundays in Ordinary Time, pp. 499-502.

Communion Antiphon
The eyes of all look to you, Lord,
and you give them their food in due season.   Psalm 144:15

or

I am the Good Shepherd,
and I lay down my life for my sheep, says the Lord.   John 10:11. 15

Prayer after Communion
Renewed and nourished
by the Sacred Body and Precious Blood of your Son,
we ask of your mercy, O Lord,
that what we celebrate with constant devotion
may be our sure pledge of redemption.
Through Christ our Lord.

THIRTEENTH SUNDAY IN ORDINARY TIME – B

Christ the giver of life.
Christ came that we might have life and have it to the full. Death came through
the power of evil, and it is to rescue us from this that Christ gave his life for
us. He tells us to wake from our sleep and turn to him that we may find life.
If we have faith, then it is life, not death, which will conquer.

Entrance Antiphon
All peoples, clap your hands.
Cry to God with shouts of joy!   Psalm 46:2

The Gloria is said or sung.

Collect
O God, who through the grace of adoption
chose us to be children of light,
grant, we pray,
that we may not be wrapped in the darkness of error
but always be seen to stand in the bright light of truth.
Through our Lord Jesus Christ, your Son,
who lives and reigns with you in the unity of the Holy Spirit,
one God, for ever and ever.

First Reading   Wisdom 1:13-15; 2:23-24
It was the devil's envy that brought death into the world.
Death was not God's doing,
he takes no pleasure in the extinction of the living.
To be – for this he created all;
the world's created things have health in them,
in them no fatal poison can be found,
and Hades holds no power on earth;
for virtue is undying.
Yet God did make man imperishable,

he made him in the image of his own nature;
it was the devil's envy that brought death into the world,
as those who are his partners will discover.

Psalm   Psalm 29

R. **I will praise you, Lord, you have rescued me.**

1. I will praise you, Lord, you have rescued me
    and have not let my enemies rejoice over me.
    O Lord, you have raised my soul from the dead,
    restored me to life from those who sink into the grave. R.

2. Sing psalms to the Lord, you who love him,
    give thanks to his holy name.
    His anger lasts but a moment; his favour through life.
    At night there are tears, but joy comes with dawn. R.

3. The Lord listened and had pity.
    The Lord came to my help.
    For me you have changed my mourning into dancing,
    O Lord my God, I will thank you for ever. R.

Second Reading   2 Corinthians 8:7. 9. 13-15

In giving relief to others, balance what happens to be your surplus now against their present need.

You always have the most of everything – of faith, of eloquence, of understanding, of keenness for any cause, and the biggest share of our affection – so we expect you to put the most into this work of mercy too. Remember how generous the Lord Jesus was: he was rich, but he became poor for your sake, to make you rich out of his poverty. This does not mean that to give relief to others you ought to make things difficult for yourselves: it is a question of balancing what happens to be your surplus now against their present need, and one day they may have something to spare that will supply your own need. That is how we strike a balance: as scripture says: The man who gathered much had none too much, the man who gathered little did not go short.

Gospel Acclamation
Alleluia, alleluia!
Your words are spirit, Lord,
and they are life:
you have the message of eternal life.
Alleluia!

cf. John 6:63. 68

or

Alleluia, alleluia!
Our Saviour Christ Jesus abolished death,
and he has proclaimed life through the Good News.
Alleluia!

cf. 2 Timothy 1:10

Gospel Mark 5:21-43
Little girl, I tell you to get up.

> When Jesus had crossed in the boat to the other side, a large crowd
> gathered round him and he stayed by the lakeside. Then one of
> the synagogue officials came up, Jairus by name, and seeing him,
> fell at his feet and pleaded with him earnestly, saying, "My little
> daughter is desperately sick. Do come and lay your hands on her
> to make her better and save her life." Jesus went with him and
> a large crowd followed him: they were pressing all around him.

Now there was a woman who had suffered from a haemorrhage
for twelve years; after long and painful treatment under various
doctors, she had spent all she had without being any the better for
it, in fact, she was getting worse. She had heard about Jesus, and
she came up behind him through the crowd and touched his cloak.
"If I can touch even his clothes," she had told herself, "I shall be
well again." And the source of the bleeding dried up instantly, and
she felt in herself that she was cured of her complaint. Immediately
aware that power had gone out from him, Jesus turned round in
the crowd and said, "Who touched my clothes?" His disciples said
to him, "You see how the crowd is pressing round you and yet you
say, 'Who touched me?'" But he continued to look all round to see
who had done it. Then the woman came forward, frightened and
trembling because she knew what had happened to her, and she

fell at his feet and told him the whole truth. "My daughter," he said, "your faith has restored you to health; go in peace and be free from your complaint."

While he was still speaking

some people arrived from the house of the synagogue official to say, "Your daughter is dead: why put the Master to any further trouble?" But Jesus had overheard this remark of theirs and he said to the official, "Do not be afraid; only have faith." And he allowed no one to go with him except Peter and James and John the brother of James. So they came to the official's house and Jesus noticed all the commotion with people weeping and wailing unrestrainedly. He went in and said to them, "Why all this commotion and crying? The child is not dead, but asleep." But they laughed at him. So he turned them all out and, taking with him the child's father and mother and his own companions, he went into the place where the child lay. And taking the child by the hand he said to her, "Talitha, kum!" which means, "Little girl, I tell you to get up." The little girl got up at once and began to walk about, for she was twelve years old. At this they were overcome with astonishment, and he ordered them strictly not to let anyone know about it, and told them to give her something to eat.

The Creed is said.

Prayer over the Offerings
O God, who graciously accomplish
the effects of your mysteries,
grant, we pray,
that the deeds by which we serve you
may be worthy of these sacred gifts.
Through Christ our Lord.

Preface I-VIII of the Sundays in Ordinary Time, pp. 499-502.

Communion Antiphon
Bless the Lord, O my soul,
and all within me, his holy name. cf. Psalm 102:1

or

O Father, I pray for them, that they may be one in us,
that the world may believe that you have sent me, says the Lord.
John 17:20-21

Prayer after Communion
May this divine sacrifice we have offered and received
fill us with life, O Lord, we pray,
so that, bound to you in lasting charity,
we may bear fruit that lasts for ever.
Through Christ our Lord.

FOURTEENTH SUNDAY IN ORDINARY TIME – B

God's grace is enough.
We are called to proclaim the kingdom of God to all people in every situation
in which we find ourselves. Whether they listen or not, we are still to live out
our lives to the full in witness to God's Spirit that has been given to us. Jesus
was himself rejected by his own people in his home town, so we can expect
rejection too. God's power is at its best in our weakness.

Entrance Antiphon
Your merciful love, O God,
we have received in the midst of your temple.
Your praise, O God, like your name,
reaches the ends of the earth;
your right hand is filled with saving justice.   cf. Psalm 47:10-11

The Gloria is said or sung.

Collect
O God, who in the abasement of your Son
have raised up a fallen world,
fill your faithful with holy joy,
for on those you have rescued from slavery to sin
you bestow eternal gladness.
Through our Lord Jesus Christ, your Son,
who lives and reigns with you in the unity of the Holy Spirit,
one God, for ever and ever.

First Reading   Ezekiel 2:2-5
The sons are defiant and obstinate and they shall know that there is
a prophet among them.
The spirit came into me and made me stand up, and I heard the
Lord speaking to me. He said, "Son of man, I am sending you to the
Israelites, to the rebels who have turned against me. Till now they

and their ancestors have been in revolt against me. The sons are defiant and obstinate; I am sending you to them, to say, 'The Lord says this.' Whether they listen or not, this set of rebels shall know there is a prophet among them."

Psalm   Psalm 122

R. **Our eyes are on the Lord**
     till he show us his mercy.

1. To you have I lifted up my eyes,
    you who dwell in the heavens:
    my eyes, like the eyes of slaves
    on the hand of their lords. R.

2. Like the eyes of a servant
    on the hand of his mistress,
    so our eyes are on the Lord our God
    till he show us his mercy. R.

3. Have mercy on us, Lord, have mercy.
    We are filled with contempt.
    Indeed all too full is our soul
    with the scorn of the rich,
    with the proud man's disdain. R.

Second Reading   2 Corinthians 12:7-10

I shall be very happy to make my weaknesses my special boast so that the power of Christ may stay over me.

In view of the extraordinary nature of these revelations, to stop me from getting too proud I was given a thorn in the flesh, an angel of Satan to beat me and stop me from getting too proud! About this thing, I have pleaded with the Lord three times for it to leave me, but he has said, "My grace is enough for you: my power is at its best in weakness." So I shall be very happy to make my weaknesses my special boast so that the power of Christ may stay over me, and that is why I am quite content with my weaknesses, and with insults, hardships, persecutions, and the agonies I go through for Christ's sake. For it is when I am weak that I am strong.

Gospel Acclamation
Alleluia, alleluia!
The Word was made flesh and lived among us;
to all who did accept him
he gave power to become children of God.
Alleluia!   John 1:12. 14

or

Alleluia, alleluia!
The Lord has sent me to bring the good news to the poor,
to proclaim liberty to captives.
Alleluia!   Luke 4:18

Gospel   Mark 6:1-6
A prophet is despised only in his own country.
Jesus went to his home town and his disciples accompanied him.
With the coming of the sabbath he began teaching in the synagogue
and most of them were astonished when they heard him. They
said, "Where did the man get all this? What is this wisdom that
has been granted him, and these miracles that are worked through
him? This is the carpenter, surely, the son of Mary, the brother of
James and Joset and Jude and Simon? His sisters, too, are they not
here with us?" And they would not accept him. And Jesus said to
them, "A prophet is only despised in his own country, among his
own relations and in his own house"; and he could work no miracle
there, though he cured a few sick people by laying his hands on
them. He was amazed at their lack of faith.

The Creed is said.

Prayer over the Offerings
May this oblation dedicated to your name
purify us, O Lord,
and day by day bring our conduct
closer to the life of heaven.
Through Christ our Lord.

Preface I-VIII of the Sundays in Ordinary Time, pp. 499-502.

Communion Antiphon
Taste and see that the Lord is good;
blessed the man who seeks refuge in him.   Psalm 33:9
or

Come to me, all who labour and are burdened,
and I will refresh you, says the Lord.   Matthew 11:28

Prayer after Communion
Grant, we pray, O Lord,
that, having been replenished by such great gifts,
we may gain the prize of salvation
and never cease to praise you.
Through Christ our Lord.

FIFTEENTH SUNDAY IN ORDINARY TIME – B

God chose us.
Before the world was made, God our Father chose us in Christ to praise the
glory of his grace, his free gift to us in the Beloved. We do not need to worry
about material things, because the Lord has set us free and given us the richness
of his grace. Like Amos, we may feel unworthy, but we are called to bring
God's message to all people. The Lord will always be near to help us.

Entrance Antiphon
As for me, in justice I shall behold your face;
I shall be filled with the vision of your glory. cf. Psalm 16:15

The Gloria is said or sung.

Collect
O God, who show the light of your truth
to those who go astray,
so that they may return to the right path,
give all who for the faith they profess
are accounted Christians
the grace to reject whatever is contrary to the name of Christ
and to strive after all that does it honour.
Through our Lord Jesus Christ, your Son,
who lives and reigns with you in the unity of the Holy Spirit,
one God, for ever and ever.

First Reading
Amos 7:12-15
Go, prophesy to my people.

Amaziah, the priest of Bethel, said to Amos, "Go away, seer; get back
to the land of Judah; earn your bread there, do your prophesying
there. We want no more prophesying in Bethel; this is the royal
sanctuary, the national temple." "I was no prophet, neither did I
belong to any of the brotherhoods of prophets," Amos replied to

Amaziah. "I was a shepherd, and looked after sycamores: but it was the Lord who took me from herding the flock, and the Lord who said, 'Go, prophesy to my people Israel.'"

Psalm   Psalm 84

R. **Let us see, O Lord, your mercy**
     and give us your saving help.

1. I will hear what the Lord God has to say,
    a voice that speaks of peace,
        peace for his people.
    His help is near for those who fear him
    and his glory will dwell in our land. R.

2. Mercy and faithfulness have met;
    justice and peace have embraced.
    Faithfulness shall spring from the earth
    and justice look down from heaven. R.

3. The Lord will make us prosper
    and our earth shall yield its fruit.
    Justice shall march before him
    and peace shall follow his steps. R.

Second Reading   Ephesians 1:3-14
Before the world was made, God chose us.

Blessed be God the Father of our Lord Jesus Christ,
who has blessed us with all the spiritual blessings of heaven in
    Christ.
Before the world was made, he chose us, chose us in Christ,
to be holy and spotless, and to live through love in his presence,
determining that we should become his adopted sons, through
    Jesus Christ
for his own kind purposes,
to make us praise the glory of his grace,
his free gift to us in the Beloved
in whom, through his blood, we gain our freedom, the forgiveness
    of our sins.

Such is the richness of the grace
which he has showered on us
in all wisdom and insight.
He has let us know the mystery of his purpose,
the hidden plan he so kindly made in Christ from the beginning
to act upon when the times had run their course to the end:
that he would bring everything together under Christ, as head,
everything in the heavens and everything on earth.

And it is in him that we were claimed as God's own,
chosen from the beginning,
under the predetermined plan of the one who guides all things
as he decides by his own will;
chosen to be,
for his greater glory,
the people who would put their hopes in Christ before he came.
Now you too, in him,
have heard the message of the truth and the good news of your
    salvation,
and have believed it:
and you too have been stamped with the seal of the Holy Spirit of
    the Promise,
the pledge of our inheritance
which brings freedom for those whom God has taken for his own,
to make his glory praised.

Gospel Acclamation
Alleluia, alleluia!
Your words are spirit, Lord,
and they are life:
you have the message of eternal life.
Alleluia!   cf. John 6:63. 68

or

Alleluia, alleluia!
May the Father of our Lord Jesus Christ
enlighten the eyes of our mind,
so that we can see what hope his call holds for us.
Alleluia!   cf. Ephesians 1:17. 18

Gospel   Mark 6:7-13
He began to send them out.

Jesus summoned the Twelve and began to send them out in pairs giving them authority over the unclean spirits. And he instructed them to take nothing for the journey except a staff – no bread, no haversack, no coppers for their purses. They were to wear sandals but, he added, "Do not take a spare tunic." And he said to them, "If you enter a house anywhere, stay there until you leave the district. And if any place does not welcome you and people refuse to listen to you, as you walk away shake off the dust from under your feet as a sign to them." So they set off to preach repentance; and they cast out many devils, and anointed many sick people with oil and cured them.

The Creed is said.

Prayer over the Offerings
Look upon the offerings of the Church, O Lord,
as she makes her prayer to you,
and grant that, when consumed by those who believe,
they may bring ever greater holiness.
Through Christ our Lord.

Preface I-VIII of the Sundays in Ordinary Time, pp. 499-502.

Communion Antiphon
The sparrow finds a home,
and the swallow a nest for her young:
by your altars, O Lord of hosts, my King and my God.
Blessed are they who dwell in your house,
for ever singing your praise.   cf. Psalm 83:4-5

or

Whoever eats my flesh and drinks my blood
remains in me and I in him, says the Lord.   John 6:57

Prayer after Communion
Having consumed these gifts, we pray, O Lord,
that, by our participation in this mystery,
its saving effects upon us may grow.
Through Christ our Lord.

SIXTEENTH SUNDAY IN ORDINARY TIME – B

Christ the shepherd of the people.
Jesus Christ looks on the people with compassion because they are like sheep
without a shepherd. He teaches the Good News that the people who have been
dispersed like lost sheep will be brought back into the fold. It is our vocation to
remind people that through his blood Christ is the peace between us.

Entrance Antiphon
See, I have God for my help.
The Lord sustains my soul.
I will sacrifice to you with willing heart,
and praise your name, O Lord, for it is good.   Psalm 53:6. 8

The Gloria is said or sung.

Collect
Show favour, O Lord, to your servants
and mercifully increase the gifts of your grace,
that, made fervent in hope, faith and charity,
they may be ever watchful in keeping your commands.
Through our Lord Jesus Christ, your Son,
who lives and reigns with you in the unity of the Holy Spirit,
one God, for ever and ever.

First Reading   Jeremiah 23:1-6
The remnant of my flock I will gather and I will raise up shepherds
to look after them.
"Doom for the shepherds who allow the flock of my pasture to be
destroyed and scattered – it is the Lord who speaks! This, therefore,
is what the Lord, the God of Israel, says about the shepherds in
charge of my people: You have let my flock be scattered and go
wandering and have not taken care of them. Right, I will take care of
you for your misdeeds – it is the Lord who speaks! But the remnant

of my flock I myself will gather from all the countries where I have dispersed them, and will bring them back to their pastures: they shall be fruitful and increase in numbers. I will raise up shepherds to look after them and pasture them; no fear, no terror for them any more; not one shall be lost – it is the Lord who speaks!

"See, the days are coming – it is the Lord who speaks –
when I will raise a virtuous Branch for David,
who will reign as true king and be wise,
practising honesty and integrity in the land.
In his days Judah will be saved
and Israel dwell in confidence.
And this is the name he will be called:
The Lord-our-integrity."

Psalm   Psalm 22

R. **The Lord is my shepherd;
    there is nothing I shall want.**

1. The Lord is my shepherd;
    there is nothing I shall want.
    Fresh and green are the pastures
    where he gives me repose.
    Near restful waters he leads me,
    to revive my drooping spirit. R.

2. He guides me along the right path;
    he is true to his name.
    If I should walk in the valley of darkness
    no evil would I fear.
    You are there with your crook and your staff;
    with these you give me comfort. R.

3. You have prepared a banquet for me
    in the sight of my foes.
    My head you have anointed with oil;
    my cup is overflowing. R.

4. Surely goodness and kindness shall follow me
   all the days of my life.
   In the Lord's own house shall I dwell
   for ever and ever. R.

Second Reading
Ephesians 2:13-18

Christ Jesus is the peace between us, and has made the two into one.

In Christ Jesus, you that used to be so far apart from us have been brought very close, by the blood of Christ. For he is the peace between us, and has made the two into one and broken down the barrier which used to keep them apart, actually destroying in his own person the hostility caused by the rules and decrees of the Law. This was to create one single New Man in himself out of the two of them and by restoring peace through the cross, to unite them both in a single Body and reconcile them with God. In his own person he killed the hostility. Later he came to bring the good news of peace, peace to you who were far away and peace to those who were near at hand. Through him, both of us have in the one Spirit our way to come to the Father.

Gospel Acclamation
Alleluia, alleluia!
The sheep that belong to me listen to my voice,
says the Lord,
I know them and they follow me.
Alleluia!   John 10:27

Gospel
Mark 6:30-34

They were like sheep without a shepherd.

The apostles rejoined Jesus and told him all they had done and taught. Then he said to them, "You must come away to some lonely place all by yourselves and rest for a while"; for there were so many coming and going that the apostles had no time even to eat. So they went off in a boat to a lonely place where they could be by themselves. But people saw them going, and many could guess where; and from every town they all hurried to the place on foot and reached it before them. So as he stepped ashore he saw

a large crowd; and he took pity on them because they were like
sheep without a shepherd, and he set himself to teach them at some
length.

The Creed is said.

Prayer over the Offerings
O God, who in the one perfect sacrifice
brought to completion varied offerings of the law,
accept, we pray, this sacrifice from your faithful servants
and make it holy, as you blessed the gifts of Abel,
so that what each has offered to the honour of your majesty
may benefit the salvation of all.
Through Christ our Lord.

Preface I-VIII of the Sundays in Ordinary Time, pp. 499-502.

Communion Antiphon
The Lord, the gracious, the merciful,
has made a memorial of his wonders;
he gives food to those who fear him.   Psalm 110:4-5

or

Behold, I stand at the door and knock, says the Lord.
If anyone hears my voice and opens the door to me,
I will enter his house and dine with him, and he with me.
                                                        Apocalypse 3:20

Prayer after Communion
Graciously be present to your people, we pray, O Lord,
and lead those you have imbued with heavenly mysteries
to pass from former ways to newness of life.
Through Christ our Lord.

SEVENTEENTH SUNDAY IN ORDINARY TIME – B

Christ feeds us.
Through the miraculous multiplication of the loaves and fishes, Jesus feeds the
hungry people, just as he feeds us daily with his word and the Eucharist. There
was plenty left over when everyone had eaten enough. We too have much to give
to others because of Christ's generosity to us. He calls us to give generously in
our turn, and so to preserve the unity of spirit given to us as children of the
same God our Father.

Entrance Antiphon
God is in his holy place,
God who unites those who dwell in his house;
he himself gives might and strength to his people.

cf. Psalm 67:6-7. 36

The Gloria is said or sung.

Collect
O God, protector of those who hope in you,
without whom nothing has firm foundation, nothing is holy,
bestow in abundance your mercy upon us
and grant that, with you as our ruler and guide,
we may use the good things that pass
in such a way as to hold fast even now
to those that ever endure.
Through our Lord Jesus Christ, your Son,
who lives and reigns with you in the unity of the Holy Spirit,
one God, for ever and ever.

First Reading   2 Kings 4:42-44
They will eat and have some left over.
A man came from Baal-shalishah, bringing Elisha, the man of God,
bread from the first-fruits, twenty barley loaves and fresh grain in
the ear. "Give it to the people to eat," Elisha said. But his servant

replied, "How can I serve this to a hundred men?" "Give it to the people to eat," he insisted, "for the Lord says this, 'They will eat and have some left over.'" He served them; they ate and had some over, as the Lord had said.

Psalm   Psalm 144

R. **You open wide your hand, O Lord,**
    and grant our desires.

1. All your creatures shall thank you, O Lord,
   and your friends shall repeat their blessing.
   They shall speak of the glory of your reign
   and declare your might, O God. R.

2. The eyes of all creatures look to you
   and you give them their food in due time.
   You open wide your hand,
   grant the desires of all who live. R.

3. The Lord is just in all his ways
   and loving in all his deeds.
   He is close to all who call him,
   who call on him from their hearts. R.

Second Reading   Ephesians 4:1-6
One Body, one Lord, one faith, one baptism.
I, the prisoner in the Lord, implore you to lead a life worthy of your vocation. Bear with one another charitably, in complete selflessness, gentleness and patience. Do all you can to preserve the unity of the Spirit by the peace that binds you together. There is one Body, one Spirit, just as you were all called into one and the same hope when you were called. There is one Lord, one faith, one baptism, and one God who is Father of all, through all and within all.

Gospel Acclamation
Alleluia, alleluia!
Your words are spirit, Lord,
and they are life:
you have the message of eternal life.
Alleluia!   cf. John 6:63. 68

or

Alleluia, alleluia!
A great prophet has appeared among us;
God has visited his people.
Alleluia!   Luke 7:16

Gospel   John 6:1-15

Jesus gave out as much as was wanted to all who were sitting ready.
Jesus went off to the other side of the Sea of Galilee – or of Tiberias
– and a large crowd followed him, impressed by the signs he gave
by curing the sick. Jesus climbed the hillside, and sat down there
with his disciples. It was shortly before the Jewish feast of Passover.
  Looking up, Jesus saw the crowds approaching and said to
Philip, "Where can we buy some bread for these people to eat?" He
only said this to test Philip; he himself knew exactly what he was
going to do. Philip answered, "Two hundred denarii would only
buy enough to give them a small piece each." One of his disciples,
Andrew, Simon Peter's brother, said, "There is a small boy here with
five barley loaves and two fish; but what is that between so many?"
Jesus said to them, "Make the people sit down." There was plenty
of grass there, and as many as five thousand men sat down. Then
Jesus took the loaves, gave thanks, and gave them out to all who
were sitting ready; he then did the same with the fish, giving out as
much as was wanted. When they had eaten enough he said to the
disciples, "Pick up the pieces left over, so that nothing gets wasted."
So they picked them up, and filled twelve hampers with scraps left
over from the meal of five barley loaves. The people, seeing this sign
that he had given, said, "This really is the prophet who is to come
into the world." Jesus, who could see they were about to come and
take him by force and make him king, escaped back to the hills by
himself.

The Creed is said.

Prayer over the Offerings
Accept, O Lord, we pray, the offerings
which we bring from the abundance of your gifts,
that through the powerful working of your grace
these most sacred mysteries may sanctify our present way of life
and lead us to eternal gladness.
Through Christ our Lord.

Preface I-VIII of the Sundays in Ordinary Time, pp. 499-502.

Communion Antiphon
Bless the Lord, O my soul,
and never forget all his benefits.   Psalm 102:2

or

Blessed are the merciful, for they shall receive mercy.
Blessed are the clean of heart, for they shall see God.

                                                        Matthew 5:7-8

Prayer after Communion
We have consumed, O Lord, this divine Sacrament,
the perpetual memorial of the Passion of your Son;
grant, we pray, that this gift,
which he himself gave us with love beyond all telling,
may profit us for salvation.
Through Christ our Lord.

EIGHTEENTH SUNDAY IN ORDINARY TIME – B

Christ the bread of life.
We do not live on bread alone. It is only Christ who can satisfy the hunger
that we all feel for God. The Lord feeds us with the Eucharist, just as in times
past he fed the people of Israel with manna from heaven. Through this act of
God's love we can learn that the Lord is indeed our God.

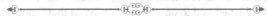

Entrance Antiphon
O God, come to my assistance;
O Lord, make haste to help me!
You are my rescuer, my help;
O Lord, do not delay.   Psalm 69:2. 6

The Gloria is said or sung.

Collect
Draw near to your servants, O Lord,
and answer their prayers with unceasing kindness,
that, for those who glory in you as their Creator and guide,
you may restore what you have created
and keep safe what you have restored.
Through our Lord Jesus Christ, your Son,
who lives and reigns with you in the unity of the Holy Spirit,
one God, for ever and ever.

First Reading   Exodus 16:2-4. 12-15
I will rain down bread for you from the heavens.
The whole community of the sons of Israel began to complain against Moses and Aaron in the wilderness and said to them, "Why did we not die at the Lord's hand in the land of Egypt, when we were able to sit down to pans of meat and could eat bread to our heart's content! As it is, you have brought us to this wilderness to starve this whole company to death!"

Then the Lord said to Moses, "Now I will rain down bread for you from the heavens. Each day the people are to go out and gather the day's portion; I propose to test them in this way to see whether they will follow my law or not.

"I have heard the complaints of the sons of Israel. Say this to them, 'Between the two evenings you shall eat meat, and in the morning you shall have bread to your heart's content. Then you will learn that I, the Lord, am your God.'" And so it came about: quails flew up in the evening, and they covered the camp; in the morning there was a coating of dew all round the camp. When the coating of dew lifted, there on the surface of the desert was a thing delicate, powdery, as fine as hoarfrost on the ground. When they saw this, the sons of Israel said to one another, "What is that?" not knowing what it was. "That", said Moses to them, "is the bread the Lord gives you to eat."

Psalm   Psalm 77

R. **The Lord gave them bread from heaven.**

1. The things we have heard and understood,
   the things our fathers have told us,
   we will tell to the next generation:
   the glories of the Lord and his might. R.

2. He commanded the clouds above
   and opened the gates of heaven.
   He rained down manna for their food,
   and gave them bread from heaven. R.

3. Mere men ate the bread of angels.
   He sent them abundance of food.
   He brought them to his holy land,
   to the mountain which his right hand had won. R.

Second Reading   Ephesians 4:17. 20-24
Put on the new self that has been created in God's way.

I want to urge you in the name of the Lord, not to go on living the aimless kind of life that pagans live. Now that is hardly the way you have learnt from Christ, unless you failed to hear him properly when you were taught what the truth is in Jesus. You must give up your old way of life; you must put aside your old self, which gets corrupted by following illusory desires. Your mind must be renewed by a spiritual revolution so that you can put on the new self that has been created in God's way, in the goodness and holiness of the truth.

Gospel Acclamation

Alleluia, alleluia!
I am the Way, the Truth and the Life, says the Lord;
no one can come to the Father except through me.
Alleluia!   John 14:5

or

Alleluia, alleluia!
Man does not live on bread alone,
but on every word that comes from the mouth of God.
Alleluia!   Matthew 4:4

Gospel   John 6:24-35

He who comes to me will never be hungry; he who believes in me will never thirst.

When the people saw that neither Jesus nor his disciples were there, they got into boats and crossed to Capernaum to look for Jesus. When they found him on the other side, they said to him, "Rabbi, when did you come here?" Jesus answered:

"I tell you most solemnly,
you are not looking for me
because you have seen the signs
but because you had all the bread you wanted to eat.
Do not work for food that cannot last,
but work for food that endures to eternal life,
the kind of food the Son of Man is offering you,
for on him the Father, God himself, has set his seal."

Then they said to him, "What must we do if we are to do the works that God wants?" Jesus gave them this answer, "This is working for God: you must believe in the one he has sent." So they said, "What sign will you give to show us that we should believe in you? What work will you do? Our fathers had manna to eat in the desert; as

scripture says: He gave them bread from heaven to eat."
Jesus answered:

"I tell you most solemnly,
it was not Moses who gave you bread from heaven,
it is my Father who gives you the bread from heaven,
the true bread;
for the bread of God
is that which comes down from heaven
and gives life to the world."

"Sir," they said, "give us that bread always." Jesus answered:

"I am the bread of life.
He who comes to me will never be hungry;
he who believes in me will never thirst."

The Creed is said.

Prayer over the Offerings
Graciously sanctify these gifts, O Lord, we pray,
and, accepting the oblation of this spiritual sacrifice,
make of us an eternal offering to you.
Through Christ our Lord.

Preface I-VIII of the Sundays in Ordinary Time, pp. 499-502.

Communion Antiphon
You have given us, O Lord, bread from heaven,
endowed with all delights and sweetness in every taste.

Wisdom 16:20

or

I am the bread of life, says the Lord;
whoever comes to me will not hunger
and whoever believes in me will not thirst.

John 6:35

Prayer after Communion
Accompany with constant protection, O Lord,
those you renew with these heavenly gifts
and, in your never-failing care for them,
make them worthy of eternal redemption.
Through Christ our Lord.

NINETEENTH SUNDAY IN ORDINARY TIME – B

Living bread.

Christ is the living bread come down from heaven. Anyone who eats this bread will live for ever. Just as Elijah the prophet was strengthened by the food given to him by God, so we too are sustained by the Eucharist as we continue our pilgrimage back to the Father. In the strength of this food, we are called to love as Christ loved us.

Entrance Antiphon

Look to your covenant, O Lord,
and forget not the life of your poor ones for ever.
Arise, O God, and defend your cause,
and forget not the cries of those who seek you.

cf. Psalm 73:20. 19. 22. 23

The Gloria is said or sung.

Collect

Almighty ever-living God,
whom, taught by the Holy Spirit,
we dare to call our Father,
bring, we pray, to perfection in our hearts
the spirit of adoption as your sons and daughters,
that we may merit to enter into the inheritance
which you have promised.
Through our Lord Jesus Christ, your Son,
who lives and reigns with you in the unity of the Holy Spirit,
one God, for ever and ever.

First Reading   1 Kings 19:4-8

Strengthened by the food he walked until he reached the mountain of God.

Elijah went into the wilderness, a day's journey, and sitting under a furze bush wished he were dead. "Lord," he said, "I have had enough.

Take my life; I am no better than my ancestors." Then he lay down and went to sleep. But an angel touched him and said, "Get up and eat." He looked round, and there at his head was a scone baked on hot stones, and a jar of water. He ate and drank and then lay down again. But the angel of the Lord came back a second time and touched him and said, "Get up and eat, or the journey will be too long for you." So he got up and ate and drank, and strengthened by that food he walked for forty days and forty nights until he reached Horeb, the mountain of God.

Psalm   Psalm 33

R. **Taste and see that the Lord is good.**

1. I will bless the Lord at all times,
    his praise always on my lips;
    in the Lord my soul shall make its boast.
    The humble shall hear and be glad. R.

2. Glorify the Lord with me.
    Together let us praise his name.
    I sought the Lord and he answered me;
    from all my terrors he set me free. R.

3. Look towards him and be radiant;
    let your faces not be abashed.
    This poor man called; the Lord heard him
    and rescued him from all his distress. R.

4. The angel of the Lord is encamped
    around those who revere him, to rescue them.
    Taste and see that the Lord is good.
    He is happy who seeks refuge in him. R.

Second Reading   Ephesians 4:30 – 5:2
Follow Christ by loving as he loved you.
Do not grieve the Holy Spirit of God who has marked you with his seal for you to be set free when the day comes. Never have grudges

against others, or lose your temper, or raise your voice to anybody, or call each other names, or allow any sort of spitefulness. Be friends with one another, and kind, forgiving each other as readily as God forgave you in Christ.

Try, then, to imitate God, as children of his that he loves, and follow Christ by loving as he loved you, giving himself up in our place as a fragrant offering and a sacrifice to God.

Gospel Acclamation
Alleluia, alleluia!
If anyone loves me he will keep my word,
and my Father will love him,
and we shall come to him.
Alleluia!   John 14:23

or

Alleluia, alleluia!
I am the living bread which has come down from heaven,
says the Lord.
Anyone who eats this bread will live for ever.
Alleluia!   John 6:51

Gospel   John 6:41-51
I am the living bread which has come down from heaven.
The Jews were complaining to each other about Jesus, because he had said, "I am the bread that came down from heaven." "Surely this is Jesus son of Joseph" they said. "We know his father and mother. How can he now say, 'I have come down from heaven'?" Jesus said in reply, "Stop complaining to each other.

"No one can come to me
unless he is drawn by the Father who sent me,
and I will raise him up at the last day.
It is written in the prophets:
They will all be taught by God,
and to hear the teaching of the Father,
and learn from it,
is to come to me.

Not that anybody has seen the Father,
except the one who comes from God:
he has seen the Father.
I tell you most solemnly,
everybody who believes has eternal life.
I am the bread of life.
Your fathers ate the manna in the desert
and they are dead;
but this is the bread that comes down from heaven,
so that a man may eat it and not die.
I am the living bread which has come down from heaven.
Anyone who eats this bread will live for ever;
and the bread that I shall give
is my flesh, for the life of the world."

The Creed is said.

Prayer over the Offerings
Be pleased, O Lord, to accept the offerings of your Church,
for in your mercy you have given them to be offered
and by your power you transform them
into the mystery of our salvation.
Through Christ our Lord.

Preface I-VIII of the Sundays in Ordinary Time, pp. 499-502.

Communion Antiphon
O Jerusalem, glorify the Lord,
who gives you your fill of finest wheat.   Psalm 147:12. 14

or

The bread that I will give, says the Lord,
is my flesh for the life of the world.   cf. John 6:51

Prayer after Communion
May the communion in your Sacrament
that we have consumed, save us, O Lord,
and confirm us in the light of your truth.
Through Christ our Lord.

TWENTIETH SUNDAY IN ORDINARY TIME – B

Eat my flesh, drink my blood.
Jesus Christ gave his life for us on the cross. Blood is a sign of life and Christ
shed it to the last drop. In the Eucharist we receive his life-giving Body and
Blood. God's Wisdom invites us to eat and drink the good gifts that God offers,
and so to receive life. We are called, in response to Christ's self-giving love, to
transform the world around us by the lives we lead.

Entrance Antiphon

Turn your eyes, O God, our shield;
and look on the face of your anointed one;
one day within your courts
is better than a thousand elsewhere.   Psalm 83:10-11

The Gloria is said or sung.

Collect

O God, who have prepared for those who love you
good things which no eye can see,
fill our hearts, we pray, with the warmth of your love,
so that, loving you in all things and above all things,
we may attain your promises,
which surpass every human desire.
Through our Lord Jesus Christ, your Son,
who lives and reigns with you in the unity of the Holy Spirit,
one God, for ever and ever.

First Reading   Proverbs 9:1-6

Eat my bread, drink the wine I have prepared for you.
Wisdom has built herself a house,
she has erected her seven pillars,
she has slaughtered her beasts, prepared her wine,
she has laid her table.

She has despatched her maidservants
and proclaimed from the city's heights:
"Who is ignorant? Let him step this way."
To the fool she says,
"Come and eat my bread,
drink the wine I have prepared!
Leave your folly and you will live,
walk in the ways of perception."

Psalm   Psalm 33

R. **Taste and see that the Lord is good.**

1. I will bless the Lord at all times,
   his praise always on my lips;
   in the Lord my soul shall make its boast.
   The humble shall hear and be glad. R.

2. Revere the Lord, you his saints.
   They lack nothing, those who revere him.
   Strong lions suffer want and go hungry
   but those who seek the Lord lack no blessing. R.

3. Come, children, and hear me
   that I may teach you the fear of the Lord.
   Who is he who longs for life
   and many days, to enjoy his prosperity? R.

4. Then keep your tongue from evil
   and your lips from speaking deceit.
   Turn aside from evil and do good;
   seek and strive after peace. R.

Second Reading   Ephesians 5:15-20
Recognise what is the will of God.
Be very careful about the sort of lives you lead, like intelligent and
not like senseless people. This may be a wicked age, but your lives
should redeem it. And do not be thoughtless but recognise what

is the will of the Lord. Do not drug yourselves with wine, this is simply dissipation; be filled with the Spirit. Sing the words and tunes of the psalms and hymns when you are together, and go on singing and chanting to the Lord in your hearts, so that always and everywhere you are giving thanks to God who is our Father in the name of our Lord Jesus Christ.

Gospel Acclamation
Alleluia, alleluia!
The Word was made flesh and lived among us;
to all who did accept him
He gave power to become children of God.   John 1:12. 14

or

Alleluia, alleluia!
He who eats my flesh and drinks my blood
lives in me, and I live in him,
says the Lord.
Alleluia!   John 6:56

Gospel   John 6:51-58
My flesh is real food and my blood is real drink.
Jesus said to the crowd:

> "I am the living bread which has come down from heaven.
> Anyone who eats this bread will live for ever;
> and the bread that I shall give
> is my flesh, for the life of the world."

Then the Jews started arguing with one another: "How can this man give us his flesh to eat?" they said. Jesus replied:

> "I tell you most solemnly,
> if you do not eat the flesh of the Son of Man
> and drink his blood,
> you will not have life in you.
> Anyone who does eat my flesh and drink my blood
> has eternal life,
> and I shall raise him up on the last day.
> For my flesh is real food

and my blood is real drink.
He who eats my flesh and drinks my blood
lives in me
and I live in him.
As I, who am sent by the living Father,
myself draw life from the Father,
so whoever eats me will draw life from me.
This is the bread come down from heaven;
not like the bread our ancestors ate:
they are dead,
but anyone who eats this bread will live for ever."

The Creed is said.

Prayer over the Offerings
Receive our oblation, O Lord,
by which is brought about a glorious exchange,
that, by offering what you have given,
we may merit to receive your very self.
Through Christ our Lord.

Preface I-VIII of the Sundays in Ordinary Time, pp. 499-502.

Communion Antiphon
With the Lord there is mercy;
in him is plentiful redemption.   Psalm 129:7

or

I am the living bread that came down from heaven, says the Lord.
Whoever eats of this bread will live for ever.   John 6:51-52

Prayer after Communion
Made partakers of Christ through these Sacraments,
we humbly implore your mercy, Lord,
that, conformed to his image on earth,
we may merit also to be his coheirs in heaven.
Who lives and reigns for ever and ever.

TWENTY-FIRST SUNDAY IN ORDINARY TIME – B

The message of eternal life.
Jesus Christ lives in his Church, and in loving the Church we love him.
However challenging the world may find Christ's teaching, we know that he
has the message of eternal life, and there is no one else to whom we want to go.
We show our love for Christ in our service of his Church.

Entrance Antiphon
Turn your ear, O Lord, and answer me;
save the servant who trusts in you, my God.
Have mercy on me, O Lord, for I cry to you all the day long.
cf. Psalm 85:1-3

The Gloria is said or sung.

Collect
O God, who cause the minds of the faithful
to unite in a single purpose,
grant your people to love what you command
and to desire what you promise,
that, amid the uncertainties of this world,
our hearts may be fixed on that place
where true gladness is found.
Through our Lord Jesus Christ, your Son,
who lives and reigns with you in the unity of the Holy Spirit,
one God, for ever and ever.

First Reading   Joshua 24:1-2. 15-18
We will serve the Lord, for he is our God.
Joshua gathered all the tribes of Israel together at Shechem; then
he called the elders, leaders, judges and scribes of Israel, and they
presented themselves before God. Then Joshua said to all the
people: "If you will not serve the Lord, choose today whom you

wish to serve, whether the gods that your ancestors served beyond the River, or the gods of the Amorites in whose land you are now living. As for me and my House, we will serve the Lord."

The people answered, "We have no intention of deserting the Lord our God who brought us and our ancestors out of the land of Egypt, the house of slavery, who worked those great wonders before our eyes and preserved us all along the way we travelled and among all the peoples through whom we journeyed. We too will serve the Lord, for he is our God."

Psalm   Psalm 33

R. **Taste and see that the Lord is good.**

1. I will bless the Lord at all times,
   his praise always on my lips;
   in the Lord my soul shall make its boast.
   The humble shall hear and be glad. R.

2. The Lord turns his face against the wicked
   to destroy their remembrance from the earth.
   The Lord turns his eyes to the just
   and his ears to their appeal. R.

3. They call and the Lord hears
   and rescues them in all their distress.
   The Lord is close to the broken-hearted;
   those whose spirit is crushed he will save. R.

4. Many are the trials of the just man
   but from them all the Lord will rescue him.
   He will keep guard over all his bones,
   not one of his bones shall be broken. R.

5. Evil brings death to the wicked;
   those who hate the good are doomed.
   The Lord ransoms the souls of his servants.
   Those who hide in him shall not be condemned. R.

Second Reading
Ephesians 5:21-32

This mystery has many implications for Christ and his Church.

Give way to one another in obedience to Christ. Wives should regard their husbands as they regard the Lord, since as Christ is head of the Church and saves the whole body, so is a husband the head of his wife; and as the Church submits to Christ, so should wives to their husbands, in everything. Husbands should love their wives just as Christ loved the Church and sacrificed himself for her to make her holy. He made her clean by washing her in water with a form of words, so that when he took her to himself she would be glorious, with no speck or wrinkle or anything like that, but holy and faultless. In the same way, husbands must love their wives as they love their own bodies; for a man to love his wife is for him to love himself. A man never hates his own body, but he feeds it and looks after it; and that is the way Christ treats the Church, because it is his body – and we are its living parts. For this reason, a man must leave his father and mother and be joined to his wife, and the two will become one body. This mystery has many implications; but I am saying it applies to Christ and the Church.

Gospel Acclamation
Alleluia, alleluia!
Your words are spirit, Lord,
and they are life:
you have the message of eternal life.
Alleluia!   cf. John 6:63. 68

Gospel
John 6:60-69

Whom shall we go to? You have the message of eternal life.

After hearing his doctrine many of the followers of Jesus said, "This is intolerable language. How could anyone accept it?" Jesus was aware that his followers were complaining about it and said, "Does this upset you? What if you should see the Son of Man ascend to where he was before?

"It is the spirit that gives life,
the flesh has nothing to offer.
The words I have spoken to you are spirit
and they are life.

"But there are some of you who do not believe." For Jesus knew from the outset those who did not believe, and who it was that would betray him. He went on, "This is why I told you that no one could come to me unless the Father allows him." After this, many of his disciples left him and stopped going with him.

Then Jesus said to the Twelve, "What about you, do you want to go away too?" Simon Peter answered, "Lord, who shall we go to? You have the message of eternal life, and we believe; we know that you are the Holy One of God."

The Creed is said.

Prayer over the Offerings

O Lord, who gained for yourself a people by adoption
through the one sacrifice offered once for all,
bestow graciously on us, we pray,
the gifts of unity and peace in your Church.
Through Christ our Lord.

Preface I-VIII of the Sundays in Ordinary Time, pp. 499-502.

Communion Antiphon

The earth is replete with the fruits of your work, O Lord;
you bring forth bread from the earth
and wine to cheer the heart.   cf. Psalm 103:13-15

or

Whoever eats my flesh and drinks my blood
has eternal life, says the Lord,
and I will raise him up on the last day.   cf. John 6:54

Prayer after Communion

Complete within us, O Lord, we pray,
the healing work of your mercy
and graciously perfect and sustain us,
so that in all things we may please you.
Through Christ our Lord.

TWENTY-SECOND SUNDAY IN ORDINARY TIME – B

The commandments of God.

Christ did not come to set aside God's commandments but to fulfil them. He shows us how we are to act in order to witness to the power of God's word within us. Faith without good works is dead, and we show we are God's people by our care of those in need, rather than by adhering to human rules and traditions.

Entrance Antiphon
Have mercy on me, O Lord, for I cry to you all the day long.
O Lord, you are good and forgiving,
full of mercy to all who call to you.   cf. Psalm 85:3. 5

The Gloria is said or sung.

Collect
God of might, giver of every good gift,
put into our hearts the love of your name,
so that, by deepening our sense of reverence,
you may nurture in us what is good
and, by your watchful care,
keep safe what you have nurtured.
Through our Lord Jesus Christ, your Son,
who lives and reigns with you in the unity of the Holy Spirit,
one God, for ever and ever.

First Reading   Deuteronomy 4:1-2. 6-8
Add nothing to what I command you, keep the commandments of
the Lord.
Moses said to the people: "Now, Israel, take notice of the laws and
customs that I teach you today, and observe them, that you may
have life and may enter and take possession of the land that the
Lord the God of your fathers is giving you. You must add nothing
to what I command you, and take nothing from it, but keep the

commandments of the Lord your God just as I lay them down for you. Keep them, observe them, and they will demonstrate to the peoples your wisdom and understanding. When they come to know of all these laws they will exclaim, 'No other people is as wise and prudent as this great nation.' And indeed, what great nation is there that has its gods so near as the Lord our God is to us whenever we call to him? And what great nation is there that has laws and customs to match this whole Law that I put before you today?"

Psalm   Psalm 14

R. **The just will live in the presence of the Lord.**

1. Lord, who shall dwell on your holy mountain?
   He who walks without fault;
   he who acts with justice
   and speaks the truth from his heart. R.

2. He who does no wrong to his brother,
   who casts no slur on his neighbour,
   who holds the godless in disdain,
   but honours those who fear the Lord. R.

3. He who keeps his pledge, come what may;
   who takes no interest on a loan
   and accepts no bribes against the innocent.
   Such a man will stand firm for ever. R.

Second Reading   James 1:17-18. 21-22. 27
You must do what the word tells you.
It is all that is good, everything that is perfect, which is given us from above; it comes down from the Father of all light; with him there is no such thing as alteration, no shadow of a change. By his own choice he made us his children by the message of the truth so that we should be a sort of first-fruits of all that he had created.

Accept and submit to the word which has been planted in you and can save your souls. But you must do what the word tells you, and not just listen to it and deceive yourselves.

Pure unspoilt religion, in the eyes of God our Father is this:

coming to the help of orphans and widows when they need it, and keeping oneself uncontaminated by the world.

Gospel Acclamation
Alleluia, alleluia!
Your words are spirit, Lord,
and they are life:
you have the message of eternal life.
Alleluia!
cf. John 6:63. 68

or

Alleluia, alleluia!
By his own choice the Father made us his children
by the message of his truth,
so that we should be a sort of first-fruits
of all that he created.
Alleluia!
James 1:18

Gospel   Mark 7:1-8. 14-15. 21-23
You put aside the commandment of God to cling to human traditions.
The Pharisees and some of the scribes who had come from Jerusalem gathered round Jesus, and they noticed that some of his disciples were eating with unclean hands, that is, without washing them. For the Pharisees, and the Jews in general, follow the tradition of the elders and never eat without washing their arms as far as the elbow; and on returning from the market place they never eat without first sprinkling themselves. There are also many other observances which have been handed down to them concerning the washing of cups and pots and bronze dishes. So these Pharisees and scribes asked him, "Why do your disciples not respect the tradition of the elders but eat their food with unclean hands?" He answered, "It was of you hypocrites that Isaiah so rightly prophesied in this passage of scripture:

This people honours me only with lip-service,
while their hearts are far from me.
The worship they offer me is worthless,
the doctrines they teach are only human regulations.

You put aside the commandment of God to cling to human traditions."

He called the people to him again and said, "Listen to me, all of you, and understand. Nothing that goes into a man from outside can make him unclean; it is the things that come out of a man that make him unclean. For it is from within, from men's hearts, that evil intentions emerge: fornication, theft, murder, adultery, avarice, malice, deceit, indecency, envy, slander, pride, folly. All these evil things come from within and make a man unclean."

The Creed is said.

Prayer over the Offerings
May this sacred offering, O Lord,
confer on us always the blessing of salvation,
that what it celebrates in mystery
it may accomplish in power.
Through Christ our Lord.

Preface I-VIII of the Sundays in Ordinary Time, pp. 499-502.

Communion Antiphon
How great is the goodness, Lord,
that you keep for those who fear you.   Psalm 30:20
or
Blessed are the peacemakers,
for they shall be called children of God.
Blessed are they who are persecuted for the sake of righteousness,
for theirs is the Kingdom of Heaven.   Matthew 5:9-10

Prayer after Communion
Renewed by this bread from the heavenly table,
we beseech you, Lord,
that, being the food of charity,
it may confirm our hearts
and stir us to serve you in our neighbour.
Through Christ our Lord.

TWENTY-THIRD SUNDAY IN ORDINARY TIME – B

Christ opens our ears and our lips.
The power of Christ helps us to understand the Gospel and to speak its
message to others. Even though in the world's eyes we may be insignificant,
nevertheless the Lord has chosen us to be heirs to his kingdom. We do not need
to be afraid. Our God is always faithful to his promises.

Entrance Antiphon

You are just, O Lord, and your judgement is right;
treat your servant in accord with your merciful love.

Psalm 118:137. 124

The Gloria is said or sung.

Collect

O God, by whom we are redeemed and receive adoption,
look graciously upon your beloved sons and daughters,
that those who believe in Christ
may receive true freedom
and an everlasting inheritance.
Through our Lord Jesus Christ, your Son,
who lives and reigns with you in the unity of the Holy Spirit,
one God, for ever and ever.

First Reading   Isaiah 35:4-7

The ears of the deaf shall be unsealed and the tongues of the dumb
shall be loosed.

Say to all faint hearts,
"Courage! Do not be afraid.

"Look, your God is coming,
vengeance is coming,
the retribution of God;
he is coming to save you."

Then the eyes of the blind shall be opened,
the ears of the deaf unsealed,
then the lame shall leap like a deer
and the tongues of the dumb sing for joy;

for water gushes in the desert,
streams in the wasteland,
the scorched earth becomes a lake,
the parched land springs of water.

Psalm   Psalm 145

R. **My soul, give praise to the Lord.**

or **Alleluia!**

1. It is the Lord who keeps faith for ever,
    who is just to those who are oppressed.
    It is he who gives bread to the hungry,
    the Lord, who sets prisoners free. R.

2. It is the Lord who gives sight to the blind,
    who raises up those who are bowed down,
    the Lord, who loves the just,
    the Lord, who protects the stranger. R.

3. The Lord upholds the widow and orphan,
    but thwarts the path of the wicked.
    The Lord will reign for ever,
    Zion's God, from age to age. R.

Second Reading   James 2:1-5
God chose the poor to be the heirs to the kingdom.
My brothers, do not try to combine faith in Jesus Christ, our
glorified Lord, with the making of distinctions between classes of
people. Now suppose a man comes into your synagogue, beautifully
dressed and with a gold ring on, and at the same time a poor man
comes in, in shabby clothes, and you take notice of the well-dressed

man, and say, "Come this way to the best seats"; then you tell the poor man, "Stand over there" or "You can sit on the floor by my foot-rest." Can't you see that you have used two different standards in your mind, and turned yourselves into judges, and corrupt judges at that?

Listen, my dear brothers: it was those who are poor according to the world that God chose, to be rich in faith and to be the heirs of the kingdom which he promised to those who love him.

Gospel Acclamation
Alleluia, alleluia!
Speak, Lord, your servant is listening:
you have the message of eternal life.
Alleluia!   1 Samuel 3:9; John 6:68

or

Alleluia, alleluia!
Jesus proclaimed the Good News of the kingdom,
and cured all kinds of sickness among the people.
Alleluia!   cf. Matthew 4:23

Gospel   Mark 7:31-37
He makes the deaf hear and the dumb speak.
Returning from the district of Tyre, Jesus went by way of Sidon towards the Sea of Galilee, right through the Decapolis region. And they brought him a deaf man who had an impediment in his speech; and they asked him to lay his hand on him. He took him aside in private, away from the crowd, put his fingers into the man's ears and touched his tongue with spittle. Then looking up to heaven he sighed; and he said to him, "Ephphatha", that is "Be opened." And his ears were opened, and the ligament of his tongue was loosened and he spoke clearly. And Jesus ordered them to tell no one about it, but the more he insisted, the more widely they published it. Their admiration was unbounded. "He has done all things well," they said, "he makes the deaf hear and the dumb speak."

The Creed is said.

Prayer over the Offerings
O God, who give us the gift of true prayer and of peace,
graciously grant that through this offering,
we may do fitting homage to your divine majesty
and, by partaking of the sacred mystery,
we may be faithfully united in mind and heart.
Through Christ our Lord.

Preface I-VIII of the Sundays in Ordinary Time, pp. 499-502.

Communion Antiphon
Like the deer that yearns for running streams,
so my soul is yearning for you, my God;
my soul is thirsting for God, the living God.   cf. Psalm 41:2-3

or

I am the light of the world, says the Lord;
whoever follows me will not walk in darkness,
but will have the light of life.   John 8:12

Prayer after Communion
Grant that your faithful, O Lord,
whom you nourish and endow with life
through the food of your Word and heavenly Sacrament,
may so benefit from your beloved Son's great gifts
that we may merit an eternal share in his life.
Who lives and reigns for ever and ever.

TWENTY-FOURTH SUNDAY IN ORDINARY TIME – B

You are the Christ.
We believe that Jesus is the Christ, the Son of God. To show his love for us,
he suffered grievously and died for us upon a cross. If we want to find life,
he tells us to be prepared to lose it. It is in the manner in which we accept
suffering that we show our love for God.

Entrance Antiphon

Give peace, O Lord, to those who wait for you,
that your prophets be found true.
Hear the prayers of your servant,
and of your people Israel.

cf. Ecclesiasticus 36:18

The Gloria is said or sung.

Collect

Look upon us, O God,
Creator and ruler of all things,
and, that we may feel the working of your mercy,
grant that we may serve you with all our heart.
Through our Lord Jesus Christ, your Son,
who lives and reigns with you in the unity of the Holy Spirit,
one God, for ever and ever.

First Reading
Isaiah 50:5-9

I offered my back to those who struck me.
The Lord has opened my ear.

For my part, I made no resistance,
neither did I turn away.
I offered my back to those who struck me,
my cheeks to those who tore at my beard;
I did not cover my face
against insult and spittle.

The Lord comes to my help,
so that I am untouched by the insults.
So, too, I set my face like flint;
I know I shall not be shamed.

My vindicator is here at hand. Does anyone start proceedings
    against me?
Then let us go to court together.
Who thinks he has a case against me?
Let him approach me.
The Lord is coming to my help,
who dare condemn me?

Psalm   Psalm 114

R. **I will walk in the presence of the Lord
    in the land of the living.**

or **Alleluia!**

1. I love the Lord for he has heard
   the cry of my appeal;
   for he turned his ear to me
   in the day when I called him. R.

2. They surrounded me, the snares of death,
   with the anguish of the tomb;
   they caught me, sorrow and distress.
   I called on the Lord's name.
   O Lord my God, deliver me! R.

3. How gracious is the Lord, and just;
   our God has compassion.
   The Lord protects the simple hearts;
   I was helpless so he saved me. R.

4. He has kept my soul from death,
   my eyes from tears
   and my feet from stumbling.
   I will walk in the presence of the Lord
   in the land of the living. R.

Second Reading   James 2:14-18

If good works do not go with faith, it is quite dead.

Take the case, my brothers, of someone who has never done a single good act but claims that he has faith. Will that faith save him? If one of the brothers or one of the sisters is in need of clothes and has not enough food to live on, and one of you says to them, "I wish you well; keep yourself warm and eat plenty," without giving them these bare necessities of life, then what good is that? Faith is like that: if good works do not go with it, it is quite dead.

This is the way to talk to people of that kind: "You say you have faith and I have good deeds; I will prove to you that I have faith by showing you my good deeds – now you prove to me that you have faith without any good deeds to show."

Gospel Acclamation

Alleluia, alleluia!

I am the Way, the Truth and the Life, says the Lord;

no one can come to the Father except through me.

Alleluia!   John 14:5

or

Alleluia, alleluia!

The only thing I can boast about is the cross of our Lord,

through whom the world is crucified to me, and I to the world.

Alleluia!   Galatians 6:14

Gospel   Mark 8:27-35

You are the Christ. The Son of Man is destined to suffer grievously.

Jesus and his disciples left for the villages round Caesarea Philippi. On the way he put this question to his disciples, "Who do people say I am?" And they told him. "John the Baptist," they said, "others Elijah; others again, one of the prophets." "But you," he asked, "who do you say I am?" Peter spoke up and said to him, "You are the Christ." And he gave them strict orders not to tell anyone about him.

And he began to teach them that the Son of Man was destined to suffer grievously, to be rejected by the elders and the chief priests and the scribes, and to be put to death, and after three days to rise again; and he said all this quite openly. Then, taking him aside, Peter started to remonstrate with him. But, turning and seeing his disciples, he rebuked Peter and said to him, "Get behind me, Satan! Because the way you think is not God's way but man's."

He called the people and his disciples to him and said, "If anyone wants to be a follower of mine, let him renounce himself and take up his cross and follow me. For anyone who wants to save his life will lose it; but anyone who loses his life for my sake, and for the sake of the gospel, will save it."

The Creed is said.

Prayer over the Offerings
Look with favour on our supplications, O Lord,
and in your kindness accept these, your servants' offerings,
that what each has offered to the honour of your name
may serve the salvation of all.
Through Christ our Lord.

Preface I-VIII of the Sundays in Ordinary Time, pp. 499-502.

Communion Antiphon
How precious is your mercy, O God!
The children of men seek shelter in the shadow of your wings.
cf. Psalm 35:8

or

The chalice of blessing that we bless
is a communion in the Blood of Christ;
and the bread that we break
is a sharing in the Body of the Lord.   cf. 1 Corinthians 10:16

Prayer after Communion
May the working of this heavenly gift, O Lord, we pray,
take possession of our minds and bodies,
so that its effects, and not our own desires,
may always prevail in us.
Through Christ our Lord.

TWENTY-FIFTH SUNDAY IN ORDINARY TIME – B

Christ must die a shameful death.
When Jesus explained to his followers that he must die a shameful death, they
did not understand him. In the same way, we do not understand suffering,
even though we are surrounded by it. When we accept and carry our cross, we
discover a peace that the world cannot give.

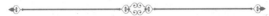

Entrance Antiphon
I am the salvation of the people, says the Lord.
Should they cry to me in any distress,
I will hear them, and I will be their Lord for ever.

The Gloria is said or sung.

Collect
O God, who founded all the commands of your sacred Law
upon love of you and of our neighbour,
grant that, by keeping your precepts,
we may merit to attain eternal life.
Through our Lord Jesus Christ, your Son,
who lives and reigns with you in the unity of the Holy Spirit,
one God, for ever and ever.

First Reading   Wisdom 2:12. 17-20
Let us condemn him to a shameful death.
The godless say to themselves,
"Let us lie in wait for the virtuous man, since he annoys us
and opposes our way of life,
reproaches us for our breaches of the law
and accuses us of playing false to our upbringing.
Let us see if what he says is true,
let us observe what kind of end he himself will have.
If the virtuous man is God's son, God will take his part

and rescue him from the clutches of his enemies.
Let us test him with cruelty and with torture,
and thus explore this gentleness of his
and put his endurance to the proof.
Let us condemn him to a shameful death
since he will be looked after – we have his word for it."

Psalm   Psalm 53

R. **The Lord upholds my life.**

1. O God, save me by your name;
   by your power, uphold my cause.
   O God, hear my prayer;
   listen to the words of my mouth. R.

2. For proud men have risen against me,
   ruthless men seek my life.
   They have no regard for God. R.

3. But I have God for my help.
   The Lord upholds my life.
   I will sacrifice to you with willing heart
   and praise your name for it is good. R.

Second Reading   James 3:16 – 4:3
Peacemakers, when they work for peace, sow the seeds which will
bear fruit in holiness.
Wherever you find jealousy and ambition, you find disharmony,
and wicked things of every kind being done; whereas the wisdom
that comes down from above is essentially something pure; it
also makes for peace, and is kindly and considerate; it is full of
compassion and shows itself by doing good; nor is there any trace
of partiality or hypocrisy in it. Peacemakers, when they work for
peace, sow the seeds which will bear fruit in holiness.

Where do these wars and battles between yourselves first start?
Isn't it precisely in the desires fighting inside your own selves? You
want something and you haven't got it; so you are prepared to kill.

You have an ambition that you cannot satisfy; so you fight to get your way by force. Why you don't have what you want is because you don't pray for it; when you do pray and don't get it, it is because you have not prayed properly, you have prayed for something to indulge your own desires.

Gospel Acclamation
Alleluia, alleluia!
I am the light of the world, says the Lord,
anyone who follows me
will have the light of life.
Alleluia!   John 8:12

or

Alleluia, alleluia!
Through the Good News God called us
to share the glory of our Lord Jesus Christ.
Alleluia!   cf. 2 Thessalonians 2:14

Gospel   Mark 9:30-37
The Son of Man will be delivered. If anyone wants to be first, he must make himself servant of all.

After leaving the mountain Jesus and his disciples made their way through Galilee; and he did not want anyone to know, because he was instructing his disciples; he was telling them, "The Son of Man will be delivered into the hands of men; they will put him to death; and three days after he has been put to death he will rise again." But they did not understand what he said and were afraid to ask him.

They came to Capernaum, and when he was in the house he asked them, "What were you arguing about on the road?" They said nothing because they had been arguing which of them was the greatest. So he sat down, called the Twelve to him and said, "If anyone wants to be first, he must make himself last of all and servant of all." He then took a little child, set him in front of them, put his arms round him, and said to them, "Anyone who welcomes one of these little children in my name, welcomes me; and anyone who welcomes me welcomes not me but the one who sent me."

The Creed is said.

Prayer over the Offerings
Receive with favour, O Lord, we pray,
the offerings of your people,
that what they profess with devotion and faith
may be theirs through these heavenly mysteries.
Through Christ our Lord.

Preface I-VIII of the Sundays in Ordinary Time, pp. 499-502.

Communion Antiphon
You have laid down your precepts to be carefully kept;
may my ways be firm in keeping your statutes.   Psalm 118:4-5

or

I am the Good Shepherd, says the Lord;
I know my sheep, and mine know me.   John 10:14

Prayer after Communion
Graciously raise up, O Lord,
those you renew with this Sacrament,
that we may come to possess your redemption
both in mystery and in the manner of our life.
Through Christ our Lord.

TWENTY-SIXTH SUNDAY IN ORDINARY TIME – B

Anyone who is not against Christ is for him.
We often tend to be exclusive, thinking that God acts only through those we
recognise as fellow believers. Yet there are many good people through whom
the Holy Spirit works, even though they may not call themselves Christians.
Rather than seeing this as a problem, we can see it as an encouragement to live
our lives of faith to the full.

Entrance Antiphon
All that you have done to us, O Lord,
you have done with true judgement,
for we have sinned against you
and not obeyed your commandments.
But give glory to your name
and deal with us according to the bounty of your mercy.

Daniel 3:31. 29. 30. 43. 42

The Gloria is said or sung.

Collect
O God, who manifest your almighty power
above all by pardoning and showing mercy,
bestow, we pray, your grace abundantly upon us
and make those hastening to attain your promises
heirs to the treasures of heaven.
Through our Lord Jesus Christ, your Son,
who lives and reigns with you in the unity of the Holy Spirit,
one God, for ever and ever.

First Reading   **Numbers 11:25-29**
Are you jealous on my account? If only the whole people of the
Lord were prophets!
The Lord came down in the Cloud. He spoke with Moses, but took
some of the spirit that was on him and put it on the seventy elders.

When the spirit came on them they prophesied, but not again.

Two men had stayed back in the camp; one was called Eldad and the other Medad. The spirit came down on them; though they had not gone to the Tent, their names were enrolled among the rest. These began to prophesy in the camp. The young man ran to tell this to Moses, "Look," he said, "Eldad and Medad are prophesying in the camp." Then said Joshua the son of Nun, who had served Moses from his youth, "My Lord Moses, stop them!" Moses answered him, "Are you jealous on my account? If only the whole people of the Lord were prophets, and the Lord gave his Spirit to them all!"

Psalm   Psalm 18

R. **The precepts of the Lord gladden the heart.**

1. The law of the Lord is perfect,
   it revives the soul.
   The rule of the Lord is to be trusted,
   it gives wisdom to the simple. R.

2. The fear of the Lord is holy,
   abiding for ever.
   The decrees of the Lord are truth
   and all of them just. R.

3. So in them your servant finds instruction;
   great reward is in their keeping.
   But who can detect all his errors?
   From hidden faults acquit me. R.

4. From presumption restrain your servant
   and let it not rule me.
   Then shall I be blameless,
   clean from grave sin. R.

Second Reading   James 5:1-6
Your wealth is all rotting.
An answer for the rich. Start crying, weep for the miseries that are coming to you. Your wealth is all rotting, your clothes are all eaten up by moths. All your gold and your silver are corroding away, and

the same corrosion will be your own sentence, and eat into your body. It was a burning fire that you stored up as your treasure for the last days. Labourers mowed your fields, and you cheated them – listen to the wages that you kept back, calling out; realise that the cries of the reapers have reached the ears of the Lord of hosts. On earth you have had a life of comfort and luxury; in the time of slaughter you went on eating to your heart's content. It was you who condemned the innocent and killed them; they offered you no resistance.

Gospel Acclamation
Alleluia, alleluia!
Your word is truth, O Lord,
consecrate us in the truth.
Alleluia!   cf. John 17:17

Gospel   Mark 9:38-43. 45. 47-48
Anyone who is not against us is for us. If your hand should cause you to sin, cut it off.

John said to Jesus, "Master, we saw a man who is not one of us casting out devils in your name; and because he was not one of us we tried to stop him." But Jesus said, "You must not stop him: no one who works a miracle in my name is likely to speak evil of me. Anyone who is not against us is for us.

"If anyone gives you a cup of water to drink just because you belong to Christ, then I tell you solemnly, he will most certainly not lose his reward.

"But anyone who is an obstacle to bring down one of these little ones who have faith, would be better thrown into the sea with a great millstone round his neck. And if your hand should cause you to sin, cut it off; it is better for you to enter into life crippled, than to have two hands and go to hell, into the fire that cannot be put out. And if your foot should cause you to sin, cut it off; it is better for you to enter into life lame, than to have two feet and be thrown into hell. And if your eye should cause you to sin, tear it out; it is better for you to enter into the kingdom of God with one eye, than to have two eyes and be thrown into hell where their worm does not die nor their fire go out."

The Creed is said.

Prayer over the Offerings
Grant us, O merciful God,
that this our offering may find acceptance with you
and that through it the wellspring of all blessing
may be laid open before us.
Through Christ our Lord.

Preface I-VIII of the Sundays in Ordinary Time, pp. 499-502.

Communion Antiphon
Remember your word to your servant, O Lord,
by which you have given me hope.
This is my comfort when I am brought low.   cf. Psalm 118:49-50

or

By this we came to know the love of God:
that Christ laid down his life for us;
so we ought to lay down our lives for one another.   1 John 3:16

Prayer after Communion
May this heavenly mystery, O Lord,
restore us in mind and body,
that we may be coheirs in glory with Christ,
to whose suffering we are united
whenever we proclaim his Death.
Who lives and reigns for ever and ever.

TWENTY-SEVENTH SUNDAY IN ORDINARY TIME – B

Marriage is a sacred bond of unity.
In marriage, a husband and wife form a unity, according to God's plan from the very beginning. A Christian marriage can be a witness to the world of the self-giving love of Christ.

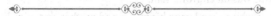

Entrance Antiphon

Within your will, O Lord, all things are established,
and there is none that can resist your will.
For you have made all things, the heaven and the earth,
and all that is held within the circle of heaven;
you are the Lord of all.   cf. Esther 4:17

The Gloria is said or sung.

Collect

Almighty ever-living God,
who in the abundance of your kindness
surpass the merits and the desires of those who entreat you,
pour out your mercy upon us
to pardon what conscience dreads
and to give what prayer does not dare to ask.
Through our Lord Jesus Christ, your Son,
who lives and reigns with you in the unity of the Holy Spirit,
one God, for ever and ever.

First Reading   Genesis 2:18-24

They become one body.

The Lord God said, "It is not good that the man should be alone. I will make him a helpmate." So from the soil the Lord God fashioned all the wild beasts and all the birds of heaven. These he brought to the man to see what he would call them; each one was to bear the name the man would give it. The man gave names to all the cattle, all the birds of heaven and all the wild beasts. But no helpmate suitable for man was found for him. So the Lord God made the man fall into a deep sleep. And while he slept, he took one of his ribs and enclosed it in flesh. The Lord God built the rib he had taken from the man into a woman, and brought her to the man. The man exclaimed:

"This at last is bone from my bones,
and flesh from my flesh!
This is to be called woman,
for this was taken from man."

This is why a man leaves his father and mother and joins himself to his wife, and they become one body.

Psalm   Psalm 127

R. **May the Lord bless us
    all the days of our life.**

1. O blessed are those who fear the Lord
    and walk in his ways!
    By the labour of your hands you shall eat.
    You will be happy and prosper. R.

2. Your wife will be like a fruitful vine
    in the heart of your house;
    your children like shoots of the olive,
    around your table. R.

3. Indeed thus shall be blessed
    the man who fears the Lord.
    May the Lord bless you from Zion
    in a happy Jerusalem
    all the days of your life!
    May you see your children's children.
    On Israel, peace! R.

Second Reading   Hebrews 2:9-11
The one who sanctifies, and the ones who are sanctified, are of the same stock.

We see in Jesus one who was for a short while made lower than the angels and is now crowned with glory and splendour because he submitted to death; by God's grace he had to experience death for all mankind.

As it was his purpose to bring a great many of his sons into glory, it was appropriate that God, for whom everything exists and through whom everything exists, should make perfect, through suffering, the leader who would take them to their salvation. For the one who sanctifies, and the ones who are sanctified, are the same stock; that is why he openly calls them brothers.

Gospel Acclamation
Alleluia, alleluia!
Your word is truth, O Lord,
consecrate us in the truth.
Alleluia!   cf. John 17:17

or

Alleluia, alleluia!
As long as we love one another
God will live in us
and his love will be complete in us.
Alleluia!   1 John 4:12

Gospel   Mark 10:2-16
What God has united, man must not divide.

Some Pharisees approached Jesus and asked, "Is it against the law for a man to divorce his wife?" They were testing him. He answered them, "What did Moses command you?" "Moses allowed us", they said, "to draw up a writ of dismissal and so to divorce." Then Jesus said to them, "It was because you were so unteachable that he wrote this commandment for you. But from the beginning of creation God made them male and female. This is why a man must leave father and mother, and the two become one body. They are no longer two, therefore, but one body. So then, what God has united, man must not divide." Back in the house the disciples questioned him again about this, and he said to them, "The man who divorces his wife and marries another is guilty of adultery against her. And if a woman divorces her husband and marries another she is guilty of adultery too."

People were bringing little children to him for him to touch them. The disciples turned them away, but when Jesus saw this he was indignant and said to them, "Let the little children come to me; do not stop them; for it is to such as these that the kingdom of God belongs. I tell you solemnly, anyone who does not welcome the kingdom of God like a little child will never enter it." Then he put his arms round them, laid his hands on them and gave them his blessing.

The Creed is said.

Prayer over the Offerings
Accept, O Lord, we pray,
the sacrifices instituted by your commands
and, through the sacred mysteries,
which we celebrate with dutiful service,
graciously complete the sanctifying work
by which you are pleased to redeem us.
Through Christ our Lord.

Preface I-VIII of the Sundays in Ordinary Time, pp. 499-502.

Communion Antiphon
The Lord is good to those who hope in him,
to the soul that seeks him.   Lamentations 3:25

or

Though many, we are one bread, one body,
for we all partake of the one Bread and one Chalice.
                                                         cf. 1 Corinthians 10:17

Prayer after Communion
Grant us, almighty God,
that we may be refreshed and nourished
by the Sacrament which we have received,
so as to be transformed into what we consume.
Through Christ our Lord.

TWENTY-EIGHTH SUNDAY IN ORDINARY TIME – B

The poverty of riches.
Rich people may be too preoccupied with their worldly possessions to follow
Christ. He tells us that those with riches find it hard to enter the kingdom of
God; but the most important thing is to be wise through God's word and see
wealth and material things in their proper perspective. Then we will come to
appreciate the richness of poverty for Christ's sake.

Entrance Antiphon
If you, O Lord, should mark iniquities,
Lord, who could stand?
But with you is found forgiveness,
O God of Israel.   Psalm 129:3-4

The Gloria is said or sung.

Collect
May your grace, O Lord, we pray,
at all times go before us and follow after
and make us always determined
to carry out good works.
Through our Lord Jesus Christ, your Son,
who lives and reigns with you in the unity of the Holy Spirit,
one God, for ever and ever.

First Reading   Wisdom 7:7-11
Compared with wisdom, I held riches as nothing.
I prayed, and understanding was given me;
I entreated, and the spirit of Wisdom came to me.
I esteemed her more than sceptres and thrones;
compared with her, I held riches as nothing.
I reckoned no priceless stone to be her peer,
for compared with her, all gold is a pinch of sand,

and beside her silver ranks as mud.
I loved her more than health or beauty,
preferred her to the light,
since her radiance never sleeps.
In her company all good things came to me,
at her hands riches not to be numbered.

Psalm   Psalm 89

R. **Fill us with your love that we may rejoice.**

1. Make us know the shortness of our life
   that we may gain wisdom of heart.
   Lord, relent! Is your anger for ever?
   Show pity to your servants. R.

2. In the morning, fill us with your love;
   we shall exult and rejoice all our days.
   Give us joy to balance our affliction
   for the years when we knew misfortune. R.

3. Show forth your work to your servants;
   let your glory shine on their children.
   Let the favour of the Lord be upon us:
   give success to the work of our hands. R.

Second Reading   Hebrews 4:12-13
The word of God can judge secret emotions and thoughts.
The word of God is something alive and active: it cuts like any
double-edged sword but more finely: it can slip through the place
where the soul is divided from the spirit, or joints from the marrow;
it can judge the secret emotions and thoughts. No created thing can
hide from him; everything is uncovered and open to the eyes of the
one to whom we must give account of ourselves.

Gospel Acclamation
Alleluia, alleluia!
Blessed are you, Father,
Lord of heaven and earth,
for revealing the mysteries of the kingdom
to mere children.
Alleluia!   cf. Matthew 11:25

or

Alleluia, alleluia!
How happy are the poor in spirit;
theirs is the kingdom of heaven.
Alleluia!   Matthew 5:3

Gospel   Mark 10:17-30
Go and sell everything you own and follow me.

Jesus was setting out on a journey when a man ran up, knelt before him and put this question to him, "Good master, what must I do to inherit eternal life?" Jesus said to him, "Why do you call me good? No one is good but God alone. You know the commandments: You must not kill; You must not commit adultery; You must not steal; You must not bring false witness; You must not defraud; Honour your father and mother." And he said to him, "Master, I have kept all these from my earliest days." Jesus looked steadily at him and loved him, and he said, "There is one thing you lack. Go and sell everything you own and give the money to the poor, and you will have treasure in heaven; then come, follow me." But his face fell at these words and he went away sad, for he was a man of great wealth.

Jesus looked round and said to his disciples, "How hard it is for those who have riches to enter the kingdom of God!" The disciples were astounded by these words, but Jesus insisted, "My children," he said to them, "how hard it is to enter the kingdom of God! It is easier for a camel to pass through the eye of a needle than for a rich man to enter the kingdom of God." They were more astonished than ever. "In that case", they said to one another, "who can be saved?" Jesus gazed at them. "For men", he said, "it is impossible, but not for God: because everything is possible for God."

Peter took this up. "What about us?" he asked him. "We have left everything and followed you." Jesus said, "I tell you solemnly, there is no one who has left house, brothers, sisters, father, children or land for my sake and for the sake of the gospel who will not be repaid a hundred times over, houses, brothers, sisters, mothers, children and land – not without persecutions – now in this present time and, in the world to come, eternal life."

The Creed is said.

Prayer over the Offerings
Accept, O Lord, the prayers of your faithful
with the sacrificial offerings,
that, through these acts of devotedness,
we may pass over to the glory of heaven.
Through Christ our Lord.

Preface I-VIII of the Sundays in Ordinary Time, pp. 499-502.

Communion Antiphon
The rich suffer want and go hungry,
but those who seek the Lord lack no blessing.   cf. Psalm 33:11

or

When the Lord appears, we shall be like him,
for we shall see him as he is.   1 John 3:2

Prayer after Communion
We entreat your majesty most humbly, O Lord,
that, as you feed us with the nourishment
which comes from the most holy Body and Blood of your Son,
so you may make us sharers of his divine nature.
Who lives and reigns for ever and ever.

TWENTY-NINTH SUNDAY IN ORDINARY TIME – B

Christ's death is our ransom.
*God our Father showed his love for us by sending his Son, not to be served but
to serve. Christ showed his love for us by giving his life in atonement for our
sins. He is our high priest who has gone through to the highest heaven but not
before experiencing the depth of human suffering.*

Entrance Antiphon

To you I call; for you will surely heed me, O God;
turn your ear to me; hear my words.
Guard me as the apple of your eye;
in the shadow of your wings protect me. *cf. Psalm 16:6. 8*

The Gloria is said or sung.

Collect

Almighty ever-living God,
grant that we may always conform our will to yours
and serve your majesty in sincerity of heart.
Through our Lord Jesus Christ, your Son,
who lives and reigns with you in the unity of the Holy Spirit,
one God, for ever and ever.

First Reading   Isaiah 53:10-11

If he offers his life in atonement, he shall see his heirs, he shall have
a long life.

The Lord has been pleased to crush his servant with suffering.
If he offers his life in atonement,
he shall see his heirs, he shall have a long life
and through him what the Lord wishes will be done.

His soul's anguish over
he shall see the light and be content.
By his sufferings shall my servant justify many,
taking their faults on himself.

Psalm   Psalm 32

R. **May your love be upon us, O Lord,**
   as we place all our hope in you.

1. The word of the Lord is faithful
   and all his works to be trusted.
   The Lord loves justice and right
   and fills the earth with his love. R.

2. The Lord looks on those who revere him,
   on those who hope in his love,
   to rescue their souls from death,
   to keep them alive in famine. R.

3. Our soul is waiting for the Lord.
   The Lord is our help and our shield.
   May your love be upon us, O Lord,
   as we place all our hope in you. R.

Second Reading   Hebrews 4:14-16
Let us be confident in approaching the throne of grace.
Since in Jesus, the Son of God, we have the supreme high priest who
has gone through to the highest heaven, we must never let go of the
faith that we have professed. For it is not as if we had a high priest
who was incapable of feeling our weaknesses with us; but we have
one who has been tempted in every way that we are, though he is
without sin. Let us be confident, then, in approaching the throne of
grace, that we shall have mercy from him and find grace when we
are in need of help.

Gospel Acclamation
Alleluia, alleluia!
I am the Way, the Truth and the Life, says the Lord;
no one can come to the Father except through me.
Alleluia!   John 14:6
or

Alleluia, alleluia!
The Son of Man came to serve,
and to give his life as a ransom for many.
Alleluia!   Mark 10:45

Gospel   Mark 10:35-45
The Son of Man came to give his life as a ransom for many.
James and John, the sons of Zebedee, approached Jesus. "Master,"
they said to him, "we want you to do us a favour." He said to them,
"What is it you want me to do for you?" They said to him, "Allow us
to sit one at your right hand and the other at your left in your glory."
"You do not know what you are asking" Jesus said to them. "Can
you drink the cup that I must drink, or be baptised with the baptism
with which I must be baptised?" They replied, "We can." Jesus said
to them, "The cup that I must drink you shall drink, and with the
baptism with which I must be baptised you shall be baptised, but as
for seats at my right hand or my left, these are not mine to grant:
they belong to those to whom they have been allotted."

When the other ten heard this they began to feel indignant with
James and John, so

> Jesus called them to him and said to them, "You know that among
> the pagans their so-called rulers lord it over them, and their great
> men make their authority felt. This is not to happen among you.
> No; anyone who wants to become great among you must be your
> servant, and anyone who wants to be first among you must be
> slave to all. For the Son of Man himself did not come to be served
> but to serve, and to give his life as a ransom for many."

The Creed is said.

Prayer over the Offerings
Grant us, Lord, we pray,
a sincere respect for your gifts,
that, through the purifying action of your grace,
we may be cleansed by the very mysteries we serve.
Through Christ our Lord.

Preface I-VIII of the Sundays in Ordinary Time, pp. 499-502.

Communion Antiphon
Behold, the eyes of the Lord
are on those who fear him,
who hope in his merciful love,
to rescue their souls from death,
to keep them alive in famine.   cf. Psalm 32:18-19

or

The Son of Man has come
to give his life as a ransom for many.   Mark 10:45

Prayer after Communion
Grant, O Lord, we pray,
that, benefiting from participation in heavenly things,
we may be helped by what you give in this present age
and prepared for the gifts that are eternal.
Through Christ our Lord.

THIRTIETH SUNDAY IN ORDINARY TIME – B

Master, let me see again.

God's gift of faith to us helps us to see the world with a new vision. Christ renews our faith so that we may see more clearly the world in which we live. We are God's children and share in Christ's priesthood; we try never to lose sight of this great privilege that has been given to us.

Entrance Antiphon

Let the hearts that seek the Lord rejoice;
turn to the Lord and his strength;
constantly seek his face.

cf. Psalm 104:3-4

The Gloria is said or sung.

Collect

Almighty ever-living God,
increase our faith, hope and charity,
and make us love what you command,
so that we may merit what you promise.
Through our Lord Jesus Christ, your Son,
who lives and reigns with you in the unity of the Holy Spirit,
one God, for ever and ever.

First Reading

Jeremiah 31:7-9

I will comfort the blind and the lame as I lead them back.

The Lord says this:

Shout with joy for Jacob!
Hail the chief of nations!
Proclaim! Praise! Shout!
"The Lord has saved his people,
the remnant of Israel!"
See, I will bring them back
from the land of the North

and gather them from the far ends of earth;
all of them: the blind and the lame,
women with child, women in labour:
a great company returning here.
They had left in tears,
I will comfort them as I lead them back;
I will guide them to streams of water,
by a smooth path where they will not stumble.
For I am a father to Israel,
and Ephraim is my first-born son.

Psalm   Psalm 125

R. **What marvels the Lord worked for us!**
    Indeed we were glad.

1. When the Lord delivered Zion from bondage,
   it seemed like a dream.
   Then was our mouth filled with laughter,
   on our lips there were songs. R.

2. The heathens themselves said: "What marvels
   the Lord worked for them!"
   What marvels the Lord worked for us!
   Indeed we were glad. R.

3. Deliver us, O Lord, from our bondage
   as streams in dry land.
   Those who are sowing in tears
   will sing when they reap. R.

4. They go out, they go out, full of tears,
   carrying seed for the sowing:
   they come back, they come back, full of song,
   carrying their sheaves. R.

Second Reading   Hebrews 5:1-6

You are a priest of the order of Melchizedek, and for ever.

Every high priest has been taken out of mankind and is appointed to
act for men in their relations with God, to offer gifts and sacrifices
for sins; and so he can sympathise with those who are ignorant or
uncertain because he too lives in the limitations of weakness. That
is why he has to make sin offerings for himself as well as for the
people. No one takes this honour on himself, but each one is called
by God, as Aaron was. Nor did Christ give himself the glory of
becoming high priest, but he had it from the one who said to him:
You are my son, today I have become your father, and in another
text: You are a priest of the order of Melchizedek, and for ever.

Gospel Acclamation
Alleluia, alleluia!
I am the light of the world, says the Lord,
anyone who follows me
will have the light of life.
Alleluia!   John 8:12

or

Alleluia, alleluia!
Our Saviour Christ Jesus abolished death,
and he has proclaimed life through the Good News.
Alleluia!   cf. 2 Timothy 1:10

Gospel   Mark 10:46-52

Master, let me see again.

As Jesus left Jericho with his disciples and a large crowd, Bartimaeus
(that is, the son of Timaeus), a blind beggar, was sitting at the side of
the road. When he heard that it was Jesus of Nazareth, he began to
shout and say, "Son of David, Jesus, have pity on me." And many of
them scolded him and told him to keep quiet, but he only shouted
all the louder, "Son of David, have pity on me." Jesus stopped and
said, "Call him here." So they called the blind man. "Courage," they
said, "get up; he is calling you." So throwing off his cloak, he jumped

up and went to Jesus. Then Jesus spoke, "What do you want me to do for you?" "Rabbuni," the blind man said to him, "Master, let me see again." Jesus said to him, "Go; your faith has saved you." And immediately his sight returned and he followed him along the road.

The Creed is said.

Prayer over the Offerings
Look, we pray, O Lord,
on the offerings we make to your majesty,
that whatever is done by us in your service
may be directed above all to your glory.
Through Christ our Lord.

Preface I-VIII of the Sundays in Ordinary Time, pp. 499-502.

Communion Antiphon
We will ring out our joy at your saving help
and exult in the name of our God.   cf. Psalm 19:6

or

Christ loved us and gave himself up for us,
as a fragrant offering to God.   Ephesians 5:2

Prayer after Communion
May your Sacraments, O Lord, we pray,
perfect in us what lies within them,
that what we now celebrate in signs
we may one day possess in truth.
Through Christ our Lord.

THIRTY-FIRST SUNDAY IN ORDINARY TIME – B

Love God, and love your neighbour as yourself.
Christ calls us to love God with all our heart, soul, mind and strength, and to love our neighbour as ourselves. Love is of the very essence of the Christian faith. This love demands nothing less than everything, and that is why it is the greatest commandment of all.

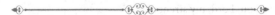

Entrance Antiphon
Forsake me not, O Lord, my God;
be not far from me!
Make haste and come to my help,
O Lord, my strong salvation!

cf. Psalm 37:22-23

The Gloria is said or sung.

Collect
Almighty and merciful God,
by whose gift your faithful offer you
right and praiseworthy service,
grant, we pray,
that we may hasten without stumbling
to receive the things you have promised.
Through our Lord Jesus Christ, your Son,
who lives and reigns with you in the unity of the Holy Spirit,
one God, for ever and ever.

First Reading   Deuteronomy 6:2-6
Listen, Israel: You shall love the Lord your God with all your heart.
Moses said to the people: "If you fear the Lord your God all the days of your life and if you keep all his laws and commandments which I lay on you, you will have a long life, you and your son and your grandson. Listen then, Israel, keep and observe what will make you prosper and give you great increase, as the Lord God of your fathers

has promised you, giving you a land where milk and honey flow.

"Listen, Israel: The Lord our God is the one Lord. You shall love the Lord your God with all your heart, with all your soul, with all your strength. Let these words I urge on you today be written on your heart."

Psalm   Psalm 17

R. **I love you, Lord, my strength.**

1. I love you, Lord, my strength,
    my rock, my fortress, my saviour.
    My God is the rock where I take refuge;
    my shield, my mighty help, my stronghold.
    The Lord is worthy of all praise:
    when I call I am saved from my foes. R.

2. Long life to the Lord, my rock!
    Praised be the God who saves me.
    He has given great victories to his king
    and shown his love for his anointed. R.

Second Reading   Hebrews 7:23-28

Because he remains for ever, Christ can never lose his priesthood.

There used to be a great number of priests under the former covenant, because death put an end to each one of them; but this one, Christ, because he remains for ever, can never lose his priesthood. It follows, then, that his power to save is utterly certain, since he is living for ever to intercede for all who come to God through him.

To suit us, the ideal high priest would have to be holy, innocent and uncontaminated, beyond the influence of sinners, and raised up above the heavens; one who would not need to offer sacrifices every day, as the other high priests do for their own sins and then for those of the people, because he has done this once and for all by offering himself. The Law appoints high priests who are men subject to weakness; but the promise on oath, which came after the Law, appointed the Son who is made perfect for ever.

Gospel Acclamation
Alleluia, alleluia!
Your words are spirit, Lord,
and they are life:
you have the message of eternal life.
Alleluia!   cf. John 6:63.68

or

Alleluia, alleluia!
If anyone loves me he will keep my word,
and my Father will love him,
and we shall come to him.
Alleluia!   John 14:23

Gospel   Mark 12:28-34
This is the first commandment. The second is like it.
One of the scribes came up and put a question to him, "Which is
the first of all the commandments?" Jesus replied, "This is the first:
Listen, Israel, the Lord our God is the one Lord, and you must love
the Lord your God with all your heart, with all your soul, with all
your mind and with all your strength. The second is this: You must
love your neighbour as yourself. There is no commandment greater
than these." The scribe said to him, "Well spoken, Master; what you
have said is true: that he is one and there is no other. To love him
with all your heart, with all your understanding and strength, and
to love your neighbour as yourself, this is far more important than
any holocaust or sacrifice." Jesus, seeing how wisely he had spoken,
said, "You are not far from the kingdom of God." And after that no
one dared to question him any more.

The Creed is said.

Prayer over the Offerings
May these sacrificial offerings, O Lord,
become for you a pure oblation,
and for us a holy outpouring of your mercy.
Through Christ our Lord.

Preface I-VIII of the Sundays in Ordinary Time, pp. 499-502.

Communion Antiphon

You will show me the path of life,
the fullness of joy in your presence, O Lord.   cf. Psalm 15:11

or

Just as the living Father sent me
and I have life because of the Father,
so whoever feeds on me
shall have life because of me, says the Lord.   John 6:58

Prayer after Communion

May the working of your power, O Lord,
increase in us, we pray,
so that, renewed by these heavenly Sacraments,
we may be prepared by your gift
for receiving what they promise.
Through Christ our Lord.

THIRTY-SECOND SUNDAY IN ORDINARY TIME – B

The widow's offering.

The widow's offering of a penny was made out of love and of the little on which she had to live. In the same way, the widow at Sidon was willing to share her little with the prophet Elijah. We are called never to be afraid to give generously to God, who will always provide for us. All our gifts are to be given lovingly and generously.

Entrance Antiphon
Let my prayer come into your presence.
Incline your ear to my cry for help, O Lord.   cf. Psalm 87:3

The Gloria is said or sung.

Collect
Almighty and merciful God,
graciously keep from us all adversity,
so that, unhindered in mind and body alike,
we may pursue in freedom of heart
the things that are yours.
Through our Lord Jesus Christ, your Son,
who lives and reigns with you in the unity of the Holy Spirit,
one God, for ever and ever.

First Reading   1 Kings 17:10-16
The widow made a little scone from her meal and brought it to Elijah.

Elijah the Prophet went off to Sidon. And when he reached the city gate, there was a widow gathering sticks; addressing her he said, "Please bring a little water in a vessel for me to drink." She was setting off to bring it when he called after her. "Please", he said, "bring me a scrap of bread in your hand." "As the Lord your God lives," she replied, "I have no baked bread, but only a handful of meal in a jar and a little oil in a jug; I am just gathering a stick or two to go and prepare this for myself and my son to eat, and then we shall die." But Elijah said to her, "Do not be afraid, go and do as you have said; but first make a little scone of it for me and bring it to me, and then make some for yourself and for your son. For thus the Lord speaks, the God of Israel:

'Jar of meal shall not be spent,
jug of oil shall not be emptied,
    before the day when the Lord sends
    rain on the face of the earth.'"

The woman went and did as Elijah told her and they ate the food, she, himself and her son. The jar of meal was not spent nor the jug of oil emptied, just as the Lord had foretold through Elijah.

Psalm   Psalm 145

R. **My soul, give praise to the Lord.**

or **Alleluia!**

1. It is the Lord who keeps faith for ever,
   who is just to those who are oppressed.
   It is he who gives bread to the hungry,
   the Lord, who sets prisoners free. R.

2. It is the Lord who gives sight to the blind,
   who raises up who are bowed down.
   It is the Lord who loves the just,
   the Lord, who protects the stranger. R.

3. The Lord upholds the widow and orphan
   but thwarts the path of the wicked.
   The Lord will reign for ever,
   Zion's God, from age to age. R.

Second Reading   Hebrews 9:24-28

Christ offers himself only once to take the faults of many on himself.

It is not as though Christ had entered a man-made sanctuary which was only modelled on the real one; but it was heaven itself, so that he could appear in the actual presence of God on our behalf. And he does not have to offer himself again and again, like the high priest going into the sanctuary year after year with the blood that is not his own, or else he would have had to suffer over and over again since the world began. Instead of that, he has made his appearance once and for all, now at the end of the last age, to do away with sin by sacrificing himself. Since men only die once, and after that comes judgement, so Christ, too, offers himself only once to take the faults of many on himself, and when he appears a second time, it will not be to deal with sin but to reward with salvation those who are waiting for him.

Gospel Acclamation

Alleluia, alleluia!
Even if you have to die, says the Lord,
keep faithful, and I will give you
the crown of life.
Alleluia!   Apocalypse 2:10

or

Alleluia, alleluia!
How happy are the poor in spirit:
theirs is the kingdom of heaven.
Alleluia!   Matthew 5:3

Gospel   Mark 12:38-44

This poor widow has put in more than all.

In his teaching Jesus said, "Beware of the scribes who like to walk about in long robes, to be greeted obsequiously in the market squares, to take the front seats in the synagogues and the places of honour at banquets; these are the men who swallow the property of widows, while making a show of lengthy prayers. The more severe will be the sentence they receive."

He sat down opposite the treasury and watched the people putting money into the treasury, and many of the rich put in a great deal. A poor widow came and put in two small coins, the equivalent of a penny. Then he called his disciples and said to them, "I tell you solemnly, this poor widow has put more in than all who have contributed to the treasury; for they have all put in money they had over, but she from the little she had has put in everything she possessed, all she had to live on."

The Creed is said.

Prayer over the Offerings
Look with favour, we pray, O Lord,
upon the sacrificial gifts offered here,
that, celebrating in mystery the Passion of your Son,
we may honour it with loving devotion.
Through Christ our Lord.

Preface I-VIII of the Sundays in Ordinary Time, pp. 499-502.

Communion Antiphon
The Lord is my shepherd; there is nothing I shall want.
Fresh and green are the pastures where he gives me repose,
near restful waters he leads me.   cf. Psalm 22:1-2

or

The disciples recognised the Lord Jesus in the breaking of bread.
                                                    cf. Luke 24:35

Prayer after Communion
Nourished by this sacred gift, O Lord,
we give you thanks and beseech your mercy,
that, by the pouring forth of your Spirit,
the grace of integrity may endure
in those your heavenly power has entered.
Through Christ our Lord.

THIRTY-THIRD SUNDAY IN ORDINARY TIME – B

The Son of Man is coming in power and glory.
Christ died once for all and then took his place at the right hand of God. We await his second coming in power and glory. On that day we will come to understand God's plan for our salvation, and we will praise the Lord for his compassion and mercy towards us.

Entrance Antiphon

The Lord said: I think thoughts of peace and not of affliction.
You will call upon me, and I will answer you,
and I will lead back your captives from every place.

Jeremiah 29:11. 12. 14

The Gloria is said or sung.

Collect

Grant us, we pray, O Lord our God,
the constant gladness of being devoted to you,
for it is full and lasting happiness
to serve with constancy
the author of all that is good.
Through our Lord Jesus Christ, your Son,
who lives and reigns with you in the unity of the Holy Spirit,
one God, for ever and ever.

First Reading   Daniel 12:1-3

When that time comes, your own people will be spared.

"At that time Michael will stand up, the great prince who mounts guard over your people. There is going to be a time of great distress, unparalleled since nations first came into existence. When that time comes, your own people will be spared, all those whose names are found written in the Book. Of those who lie sleeping in the dust of the earth many will awake, some to everlasting life, some to shame and everlasting disgrace. The learned will shine as brightly as the vault of heaven, and those who have instructed many in virtue, as bright as stars for all eternity."

Psalm   Psalm 15

R. **Preserve me, God, I take refuge in you.**

1. O Lord, it is you who are my portion and cup;
   it is you yourself who are my prize.
   I keep the Lord ever in my sight:
   since he is at my right hand, I shall stand firm. R.

2. And so my heart rejoices, my soul is glad;
   even my body shall rest in safety.
   For you will not leave my soul among the dead,
   nor let your beloved know decay. R.

3. You will show me the path of life,
   the fullness of joy in your presence,
   at your right hand happiness for ever. R.

Second Reading   Hebrews 10:11-14. 18
By virtue of one single offering, he has achieved the eternal perfection of all whom he is sanctifying.
All the priests stand at their duties every day, offering over and over again the same sacrifices which are quite incapable of taking sins away. Christ, on the other hand, has offered one single sacrifice for sins, and then taken his place for ever, at the right hand of God, where he is now waiting until his enemies are made into a footstool for him. By virtue of that one single offering, he has achieved the eternal perfection of all whom he is sanctifying. When all sins have been forgiven, there can be no more sin offerings.

Gospel Acclamation

Alleluia, alleluia!
Stay awake and stand ready,
because you do not know the hour
when the Son of Man is coming.
Alleluia!   Matthew 24:42. 44

or

Alleluia, alleluia!
Stay awake, praying at all times
for the strength to stand with confidence
before the Son of Man.
Alleluia!   Luke 21:36

Gospel   Mark 13:24-32

He will gather his chosen from the four winds.

Jesus said to his disciples: "In those days, after the time of distress,
the sun will be darkened, the moon will lose its brightness, the stars
will come falling from heaven and the powers in the heavens will
be shaken. And then they will see the Son of Man coming in the
clouds with great power and glory; then too he will send the angels
to gather his chosen from the four winds, from the ends of the
world to the ends of heaven.

"Take the fig tree as a parable: as soon as its twigs grow supple
and its leaves come out, you know that summer is near. So with
you, when you see these things happening: know that he is near, at
the very gates. I tell you solemnly, before this generation has passed
away all these things will have taken place. Heaven and earth will
pass away, but my words will not pass away.

"But as for that day or hour, nobody knows it, neither the angels
of heaven, nor the Son; no one but the Father."

The Creed is said.

Prayer over the Offerings
Grant, O Lord, we pray,
that what we offer in the sight of your majesty
may obtain for us the grace of being devoted to you
and gain us the prize of everlasting happiness.
Through Christ our Lord.

Preface I-VIII of the Sundays in Ordinary Time, pp. 499-502.

Communion Antiphon
To be near God is my happiness,
to place my hope in God the Lord.   Psalm 72:28

or

Amen, I say to you: Whatever you ask in prayer,
believe that you will receive,
and it shall be given to you, says the Lord.   Mark 11:23-24

Prayer after Communion
We have partaken of the gifts of this sacred mystery,
humbly imploring, O Lord,
that what your Son commanded us to do
in memory of him
may bring us growth in charity.
Through Christ our Lord.

Last Sunday in Ordinary Time

OUR LORD JESUS CHRIST, KING OF THE UNIVERSE – B

Christ's kingdom is not of this world.
Christ's kingship is very different from what we are used to seeing in the
rulers of our world. It is a kingship of love and service. Christ's sovereignty
will never pass away, since his power comes from God and not from human
means. He has made us a line of kings and priests to serve God until the end
of time.

Entrance Antiphon

How worthy is the Lamb who was slain,
to receive power and divinity,
and wisdom and strength and honour.
To him belong glory and power for ever and ever.

Apocalypse 5:12; 1:6

The Gloria is said or sung.

Collect

Almighty ever-living God,
whose will is to restore all things
in your beloved Son, the King of the universe,
grant, we pray,
that the whole creation, set free from slavery,
may render your majesty service
and ceaselessly proclaim your praise.
Through our Lord Jesus Christ, your Son,
who lives and reigns with you in the unity of the Holy Spirit,
one God, for ever and ever.

First Reading   Daniel 7:13-14

His sovereignty is an eternal sovereignty.

I gazed into the visions of the night.
And I saw, coming on the clouds of heaven,
one like a son of man.
He came to the one of great age
and was led into his presence.
On him was conferred sovereignty,
glory and kingship,
and men of all peoples, nations and languages became his servants.
His sovereignty is an eternal sovereignty,
which shall never pass away,
nor will his empire be destroyed.

Psalm   Psalm 92

R.   **The Lord is king, with majesty enrobed.**

1. The Lord is king, with majesty enrobed;
    the Lord has robed himself with might,
    he has girded himself with power. R.

2. The world you made firm, not to be moved;
    your throne has stood firm from of old.
    From all eternity, O Lord, you are. R.

3. Truly your decrees are to be trusted.
    Holiness is fitting to your house,
    O Lord, until the end of time. R.

Second Reading   Apocalypse 1:5-8

*Ruler of the kings of the earth… he made us a line of kings, priests
to serve his God.*

Jesus Christ is the faithful witness, the First-born from the dead, the
Ruler of the kings of the earth. He loves us and has washed away
our sins with his blood, and made us a line of kings, priests to serve
his God and Father; to him, then, be glory and power for ever and

ever. Amen. It is he who is coming on the clouds; everyone will see him, even those who pierced him, and all the races of the earth will mourn over him. This is the truth. Amen. "I am the Alpha and the Omega" says the Lord God, who is, who was, and who is to come, the Almighty.

Gospel Acclamation
Alleluia, alleluia!
Blessings on him who comes in the name of the Lord!
Blessings on the coming kingdom of our father David!
Alleluia!   Mark 11:9. 10

Gospel   John 18:33-37
It is you who say that I am a king.
"Are you the king of the Jews?" Pilate asked. Jesus replied, "Do you ask this of your own accord, or have others spoken to you about me?" Pilate answered, "Am I a Jew? It is your own people and the chief priests who have handed you over to me: what have you done?" Jesus replied, "Mine is not a kingdom of this world; if my kingdom were of this world, my men would have fought to prevent my being surrendered to the Jews. But my kingdom is not of this kind." "So you are a king then?" said Pilate. "It is you who say it" answered Jesus. "Yes, I am a king. I was born for this, I came into the world for this: to bear witness to the truth; and all who are on the side of truth listen to my voice."

The Creed is said.

Prayer over the Offerings
As we offer you, O Lord, the sacrifice
by which the human race is reconciled to you,
we humbly pray,
that your Son himself may bestow on all nations
the gifts of unity and peace.
Through Christ our Lord.

Preface

It is truly right and just, our duty and our salvation,
always and everywhere to give you thanks,
Lord, holy Father, almighty and eternal God.

For you anointed your Only Begotten Son,
our Lord Jesus Christ, with the oil of gladness
as eternal Priest and King of all creation,
so that, by offering himself on the altar of the Cross
as a spotless sacrifice to bring us peace,
he might accomplish the mysteries of human redemption
and, making all created things subject to his rule,
he might present to the immensity of your majesty
an eternal and universal kingdom,
a kingdom of truth and life,
a kingdom of holiness and grace,
a kingdom of justice, love and peace.

And so, with Angels and Archangels,
with Thrones and Dominions,
and with all the hosts and Powers of heaven,
we sing the hymn of your glory,
as without end we acclaim:

Holy, Holy, Holy Lord God of hosts…

Communion Antiphon

The Lord sits as King for ever.
The Lord will bless his people with peace.   Psalm 28:10-11

Prayer after Communion

Having received the food of immortality,
we ask, O Lord,
that, glorying in obedience
to the commands of Christ, the King of the universe,
we may live with him eternally in his heavenly Kingdom.
Who lives and reigns for ever and ever.

SECOND SUNDAY IN ORDINARY TIME – C

Christ is the bridegroom of the Church.
Just as the bridegroom rejoices in his bride, so Christ rejoices in his Church. In the Eucharist, by the power of his Holy Spirit, he transforms bread and wine into his Body and Blood for us. The Holy Spirit gives us a variety of gifts, which we are to use for the mission of the Church.

Entrance Antiphon

All the earth shall bow down before you, O God,
and shall sing to you,
shall sing to your name, O Most High!   Psalm 65:4

The Gloria is said or sung.

Collect

Almighty ever-living God,
who govern all things,
both in heaven and on earth,
mercifully hear the pleading of your people
and bestow your peace on our times.
Through our Lord Jesus Christ, your Son,
who lives and reigns with you in the unity of the Holy Spirit,
one God, for ever and ever.

First Reading   Isaiah 62:1-5

The bridegroom rejoices in his bride.
About Zion I will not be silent,
about Jerusalem I will not grow weary,
until her integrity shines out like the dawn
and her salvation flames like a torch.

The nations then will see your integrity,
all the kings your glory,
and you will be called by a new name,
one which the mouth of the Lord will confer.

You are to be a crown of splendour in the hand of the Lord,
a princely diadem in the hand of your God;
no longer are you to be named "Forsaken",
nor your land "Abandoned",
but you shall be called "My Delight"
and your land "The Wedded";
for the Lord takes delight in you
and your land will have its wedding.
Like a young man marrying a virgin,
so will the one who built you wed you,
and as the bridegroom rejoices in his bride,
so will your God rejoice in you.

Psalm   Psalm 95

R. **Proclaim the wonders of the Lord
     among all the peoples.**

1. O sing a new song to the Lord,
   sing to the Lord all the earth.
   O sing to the Lord, bless his name. R.

2. Proclaim his help day by day,
   tell among the nations his glory
   and his wonders among all the peoples. R.

3. Give the Lord, you families of peoples,
   give the Lord glory and power,
   give the Lord the glory of his name. R.

4. Worship the Lord in his temple.
   O earth, tremble before him.
   Proclaim to the nations: "God is king."
   He will judge the peoples in fairness. R.

Second Reading   1 Corinthians 12:4-11
One and the same Spirit, who distributes gifts to different people
just as he chooses.
There is a variety of gifts but always the same Spirit; there are all
sorts of service to be done, but always to the same Lord; working in

all sorts of different ways in different people, it is the same God who is working in all of them. The particular way in which the Spirit is given to each person is for a good purpose. One may have the gift of preaching with wisdom given him by the Spirit; another may have the gift of preaching instruction given him by the same Spirit; and another the gift of faith given by the same Spirit; another again the gift of healing, through this one Spirit; one, the power of miracles; another, prophecy; another the gift of recognising spirits; another the gift of tongues and another the ability to interpret them. All these are the work of one and the same Spirit, who distributes different gifts to different people just as he chooses.

Gospel Acclamation
Alleluia, alleluia!
Your words are spirit, Lord,
and they are life:
you have the message of eternal life.
Alleluia!   cf. John 6:63. 68

or

Alleluia, alleluia!
Through the Good News God called us
to share the glory of our Lord Jesus Christ.
Alleluia!   cf. 2 Thessalonians 2:14

Gospel   John 2:1-11
This was the first of the signs given by Jesus: it was given at Cana in Galilee.
There was a wedding at Cana in Galilee. The mother of Jesus was there, and Jesus and his disciples had also been invited. When they ran out of wine, since the wine provided for the wedding was all finished, the mother of Jesus said to him, "They have no wine." Jesus said, "Woman, why turn to me? My hour has not come yet." His mother said to the servants, "Do whatever he tells you." There were six stone water jars standing there, meant for the ablutions that are customary among the Jews; each could hold twenty or thirty gallons. Jesus said to the servants, "Fill the jars with water,"

and they filled them to the brim. "Draw some out now", he told them, "and take it to the steward." They did this; the steward tasted the water, and it had turned into wine. Having no idea where it came from – only the servants who had drawn the water knew – the steward called the bridegroom and said, "People generally serve the best wine first, and keep the cheaper sort till the guests have had plenty to drink; but you have kept the best wine till now."

This was the first of the signs given by Jesus: it was given at Cana in Galilee. He let his glory be seen, and his disciples believed in him.

The Creed is said.

Prayer over the Offerings
Grant us, O Lord, we pray,
that we may participate worthily in these mysteries,
for whenever the memorial of this sacrifice is celebrated
the work of our redemption is accomplished.
Through Christ our Lord.

Preface I-VIII of the Sundays in Ordinary Time, pp. 499-502.

Communion Antiphon
You have prepared a table before me,
and how precious is the chalice that quenches my thirst.

cf. Psalm 22:5

or

We have come to know and to believe
in the love that God has for us.   1 John 4:16

Prayer after Communion
Pour on us, O Lord, the Spirit of your love,
and in your kindness
make those you have nourished
by this one heavenly Bread
one in mind and heart.
Through Christ our Lord.

THIRD SUNDAY IN ORDINARY TIME – C

Together we are Christ's body.
We belong to the Church of which the head is Christ. Just as the human body
is made up of many parts, all of which are interdependent, so we too are
dependent on each other and ultimately on Christ. The Holy Spirit is given to
us so that we may bring the Good News to those who are poor. In our lives we
witness to the fulfilling of God's promises.

Entrance Antiphon
O sing a new song to the Lord;
sing to the Lord, all the earth.
In his presence are majesty and splendour,
strength and honour in his holy place. cf. Psalm 95:1. 6

The Gloria is said or sung.

Collect
Almighty ever-living God,
direct our actions according to your good pleasure,
that in the name of your beloved Son
we may abound in good works.
Through our Lord Jesus Christ, your Son,
who lives and reigns with you in the unity of the Holy Spirit,
one God, for ever and ever.

First Reading Nehemiah 8:2-6. 8-10
Ezra read from the law of God and the people understood what
was read.
Ezra the priest brought the Law before the assembly, consisting of
men, women, and children old enough to understand. This was the
first day of the seventh month. On the square before the Water Gate,
in the presence of the men and women, and children old enough to
understand, he read from the book from early morning till noon;

all the people listened attentively to the Book of the Law.

Ezra the scribe stood on a wooden dais erected for the purpose. In full view of all the people – since he stood higher than all the people – Ezra opened the book; and when he opened it all the people stood up. Then Ezra blessed the Lord, the great God, and all the people raised their hands and answered, "Amen! Amen!"; then they bowed down and, face to the ground, prostrated themselves before the Lord. And Ezra read from the Law of God, translating and giving the sense, so that the people understood what was read.

Then Nehemiah – His Excellency – and Ezra, priest and scribe (and the Levites who were instructing the people) said to all the people, "This day is sacred to the Lord your God. Do not be mournful, do not weep." For the people were all in tears as they listened to the words of the Law.

He then said, "Go, eat the fat, drink the sweet wine, and send a portion to the man who has nothing prepared ready. For this day is sacred to our Lord. Do not be sad: the joy of the Lord is your stronghold."

Psalm   Psalm 18

R. **Your words are spirit, Lord,
      and they are life.**

1. The law of the Lord is perfect,
   it revives the soul.
   The rule of the Lord is to be trusted,
   it gives wisdom to the simple. R.

2. The precepts of the Lord are right,
   they gladden the heart.
   The command of the Lord is clear,
   it gives light to the eyes. R.

3. The fear of the Lord is holy,
   abiding for ever.
   The decrees of the Lord are truth
   and all of them just. R.

4. May the spoken words of my mouth,
   the thoughts of my heart,
   win favour in your sight, O Lord,
   my rescuer, my rock! R.

Second Reading   1 Corinthians 12:12-30

You together are Christ's body; but each of you is a different part of it.

Just as a human body, though it is made up of many parts, is a single unit because all these parts, though many, make one body, so it is with Christ. In the one Spirit we were all baptised, Jews as well as Greeks, slaves as well as citizens, and one Spirit was given to us all to drink.

Nor is the body to be identified with any one of its many parts.

If the foot were to say, "I am not a hand and so I do not belong to the body," would that mean that it stopped being part of the body? If the ear were to say, "I am not an eye, and so I do not belong to the body," would that mean it was not part of the body? If your whole body was just one eye, how would you hear anything? If it was just one ear, how would you smell anything?

Instead of that, God put all the separate parts into the body on purpose. If all the parts were the same, how could it be a body? As it is, the parts are many but the body is one. The eye cannot say to the hand, "I do not need you," nor can the head say to the feet, "I do not need you."

What is more, it is precisely the parts of the body that seem to be the weakest which are the indispensable ones; and it is the least honourable parts of the body that we clothe with the greatest care. So our more improper parts get decorated in a way that our more proper parts do not need. God has arranged the body so that more dignity is given to the parts which are without it, and so that there may not be disagreements inside the body, but that each part may be equally concerned for all the others. If one part is hurt, all parts are hurt with it. If one part is given special honour, all parts enjoy it.

Now you together are Christ's body; but each of you is a different part of it.

In the Church, God has given the first place to apostles, the second to prophets, the third to teachers; after them, miracles, and after them the gift of healing; helpers, good leaders, those with many languages. Are all of them apostles, or all of them prophets, or all of them teachers? Do they all have the gift of miracles, or all have the gift of healing? Do all speak strange languages, and all interpret them?

Gospel Acclamation
Alleluia, alleluia!
The Lord has sent me to bring the good news to the poor,
to proclaim liberty to captives.
Alleluia!   Luke 4:18

Gospel   Luke 1:1-4; 4:14-21
This text is being fulfilled today.
Seeing that many others have undertaken to draw up accounts of the events that have taken place among us, exactly as these were handed down to us by those who from the outset were eyewitnesses and ministers of the word, I in my turn, after carefully going over the whole story from the beginning, have decided to write an ordered account for you, Theophilus, so that your Excellency may learn how well founded the teaching is that you have received.

Jesus, with the power of the Spirit in him, returned to Galilee; and his reputation spread throughout the countryside. He taught in their synagogues and everyone praised him.

He came to Nazara, where he had been brought up, and went into the synagogue on the sabbath day as he usually did. He stood up to read, and they handed him the scroll of the prophet Isaiah. Unrolling the scroll he found the place where it is written:

The spirit of the Lord has been given to me, for he has anointed me.
He has sent me to bring the good news to the poor,
to proclaim liberty to captives
and to the blind new sight,
to set the downtrodden free,
to proclaim the Lord's year of favour.

He then rolled up the scroll, gave it back to the assistant and sat down. And all eyes in the synagogue were fixed on him. Then he began to speak to them, "This text is being fulfilled today even as you listen."

The Creed is said.

Prayer over the Offerings
Accept our offerings, O Lord, we pray,
and in sanctifying them
grant that they may profit us for salvation.
Through Christ our Lord.

Preface I-VIII of the Sundays in Ordinary Time, pp. 499-502.

Communion Antiphon
Look toward the Lord and be radiant;
let your faces not be abashed.   cf. Psalm 33:6

or

I am the light of the world, says the Lord;
whoever follows me will not walk in darkness,
but will have the light of life.   John 8:12

Prayer after Communion
Grant, we pray, almighty God,
that, receiving the grace
by which you bring us to new life,
we may always glory in your gift.
Through Christ our Lord.

FOURTH SUNDAY IN ORDINARY TIME – C

The greatest gift is love.
We are a people not only of faith and hope but especially of love. Love is the greatest gift that the Spirit gives to the members of Christ's Church. This gift is also given to those outside the Church, which is something for which we can thank God. Love breaks down human barriers and divisions. Love will bring about greater unity among Christians and thus a better witness to the Gospel if we are open to the Spirit.

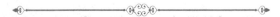

Entrance Antiphon
Save us, O Lord our God!
And gather us from the nations,
to give thanks to your holy name,
and make it our glory to praise you.

Psalm 105:47

The Gloria is said or sung.

Collect
Grant us, Lord our God,
that we may honour you with all our mind,
and love everyone in truth of heart.
Through our Lord Jesus Christ, your Son,
who lives and reigns with you in the unity of the Holy Spirit,
one God, for ever and ever.

First Reading   Jeremiah 1:4-5. 17-19
I have appointed you as prophet to the nations.
In the days of Josiah, the word of the Lord was addressed to me, saying,

> "Before I formed you in the womb I knew you;
> before you came to birth I consecrated you;
> I have appointed you as prophet to the nations.

So now brace yourself for action.
Stand up and tell them
all I command you.
Do not be dismayed at their presence,
or in their presence I will make you dismayed.
I, for my part, today will make you
into a fortified city,
a pillar of iron,
and a wall of bronze
to confront all this land:
the kings of Judah, its princes,
its priests and the country people.
They will fight against you
but shall not overcome you,
for I am with you to deliver you –
it is the Lord who speaks."

Psalm   Psalm 70

R. **My lips will tell of your help.**

1. In you, O Lord, I take refuge;
    let me never be put to shame.
    In your justice rescue me, free me:
    pay heed to me and save me. R.

2. Be a rock where I can take refuge,
    a mighty stronghold to save me;
    for you are my rock, my stronghold.
    Free me from the hand of the wicked. R.

3. It is you, O Lord, who are my hope,
    my trust, O Lord, since my youth.
    On you I have leaned from my birth,
    from my mother's womb you have been my help. R.

4. My lips will tell of your justice
    and day by day of your help.
    O God, you have taught me from my youth
    and I proclaim your wonders still. R.

Second Reading   1 Corinthians 12:31 – 13:13

There are three things that last: faith, hope and love; and the greatest of these is love.

Be ambitious for the higher gifts. And I am going to show you a way that is better than any of them.

If I have all the eloquence of men or of angels, but speak without love, I am simply a gong booming or a cymbal clashing. If I have the gift of prophecy, understanding all the mysteries there are, and knowing everything, and if I have faith in all its fulness, to move mountains, but without love, then I am nothing at all. If I give away all that I possess, piece by piece, and if I even let them take my body to burn it, but am without love, it will do me no good whatever.

Love is always patient and kind: it is never jealous; love is never boastful or conceited; it is never rude or selfish; it does not take offence, and is not resentful. Love takes no pleasure in other people's sins but delights in the truth; it is always ready to excuse, to trust, to hope, and to endure whatever comes.

Love does not come to an end. But if there are gifts of prophecy, the time will come when they must fail; or the gift of languages, it will not continue for ever; and knowledge – for this, too, the time will come when it must fail. For our knowledge is imperfect and our prophesying is imperfect; but once perfection comes, all imperfect things will disappear. When I was a child, I used to talk like a child, and think like a child, and argue like a child, but now I am a man, all childish ways are put behind me. Now we are seeing a dim reflection in a mirror; but then we shall be seeing face to face. The knowledge that I have now is imperfect; but then I shall know as fully as I am known.

In short, there are three things that last: faith, hope and love; and the greatest of these is love.

Gospel Acclamation

Alleluia, alleluia!
I am the Way, the Truth and the Life, says the Lord;
no one can come to the Father except through me.
Alleluia!

                                                        John 14:6

or

Alleluia, alleluia!
The Lord has sent me to bring the good news to the poor,
to proclaim liberty to captives.
Alleluia!   Luke 4:18

Gospel   Luke 4:21-30
Like Elijah and Elisha, Jesus is not sent to the Jews only.

Jesus began to speak in the synagogue, "This text is being fulfilled today even as you listen." And he won the approval of all, and they were astonished by the gracious words that came from his lips.

They said, "This is Joseph's son, surely?" But he replied, "No doubt you will quote me the saying, 'Physician, heal yourself' and tell me, 'We have heard all that happened in Capernaum, do the same here in your own countryside.'" And he went on, "I tell you solemnly, no prophet is ever accepted in his own country.

"There were many widows in Israel, I can assure you, in Elijah's day, when heaven remained shut for three years and six months and a great famine raged throughout the land, but Elijah was not sent to any one of these: he was sent to a widow at Zarephath, a Sidonian town. And in the prophet Elisha's time there were many lepers in Israel, but none of these was cured, except the Syrian, Naaman."

When they heard this everyone in the synagogue was enraged. They sprang to their feet and hustled him out of the town; and they took him up to the brow of the hill their town was built on, intending to throw him down the cliff, but he slipped through the crowd and walked away.

The Creed is said.

Prayer over the Offerings
O Lord, we bring to your altar
these offerings of our service:
be pleased to receive them, we pray,
and transform them
into the Sacrament of our redemption.
Through Christ our Lord.

Preface I-VIII of the Sundays in Ordinary Time, pp. 499-502.

Communion Antiphon
Let your face shine on your servant.
Save me in your merciful love.
O Lord, let me never be put to shame, for I call on you.

cf. Psalm 30:17-18

or

Blessed are the poor in spirit,
for theirs is the Kingdom of Heaven.
Blessed are the meek, for they shall possess the land.

Matthew 5:3-4

Prayer after Communion
Nourished by these redeeming gifts,
we pray, O Lord,
that through this help to eternal salvation
true faith may ever increase.
Through Christ our Lord.

FIFTH SUNDAY IN ORDINARY TIME – C

Here I am, send me.
Jesus Christ calls his apostles. He transforms them from fishermen into "fishers
of men". We are all apostles and prophets to proclaim the saving power of God.
Like Isaiah, we are touched with the burning fire of the Holy Spirit. When the
Lord asks who will be his messenger, we reply: "Here I am, Lord, send me."

Entrance Antiphon
O come, let us worship God
and bow low before the God who made us,
for he is the Lord our God. Psalm 94:6-7

The Gloria is said or sung.

Collect
Keep your family safe, O Lord, with unfailing care,
that, relying solely on the hope of heavenly grace,
they may be defended always by your protection.
Through our Lord Jesus Christ, your Son,
who lives and reigns with you in the unity of the Holy Spirit,
one God, for ever and ever.

First Reading Isaiah 6:1-8
Here I am, send me.
In the year of King Uzziah's death I saw the Lord seated on a high
throne; his train filled the sanctuary; above him stood seraphs, each
one with six wings.

And they cried out one to another in this way,

"Holy, holy, holy is the Lord of hosts.
His glory fills the whole earth."

The foundations of the threshold shook with the voice of the one
who cried out, and the Temple was filled with smoke. I said:

"What a wretched state I am in! I am lost,
for I am a man of unclean lips
and I live among a people of unclean lips,
and my eyes have looked at the King, the Lord of hosts."

Then one of the seraphs flew to me, holding in his hand a live coal
which he had taken from the altar with a pair of tongs. With this he
touched my mouth and said:

"See now, this has touched your lips,
your sin is taken away,
your iniquity is purged."

Then I heard the voice of the Lord saying:

"Whom shall I send? Who will be our messenger?"

I answered, "Here I am, send me."

Psalm   Psalm 137

R. **Before the angels I will bless you, O Lord.**

1. I thank you, Lord, with all my heart,
      you have heard the words of my mouth.
      Before the angels I will bless you.
      I will adore before your holy temple. R.

2. I thank you for your faithfulness and love
      which excel all we ever knew of you.
      On the day I called, you answered;
      you increased the strength of my soul. R.

3. All earth's kings shall thank you
      when they hear the words of your mouth.
      They shall sing of the Lord's ways:
      "How great is the glory of the Lord!" R.

4. You stretch out your hand and save me,
      your hand will do all things for me.
      Your love, O Lord, is eternal,
      discard not the work of your hands. R.

Second Reading   1 Corinthians 15:1-11

I preach what they preach, and this is what you all believed.

Brothers, I want to remind you of the gospel I preached to you, the gospel that you received and in which you are firmly established; because the gospel will save you only if you keep believing exactly what I preached to you – believing anything else will not lead to anything.

Well then,

in the first place, I taught you what I had been taught myself, namely that Christ died for our sins, in accordance with the scriptures; that he was buried; and that he was raised to life on the third day, in accordance with the scriptures; that he appeared first to Cephas and secondly to the Twelve. Next he appeared to more than five hundred of the brothers at the same time, most of whom are still alive, though some have died; then he appeared to James, and then to all the apostles; and last of all he appeared to me too; it was as though I was born when no one expected it.

I am the least of the apostles; in fact, since I persecuted the Church of God, I hardly deserve the name apostle; but by God's grace that is what I am, and the grace that he gave me has not been fruitless. On the contrary, I, or rather the grace of God that is with me, have worked harder than any of the others;

but what matters is that I preach what they preach, and this is what you all believed.

Gospel Acclamation
Alleluia, alleluia!
I call you friends, says the Lord,
because I have made known to you
everything I have learnt from my Father.
Alleluia!   John 15:15

or

Alleluia, alleluia!
Follow me, says the Lord,
and I will make you fishers of men.
Alleluia!   Matthew 4:19

Gospel   Luke 5:1-11
They left everything and followed him.

Jesus was standing one day by the lake of Gennesaret, with the crowd pressing round him listening to the word of God, when he caught sight of two boats close to the bank. The fishermen had gone out of them and were washing their nets. He got into one of the boats – it was Simon's – and asked him to put out a little from the shore. Then he sat down and taught the crowds from the boat.

When he had finished speaking he said to Simon, "Put out into deep water and pay out your nets for a catch." "Master," Simon replied "we worked hard all night long and caught nothing, but if you say so, I will pay out the nets." And when they had done this they netted such a huge number of fish that their nets began to tear, so they signalled to their companions in the other boat to come and help them; when these came, they filled the two boats to sinking point.

When Simon Peter saw this he fell at the knees of Jesus saying, "Leave me, Lord; I am a sinful man." For he and all his companions were completely overcome by the catch they had made; so also were James and John, sons of Zebedee, who were Simon's partners. But Jesus said to Simon, "Do not be afraid; from now on it is men you will catch." Then, bringing their boats back to land, they left everything and followed him.

The Creed is said.

Prayer over the Offerings
O Lord, our God,
who once established these created things
to sustain us in our frailty,
grant, we pray,
that they may become for us now
the Sacrament of eternal life.
Through Christ our Lord.

Preface I-VIII of the Sundays in Ordinary Time, pp. 499-502.

Communion Antiphon
Let them thank the Lord for his mercy,
his wonders for the children of men,
for he satisfies the thirsty soul,
and the hungry he fills with good things.   cf. Psalm 106:8-9

or

Blessed are those who mourn, for they shall be consoled.
Blessed are those who hunger and thirst for righteousness,
for they shall have their fill.   Matthew 5:5-6

Prayer after Communion
O God, who have willed that we be partakers
in the one Bread and the one Chalice,
grant us, we pray, so to live
that, made one in Christ,
we may joyfully bear fruit
for the salvation of the world.
Through Christ our Lord.

SIXTH SUNDAY IN ORDINARY TIME – C

Blessed are those who trust in the Lord.
We can place all our hope in the Resurrection of Christ. Christ is risen from the dead and is the source of our happiness. Even those who know poverty and suffering in this life are blessed by him. In Christ we can put our trust and ask for nothing more.

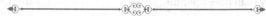

Entrance Antiphon
Be my protector, O God,
a mighty stronghold to save me.
For you are my rock, my stronghold!
Lead me, guide me, for the sake of your name.   cf. Psalm 30:3-4

The Gloria is said or sung.

Collect
O God, who teach us that you abide
in hearts that are just and true,
grant that we may be so fashioned by your grace
as to become a dwelling pleasing to you.
Through our Lord Jesus Christ, your Son,
who lives and reigns with you in the unity of the Holy Spirit,
one God, for ever and ever.

First Reading   Jeremiah 17:5-8
A curse on the man who puts his trust in man, a blessing on the man who puts his trust in the Lord.
The Lord says this:

"A curse on the man who puts his trust in man,
who relies on things of flesh,
whose heart turns from the Lord.
He is like dry scrub in the wastelands:
if good comes, he has no eyes for it,
he settles in the parched places of the wilderness,
a salt land, uninhabited.

"A blessing on the man who puts his trust in the Lord,
with the Lord for his hope.
He is like a tree by the waterside
that thrusts its roots to the stream:
when the heat comes it feels no alarm,
its foliage stays green;
it has no worries in a year of drought,
and never ceases to bear fruit."

Psalm   Psalm 1

R. **Happy the man who has placed
his trust in the Lord.**

1. Happy indeed is the man
   who follows not the counsel of the wicked;
   nor lingers in the way of sinners
   nor sits in the company of scorners,
   but whose delight is the law of the Lord
   and who ponders his law day and night. R.

2. He is like a tree that is planted
   beside the flowing waters,
   that yields its fruit in due season
   and whose leaves shall never fade;
   and all that he does shall prosper. R.

3. Not so are the wicked, not so!
   For they like winnowed chaff
   shall be driven away by the wind.
   For the Lord guards the way of the just
   but the way of the wicked leads to doom. R.

Second Reading   1 Corinthians 15:12. 16-20
If Christ has not been raised, your believing is useless.
If Christ raised from the dead is what has been preached, how can
some of you be saying that there is no resurrection of the dead? For
if the dead are not raised, Christ has not been raised, and if Christ

has not been raised, you are still in your sins. And what is more serious, all who have died in Christ have perished. If our hope in Christ has been for this life only, we are the most unfortunate of all people.

But Christ has in fact been raised from the dead, the first-fruits of all who have fallen asleep.

Gospel Acclamation
Alleluia, alleluia!
Blessed are you, Father,
Lord of heaven and earth,
for revealing the mysteries of the kingdom
to mere children.
Alleluia!

cf. Matthew 11:25

or

Alleluia, alleluia!
Rejoice and be glad:
your reward will be great in heaven.
Alleluia!

Luke 6:23

Gospel   Luke 6:17. 20-26
How happy are you who are poor. Alas for you who are rich.
Jesus came down with the Twelve and stopped at a piece of level ground where there was a large gathering of his disciples with a great crowd of people from all parts of Judaea and from Jerusalem and from the coastal region of Tyre and Sidon who had come to hear him and to be cured of their diseases.

Then fixing his eyes on his disciples he said:

"How happy are you who are poor: yours is the kingdom of God.
Happy you who are hungry now: you shall be satisfied.
Happy you who weep now: you shall laugh.

"Happy are you when people hate you, drive you out, abuse you, denounce your name as criminal, on account of the Son of Man. Rejoice when that day comes and dance for joy, for then your reward will be great in heaven. This was the way their ancestors treated the prophets.

"But alas for you who are rich: you are having your consolation
now.
 Alas for you who have your fill now: you shall go hungry.
 Alas for you who laugh now: you shall mourn and weep.
 "Alas for you when the world speaks well of you! This was the
way their ancestors treated the false prophets."

The Creed is said.

Prayer over the Offerings
May this oblation, O Lord, we pray,
cleanse and renew us
and may it become for those who do your will
the source of eternal reward.
Through Christ our Lord.

Preface I-VIII of the Sundays in Ordinary Time, pp. 499-502.

Communion Antiphon
They ate and had their fill,
and what they craved the Lord gave them;
they were not disappointed in what they craved.   cf. Psalm 77:29-30

or

God so loved the world
that he gave his Only Begotten Son,
so that all who believe in him may not perish,
but may have eternal life.   John 3:16

Prayer after Communion
Having fed upon these heavenly delights,
we pray, O Lord,
that we may always long
for that food by which we truly live.
Through Christ our Lord.

SEVENTH SUNDAY IN ORDINARY TIME – C

Be compassionate as your Father is compassionate.
Our hope of salvation lies in God's mercy. Jesus teaches us to be compassionate
as our heavenly Father is compassionate. If we learn to love our enemies, we
will be modelling ourselves on Christ the new Adam, who will teach us how to
lead the life of the Spirit.

Entrance Antiphon

O Lord, I trust in your merciful love.
My heart will rejoice in your salvation.
I will sing to the Lord who has been bountiful with me.   Psalm 12:6

The Gloria is said or sung.

Collect

Grant, we pray, almighty God,
that, always pondering spiritual things,
we may carry out in both word and deed
that which is pleasing to you.
Through our Lord Jesus Christ, your Son,
who lives and reigns with you in the unity of the Holy Spirit,
one God, for ever and ever.

First Reading   1 Samuel 26:2. 7-9. 12-13. 22-23

The Lord put you in my power, but I would not raise my hand.

Saul set off and went down to the wilderness of Ziph, accompanied
by three thousand men chosen from Israel to search for David in the
wilderness of Ziph.

So in the dark David and Abishai made their way towards the force,
where they found Saul asleep inside the camp, his spear stuck in the
ground beside his head, with Abner and the troops lying round him.

Then Abishai said to David, "Today God has put your enemy in
your power; so now let me pin him to the ground with his own spear.
Just one stroke! I will not need to strike him twice." David answered
Abishai, "Do not kill him, for who can lift his hand against the Lord's

anointed and be without guilt?" David took the spear and the pitcher of water from beside Saul's head, and they made off. No one saw, no one knew, no one woke up; they were all asleep, for a deep sleep from the Lord had fallen on them.

David crossed to the other side and halted on the top of the mountain a long way off; there was a wide space between them. David then called out, "Here is the king's spear. Let one of the soldiers come across and take it. The Lord repays everyone for his uprightness and loyalty. Today the Lord put you in my power, but I would not raise my hand against the Lord's anointed."

Psalm   Psalm 102

R. **The Lord is compassion and love.**

1. My soul, give thanks to the Lord,
   all my being, bless his holy name.
   My soul, give thanks to the Lord
   and never forget all his blessings. R.

2. It is he who forgives all your guilt,
   who heals every one of your ills,
   who redeems your life from the grave,
   who crowns you with love and compassion. R.

3. The Lord is compassion and love,
   slow to anger and rich in mercy.
   He does not treat us according to our sins
   nor repay us according to our faults. R.

4. As far as the east is from the west
   so far does he remove our sins.
   As a father has compassion on his sons,
   the Lord has pity on those who fear him. R.

Second Reading   1 Corinthians 15:45-49
We who have been modelled on the earthly man will be modelled on the heavenly man.

The first man, Adam, as scripture says, became a living soul; but the last Adam has become a life-giving spirit. That is, first the one with the soul, not the spirit, and after that, the one with the spirit.

The first man, being from the earth, is earthly by nature; the second man is from heaven. As this earthly man was, so are we on earth; and as the heavenly man is, so are we in heaven. And we, who have been modelled on the earthly man, will be modelled on the heavenly man.

Gospel Acclamation
Alleluia, alleluia!
Open our heart, O Lord,
to accept the words of your Son.
Alleluia!

cf. Acts 16:14

or

Alleluia, alleluia!
I give you a new commandment:
love one another,
just as I have loved you,
says the Lord.
Alleluia!

John 13:34

Gospel   Luke 6:27-38
Be compassionate as your Father is compassionate.
Jesus said to his disciples: "I say this to you who are listening: Love your enemies, do good to those who hate you, bless those who curse you, pray for those who treat you badly. To the man who slaps you on one cheek, present the other cheek too; to the man who takes your cloak from you, do not refuse your tunic. Give to everyone who asks you, and do not ask for your property back from the man who robs you. Treat others as you would like them to treat you. If you love those who love you, what thanks can you expect? Even sinners love those who love them. And if you do good to those who do good to you, what thanks can you expect? For even sinners do that much. And if you lend to those from whom you hope to receive, what thanks can you expect? Even sinners lend to sinners to get back the same amount. Instead, love your enemies and do good, and lend without any hope of return. You will have a great reward, and you will be sons of the Most High, for he himself is kind to the ungrateful and the wicked.

"Be compassionate as your Father is compassionate. Do not judge, and you will not be judged yourselves; do not condemn, and you will not be condemned yourselves; grant pardon, and you will be pardoned. Give, and there will be gifts for you: a full measure, pressed down, shaken together, and running over, will be poured into your lap; because the amount you measure out is the amount you will be given back."

The Creed is said.

Prayer over the Offerings
As we celebrate your mysteries, O Lord,
with the observance that is your due,
we humbly ask you,
that what we offer to the honour of your majesty
may profit us for salvation.
Through Christ our Lord.

Preface I-VIII of the Sundays in Ordinary Time, pp. 499-502.

Communion Antiphon
I will recount all your wonders,
I will rejoice in you and be glad,
and sing psalms to your name, O Most High.   Psalm 9:2-3

or

Lord, I have come to believe that you are the Christ,
the Son of the living God, who is coming into this world.
                                                    John 11:27

Prayer after Communion
Grant, we pray, almighty God,
that we may experience the effects of the salvation
which is pledged to us by these mysteries.
Through Christ our Lord.

EIGHTH SUNDAY IN ORDINARY TIME – C

Words flow from what is in the heart.
If we are filled with the love of God, then we will judge mercifully. Too often
we are negative in our criticism of the petty faults of others, forgetting that we
too are imperfect. We can turn to Christ in our weakness, knowing that in the
Lord we can never labour in vain.

Entrance Antiphon
The Lord became my protector.
He brought me out to a place of freedom;
he saved me because he delighted in me.   cf. Psalm 17:19-20

The Gloria is said or sung.

Collect
Grant us, O Lord, we pray,
that the course of our world
may be directed by your peaceful rule
and that your Church may rejoice,
untroubled in her devotion.
Through our Lord Jesus Christ, your Son,
who lives and reigns with you in the unity of the Holy Spirit,
one God, for ever and ever.

First Reading   Ecclesiasticus 27:4-7
Do not praise a man before he has spoken.
In a shaken sieve the rubbish is left behind,
so too the defects of a man appear in his talk.
The kiln tests the work of the potter,
the test of a man is in his conversation.
The orchard where the tree grows is judged on the quality of its
   fruit,
similarly a man's words betray what he feels.
Do not praise a man before he has spoken,
since this is the test of men.

Psalm   Psalm 91

R. **It is good to give you thanks, O Lord.**

1. It is good to give thanks to the Lord,
    to make music to your name, O Most High,
    to proclaim your love in the morning
    and your truth in the watches of the night. R.

2. The just will flourish like the palm-tree
    and grow like a Lebanon cedar. R.

3. Planted in the house of the Lord
    they will flourish in the courts of our God,
    still bearing fruit when they are old,
    still full of sap, still green,
    to proclaim that the Lord is just.
    In him, my rock, there is no wrong. R.

Second Reading   1 Corinthians 15:54-58
He has given us the victory through our Lord Jesus Christ.
When this perishable nature has put on imperishability, and when
this mortal nature has put on immortality, then the words of
scripture will come true: Death is swallowed up in victory. Death,
where is your victory? Death, where is your sting? Now the sting
of death is sin, and sin gets its power from the Law. So let us thank
God for giving us the victory through our Lord Jesus Christ.

   Never give in then, my dear brothers, never admit defeat; keep on
working at the Lord's work always, knowing that, in the Lord, you
cannot be labouring in vain.

Gospel Acclamation
Alleluia, alleluia!
Open our heart, O Lord,
to accept the words of your Son.
Alleluia!   cf. Acts 16:14

or

Alleluia, alleluia!
You will shine in the world like bright stars
because you are offering it the word of life.
Alleluia!

Philippians 2:15-16

Gospel   Luke 6:39-45
A man's words flow out of what fills his heart.

Jesus told a parable to his disciples, "Can one blind man guide another? Surely both will fall into a pit? The disciple is not superior to his teacher; the fully trained disciple will always be like his teacher. Why do you observe the splinter in your brother's eye and never notice the plank in your own? How can you say to your brother, 'Brother, let me take out the splinter that is in your eye,' when you cannot see the plank in your own? Hypocrite! Take the plank out of your own eye first, and then you will see clearly enough to take out the splinter that is in your brother's eye.

"There is no sound tree that produces rotten fruit, nor again a rotten tree that produces sound fruit. For every tree can be told by its own fruit: people do not pick figs from thorns, nor gather grapes from brambles. A good man draws what is good from the store of goodness in his heart; a bad man draws what is bad from the store of badness. For a man's words flow out of what fills his heart."

The Creed is said.

Prayer over the Offerings
O God, who provide gifts to be offered to your name
and count our oblations as signs
of our desire to serve you with devotion,
we ask of your mercy
that what you grant as the source of merit
may also help us to attain merit's reward.
Through Christ our Lord.

Preface I-VIII of the Sundays in Ordinary Time, pp. 499-502.

Communion Antiphon
I will sing to the Lord who has been bountiful with me,
sing psalms to the name of the Lord Most High.   cf. Psalm 12:6

or

Behold, I am with you always,
even to the end of the age, says the Lord.   Matthew 28:20

Prayer after Communion
Nourished by your saving gifts,
we beseech your mercy, Lord,
that by this same Sacrament
with which you feed us in the present age,
you may make us partakers of life eternal.
Through Christ our Lord.

NINTH SUNDAY IN ORDINARY TIME – C

God has no favourites.
The Holy Spirit pours God's grace not only upon Christians but also on people outside the Church. God loves everyone, and wants all to be saved. Just as Jesus did not find faith among his own people of such quality and depth as that of the centurion, so too we find Christian virtues outside the fold of the Church. We praise the Lord for his goodness to all people.

Entrance Antiphon
Turn to me and have mercy on me, O Lord,
for I am alone and poor.
See my lowliness and suffering
and take away all my sins, my God. cf. Psalm 24:16. 18

The Gloria is said or sung.

Collect
O God, whose providence never fails in its design,
keep from us, we humbly beseech you,
all that might harm us
and grant all that works for our good.
Through our Lord Jesus Christ, your Son,
who lives and reigns with you in the unity of the Holy Spirit,
one God, for ever and ever.

First Reading 1 Kings 8:41-43
If a foreigner comes, grant all he asks.
Solomon stood before the altar of the Lord and, stretching out his hands towards heaven, said:
"If a foreigner, not belonging to your people Israel, comes from a distant country for the sake of your name – for men will hear of your name, of your mighty hand and outstretched arm – if he comes and prays in this Temple, hear from heaven where your home is,

and grant all the foreigner asks, so that all the peoples of the earth may come to know your name and, like your people Israel, revere you, and know that your name is given to the Temple I have built."

Psalm   Psalm 116

R. **Go out to the whole world**
   and proclaim the Good News.

or **Alleluia!**

1. O praise the Lord, all you nations,
   acclaim him all you peoples! R.

2. Strong is his love for us;
   he is faithful for ever. R.

Second Reading   Galatians 1:1-2. 6-10

If I still wanted men's approval, I should not be a servant of Christ.

From Paul to the churches of Galatia, and from all the brothers who are here with me, an apostle who does not owe his authority to men or his appointment to any human being but who has been appointed by Jesus Christ and by God the Father who raised Jesus from the dead.

I am astonished at the promptness with which you have turned away from the one who called you and have decided to follow a different version of the Good News. Not that there can be more than one Good News; it is merely that some troublemakers among you want to change the Good News of Christ; and let me warn you that if anyone preaches a version of the Good News different from the one we have already preached to you, whether it be ourselves or an angel from heaven, he is to be condemned. I am only repeating what we told you before: if anyone preaches a version of the Good News different from the one you have already heard, he is to be condemned. So now whom am I trying to please – man, or God? Would you say it is men's approval I am looking for? If I still wanted that, I should not be what I am – a servant of Christ.

Gospel Acclamation

Alleluia, alleluia!
The Word was made flesh and lived among us;
to all who did accept him
he gave power to become children of God.
Alleluia!

John 1:14. 12

or

Alleluia, alleluia!
God loved the world so much
that he gave his only Son
so that anyone who believes in him
may have eternal life.
Alleluia!

John 3:16

Gospel   Luke 7:1-10

Not even in Israel have I found faith like this.

When Jesus had come to the end of all he wanted the people to hear, he went into Capernaum. A centurion there had a servant, a favourite of his, who was sick and near death. Having heard about Jesus he sent some Jewish elders to him to ask him to come and heal his servant. When they came to Jesus they pleaded earnestly with him. "He deserves this of you," they said, "because he is friendly towards our people; in fact, he is the one who built the synagogue." So Jesus went with them, and was not very far from the house when the centurion sent word to him by some friends: "Sir," he said, "do not put yourself to trouble; because I am not worthy to have you under my roof; and for this same reason I did not presume to come to you myself; but give the word and let my servant be cured. For I am under authority myself, and have soldiers under me; and I say to one man: Go, and he goes; to another: Come here, and he comes; to my servant: Do this, and he does it." When Jesus heard these words he was astonished at him and, turning round, said to the crowd following him, "I tell you, not even in Israel have I found faith like this." And when the messengers got back to the house they found the servant in perfect health.

The Creed is said.

Prayer over the Offerings
Trusting in your compassion, O Lord,
we come eagerly with our offerings to your sacred altar,
that, through the purifying action of your grace,
we may be cleansed by the very mysteries we serve.
Through Christ our Lord.

Preface I-VIII of the Sundays in Ordinary Time, pp. 499-502.

Communion Antiphon
To you I call, for you will surely heed me, O God;
turn your ear to me; hear my words.   cf. Psalm 16:6

or

Amen, I say to you: Whatever you ask for in prayer,
believe you will receive it,
and it will be yours, says the Lord.   Mark 11:23. 24

Prayer after Communion
Govern by your Spirit, we pray, O Lord,
those you feed with the Body and Blood of your Son,
that, professing you not just in word or in speech,
but also in works and in truth,
we may merit to enter the Kingdom of Heaven.
Through Christ our Lord.

TENTH SUNDAY IN ORDINARY TIME – C

Christ the restorer of life.
Christ restores us to life through his own Death and Resurrection. He has
pity on our human nature, weakened by sin. In response to his words, like
the young man at Nain, we rise up to live the new life of grace. The Lord's
kindness to us is what we preach to those who do not believe in him. We praise
the Lord who has rescued us from sin and death.

Entrance Antiphon

The Lord is my light and my salvation; whom shall I fear?
The Lord is the stronghold of my life; whom should I dread?
When those who do evil draw near, they stumble and fall.

cf. Psalm 26:1-2

The Gloria is said or sung.

Collect

O God, from whom all good things come,
grant that we, who call on you in our need,
may at your prompting discern what is right,
and by your guidance do it.
Through our Lord Jesus Christ, your Son,
who lives and reigns with you in the unity of the Holy Spirit,
one God, for ever and ever.

First Reading   1 Kings 17:17-24

Look, your son is alive.

The son of the mistress of the house fell sick; his illness was so
severe that in the end he had no breath left in him. And the woman
said to Elijah, "What quarrel have you with me, man of God? Have
you come here to bring my sins home to me and to kill my son?"
"Give me your son," he said, and taking him from her lap, carried
him to the upper room where he was staying and laid him on his

own bed. He cried out to the Lord, "Lord my God, do you mean to bring grief to the widow who is looking after me by killing her son?" He stretched himself on the child three times and cried out to the Lord, "Lord my God, may the soul of this child, I beg you, come into him again!" The Lord heard the prayer of Elijah and the soul of the child returned to him again and he revived. Elijah took the child, brought him down from the upper room into the house, and gave him to his mother. "Look," Elijah said, "your son is alive." And the woman replied, "Now I know you are a man of God and the word of the Lord in your mouth is truth itself."

Psalm   Psalm 29

R. **I will praise you, Lord,**
      you have rescued me.

1. I will praise you, Lord, you have rescued me
   and have not let my enemies rejoice over me.
   O Lord, you have raised my soul from the dead,
   restored me to life from those who sink into the grave. R.

2. Sing psalms to the Lord, you who love him,
   give thanks to his holy name.
   His anger lasts a moment; his favour all through life.
   At night there are tears, but joy comes with dawn. R.

3. The Lord listened and had pity.
   The Lord came to my help.
   For me you have changed my mourning into dancing;
   O Lord my God, I will thank you for ever. R.

Second Reading   Galatians 1:11-19
God revealed his Son to me, so that I might preach the Good News about him to the pagans.
The Good News I preached is not a human message that I was given by men, it is something I learnt only through a revelation of Jesus Christ. You must have heard of my career as a practising Jew, how merciless I was in persecuting the Church of God, how

much damage I did to it, how I stood out among other Jews of my generation, and how enthusiastic I was for the traditions of my ancestors.

Then God, who had specially chosen me while I was still in my mother's womb, called me through his grace and chose to reveal his Son in me, so that I might preach the Good News about him to the pagans. I did not stop to discuss this with any human being, nor did I go up to Jerusalem to see those who were already apostles before me, but I went off to Arabia at once and later went straight back from there to Damascus. Even when after three years I went up to Jerusalem to visit Cephas and stayed with him for fifteen days, I did not see any of the other apostles; I only saw James, the brother of the Lord.

Gospel Acclamation
Alleluia, alleluia!
May the Father of our Lord Jesus Christ
enlighten the eyes of our mind,
so that we can see what hope his call holds for us.
Alleluia!   cf. Ephesians 1:17. 18

or

Alleluia, alleluia!
A great prophet has appeared among us;
God has visited his people.
Alleluia!   Luke 7:16

Gospel   Luke 7:11-17
Young man, I tell you to get up.
Jesus went to a town called Nain, accompanied by his disciples and a great number of people. When he was near the gate of the town it happened that a dead man was being carried out for burial, the only son of his mother, and she was a widow. And a considerable number of the townspeople were with her. When the Lord saw her he felt sorry for her. "Do not cry," he said. Then he went up and put his hand on the bier and the bearers stood still, and he said, "Young man, I tell you to get up." And the dead man sat up and began to

walk, and Jesus gave him to his mother. Everyone was filled with awe and praised God saying, "A great prophet has appeared among us; God has visited his people." And this opinion of him spread throughout Judaea and all over the countryside.

The Creed is said.

Prayer over the Offerings
Look kindly upon our service, O Lord, we pray,
that what we offer
may be an acceptable oblation to you
and lead us to grow in charity.
Through Christ our Lord.

Preface I-VIII of the Sundays in Ordinary Time, pp. 499-502.

Communion Antiphon
The Lord is my rock, my fortress, and my deliverer;
my God is my saving strength.   Psalm 17:3

or

God is love, and whoever abides in love
abides in God, and God in him.   1 John 4:16

Prayer after Communion
May your healing work, O Lord,
free us, we pray, from doing evil
and lead us to what is right.
Through Christ our Lord.

ELEVENTH SUNDAY IN ORDINARY TIME – C

Christ the forgiver of sins.
We are all sinners and come to Christ for forgiveness. It is faith in Christ's
saving power, rather than any observance of the law, which brings pardon for
sins. Forgiveness is given to those who love, and if we love Christ then we are
living a life of peace with God. Once we die to sin, then Christ lives in us.

Entrance Antiphon
O Lord, hear my voice, for I have called to you; be my help.
Do not abandon or forsake me, O God, my Saviour!

cf. Psalm 26:7. 9

The Gloria is said or sung.

Collect
O God, strength of those who hope in you,
graciously hear our pleas,
and, since without you mortal frailty can do nothing,
grant us always the help of your grace,
that in following your commands
we may please you by our resolve and our deeds.
Through our Lord Jesus Christ, your Son,
who lives and reigns with you in the unity of the Holy Spirit,
one God, for ever and ever.

First Reading   2 Samuel 12:7-10. 13
The Lord forgives your sin; you are not to die.
Nathan said to David, "The Lord the God of Israel says this, 'I
anointed you king over Israel; I delivered you from the hands of
Saul; I gave your master's house to you, his wives into your arms;
I gave you the House of Israel and of Judah; and if this were not
enough, I would add as much again for you. Why have you shown
contempt for the Lord, doing what displeases him? You have struck

down Uriah the Hittite with the sword, taken his wife for your own, and killed him with the sword of the Ammonites. So now the sword will never be far from your House, since you have shown contempt for me and taken the wife of Uriah the Hittite to be your wife.'"

David said to Nathan, "I have sinned against the Lord." Then Nathan said to David, "The Lord, for his part, forgives your sin; you are not to die."

Psalm   **Psalm 31**

R. **Forgive, Lord, the guilt of my sin.**

1. Happy the man whose offence is forgiven,
   whose sin is remitted.
   O happy the man to whom the Lord
   imputes no guilt,
   in whose spirit is no guile. R.

2. But now I have acknowledged my sins:
   my guilt I did not hide.
   I said: "I will confess
   my offence to the Lord."
   And you, Lord, have forgiven
   the guilt of my sin. R.

3. You are my hiding place, O Lord;
   you save me from distress.
   You surround me with cries of deliverance. R.

4. Rejoice, rejoice in the Lord,
   exult, you just!
   O come, ring out your joy,
   all you upright of heart. R.

Second Reading   **Galatians 2:16. 19-21**
I live now, not with my own life but with the life of Christ who lives in me.

We acknowledge that what makes a man righteous is not obedience to the Law, but faith in Jesus Christ. We had to become believers in Christ Jesus no less than you had, and now we hold that faith in Christ rather than fidelity to the Law is what justifies us, and that no one can be justified by keeping the Law. In other words, through the Law I am dead to the Law, so that now I can live for God. I have been crucified with Christ, and I live now not with my own life but with the life of Christ who lives in me. The life I now live in this body I live in faith: faith in the Son of God who loved me and who sacrificed himself for my sake. I cannot bring myself to give up God's gift: if the Law can justify us, there is no point in the death of Christ.

Gospel Acclamation
Alleluia, alleluia!
I am the Way, the Truth and the Life, says the Lord;
no one can come to the Father except through me.
Alleluia!   John 14:6

or

Alleluia, alleluia!
God so loved us when he sent his Son
to be the sacrifice that takes our sins away.
Alleluia!   1 John 4:10

Gospel   Luke 7:36 – 8:3
Her many sins have been forgiven, or she would not have shown such great love.

One of the Pharisees invited Jesus to a meal. When he arrived at the Pharisee's house and took his place at table, a woman came in, who had a bad name in the town. She had heard he was dining with the Pharisee and had brought with her an alabaster jar of ointment. She waited behind him at his feet, weeping, and her tears fell on his feet, and she wiped them away with her hair; then she covered his feet with kisses and anointed them with the ointment.

When the Pharisee who had invited him saw this, he said to himself, "If this man were a prophet, he would know who this woman is that is touching him and what a bad name she has." Then Jesus took him up and said, "Simon, I have something to say to you." "Speak, Master," was the reply. "There was once a creditor who had two men in his debt; one owed him five hundred denarii, the other fifty. They were unable to pay, so he pardoned them both. Which of them will love him more?" "The one who was pardoned more, I suppose," answered Simon. Jesus said, "You are right."

Then he turned to the woman. "Simon," he said, "you see this woman? I came into your house, and you poured no water over my feet, but she has poured out her tears over my feet and wiped them away with her hair. You gave me no kiss, but she has been covering my feet with kisses ever since I came in. You did not anoint my head with oil, but she has anointed my feet with ointment. For this reason I tell you that her sins, her many sins, must have been forgiven her, or she would not have shown such great love. It is the man who is forgiven little who shows little love." Then he said to her, "Your sins are forgiven." Those who were with him at table began to say to themselves, "Who is this man, that he even forgives sins?" But he said to the woman, "Your faith has saved you; go in peace."

Now after this he made his way through towns and villages, preaching, and proclaiming the Good News of the kingdom of God. With him went the Twelve, as well as certain women who had been cured of evil spirits and ailments: Mary surnamed the Magdalene, from whom seven demons had gone out, Joanna the wife of Herod's steward Chuza, Susanna, and several others who provided for them out of their own resources.

The Creed is said.

Prayer over the Offerings
O God, who in the offerings presented here
provide for the twofold needs of human nature,
nourishing us with food
and renewing us with your Sacrament,
grant, we pray,
that the sustenance they provide
may not fail us in body or in spirit.
Through Christ our Lord.

Preface I-VIII of the Sundays in Ordinary Time, pp. 499-502.

Communion Antiphon
There is one thing I ask of the Lord, only this do I seek:
to live in the house of the Lord all the days of my life.   Psalm 26:4

or

Holy Father, keep in your name those you have given me,
that they may be one as we are one, says the Lord.   John 17:11

Prayer after Communion
As this reception of your Holy Communion, O Lord,
foreshadows the union of the faithful in you,
so may it bring about unity in your Church.
Through Christ our Lord.

TWELFTH SUNDAY IN ORDINARY TIME – C

The Son of Man is destined to suffer.
All followers of Jesus Christ can expect to suffer in this world. In this way
we unite ourselves with his sufferings and live out our baptism, which makes
us one with Christ. We may appear to lose our lives for Christ's sake but in
fact we are saving them for eternity. That is the paradox of Christian faith.

Entrance Antiphon

The Lord is the strength of his people,
a saving refuge for the one he has anointed.
Save your people, Lord, and bless your heritage,
and govern them for ever.   cf. Psalm 27:8-9

The Gloria is said or sung.

Collect

Grant, O Lord,
that we may always revere and love your holy name,
for you never deprive of your guidance
those you set firm on the foundation of your love.
Through our Lord Jesus Christ, your Son,
who lives and reigns with you in the unity of the Holy Spirit,
one God, for ever and ever.

First Reading   Zechariah 12:10-11; 13:1
They will look on the one whom they have pierced.
It is the Lord who speaks: "Over the House of David and the citizens
of Jerusalem I will pour out a spirit of kindness and prayer. They
will look on the one whom they have pierced; they will mourn for
him as for an only son, and weep for him as people weep for a first-
born child. When that day comes, there will be great mourning
in Judah, like the mourning of Hadad-rimmon in the plain of
Megiddo. When that day comes, a fountain will be opened for the
House of David and the citizens of Jerusalem, for sin and impurity."

Psalm   Psalm 62

R. **For you my soul is thirsting,**
     O God, my God.

1. O God, you are my God, for you I long;
   for you my soul is thirsting.
   My body pines for you
   like a dry, weary land without water. R.

2. So I gaze on you in the sanctuary
   to see your strength and your glory.
   For your love is better than life,
   my lips will speak your praise. R.

3. So I will bless you all my life,
   in your name I will lift up my hands.
   My soul shall be filled as with a banquet,
   my mouth shall praise you with joy. R.

4. For you have been my help;
   in the shadow of your wings I rejoice.
   My soul clings to you;
   your right hand holds me fast. R.

Second Reading   Galatians 3:26-29
All baptised in Christ, you have all clothed yourselves in Christ.
You are, all of you, sons of God through faith in Christ Jesus. All
baptised in Christ, you have all clothed yourselves in Christ, and
there are no more distinctions between Jew and Greek, slave and
free, male and female, but all of you are one in Christ Jesus. Merely
by belonging to Christ you are the posterity of Abraham, the heirs
he was promised.

Gospel Acclamation
Alleluia, alleluia!
I am the light of the world, says the Lord,
anyone who follows me
will have the light of life.
Alleluia!   John 8:12

or

Alleluia, alleluia!
The sheep that belong to me listen to my voice,
says the Lord.
I know them and they follow me.
Alleluia.   John 10:27

Gospel   Luke 9:18-24
You are the Christ of God. The Son of Man is destined to suffer
grievously.
One day when Jesus was praying alone in the presence of his
disciples he put this question to them, "Who do the crowds say
I am?" And they answered, "John the Baptist; others Elijah; and
others say one of the ancient prophets come back to life." "But you,"
he said, "who do you say I am?" It was Peter who spoke up. "The
Christ of God," he said. But he gave them strict orders not to tell
anyone anything about this.

"The Son of Man", he said, "is destined to suffer grievously, to be
rejected by the elders and chief priests and scribes and to be put to
death, and to be raised up on the third day."

Then to all he said, "If anyone wants to be a follower of mine, let
him renounce himself and take up his cross every day and follow
me. For anyone who wants to save his life will lose it; but anyone
who loses his life for my sake, that man will save it."

The Creed is said.

Prayer over the Offerings

Receive, O Lord, the sacrifice of conciliation and praise
and grant that, cleansed by its action,
we may make offering of a heart pleasing to you.
Through Christ our Lord.

Preface I-VIII of the Sundays in Ordinary Time, pp. 499-502.

Communion Antiphon

The eyes of all look to you, Lord,
and you give them their food in due season.   Psalm 144:15

or

I am the Good Shepherd,
and I lay down my life for my sheep, says the Lord.   John 10:11. 15

Prayer after Communion

Renewed and nourished
by the Sacred Body and Precious Blood of your Son,
we ask of your mercy, O Lord,
that what we celebrate with constant devotion
may be our sure pledge of redemption.
Through Christ our Lord.

THIRTEENTH SUNDAY IN ORDINARY TIME – C

I will follow you wherever you go.
When Christ calls us to follow him, he wants us to make no excuses but to
follow immediately. His service is perfect freedom and it is in the service of
each other through the love of Christ that we discover the true meaning of
liberty. God's Spirit will keep us close to Christ. We have nothing to fear, since
love casts out fear.

Entrance Antiphon
All peoples, clap your hands.
Cry to God with shouts of joy!   Psalm 46:2

The Gloria is said or sung.

Collect
O God, who through the grace of adoption
chose us to be children of light,
grant, we pray,
that we may not be wrapped in the darkness of error
but always be seen to stand in the bright light of truth.
Through our Lord Jesus Christ, your Son,
who lives and reigns with you in the unity of the Holy Spirit,
one God, for ever and ever.

First Reading   1 Kings 19:16. 19-21
Elisha rose and followed Elijah.

The Lord said to Elijah: "Go, you are to anoint Elisha son of Shaphat,
of Abel Meholah, as prophet to succeed you."

Leaving there, Elijah came on Elisha son of Shaphat as he was
ploughing behind twelve yoke of oxen, he himself being with the
twelfth. Elijah passed near to him and threw his cloak over him.
Elisha left his oxen and ran after Elijah. "Let me kiss my father and
mother, then I will follow you," he said. Elijah answered, "Go, go

back; for have I done anything to you?" Elisha turned away, took the pair of oxen and slaughtered them. He used the plough for cooking the oxen, then gave to his men, who ate. He then rose, and followed Elijah and became his servant.

Psalm   Psalm 15

R. **O Lord, it is you who are my portion.**

1. Preserve me, God, I take refuge in you.
   I say to the Lord: "You are my God."
   O Lord, it is you who are my portion and cup;
   it is you yourself who are my prize. R.

2. I will bless the Lord who gives me counsel,
   who even at night directs my heart.
   I keep the Lord ever in my sight:
   since he is at my right hand, I shall stand firm. R.

3. And so my heart rejoices, my soul is glad;
   even my body shall rest in safety.
   For you will not leave my soul among the dead,
   nor let your beloved know decay. R.

4. You will show me the path of life,
   the fullness of joy in your presence,
   at your right hand happiness for ever. R.

Second Reading   Galatians 5:1. 13-18
You were called to liberty.

When Christ freed us, he meant us to remain free. Stand firm, therefore, and do not submit again to the yoke of slavery.

My brothers, you were called, as you know, to liberty; but be careful, or this liberty will provide an opening for self-indulgence. Serve one another, rather, in works of love, since the whole of the Law is summarised in a single command: Love your neighbour as yourself. If you go snapping at each other and tearing each other to pieces, you had better watch or you will destroy the whole community.

Let me put it like this: if you are guided by the Spirit you will be in no danger of yielding to self-indulgence, since self-indulgence is the opposite of the Spirit, the Spirit is totally against such a thing, and it is precisely because the two are so opposed that you do not always carry out your good intentions. If you are led by the Spirit, no law can touch you.

Gospel Acclamation
Alleluia, alleluia!
Speak, Lord, your servant is listening:
you have the message of eternal life.
Alleluia!   1 Samuel 3:9; John 6:68

Gospel   Luke 9:51-62
Jesus resolutely took the road for Jerusalem. I will follow you wherever you go.

As the time drew near for him to be taken up to heaven, Jesus resolutely took the road for Jerusalem and sent messengers ahead of him. These set out, and they went into a Samaritan village to make preparations for him, but the people would not receive him because he was making for Jerusalem. Seeing this, the disciples James and John said, "Lord, do you want us to call down fire from heaven to burn them up?" But he turned and rebuked them, and they went off to another village.

As they travelled along they met a man on the road who said to him, "I will follow you wherever you go." Jesus answered, "Foxes have holes and the birds of the air have nests, but the Son of Man has nowhere to lay his head."

Another to whom he said, "Follow me," replied, "Let me go and bury my father first." But he answered, "Leave the dead to bury their dead; your duty is to go and spread the news of the kingdom of God."

Another said, "I will follow you, sir, but first let me go and say good-bye to my people at home." Jesus said to him, "Once the hand is laid on the plough, no one who looks back is fit for the kingdom of God."

The Creed is said.

Prayer over the Offerings

O God, who graciously accomplish
the effects of your mysteries,
grant, we pray,
that the deeds by which we serve you
may be worthy of these sacred gifts.
Through Christ our Lord.

Preface I-VIII of the Sundays in Ordinary Time, pp. 499-502.

Communion Antiphon

Bless the Lord, O my soul,
and all within me, his holy name.   cf. Psalm 102:1

or

O Father, I pray for them, that they may be one in us,
that the world may believe that you have sent me, says the Lord.
                                                     John 17:20-21

Prayer after Communion

May this divine sacrifice we have offered and received
fill us with life, O Lord, we pray,
so that, bound to you in lasting charity,
we may bear fruit that lasts for ever.
Through Christ our Lord.

FOURTEENTH SUNDAY IN ORDINARY TIME – C

Christ is our peace.
The Gospel message is one of peace. Wherever we go, we are to bring the peace of Christ with us but we can only do this when we have learned to suffer like him. Then we will lead an entirely new life and peace will flow like a river from us to everyone around us.

Entrance Antiphon
Your merciful love, O God,
we have received in the midst of your temple.
Your praise, O God, like your name,
reaches the ends of the earth;
your right hand is filled with saving justice.   cf. Psalm 47:10-11

The Gloria is said or sung.

Collect
O God, who in the abasement of your Son
have raised up a fallen world,
fill your faithful with holy joy,
for on those you have rescued from slavery to sin
you bestow eternal gladness.
Through our Lord Jesus Christ, your Son,
who lives and reigns with you in the unity of the Holy Spirit,
one God, for ever and ever.

First Reading   Isaiah 66:10-14
Towards her I send flowing peace, like a river.

Rejoice, Jerusalem,
be glad for her, all you who love her!
Rejoice, rejoice for her,
all you who mourned her!

That you may be suckled, filled,
from her consoling breast,
that you may savour with delight
her glorious breasts.

For thus says the Lord:
Now towards her I send flowing
peace, like a river,
and like a stream in spate
the glory of the nations.

At her breast will her nurslings be carried
and fondled in her lap.
Like a son comforted by his mother
will I comfort you.
And by Jerusalem you will be comforted.

At the sight your heart will rejoice,
and your bones flourish like the grass.
To his servants the Lord will reveal his hand.

Psalm   Psalm 65

R. **Cry out with joy to God all the earth.**

1. Cry out with joy to God all the earth,
   O sing to the glory of his name.
   O render him glorious praise.
   Say to God: "How tremendous your deeds!" R.

2. "Before you all the earth shall bow;
   shall sing to you, sing to your name!"
   Come and see the works of God,
   tremendous his deeds among men. R.

3. He turned the sea into dry land,
   they passed through the river dry-shod.
   Let our joy then be in him;
   he rules for ever by his might. R.

4. Come and hear, all who fear God.
   I will tell what he did for my soul.
   Blessed be God who did not reject my prayer
   nor withhold his love from me. R.

Second Reading   **Galatians 6:14-18**

The marks on my body are those of the Lord Jesus.

The only thing I can boast about is the cross of our Lord Jesus Christ, through whom the world is crucified to me, and I to the world. It does not matter if a person is circumcised or not; what matters is for him to become an altogether new creature. Peace and mercy to all who follow this rule, who form the Israel of God.

I want no more trouble from anybody after this; the marks on my body are those of Jesus. The grace of our Lord Jesus Christ be with your spirit, my brothers. Amen.

Gospel Acclamation

Alleluia, alleluia!

I call you friends, says the Lord,

because I have made known to you

everything I have learnt from my Father.

Alleluia!   John 15:15

or

Alleluia, alleluia!

May the peace of Christ

reign in your hearts,

because it is for this that you were called together

as parts of one body.

Alleluia!   Colossians 3:15, 16

Gospel   **Luke 10:1-12. 17-20**

Your peace will rest on that man.

The Lord appointed seventy-two others and sent them out ahead of him, in pairs, to all the towns and places he himself was to visit. He said to them, "The harvest is rich but the labourers are few, so ask the Lord of the harvest to send labourers to his harvest. Start off now, but remember, I am sending you out like lambs among wolves. Carry no purse, no haversack, no sandals. Salute no one on the road. Whatever house you go into, let your first words be, 'Peace to this house!' And if a man of peace lives there, your peace will go and rest on him; if not, it will come back to you. Stay in the same house, taking what food and drink they have to offer, for the labourer deserves his wages; do not move from house to house.

Whenever you go into a town where they make you welcome, eat what is set before you. Cure those in it who are sick, and say, 'The kingdom of God is very near to you.'

But whenever you enter a town and they do not make you welcome, go out into its streets and say, 'We wipe off the very dust of your town that clings to our feet, and leave it with you. Yet be sure of this: the kingdom of God is very near.' I tell you, on that day it will not go as hard with Sodom as with that town."

The seventy-two came back rejoicing. "Lord," they said, "even the devils submit to us when we use your name." He said to them, "I watched Satan fall like lightning from heaven. Yes, I have given you power to tread underfoot serpents and scorpions and the whole strength of the enemy; nothing shall ever hurt you. Yet do not rejoice that the spirits submit to you; rejoice rather that your names are written in heaven."

The Creed is said.

Prayer over the Offerings
May this oblation dedicated to your name
purify us, O Lord,
and day by day bring our conduct
closer to the life of heaven.
Through Christ our Lord.

Preface I-VIII of the Sundays in Ordinary Time, pp. 499-502.

Communion Antiphon
Taste and see that the Lord is good;
blessed the man who seeks refuge in him.   Psalm 33:9
or
Come to me, all who labour and are burdened,
and I will refresh you, says the Lord.   Matthew 11:28

Prayer after Communion
Grant, we pray, O Lord,
that, having been replenished by such great gifts,
we may gain the prize of salvation
and never cease to praise you.
Through Christ our Lord.

FIFTEENTH SUNDAY IN ORDINARY TIME – C

Love your neighbour as yourself.

God is as near to us as our own heart. If we wish to become like Christ then we will serve all people without distinction of race, colour or creed. We will become reconcilers and love God with all our heart. In this way we will become the Good Samaritans of a wounded world.

Entrance Antiphon

As for me, in justice I shall behold your face;
I shall be filled with the vision of your glory. cf. Psalm 16:15

The Gloria is said or sung.

Collect

O God, who show the light of your truth
to those who go astray,
so that they may return to the right path,
give all who for the faith they profess
are accounted Christians
the grace to reject whatever is contrary to the name of Christ
and to strive after all that does it honour.
Through our Lord Jesus Christ, your Son,
who lives and reigns with you in the unity of the Holy Spirit,
one God, for ever and ever.

First Reading   Deuteronomy 30:10-14

The Word is very near to you for your observance.

Moses said to the people: "Obey the voice of the Lord your God, keeping those commandments and laws of his that are written in the Book of this Law, and you shall return to the Lord your God with all your heart and soul.

"For this Law that I enjoin on you today is not beyond your strength or beyond your reach. It is not in heaven, so that you need to wonder, 'Who will go up to heaven for us and bring it down to us, so that we may hear it and keep it?' Nor is it beyond the seas, so that you need to wonder, 'Who will cross the seas for us and bring it back to us, so that we may hear it and keep it?' No, the Word is very near to you, it is in your mouth and in your heart for your observance."

Psalm   Psalm 68

R. **Seek the Lord, you who are poor,**
      and your hearts will revive.

1. This is my prayer to you,
    my prayer for your favour.
    In your great love, answer me, O God,
    with your help that never fails:
    Lord, answer, for your love is kind;
    in your compassion, turn towards me. R.

2. As for me in my poverty and pain
    let your help, O God, lift me up.
    I will praise God's name with a song;
    I will glorify him with thanksgiving. R.

3. The poor when they see it will be glad
    and God-seeking hearts will revive;
    for the Lord listens to the needy
    and does not spurn his servants in their chains. R.

4. For God will bring help to Zion
    and rebuild the cities of Judah.
    The sons of his servants shall inherit it;
    those who love his name shall dwell there. R.

or   Psalm 18

R. **The precepts of the Lord**
      gladden the heart.

1. The law of the Lord is perfect,
    it revives the soul.
    The rule of the Lord is to be trusted,
    it gives wisdom to the simple. R.

2. The precepts of the Lord are right,
   they gladden the heart.
   The command of the Lord is clear,
   it gives light to the eyes. R.

3. The fear of the Lord is holy,
   abiding for ever.
   The decrees of the Lord are truth
   and all of them just. R.

4. They are more to be desired than gold,
   than the purest of gold
   and sweeter are they than honey,
   than honey from the comb. R.

Second Reading   Colossians 1:15-20

All things were created through Christ and for him.

Christ Jesus is the image of the unseen God
and the first-born of all creation,
for in him were created
all things in heaven and on earth:
everything visible and everything invisible,
Thrones, Dominations, Sovereignties, Powers –
all things were created through him and for him.
Before anything was created, he existed,
and he holds all things in unity.
Now the Church is his body,
he is its head.
As he is the Beginning,
he was first to be born from the dead,
so that he should be first in every way;
because God wanted all perfection
to be found in him
and all things to be reconciled through him and for him,
everything in heaven and everything on earth,
when he made peace
by his death on the cross.

Gospel Acclamation
Alleluia, alleluia!
The sheep that belong to me listen to my voice,
says the Lord,
I know them and they follow me.
Alleluia!   John 10:27

or

Alleluia, alleluia!
Your words are spirit, Lord,
and they are life:
you have the message of eternal life.
Alleluia!   cf. John 6:63. 68

Gospel   Luke 10:25-37
Who is my neighbour?

There was a lawyer who, to disconcert Jesus, stood up and said to him, "Master, what must I do to inherit eternal life?" He said to him, "What is written in the Law? What do you read there?" He replied, "You must love the Lord your God with all your heart, with all your soul, with all your strength, and with all your mind, and your neighbour as yourself." "You have answered right," said Jesus, "do this and life is yours."

But the man was anxious to justify himself and said to Jesus, "And who is my neighbour?" Jesus replied, "A man was once on his way down from Jerusalem to Jericho and fell into the hands of brigands; they took all he had, beat him and then made off, leaving him half dead. Now a priest happened to be travelling down the same road, but when he saw the man, he passed by on the other side. In the same way a Levite who came to the place saw him, and passed by on the other side. But a Samaritan traveller who came upon him was moved with compassion when he saw him. He went up and bandaged his wounds, pouring oil and wine on them. He then lifted him on to his mount, carried him to the inn and looked after him. Next day, he took out two denarii and handed them to the innkeeper. 'Look after him,' he said, 'and on my way back I will make good any extra expense you have.' Which of these three, do you think, proved himself a neighbour to the man who fell into the brigands' hands?" "The one who took pity on him," he replied. Jesus said to him, "Go, and do the same yourself."

The Creed is said.

Prayer over the Offerings
Look upon the offerings of the Church, O Lord,
as she makes her prayer to you,
and grant that, when consumed by those who believe,
they may bring ever greater holiness.
Through Christ our Lord.

Preface I-VIII of the Sundays in Ordinary Time, pp. 499-502.

Communion Antiphon
The sparrow finds a home,
and the swallow a nest for her young:
by your altars, O Lord of hosts, my King and my God.
Blessed are they who dwell in your house,
for ever singing your praise.   cf. Psalm 83:4-5

or

Whoever eats my flesh and drinks my blood
remains in me and I in him, says the Lord.   John 6:57

Prayer after Communion
Having consumed these gifts, we pray, O Lord,
that, by our participation in this mystery,
its saving effects upon us may grow.
Through Christ our Lord.

SIXTEENTH SUNDAY IN ORDINARY TIME – C

Christ our welcome guest.

Jesus Christ was welcomed by Martha and Mary in different ways. Martha was anxious to prepare a meal for him, while Mary kept him company, listening to all he had to say. Christ calls us to listen to him with love. It is love that opens our heart to his message when he comes to share his life with us.

Entrance Antiphon
See, I have God for my help.
The Lord sustains my soul.
I will sacrifice to you with willing heart,
and praise your name, O Lord, for it is good.   Psalm 53:6. 8

The Gloria is said or sung.

Collect
Show favour, O Lord, to your servants
and mercifully increase the gifts of your grace,
that, made fervent in hope, faith and charity,
they may be ever watchful in keeping your commands.
Through our Lord Jesus Christ, your Son,
who lives and reigns with you in the unity of the Holy Spirit,
one God, for ever and ever.

First Reading   Genesis 18:1-10
Lord, do not pass your servant by.

The Lord appeared to Abraham at the Oak of Mamre while he was sitting by the entrance of the tent during the hottest part of the day. He looked up, and there he saw three men standing near him. As soon as he saw them he ran from the entrance of the tent to meet them, and bowed to the ground. "My Lord," he said, "I beg you, if I find favour with you, kindly do not pass your servant by. A little water shall be brought; you shall wash your feet and lie down under the tree. Let me fetch a little bread and you shall refresh yourselves before going further. That is why you have come in your servant's direction." They replied, "Do as you say."

Abraham hastened to the tent to find Sarah. "Hurry," he said, "knead three bushels of flour and make loaves." Then running to the cattle Abraham took a fine and tender calf and gave it to the servant, who hurried to prepare it. Then taking cream, milk and the calf he had prepared, he laid all before them, and they ate while he remained standing near them under the tree.

"Where is your wife Sarah?" they asked him. "She is in the tent," he replied. Then his guest said, "I shall visit you again next year without fail, and your wife will then have a son."

Psalm   Psalm 14

R. **The just will live in the presence of the Lord.**

1. Lord, who shall dwell on your holy mountain?
   He who walks without fault;
   he who acts with justice
   and speaks the truth from his heart;
   he who does not slander with his tongue. R.

2. He who does no wrong to his brother,
   who casts no slur on his neighbour,
   who holds the godless in disdain,
   but honours those who fear the Lord. R.

3. He who keeps his pledge, come what may;
   who takes no interest on a loan
   and accepts no bribes against the innocent.
   Such a man will stand firm for ever. R.

Second Reading   Colossians 1:24-28
A mystery hidden for centuries has now been revealed to God's saints.

It makes me happy to suffer for you, as I am suffering now, and in my body to do what I can to make up all that has still to be undergone by Christ for the sake of his body, the Church. I became the servant of the Church when God made me responsible for delivering God's message to you, the message which was a mystery hidden for generations and centuries and has now been revealed to his saints. It was God's purpose to reveal it to them and to show all the rich glory of this mystery to pagans. The mystery is Christ among you, your hope of glory: this is the Christ we proclaim, this is the wisdom in which we thoroughly train everyone and instruct everyone, to make them all perfect in Christ.

Gospel Acclamation
Alleluia, alleluia!
Open our heart, O Lord,
to accept the words of your Son.
Alleluia!   cf. Acts 16:14

or

Alleluia, alleluia!
Blessed are those who,
with a noble and generous heart,
take the word of God to themselves
and yield a harvest through their perseverance.
Alleluia!   cf. Luke 8:15

Gospel   Luke 10:38-42
Martha welcomed Jesus into her house. Mary has chosen the better part.

Jesus came to a village, and a woman named Martha welcomed him into her house. She had a sister called Mary, who sat down at the Lord's feet and listened to him speaking. Now Martha who was distracted with all the serving said, "Lord, do you not care that my sister is leaving me to do the serving all by myself? Please tell her to help me." But the Lord answered: "Martha, Martha," he said, "you worry and fret about so many things, and yet few are needed, indeed only one. It is Mary who has chosen the better part; it is not to be taken from her."

The Creed is said.

Prayer over the Offerings
O God, who in the one perfect sacrifice
brought to completion varied offerings of the law,
accept, we pray, this sacrifice from your faithful servants
and make it holy, as you blessed the gifts of Abel,
so that what each has offered to the honour of your majesty
may benefit the salvation of all.
Through Christ our Lord.

Preface I-VIII of the Sundays in Ordinary Time, pp. 499-502.

Communion Antiphon
The Lord, the gracious, the merciful,
has made a memorial of his wonders;
he gives food to those who fear him.   Psalm 110:4-5

or

Behold, I stand at the door and knock, says the Lord.
If anyone hears my voice and opens the door to me,
I will enter his house and dine with him, and he with me.
                                                    Apocalypse 3:20

Prayer after Communion
Graciously be present to your people, we pray, O Lord,
and lead those you have imbued with heavenly mysteries
to pass from former ways to newness of life.
Through Christ our Lord.

SEVENTEENTH SUNDAY IN ORDINARY TIME – C

God is our Father.

Jesus teaches us to call God "Father" when we pray. Through Baptism we are made one with Christ; we too are children of God. We are taught to persist in our prayers, assured that God will answer us because he is our Father. Jesus tells us to ask until we receive and to seek until we find.

Entrance Antiphon

God is in his holy place,
God who unites those who dwell in his house;
he himself gives might and strength to his people.

cf. Psalm 67:6-7. 36

The Gloria is said or sung.

Collect

O God, protector of those who hope in you,
without whom nothing has firm foundation, nothing is holy,
bestow in abundance your mercy upon us
and grant that, with you as our ruler and guide,
we may use the good things that pass
in such a way as to hold fast even now
to those that ever endure.
Through our Lord Jesus Christ, your Son,
who lives and reigns with you in the unity of the Holy Spirit,
one God, for ever and ever.

First Reading   Genesis 18:20-32

I trust my Lord will not be angry, but give me leave to speak.

The Lord said, "How great an outcry there is against Sodom and Gomorrah! How grievous is their sin! I propose to go down and see whether or not they have done all that is alleged in the outcry against them that has come up to me. I am determined to know."

The men left there and went to Sodom while Abraham remained standing before the Lord. Approaching him he said, "Are you really going to destroy the just man with the sinner? Perhaps there are fifty just men in the town. Will you really overwhelm them, will you not spare the place for the fifty just men in it? Do not think of doing such a thing: to kill the just man with the sinner, treating just and sinner alike! Do not think of it! Will the judge of the whole earth not administer justice?" The Lord replied, "If at Sodom I find fifty just men in the town, I will spare the whole place because of them."

Abraham replied, "I am bold indeed to speak like this to my Lord, I who am dust and ashes. But perhaps the fifty just men lack five: will you destroy the whole city for five?" "No," he replied. "I will not destroy it if I find forty-five just men there." Again Abraham said to him, "Perhaps there will only be forty there." "I will not do it," he replied, "for the sake of the forty."

Abraham said, "I trust my Lord will not be angry, but give me leave to speak: perhaps there will only be thirty there." "I will not do it," he replied, "if I find thirty there." He said, "I am bold indeed to speak like this, but perhaps there will only be twenty there." "I will not destroy it," he replied, "for the sake of the twenty." He said, "I trust my Lord will not be angry if I speak once more: perhaps there will only be ten." "I will not destroy it," he replied, "for the sake of the ten."

Psalm   Psalm 137

R. **On the day I called,**
    you answered me, O Lord.

1. I thank you, Lord, with all my heart,
    you have heard the words of my mouth.
    Before the angels I will bless you.
    I will adore before your holy temple. R.

2. I thank you for your faithfulness and love
    which excel all we ever knew of you.
    On the day I called, you answered;
    you increased the strength of my soul. R.

3. The Lord is high yet he looks on the lowly
   and the haughty he knows from afar.
   Though I walk in the midst of affliction
   you give me life and frustrate my foes. R.

4. You stretch out your hand and save me,
   your hand will do all things for me.
   Your love, O Lord, is eternal.
   discard not the work of your hands. R.

Second Reading   Colossians 2:12-14

He has brought you to life with him, he has forgiven us all our sins.

You have been buried with Christ, when you were baptised; and by baptism, too, you have been raised up with him through your belief in the power of God who raised him from the dead. You were dead, because you were sinners and had not been circumcised: he has brought you to life with him, he has forgiven us all our sins.

He has overridden the Law, and cancelled every record of the debt that we had to pay; he has done away with it by nailing it to the cross.

Gospel Acclamation
Alleluia, alleluia!
The Word was made flesh and lived among us;
to all who did accept him
he gave power to become children of God.
Alleluia!   John 1:12. 14

or

Alleluia, alleluia!
The spirit you received is the spirit of sons,
and it makes us cry out, "Abba, Father!"
Alleluia!   Romans 8:15

Gospel   Luke 11:1-13

Ask, and it will be given to you.

Once Jesus was in a certain place praying, and when he had finished, one of his disciples said, "Lord, teach us to pray, just as John taught his disciples," He said to them, "Say this when you pray:

'Father, may your name be held holy,
your kingdom come;
give us each day our daily bread,
and forgive us our sins,
for we ourselves forgive each one who is in debt to us.
And do not put us to the test.'"

He also said to them, "Suppose one of you has a friend and goes to him in the middle of the night to say, 'My friend, lend me three loaves, because a friend of mine on his travels has just arrived at my house and I have nothing to offer him'; and the man answers from inside the house, 'Do not bother me. The door is bolted now, and my children and I are in bed; I cannot get up to give it to you.' I tell you, if the man does not get up and give it him for friendship's sake, persistence will be enough to make him get up and give his friend all he wants.

"So I say to you: Ask, and it will be given to you; search, and you will find; knock, and the door will be opened to you. For the one who asks always receives; the one who searches always finds; the one who knocks will always have the door opened to him. What father among you would hand his son a stone when he asked for bread? Or hand him a snake instead of a fish? Or hand him a scorpion if he asked for an egg? If you then, who are evil, know how to give your children what is good, how much more will the heavenly Father give the Holy Spirit to those who ask him!"

The Creed is said.

Prayer over the Offerings

Accept, O Lord, we pray, the offerings
which we bring from the abundance of your gifts,
that through the powerful working of your grace
these most sacred mysteries may sanctify our present way of life
and lead us to eternal gladness.
Through Christ our Lord.

Preface I-VIII of the Sundays in Ordinary Time, pp. 499-502.

Communion Antiphon
Bless the Lord, O my soul,
and never forget all his benefits. *Psalm 102:2*

or

Blessed are the merciful, for they shall receive mercy.
Blessed are the clean of heart, for they shall see God.
Matthew 5:7-8

Prayer after Communion
We have consumed, O Lord, this divine Sacrament,
the perpetual memorial of the Passion of your Son;
grant, we pray, that this gift,
which he himself gave us with love beyond all telling,
may profit us for salvation.
Through Christ our Lord.

EIGHTEENTH SUNDAY IN ORDINARY TIME – C

There is more to life than wealth and riches.
We can become obsessive about looking for material security in this life. Yet we
cannot take our riches with us when we die. We are called to live as people who
have died to the things of this world, in order to focus on the spiritual riches
of a life given to Christ. In this way we will get our priorities right, and our
lives will be full of true happiness.

Entrance Antiphon
O God, come to my assistance;
O Lord, make haste to help me!
You are my rescuer, my help;
O Lord, do not delay.

Psalm 69:2. 6

The Gloria is said or sung.

Collect
Draw near to your servants, O Lord,
and answer their prayers with unceasing kindness,
that, for those who glory in you as their Creator and guide,
you may restore what you have created
and keep safe what you have restored.
Through our Lord Jesus Christ, your Son,
who lives and reigns with you in the unity of the Holy Spirit,
one God, for ever and ever.

First Reading   Ecclesiastes 1:2; 2:21-23
What does a man gain for all his toil?
Vanity of vanities, the Preacher says. Vanity of vanities. All is vanity!
   For so it is that a man who has laboured wisely, skilfully and successfully must leave what is his own to someone who has not toiled for it at all. This, too, is vanity and great injustice; for what does he gain for all the toil and strain that he has undergone under the sun? What of all his laborious days, his cares of office, his restless nights? This, too, is vanity.

Psalm   Psalm 89

R. **O Lord, you have been our refuge**
    from one generation to the next.

1. You turn men back into dust
    and say: "Go back, sons of men."
    To your eyes a thousand years
    are like yesterday, come and gone,
    no more than a watch in the night. R.

2. You sweep men away like a dream,
    like grass which springs up in the morning.
    In the morning it springs up and flowers:
    by evening it withers and fades. R.

3. Make us know the shortness of our life
    that we may gain wisdom of heart.
    Lord, relent! Is your anger for ever?
    Show pity to your servants. R.

4. In the morning, fill us with your love;
    we shall exult and rejoice all our days.
    Let the favour of the Lord be upon us:
    give success to the work of our hands. R.

or   Psalm 94

R. **O that today you would listen to his voice!**
    Harden not your hearts.

1. Come, ring out our joy to the Lord;
    hail the rock who saves us.
    Let us come before him, giving thanks,
    with songs let us hail the Lord. R.

2. Come in; let us bow and bend low;
let us kneel before the God who made us
for he is our God and we
the people who belong to his pasture,
the flock that is led by his hand. R.

3. O that today you would listen to his voice!
"Harden not your hearts at Meribah,
as on that day at Massah in the desert
when your fathers put me to the test;
when they tried me, though they saw my work." R.

Second Reading   Colossians 3:1-5. 9-11
You must look for the things that are in heaven, where Christ is.
Since you have been brought back to true life with Christ, you must
look for the things that are in heaven, where Christ is, sitting at
God's right hand. Let your thoughts be on heavenly things, not on
the things that are on the earth, because you have died, and now
the life you have is hidden with Christ in God. But when Christ is
revealed – and he is your life – you too will be revealed in all your
glory with him.

That is why you must kill everything in you that belongs only
to earthly life: fornication, impurity, guilty passion, evil desires
and especially greed, which is the same thing as worshipping a
false god; and never tell each other lies. You have stripped off your
old behaviour with your old self, and you have put on a new self
which will progress towards true knowledge the more it is renewed
in the image of its creator; and in that image there is no room for
distinction between Greek and Jew, between the circumcised or the
uncircumcised, or between barbarian and Scythian, slave and free
man. There is only Christ: he is everything and he is in everything.

Gospel Acclamation
Alleluia, alleluia!
Your word is truth, O Lord,
consecrate us in the truth.
Alleluia!   cf. John 17:17

or

Alleluia, alleluia!
How happy are the poor in spirit;
theirs is the kingdom of heaven.
Alleluia!

Matthew 5:3

Gospel   Luke 12:13-21
This hoard of yours, whose will it be?
A man in the crowd said to Jesus, "Master, tell my brother to give me
a share of our inheritance." "My friend," he replied, "who appointed
me your judge, or the arbitrator of your claims?" Then he said to
them, "Watch, and be on your guard against avarice of any kind, for
a man's life is not made secure by what he owns, even when he has
more than he needs."

   Then he told them a parable: "There was once a rich man who,
having had a good harvest from his land, thought to himself, 'What
am I to do? I have not enough room to store my crops.' Then he
said, 'This is what I will do; I will pull down my barns and build
bigger ones, and store all my grain and my goods in them, and I will
say to my soul: My soul, you have plenty of good things laid by for
many years to come; take things easy, eat, drink, have a good time.'
But God said to him, 'Fool! This very night the demand will be
made for your soul; and this hoard of yours, whose will it be then?'
So it is when a man stores up treasure for himself in place of making
himself rich in the sight of God."

The Creed is said.

Prayer over the Offerings
Graciously sanctify these gifts, O Lord, we pray,
and, accepting the oblation of this spiritual sacrifice,
make of us an eternal offering to you.
Through Christ our Lord.

Preface I-VIII of the Sundays in Ordinary Time, pp. 499-502.

Communion Antiphon
You have given us, O Lord, bread from heaven,
endowed with all delights and sweetness in every taste.

Wisdom 16:20

or

I am the bread of life, says the Lord;
whoever comes to me will not hunger
and whoever believes in me will not thirst.

John 6:35

Prayer after Communion
Accompany with constant protection, O Lord,
those you renew with these heavenly gifts
and, in your never-failing care for them,
make them worthy of eternal redemption.
Through Christ our Lord.

NINETEENTH SUNDAY IN ORDINARY TIME – C

Be ready.

Jesus teaches us to be ready when the Lord comes to call us to our heavenly home. A good life is the best preparation we can make. We will enter into a kingdom promised to us by our heavenly Father, who through his own kindness and generosity has chosen us as his own.

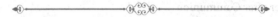

Entrance Antiphon
Look to your covenant, O Lord,
and forget not the life of your poor ones for ever.
Arise, O God, and defend your cause,
and forget not the cries of those who seek you.

cf. Psalm 73:20. 19. 22. 23

The Gloria is said or sung.

Collect
Almighty ever-living God,
whom, taught by the Holy Spirit,
we dare to call our Father,
bring, we pray, to perfection in our hearts
the spirit of adoption as your sons and daughters,
that we may merit to enter into the inheritance
which you have promised.
Through our Lord Jesus Christ, your Son,
who lives and reigns with you in the unity of the Holy Spirit,
one God, for ever and ever.

First Reading   Wisdom 18:6-9
By the same act with which you took vengeance on our foes you
made us glorious by calling us to you.
That night had been foretold to our ancestors, so that,
once they saw what kind of oaths they had put their trust in

they would joyfully take courage.
This was the expectation of your people,
the saving of the virtuous and the ruin of their enemies;
for by the same act with which you took vengeance on our foes
you made us glorious by calling us to you.
The devout children of worthy men offered sacrifice in secret
and this divine pact they struck with one accord:
that the saints would share the same blessings and dangers alike;
and forthwith they had begun to chant the hymns of the fathers.

Psalm   **Psalm 32**

R. **Happy are the people the Lord has chosen as his own.**

1. Ring out your joy to the Lord, O you just;
   for praise is fitting for loyal hearts.
   They are happy, whose God is the Lord,
   the people he has chosen as his own. R.

2. The Lord looks on those who revere him,
   on those who hope in his love,
   to rescue their souls from death,
   to keep them alive in famine. R.

3. Our soul is waiting for the Lord.
   The Lord is our help and our shield,
   May your love be upon us, O Lord,
   as we place all our hope in you. R.

Second Reading   Hebrews 11:1-2. 8-19
Abraham looked forward to a city founded, designed and built by
God.

Only faith can guarantee the blessings that we hope for, or prove
the existence of the realities that at present remain unseen. It was
for faith that our ancestors were commended.

It was by faith that Abraham obeyed the call to set out for a
country that was the inheritance given to him and his descendants,

and that he set out without knowing where he was going. By faith he arrived, as a foreigner, in the Promised Land, and lived there as if in a strange country, with Isaac and Jacob, who were heirs with him of the same promise. They lived there in tents while he looked forward to a city founded, designed and built by God.

It was equally by faith that Sarah, in spite of being past the age, was made able to conceive, because she believed that he who had made the promise would be faithful to it. Because of this, there came from one man, and one who was already as good as dead himself, more descendants than could be counted, as many as the stars of heaven or the grains of sand on the seashore.

All these died in faith, before receiving any of the things that had been promised, but they saw them in the far distance and welcomed them, recognising that they were only strangers and nomads on earth. People who use such terms about themselves make it quite plain that they are in search of their real homeland. They can hardly have meant the country they came from, since they had the opportunity to go back to it; but in fact they were longing for a better homeland, their heavenly homeland. That is why God is not ashamed to be called their God, since he has founded the city for them.

It was by faith that Abraham, when put to the test, offered up Isaac. He offered to sacrifice his only son even though the promises had been made to him and he had been told: It is through Isaac that your name will be carried on. He was confident that God had the power even to raise the dead; and so, figuratively speaking, he was given back Isaac from the dead.

Gospel Acclamation
Alleluia, alleluia!
Blessed are you, Father,
Lord of heaven and earth,
for revealing the mysteries of the kingdom
to mere children.
Alleluia!   cf. Matthew 11:25

or

Alleluia, alleluia!
Stay awake and stand ready,
because you do not know the hour
when the Son of Man is coming.
Alleluia!   Matthew 24:42, 44

Gospel   Luke 12:32-48
You too must stand ready.

| Jesus said to his disciples:

"There is no need to be afraid, little flock, for it has pleased your
Father to give you the kingdom.

"Sell your possessions and give alms. Get yourselves purses that
do not wear out, treasure that will not fail you, in heaven where no
thief can reach it and no moth destroy it. For where your treasure
is, there will your heart be also.

"See that you are dressed for action and have your lamps lit. Be
like men waiting for their master to return from the wedding feast,
ready to open the door as soon as he comes and knocks. Happy
those servants whom the master finds awake when he comes. I
tell you solemnly, he will put on an apron, sit them down at table
and wait on them. It may be in the second watch he comes, or in
the third, but happy those servants if he finds them ready. You
may be quite sure of this, that if the householder had known at
what hour the burglar would come, he would not have let anyone
break through the wall of his house. You too must stand ready,
because the Son of Man is coming at an hour you do not expect."

Peter said, "Lord, do you mean this parable for us, or for
everyone?" The Lord replied, "What sort of steward, then, is faithful
and wise enough for the master to place him over his household to
give them their allowance of food at the proper time? Happy that
servant if his master's arrival finds him at this employment. I tell
you truly, he will place him over everything he owns. But as for the
servant who says to himself, 'My master is taking his time coming,'
and sets about beating the menservants and the maids, and eating
and drinking and getting drunk, his master will come on a day he
does not expect and at an hour he does not know. The master will
cut him off and send him to the same fate as the unfaithful.

"The servant who knows what his master wants, but has not even started to carry out those wishes, will receive very many strokes of the lash. The one who did not know, but deserves to be beaten for what he has done, will receive fewer strokes. When a man has had a great deal given him, a great deal will be demanded of him; when a man has had a great deal given him on trust, even more will be expected of him."

The Creed is said.

Prayer over the Offerings
Be pleased, O Lord, to accept the offerings of your Church,
for in your mercy you have given them to be offered
and by your power you transform them
into the mystery of our salvation.
Through Christ our Lord.

Preface I-VIII of the Sundays in Ordinary Time, pp. 499-502.

Communion Antiphon
O Jerusalem, glorify the Lord,
who gives you your fill of finest wheat.   Psalm 147:12. 14

or

The bread that I will give, says the Lord,
is my flesh for the life of the world.   cf. John 6:51

Prayer after Communion
May the communion in your Sacrament
that we have consumed, save us, O Lord,
and confirm us in the light of your truth.
Through Christ our Lord.

TWENTIETH SUNDAY IN ORDINARY TIME – C

Do not lose sight of Jesus.

The path to heaven is likened to a race in which we are to keep our eyes on Jesus our leader. The saints are praying for us to reach the finishing line. With so many cheering us on, how can we fail? We are called never to give up, even when the going is hard. We are bound to suffer for our faith, just as Jeremiah the prophet did, but the Lord will deliver us.

Entrance Antiphon
Turn your eyes, O God, our shield;
and look on the face of your anointed one;
one day within your courts
is better than a thousand elsewhere.   Psalm 83:10-11

The Gloria is said or sung.

Collect
O God, who have prepared for those who love you
good things which no eye can see,
fill our hearts, we pray, with the warmth of your love,
so that, loving you in all things and above all things,
we may attain your promises,
which surpass every human desire.
Through our Lord Jesus Christ, your Son,
who lives and reigns with you in the unity of the Holy Spirit,
one God, for ever and ever.

First Reading   Jeremiah 38:4-6. 8-10
You have borne me to be a man of dissension for all the land.
The king's leading men spoke to the king. "Let Jeremiah be put to death: he is unquestionably disheartening the remaining soldiers in the city, and all the people too, by talking like this. The fellow does not have the welfare of this people at heart so much as its ruin." "He

is in your hands as you know," King Zedekiah answered, "for the king is powerless against you." So they took Jeremiah and threw him into the well of Prince Malchiah in the Court of the Guard, letting him down with ropes. There was no water in the well, only mud, and into the mud Jeremiah sank.

Ebed-melech came out from the palace and spoke to the king. "My lord king," he said, "these men have done a wicked thing by treating the prophet Jeremiah like this: they have thrown him into the well where he will die." At this the king gave Ebed-melech the Cushite the following order: "Take three men with you from here and pull the prophet Jeremiah out of the well before he dies."

Psalm   Psalm 39

R. **Lord, come to my aid!**

1. I waited, I waited for the Lord
   and he stooped down to me;
   he heard my cry. R.

2. He drew me from the deadly pit,
   from the miry clay.
   He set my feet upon a rock
   and made my footsteps firm. R.

3. He put a new song into my mouth,
   praise of our God.
   Many shall see and fear
   and shall trust in the Lord. R.

4. As for me, wretched and poor,
   the Lord thinks of me.
   You are my rescuer, my help,
   O God, do not delay. R.

Second Reading   Hebrews 12:1-4
We shall keep running steadily in the race we have started.

With so many witnesses in a great cloud on every side of us, we too, then, should throw off everything that hinders us, especially the sin that clings so easily, and keep running steadily in the race we have started. Let us not lose sight of Jesus, who leads us in our faith and brings it to perfection: for the sake of the joy which was still in the future, he endured the cross, disregarding the shamefulness of it, and from now on has taken his place at the right of God's throne. Think of the way he stood such opposition from sinners and then you will not give up for want of courage. In the fight against sin, you have not yet had to keep fighting to the point of death.

Gospel Acclamation
Alleluia, alleluia!
Open our heart, O Lord,
to accept the words of your Son.
Alleluia!   cf. Acts 16:14

or

Alleluia, alleluia!
The sheep that belong to me listen to my voice,
says the Lord,
I know them and they follow me.
Alleluia!   John 10:27

Gospel   Luke 12:49-53
I am not here to bring peace, but rather division.

Jesus said to his disciples: "I have come to bring fire to the earth, and how I wish it were blazing already! There is a baptism I must still receive, and how great is my distress till it is over!

"Do you suppose that I am here to bring peace on earth? No, I tell you, but rather division. For from now on a household of five will be divided: three against two and two against three; the father divided against the son, son against father, mother against daughter, daughter against mother, mother-in-law against daughter-in-law, daughter-in-law against mother-in-law."

The Creed is said.

Prayer over the Offerings
Receive our oblation, O Lord,
by which is brought about a glorious exchange,
that, by offering what you have given,
we may merit to receive your very self.
Through Christ our Lord.

Preface I-VIII of the Sundays in Ordinary Time, pp. 499-502.

Communion Antiphon
With the Lord there is mercy;
in him is plentiful redemption.   Psalm 129:7

or

I am the living bread that came down from heaven, says the Lord.
Whoever eats of this bread will live for ever.   John 6:51-52

Prayer after Communion
Made partakers of Christ through these Sacraments,
we humbly implore your mercy, Lord,
that, conformed to his image on earth,
we may merit also to be his coheirs in heaven.
Who lives and reigns for ever and ever.

TWENTY-FIRST SUNDAY IN ORDINARY TIME – C

The last shall be first.

Jesus teaches us never to think of ourselves as better than others, just because we profess our faith in him. Many people of other faiths and nations will find their way into God's kingdom before us. We are called to set ourselves high standards and to try our best to enter the kingdom by the narrow door.

Entrance Antiphon
Turn your ear, O Lord, and answer me;
save the servant who trusts in you, my God.
Have mercy on me, O Lord, for I cry to you all the day long.

cf. Psalm 85:1-3

The Gloria is said or sung.

Collect
O God, who cause the minds of the faithful
to unite in a single purpose,
grant your people to love what you command
and to desire what you promise,
that, amid the uncertainties of this world,
our hearts may be fixed on that place
where true gladness is found.
Through our Lord Jesus Christ, your Son,
who lives and reigns with you in the unity of the Holy Spirit,
one God, for ever and ever.

First Reading   Isaiah 66:18-21
They will bring all your brothers from all the nations.
The Lord says this: I am coming to gather the nations of every language. They shall come to witness my glory. I will give them a sign and send some of their survivors to the nations: to Tarshish, Put, Lud, Moshech, Rosh, Tubal, and Javan, to the distant islands

that have never heard of me or seen my glory. They will proclaim my glory to the nations. As an offering to the Lord they will bring all your brothers, on horses, in chariots, in litters, on mules, on dromedaries, from all the nations to my holy mountain in Jerusalem, says the Lord, like Israelites bringing oblations in clean vessels to the Temple of the Lord. And of some of them I will make priests and Levites, says the Lord.

Psalm   Psalm 116

R. **Go out to the whole world;**
    proclaim the Good News.

or **Alleluia!**

1. O praise the Lord, all you nations,
    acclaim him all you peoples! R.

2. Strong is his love for us;
    he is faithful for ever. R.

Second Reading   Hebrews 12:5-7. 11-13
The Lord trains the one that he loves.
Have you forgotten that encouraging text in which you are addressed as sons? My son, when the Lord corrects you, do not treat it lightly; but do not get discouraged when he reprimands you. For the Lord trains the ones that he loves and he punishes all those that he acknowledges as his sons. Suffering is part of your training; God is treating you as his sons. Has there ever been any son whose father did not train him? Of course, any punishment is most painful at the time, and far from pleasant; but later, in those on whom it has been used, it bears fruit in peace and goodness. So hold up your limp arms and steady your trembling knees and smooth out the path you tread; then the injured limb will not be wrenched, it will grow strong again.

Gospel Acclamation
Alleluia, alleluia!
If anyone loves me he will keep my word,
and my Father will love him,
and we shall come to him.
Alleluia!   John 14:23

or

Alleluia, alleluia!
I am the Way, the Truth and the Life, says the Lord;
no one can come to the Father except through me.
Alleluia!   John 14:6

Gospel   Luke 13:22-30
Men from east and west will come to take their places at the feast in
the kingdom of God.

Through towns and villages Jesus went teaching, making his way
to Jerusalem. Someone said to him, "Sir, will there be only a few
saved?" He said to them, "Try your best to enter by the narrow door,
because, I tell you, many will try to enter and will not succeed.

"Once the master of the house has got up and locked the door,
you may find yourself knocking on the door, saying, 'Lord, open
to us,' but he will answer, 'I do not know where you come from.'
Then you will find yourself saying, 'We once ate and drank in your
company; you taught in our streets,' but he will reply, 'I do not know
where you come from. Away from me, all you wicked men!'

"Then there will be weeping and grinding of teeth, when you see
Abraham and Isaac and Jacob and all the prophets in the kingdom
of God, and yourselves turned outside. And men from east and
west, from north and south, will come to take their places at the
feast in the kingdom of God.

"Yes, there are those now last who will be first, and those now
first who will be last."

The Creed is said.

Prayer over the Offerings
O Lord, who gained for yourself a people by adoption
through the one sacrifice offered once for all,
bestow graciously on us, we pray,
the gifts of unity and peace in your Church.
Through Christ our Lord.

Preface I-VIII of the Sundays in Ordinary Time, pp. 499-502.

Communion Antiphon
The earth is replete with the fruits of your work, O Lord;
you bring forth bread from the earth
and wine to cheer the heart.   cf. Psalm 103:13-15
or

Whoever eats my flesh and drinks my blood
has eternal life, says the Lord,
and I will raise him up on the last day.   cf. John 6:54

Prayer after Communion
Complete within us, O Lord, we pray,
the healing work of your mercy
and graciously perfect and sustain us,
so that in all things we may please you.
Through Christ our Lord.

TWENTY-SECOND SUNDAY IN ORDINARY TIME – C

Being humble.

God's blessing comes to those who behave humbly. Jesus teaches us not to seek status and honours from other people. It is in being humble like him that we will find favour with God. Christ will lead us to the heavenly Jerusalem, the city of the living God, if we will only follow him in humility.

Entrance Antiphon

Have mercy on me, O Lord, for I cry to you all the day long.
O Lord, you are good and forgiving,
full of mercy to all who call to you.   cf. Psalm 85:3. 5

The Gloria is said or sung.

Collect

God of might, giver of every good gift,
put into our hearts the love of your name,
so that, by deepening our sense of reverence,
you may nurture in us what is good
and, by your watchful care,
keep safe what you have nurtured.
Through our Lord Jesus Christ, your Son,
who lives and reigns with you in the unity of the Holy Spirit,
one God, for ever and ever.

First Reading   Ecclesiasticus 3:17-20. 28-29

Behave humbly, and then you will find favour with the Lord.

My son, be gentle in carrying out your business,
and you will be better loved than a lavish giver.
The greater you are, the more you should behave humbly,
and then you will find favour with the Lord;
for great though the power of the Lord is,
he accepts the homage of the humble.

There is no cure for the proud man's malady,
since an evil growth has taken root in him.
The heart of a sensible man will reflect on parables,
an attentive ear is the sage's dream.

Psalm   Psalm 67

R. **In your goodness, O God,
    you prepared a home for the poor.**

1. The just shall rejoice at the presence of God,
   they shall exult and dance for joy.
   O sing to the Lord, make music to his name;
   rejoice in the Lord, exult at his presence. R.

2. Father of the orphan, defender of the widow,
   such is God in his holy place.
   God gives the lonely a home to live in;
   he leads the prisoners forth into freedom. R.

3. You poured down, O God, a generous rain:
   when your people were starved you gave them new life.
   It was there that your people found a home,
   prepared in your goodness, O God, for the poor. R.

Second Reading   Hebrews 12:18-19. 22-24
You have to come to Mount Zion and to the city of the living God.
What you have come to is nothing known to the senses: not a
blazing fire, or a gloom turning to total darkness, or a storm; or
trumpeting thunder or the great voice speaking which made
everyone that heard it beg that no more should be said to them.
But what you have come to is Mount Zion and the city of the living
God, the heavenly Jerusalem where the millions of angels have
gathered for the festival, with the whole Church in which everyone
is a "first-born son" and a citizen of heaven. You have come to God
himself, the supreme Judge, and been placed with the spirits of the
saints who have been made perfect; and to Jesus, the mediator who
brings a new covenant.

Gospel Acclamation
Alleluia, alleluia!
If anyone loves me he will keep my word,
and my Father will love him,
and we shall come to him.
Alleluia!   John 14:23

or

Alleluia, alleluia!
Shoulder my yoke and learn from me,
for I am gentle and humble in heart.
Alleluia!   Matthew 11:29

Gospel   Luke 14:1. 7-14
Everyone who exalts himself will be humbled, and the man who
humbles himself will be exalted.

On a sabbath day Jesus had gone for a meal to the house of one
of the leading Pharisees; and they watched him closely. He then
told the guests a parable, because he had noticed how they picked
the places of honour. He said this, "When someone invites you to
a wedding feast, do not take your seat in the place of honour. A
more distinguished person than you may have been invited, and the
person who invited you both may come and say, 'Give up your place
to this man.' And then, to your embarrassment, you would have to
go and take the lowest place. No; when you are a guest, make your
way to the lowest place and sit there, so that, when your host comes,
he may say, 'My friend, move up higher.' In that way, everyone with
you at the table will see you honoured. For everyone who exalts
himself will be humbled, and the man who humbles himself will
be exalted."

   Then he said to his host, "When you give a lunch or a dinner, do
not ask your friends, brothers, relations or rich neighbours, for fear
they repay your courtesy by inviting you in return. No; when you
have a party, invite the poor, the crippled, the lame, the blind; that
they cannot pay you back means that you are fortunate, because
repayment will be made to you when the virtuous rise again."

The Creed is said.

Prayer over the Offerings
May this sacred offering, O Lord,
confer on us always the blessing of salvation,
that what it celebrates in mystery
it may accomplish in power.
Through Christ our Lord.

Preface I-VIII of the Sundays in Ordinary Time, pp. 499-502.

Communion Antiphon
How great is the goodness, Lord,
that you keep for those who fear you.   Psalm 30:20

or

Blessed are the peacemakers,
for they shall be called children of God.
Blessed are they who are persecuted for the sake of righteousness,
for theirs is the Kingdom of Heaven.   Matthew 5:9-10

Prayer after Communion
Renewed by this bread from the heavenly table,
we beseech you, Lord,
that, being the food of charity,
it may confirm our hearts
and stir us to serve you in our neighbour.
Through Christ our Lord.

TWENTY-THIRD SUNDAY IN ORDINARY TIME – C

The cost of following Christ.
God has created us free. Nothing must come between us and God. Yet we are
often distracted by worldly things and possessions. Jesus teaches us that we
will need commitment and dedication if we are to follow him. In this we will
discover the true freedom for which God made us.

Entrance Antiphon
You are just, O Lord, and your judgement is right;
treat your servant in accord with your merciful love.

Psalm 118:137. 124

The Gloria is said or sung.

Collect
O God, by whom we are redeemed and receive adoption,
look graciously upon your beloved sons and daughters,
that those who believe in Christ
may receive true freedom
and an everlasting inheritance.
Through our Lord Jesus Christ, your Son,
who lives and reigns with you in the unity of the Holy Spirit,
one God, for ever and ever.

First Reading
Wisdom 9:13-18

Who can divine the will of the Lord?

What man can know the intentions of God?
Who can divine the will of the Lord?
The reasonings of mortals are unsure
and our intentions unstable;
for a perishable body presses down the soul,
and this tent of clay weighs down the teeming mind.
It is hard enough for us to work out what is on earth,

laborious to know what lies within our reach;
who, then, can discover what is in the heavens?
As for your intention, who could have learnt it, had you not granted
 Wisdom
and sent your holy spirit from above?
Thus have the paths of those on earth been straightened
and men been taught what pleases you,
and saved, by Wisdom.

Psalm   Psalm 89

R. **O Lord, you have been our refuge
     from one generation to the next.**

1. You turn men back into dust
   and say: "Go back, sons of men."
   To your eyes a thousand years
   are like yesterday, come and gone,
   no more than a watch in the night. R.

2. You sweep men away like a dream,
   like grass which springs up in the morning.
   In the morning it springs up and flowers:
   by evening it withers and fades. R.

3. Make us know the shortness of our life
   that we may gain wisdom of heart.
   Lord, relent! Is your anger for ever?
   Show pity to your servants. R.

4. In the morning, fill us with your love;
   we shall exult and rejoice all our days.
   Let the favour of the Lord be upon us:
   give success to the work of our hands. R.

Second Reading   Philemon 9-10. 12-17
Have him back, not as a slave any more, but as a dear brother.
This is Paul writing, an old man now and, what is more, still
a prisoner of Christ Jesus. I am appealing to you for a child of
mine, whose father I became while wearing these chains: I mean

Onesimus. I am sending him back to you, and with him – I could say – a part of my own self. I should have liked to keep him with me; he could have been a substitute for you, to help me while I am in the chains that the Good News has brought me. However, I did not want to do anything without your consent; it would have been forcing your act of kindness, which should be spontaneous. I know you have been deprived of Onesimus for a time, but it was only so that you could have him back for ever, not as a slave any more, but something much better than a slave, a dear brother; especially dear to me, but how much more to you, as a blood-brother as well as a brother in the Lord. So if all that we have in common means anything to you, welcome him as you would me.

Gospel Acclamation
Alleluia, alleluia!
I call you friends, says the Lord,
because I have made known to you
everything I have learnt from my Father.
Alleluia!   John 15:15

or

Alleluia, alleluia!
Let your face shine on your servant,
and teach me your decrees.
Alleluia!   Psalm 118:135

Gospel   Luke 14:25-33
None of you can be my disciple unless he gives up all his possessions.
Great crowds accompanied Jesus on his way and he turned and spoke to them. "If any man comes to me without hating his father, mother, wife, children, brothers, sisters, yes and his own life too, he cannot be my disciple. Anyone who does not carry his cross and come after me cannot be my disciple.

"And indeed, which of you here, intending to build a tower, would not first sit down and work out the cost to see if he had enough to complete it? Otherwise, if he laid the foundation and then found himself unable to finish the work, the onlookers would all start making fun of him and saying, 'Here is a man who started to build and was unable to finish.' Or again, what king marching to war against another king would not first sit down and consider whether with ten thousand men he could stand up to the other who advanced against him with twenty thousand? If not, then while the other king was still a long way off, he would send envoys to sue for peace. So in the same way, none of you can be my disciple unless he gives up all his possessions."

The Creed is said.

Prayer over the Offerings
O God, who give us the gift of true prayer and of peace,
graciously grant that through this offering,
we may do fitting homage to your divine majesty
and, by partaking of the sacred mystery,
we may be faithfully united in mind and heart.
Through Christ our Lord.

Preface I-VIII of the Sundays in Ordinary Time, pp. 499-502.

Communion Antiphon
Like the deer that yearns for running streams,
so my soul is yearning for you, my God;
my soul is thirsting for God, the living God.   cf. Psalm 41:2-3

or

I am the light of the world, says the Lord;
whoever follows me will not walk in darkness,
but will have the light of life.   John 8:12

Prayer after Communion
Grant that your faithful, O Lord,
whom you nourish and endow with life
through the food of your Word and heavenly Sacrament,
may so benefit from your beloved Son's great gifts
that we may merit an eternal share in his life.
Who lives and reigns for ever and ever.

TWENTY-FOURTH SUNDAY IN ORDINARY TIME – C

Christ welcomes sinners.

Jesus' story of the prodigal son is one of the most famous ever told. The father in the story is merciful to his wayward son because he loves him. God is our Father and forgives us because he loves us. The parable teaches us to have no fear in returning to God, no matter what we have done in the past. Our Father loves us so much that he sent Christ into this world to forgive sinners.

Entrance Antiphon
Give peace, O Lord, to those who wait for you,
that your prophets be found true.
Hear the prayers of your servant,
and of your people Israel. cf. Ecclesiasticus 36:18

The Gloria is said or sung.

Collect
Look upon us, O God,
Creator and ruler of all things,
and, that we may feel the working of your mercy,
grant that we may serve you with all our heart.
Through our Lord Jesus Christ, your Son,
who lives and reigns with you in the unity of the Holy Spirit,
one God, for ever and ever.

First Reading Exodus 32:7-11. 13-14
The Lord relented and did not bring on his people the disaster he had threatened.
The Lord spoke to Moses, "Go down now, because your people whom you brought out of Egypt have apostasised. They have been quick to leave the way I marked out for them; they have made themselves a calf of molten metal and have worshipped it and offered it sacrifice. 'Here is your God, Israel,' they have cried, 'who

brought you up from the land of Egypt!' I can see how headstrong these people are! Leave me, now, my wrath shall blaze out against them and devour them; of you, however, I will make a great nation."

But Moses pleaded with the Lord his God. "Lord," he said, "why should your wrath blaze out against this people of yours whom you brought out of the land of Egypt with arm outstretched and mighty hand? Remember Abraham, Isaac and Jacob, your servants to whom by your own self you swore and made this promise: I will make your offspring as many as the stars of heaven, and all this land which I promised I will give to your descendants, and it shall be their heritage for ever." So the Lord relented and did not bring on his people the disaster he had threatened.

Psalm   Psalm 50

R. **I will leave this place and go to my father.**

1. Have mercy on me, God, in your kindness.
    In your compassion blot out my offence.
    O wash me more and more from my guilt
    and cleanse me from my sin. R.

2. A pure heart create for me, O God,
    put a steadfast spirit within me.
    Do not cast me away from your presence,
    nor deprive me of your holy spirit. R.

3. O Lord, open my lips
    and my mouth shall declare your praise.
    My sacrifice is a contrite spirit;
    a humbled, contrite heart you will not spurn. R.

Second Reading   1 Timothy 1:12-17
Christ Jesus came into the world to save sinners.
I thank Christ Jesus our Lord, who has given me strength, and who judged me faithful enough to call me into his service even though I used to be a blasphemer and did all I could to injure and discredit the faith. Mercy, however, was shown me, because until I became a believer I had been acting in ignorance; and the grace of our Lord

filled me with faith and with the love that is in Christ Jesus. Here is a saying that you can rely on and nobody should doubt: that Christ Jesus came into the world to save sinners. I myself am the greatest of them; and if mercy has been shown to me, it is because Jesus Christ meant to make me the greatest evidence of his inexhaustible patience for all the other people who would later have to trust in him to come to eternal life. To the eternal King, the undying, invisible and only God, be honour and glory for ever and ever. Amen.

Gospel Acclamation
Alleluia, alleluia!
May the Father of our Lord Jesus Christ
enlighten the eyes of our mind,
so that we can see what hope his call holds for us.
Alleluia!   cf. Ephesians 1:17. 18

or

Alleluia, alleluia!
God in Christ was reconciling the world to himself,
and he has entrusted to us the news that they are reconciled.
Alleluia!   2 Corinthians 5:19

Gospel   Luke 15:1-32
There will be rejoicing in heaven over one repentant sinner.

The tax collectors and the sinners were all seeking the company of Jesus to hear what he had to say, and the Pharisees and the scribes complained. "This man", they said, "welcomes sinners and eats with them." So he spoke this parable to them:

"What man among you with a hundred sheep, losing one, would not leave the ninety-nine in the wilderness and go after the missing one till he found it? And when he found it, would he not joyfully take it on his shoulders and then, when he got home, call together his friends and neighbours? 'Rejoice with me,' he would say, 'I have found my sheep that was lost.' In the same way, I tell you, there will be more rejoicing in heaven over one repentant sinner than over ninety-nine virtuous men who have no need of repentance.

"Or again, what woman with ten drachmas would not, if she lost one, light a lamp and sweep out the house and search thoroughly till she found it? And then, when she had found it, call together her friends and neighbours? 'Rejoice with me,' she would say, 'I have found the drachma I lost.' In the same way, I tell you, there is rejoicing among the angels of God over one repentant sinner."

He also said, "A man had two sons. The younger said to his father, 'Father, let me have the share of the estate that would come to me.' So the father divided the property between them. A few days later, the younger son got together everything he had and left for a distant country where he squandered his money on a life of debauchery.

"When he had spent it all, that country experienced a severe famine, and now he began to feel the pinch, so he hired himself out to one of the local inhabitants who put him on his farm to feed the pigs. And he would willingly have filled his belly with the husks the pigs were eating but no one offered him anything. Then he came to his senses and said, 'How many of my father's paid servants have more food than they want, and here am I dying of hunger! I will leave this place and go to my father and say: Father, I have sinned against heaven and against you; I no longer deserve to be called your son; treat me as one of your paid servants.' So he left the place and went back to his father.

"While he was still a long way off, his father saw him and was moved with pity. He ran to the boy, clasped him in his arms and kissed him tenderly. Then his son said, 'Father, I have sinned against heaven and against you. I no longer deserve to be called your son.' But the father said to his servants, 'Quick! Bring out the best robe and put it on him; put a ring on his finger and sandals on his feet. Bring the calf we have been fattening, and kill it; we are going to have a feast, a celebration, because this son of mine was dead and has come back to life; he was lost and is found.' And they began to celebrate.

"Now the elder son was out in the fields, and on his way back, as he drew near the house, he could hear music and dancing. Calling one of the servants, he asked what it was all about. 'Your brother has come,' replied the servant, 'and your father has killed the calf we had fattened because he has got him back safe and sound.' He was angry then and refused to go in, and his father came out to plead with him; but he answered his father, 'Look, all these years I have slaved for you and never once disobeyed your orders, yet you never offered me so much as a kid for me to celebrate with my friends. But, for this son of yours, when he comes back after swallowing up your property – he and his women – you kill the calf we had been fattening.'

"The father said, 'My son, you are with me always and all I have is yours. But it was only right we should celebrate and rejoice, because your brother here was dead and has come to life; he was lost and is found.'"

The Creed is said.

Prayer over the Offerings

Look with favour on our supplications, O Lord,
and in your kindness accept these, your servants' offerings,
that what each has offered to the honour of your name
may serve the salvation of all.
Through Christ our Lord.

Preface I-VIII of the Sundays in Ordinary Time, pp. 499-502.

Communion Antiphon

How precious is your mercy, O God!
The children of men seek shelter in the shadow of your wings.

cf. Psalm 35:8

or

The chalice of blessing that we bless
is a communion in the Blood of Christ;
and the bread that we break
is a sharing in the Body of the Lord.   cf. 1 Corinthians 10:16

Prayer after Communion

May the working of this heavenly gift, O Lord, we pray,
take possession of our minds and bodies,
so that its effects, and not our own desires,
may always prevail in us.
Through Christ our Lord.

TWENTY-FIFTH SUNDAY IN ORDINARY TIME – C

The call to social justice and peace.
We are called to be people who are on the side of those who are oppressed. We are to stand up for those who are poor, who are so often exploited by rich people for the sake of material gain. It is vital to put money and power into proper perspective in our lives. We cannot serve both God and money.

Entrance Antiphon
I am the salvation of the people, says the Lord.
Should they cry to me in any distress,
I will hear them, and I will be their Lord for ever.

The Gloria is said or sung.

Collect
O God, who founded all the commands of your sacred Law
upon love of you and of our neighbour,
grant that, by keeping your precepts,
we may merit to attain eternal life.
Through our Lord Jesus Christ, your Son,
who lives and reigns with you in the unity of the Holy Spirit,
one God, for ever and ever.

First Reading   Amos 8:4-7
Against those who "buy up the poor for money".
Listen to this, you who trample on the needy
and try to suppress the poor people of the country,
you who say, "When will New Moon be over
so that we can sell our corn,
and sabbath, so that we can market our wheat?
Then by lowering the bushel, raising the shekel,
by swindling and tampering with the scales,
we can buy up the poor for money,

and the needy for a pair of sandals,
and get a price even for the sweepings of the wheat."
The Lord swears it by the pride of Jacob,
"Never will I forget a single thing you have done."

Psalm   Psalm 112

R. **Praise the Lord, who raises the poor.**

or **Alleluia!**

1. Praise, O servants of the Lord,
    praise the name of the Lord!
    May the name of the Lord be blessed
    both now and for evermore! R.

2. High above all nations is the Lord,
    above the heavens his glory.
    Who is like the Lord, our God,
    who has risen on high to his throne
    yet stoops from the heights to look down,
    to look down upon heaven and earth? R.

3. From the dust he lifts up the lowly,
    from the dungheap he raises the poor
    to set him in the company of princes,
    yes, with the princes of his people. R.

Second Reading   1 Timothy 2:1-8
There should be prayers offered for everyone to God, who wants
everyone to be saved.
My advice is that, first of all, there should be prayers offered
for everyone – petitions, intercessions and thanksgiving – and
especially for kings and others in authority, so that we may be able
to live religious and reverent lives in peace and quiet. To do this
is right, and will please God our saviour: he wants everyone to be
saved and reach full knowledge of the truth. For there is only one

God, and there is only one mediator between God and mankind, himself a man, Christ Jesus, who sacrificed himself as a ransom for them all. He is the evidence of this, sent at the appointed time, and I have been named a herald and apostle of it and – I am telling the truth and no lie – a teacher of the faith and the truth to the pagans.

In every place, then, I want the men to lift their hands up reverently in prayer, with no anger or argument.

Gospel Acclamation
Alleluia, alleluia!
Open our heart, O Lord,
to accept the words of your Son.
Alleluia!   cf. Acts 16:14

or

Alleluia, alleluia!
Jesus Christ was rich,
but he became poor for your sake,
to make you rich out of his poverty.
Alleluia!   2 Corinthians 8:9

Gospel   Luke 16:1-13
You cannot be the slave both of God and of money.

| Jesus said to his disciples,

"There was a rich man and he had a steward who was denounced to him for being wasteful with his property. He called for the man and said, 'What is this I hear about you? Draw me up an account of your stewardship because you are not to be my steward any longer.' Then the steward said to himself, 'Now that my master is taking the stewardship from me, what am I to do? Dig? I am not strong enough. Go begging? I should be too ashamed. Ah, I know what I will do to make sure that when I am dismissed from office there will be some to welcome me into their homes.'

"Then he called his master's debtors one by one. To the first he said, 'How much do you owe my master?' 'One hundred measures of oil' was the reply. The steward said, 'Here, take your bond; sit down straight away and write fifty.' To another he said, 'And you, sir, how much do you owe?' 'One hundred measures of wheat' was the reply. The steward said, 'Here, take your bond and write eighty.'

"The master praised the dishonest steward for his astuteness. For the children of this world are more astute in dealing with their own kind than are the children of light.

"And so I tell you this: use money, tainted as it is, to win you friends, and thus make sure that when it fails you, they will welcome you into the tents of eternity.

The man who can be trusted in little things can be trusted in great; the man who is dishonest in little things will be dishonest in great. If then you cannot be trusted with money, that tainted thing, who will trust you with genuine riches? And if you cannot be trusted with what is not yours, who will give you what is your very own?

"No servant can be the slave of two masters; he will either hate the first and love the second, or treat the first with respect and the second with scorn. You cannot be the slave both of God and of money."

The Creed is said.

Prayer over the Offerings
Receive with favour, O Lord, we pray,
the offerings of your people,
that what they profess with devotion and faith
may be theirs through these heavenly mysteries.
Through Christ our Lord.

Preface I-VIII of the Sundays in Ordinary Time, pp. 499-502.

Communion Antiphon
You have laid down your precepts to be carefully kept;
may my ways be firm in keeping your statutes.   Psalm 118:4-5

or

I am the Good Shepherd, says the Lord;
I know my sheep, and mine know me.   John 10:14

Prayer after Communion
Graciously raise up, O Lord,
those you renew with this Sacrament,
that we may come to possess your redemption
both in mystery and in the manner of our life.
Through Christ our Lord.

TWENTY-SIXTH SUNDAY IN ORDINARY TIME – C

Rich and poor.

Jesus teaches about the dangers of inequality in the distribution of wealth. The rich man will be punished in the next life because of his indifference to the poor man who lay hungry at the gate of his house. Luxury and holiness are rarely found together. We are called to share our goods, just as we are called to share our faith in Christ with others through the way in which we live.

Entrance Antiphon

All that you have done to us, O Lord,
you have done with true judgement,
for we have sinned against you
and not obeyed your commandments.
But give glory to your name
and deal with us according to the bounty of your mercy.

Daniel 3:31. 29. 30. 43. 42

The Gloria is said or sung.

Collect

O God, who manifest your almighty power
above all by pardoning and showing mercy,
bestow, we pray, your grace abundantly upon us
and make those hastening to attain your promises
heirs to the treasures of heaven.
Through our Lord Jesus Christ, your Son,
who lives and reigns with you in the unity of the Holy Spirit,
one God, for ever and ever.

First Reading   Amos 6:1. 4-7

Those who sprawl and those who bawl will be exiled.

The almighty Lord says this:

Woe to those ensconced so snugly in Zion
and to those who feel so safe on the mountain of Samaria.
Lying on ivory beds
and sprawling on their divans,

they dine on lambs from the flock,
and stall-fattened veal;
they brawl to the sound of the harp,
they invent new instruments of music like David,
they drink wine by the bowlful,
and use the finest oil for anointing themselves,
but about the ruin of Joseph they do not care at all.
That is why they will be the first to be exiled;
the sprawlers' revelry is over.

Psalm   Psalm 145

R. **My soul, give praise to the Lord.**

or **Alleluia!**

1. It is the Lord who keeps faith for ever,
   who is just to those who are oppressed.
   It is he who gives bread to the hungry,
   the Lord, who sets prisoners free. R.

2. It is the Lord who gives sight to the blind,
   who raises up those who are bowed down.
   It is the Lord who loves the just,
   the Lord, who protects the stranger. R.

3. He upholds the widow and orphan
   but thwarts the path of the wicked.
   The Lord will reign for ever,
   Zion's God, from age to age. R.

Second Reading   1 Timothy 6:11-16

Do all that you have been told until the Appearing of the Lord.

As a man dedicated to God, you must aim to be saintly and religious, filled with faith and love, patient and gentle. Fight the good fight of the faith and win for yourself the eternal life to which you were called when you made your profession and spoke up for the truth in front of many witnesses. Now, before God the source of all life and before Jesus Christ, who spoke up as a witness for the truth in front of Pontius Pilate, I put to you the duty of doing all that you have been told, with no faults or failures, until the Appearing of our Lord Jesus Christ,

who at the due time will be revealed
by God, the blessed and only Ruler of all,
the King of kings and the Lord of lords,
who alone is immortal,
whose home is in inaccessible light,
whom no man has seen and no man is able to see:
to him be honour and everlasting power. Amen.

Gospel Acclamation

Alleluia, alleluia!
The sheep that belong to me listen to my voice,
says the Lord,
I know them and they follow me.
Alleluia!   John 10:27

or

Alleluia, alleluia!
Jesus Christ was rich,
but he became poor for your sake,
to make you rich out of his poverty.
Alleluia!   2 Corinthians 8:9

Gospel   Luke 16:19-31

Good things come your way, just as bad things came the way of
Lazarus. Now he is being comforted here while you are in agony.

Jesus said to the Pharisees: "There was a rich man who used to dress
in purple and fine linen and feast magnificently every day. And at his
gate there lay a poor man called Lazarus, covered with sores, who
longed to fill himself with the scraps that fell from the rich man's
table. Dogs even came and licked his sores. Now the poor man died
and was carried away by the angels to the bosom of Abraham. The
rich man also died and was buried.

"In his torment in Hades he looked up and saw Abraham a long
way off with Lazarus in his bosom. So he cried out, 'Father Abraham,
pity me and send Lazarus to dip the tip of his finger in water and cool
my tongue, for I am in agony in these flames.' 'My son,' Abraham
replied, 'remember that during your life good things came your
way, just as bad things came the way of Lazarus. Now he is being
comforted here while you are in agony. But that is not all: between us

and you a great gulf has been fixed, to stop anyone, if he wanted to, crossing from our side to yours, and to stop any crossing from your side to ours.'

"The rich man replied, 'Father, I beg you then to send Lazarus to my father's house, since I have five brothers, to give them warning so that they do not come to this place of torment too.' 'They have Moses and the prophets,' said Abraham, 'let them listen to them.' 'Ah no, father Abraham,' said the rich man, 'but if someone comes to them from the dead, they will repent.' Then Abraham said to him, 'If they will not listen either to Moses or to the prophets, they will not be convinced even if someone should rise from the dead.'"

The Creed is said.

Prayer over the Offerings

Grant us, O merciful God,
that this our offering may find acceptance with you
and that through it the wellspring of all blessing
may be laid open before us.
Through Christ our Lord.

Preface I-VIII of the Sundays in Ordinary Time, pp. 499-502.

Communion Antiphon

Remember your word to your servant, O Lord,
by which you have given me hope.
This is my comfort when I am brought low.   cf. Psalm 118:49-50

or

By this we came to know the love of God:
that Christ laid down his life for us;
so we ought to lay down our lives for one another.   1 John 3:16

Prayer after Communion

May this heavenly mystery, O Lord,
restore us in mind and body,
that we may be coheirs in glory with Christ,
to whose suffering we are united
whenever we proclaim his Death.
Who lives and reigns for ever and ever.

TWENTY-SEVENTH SUNDAY IN ORDINARY TIME – C

Increase our faith.
We are called to continue professing and practising our faith in God, even
in the midst of a materialistic world. It will not be easy, and so we require
Christ's help. We are never to be ashamed of witnessing to the Lord; we have
his Spirit with us, and can rely on his power.

Entrance Antiphon

Within your will, O Lord, all things are established,
and there is none that can resist your will.
For you have made all things, the heaven and the earth,
and all that is held within the circle of heaven;
you are the Lord of all.   cf. Esther 4:17

The Gloria is said or sung.

Collect

Almighty ever-living God,
who in the abundance of your kindness
surpass the merits and the desires of those who entreat you,
pour out your mercy upon us
to pardon what conscience dreads
and to give what prayer does not dare to ask.
Through our Lord Jesus Christ, your Son,
who lives and reigns with you in the unity of the Holy Spirit,
one God, for ever and ever.

First Reading   Habakkuk 1:2-3; 2:2-4

The upright man will live by his faithfulness.

How long, Lord, am I to cry for help
while you will not listen;
to cry "Oppression!" in your ear
and you will not save?

Why do you set injustice before me,
why do you look on where there is tyranny?
Outrage and violence, this is all I see,
all is contention, and discord flourishes.
Then the Lord answered and said,

> "Write the vision down,
> inscribe it on tablets
> to be easily read,
> since this vision is for its own time only:
> eager for its own fulfilment, it does not deceive;
> if it comes slowly, wait,
> for come it will, without fail.
> See how he flags, he whose soul is not at rights,
> but the upright man will live by his faithfulness."

Psalm   Psalm 94

R.   **O that today you would listen to his voice!**
     Harden not your hearts.

1. Come, ring out our joy to the Lord;
    hail the rock who saves us.
    Let us come before him, giving thanks,
    with songs let us hail the Lord. R.

2. Come in; let us bow and bend low;
    let us kneel before the God who made us
    for he is our God and we
    the people who belong to his pasture,
    the flock that is led by his hand. R.

3. O that today you would listen to his voice!
    "Harden not your hearts as at Meribah,
    as on that day at Massah in the desert
    when your fathers put me to the test;
    when they tried me, though they saw my work." R.

Second Reading   2 Timothy 1:6-8. 13-14
Never be ashamed of witnessing to the Lord.

I am reminding you to fan into a flame the gift that God gave you when I laid my hands on you. God's gift was not a spirit of timidity, but the Spirit of power, and love, and self-control. So you are never to be ashamed of witnessing to the Lord, or ashamed of me for being his prisoner; but with me, bear the hardships for the sake of the Good News, relying on the power of God.

Keep as your pattern the sound teaching you have heard from me, in the faith and love that are in Christ Jesus. You have been trusted to look after something precious; guard it with the help of the Holy Spirit who lives in us.

Gospel Acclamation
Alleluia, alleluia!
Speak, Lord, your servant is listening:
you have the message of eternal life.
Alleluia!   1 Samuel 3:9; John 6:68

or

Alleluia, alleluia!
The word of the Lord remains for ever:
What is this word?
It is the Good News that has been brought to you.
Alleluia!   1 Peter 1:25

Gospel   Luke 17:5-10
If only you had faith!

The apostles said to the Lord, "Increase our faith." The Lord replied, "Were your faith the size of a mustard seed you could say to this mulberry tree, 'Be uprooted and planted in the sea,' and it would obey you.

"Which of you, with a servant ploughing or minding sheep, would say to him when he returned from the fields, 'Come and have your meal immediately?' Would he not be more likely to say, 'Get my supper laid; make yourself tidy and wait on me while I eat and drink. You can eat and drink yourself afterwards'? Must he be grateful to the servant for doing what he was told? So with you: when you have done all you have been told to do, say, 'We are merely servants: we have done no more than our duty.'"

The Creed is said.

Prayer over the Offerings
Accept, O Lord, we pray,
the sacrifices instituted by your commands
and, through the sacred mysteries,
which we celebrate with dutiful service,
graciously complete the sanctifying work
by which you are pleased to redeem us.
Through Christ our Lord.

Preface I-VIII of the Sundays in Ordinary Time, pp. 499-502.

Communion Antiphon
The Lord is good to those who hope in him,
to the soul that seeks him. Lamentations 3:25

or

Though many, we are one bread, one body,
for we all partake of the one Bread and one Chalice.
cf. 1 Corinthians 10:17

Prayer after Communion
Grant us, almighty God,
that we may be refreshed and nourished
by the Sacrament which we have received,
so as to be transformed into what we consume.
Through Christ our Lord.

TWENTY-EIGHTH SUNDAY IN ORDINARY TIME – C

Give thanks to the Lord.
It is right always to give thanks to the Lord for his constant goodness to us. He gives us new life through the Death and Resurrection of his Son, Jesus Christ. If we die with him, we shall also live with him. We were like lepers through sin; but now we are made new through Christ's saving power, which cleanses and heals us.

Entrance Antiphon
If you, O Lord, should mark iniquities,
Lord, who could stand?
But with you is found forgiveness,
O God of Israel.

Psalm 129:3-4

The Gloria is said or sung.

Collect
May your grace, O Lord, we pray,
at all times go before us and follow after
and make us always determined
to carry out good works.
Through our Lord Jesus Christ, your Son,
who lives and reigns with you in the unity of the Holy Spirit,
one God, for ever and ever.

First Reading   **2 Kings 5:14-17**
Naaman returned to Elisha and acknowledged the Lord.
Naaman the leper went down and immersed himself seven times in the Jordan, as Elisha had told him to do. And his flesh became clean once more like the flesh of a little child.

Returning to Elisha with his whole escort, he went in and stood before him. "Now I know", he said, "that there is no God in all the earth except in Israel. Now, please, accept a present from your servant." But Elisha replied, "As the Lord lives, whom I serve, I will accept nothing." Naaman pressed him to accept, but he refused. Then Naaman said, "Since your answer is 'No,' allow your servant to be given as much earth as two mules may carry, because your servant will no longer offer holocaust or sacrifice to any god except the Lord."

Psalm   **Psalm 97**

R. **The Lord has shown his salvation to the nations.**

1. Sing a new song to the Lord
   for he has worked wonders.
   His right hand and his holy arm
   have brought salvation. R.

2. The Lord has made known his salvation;
   has shown his justice to the nations.
   He has remembered his truth and love
   for the house of Israel. R.

3. All the ends of the earth have seen
   the salvation of our God.
   Shout to the Lord all the earth,
   ring out your joy. R.

Second Reading   2 Timothy 2:8-13
If we hold firm, then we shall reign with Christ.
Remember the Good News that I carry, "Jesus Christ risen from the dead, sprung from the race of David"; it is on account of this that I have my own hardships to bear, even to being chained like a criminal – but they cannot chain up God's news. So I bear it all for the sake of those who are chosen, so that in the end they may have the salvation that is in Christ Jesus and the eternal glory that comes with it.

Here is a saying that you can rely on:

If we have died with him, then we shall live with him.
If we hold firm, then we shall reign with him.

If we disown him, then he will disown us.
We may be unfaithful, but he is always faithful,
for he cannot disown his own self.

Gospel Acclamation
Alleluia, alleluia!
Your words are spirit, Lord,
and they are life:
you have the message of eternal life.
Alleluia!   cf. John 6:63. 68

or

Alleluia, alleluia!
For all things give thanks,
because this is what God expects you to do in Christ Jesus.
Alleluia!   1 Thessalonians 5:18

Gospel   Luke 17:11-19
No one has come back to give praise to God, except this foreigner.
On the way to Jerusalem Jesus travelled along the border between
Samaria and Galilee. As he entered one of the villages, ten lepers
came to meet him. They stood some way off and called to him,
"Jesus! Master! Take pity on us." When he saw them he said, "Go
and show yourselves to the priests." Now as they were going away
they were cleansed. Finding himself cured, one of them turned back
praising God at the top of his voice and threw himself at the feet of
Jesus and thanked him. The man was a Samaritan. This made Jesus
say, "Were not all ten made clean? The other nine, where are they? It
seems that no one has come back to give praise to God, except this
foreigner." And he said to the man, "Stand up and go on your way.
Your faith has saved you."

The Creed is said.

Prayer over the Offerings
Accept, O Lord, the prayers of your faithful
with the sacrificial offerings,
that, through these acts of devotedness,
we may pass over to the glory of heaven.
Through Christ our Lord.

Preface I-VIII of the Sundays in Ordinary Time, pp. 499-502.

Communion Antiphon
The rich suffer want and go hungry,
but those who seek the Lord lack no blessing.   cf. Psalm 33:11

or

When the Lord appears, we shall be like him,
for we shall see him as he is.   1 John 3:2

Prayer after Communion
We entreat your majesty most humbly, O Lord,
that, as you feed us with the nourishment
which comes from the most holy Body and Blood of your Son,
so you may make us sharers of his divine nature.
Who lives and reigns for ever and ever.

TWENTY-NINTH SUNDAY IN ORDINARY TIME – C

Pray continually and never lose heart.

When we pray, we sometimes are tempted to give up if God does not seem to answer us immediately. Christ teaches us to persevere, and we can know that he is always interceding for us to his Father. As long as we pray in faith, we will never be beaten by those who are against us.

Entrance Antiphon

To you I call; for you will surely heed me, O God;
turn your ear to me; hear my words.
Guard me as the apple of your eye;
in the shadow of your wings protect me. cf. Psalm 16:6. 8

The Gloria is said or sung.

Collect

Almighty ever-living God,
grant that we may always conform our will to yours
and serve your majesty in sincerity of heart.
Through our Lord Jesus Christ, your Son,
who lives and reigns with you in the unity of the Holy Spirit,
one God, for ever and ever.

First Reading Exodus 17:8-13

As long as Moses kept his arms raised, Israel had the advantage.

The Amalekites came and attacked Israel at Rephidim. Moses said to Joshua, "Pick out men for yourself, and tomorrow morning march out to engage Amalek. I, meanwhile, will stand on the hilltop, the staff of God in my hand." Joshua did as Moses told him and marched out to engage Amalek, while Moses and Aaron and Hur went up to the top of the hill. As long as Moses kept his arms raised, Israel had the advantage; when he let his arms fall, the advantage went to Amalek. But Moses' arms grew heavy, so they took a stone and put it under him and on this he sat, Aaron and Hur supporting his arms, one on one side, one on the other; and his arms remained firm till sunset. With the edge of the sword Joshua cut down Amalek and his people.

Psalm   Psalm 120

R. **Our help is in the name of the Lord**
    who made heaven and earth.

1. I lift up my eyes to the mountains:
   from where shall come my help?
   My help shall come from the Lord
   who made heaven and earth. R.

2. May he never allow you to stumble!
   Let him sleep not, your guard.
   No, he sleeps not nor slumbers,
   Israel's guard. R.

3. The Lord is your guard and your shade;
   at your right side he stands.
   By day the sun shall not smite you
   nor the moon in the night. R.

4. The Lord will guard you from evil,
   he will guard your soul.
   The Lord will guard your going and coming
   both now and for ever. R.

Second Reading   2 Timothy 3:14 – 4:2
The man who is dedicated to God becomes fully equipped and ready for any good work.
You must keep to what you have been taught and know to be true; remember who your teachers were, and how, ever since you were a child, you have known the holy scriptures – from these you can learn the wisdom that leads to salvation through faith in Christ Jesus. All scripture is inspired by God and can profitably be used for teaching, for refuting error, for guiding people's lives and teaching them to be holy. This is how the man who is dedicated to God

becomes fully equipped and ready for any good work.

Before God and before Christ Jesus who is to be judge of the living and the dead, I put this duty to you, in the name of his Appearing and of his kingdom: proclaim the message and, welcome or unwelcome, insist on it. Refute falsehood, correct error, call to obedience – but do all with patience and with the intention of teaching.

Gospel Acclamation
Alleluia, alleluia!
May the Father of our Lord Jesus Christ
enlighten the eyes of our mind,
so that we can see what hope his call holds for us.
Alleluia!   cf. Ephesians 1:17. 18

or

Alleluia, alleluia!
The word of God is something alive and active;
it can judge secret emotions and thoughts.
Allelluia!   Hebrews 4:12

Gospel   Luke 18:1-8
God will see justice done to his chosen who cry to him.

Jesus told his disciples a parable about the need to pray continually and never lose heart. "There was a judge in a certain town", he said, "who had neither fear of God nor respect for man. In the same town there was a widow who kept on coming to him and saying, 'I want justice from you against my enemy!' For a long time he refused, but at last he said to himself, 'Maybe I have neither fear of God nor respect for man, but since she keeps pestering me I must give this widow her just rights, or she will persist in coming and worry me to death.' "

And the Lord said, "You notice what the unjust judge has to say? Now will not God see justice done to his chosen who cry to him day and night even when he delays to help them? I promise you, he will see justice done to them, and done speedily. But when the Son of Man comes, will he find any faith on earth?"

The Creed is said.

Prayer over the Offerings
Grant us, Lord, we pray,
a sincere respect for your gifts,
that, through the purifying action of your grace,
we may be cleansed by the very mysteries we serve.
Through Christ our Lord.

Preface I-VIII of the Sundays in Ordinary Time, pp. 499-502.

Communion Antiphon
Behold, the eyes of the Lord
are on those who fear him,
who hope in his merciful love,
to rescue their souls from death,
to keep them alive in famine.   cf. Psalm 32:18-19

or

The Son of Man has come
to give his life as a ransom for many.   Mark 10:45

Prayer after Communion
Grant, O Lord, we pray,
that, benefiting from participation in heavenly things,
we may be helped by what you give in this present age
and prepared for the gifts that are eternal.
Through Christ our Lord.

THIRTIETH SUNDAY IN ORDINARY TIME – C

The prayer of the humble.
Like the Pharisee, those who are self-righteous have closed minds and hearts;
they consider themselves superior to others. In contrast, those who are humble
recognise that they are sinners before God; it is their prayer that will be
answered. When we recognise that we need help we will receive it because we
know that the answer to our prayer is due to God's mercy and not
to our own goodness.

Entrance Antiphon
Let the hearts that seek the Lord rejoice;
turn to the Lord and his strength;
constantly seek his face.

cf. Psalm 104:3-4

The Gloria is said or sung.

Collect
Almighty ever-living God,
increase our faith, hope and charity,
and make us love what you command,
so that we may merit what you promise.
Through our Lord Jesus Christ, your Son,
who lives and reigns with you in the unity of the Holy Spirit,
one God, for ever and ever.

First Reading   Ecclesiasticus 35:12-14. 16-19
The humble man's prayer pierces the clouds.
The Lord is a judge
who is no respecter of personages.
He shows no respect of personages to the detriment of a poor man,
he listens to the plea of the injured party.
He does not ignore the orphan's supplication,
nor the widow's as she pours out her story.

The man who with his whole heart serves God will be accepted,
his petitions will carry to the clouds.
The humble man's prayer pierces the clouds,
until it arrives he is inconsolable,
nor will he desist until the Most High takes notice of him,
acquits the virtuous and delivers judgement.
And the Lord will not be slow,
nor will he be dilatory on their behalf.

Psalm   Psalm 32

R. **This poor man called; the Lord heard him.**

1. I will bless the Lord at all times,
   his praise always on my lips;
   in the Lord my soul shall make its boast.
   The humble shall hear and be glad. R.

2. The Lord turns his face against the wicked
   to destroy their remembrance from the earth.
   The just call and the Lord hears
   and rescues them in all their distress. R.

3. The Lord is close to the broken-hearted;
   those whose spirit is crushed he will save.
   The Lord ransoms the souls of his servants.
   Those who hide in him shall not be condemned. R.

Second Reading   2 Timothy 4:6-8. 16-18
All there is to come now is the crown of righteousness reserved for
me.
My life is already being poured away as a libation, and the time has
come for me to be gone. I have fought the good fight to the end; I
have run the race to the finish; I have kept the faith; all there is to
come now is the crown of righteousness reserved for me, which the
Lord, the righteous judge, will give to me on that Day; and not only
to me but to all those who have longed for his Appearing.

The first time I had to present my defence, there was not a single witness to support me. Every one of them deserted me – may they not be held accountable for it. But the Lord stood by me and gave me power, so that through me the whole message might be proclaimed for all the pagans to hear; and so I was rescued from the lion's mouth. The Lord will rescue me from all evil attempts on me, and bring me safely to his heavenly kingdom. To him be glory for ever and ever. Amen.

Gospel Acclamation
Alleluia, alleluia!
Blessed are you, Father,
Lord of heaven and earth,
for revealing the mysteries of the kingdom
to mere children.
Alleluia!   cf. Matthew 11:25

or

Alleluia, alleluia!
God in Christ was reconciling the world to himself,
and he has entrusted to us the news that they are reconciled.
Alleluia!   2 Corinthians 5:19

Gospel   Luke 18:9-14
The publican went home at rights with God; the Pharisee did not.
Jesus spoke the following parable to some people who prided themselves on being virtuous and despised everyone else. "Two men went up to the Temple to pray, one a Pharisee, the other a tax collector. The Pharisee stood there and said this prayer to himself, 'I thank you, God, that I am not grasping, unjust, adulterous like the rest of mankind, and particularly that I am not like this tax collector here. I fast twice a week; I pay tithes on all I get.' The tax collector stood some distance away, not daring even to raise his eyes to heaven; but he beat his breast and said, 'God, be merciful to me, a sinner.' This man, I tell you, went home again at rights with God; the other did not. For everyone who exalts himself will be humbled, but the man who humbles himself will be exalted."

The Creed is said.

Prayer over the Offerings

Look, we pray, O Lord,
on the offerings we make to your majesty,
that whatever is done by us in your service
may be directed above all to your glory.
Through Christ our Lord.

Preface I-VIII of the Sundays in Ordinary Time, pp. 499-502.

Communion Antiphon

We will ring out our joy at your saving help
and exult in the name of our God.   cf. Psalm 19:6

or

Christ loved us and gave himself up for us,
as a fragrant offering to God.   Ephesians 5:2

Prayer after Communion

May your Sacraments, O Lord, we pray,
perfect in us what lies within them,
that what we now celebrate in signs
we may one day possess in truth.
Through Christ our Lord.

THIRTY-FIRST SUNDAY IN ORDINARY TIME – C

Today salvation has come to this house.
The Lord is the lover of life and his imperishable Spirit is in all things. He
overlooks our sins so that we can repent. God's love reaches its fulfilment in
Christ who has come to save everybody, if only, like Zacchaeus, they will meet
him and accept him into their lives. Today salvation has come to us too if we
are prepared to welcome Christ into our hearts.

Entrance Antiphon
Forsake me not, O Lord, my God;
be not far from me!
Make haste and come to my help,
O Lord, my strong salvation!   cf. Psalm 37:22-23

The Gloria is said or sung.

Collect
Almighty and merciful God,
by whose gift your faithful offer you
right and praiseworthy service,
grant, we pray,
that we may hasten without stumbling
to receive the things you have promised.
Through our Lord Jesus Christ, your Son,
who lives and reigns with you in the unity of the Holy Spirit,
one God, for ever and ever.

First Reading   Wisdom 11:22 – 12:2
You are merciful to all because you love all that exists.
In your sight, Lord, the whole world is like a grain of dust that tips
    the scales,
like a drop of morning dew falling on the ground.
Yet you are merciful to all, because you can do all things

and overlook men's sins so that they can repent.
Yes, you love all that exists, you hold nothing of what you have
    made in abhorrence,
for had you hated anything, you would not have formed it.
And how, had you not willed it, could a thing persist,
how be conserved if not called forth by you?
You spare all things because all things are yours, Lord, lover of life,
you whose imperishable spirit is in all.
Little by little, therefore, you correct those who offend,
you admonish and remind them of how they have sinned,
so that they may abstain from evil and trust in you, Lord.

Psalm   Psalm 144

R. **I will bless your name for ever,**
    O God my King.

1. I will give you glory, O God my King,
   I will bless your name for ever.
   I will bless you day after day
   and praise your name for ever. R.

2. The Lord is kind and full of compassion,
   slow to anger, abounding in love.
   How good is the Lord to all,
   compassionate to all his creatures. R.

3. All your creatures shall thank you, O Lord,
   and your friends shall repeat their blessing.
   They shall speak of the glory of your reign
   and declare your might, O God. R.

4. The Lord is faithful in all his words
   and loving in all his deeds.
   The Lord supports all who fall
   and raises all who are bowed down. R.

Second Reading   2 Thessalonians 1:11 – 2:2
The name of Christ will be glorified in you and you in him.

We pray continually that our God will make you worthy of his call,
and by his power fulfil all your desires for goodness and complete
all that you have been doing through faith; because in this way the
name of our Lord Jesus Christ will be glorified in you and you in
him, by the grace of our God and the Lord Jesus Christ.

To turn now, brothers, to the coming of our Lord Jesus Christ and
how we shall all be gathered round him: please do not get excited
too soon or alarmed by any prediction or rumour or any letter
claiming to come from us, implying that the Day of the Lord has
already arrived.

Gospel Acclamation
Alleluia, alleluia!
Blessings on the King who comes,
in the name of the Lord!
Peace in heaven
and glory in the highest heavens!
Alleluia!   Luke 19:38

or

Alleluia, alleluia!
God loved the world so much
that he gave his only Son
so that anyone who believes in him
may have eternal life.
Alleluia!   John 3:16

Gospel   Luke 19:1-10
The Son of Man has come to seek out and save what was lost.

Jesus entered Jericho and was going through the town when a man
whose name was Zacchaeus made his appearance; he was one of the
senior tax collectors and a wealthy man. He was anxious to see what
kind of man Jesus was, but he was too short and could not see him
for the crowd; so he ran ahead and climbed a sycamore tree to catch
a glimpse of Jesus who was to pass that way. When Jesus reached

the spot he looked up and spoke to him: "Zacchaeus, come down. Hurry, because I must stay at your house today." And he hurried down and welcomed him joyfully. They all complained when they saw what was happening. "He has gone to stay at a sinner's house," they said. But Zacchaeus stood his ground and said to the Lord, "Look, sir, I am going to give half my property to the poor, and if I have cheated anybody I will pay him back four times the amount." And Jesus said to him, "Today salvation has come to this house, because this man too is a son of Abraham; for the Son of Man has come to seek out and save what was lost."

The Creed is said.

Prayer over the Offerings
May these sacrificial offerings, O Lord,
become for you a pure oblation,
and for us a holy outpouring of your mercy.
Through Christ our Lord.

Preface I-VIII of the Sundays in Ordinary Time, pp. 499-502.

Communion Antiphon
You will show me the path of life,
the fullness of joy in your presence, O Lord.   cf. Psalm 15:11

or

Just as the living Father sent me
and I have life because of the Father,
so whoever feeds on me
shall have life because of me, says the Lord.   John 6:58

Prayer after Communion
May the working of your power, O Lord,
increase in us, we pray,
so that, renewed by these heavenly Sacraments,
we may be prepared by your gift
for receiving what they promise.
Through Christ our Lord.

THIRTY-SECOND SUNDAY IN ORDINARY TIME – C

God of the living.
In the midst of all the troubles of this life, God is at our side constantly
strengthening us through Jesus Christ. We believe in the resurrection of the dead
and so are called as children of God to the hope of eternal life. Our God is not
God of the dead but of the living.

Entrance Antiphon
Let my prayer come into your presence.
Incline your ear to my cry for help, O Lord.

cf. Psalm 87:3

The Gloria is said or sung.

Collect
Almighty and merciful God,
graciously keep from us all adversity,
so that, unhindered in mind and body alike,
we may pursue in freedom of heart
the things that are yours.
Through our Lord Jesus Christ, your Son,
who lives and reigns with you in the unity of the Holy Spirit,
one God, for ever and ever.

First Reading

2 Maccabees 7:1-2. 9-14

The King of the world will raise us up to live again for ever.
There were seven brothers who were arrested with their mother. The
king tried to force them to taste pig's flesh, which the Law forbids,
by torturing them with whips and scourges. One of them, acting
as spokesman for the others, said, "What are you trying to find out
from us? We are prepared to die rather than break the Law of our
ancestors."

With his last breath the second brother exclaimed, "Inhuman
fiend, you may discharge us from this present life, but the King of

the world will raise us up, since it is for his laws that we die, to live again for ever."

After him, they amused themselves with the third, who on being asked for his tongue promptly thrust it out and boldly held out his hands, with these honourable words, "It was heaven that gave me these limbs; for the sake of his laws I disdain them; from him I hope to receive them again." The king and his attendants were astounded at the young man's courage and his utter indifference to suffering.

When this one was dead they subjected the fourth to the same savage torture. When he neared his end he cried, "Ours is the better choice, to meet death at men's hands, yet relying on God's promise that we shall be raised up by him; whereas for you there can be no resurrection, no new life."

Psalm   Psalm 16

R. **I shall be filled, when I awake,
     with the sight of your glory, O Lord.**

1. Lord, hear a cause that is just,
    pay heed to my cry.
    Turn your ear to my prayer:
    no deceit is on my lips. R.

2. I kept my feet firmly in your paths;
    there was no faltering in my steps.
    I am here and I call, you will hear me, O God.
    Turn your ear to me; hear my words. R.

3. Guard me as the apple of your eye.
    Hide me in the shadow of your wings.
    As for me, in my justice I shall see your face
    and be filled, when I awake, with the sight of your glory. R.

Second Reading   2 Thessalonians 2:16 – 3:5
May the Lord strengthen you in everything good that you do or say.
May our Lord Jesus Christ himself, and God our Father who has given us his love and, through his grace, such inexhaustible comfort and such sure hope, comfort you and strengthen you in everything good that you do or say.

Finally, brothers, pray for us; pray that the Lord's message may spread quickly, and be received with honour as it was among you; and pray that we may be preserved from the interference of bigoted and evil people, for faith is not given to everyone. But the Lord is faithful, and he will give you strength and guard you from the evil one, and we, in the Lord, have every confidence that you are doing and will go on doing all that we tell you. May the Lord turn your hearts towards the love of God and the fortitude of Christ.

Gospel Acclamation
Alleluia, alleluia!
Stay awake, praying at all times
for the strength to stand with confidence before the Son of Man.
Alleluia!   Luke 21:36

or

Alleluia, alleluia!
Jesus Christ is the First-born from the dead;
to him be glory and power for ever and ever.
Alleluia!   Apocalypse 1:5. 6

Gospel   Luke 20:27-38
He is God, not of the dead, but of the living.

Some Sadducees – those who say that there is no resurrection – approached Jesus and they put this* question to him,

"Master, we have it from Moses in writing, that if a man's married brother dies childless, the man must marry the widow to raise up children for his brother. Well, then, there were seven brothers. The first, having married a wife, died childless. The second and then the third married the widow. And the same with all seven, they died leaving no children. Finally the woman herself died. Now, at the resurrection, to which of them will she be wife since she had been married to all seven?"

Jesus replied, "The children of this world take wives and husbands, but those who are judged worthy of a place in the other world and in the resurrection from the dead do not marry because they can no longer die, for they are the same as the angels, and being children of the resurrection they are sons of God. And Moses himself implies that the dead rise again, in the passage about the bush where he calls the Lord the God of Abraham, the God of Isaac and the God of Jacob. Now he is God, not of the dead, but of the living; for to him all men are in fact alive."

* In the shorter form, for "this" read "a".

The Creed is said.

Prayer over the Offerings
Look with favour, we pray, O Lord,
upon the sacrificial gifts offered here,
that, celebrating in mystery the Passion of your Son,
we may honour it with loving devotion.
Through Christ our Lord.

Preface I-VIII of the Sundays in Ordinary Time, pp. 499-502.

Communion Antiphon
The Lord is my shepherd; there is nothing I shall want.
Fresh and green are the pastures where he gives me repose,
near restful waters he leads me.   cf. Psalm 22:1-2

or

The disciples recognised the Lord Jesus in the breaking of bread.
                                                    cf. Luke 24:35

Prayer after Communion
Nourished by this sacred gift, O Lord,
we give you thanks and beseech your mercy,
that, by the pouring forth of your Spirit,
the grace of integrity may endure
in those your heavenly power has entered.
Through Christ our Lord.

THIRTY-THIRD SUNDAY IN ORDINARY TIME – C

Patient endurance.
We will suffer because of our belief in Jesus Christ. Jesus teaches us not to be afraid or to lose heart, because God will vindicate us. By patiently enduring suffering, we will gain life without end. This hope of ultimate victory can keep us firm in times of trial.

Entrance Antiphon
The Lord said: I think thoughts of peace and not of affliction.
You will call upon me, and I will answer you,
and I will lead back your captives from every place.

Jeremiah 29:11. 12. 14

The Gloria is said or sung.

Collect
Grant us, we pray, O Lord our God,
the constant gladness of being devoted to you,
for it is full and lasting happiness
to serve with constancy
the author of all that is good.
Through our Lord Jesus Christ, your Son,
who lives and reigns with you in the unity of the Holy Spirit,
one God, for ever and ever.

First Reading   Malachi 3:19-20
For you the sun of righteousness will shine out.
The day is coming now, burning like a furnace; and all the arrogant and the evil-doers will be like stubble. The day that is coming is going to burn them up, says the Lord of hosts, leaving them neither root nor stalk. But for you who fear my name, the sun of righteousness will shine out with healing in its rays.

Psalm   Psalm 97

R. **The Lord comes to rule the peoples with fairness.**

1. Sing psalms to the Lord with the harp
   with the sound of music.
   With trumpets and the sound of the horn
   acclaim the King, the Lord. R.

2. Let the sea and all within it, thunder;
   the world, and all its peoples.
   Let the rivers clap their hands
   and the hills ring out their joy
   at the presence of the Lord. R.

3. For the Lord comes,
   he comes to rule the earth.
   He will rule the world with justice
   and the peoples with fairness. R.

Second Reading   2 Thessalonians 3:7-12
Do not let anyone have food if he refuses to work.

You know how you are supposed to imitate us: now we were not idle
when we were with you, nor did we ever have our meals at anyone's
table without paying for them; no, we worked night and day, slaving
and straining, so as not to be a burden on any of you. This was not
because we had no right to be, but in order to make ourselves an
example for you to follow.

   We gave you a rule when we were with you: not to let anyone have
any food if he refused to do any work. Now we hear that there are
some of you who are living in idleness, doing no work themselves
but interfering with everyone else's. In the Lord Jesus Christ, we
order and call on people of this kind to go on quietly working and
earning the food that they eat.

Gospel Acclamation
Alleluia, alleluia!
Stay awake, praying at all times
for the strength to stand with confidence
before the Son of Man.
Alleluia!

Luke 21:36

or

Alleluia, alleluia!
Stand erect, hold your heads high,
because your liberation is near at hand.
Alleluia!

Luke 21:28

Gospel

Luke 21:5-19

Your endurance will win you your lives.

When some were talking about the Temple, remarking how it was adorned with fine stonework and votive offerings, Jesus said, "All these things you are staring at now – the time will come when not a single stone will be left on another: everything will be destroyed." And they put to him this question: "Master," they said, "when will this happen, then, and what sign will there be that this is about to take place?"

"Take care not to be deceived," he said, "because many will come using my name and saying, 'I am he,' and, 'The time is near at hand.' Refuse to join them. And when you hear of wars and revolutions, do not be frightened, for this is something that must happen but the end is not so soon." Then he said to them, "Nation will fight against nation, and kingdom against kingdom. There will be great earthquakes and plagues and famines here and there; there will be fearful sights and great signs from heaven.

"But before all this happens, men will seize you and persecute you; they will hand you over to the synagogues and to imprisonment, and bring you before kings and governors because of my name – and that will be your opportunity to bear witness. Keep this carefully in mind: you are not to prepare your defence, because I myself shall give you an eloquence and a wisdom that none of your opponents will be able to resist or contradict. You will be betrayed

even by parents and brothers, relations and friends; and some of
you will be put to death. You will be hated by all men on account of
my name, but not a hair of your head will be lost. Your endurance
will win you your lives."

The Creed is said.

Prayer over the Offerings
Grant, O Lord, we pray,
that what we offer in the sight of your majesty
may obtain for us the grace of being devoted to you
and gain us the prize of everlasting happiness.
Through Christ our Lord.

Preface I-VIII of the Sundays in Ordinary Time, pp. 499-502.

Communion Antiphon
To be near God is my happiness,
to place my hope in God the Lord.   Psalm 72:28

or

Amen, I say to you: Whatever you ask in prayer,
believe that you will receive,
and it shall be given to you, says the Lord.   Mark 11:23-24

Prayer after Communion
We have partaken of the gifts of this sacred mystery,
humbly imploring, O Lord,
that what your Son commanded us to do
in memory of him
may bring us growth in charity.
Through Christ our Lord.

Last Sunday in Ordinary Time

OUR LORD JESUS CHRIST, KING OF THE UNIVERSE – C

The promise of the kingdom.
On the cross, Christ the King promises his kingdom to a penitent thief. We, like the repentant criminal, receive redemption and forgiveness of our sins through Christ, who gives us the strength to bear all things joyfully. If we suffer with him, we will reign with him. He is the firstborn from the dead, never to die again.

Entrance Antiphon
How worthy is the Lamb who was slain,
to receive power and divinity,
and wisdom and strength and honour.
To him belong glory and power for ever and ever.

Apocalypse 5:12; 1:6

The Gloria is said or sung.

Collect
Almighty ever-living God,
whose will is to restore all things
in your beloved Son, the King of the universe,
grant, we pray,
that the whole creation, set free from slavery,
may render your majesty service
and ceaselessly proclaim your praise.
Through our Lord Jesus Christ, your Son,
who lives and reigns with you in the unity of the Holy Spirit,
one God, for ever and ever.

First Reading   2 Samuel 5:1-3
They anointed David king of Israel.
All the tribes of Israel came to David at Hebron. "Look," they said,
"we are your own flesh and blood. In days past when Saul was our
king, it was you who led Israel in all their exploits; and the Lord said

to you, 'You are the man who shall be shepherd of my people Israel,
you shall be the leader of Israel.'" So all the elders of Israel came
to the king at Hebron, and King David made a pact with them at
Hebron in the presence of the Lord, and they anointed David king
of Israel.

Psalm   Psalm 121

R. **I rejoiced when I heard them say:**
    "Let us go to God's house."

1. I rejoiced when I heard them say:
   "Let us go to God's house."
   And now our feet are standing
   within your gates, O Jerusalem. R.

2. Jerusalem is built as a city
   strongly compact.
   It is there that the tribes go up,
   the tribes of the Lord. R.

3. For Israel's law it is,
   there to praise the Lord's name.
   There were set the thrones of judgement
   of the house of David. R.

Second Reading   Colossians 1:12-20
He has created a place for us in the kingdom of the Son that he
loves.
We give thanks to the Father who has made it possible for you to
join the saints and with them to inherit the light.

   Because that is what he has done: he has taken us out of the
power of darkness and created a place for us in the kingdom of the
Son that he loves, and in him, we gain our freedom, the forgiveness
of our sins.

   He is the image of the unseen God
   and the first-born of all creation,

for in him were created
all things in heaven and on earth:
everything visible and everything invisible,
Thrones, Dominations, Sovereignties, Powers –
all things were created through him and for him.
Before anything was created, he existed,
and he holds all things in unity.
Now the Church is his body,
he is its head.
As he is the Beginning,
he was first to be born from the dead,
so that he should be first in every way;
because God wanted all perfection
to be found in him
and all things to be reconciled through him and for him,
everything in heaven and everything on earth,
when he made peace
by his death on the cross.

Gospel Acclamation
Alleluia, alleluia!
Blessings on him who comes in the name of the Lord!
Blessings on the coming kingdom of our father David!
Alleluia!   Mark 11:9. 10

Gospel   Luke 23:35-43
Lord, remember me when you come into your kingdom.
The people stayed there before the cross watching Jesus. As for
the leaders, they jeered at him. "He saved others," they said, "let
him save himself if he is the Christ of God, the Chosen One." The
soldiers mocked him too, and when they approached to offer him
vinegar they said, "If you are the king of the Jews, save yourself."
Above him there was an inscription: "This is the King of the Jews."

   One of the criminals hanging there abused him. "Are you not the
Christ?" he said. "Save yourself and us as well." But the other spoke
up and rebuked him. "Have you no fear of God at all?" he said. "You
got the same sentence as he did, but in our case we deserved it: we

are paying for what we did. But this man has done nothing wrong.
Jesus," he said, "remember me when you come into your kingdom."
"Indeed, I promise you," he replied, "today you will be with me in
paradise."

The Creed is said.

Prayer over the Offerings

As we offer you, O Lord, the sacrifice
by which the human race is reconciled to you,
we humbly pray,
that your Son himself may bestow on all nations
the gifts of unity and peace.
Through Christ our Lord.

Preface

It is truly right and just, our duty and our salvation,
always and everywhere to give you thanks,
Lord, holy Father, almighty and eternal God.

For you anointed your Only Begotten Son,
our Lord Jesus Christ, with the oil of gladness
as eternal Priest and King of all creation,
so that, by offering himself on the altar of the Cross
as a spotless sacrifice to bring us peace,
he might accomplish the mysteries of human redemption
and, making all created things subject to his rule,
he might present to the immensity of your majesty
an eternal and universal kingdom,
a kingdom of truth and life,
a kingdom of holiness and grace,
a kingdom of justice, love and peace.

And so, with Angels and Archangels,
with Thrones and Dominions,
and with all the hosts and Powers of heaven,
we sing the hymn of your glory,
as without end we acclaim:
Holy, Holy, Holy Lord God of hosts…

Communion Antiphon
The Lord sits as King for ever.
The Lord will bless his people with peace.   Psalm 28:10-11

Prayer after Communion
Having received the food of immortality,
we ask, O Lord,
that, glorying in obedience
to the commands of Christ, the King of the universe,
we may live with him eternally in his heavenly Kingdom.
Who lives and reigns for ever and ever.

SOLEMNITIES AND FEASTS

2 February

THE PRESENTATION OF
THE LORD

Feast

Christ the light of the nations.
Jesus Christ brings God's light into a world darkened by sin. He calls us to
share in his mission to let this light shine out to all people in our world today.
He was born as one of us, and because he has himself been through temptation
he is able to help us when we are tempted. Christ was rejected by many in his
day, yet through his Death and Resurrection he took away the power of evil.

THE BLESSING OF CANDLES AND THE PROCESSION

First Form: The Procession

The people gather in a chapel or other suitable place outside the church where the Mass will be celebrated. They carry unlighted candles. While the candles are being lit, the following antiphon or another appropriate hymn is sung.

Behold, our Lord will come with power,
to enlighten the eyes of his servants, alleluia.

Then the priest makes the Sign of the Cross, greets the people in the usual way and introduces the liturgy of the day. He may use these or similar words:

Dear brethren (brothers and sisters),
forty days have passed since we celebrated the joyful feast
of the Nativity of the Lord.
Today is the blessed day
when Jesus was presented in the Temple by Mary and Joseph.
Outwardly he was fulfilling the Law,
but in reality he was coming to meet his believing people.
Prompted by the Holy Spirit,
Simeon and Anna came to the Temple.
Enlightened by the same Spirit,
they recognised the Lord

and confessed him with exultation.
So let us also, gathered together by the Holy Spirit,
proceed to the house of God to encounter Christ.
There we shall find him
and recognise him in the breaking of the bread,
until he comes again, revealed in glory.

Then the priest blesses the candles, saying:

Let us pray.

O God, source and origin of all light,
who on this day showed to the just man Simeon
the Light for revelation to the Gentiles,
we humbly ask that,
in answer to your people's prayers,
you may be pleased to sanctify with your blessing ✠ these candles,
which we are eager to carry in praise of your name,
so that, treading the path of virtue,
we may reach that light which never fails.
Through Christ our Lord.

or

O God, true light, who create light eternal,
spreading it far and wide,
pour, we pray, into the hearts of the faithful
the brilliance of perpetual light,
so that all who are brightened in your holy temple
by the splendour of these candles
may happily reach the light of your glory.
Through Christ our Lord.

The priest sprinkles the candles with holy water. He then takes the lighted candle prepared for him and the procession begins with the acclamation:

Let us go in peace to meet the Lord.

or

Let us go forth in peace.
In the name of Christ. Amen.

All carry lighted candles. As the procession moves forward, one or other of the antiphons that follow, or another appropriate hymn, is sung.

I. Antiphon

R. **A light for revelation to the Gentiles
and the glory of your people Israel.**

Lord, now you let your servant go in peace,
in accordance with your word. R.

For my eyes have seen your salvation. R.

Which you have prepared in the sight of all the peoples. R.

Luke 2:29-32

II. Antiphon

Sion, adorn your bridal chamber and welcome Christ the King; take Mary in your arms, who is the gate of heaven, for she herself is carrying the King of glory and new light. A Virgin she remains, though bringing in her hands the Son before the morning star begotten, whom Simeon, taking in his arms announced to the peoples as Lord of life and death and Saviour of the world.

As the procession enters the church, the Entrance Antiphon of the Mass is sung. The Gloria is said or sung, and the Mass continues as usual.

Second Form: The Solemn Entrance

If a procession cannot take place, the people gather in the church, carrying unlighted candles in their hands. The priest, accompanied by the ministers and a representative group of the faithful, goes to a suitable place, either in front of the church door or inside the church itself, where most of the people can easily participate in the rite.

The candles are lit while the antiphon **Behold, our Lord** (p. 974) or another appropriate hymn is sung.

Then, after the greeting and introduction, the priest blesses the candles, as above (p. 975); and then the procession to the altar takes place, while all sing one of the antiphons above or another appropriate hymn.

The Mass continues as usual.

THE MASS

Entrance Antiphon
Your merciful love, O God,
we have received in the midst of your temple.
Your praise, O God, like your name,
reaches the ends of the earth;
your right hand is filled with saving justice.

cf. Psalm 47:10-11

The Gloria is said or sung.

Collect
Almighty ever-living God,
we humbly implore your majesty
that, just as your Only Begotten Son
was presented on this day in the Temple
in the substance of our flesh,
so, by your grace,
we may be presented to you with minds made pure.
Through our Lord Jesus Christ, your Son,
who lives and reigns with you in the unity of the Holy Spirit,
one God, for ever and ever.

First Reading   Malachi 3:1-4
The Lord you are seeking will suddenly enter his Temple.
The Lord God says this: Look, I am going to send my messenger
to prepare a way before me. And the Lord you are seeking will
suddenly enter his Temple; and the angel of the covenant whom you
are longing for, yes, he is coming, says the Lord of hosts. Who will
be able to resist the day of his coming? Who will remain standing
when he appears? For he is like the refiner's fire and the fullers'
alkali. He will take his seat as refiner and purifier; he will purify the
sons of Levi and refine them like gold and silver, and then they will
make the offering to the Lord as it should be made. The offering
of Judah and Jerusalem will then be welcomed by the Lord as in
former days, as in the years of old.

Psalm   Psalm 23

R. **Who is the king of glory?**
    It is the Lord.

1. O gates, lift up your heads;
   grow higher, ancient doors.
   Let him enter, the king of glory! R.

2. Who is the king of glory?
   The Lord, the mighty, the valiant,
   the Lord, the valiant in war. R.

3. O gates, lift high your heads;
   grow higher, ancient doors.
   Let him enter, the king of glory! R.

4. Who is he, the king of glory?
   He, the Lord of armies,
   he is the king of glory. R.

Second Reading   Hebrews 2:14-18

It was essential that he should in this way become completely like
his brothers.

Since all the children share the same blood and flesh, Jesus too
shared equally in it, so that by his death he could take away all
the power of the devil, who had power over death, and set free
all those who had been held in slavery all their lives by the fear of
death. For it was not the angels that he took to himself; he took to
himself descent from Abraham. It was essential that he should in
this way become completely like his brothers so that he could be a
compassionate and trustworthy high priest of God's religion, able to
atone for human sins. That is, because he has himself been through
temptation he is able to help others who are tempted.

Gospel Acclamation
Alleluia, alleluia!
The light to enlighten the Gentiles
and give glory to Israel, your people.
Alleluia!
                                                          Luke 2:32

Gospel   Luke 2:22-40

My eyes have seen your salvation.

When the day came for them to be purified as laid down by the Law of Moses, the parents of Jesus took him up to Jerusalem to present him to the Lord – observing what stands written in the Law of the Lord: Every first-born male must be consecrated to the Lord – and also to offer in sacrifice, in accordance with what is said in the Law of the Lord, a pair of turtle-doves or two young pigeons. Now in Jerusalem there was a man named Simeon. He was an upright and devout man; he looked forward to Israel's comforting and the Holy Spirit rested on him. It had been revealed to him by the Holy Spirit that he would not see death until he had set eyes on the Christ of the Lord. Prompted by the Spirit he came to the Temple: and when the parents brought in the child Jesus to do for him what the Law required, he took him into his arms and blessed God; and he said:

"Now, Master, you can let your servant go in peace,
just as you promised;
because my eyes have seen the salvation
which you have prepared for all the nations to see,
a light to enlighten the pagans
and the glory of your people Israel."

As the child's father and mother stood there wondering at the things that were being said about him, Simeon blessed them and said to Mary his mother, "You see this child: he is destined for the fall and for the rising of many in Israel, destined to be a sign that is rejected – and a sword will pierce your own soul too – so that the secret thoughts of many may be laid bare."

There was a prophetess also, Anna the daughter of Phanuel, of the tribe of Asher. She was well on in years. Her days of girlhood over, she had been married for seven years before becoming a widow. She was now eighty-four years old and never left the Temple, serving God night and day with fasting and prayer. She came by just at that moment and began to praise God; and she spoke of the child to all who looked forward to the deliverance of Jerusalem.

When they had done everything the Law of the Lord required, they went back to Galilee, to their own town of Nazareth. Meanwhile the child grew to maturity, and he was filled with wisdom; and God's favour was with him.

When this feast falls on a Sunday, the Creed is said.

Prayer over the Offerings
May the offering made with exultation by your Church
be pleasing to you, O Lord, we pray,
for you willed that your Only Begotten Son
be offered to you for the life of the world
as the Lamb without blemish.
Who lives and reigns for ever and ever.

Preface
It is truly right and just, our duty and our salvation,
always and everywhere to give you thanks,
Lord, holy Father, almighty and eternal God.

For your co-eternal Son was presented on this day in the Temple
and revealed by the Spirit
as the glory of Israel and Light of the nations.

And so, we, too, go forth, rejoicing to encounter your Salvation,
and with the Angels and Saints
praise you, as without end we acclaim:
Holy, Holy, Holy Lord God of hosts...

Communion Antiphon
My eyes have seen your salvation,
which you prepared in the sight of all the peoples.   Luke 2:30-31

Prayer after Communion
By these holy gifts which we have received, O Lord,
bring your grace to perfection within us,
and, as you fulfilled Simeon's expectation
that he would not see death
until he had been privileged to welcome the Christ,
so may we, going forth to meet the Lord,
obtain the gift of eternal life.
Through Christ our Lord.

SAINT DAVID, BISHOP

1 March

SAINT DAVID, BISHOP

Patron of Wales
Solemnity in Wales

You are the salt of the earth and the light of the world.
The lives of the saints were based on Christ. We are called, like Saint David
and all the saints, to follow in Christ's way. Like them, our mission is to
reflect Christ's light in the world in which we live, and to encourage the world
to taste and see that the Lord is good.

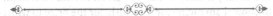

Entrance Antiphon

How beautiful upon the mountains are the feet of him
who brings glad tidings of peace,
bearing good news, announcing salvation!   Isaiah 52:7

The Gloria is said or sung.

Collect

O God, who graciously bestowed on your
   Bishop Saint David of Wales
the virtue of wisdom and the gift of eloquence,
and made him an example of prayer and pastoral zeal;
grant that, through his intercession
your Church may ever prosper and render you joyful praise.
Through our Lord Jesus Christ, your Son,
who lives and reigns with you in the unity of the Holy Spirit,
one God, for ever and ever.

Other readings may be used instead of those given here.

First Reading   Philippians 3:8-14

I am racing for the finish, for the prize to which God calls us
upwards to receive in Christ Jesus.

I believe nothing can happen that will outweigh the supreme
advantage of knowing Christ Jesus my Lord. For him I have accepted

the loss of everything, and I look on everything as so much rubbish if only I can have Christ and be given a place in him. I am no longer trying for perfection by my own efforts, the perfection that comes from the Law, but I want only the perfection that comes through faith in Christ, and is from God and based on faith. All I want is to know Christ and the power of his resurrection and to share his sufferings by reproducing the pattern of his death. That is the way I can hope to take my place in the resurrection of the dead. Not that I have become perfect yet: I have not yet won, but I am still running, trying to capture the prize for which Christ Jesus captured me. I can assure you my brothers, I am far from thinking that I have already won. All I can say is that I forget the past and I strain ahead for what is still to come; I am racing for the finish, for the prize to which God calls us upwards to receive in Christ Jesus.

Psalm   Psalm 1

R. **Happy the man who has placed
      his trust in the Lord.**

1. Happy indeed is the man
    who follows not the counsel of the wicked;
    nor lingers in the way of sinners
    nor sits in the company of scorners,
    but whose delight is the law of the Lord
    and who ponders his law day and night. R.

2. He is like a tree that is planted
    beside the flowing waters,
    that yields its fruit in due season
    and whose leaves shall never fade;
    and all that he does shall prosper. R.

3. Not so are the wicked, not so!
    for they like winnowed chaff
    shall be driven away by the wind;
    for the Lord guards the way of the just
    but the way of the wicked leads to doom. R.

Gospel Acclamation
(Alleluia, alleluia!)
If you make my word your home
you will indeed be my disciples,
and you will learn the truth, says the Lord.
(Alleluia!)   John 8:31-32

Gospel   Matthew 5:13-16
You are the light of the world.
Jesus said to his disciples, "You are the salt of the earth. But if salt
becomes tasteless, what can make it salty again? It is good for nothing,
and can only be thrown out to be trampled underfoot by men.

   "You are the light of the world. A city built on a hill-top cannot be
hidden. No one lights a lamp to put it under a tub; they put it on the
lamp-stand where it shines for everyone in the house. In the same
way your light must shine in the sight of men, so that, seeing your
good works, they may give the praise to your Father in heaven."

Where this day is kept as a Solemnity, the Creed is said.

Prayer over the Offerings
Look with favour, O Lord, we pray,
on the offerings we set upon this sacred altar
on the feast day of the Bishop Saint David,
that, bestowing on us your pardon
our oblations may give honour to your name.
Through Christ our Lord.

Preface
It is truly right and just, our duty and our salvation,
always and everywhere to give you thanks,
Lord, holy Father, almighty and eternal God,
through Christ our Lord.

For, as on the festival of Saint David you bid your Church rejoice,
so, too, you strengthen her by the example of his holy life,
teach her by his words of preaching,
and keep her safe in answer to his prayers.

And so, with the company of Angels and Saints,
we sing the hymn of your praise,
as without end we acclaim:
Holy, Holy, Holy Lord God of hosts…

Communion Antiphon
We proclaim Christ crucified,
Christ, the power of God, and the wisdom of God.

1 Corinthians 1:23-24

Prayer after Communion
We pray, almighty God,
that we, who are fortified by the power of this Sacrament,
may learn through the example of your Bishop Saint David
to seek you always above all things
and to bear in this world the likeness of the New Man.
Who lives and reigns for ever and ever.

17 March

SAINT PATRICK, BISHOP

Principal Patron of Ireland
Solemnity in Ireland

Nations will proclaim his wisdom.
Throughout the ages the Lord calls men and women to witness to the power of
his name. Some, like Saint Patrick, are called to leave their homes and become
missionaries, confessing their faith among the people of other lands. In this
way the seed of God's word is sown. As we honour Saint Patrick, we ask the
Lord's help that we too may fulfil his calling in our lives and run the race to
the finish.

Entrance Antiphon
Go from your country and your kindred and your father's house to
the land that I will show you.
I will make of you a great nation, and I will bless you,
and make your name great, so that you will be a blessing.

Genesis 12:1-2

The Gloria is said or sung.

Collect
Lord, through the work of Saint Patrick in Ireland
we have come to acknowledge the mystery of the one true God
and give thanks for our salvation in Christ;
grant by his prayers
that we who celebrate this festival
may keep alive the fire of faith he kindled.
Through our Lord Jesus Christ, your Son,
who lives and reigns with you and the Holy Spirit,
one God, for ever and ever.

Other readings may be used instead of those given here.

First Reading   Ecclesiasticus 39:6-10

His memory will not disappear, generation after generation his name will live.

If it is the will of the great Lord,
the scholar will be filled with the spirit of understanding,
he will shower forth words of wisdom,
and in prayer give thanks to the Lord.
He will grow upright in purpose and learning,
he will ponder the Lord's hidden mysteries.
He will display the instruction he has received,
taking his pride in the Law of the Lord's covenant.
Many will praise his understanding,
and it will never be forgotten.
His memory will not disappear,
generation after generation his name will live.
Nations will proclaim his wisdom,
the assembly will celebrate his praises.

Psalm   Psalm 115

R. **How can I repay the Lord for his goodness to me?**

1. How can I repay the Lord
   for his goodness to me?
   The cup of salvation I will raise;
   I will call on the Lord's name. R.

2. My vows to the Lord I will fulfil
   before all his people.
   O precious in the eyes of the Lord
   is the death of his faithful. R.

3. Your servant, Lord, your servant am I;
   you have loosened my bonds.
   A thanksgiving sacrifice I make;
   I will call on the Lord's name. R.

4. My vows to the Lord I will fulfil
   before all his people,
   in the courts of the house of the Lord,
   in your midst, O Jerusalem. R.

Second Reading   2 Timothy 4:1-8

Refute falsehood, correct error, call to obedience – but do all with patience and with the intention of teaching.

Before God and before Christ Jesus who is to be judge of the living and the dead, I put this duty to you, in the name of his Appearing and of his kingdom: proclaim the message and, welcome or unwelcome, insist on it. Refute falsehood, correct error, call to obedience – but do all with patience and with the intention of teaching. The time is sure to come when, far from being content with sound teaching, people will be avid for the latest novelty and collect themselves a whole series of teachers according to their own tastes; and then, instead of listening to the truth, they will turn to myths. Be careful always to choose the right course; be brave under trials; make the preaching of the Good News your life's work, in thoroughgoing service.

As for me, my life is already being poured away as a libation, as the time has come for me to be gone. I have fought the good fight to the end; I have run the race to the finish; I have kept the faith; all there is to come now is the crown of righteousness reserved for me, which the Lord, the righteous judge, will give me on that Day; and not only to me but to all those who have longed for his Appearing.

Gospel Acclamation

Glory to you, O Christ, you are the Word of God!
Accept and submit to the word
which has been planted in you
and can save your souls.
Glory to you, O Christ, you are the Word of God!   James 1:21

Gospel   Matthew 13:24-32

It is the smallest of all the seeds, but when it has grown it is the greatest of shrubs.

Jesus put a parable before the crowds: "The kingdom of heaven may be compared to a man who sowed good seed in his field. While everybody was asleep his enemy came, sowed darnel all among the wheat and made off. When the new wheat sprouted and ripened, the darnel appeared as well. The owner's servants went to him and said, 'Sir, was it not good seed that you sowed in your field? If so, where does the darnel come from?' 'Some enemy has done this,' he answered. And the servants said, 'Do you want us to go and weed it out?' But he said, 'No, because when you weed out the darnel you might pull up the wheat with it. Let them both grow till the harvest; and at harvest time I shall say to the reapers: First collect the darnel and tie it in bundles to be burnt, then gather the wheat into my barn.' "

He put another parable before them: "The kingdom of heaven is like a mustard seed which a man took and sowed in his field. It is the smallest of all the seeds, but when it has grown it is the biggest of shrubs and becomes a tree, so that the birds of the air can come and shelter in its branches."

Where this day is kept as a Solemnity, the Creed is said.

Prayer over the Offerings
Lord, accept this pure sacrifice
which, through the labours of Saint Patrick,
your grateful people make
to the glory of your name.
Through Christ our Lord.

Preface
It is truly right and just, our duty and our salvation,
always and everywhere to give you thanks,
Lord, holy Father, almighty and eternal God,
and to proclaim your greatness with due praise
as we honour Saint Patrick.

For you drew him through daily prayer
in captivity and hardship
to know you as a loving Father.

You chose him out of all the world
to return to the land of his captors,
that they might acknowledge Jesus Christ, their Redeemer.

In the power of your Spirit you directed his paths
to win the sons and daughters of the Irish
to the service of the Triune God.

And so, with the Angels and Archangels,
and with the great multitude of the Saints,
we sing the hymn of your praise,
as without end we acclaim:
Holy, Holy, Holy Lord God of hosts…

Communion Antiphon
Many will come from east and west
and sit down with Abraham, Isaac and Jacob
at the feast in the kingdom of heaven, says the Lord.

cf. Matthew 8:11

Prayer after Communion
Strengthen us, O Lord, by this sacrament
so that we may profess the faith taught by Saint Patrick
and proclaim it in our way of living.
Through Christ our Lord.

Solemn Blessing
May God the Father, who called us together
to celebrate this feast of Saint Patrick,
bless you, protect you and keep you faithful.
Amen.

May Christ the Lord, the High King of Heaven,
be near you at all times and shield you from evil.
Amen.

May the Holy Spirit, who is the source of all holiness,
make you rich in the love of God's people.
Amen.

And may the blessing of almighty God,
the Father, and the Son, ✠ and the Holy Spirit,
come down on you and remain for ever.
Amen.

SAINT JOSEPH, SPOUSE OF THE BLESSED VIRGIN MARY

Solemnity

Joseph did what the Lord had told him to do.

Joseph, the husband of Mary, is a perfect example of faith. Through faith he is open to whatever God asks of him. He is like Abraham, who believed in God's promise that he would have many descendants even though he did not see how this could be achieved. The promise made to David, that his throne would be secure for ever, is fulfilled through Jesus because Joseph comes from the line of David. Through our faith many things can be achieved without our knowing, if only we trust that the Lord will fulfil his promises.

⬧━━━━━━━━⬧⬧⬧━━━━━━━━⬧

Entrance Antiphon

Behold, a faithful and prudent steward,
whom the Lord set over his household.   cf. Luke 12:42

The Gloria is said or sung.

Collect

Grant, we pray, almighty God,
that by Saint Joseph's intercession
your Church may constantly watch over
the unfolding of the mysteries of human salvation,
whose beginnings you entrusted to his faithful care.
Through our Lord Jesus Christ, your Son,
who lives and reigns with you in the unity of the Holy Spirit,
one God, for ever and ever.

First Reading   2 Samuel 7:4-5. 12-14. 16

The Lord will give him the throne of his ancestor David.

The word of the Lord came to Nathan:

"Go and tell my servant David, 'Thus the Lord speaks: When your days are ended and you are laid to rest with your ancestors, I will preserve the offspring of your body after you and make his sovereignty secure. (It is he who shall build a house for my name, and I will make his royal throne secure for ever.) I will be a father to him and he a son to me. Your House and your sovereignty will always stand secure before me and your throne be established for ever.'"

Psalm   Psalm 88

R. **His dynasty shall last for ever.**

1. I will sing for ever of your love, O Lord;
    through all ages my mouth will proclaim your truth.
    Of this I am sure, that your love lasts for ever,
    that your truth is firmly established as the heavens. R.

2. "I have made a covenant with my chosen one;
    I have sworn to David my servant:
    I will establish your dynasty for ever
    and set up your throne through all ages." R.

3. He will say to me: "You are my father,
    my God, the rock who saves me."
    I will keep my love for him always;
    with him my covenant shall endure. R.

Second Reading   Romans 4:13. 16-18. 22
Though it seemed Abraham's hope could not be fulfilled, he hoped and he believed.
The promise of inheriting the world was not made to Abraham and his descendants on account of any law but on account of the righteousness which consists in faith. That is why what fulfils the promise depends on faith, so that it may be a free gift and be available to all of Abraham's descendants, not only those who belong to the Law but also those who belong to the faith of Abraham who is the Father of all of us. As scripture says: I have made you the ancestor of many nations – Abraham is our father in the eyes of God, in whom he put his faith, and who brings the dead to life and calls into being what does not exist.

  Though it seemed Abraham's hope could not be fulfilled, he hoped and he believed, and through doing so he did become the father of many nations exactly as he had been promised: Your descendants will be as many as the stars. This is the faith that was "considered as justifying him".

Gospel Acclamation
Glory and praise to you, O Christ!
They are happy who dwell in your house, O Lord,
for ever singing your praise.
Glory and praise to you, O Christ!   Psalm 83:5

Gospel   Matthew 1:16. 18-21. 24
Joseph did what the angel of the Lord had told him to do.
Jacob was the father of Joseph the husband of Mary; of her was born Jesus who is called Christ.

This is how Jesus Christ came to be born. His mother Mary was betrothed to Joseph; but before they came to live together she was found to be with child through the Holy Spirit. Her husband Joseph, being a man of honour and wanting to spare her publicity, decided to divorce her informally. He had made up his mind to do this when the angel of the Lord appeared to him in a dream and said, "Joseph son of David, do not be afraid to take Mary home as your wife, because she has conceived what is in her by the Holy Spirit. She will give birth to a son and you must name him Jesus, because he is the one who is to save his people from their sins." When Joseph woke up he did what the angel of the Lord had told him to do.

or

Gospel   Luke 2:41-51
See how worried your father and I have been, looking for you.
Every year the parents of Jesus used to go to Jerusalem for the feast of the Passover. When he was twelve years old, they went up for the feast as usual. When they were on their way home after the feast, the boy Jesus stayed behind in Jerusalem without his parents knowing it. They assumed he was with the caravan, and it was only after a day's journey that they went to look for him among their relations and acquaintances. When they failed to find him they went back to Jerusalem looking for him everywhere.

Three days later, they found him in the Temple, sitting among the doctors, listening to them, and asking them questions; and all those who heard him were astounded at his intelligence and his replies. They were overcome when they saw him, and his mother said to him, "My child, why have you done this to us? See how worried your father and I have been, looking for you." "Why were you looking for me?" he replied "Did you not know that I must be busy with my Father's affairs?" But they did not understand what he meant.

He then went down with them and came to Nazareth and lived under their authority.

The Creed is said.

Prayer over the Offerings

We pray, O Lord,
that, just as Saint Joseph served with loving care
your Only Begotten Son, born of the Virgin Mary,
so we may be worthy to minister
with a pure heart at your altar.
Through Christ our Lord.

Preface

It is truly right and just, our duty and our salvation,
always and everywhere to give you thanks,
Lord, holy Father, almighty and eternal God,
and on the Solemnity of Saint Joseph
to give you fitting praise,
to glorify you and bless you.

For this just man was given by you
as spouse to the Virgin Mother of God
and set as a wise and faithful servant
in charge of your household,
to watch like a father over your Only Begotten Son,
who was conceived by the overshadowing of the Holy Spirit,
our Lord Jesus Christ.

Through him the Angels praise your majesty,
Dominions adore and Powers tremble before you.

Heaven and the Virtues of heaven and the blessed Seraphim
worship together with exultation.
May our voices, we pray, join with theirs
in humble praise, as we acclaim:
Holy, Holy, Holy Lord God of hosts…

Communion Antiphon
Well done, good and faithful servant.
Come, share your master's joy. Matthew 25:21

Prayer after Communion
Defend with unfailing protection,
O Lord, we pray,
the family you have nourished
with food from this altar,
as they rejoice at the Solemnity of Saint Joseph,
and graciously keep safe your gifts among them.
Through Christ our Lord.

25 March

THE ANNUNCIATION OF THE LORD

Solemnity

Let what you have said be done to me.
Mary said "yes" to God and so became the mother of our Saviour. All things
are possible through the power of God's Holy Spirit for those who truly believe.
We too are called to say "yes" to God's plan for our lives. In this way Christ,
through faith, will live in us. Like Mary, we bring Jesus into our world.

Entrance Antiphon

The Lord said, as he entered the world:
Behold, I come to do your will, O God.   Hebrews 10:5. 7

The Gloria is said or sung.

Collect

O God, who willed that your Word
should take on the reality of human flesh
in the womb of the Virgin Mary,
grant, we pray,
that we, who confess our Redeemer to be God and man,
may merit to become partakers even in his divine nature.
Who lives and reigns with you in the unity of the Holy Spirit,
one God, for ever and ever.

First Reading   Isaiah 7:10-14; 8:10

The maiden is with child.

The Lord spoke to Ahaz and said, "Ask the Lord your God for a sign for
yourself coming either from the depths of Sheol or from the heights
above." "No," Ahaz answered, "I will not put the Lord to the test."

Then Isaiah said:

Listen now, House of David:
are you not satisfied with trying the patience of men
without trying the patience of my God, too?
The Lord himself, therefore,

will give you a sign.
It is this: the maiden is with child
and will soon give birth to a son
whom she will call Immanuel,
a name which means "God-is-with-us".

Psalm   Psalm 39

R. **Here I am, Lord!**
    I come to do your will.

1. You do not ask for sacrifice and offerings,
   but an open ear.
   You do not ask for holocaust and victim.
   Instead, here am I. R.

2. In the scroll of the book it stands written
   that I should do your will.
   My God, I delight in your law
   in the depth of my heart. R.

3. Your justice I have proclaimed
   in the great assembly.
   My lips I have not sealed;
   you know it, O Lord. R.

4. I have not hidden your justice in my heart
   but declared your faithful help.
   I have not hidden your love and your truth
   from the great assembly. R.

Second Reading   Hebrews 10:4-10

I was commanded in the scroll of the book, "God, here I am! I am coming to obey your will."
Bulls' blood and goats' blood are useless for taking away sins, and this is what Christ said, on coming into the world:

You who wanted no sacrifice or oblation,
prepared a body for me.
You took no pleasure in holocausts or sacrifices for sin;
then I said,
just as I was commanded in the scroll of the book,
"God, here I am! I am coming to obey your will."

Notice that he says first: You did not want what the Law lays down as the things to be offered, that is: the sacrifices, the oblations, the holocausts and the sacrifices for sin, and you took no pleasure in them; and then he says: Here I am! I am coming to obey your will. He is abolishing the first sort to replace it with the second. And this will was for us to be made holy by the offering of his body made once and for all by Jesus Christ.

Gospel Acclamation
[Alleluia, alleluia!]
The Word was made flesh,
he lived among us,
and we saw his glory.
[Alleluia!]   John 1:14

Gospel   Luke 1:26-38
Listen! You are to conceive and bear a son.
The angel Gabriel was sent by God to a town in Galilee called Nazareth, to a virgin betrothed to a man named Joseph, of the House of David; and the virgin's name was Mary. He went in and said to her, "Rejoice, so highly favoured! The Lord is with you." She was deeply disturbed by these words and asked herself what this greeting could mean, but the angel said to her, "Mary, do not be afraid; you have won God's favour. Listen! You are to conceive and bear a son, and you must name him Jesus. He will be great and will be called Son of the Most High. The Lord God will give him the throne of his ancestor David; he will rule over the House of Jacob for ever and his reign will have no end." Mary said to the angel. "But how can this come about, since I am a virgin?" "The Holy Spirit will come upon you," the angel answered, "and the power of the Most High will cover you with its shadow. And so the child will be holy and will be called Son of God. Know this too: your kinswoman Elizabeth has, in her old age, herself conceived a son, and she whom people called barren is now in her sixth month, for nothing is impossible to God." "I am the handmaid of the Lord," said Mary, "let what you have said be done to me." And the angel left her.

The Creed is said. All kneel at the words *and by the Holy Spirit was incarnate.*

Prayer over the Offerings
Be pleased, almighty God,
to accept your Church's offering,
so that she, who is aware that her beginnings
lie in the Incarnation of your Only Begotten Son,
may rejoice to celebrate his mysteries on this Solemnity.
Who lives and reigns for ever and ever.

Preface
It is truly right and just, our duty and our salvation,
always and everywhere to give you thanks,
Lord, holy Father, almighty and eternal God,
through Christ our Lord.

For the Virgin Mary heard with faith
that the Christ was to be born among men and for men's sake
by the overshadowing power of the Holy Spirit.
Lovingly she bore him in her immaculate womb,
that the promises to the children of Israel might come about
and the hope of nations be accomplished beyond all telling.

Through him the host of Angels adores your majesty
and rejoices in your presence for ever.
May our voices, we pray, join with theirs
in one chorus of exultant praise, as we acclaim:
Holy, Holy, Holy Lord God of hosts...

Communion Antiphon
Behold, a Virgin shall conceive and bear a son;
and his name will be called Emmanuel.   Isaiah 7:14

Prayer after Communion
Confirm in our minds the mysteries of the true faith,
we pray, O Lord,
so that, confessing that he who was conceived of the Virgin Mary
is true God and true man,
we may, through the saving power of his Resurrection,
merit to attain eternal joy.
Through Christ our Lord.

23 April

SAINT GEORGE, MARTYR

Patron of England
Solemnity in England

Those who sow in tears will reap in joy.
Saint George and all the martyrs witness to a life that conquers death. Their lives are a contradiction to the world that persecuted them for their faith. They have paid the ultimate price by giving their lives in witness to Christ. Now they triumph through the blood of the Lamb. They are an example and an inspiration to us.

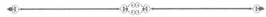

Entrance Antiphon
Rejoice, you Saints, in the presence of the Lamb;
a kingdom has been prepared for you
from the foundation of the world, alleluia.   cf. Matthew 25:34

or

On the asp and the viper you will tread,
and trample the young lion and the dragon, alleluia.   Psalm 90:13

The Gloria is said or sung.

Collect
God of hosts,
who so kindled the fire of charity
in the heart of Saint George your martyr,
that he bore witness to the risen Lord
both by his life and by his death;
grant us through his intercession, we pray,
the same faith and power of love,
that we who rejoice in his triumph
may be led to share with him
in the fullness of the resurrection.
Through our Lord Jesus Christ, your Son,
who lives and reigns with you in the unity of the Holy Spirit,
one God, for ever and ever.

Other readings may be used instead of those given here.

First Reading   Apocalypse 12:10-12
In the face of death they would not cling to life.
I, John, heard a voice shout from heaven, "Victory and power and
empire for ever have been won by our God, and all authority for
his Christ, now that the persecutor, who accused our brothers day
and night before our God, has been brought down. They have
triumphed over him by the blood of the Lamb and by the witness of
their martyrdom, because even in the face of death they would not
cling to life. Let the heavens rejoice and all who live there."

Psalm   Psalm 125

R. **Those who are sowing in tears**
   will sing when they reap.

1. When the Lord delivered Zion from bondage,
   it seemed like a dream.
   Then was our mouth filled with laughter,
   on our lips there were songs. R.

2. The heathens themselves said: "What marvels
   the Lord worked for them!"
   What marvels the Lord worked for us!
   Indeed we were glad. R.

3. Deliver us, O Lord, from our bondage
   as streams in dry land.
   Those who are sowing in tears
   will sing when they reap. R.

4. They go out, they go out, full of tears,
   carrying seed for the sowing:
   they come back, they come back, full of song,
   carrying their sheaves. R.

Gospel Acclamation
Alleluia, alleluia!
Happy the man who stands firm.
For he has proved himself,
and will win the crown of life.
Allelluia!   James 1:12

Gospel   John 15:18-21
If they persecuted me, they will persecute you too.
Jesus said to his disciples:

"If the world hates you,
remember that it hated me before you.
If you belonged to the world,
the world would love you as its own;
but because you do not belong to the world,
because my choice withdrew you from the world,
therefore the world hates you.
Remember the words I said to you:
A servant is not greater than his master.
If they persecuted me,
they will persecute you too;
if they kept my word,
they will keep yours as well.
But it will be on my account that they will do all this,
because they do not know the one who sent me."

or

Gospel   John 15:1-8
Whoever remains in me, with me in him, bears fruit in plenty.
Jesus said to his disciples:

"I am the true vine
and my Father is the vinedresser.
Every branch in me that bears no fruit
he cuts away,
and every branch that does bear fruit he prunes
to make it bear even more.
You are pruned already,
by means of the word that I have spoken to you.

Make your home in me, as I make mine in you.
As a branch cannot bear fruit all by itself,
but must remain part of the vine,
neither can you unless you remain in me.
I am the vine,
you are the branches.
Whoever remains in me, with me in him.
bears fruit in plenty;
for cut off from me you can do nothing.
Anyone who does not remain in me
is like a branch that has been thrown away
– he withers;
these branches are collected and thrown on the fire,
and they are burnt.
If you remain in me
and my words remain in you,
you may ask what you will
and you shall get it.
It is to the glory of my Father that you should bear much fruit,
and then you will be my disciples.

Where this day is kept as a Solemnity, the Creed is said.

Prayer over the Offerings
Receive, we pray, O Lord,
the sacrifice of conciliation and praise,
which we offer to your majesty
in commemoration of the blessed Martyr Saint George,
that it may lead us to forgiveness
and confirm us in constant thanksgiving.
Through Christ our Lord.

Preface
It is truly right and just, our duty and our salvation,
always and everywhere to give you thanks,
Lord, holy Father, almighty and eternal God.

For the blood of your blessed Martyr George,
poured out like Christ's to glorify your name,
shows forth your marvellous works,

by which in our weakness you perfect your power
and on the feeble bestow strength to bear you witness,
through Christ our Lord.

And so, with the Powers of heaven,
we worship you constantly on earth,
and before your majesty
without end we acclaim:
Holy, Holy, Holy Lord God of hosts…

or

It is truly right and just, our duty and our salvation,
always and everywhere to give you thanks,
Lord, holy Father, almighty and eternal God.

For you are glorified when your Saints are praised;
their very sufferings are but wonders of your might:
in your mercy you give ardour to their faith,
to their endurance you grant firm resolve,
and in their struggle the victory is yours, through Christ our Lord.

Therefore, all creatures of heaven and earth
sing a new song in adoration,
and we, with all the host of Angels,
cry out, and without end we acclaim:
Holy, Holy, Holy Lord God of hosts…

Communion Antiphon
If we have died with Christ, we shall also live with him;
if we persevere, we shall also reign with him, alleluia.

cf. 2 Timothy 2:11-12

Prayer after Communion
Rejoicing on this festival day, O Lord,
we have received your heavenly gifts;
grant, we pray,
that we who in this divine banquet
proclaim the death of your Son
may merit with Saint George to be partakers
in his resurrection and glory.
Through Christ our Lord.

24 June

THE NATIVITY OF SAINT JOHN THE BAPTIST

Solemnity

Prepare the way of the Lord.

From before his birth, John the Baptist was called by God to be the prophet specially chosen to prepare the people for the coming of Christ. We too are called, through our rebirth in Baptism, to prepare the people of our day to receive Christ into their lives. Through God's grace, we are the light of the nations today.

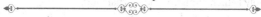

Entrance Antiphon

A man was sent from God, whose name was John.
He came to testify to the light,
to prepare a people fit for the Lord.   John 1:6-7; Luke 1:17

The Gloria is said or sung.

Collect

O God, who raised up Saint John the Baptist
to make ready a nation fit for Christ the Lord,
give your people, we pray,
the grace of spiritual joys
and direct the hearts of all the faithful
into the way of salvation and peace.
Through our Lord Jesus Christ, your Son,
who lives and reigns with you in the unity of the Holy Spirit,
one God, for ever and ever.

First Reading   Isaiah 49:1-6

I will make you the light of the nations so that my salvation may reach to the ends of the earth.

Islands, listen to me,
pay attention, remotest peoples.
The Lord called me before I was born,
from my mother's womb he pronounced my name.

He made my mouth a sharp sword,

and hid me in the shadow of his hand.
He made me into a sharpened arrow,
and concealed me in his quiver.

He said to me, "You are my servant (Israel)
in whom I shall be glorified";
while I was thinking, "I have toiled in vain,
I have exhausted myself for nothing";
and all the while my cause was with the Lord,
my reward with my God.
I was honoured in the eyes of the Lord,
my God was my strength.

And now the Lord has spoken,
he who formed me in the womb to be his servant,
to bring Jacob back to him,
to gather Israel to him:

"It is not enough for you to be my servant,
to restore the tribes of Jacob and bring back the survivors of Israel;
I will make you the light of the nations
so that my salvation may reach to the ends of the earth."

Psalm   Psalm 138

R. **I thank you for the wonder of my being.**

1. O Lord, you search me and you know me,
   you know my resting and my rising,
   you discern my purpose from afar.
   You mark when I walk or lie down,
   all my ways lie open to you. R.

2. For it was you who created my being,
   knit me together in my mother's womb.
   I thank you for the wonder of my being,
   for the wonders of all your creation. R.

3. Already you knew my soul,
   my body held no secret from you
   when I was being fashioned in secret
   and moulded in the depths of the earth. R.

Second Reading   Acts 13:22-26

Jesus, whose coming was heralded by John.

Paul said: "God made David the king of our ancestors, of whom he approved in these words, 'I have selected David son of Jesse, a man after my own heart, who will carry out my whole purpose.' To keep his promise, God has raised up for Israel one of David's descendants, Jesus, as Saviour, whose coming was heralded by John when he proclaimed a baptism of repentance for the whole people of Israel. Before John ended his career he said, 'I am not the one you imagine me to be; that one is coming after me and I am not fit to undo his sandal.'

"My brothers, sons of Abraham's race, and all you who fear God, this message of salvation is meant for you."

Gospel Acclamation

Alleluia, alleluia!
As for you, little child, you shall be called
a prophet of God, the Most High.
You shall go ahead of the Lord
to prepare his ways before him.
Alleluia!   cf. Luke 1:76

Gospel   Luke 1:57-66. 80

His name is John.

The time came for Elizabeth to have her child, and she gave birth to a son; and when her neighbours and relations heard that the Lord had shown her so great a kindness, they shared her joy.

Now on the eighth day they came to circumcise the child; they were going to call him Zechariah after his father, but his mother spoke up. "No," she said, "he is to be called John." They said to her, "But no one in your family has that name", and made signs to his father to find out what he wanted him called. The father asked for a writing tablet and wrote, "His name is John." And they were all astonished. At that instant his power of speech returned and he spoke and praised God. All their neighbours were filled with awe and the whole affair was talked about throughout the hill country of Judaea. All those who heard it treasured it in their hearts. "What will this child turn out to be?" they wondered. And indeed the hand of the Lord was with him. The child grew up and his spirit matured. And he lived out in the wilderness until the day he appeared openly to Israel.

The Creed is said.

Prayer over the Offerings
We place these offerings on your altar, O Lord,
to celebrate with fitting honour the nativity of him
who both foretold the coming of the world's Saviour
and pointed him out when he came.
Who lives and reigns for ever and ever.

Preface
It is truly right and just, our duty and our salvation,
always and everywhere to give you thanks,
Lord, holy Father, almighty and eternal God,
through Christ our Lord.

In his Precursor, Saint John the Baptist,
we praise your great glory,
for you consecrated him for a singular honour
among those born of women.

His birth brought great rejoicing;
even in the womb he leapt for joy
at the coming of human salvation.
He alone of all the prophets
pointed out the Lamb of redemption.

And to make holy the flowing waters,
he baptised the very author of Baptism
and was privileged to bear him supreme witness
by the shedding of his blood.

And so, with the Powers of heaven,
we worship you constantly on earth,
and before your majesty
without end we acclaim:
Holy, Holy, Holy Lord God of hosts…

Communion Antiphon

Through the tender mercy of our God,
the Dawn from on high will visit us. cf. Luke 1:78

Prayer after Communion

Having feasted at the banquet of the heavenly Lamb,
we pray, O Lord,
that, finding joy in the nativity of Saint John the Baptist,
your Church may know as the author of her rebirth
the Christ whose coming John foretold.
Who lives and reigns for ever and ever.

29 June

SAINTS PETER AND PAUL, APOSTLES

Solemnity

Pillars of the Church.

Christ promised to build his Church on Peter, the rock, and assures us that the power of evil will never overcome it. Paul became the apostle to the Gentiles, so that the Good News spread throughout the whole world. Through these two great apostles the Church was gathered as the one family of Christ. Christ is still with us today as we witness to his power in our lives, that the world may come to believe in him.

Entrance Antiphon

These are the ones who, living in the flesh,
planted the Church with their blood;
they drank the chalice of the Lord
and became the friends of God.

The Gloria is said or sung.

Collect

O God, who on the Solemnity of the Apostles Peter and Paul
give us the noble and holy joy of this day,
grant, we pray, that your Church
may in all things follow the teaching
of those through whom she received
the beginnings of right religion.
Through our Lord Jesus Christ, your Son,
who lives and reigns with you in the unity of the Holy Spirit,
one God, for ever and ever.

First Reading   Acts 12:1-11

Now I know the Lord really did save me from Herod.

King Herod started persecuting certain members of the Church.
He beheaded James the brother of John, and when he saw that

this pleased the Jews he decided to arrest Peter as well. This was during the days of Unleavened Bread, and he put Peter in prison, assigning four squads of four soldiers each to guard him in turns. Herod meant to try Peter in public after the end of Passover week. All the time Peter was under guard the Church prayed to God for him unremittingly.

On the night before Herod was to try him, Peter was sleeping between two soldiers, fastened with double chains, while guards kept watch at the main entrance to the prison. Then suddenly the angel of the Lord stood there, and the cell was filled with light. He tapped Peter on the side and woke him. "Get up!" he said "Hurry!" – and the chains fell from his hands. The angel then said, "Put on your belt and sandals." After he had done this, the angel next said, "Wrap your cloak round you and follow me." Peter followed him, but had no idea that what the angel did was all happening in reality; he thought he was seeing a vision. They passed through two guard posts one after the other, and reached the iron gate leading to the city. This opened of its own accord; they went through it and had walked the whole length of one street when suddenly the angel left him. It was only then that Peter came to himself. "Now I know it is all true," he said. "The Lord really did send his angel and has saved me from Herod and from all that the Jewish people were so certain would happen to me."

Psalm   Psalm 33

R. **From all my terrors the Lord set me free.**

or

R. **The angel of the Lord rescues those who revere him.**

1. I will bless the Lord at all times,
   his praise always on my lips;
   in the Lord my soul shall make its boast.
   The humble shall hear and be glad. R.

2. Glorify the Lord with me.
   Together let us praise his name.
   I sought the Lord and he answered me;
   from all my terrors he set me free. R.

3. Look towards him and be radiant;
    let your faces not be abashed.
    This poor man called; the Lord heard him
    and rescued him from all his distress. R.

4. The angel of the Lord is encamped
    around those who revere him, to rescue them.
    Taste and see that the Lord is good.
    He is happy who seeks refuge in him. R.

Second Reading   2 Timothy 4:6-8. 17-18

All there is to come now is the crown of righteousness reserved for me.

My life is already being poured away as a libation, and the time has
come for me to be gone. I have fought the good fight to the end; I
have run the race to the finish; I have kept the faith; all there is to
come now is the crown of righteousness reserved for me, which the
Lord, the righteous judge, will give to me on that Day; and not only
to me but to all those who have longed for his Appearing.

The Lord stood by me and gave me power, so that through me
the whole message might be proclaimed for all the pagans to hear;
and so I was rescued from the lion's mouth. The Lord will rescue
me from all evil attempts on me, and bring me safely to his heavenly
kingdom. To him be glory for ever and ever. Amen.

Gospel Acclamation
Alleluia, alleluia!
You are Peter and on this rock I will build my Church.
And the gates of the underworld can never hold out against it.
Alleluia!   Matthew 16:18

Gospel   Matthew 16:13-19

You are Peter, and I will give you the keys of the kingdom of heaven.

When Jesus came to the region of Caesarea Philippi he put this
question to his disciples, "Who do people say the Son of Man is?"
And they said, "Some say he is John the Baptist, some Elijah, and
others Jeremiah or one of the prophets." "But you," he said, "who do
you say I am?" Then Simon Peter spoke up, "You are the Christ,"

he said, "the Son of the living God." Jesus replied, "Simon son of
Jonah, you are a happy man! Because it was not flesh and blood that
revealed this to you but my Father in heaven. So I now say to you:
You are Peter and on this rock I will build my Church. And the gates
of the underworld can never hold out against it. I will give you the
keys of the kingdom of heaven: whatever you bind on earth shall be
considered bound in heaven; whatever you loose on earth shall be
considered loosed in heaven."

The Creed is said.

Prayer over the Offerings
May the prayer of the Apostles, O Lord,
accompany the sacrificial gift
that we present to your name for consecration,
and may their intercession make us devoted to you
in celebration of the sacrifice.
Through Christ our Lord.

Preface
It is truly right and just, our duty and our salvation,
always and everywhere to give you thanks,
Lord, holy Father, almighty and eternal God.

For by your providence
the blessed Apostles Peter and Paul bring us joy:
Peter, foremost in confessing the faith,
Paul, its outstanding preacher,
Peter, who established the early Church from the remnant of Israel,
Paul, master and teacher of the Gentiles that you call.

And so, each in a different way
gathered together the one family of Christ;
and revered together throughout the world,
they share one Martyr's crown.

And therefore, with all the Angels and Saints,
we praise you, as without end we acclaim:
Holy, Holy, Holy Lord God of hosts...

Communion Antiphon
Peter said to Jesus: You are the Christ, the Son of the living God.
And Jesus replied: You are Peter,
and upon this rock I will build my Church.   cf. Matthew 16:16. 18

Prayer after Communion
Grant us, O Lord,
who have been renewed by this Sacrament,
so to live in the Church,
that, persevering in the breaking of the Bread
and in the teaching of the Apostles,
we may be one heart and one soul,
made steadfast in your love.
Through Christ our Lord.

The Solemn Blessing for Saints Peter and Paul, Apostles, may be used, p. 516.

6 August

THE TRANSFIGURATION OF THE LORD

Feast

Jesus in his glory.
Jesus was seen by Peter, James and John in his glory as the Son of God. It was
wonderful for them to be there and witness his power, even though they were
overcome by fear at what they saw. God reveals Christ to us too, and we look
forward in joy and hope to sharing fully in his glory. We have no need to fear.

Entrance Antiphon
In a resplendent cloud the Holy Spirit appeared.
The Father's voice was heard: This is my beloved Son,
with whom I am well pleased. Listen to him.   cf. Matthew 17:5

The Gloria is said or sung.

Collect
O God, who in the glorious Transfiguration
of your Only Begotten Son
confirmed the mysteries of faith by the witness of the Fathers
and wonderfully prefigured our full adoption to sonship,
grant, we pray, to your servants,
that, listening to the voice of your beloved Son,
we may merit to become coheirs with him.
Who lives and reigns with you in the unity of the Holy Spirit,
one God, for ever and ever.

First Reading   Daniel 7:9-10. 13-14
His robe was white as snow.
As I watched:
Thrones were set in place
and one of great age took his seat.
His robe was white as snow,

the hair of his head as pure as wool.
His throne was a blaze of flames,
its wheels were a burning fire.
A stream of fire poured out,
issuing from his presence.
A thousand thousand waited on him,
ten thousand times ten thousand stood before him.
A court was held and the books were opened.
I gazed into the visions of the night.
And I saw, coming on the clouds of heaven,
one like a son of man.
He came to the one of great age
and was led into his presence.
On him was conferred sovereignty,
glory and kingship,
and men of all peoples, nations and languages became his servants.
His sovereignty is an eternal sovereignty
which shall never pass away,
nor will his empire ever be destroyed.

Psalm   Psalm 96

R. **The Lord is king,**
    most high above all the earth.

1. The Lord is king, let earth rejoice,
   let all the coastlands be glad.
   Cloud and darkness are his raiment;
   his throne, justice and right. R.

2. The mountains melt like wax
   before the Lord of all the earth.
   The skies proclaim his justice;
   all peoples see his glory. R.

3. For you indeed are the Lord
   most high above all the earth
   exalted far above all spirits. R.

Second Reading   **2 Peter 1:16-19**

We heard this ourselves, spoken from heaven.

It was not any cleverly invented myths that we were repeating when we brought you the knowledge of the power and the coming of our our Lord Jesus Christ; we had seen his majesty for ourselves. He was honoured and glorified by God the Father, when the Sublime Glory itself spoke to him and said, "This is my Son, the Beloved; he enjoys my favour." We heard this ourselves, spoken from heaven, when we were with him on the holy mountain.

So we have confirmation of what was said in prophecies; and you will be right to depend on prophecy and take it as a lamp for lighting a way through the dark until the dawn comes and the morning star rises in your minds.

Gospel Acclamation

Alleluia, alleluia!
This is my Son, the Beloved,
he enjoys my favour;
listen to him.
Alleluia!   Matthew 17:5

Gospel A, B or C is read according to the cycle for the year.

A

Gospel   **Matthew 17:1-9**

His face shone like the sun.

Jesus took with him Peter and James and his brother John and led them up a high mountain where they could be alone. There in their presence he was transfigured: his face shone like the sun and his clothes became as white as the light. Suddenly Moses and Elijah appeared to them; they were talking with him. Then Peter spoke to Jesus. "Lord," he said, "it is wonderful for us to be here; if you wish, I will make three tents here, one for you, one for Moses and one for Elijah." He was still speaking when suddenly a bright cloud covered them with shadow, and from the cloud there came a voice which said, "This is my Son, the Beloved; he enjoys my favour. Listen to him." When they heard this, the disciples fell on their faces, overcome with fear. But Jesus came up and touched them. "Stand up," he said, "do not be afraid." And when they raised their eyes they saw no one but only Jesus.

As they came down from the mountain Jesus gave them this order, "Tell no one about the vision until the Son of Man has risen from the dead."

B

Gospel   Mark 9:2-10

This is my Son, the Beloved.

Jesus took with him Peter and James and John and led them up a high mountain where they could be alone by themselves. There in their presence he was transfigured: his clothes became dazzlingly white, whiter than any earthly bleacher could make them. Elijah appeared to them with Moses; and they were talking with Jesus. Then Peter spoke to Jesus: "Rabbi," he said, "it is wonderful for us to be here; so let us make three tents, one for you, one for Moses and one for Elijah." He did not know what to say; they were so frightened. And a cloud came, covering them in shadow; and there came a voice from the cloud, "This is my Son, the Beloved. Listen to him." Then suddenly, when they looked round, they saw no one with them any more but only Jesus.

As they came down from the mountain he warned them to tell no one what they had seen, until after the Son of Man had risen from the dead. They observed the warning faithfully, though among themselves they discussed what "rising from the dead" could mean.

C

Gospel   Luke 9:28-36

Moses and Elijah were talking about his death.

Jesus took with him Peter and John and James and went up the mountain to pray. As he prayed, the aspect of his face was changed and his clothing became brilliant as lightning. Suddenly there were two men there talking to him; they were Moses and Elijah appearing in glory, and they were speaking of his passing which he was to accomplish in Jerusalem. Peter and his companions were heavy with sleep, but they kept awake and saw his glory and the two men standing with him. As these were leaving him, Peter said to Jesus, "Master, it is wonderful for us to be here; so let us make three tents, one for you, one for Moses and one for Elijah." – He did not know what he was saying. As he spoke, a cloud came and covered them with shadow; and when they went into the cloud the disciples were afraid. And a voice came from the cloud, saying, "This is my Son, the Chosen One. Listen to him." And after the voice had spoken, Jesus was found alone. The disciples kept silence and, at that time, told no one what they had seen.

When this feast falls on a Sunday, the Creed is said.

Prayer over the Offerings
Sanctify, O Lord, we pray,
these offerings here made to celebrate
the glorious Transfiguration of your Only Begotten Son,
and by his radiant splendour
cleanse us from the stains of sin.
Through Christ our Lord.

Preface
It is truly right and just, our duty and our salvation,
always and everywhere to give you thanks,
Lord, holy Father, almighty and eternal God,
through Christ our Lord.

For he revealed his glory in the presence of chosen witnesses
and filled with the greatest splendour that bodily form
which he shares with all humanity,
that the scandal of the Cross
might be removed from the hearts of his disciples
and that he might show
how in the Body of the whole Church is to be fulfilled
what so wonderfully shone forth first in its Head.

And so, with the Powers of heaven,
we worship you constantly on earth,
and before your majesty
without end we acclaim:
Holy, Holy, Holy Lord God of hosts…

Communion Antiphon
When Christ appears, we shall be like him,
for we shall see him as he is.

cf. 1 John 3:2

Prayer after Communion
May the heavenly nourishment we have received,
O Lord, we pray,
transform us into the likeness of your Son,
whose radiant splendour you willed to make manifest
in his glorious Transfiguration.
Who lives and reigns for ever and ever.

1020

15 August
THE ASSUMPTION
OF THE BLESSED VIRGIN MARY
Solemnity

The Almighty has done great things for me.
Through the Resurrection of Christ, God has assured us of the victory over sin
and death. Our Lady is assumed into glory through the power of her Son and
we pray that one day the fulfilment of glory will be ours too. We are destined
for heaven, where Mary is now with her glorified Son. Mary's Assumption
gives glory to God the Father who has done great things for her.

Entrance Antiphon
A great sign appeared in heaven:
a woman clothed with the sun, and the moon beneath her feet,
and on her head a crown of twelve stars.   cf. Apocalypse 12:1

or

Let us all rejoice in the Lord,
as we celebrate the feast day in honour of the Virgin Mary,
at whose Assumption the Angels rejoice
and praise the Son of God.

The Gloria is said or sung.

Collect
Almighty ever-living God,
who assumed the Immaculate Virgin Mary, the Mother of your Son,
body and soul into heavenly glory,
grant, we pray,
that, always attentive to the things that are above,
we may merit to be sharers of her glory.
Through our Lord Jesus Christ, your Son,
who lives and reigns with you in the unity of the Holy Spirit,
one God, for ever and ever.

First Reading Apocalypse 11:19; 12:1-6. 10

A woman adorned with the sun, standing on the moon.

The sanctuary of God in heaven opened, and the ark of the covenant could be seen inside it.

Now a great sign appeared in heaven: a woman, adorned with the sun, standing on the moon, and with the twelve stars on her head for a crown. She was pregnant, and in labour, crying aloud in the pangs of childbirth. Then a second sign appeared in the sky, a huge red dragon which had seven heads and ten horns, and each of the seven heads crowned with a coronet. Its tail dragged a third of the stars from the sky and dropped them to the earth, and the dragon stopped in front of the woman as she was having the child, so that he could eat it as soon as it was born from its mother. The woman brought a male child into the world, the son who was to rule all the nations with an iron sceptre, and the child was taken straight up to God and to his throne, while the woman escaped into the desert, where God had made a place of safety ready. Then I heard a voice shout from heaven, "Victory and power and empire for ever have been won by our God, and all authority for his Christ."

Psalm Psalm 44

R. **On your right stands the queen,
in garments of gold.**

1. The daughters of kings are among your loved ones.
   On your right stands the queen in gold of Ophir.
   Listen, O daughter, give ear to my words:
   forget your own people and your father's house. R.

2. So will the king desire your beauty:
   he is your lord, pay homage to him.
   They are escorted amid gladness and joy;
   they pass within the palace of the king. R.

Second Reading 1 Corinthians 15:20-26

Christ as the first-fruits and then those who belong to him.

Christ has been raised from the dead, the first-fruits of all who have fallen asleep. Death came through one man and in the same way the resurrection of the dead has come through one man. Just as all men die in Adam, so all men will be brought to life in Christ; but all of them in their proper order: Christ as the first-fruits and then, after the coming of Christ, those who belong to him. After that will come the end, when he hands over the kingdom to God the Father, having done away with every sovereignty, authority and power. For he must be king until he has put all his enemies under his feet and the last of the enemies to be destroyed is death, for everything is to be put under his feet.

Gospel Acclamation

Alleluia, alleluia!
Mary has been taken up into heaven;
all the choirs of angels are rejoicing.
Alleluia!

Gospel   Luke 1:39-56

The Almighty has done great things for me, he has exalted the lowly.
Mary set out and went as quickly as she could to a town in the hill country of Judah. She went into Zechariah's house and greeted Elizabeth. Now as soon as Elizabeth heard Mary's greeting, the child leapt in her womb and Elizabeth was filled with the Holy Spirit. She gave a loud cry and said, "Of all women you are the most blessed, and blessed is the fruit of your womb. Why should I be honoured with a visit from the mother of my Lord? For the moment your greeting reached my ears, the child in my womb leapt for joy. Yes, blessed is she who believed that the promise made her by the Lord would be fulfilled."

And Mary said:

"My soul proclaims the greatness of the Lord
and my spirit exults in God my saviour;
because he has looked upon his lowly handmaid.
Yes, from this day forward all generations will call me blessed,
for the Almighty has done great things for me.
Holy is his name,
and his mercy reaches from age to age for those who fear him.
He has shown the power of his arm,
he has routed the proud of heart.
He has pulled down princes from their thrones and exalted the
    lowly.

The hungry he has filled with good things, the rich sent empty
away.
He has come to the help of Israel his servant, mindful of his mercy
– according to the promise he made to our ancestors –
of his mercy to Abraham and to his descendants for ever."

Mary stayed with Elizabeth about three months and then went back
home.

The Creed is said.

Prayer over the Offerings
May this oblation, our tribute of homage,
rise up to you, O Lord,
and, through the intercession of the most Blessed Virgin Mary,
whom you assumed into heaven,
may our hearts, aflame with the fire of love,
constantly long for you.
Through Christ our Lord.

Preface
It is truly right and just, our duty and our salvation,
always and everywhere to give you thanks,
Lord, holy Father, almighty and eternal God,
through Christ our Lord.

For today the Virgin Mother of God
was assumed into heaven
as the beginning and image
of your Church's coming to perfection
and a sign of sure hope and comfort to your pilgrim people;
rightly you would not allow her
to see the corruption of the tomb
since from her own body she marvellously brought forth
your incarnate Son, the Author of all life.

And so, in company with the choirs of Angels,
we praise you, and with joy we proclaim:
Holy, Holy, Holy Lord God of hosts…

Communion Antiphon
All generations will call me blessed,
for he who is mighty has done great things for me.   Luke 1:48-49

Prayer after Communion
Having received the Sacrament of salvation,
we ask you to grant, O Lord,
that, through the intercession of the Blessed Virgin Mary,
whom you assumed into heaven,
we may be brought to the glory of the resurrection.
Through Christ our Lord.

The Solemn Blessing for the Blessed Virgin Mary may be used,
p. 515.

14 September

THE EXALTATION OF THE HOLY CROSS
Feast

God the Father gave his only Son.
The cross is the sign of salvation because when he was lifted up on it Jesus drew everyone to himself. He humbled himself even to the death of a criminal on a cross to show his love for his Father and for each one of us, and to bring us eternal life. Now we acclaim Jesus as Lord to the glory of the Father.

Entrance Antiphon
We should glory in the Cross of our Lord Jesus Christ,
in whom is our salvation, life and resurrection,
through whom we are saved and delivered.　　　cf. Galatians 6:14

The Gloria is said or sung.

Collect
O God, who willed that your Only Begotten Son
should undergo the Cross to save the human race,
grant, we pray,
that we, who have known his mystery on earth,
may merit the grace of his redemption in heaven.
Through our Lord Jesus Christ, your Son,
who lives and reigns with you in the unity of the Holy Spirit,
one God, for ever and ever.

First Reading　　　　　　　　　　　　　　　　Numbers 21:4-9
If anyone was bitten by a serpent, he looked at the bronze serpent
and lived.
On the way through the wilderness, the Israelites lost patience.
They spoke against God and against Moses, "Why did you bring us
out of Egypt to die in this wilderness? For there is neither bread nor
water here; we are sick of this unsatisfying food."

At this God sent fiery serpents among the people; their bite brought death to many in Israel. The people came and said to Moses, "We have sinned by speaking against the Lord and against you. Intercede for us with the Lord to save us from these serpents." Moses interceded for the people, and the Lord answered him, "Make a fiery serpent and put it on a standard. If anyone is bitten and looks at it, he shall live." So Moses fashioned a bronze serpent which he put on a standard, and if anyone was bitten by a serpent, he looked at the bronze serpent and lived.

Psalm   Psalm 77

R. **Never forget the deeds of the Lord.**

1. Give heed, my people, to my teaching;
   turn your ear to the words of my mouth.
   I will open my mouth in a parable
   and reveal hidden lessons of the past. R.

2. When he slew them then they would seek him,
   return and seek him in earnest.
   They would remember that God was their rock,
   God the Most High their redeemer. R.

3. But the words they spoke were mere flattery;
   they lied to him with their lips.
   For their hearts were not truly with him;
   they were not faithful to his covenant. R.

4. Yet he who is full of compassion
   forgave their sin and spared them.
   So often he held back his anger
   when he might have stirred up his rage. R.

Second Reading   Philippians 2:6-11
He humbled himself, therefore God raised him high.
The state of Jesus Christ was divine,
yet he did not cling
to his equality with God
but emptied himself

to assume the condition of a slave,
and became as men are;
and being as all men are,
he was humbler yet,
even to accepting death,
death on a cross.
But God raised him high
and gave him the name
which is above all other names
so that all beings
in the heavens, on earth and in the underworld,
should bend the knee at the name of Jesus
and that every tongue should acclaim
Jesus Christ as Lord,
to the glory of God the Father.

Gospel Acclamation
Alleluia, alleluia!
We adore you, O Christ,
and we bless you;
because by your cross
you have redeemed the world.
Alleluia!

Gospel   **John 3:13-17**
The Son of Man must be lifted up.

Jesus said to Nicodemus:

"No one has gone up to heaven
except the one who came down from heaven,
the Son of Man who is in heaven;
and the Son of Man must be lifted up
as Moses lifted up the serpent in the desert,
so that everyone who believes may have eternal life in him.
Yes, God loved the world so much
that he gave his only Son,
so that everyone who believes in him may not be lost
but may have eternal life.

For God sent his Son into the world
not to condemn the world,
but so that through him the world might be saved."

When this feast falls on a Sunday, the Creed is said.

Prayer over the Offerings
May this oblation, O Lord,
which on the altar of the Cross
cancelled the offence of the whole world,
cleanse us, we pray, of all our sins.
Through Christ our Lord.

Preface
It is truly right and just, our duty and our salvation,
always and everywhere to give you thanks,
Lord, holy Father, almighty and eternal God.

For you placed the salvation of the human race
on the wood of the Cross,
so that, where death arose,
life might again spring forth
and the evil one, who conquered on a tree,
might likewise on a tree be conquered,
through Christ our Lord.

Through him the Angels praise your majesty,
Dominions adore and Powers tremble before you.
Heaven and the Virtues of heaven and the blessed Seraphim
worship together with exultation.
May our voices, we pray, join with theirs
in humble praise, as we acclaim:
Holy, Holy, Holy Lord God of hosts…

or

It is truly right and just, our duty and our salvation,
always and everywhere to give you thanks,
Lord, holy Father, almighty and eternal God.

For through the saving Passion of your Son

the whole world has received a heart
to confess the infinite power of your majesty,
since by the wondrous power of the Cross
your judgement on the world is now revealed
and the authority of Christ crucified.

And so, Lord, with all the Angels and Saints,
we, too, give you thanks, as in exultation we acclaim:
Holy, Holy, Holy Lord God of hosts…

Communion Antiphon

When I am lifted up from the earth,
I will draw everyone to myself, says the Lord.

John 12:32

Prayer after Communion

Having been nourished by your holy banquet,
we beseech you, Lord Jesus Christ,
to bring those you have redeemed
by the wood of your life-giving Cross
to the glory of the resurrection.
Who live and reign for ever and ever.

1 November

ALL SAINTS

Solemnity

Your reward will be great in heaven.
The saints praise God's glory in heaven forever. In their lives on earth they
lived out the Beatitudes preached by Jesus in his Sermon on the Mount. We are
called to model our lives on them so that where they are we may one day be.
Like them, we too will see God face to face.

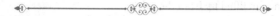

Entrance Antiphon
Let us all rejoice in the Lord,
as we celebrate the feast day in honour of all the Saints,
at whose festival the Angels rejoice
and praise the Son of God.

The Gloria is said or sung.

Collect
Almighty ever-living God,
by whose gift we venerate in one celebration
the merits of all the Saints,
bestow on us, we pray,
through the prayers of so many intercessors,
an abundance of the reconciliation with you
for which we earnestly long.
Through our Lord Jesus Christ, your Son,
who lives and reigns with you in the unity of the Holy Spirit,
one God, for ever and ever.

First Reading   Apocalypse 7:2-4. 9-14
I saw a huge number, impossible to count, of people from every
nation, race, tribe and language.
I, John, saw another angel rising where the sun rises, carrying the
seal of the living God; he called in a powerful voice to the four
angels whose duty it was to devastate land and sea, "Wait before

you do any damage on land or at sea or to the trees, until we have put the seal on the foreheads of the servants of our God." Then I heard how many were sealed: a hundred and forty-four thousand, out of all the tribes of Israel.

After that I saw a huge number, impossible to count, of people from every nation, race, tribe and language; they were standing in front of the throne and in front of the Lamb, dressed in white robes and holding palms in their hands. They shouted aloud, "Victory to our God, who sits on the throne, and to the Lamb!" And all the angels who were standing in a circle round the throne, surrounding the elders and the four animals, prostrated themselves before the throne, and touched the ground with their foreheads, worshipping God with these words: "Amen. Praise and glory and wisdom and thanksgiving and honour and power and strength to our God for ever and ever. Amen."

One of the elders then spoke, and asked me, "Do you know who these people are, dressed in white robes, and where they have come from?" I answered him, "You can tell me, my lord." Then he said, "These are the people who have been through the great persecution, and they have washed their robes white again in the blood of the Lamb."

Psalm   Psalm 23

R. **Such are the men who seek your face, O Lord.**

1. The Lord's is the earth and its fullness,
    the world and all its peoples.
    It is he who set it on the seas;
    on the waters he made it firm. R.

2. Who shall climb the mountain of the Lord?
    Who shall stand in his holy place?
    The man with clean hands and pure heart,
    who desires not worthless things. R.

3. He shall receive blessings from the Lord
    and reward from the God who saves him.
    Such are the men who seek him,
    seek the face of the God of Jacob. R.

Second Reading 1 John 3:1-3

We shall see God as he really is.

Think of the love that the Father has lavished on us,
by letting us be called God's children;
and that is what we are.
Because the world refused to acknowledge him,
therefore it does not acknowledge us.
My dear people, we are already the children of God
but what we are to be in the future has not yet been revealed;
all we know is, that when it is revealed
we shall be like him
because we shall see him as he really is.
Surely everyone who entertains this hope
must purify himself, must try to be as pure as Christ.

Gospel Acclamation

Alleluia, alleluia!
Come to me, all you who labour and are overburdened,
and I will give you rest, says the Lord.
Alleluia! Matthew 11:28

Gospel Matthew 5:1-12

Rejoice and be glad, for your reward will be great in heaven.

Seeing the crowds, Jesus went up the hill. There he sat down and
was joined by his disciples. Then he began to speak. This is what
he taught them:

"How happy are the poor in spirit;
theirs is the kingdom of heaven.
Happy the gentle:
they shall have the earth for their heritage.
Happy those who mourn:
they shall be comforted.
Happy those who hunger and thirst for what is right:
they shall be satisfied.
Happy the merciful:
they shall have mercy shown them.
Happy the pure in heart:

they shall see God.
Happy the peacemakers:
they shall be called sons of God.
Happy those who are persecuted in the cause of right:
theirs is the kingdom of heaven.

"Happy are you when people abuse you and persecute you and speak all kinds of calumny against you on my account. Rejoice and be glad, for your reward will be great in heaven."

The Creed is said.

Prayer over the Offerings

May these offerings we bring in honour of all the Saints
be pleasing to you, O Lord,
and grant that, just as we believe the Saints
to be already assured of immortality,
so we may experience their concern for our salvation.
Through Christ our Lord.

Preface

It is truly right and just, our duty and our salvation,
always and everywhere to give you thanks,
Lord, holy Father, almighty and eternal God.

For today by your gift we celebrate the festival of your city,
the heavenly Jerusalem, our mother,
where the great array of our brothers and sisters
already gives you eternal praise.

Towards her, we eagerly hasten, as pilgrims advancing by faith,
rejoicing in the glory bestowed upon those exalted
    members of the Church
through whom you give us, in our frailty,
    both strength and good example.

And so, we glorify you with the multitude of Saints and Angels,
as with one voice of praise we acclaim:
Holy, Holy, Holy Lord God of hosts…

Communion Antiphon

Blessed are the clean of heart, for they shall see God.
Blessed are the peacemakers,
for they shall be called children of God.
Blessed are they who are persecuted for the sake of righteousness,
for theirs is the Kingdom of Heaven.   Matthew 5:8-10

Prayer after Communion

As we adore you, O God, who alone are holy
and wonderful in all your Saints,
we implore your grace,
so that, coming to perfect holiness in the fullness of your love,
we may pass from this pilgrim table
to the banquet of our heavenly homeland.
Through Christ our Lord.

The Solemn Blessing for All Saints may be used, p. 517.

2 November

THE COMMEMORATION
OF ALL THE FAITHFUL DEPARTED
(ALL SOULS)

Christ will raise them up.

We are a people who have put our hope in Christ and his Resurrection. Many of God's people, known and unknown to us, have gone before us, and we pray for their eternal happiness. Life is an ongoing process through death into eternal life. One day we will all be united as one family in our heavenly home.

FIRST MASS

Entrance Antiphon
Just as Jesus died and has risen again,
so through Jesus God will bring with him
those who have fallen asleep;
and as in Adam all die,
so also in Christ will all be brought to life.

cf. 1 Thessalonians 4:14; 1 Corinthians 15:22

Collect
Listen kindly to our prayers, O Lord,
and, as our faith in your Son,
raised from the dead, is deepened,
so may our hope of resurrection for your departed servants
also find new strength.
Through our Lord Jesus Christ, your Son,
who lives and reigns with you in the unity of the Holy Spirit,
one God, for ever and ever.

Other readings may be used instead of those given here.

First Reading   Isaiah 25:6-9
The Lord will destroy Death for ever.
On this mountain,
the Lord of hosts will prepare for all peoples
a banquet of rich food.

On this mountain he will remove
the mourning veil covering all peoples,
and the shroud enwrapping all nations,
he will destroy Death for ever.
The Lord will wipe away
the tears from every cheek;
he will take away his people's shame
everywhere on earth,
for the Lord has said so.
That day, it will be said: See, this is our God
in whom we hoped for salvation;
the Lord is the one in whom we hoped.
We exult and we rejoice
that he has saved us.

Psalm   Psalm 26

R. **The Lord is my light and my help.**

or

R. **I believe that I shall see the Lord's goodness
     in the land of the living.**

1. The Lord is my light and my help
    whom shall I fear?
    The Lord is the stronghold of my life;
    before whom shall I shrink? R.

2. There is one thing I ask of the Lord,
    for this I long,
    to live in the house of the Lord,
    all the days of my life,
    to savour the sweetness of the Lord,
    to behold his temple. R.

3. O Lord, hear my voice when I call;
    have mercy and answer.
    It is your face, O Lord, that I seek;
    hide not your face. R.

4. I am sure I shall see the Lord's goodness
   in the land of the living.
   Hope in him, hold firm and take heart.
   Hope in the Lord! R.

Second Reading   **Romans 5:5-11**
Having died to make us righteous, is it likely that he would now fail
to save us from God's anger?
Hope is not deceptive, because the love of God has been poured
into our hearts by the Holy Spirit which has been given us. We were
still helpless when at his appointed moment Christ died for sinful
men. It is not easy to die even for a good man – though of course for
someone really worthy, a man might be prepared to die – but what
proves that God loves us is that Christ died for us while we were still
sinners. Having died to make us righteous, is it likely that he would
now fail to save us from God's anger? When we were reconciled to
God by the death of his Son, we were still enemies; now that we have
been reconciled, surely we may count on being saved by the life of
his Son? Not merely because we have been reconciled but because
we are filled with joyful trust in God, through our Lord Jesus Christ,
through whom we have already gained our reconciliation.

Gospel Acclamation
Alleluia, alleluia!
It is my Father's will, says the Lord,
that I should lose nothing
of all that he has given to me,
and that I should raise it up on the last day.
Alleluia!   John 6:39

Gospel A, B or C is read according to the cycle for the year.

A
Gospel   **Matthew 11:25-30**
You have hidden these things from the learned and have revealed
them to mere children.
Jesus exclaimed, "I bless you, Father, Lord of heaven and of earth, for
hiding these things from the learned and the clever and revealing

them to mere children. Yes, Father, for that is what it pleased you to do. Everything has been entrusted to me by my Father; and no one knows the Son except the Father, just as no one knows the Father except the Son and those to whom the Son chooses to reveal him.

"Come to me, all you who labour and are overburdened, and I will give you rest. Shoulder my yoke and learn from me, for I am gentle and humble in heart, and you will find rest for your souls. Yes, my yoke is easy and my burden light."

B

Gospel   Mark 15:33-39; 16:1-6

Jesus gave a loud cry and breathed his last.

When the sixth hour came there was darkness over the whole land until the ninth hour. And at the ninth hour Jesus cried out in a loud voice, "Eloi, Eloi, lama sabachthani?" which means, "My God, my God, why have you deserted me?" When some of those who stood by heard this, they said, "Listen, he is calling on Elijah". Someone ran and soaked a sponge in vinegar and, putting it on a reed, gave it him to drink saying, "Wait and see if Elijah will come to take him down." But Jesus gave a loud cry and breathed his last. And the veil of the Temple was torn in two from top to bottom. The centurion, who was standing in front of him, had seen how he had died, and he said, "In truth this man was a son of God."

When the sabbath was over, Mary of Magdala, Mary the mother of James, and Salome, bought spices with which to go and anoint him. And very early in the morning on the first day of the week they went to the tomb, just as the sun was rising.

They had been saying to one another, "Who will roll away the stone for us from the entrance to the tomb?" But when they looked they could see that the stone – which was very big – had already been rolled back. On enterering the tomb they saw a young man in a white robe seated on the right-hand side, and they were struck with amazement. But he said to them, "There is no need for alarm. You are looking for Jesus of Nazareth, who was crucified: he has risen, he is not here. See, here is the place where they laid him."

C

Gospel   Luke 7:11-17

Young man, I tell you to get up.

Jesus went to a town called Nain, accompanied by his disciples and a great number of people. When he was near the gate of the town it happened that a dead man was being carried out for burial, the only son of his mother, and she was a widow. And a considerable number of the townspeople were with her. When the Lord saw her he felt sorry for her. "Do not cry," he said. Then he went up and put his hand on the bier and the bearers stood still, and he said, "Young man, I tell you to get up." And the dead man sat up and began to talk, and Jesus gave him to his mother. Everyone was filled with awe and praised God saying, "A great prophet has appeared among us; God has visited his people." And this opinion of him spread throughout Judaea and all over the countryside.

Prayer over the Offerings

Look favourably on our offerings, O Lord,
so that your departed servants
may be taken up into glory with your Son,
in whose great mystery of love we are all united.
Who lives and reigns for ever and ever.

Preface I-V for the Dead, pp. 505-507.

Communion Antiphon

I am the Resurrection and the Life, says the Lord.
Whoever believes in me, even though he dies, will live,
and everyone who lives and believes in me will not die for ever.

                                                          cf. John 11:25-26

Prayer after Communion

Grant we pray, O Lord, that your departed servants,
for whom we have celebrated this paschal Sacrament,
may pass over to a dwelling place of light and peace.
Through Christ our Lord.

The Solemn Blessing for Celebrations for the Dead may be used, p. 518.

Second Mass

Entrance Antiphon
Eternal rest grant unto them, O Lord,
and let perpetual light shine upon them. *cf. 4 Esdras 2:34-35*

Collect
O God, glory of the faithful and life of the just,
by the Death and Resurrection of whose Son
we have been redeemed,
look mercifully on your departed servants,
that, just as they professed the mystery of our resurrection,
so they may merit to receive the joys of eternal happiness.
Through our Lord Jesus Christ, your Son,
who lives and reigns with you in the unity of the Holy Spirit,
one God, for ever and ever.

The readings from the First Mass, pp. 1035-1039, may be used, or
other readings from the Lectionary.

Prayer over the Offerings
Almighty and merciful God,
by means of these sacrificial offerings
wash away, we pray, in the Blood of Christ,
the sins of your departed servants,
for you purify unceasingly by your merciful forgiveness
those you once cleansed in the waters of Baptism.
Through Christ our Lord.

Preface I-V for the Dead, pp. 505-507.

Communion Antiphon
Let perpetual light shine upon them, O Lord,
with your Saints for ever, for you are merciful. *cf. 4 Esdras 2:35. 34*

Prayer after Communion
Having received the Sacrament of your Only Begotten Son,
who was sacrificed for us and rose in glory,
we humbly implore you, O Lord,
for your departed servants,
that, cleansed by the paschal mysteries,
they may glory in the gift of the resurrection to come.
Through Christ our Lord.

The Solemn Blessing for Celebrations for the Dead may be used,
p. 518.

THIRD MASS

Entrance Antiphon
God, who raised Jesus from the dead,
will give life also to your mortal bodies,
through his Spirit that dwells in you.   cf. Romans 8:11

Collect
O God, who willed that your Only Begotten Son,
having conquered death,
should pass over into the realm of heaven,
grant, we pray, to your departed servants
that, with the mortality of this life overcome,
they may gaze eternally on you,
their Creator and Redeemer.
Through our Lord Jesus Christ, your Son,
who lives and reigns with you in the unity of the Holy Spirit,
one God, for ever and ever.

The readings from the First Mass, pp. 1035-1039, may be used, or
other readings from the Lectionary.

Prayer over the Offerings
Receive, Lord, in your kindness,
the sacrificial offering we make
for all your servants who sleep in Christ,
that, set free from the bonds of death
by this singular sacrifice,
they may merit eternal life.
Through Christ our Lord.

Preface I-V for the Dead, pp. 505-507.

Communion Antiphon
We await a saviour, the Lord Jesus Christ,
who will change our mortal bodies,
to conform with his glorified body.   cf. Philippians 3:20-21

Prayer after Communion
Through these sacrificial gifts
which we have received, O Lord,
bestow on your departed servants your great mercy
and, to those you have endowed with the grace of Baptism,
grant also the fullness of eternal joy.
Through Christ our Lord.

The Solemn Blessing for Celebrations for the Dead may be used,
p. 518.

9 November

THE DEDICATION
OF THE LATERAN BASILICA

Feast

Living stones.
The normal place for the Christian community to gather together is the
building called the church. This is the symbol of the spiritual temple which
Christ is building up, little by little, through us. We are the living stones and
Christ himself is the corner stone. The Basilica of St John Lateran is the
cathedral church of the Pope as Bishop of Rome, and as such is regarded as the
mother of all the churches throughout the world.

Entrance Antiphon
I saw the holy city, a new Jerusalem,
coming down out of heaven from God,
prepared like a bride adorned for her husband.   cf. Apocalypse 21:2

or

Behold God's dwelling with the human race.
He will dwell with them and they will be his people,
and God himself with them will be their God.   cf. Apocalypse 21:3

The Gloria is said or sung.

Collect
O God, who from living and chosen stones
prepare an eternal dwelling for your majesty,
increase in your Church the spirit of grace you have bestowed,
so that by new growth your faithful people
may build up the heavenly Jerusalem.
Through our Lord Jesus Christ, your Son,
who lives and reigns with you in the unity of the Holy Spirit,
one God, for ever and ever.

or

O God, who were pleased to call your Church the Bride,
grant that the people that serves your name
may revere you, love you and follow you,
and may be led by you
to attain your promises in heaven.
Through our Lord Jesus Christ, your Son,
who lives and reigns with you in the unity of the Holy Spirit,
one God, for ever and ever.

First Reading   Ezekiel 47:1-2. 8-9. 12

I saw a stream of water coming from the Temple, bringing life to all wherever it flowed.

The angel brought me to the entrance of the Temple, where a stream came out from under the Temple threshold and flowed eastwards, since the Temple faced east. The water flowed from under the right side of the Temple, south of the altar. He took me out by the north gate and led me right round outside as far as the outer east gate where the water flowed out on the right-hand side. The man went to the east holding his measuring line and measured off a thousand cubits; he then made me wade across the stream; the water reached my ankles. He measured off another thousand and made me wade across the stream again; the water reached my knees. He measured off another thousand and made me wade across again; the water reached my waist. He measured off another thousand; it was now a river which I could not cross; the stream had swollen and was now deep water, a river impossible to cross. He then said, "Do you see, son of man?" He took me further, then brought me back to the bank of the river. When I got back, there were many trees on each bank of the river. He said, "This water flows east down to the Arabah and to the sea; and flowing into the sea it makes its waters wholesome. Wherever the river flows, all living creatures teeming in it will live. Fish will be very plentiful, for wherever the water goes it brings health, and life teems wherever the river flows. Along the river, on either bank, will grow every kind of fruit tree with leaves that never wither and fruit that never fails; they will bear new fruit every month, because this water comes from the sanctuary. And their fruit will be good to eat and the leaves medicinal."

Psalm   Psalm 45

R. **The waters of a river give joy to God's city,
the holy place where the Most High dwells.**

1. God is for us a refuge and strength,
a helper close at hand, in time of distress:
so we shall not fear though the earth should rock,
though the mountains fall into the depths of the sea. R.

2. The waters of a river give joy to God's city,
the holy place where the Most High dwells.
God is within, it cannot be shaken;
God will help it at the dawning of the day. R.

3. The Lord of hosts is with us:
the God of Jacob is our stronghold.
Come, consider the works of the Lord,
the redoubtable deeds he has done on the earth. R.

Second Reading   1 Corinthians 3:9-11. 16-17
You are the temple of God.

You are God's building. By the grace God gave me, I succeeded as an architect and laid the foundations, on which someone else is doing the building. Everyone doing the building must work carefully. For the foundation, nobody can lay any other than the one which has already been laid, that is Jesus Christ.

Didn't you realise that you were God's temple and that the Spirit of God was living among you? If anybody should destroy the temple of God, God will destroy him, because the temple of God is sacred; and you are that temple.

Gospel Acclamation
Alleluia, alleluia!
I have chosen and consecrated this house, says the Lord,
for my name to be there for ever.
Alleluia!   2 Chronicles 7:16

Gospel John 2:13-22

He was speaking of the sanctuary that was his body.

Just before the Jewish Passover Jesus went up to Jerusalem, and in the Temple he found people selling cattle and sheep and pigeons, and the money changers sitting at their counters there. Making a whip out of some cord, he drove them all out of the Temple, cattle and sheep as well, scattered the money changers' coins, knocked their tables over and said to the pigeon-sellers, "Take all this out of here and stop turning my Father's house into a market." Then his disciples remembered the words of scripture: Zeal for your house will devour me. The Jews intervened and said, "What sign can you show us to justify what you have done?" Jesus answered, "Destroy this sanctuary, and in three days I will raise it up." The Jews replied, "It has taken forty-six years to build this sanctuary: are you going to raise it up in three days?" But he was speaking of the sanctuary that was his body, and when Jesus rose from the dead, his disciples remembered that he had said this, and they believed the scripture and the words he had said.

When this feast falls on a Sunday, the Creed is said.

Prayer over the Offerings
Accept, we pray, O Lord, the offering made here
and grant that by it those who seek your favour
may receive in this place
the power of the Sacraments
and the answer to their prayers.
Through Christ our Lord.

Preface
It is truly right and just, our duty and our salvation,
always and everywhere to give you thanks,
Lord, holy Father, almighty and eternal God.

For in your benevolence you are pleased
to dwell in this house of prayer
in order to perfect us as the temple of the Holy Spirit,

supported by the perpetual help of your grace
and resplendent with the glory of a life acceptable to you.

Year by year you sanctify the Church, the Bride of Christ,
foreshadowed in visible buildings,
so that, rejoicing as the mother of countless children,
she may be given her place in your heavenly glory.

And so, with all the Angels and Saints,
we praise you, as without end we acclaim:
Holy, Holy, Holy Lord God of hosts...

Communion Antiphon
Be built up like living stones,
into a spiritual house, a holy priesthood.   cf. 1 Peter 2:5

Prayer after Communion
O God, who chose to foreshadow for us
the heavenly Jerusalem
through the sign of your Church on earth,
grant, we pray,
that, by our partaking of this Sacrament,
we may be made the temple of your grace
and may enter the dwelling place of your glory.
Through Christ our Lord.

The Solemn Blessing for the Dedication of a Church may be used,
pp. 517-518.

30 November

SAINT ANDREW, APOSTLE

Patron of Scotland; Solemnity in Scotland

*Come, follow me. Jesus Christ did not only call his first apostles to follow him
and become "fishers of men"; he also called us in Baptism to be missionaries
of his Gospel. It is our task today, in the footsteps of the apostles, to make
Christ's Good News known in the world, to bring him to others.*

Entrance Antiphon
Beside the Sea of Galilee,
the Lord saw two brothers, Peter and Andrew,
and he said to them:
Come after me and I will make you fishers of men.   cf. Matthew 4:18-19

The Gloria is said or sung.

Collect
We humbly implore your majesty, O Lord,
that, just as the blessed Apostle Andrew
was for your Church a preacher and pastor,
so he may be for us a constant intercessor before you.
Through our Lord Jesus Christ, your Son,
who lives and reigns with you in the unity of the Holy Spirit,
one God, for ever and ever.

First Reading   Wisdom 3:1-9
He accepted them as a holocaust.
The souls of the virtuous are in the hands of God,
no torment shall ever touch them.
In the eyes of the unwise, they did appear to die,
their going looked like a disaster,
their leaving us, like annihilation;
but they are in peace.
If they experienced punishment as men see it,
their hope was rich with immortality;
slight was their affliction, great will their blessings be.
God has put them to the test
and proved them worthy to be with him;
he has tested them like gold in a furnace,

and accepted them as a holocaust.
When the time comes for his visitation they will shine out;
as sparks run through the stubble, so will they.
They shall judge nations, rule over peoples,
and the Lord will be their king for ever.
They who trust in him will understand the truth,
those who are faithful will live with him in love;
for grace and mercy await those he has chosen.

Psalm   Psalm 30

R. **Into your hands, O Lord,**
I commend my spirit.

1. Be a rock of refuge for me,
   a mighty stronghold to save me,
   for you are my rock, my stronghold.
   For your name's sake, lead me and guide me. R.

2. Into your hands I commend my spirit.
   It is you who will redeem me, Lord.
   As for me, I trust in the Lord:
   let me be glad and rejoice in your love. R.

3. Let your face shine on your servant.
   Save me in your love.
   You hide them in the shelter of your presence
   from the plotting of men. R.

Second Reading   Romans 10:9-18

Faith comes from what is preached, and what is preached comes
from the word of Christ.

If your lips confess that Jesus is Lord and if you believe in your
heart that God raised him from the dead, then you will be saved. By
believing from the heart you are made righteous; by confessing with
your lips you are saved. When scripture says: those who believe in
him will have no cause for shame, it makes no distinction between
Jew and Greek: all belong to the same Lord who is rich enough,
however many ask his help, for everyone who calls on the name of
the Lord will be saved.

But they will not ask his help unless they believe in him, and
they will not believe in him unless they have heard of him, and

they will not hear of him unless they get a preacher, and they will never have a preacher unless one is sent, but as scripture says: The footsteps of those who bring good news are a welcome sound. Not everyone, of course, listens to the Good News. As Isaiah says: Lord, how many believed what we proclaimed? So faith comes from what is preached, and what is preached comes from the word of Christ.

Let me put the question: is it possible that they did not hear? Indeed they did; in the words of the psalm, their voice has gone out through all the earth, and their message to the ends of the world.

Gospel Acclamation
Alleluia, alleluia!
Follow me, says the Lord,
and I will make you fishers of men.
Alleluia!   Matthew 4:19

Gospel   Matthew 4:18-22
And they left their nets at once and followed him.
As Jesus was walking by the Sea of Galilee he saw two brothers, Simon, who was called Peter, and his brother Andrew; they were making a cast in the lake with their net, for they were fishermen. And he said to them, "Follow me and I will make you fishers of men." And they left their nets at once and followed him.

Going on from there he saw another pair of brothers, James son of Zebedee and his brother John; they were in their boat with their father Zebedee, mending their nets, and he called them. At once, leaving the boat and their father, they followed him.

Where this day is kept as a Solemnity, the Creed is said.

Prayer over the Offerings
Grant us, almighty God, that through these offerings,
which we bring on the feast day of Saint Andrew,
we may please you by what we have brought
and be given life by what you have accepted.
Through Christ our Lord.

Preface
It is truly right and just, our duty and our salvation,
always and everywhere to give you thanks,
Lord, holy Father, almighty and eternal God.

For you, eternal Shepherd, do not desert your flock,
but through the blessed Apostles
watch over it and protect it always,
so that it may be governed
by those you have appointed shepherds
to lead it in the name of your Son.

And so, with Angels and Archangels,
with Thrones and Dominions,
and with all the hosts and Powers of heaven,
we sing the hymn of your glory,
as without end we acclaim:

Holy, Holy, Holy Lord God of hosts…

or

It is truly right and just, our duty and our salvation,
always and everywhere to give you thanks,
Lord, holy Father, almighty and eternal God,
through Christ our Lord.

For you have built your Church
to stand firm on apostolic foundations,
to be a lasting sign of your holiness on earth
and offer all humanity your heavenly teaching.

Therefore, now and for ages unending,
with all the host of Angels,
we sing to you with all our hearts,
crying out as we acclaim:

Holy, Holy, Holy Lord God of hosts…

Communion Antiphon

Andrew told his brother Simon:
We have found the Messiah, the Christ,
and he brought him to Jesus.   cf. John 1:41-42

Prayer after Communion

May communion in your Sacrament strengthen us, O Lord,
so that by the example of the blessed Apostle Andrew
we, who carry in our body the Death of Christ,
may merit to live with him in glory.
Who lives and reigns for ever and ever.

The Solemn Blessing for the Apostles may be used, pp. 516-517.

8 December

THE IMMACULATE CONCEPTION
OF THE BLESSED VIRGIN MARY

Solemnity

Hail, Mary, full of grace.
The Lord chose Mary to be the mother of his Son. From her conception, she
who was to bear the sinless one was herself free from sin. This shows God's
special love for Mary, who was indeed full of grace. Mary shows us how to
respond to God's will promptly and with faith in God's word. We are called to
do likewise.

Entrance Antiphon

I rejoice heartily in the Lord,
in my God is the joy of my soul;
for he has clothed me with a robe of salvation,
and wrapped me in a mantle of justice,
like a bride adorned with her jewels.   Isaiah 61:10

The Gloria is said or sung.

Collect

O God, who by the Immaculate Conception of the Blessed Virgin
prepared a worthy dwelling for your Son,
grant, we pray,
that, as you preserved her from every stain
by virtue of the Death of your Son, which you foresaw,
so, through her intercession,
we, too, may be cleansed and admitted to your presence.
Through our Lord Jesus Christ, your Son,
who lives and reigns with you in the unity of the Holy Spirit,
one God, for ever and ever.

First Reading   Genesis 3:9-15. 20

I will make you enemies of each other: your offspring and her
offspring.

After Adam had eaten of the tree, the Lord God called to him.
"Where are you?" he asked. "I heard the sound of you in the garden,"

he replied. "I was afraid because I was naked, so I hid." "Who told you that you were naked?" he asked. "Have you been eating of the tree I forbade you to eat?" The man replied, "It was the woman you put with me; she gave me the fruit, and I ate it." Then the Lord God asked the woman, "What is this you have done?" The woman replied, "The serpent tempted me and I ate."

Then the Lord God said to the serpent, "Because you have done this,

"Be accursed beyond all cattle,
all wild beasts.
You shall crawl on your belly and eat dust
every day of your life.
I will make you enemies of each other:
you and the woman,
your offspring and her offspring.
It will crush your head
and you will strike its heel."

The man named his wife "Eve" because she was the mother of all those who live.

Psalm   Psalm 97

R. **Sing a new song to the Lord**
    for he has worked wonders.

1. Sing a new song to the Lord
    for he has worked wonders.
    His right hand and his holy arm
    have brought salvation. R.

2. The Lord has made known his salvation;
    has shown his justice to the nations.
    He has remembered his truth and love
    for the house of Israel. R.

3. All the ends of the earth have seen
    the salvation of our God.
    Shout to the Lord all the earth,
    ring out your joy. R.

Second Reading   Ephesians 1:3-6. 11-12

Before the world was made, God chose us in Christ.

Blessed be God the Father of our Lord Jesus Christ,
who has blessed us with all the spiritual blessings of heaven in Christ.
Before the world was made, he chose us, chose us in Christ,
to be holy and spotless, and to live through love in his presence,
determining that we should become his adopted sons, through Jesus
    Christ
for his own kind purposes,
to make us praise the glory of his grace,
his free gift to us in the Beloved.
And it is in him that we were claimed as God's own,
chosen from the beginning,
under the predetermined plan of the one who guides all things
as he decides by his own will;
chosen to be,
for his greater glory,
the people who would put their hopes in Christ before he came.

Gospel Acclamation

Alleluia, alleluia!
Hail, Mary, full of grace; the Lord is with thee!
Blessed art thou among women.
Alleluia!   cf. Luke 1:28

Gospel   Luke 1:26-38

You are to conceive and bear a son.

The angel Gabriel was sent by God to a town in Galilee called
Nazareth, to a virgin betrothed to a man named Joseph, of the House
of David; and the virgin's name was Mary. He went in and said to her,
"Rejoice, so highly favoured! The Lord is with you." She was deeply
disturbed by these words and asked herself what this greeting could
mean, but the angel said to her, "Mary, do not be afraid; you have
won God's favour. Listen! You are to conceive and bear a son, and
you must name him Jesus. He will be great and will be called Son of
the Most High. The Lord God will give him the throne of his ancestor
David; he will rule over the House of Jacob for ever and his reign will

have no end." Mary said to the angel, "But how can this come about, since I am a virgin?" "The Holy Spirit will come upon you," the angel answered, "and the power of the Most High will cover you with its shadow. And so the child will be holy and will be called Son of God. Know this too: your kinswoman Elizabeth has, in her old age, herself conceived a son, and she whom people called barren is now in her sixth month, for nothing is impossible to God." "I am the handmaid of the Lord," said Mary, "let what you have said be done to me." And the angel left her.

The Creed is said.

Prayer over the Offerings
Graciously accept the saving sacrifice
which we offer you, O Lord,
on the Solemnity of the Immaculate Conception
of the Blessed Virgin Mary,
and grant that, as we profess her,
on account of your prevenient grace,
to be untouched by any stain of sin,
so, through her intercession,
we may be delivered from all our faults.
Through Christ our Lord.

Preface
It is truly right and just, our duty and our salvation,
always and everywhere to give you thanks,
Lord, holy Father, almighty and eternal God.

For you preserved the most Blessed Virgin Mary
from all stain of original sin,
so that in her, endowed with the rich fullness of your grace,
you might prepare a worthy Mother for your Son
and signify the beginning of the Church,
his beautiful Bride without spot or wrinkle.

She, the most pure Virgin, was to bring forth a Son,
the innocent Lamb who would wipe away our offences;
you placed her above all others

to be for your people an advocate of grace
and a model of holiness.

And so, in company with the choirs of Angels,
we praise you, and with joy we proclaim:
Holy, Holy, Holy Lord God of hosts…

Communion Antiphon
Glorious things are spoken of you, O Mary,
for from you arose the sun of justice,
Christ our God.

Prayer after Communion
May the Sacrament we have received,
O Lord our God,
heal in us the wounds of that fault
from which in a singular way
you preserved Blessed Mary in her Immaculate Conception.
Through Christ our Lord.

The Solemn Blessing for the Blessed Virgin Mary may be used,
p. 515.

LITANIES

A litany is a prayer of supplication, usually recited communally, consisting of a series of petitions recited by a leader with a fixed response by the congregation. Used in both liturgical services and private devotions, the litany has its origin in prayers like Psalm 135 with its repetitive form:

> O give thanks to the Lord for he is good.
> **For his great love is without end.**
> Give thanks to the God of gods.
> **For his great love is without end.**
> Give thanks to the Lord of lords:
> **For his great love is without end.**

Litany of the Saints

The Litany of the Saints is the oldest litany used in the Church, dating from AD 595. It is a prayer of invocation, sung during the Easter Vigil and in other celebrations, such as the sacraments of Baptism and Holy Orders.

Lord, have mercy.	**Lord, have mercy.**
Christ, have mercy.	**Christ, have mercy.**
Lord, have mercy.	**Lord, have mercy.**
Holy Mary, Mother of God,	**pray for us.**
Saint Michael,	**pray for us.**
Holy Angels of God,	**pray for us.**
Saint John the Baptist,	**pray for us.**
Saint Joseph,	**pray for us.**
Saint Peter and Saint Paul,	**pray for us.**
Saint Andrew,	**pray for us.**
Saint John,	**pray for us.**
Saint Mary Magdalene,	**pray for us.**
Saint Stephen,	**pray for us.**
Saint Ignatius of Antioch,	**pray for us.**
Saint Lawrence,	**pray for us.**
Saint Perpetua and Saint Felicity,	**pray for us.**
Saint Agnes,	**pray for us.**
Saint Gregory,	**pray for us.**
Saint Augustine,	**pray for us.**

Saint Athanasius,	**pray for us.**
Saint Basil,	**pray for us.**
Saint Martin,	**pray for us.**
Saint Benedict,	**pray for us.**
Saint Francis and Saint Dominic,	**pray for us.**
Saint Francis Xavier,	**pray for us.**
Saint John Vianney,	**pray for us.**
Saint Catherine of Siena,	**pray for us.**
Saint Teresa of Jesus,	**pray for us.**
All holy men and women, Saints of God,	**pray for us.**
Lord, be merciful,	**Lord, deliver us, we pray.**
From all evil,	**Lord, deliver us, we pray.**
From every sin,	**Lord, deliver us, we pray.**
From everlasting death,	**Lord, deliver us, we pray.**
By your Incarnation,	**Lord, deliver us, we pray.**
By your Death and Resurrection,	**Lord, deliver us, we pray.**
By the outpouring of the Holy Spirit,	**Lord, deliver us, we pray.**
Be merciful to us sinners,	**Lord, we ask you, hear our prayer.**
Jesus, Son of the living God,	**Lord, hear our prayer.**
Christ, hear us,	**Christ, hear us.**
Christ, graciously hear us,	**Christ, graciously hear us.**

Litany of the Sacred Heart of Jesus

The Litany of the Sacred Heart of Jesus is a sign of Jesus' great love for us. Jesus said: "Come to me, all you who labour and are overburdened, and I will give you rest. Shoulder my yoke and learn from me, for I am gentle and humble in heart, and you will find rest for your souls" (Matthew 11:28-29).

Lord, have mercy.	**Lord, have mercy.**
Christ, have mercy.	**Christ, have mercy.**
Lord, have mercy.	**Lord, have mercy.**
Christ, hear us.	**Christ, graciously hear us.**

God the Father of heaven,	**have mercy on us.**
God the Son, Redeemer of the world,	**have mercy on us.**
God the Holy Spirit,	**have mercy on us.**
Holy Trinity, one God,	**have mercy on us.**

Heart of Jesus, Son of the Eternal Father,	**have mercy on us.**
Heart of Jesus, formed by the Holy Spirit in the womb of the Virgin Mother,	**have mercy on us.**
Heart of Jesus, united substantially to the Eternal Word,	**have mercy on us.**
Heart of Jesus, of infinite majesty,	**have mercy on us.**
Heart of Jesus, holy temple of God,	**have mercy on us.**
Heart of Jesus, tabernacle of the Most High,	**have mercy on us.**
Heart of Jesus, house of God and gate of heaven,	**have mercy on us.**
Heart of Jesus, burning furnace of charity,	**have mercy on us.**
Heart of Jesus, vessel of justice and love,	**have mercy on us.**
Heart of Jesus, full of goodness and love,	**have mercy on us.**
Heart of Jesus, abyss of all virtues,	**have mercy on us.**
Heart of Jesus, most worthy of all praise,	**have mercy on us.**
Heart of Jesus, king and centre of all hearts,	**have mercy on us.**
Heart of Jesus, in whom are all the treasures of wisdom and knowledge,	**have mercy on us.**
Heart of Jesus, in whom dwells all the fullness of the divinity,	**have mercy on us.**
Heart of Jesus, in whom the Father is well pleased,	**have mercy on us.**
Heart of Jesus, of whose fullness we have all received,	**have mercy on us.**
Heart of Jesus, desire of the everlasting hills,	**have mercy on us.**
Heart of Jesus, patient and abounding in mercy,	**have mercy on us.**
Heart of Jesus, rich to all that call upon you,	**have mercy on us.**
Heart of Jesus, fountain of life and holiness,	**have mercy on us.**
Heart of Jesus, propitiation for our sins,	**have mercy on us.**

Heart of Jesus, filled with reproaches,	**have mercy on us.**
Heart of Jesus, bruised for our sins,	**have mercy on us.**
Heart of Jesus, made obedient unto death,	**have mercy on us.**
Heart of Jesus, pierced with a lance,	**have mercy on us.**
Heart of Jesus, source of all consolation,	**have mercy on us.**
Heart of Jesus, our life and resurrection,	**have mercy on us.**
Heart of Jesus, our peace and reconciliation,	**have mercy on us.**
Heart of Jesus, victim for our sins,	**have mercy on us.**
Heart of Jesus, salvation of those that hope in you,	**have mercy on us.**
Heart of Jesus, hope of those that die in you,	**have mercy on us.**
Heart of Jesus, delight of all the saints,	**have mercy on us.**
Lamb of God, you take away the sins of the world,	**spare us, O Lord.**
Lamb of God, you take away the sins of the world,	**graciously hear us, O Lord.**
Lamb of God, you take away the sins of the world,	**have mercy on us.**
Jesus, meek and humble of heart,	**make our hearts like unto yours.**

Let us pray. Almighty and eternal God, consider the heart of your well-beloved Son and the praises and satisfaction he offers you in the name of sinners; and to those who implore your mercy, in your great goodness, grant forgiveness in the name of the same Jesus Christ your Son who lives and reigns with you in the unity of the Holy Spirit, one God for ever and ever. **Amen.**

Litany of the Most Holy Name of Jesus

The name Jesus has always been held in special veneration by Christians. The angel Gabriel announced to Mary, "You are to conceive and bear a son, and you must name him Jesus" (Luke 1:31).

Jesus died for us to take away our sins, "But God raised him high and gave him the name which is above all other names so that all beings in the heavens, on earth and in the underworld, should bend the knee at the name of Jesus and that every tongue should acclaim Jesus Christ as Lord, to the glory of God the Father" (Philippians 2:9-11).

Lord, have mercy on us.	**Lord, have mercy on us.**
Christ, have mercy on us.	**Christ, have mercy on us.**
Lord, have mercy on us.	**Lord, have mercy on us.**
Jesus, hear us.	**Jesus, graciously hear us.**
God the Father of heaven,	**have mercy on us.**
God the Son, Redeemer of the world,	**have mercy on us.**
God the Holy Spirit,	**have mercy on us.**
Holy Trinity, one God,	**have mercy on us.**
Jesus, Son of the living God,	**have mercy on us.**
Jesus, splendour of the Father,	**have mercy on us.**
Jesus, brightness of eternal light,	**have mercy on us.**
Jesus, king of glory,	**have mercy on us.**
Jesus, sun of justice,	**have mercy on us.**
Jesus, son of the Virgin Mary,	**have mercy on us.**
Jesus, most amiable,	**have mercy on us.**
Jesus, most admirable,	**have mercy on us.**
Jesus, mighty God,	**have mercy on us.**
Jesus, father of the world to come,	**have mercy on us.**
Jesus, angel of great counsel,	**have mercy on us.**
Jesus, most powerful,	**have mercy on us.**
Jesus, most patient,	**have mercy on us.**
Jesus, most obedient,	**have mercy on us.**
Jesus, meek and humble of heart,	**have mercy on us.**
Jesus, lover of chastity,	**have mercy on us.**
Jesus, lover of us,	**have mercy on us.**
Jesus, God of peace,	**have mercy on us.**
Jesus, author of life,	**have mercy on us.**
Jesus, example of virtues,	**have mercy on us.**
Jesus, zealous lover of souls,	**have mercy on us.**
Jesus, our God,	**have mercy on us.**
Jesus, our refuge,	**have mercy on us.**

Jesus, father of the poor,	**have mercy on us.**
Jesus, treasure of the faithful,	**have mercy on us.**
Jesus, good shepherd,	**have mercy on us.**
Jesus, true light,	**have mercy on us.**
Jesus, eternal wisdom,	**have mercy on us.**
Jesus, infinite goodness,	**have mercy on us.**
Jesus, our way and our life,	**have mercy on us.**
Jesus, joy of angels,	**have mercy on us.**
Jesus, king of patriarchs,	**have mercy on us.**
Jesus, master of the apostles,	**have mercy on us.**
Jesus, teacher of the evangelists,	**have mercy on us.**
Jesus, strength of martyrs,	**have mercy on us.**
Jesus, light of confessors,	**have mercy on us.**
Jesus, purity of virgins,	**have mercy on us.**
Jesus, crown of all saints,	**have mercy on us.**
Be merciful unto us,	**Jesus, spare us.**
Be merciful unto us,	**Jesus, spare us.**
From all evil,	**Jesus, deliver us.**
From all sin,	**Jesus, deliver us.**
From your wrath,	**Jesus, deliver us.**
From the snares of the devil,	**Jesus, deliver us.**
From the spirit of uncleanness,	**Jesus, deliver us.**
From everlasting death,	**Jesus, deliver us.**
From the neglect of your inspirations,	**Jesus, deliver us.**
Through the mystery of your holy incarnation,	**Jesus, deliver us.**
Through your nativity,	**Jesus, deliver us.**
Through your infancy,	**Jesus, deliver us.**
Through your most divine life,	**Jesus, deliver us.**
Through your labours,	**Jesus, deliver us.**
Through your agony and passion,	**Jesus, deliver us.**
Through your cross and dereliction,	**Jesus, deliver us.**
Through your faintness and weariness,	**Jesus, deliver us.**
Through your death and burial,	**Jesus, deliver us.**
Through your resurrection,	**Jesus, deliver us.**
Through your ascension,	**Jesus, deliver us.**

Through your institution of the most Holy Eucharist,	**Jesus, deliver us.**
Through your joys,	**Jesus, deliver us.**
Through your glory,	**Jesus, deliver us.**
Lamb of God, you take away the sins of the world,	**spare us, O Jesus.**
Lamb of God, you take away the sins of the world,	**graciously hear us, O Jesus.**
Lamb of God, you take away the sins of the world,	**have mercy on us, O Jesus.**
Jesus, hear us.	**Jesus, graciously hear us.**

Let us pray. O Lord Jesus Christ, who said: "Ask and you shall receive, seek and you shall find, knock and it shall be opened to you"; grant, we beseech you, to us your supplicants, the gifts of your most divine love, that we may love you with our whole heart, and in all our words and works, and never cease from praising you.

O Lord, give us a perpetual fear as well as love of your holy name, for you never cease to govern those you founded upon the strength of your love. You who live and reign, world without end. **Amen.**

Litany of the Blessed Virgin Mary

This litany, also known as the Litany of Loreto from its place of first recital in Italy, is one of the oldest used in public and private devotion.

Lord, have mercy.	**Lord, have mercy.**
Christ, have mercy.	**Christ, have mercy.**
Lord, have mercy.	**Lord, have mercy.**
Christ, hear us.	**Christ, graciously hear us.**
God the Father of heaven,	**have mercy on us.**
God the Son, Redeemer of the world,	**have mercy on us.**
God the Holy Spirit,	**have mercy on us.**
Holy Trinity, one God,	**have mercy on us.**
Holy Mary,	**pray for us.**

Holy Mother of God,	**pray for us.**
Holy Virgin of virgins,	**pray for us.**
Mother of Christ,	**pray for us.**
Mother of the Church,	**pray for us.**
Mother of divine grace,	**pray for us.**
Mother most pure,	**pray for us.**
Mother most chaste,	**pray for us.**
Mother inviolate,	**pray for us.**
Mother undefiled,	**pray for us.**
Mother most lovable,	**pray for us.**
Mother most admirable,	**pray for us.**
Mother of good counsel,	**pray for us.**
Mother of our Creator,	**pray for us.**
Mother of our Saviour,	**pray for us.**
Virgin most prudent,	**pray for us.**
Virgin most venerable,	**pray for us.**
Virgin most renowned,	**pray for us.**
Virgin most powerful,	**pray for us.**
Virgin most merciful,	**pray for us.**
Virgin most faithful,	**pray for us.**
Mirror of justice,	**pray for us.**
Seat of wisdom,	**pray for us.**
Cause of our joy,	**pray for us.**
Spiritual vessel,	**pray for us.**
Vessel of honour,	**pray for us.**
Singular vessel of devotion,	**pray for us.**
Mystical rose,	**pray for us.**
Tower of David,	**pray for us.**
Tower of ivory,	**pray for us.**
House of gold,	**pray for us.**
Ark of the covenant,	**pray for us.**
Gate of heaven,	**pray for us.**
Morning star,	**pray for us.**
Health of the sick,	**pray for us.**
Refuge of sinners,	**pray for us.**
Comforter of the afflicted,	**pray for us.**
Help of Christians,	**pray for us.**

Queen of angels,	**pray for us.**
Queen of patriarchs,	**pray for us.**
Queen of prophets,	**pray for us.**
Queen of apostles,	**pray for us.**
Queen of martyrs,	**pray for us.**
Queen of confessors,	**pray for us.**
Queen of virgins,	**pray for us.**
Queen of all saints,	**pray for us.**
Queen conceived without original sin,	**pray for us.**
Queen assumed into heaven,	**pray for us.**
Queen of the most holy rosary,	**pray for us.**
Queen of families,	**pray for us.**
Queen of peace,	**pray for us.**

Lamb of God, you take away the sins of the world,	**spare us, O Lord.**
Lamb of God, you take away the sins of the world,	**graciously hear us, O Lord.**
Lamb of God, you take away the sins of the world,	**have mercy on us.**

Pray for us, O holy Mother of God.
That we may be made worthy of the promises of Christ.

Let us pray. Grant that we your servants, Lord, may enjoy unfailing health of mind and body, and through the prayers of the ever-blessed Virgin Mary in her glory, free us from our sorrows in this world and give us eternal happiness in the next. Through Christ our Lord. **Amen**.

THE ROSARY

The rosary is a vocal and contemplative form of prayer which has been very much part of Catholic devotional practice since before the thirteenth century. The rosary uses words like a mantra so that we can meditate deeply and in peace. It is a simple and effective way of leading us step by step through the essential mysteries of our faith. The love of God for us is revealed in Christ, and the mysteries of the rosary are arranged in groups of five decades (known as chaplets) and follow the sequence of the life of Our Lord and Mary, his mother. For many centuries in the life of the Church there have been three sets of mysteries of the rosary, known as the joyful, sorrowful and glorious mysteries; in 2002, Blessed Pope John Paul II added a new set, known as the luminous mysteries.

A traditional rosary consists of five groups of ten beads (a decade), with a separate bead between each decade. Attached to the rosary is a shorter strand consisting of a group of three beads, with another separate bead on either side of the group. There is usually a crucifix at the end of the rosary chain. The beads are used as a physical way of keeping count of the prayers as we say them. To pray the rosary, we normally begin by reciting the Apostles' Creed at the crucifix, then on the shorter part of the chain we say an Our Father on the first bead, a Hail Mary on each of the next three beads, followed by a Glory be to the Father on the next bead.

We then begin to pray the decades, counting the prayers on the beads, while focusing on whichever set of mysteries has been chosen. Each decade of the rosary is composed of one Our Father, ten Hail Marys and one Glory be to the Father. The rhythm of the prayers helps us to grow in contemplation and brings a stillness that is essential to our growth in prayer life.

The scriptural readings provided here are intended to help our thoughts and prayers as we contemplate the mysteries. They enable us to lift our minds and hearts to the Lord in gratitude for all he has done for us. Prayer is not so much a matter of talking a great deal but of loving a great deal. Our words in the rosary are the background music of our loving dialogue with God.

THE JOYFUL MYSTERIES

The Annunciation

In the sixth month the angel Gabriel was sent by God to a town in Galilee called Nazareth, to a virgin betrothed to a man named Joseph, of the House of David; and the virgin's name was Mary. He went in and said to her, "Rejoice, so highly favoured! The Lord is with you." She was deeply disturbed by these words and asked herself what this greeting could mean, but the angel said to her, "Mary, do not be afraid; you have won God's favour. Listen! You are to conceive and bear a son, and you must name him Jesus. He will be great and will be called Son of the Most High. The Lord God will give him the throne of his ancestor David; he will rule over the House of Jacob for ever and his reign will have no end." Mary said to the angel, "But how can this come about, since I am a virgin?" "The Holy Spirit will come upon you," the angel answered, "and the power of the Most High will cover you with its shadow. And so the child will be holy and will be called Son of God. Know this too: your kinswoman Elizabeth has, in her old age, herself conceived a son, and she whom people called barren is now in her sixth month, for nothing is impossible to God." "I am the handmaid of the Lord," said Mary, "let what you have said be done to me." And the angel left her.   Luke 1:26-38

The Visitation

Mary set out at that time and went as quickly as she could to a town in the hill country of Judah. She went into Zechariah's house and greeted Elizabeth. Now as soon as Elizabeth heard Mary's greeting, the child leapt in her womb and Elizabeth was filled with the Holy Spirit. She gave a loud cry and said, "Of all women you are the most blessed, and blessed is the fruit of your womb. Why should I be honoured with a visit from the mother of my Lord? For the moment your greeting reached my ears, the child in my womb leapt for joy. Yes, blessed is she who believed that the promise made by the Lord would be fulfilled."

And Mary said:

"My soul proclaims the greatness of the Lord
and my spirit exults in God my saviour;
because he has looked upon his lowly handmaid.
Yes, from this day forward all generations will call me blessed,
for the Almighty has done great things for me.
Holy is his name,
and his mercy reaches from age to age for those who fear him.
He has shown the power of his arm,
he has routed the proud of heart.
He has pulled down princes from their thrones and exalted the
    lowly.
The hungry he has filled with good things, the rich sent empty away.
He has come to the help of Israel his servant, mindful of his mercy
 – according to the promise he made to our ancestors –
of his mercy to Abraham and to his descendants for ever."

Mary stayed with Elizabeth about three months and then went back
home.   Luke 1:39-56

The Nativity

Now at this time Caesar Augustus issued a decree for a census of the
whole world to be taken. This census – the first – took place while
Quirinius was governor of Syria, and everyone went to his own town
to be registered. So Joseph set out from the town of Nazareth in Galilee
and travelled up to Judaea, to the town of David called Bethlehem,
since he was of David's House and line, in order to be registered
together with Mary, his betrothed, who was with child. While they
were there the time came for her to have her child, and she gave birth
to a son, her first-born. She wrapped him in swaddling clothes, and
laid him in a manger because there was no room for them at the inn.
In the countryside close by there were shepherds who lived in the
fields and took it in turns to watch their flocks during the night. The
angel of the Lord appeared to them and the glory of the Lord shone
round them. They were terrified, but the angel said, "Do not be afraid.
Listen, I bring you news of great joy, a joy to be shared by the whole
people. Today in the town of David a saviour has been born to you;
he is Christ the Lord. And here is a sign for you: you will find a baby

wrapped in swaddling clothes and lying in a manger." And suddenly with the angel there was a great throng of the heavenly host, praising God and singing:

"Glory to God in the highest heaven,
and peace to men who enjoy his favour".

Luke 2:1-14

The Presentation of Christ in the Temple

And when the day came for them to be purified as laid down by the Law of Moses, Mary and Joseph took him up to Jerusalem to present him to the Lord – observing what stands written in the Law of the Lord: Every first-born male must be consecrated to the Lord – and also to offer in sacrifice, in accordance with what is said in the Law of the Lord, a pair of turtledoves or two young pigeons. Now in Jerusalem there was a man named Simeon. He was an upright and devout man; he looked forward to Israel's comforting and the Holy Spirit rested on him. It had been revealed to him by the Holy Spirit that he would not see death until he had set eyes on the Christ of the Lord. Prompted by the Spirit he came to the Temple; and when the parents brought in the child Jesus to do for him what the Law required, he took him into his arms and blessed God; and he said:

"Now, Master, you can let your servant go in peace,
just as you promised;
because my eyes have seen the salvation
which you have prepared for all the nations to see,
a light to enlighten the pagans
and the glory of your people Israel."

As the child's father and mother stood there wondering at the things that were being said about him, Simeon blessed them and said to Mary his mother, "You see this child: he is destined for the fall and for the rising of many in Israel, destined to be a sign that is rejected – and a sword will pierce your own soul too – so that the secret thoughts of many may be laid bare."

Luke 2:22-35

The Finding of Jesus in the Temple

Every year Jesus' parents used to go to Jerusalem for the feast of the Passover. When he was twelve years old, they went up for the feast as usual. When they were on their way home after the feast, the boy Jesus stayed behind in Jerusalem without his parents knowing it. They assumed he was with the caravan, and it was only after a day's journey that they went to look for him among their relations and acquaintances. When they failed to find him they went back to Jerusalem looking for him everywhere.

Three days later, they found him in the Temple, sitting among the doctors, listening to them, and asking them questions; and all those who heard him were astounded at his intelligence and his replies. They were overcome when they saw him, and his mother said to him, "My child, why have you done this to us? See how worried your father and I have been, looking for you." "Why were you looking for me?" he replied "Did you not know that I must be busy with my Father's affairs?' But they did not understand what he meant.

Luke 2:41-50

THE LUMINOUS MYSTERIES

The Baptism of Jesus

In due course John the Baptist appeared; he preached in the wilderness of Judaea and this was his message: "Repent, for the kingdom of heaven is close at hand". This was the man the prophet Isaiah spoke of when he said:

A voice cries in the wilderness:
Prepare a way for the Lord,
make his paths straight.

This man John wore a garment made of camel-hair with a leather belt round his waist, and his food was locusts and wild honey. Then Jerusalem and all Judaea and the whole Jordan district made their way to him, and as they were baptised by him in the river Jordan they confessed their sins...

Then Jesus appeared: he came from Galilee to the Jordan to be baptised by John. John tried to dissuade him. "It is I who need baptism from you", he said, "and yet you come to me!" But Jesus replied, "Leave it like this for the time being; it is fitting that we should, in this way, do all that righteousness demands". At this, John gave in to him.

As soon as Jesus was baptised he came up from the water, and suddenly the heavens opened and he saw the Spirit of God descending like a dove and coming down on him. And a voice spoke from heaven, "This is my Son, the Beloved; my favour rests on him".   Matthew 3:1-6, 13-17

The Wedding at Cana

Three days later there was a wedding at Cana in Galilee. The mother of Jesus was there, and Jesus and his disciples had also been invited. When they ran out of wine, since the wine provided for the wedding was all finished, the mother of Jesus said to him, "They have no wine". Jesus said, "Woman, why turn to me? My hour has not come yet." His mother said to the servants, "Do whatever he tells you." There were six stone water jars standing there, meant for the ablutions that are customary among the Jews: each could hold twenty or thirty gallons. Jesus said to the servants, "Fill the jars with water," and they filled them to the brim. "Draw some out now", he told them, "and take it to the steward." They did this; the steward tasted the water, and it had turned into wine. Having no idea where it came from – only the servants who had drawn the water knew – the steward called the bridegroom and said, "People generally serve the best wine first, and keep the cheaper sort till the guests have had plenty to drink; but you have kept the best wine till now."

This was the first of the signs given by Jesus: it was given at Cana in Galilee. He let his glory be seen, and his disciples believed in him.

John 2:1-11

The Proclamation of the Kingdom of God

Jesus began his preaching with the message, "Repent, for the kingdom of heaven is close at hand."

As he was walking by the Sea of Galilee he saw two brothers, Simon, who was called Peter, and his brother Andrew; they were making a cast in the lake with their net, for they were fishermen. And he said to them, "Follow me and I will make you fishers of men." And they left their nets at once and followed him…

He went round the whole of Galilee teaching in their synagogues, proclaiming the Good News of the kingdom and curing all kinds of diseases and sickness among the people… Large crowds followed him, coming from Galilee, the Decapolis, Jerusalem, Judaea and Transjordania.

Seeing the crowds, he went up the hill. There he sat down and was joined by his disciples. Then he began to speak. This is what he taught them:

> "How happy are the poor in spirit;
> theirs is the kingdom of heaven."   Matthew 4:17-20. 23. 25; 5:1-3

The Transfiguration

Six days later, Jesus took with him Peter and James and John and led them up a high mountain where they could be alone by themselves. There in their presence he was transfigured: his clothes became dazzlingly white, whiter than any earthly bleacher could make them. Elijah appeared to them with Moses; and they were talking with Jesus. Then Peter spoke to Jesus: "Rabbi," he said, "it is wonderful for us to be here; so let us make three tents, one for you, one for Moses and one for Elijah." He did not know what to say; they were so frightened. And a cloud came, covering them in shadow; and there came a voice from the cloud, "This is my Son, the Beloved. Listen to him." Then suddenly, when they looked around, they saw no one with them any more but only Jesus.

As they came down from the mountain he warned them to tell no one what they had seen, until after the Son of Man had risen from the dead.   Mark 9:2-9

The Institution of the Eucharist

Now as they were eating, Jesus took some bread, and when he had said the blessing he broke it and gave it to the disciples. "Take it and eat," he said, "this is my body." Then he took a cup, and when he had returned thanks he gave it to them. "Drink all of you from this," he said, "for this is my blood, the blood of the covenant, which is to be poured out for many for the forgiveness of sins. From now on, I tell you, I shall not drink wine until the day I drink the new wine with you in the kingdom of my Father."

Matthew 26:26-29

"Anyone who does eat my flesh and drink my blood
has eternal life,
and I shall raise him up on the last day.
For my flesh is real food
and my blood is real drink.
He who eats my flesh and drinks my blood
lives in me
and I live in him."

John 6:54-56

THE SORROWFUL MYSTERIES

The Agony in the Garden

Then Jesus came with them to a small estate called Gethsemane; and he said to his disciples, "Stay here while I go over there to pray." He took Peter and the two sons of Zebedee with him. And sadness came over him, and great distress. Then he said to them, "My soul is sorrowful to the point of death. Wait here and keep awake with me." And going on a little further he fell on his face and prayed. "My Father," he said, "if it is possible, let this cup pass me by. Nevertheless, let it be as you, not I, would have it." He came back to his disciples and found them sleeping, and he said to Peter, "So you had not the strength to keep awake with me one hour? You should be awake, and praying not to be put to the test. The spirit is willing, but the flesh is weak." Again, a second time, he went away and prayed: "My Father," he said, "if this cup cannot pass by without my drinking it, your will be done!" And he came back again and found them sleeping, their eyes were so heavy. Leaving them there, he went away again and prayed for the third time, repeating the same words. Then he came back to the disciples and said to them, "You can sleep on now and take your rest. Now the hour has come when the Son of Man is to be betrayed into the hands of sinners. Get up! Let us go! My betrayer is already close at hand."

Matthew 26:36-46

The Scourging at the Pillar

At festival time Pilate used to release a prisoner for them, anyone they asked for. Now a man called Barabbas was then in prison with the rioters who had committed murder during the uprising. When the crowd went up and began to ask Pilate the customary favour, Pilate answered them, "Do you want me to release for you the king of the Jews?" For he realised it was out of jealousy that the chief priests had handed Jesus over. The chief priests, however, had incited the crowd to demand that he should release Barabbas for them instead. Then Pilate spoke again. "But in that case," he said to them, "what am I to do with the man you call king of the Jews?" They shouted back, "Crucify him!" "Why?" Pilate asked them "What harm has he done?" But they shouted all the louder, "Crucify him!" So Pilate, anxious to placate the crowd, released Barabbas for them and, having ordered Jesus to be scourged, handed him over to be crucified.

Mark 15:6-15

The Crowning with Thorns

Pilate then had Jesus taken away and scourged; and after this, the soldiers twisted some thorns into a crown and put it on his head, and dressed him in a purple robe. They kept coming up to him and saying, "Hail, king of the Jews!"; and they slapped him in the face.

Pilate came outside again and said to them, "Look, I am going to bring him out to you to let you see that I find no case." Jesus then came out wearing the crown of thorns and the purple robe. Pilate said, "Here is the man." When they saw him the chief priests and the guards shouted, "Crucify him! Crucify him!" Pilate said, "Take him yourselves and crucify him: I can find no case against him." "We have a Law," the Jews replied, "and according to that Law he ought to die, because he has claimed to be the Son of God." John 19:1-7

The Carrying of the Cross

As they were leading him away they seized on a man, Simon from Cyrene, who was coming in from the country, and made him shoulder the cross and carry it behind Jesus. Large numbers of people followed him, and of women too, who mourned and lamented for him. But Jesus turned to them and said, "Daughters of Jerusalem, do not weep for me; weep rather for yourselves and for your children. For the days will surely come when people will say, 'Happy are those who are barren, the wombs that have never borne, the breasts that have never suckled!' Then they will begin to say to the mountains, 'Fall on us!'; to the hills, 'Cover us!' For if men use the green wood like this, what will happen when it is dry?" Now with him they were also leading out two other criminals to be executed. Luke 23:26-32

The Crucifixion

When they reached the place called The Skull, they crucified him there and the two criminals also, one on the right, the other on the left. Jesus said, "Father, forgive them; they do not know what they are doing." Then they cast lots to share out his clothing.

The people stayed there watching him. As for the leaders, they jeered at him. "He saved others," they said, "let him save himself if he is the Christ of God, the Chosen One." The soldiers mocked him too, and when they approached to offer him vinegar they said, "If you are the king of the Jews, save yourself." Above him there was an inscription: "This is the King of the Jews."

One of the criminals hanging there abused him. "Are you not the Christ?" he said. "Save yourself and us as well." But the other spoke up and rebuked him. "Have you no fear of God at all?" he said. "You got the same sentence as he did, but in our case we deserved it: we are paying for what we did. But this man has done nothing wrong. Jesus," he said, "remember me when you come into your kingdom." "Indeed, I promise you," he replied "today you will be with me in paradise."

It was now about the sixth hour and, with the sun eclipsed, a darkness came over the whole land until the ninth hour. The veil of the Temple was torn right down the middle; and when Jesus had cried out in a loud voice, he said, "Father, into your hands I commit my spirit." With these words he breathed his last.

Luke 23:33-46

THE GLORIOUS MYSTERIES

The Resurrection

When the sabbath was over, Mary of Magdala, Mary the mother of James, and Salome, bought spices with which to go and anoint him. And very early in the morning on the first day of the week they went to the tomb, just as the sun was rising.

They had been saying to one another, "Who will roll away the stone for us from the entrance to the tomb?" But when they looked they could see that the stone – which was very big – had already been rolled back. On entering the tomb they saw a young man in a white robe seated on the right-hand side, and they were struck with amazement. But he said to them, "There is no need for alarm. You are looking for Jesus of Nazareth, who was crucified: he has risen, he is not here. See, here is the place where they laid him. But you must go and tell his disciples and Peter, 'He is going before you to Galilee; it is there you will see him, just as he told you'."

Mark 16:1-7

The Ascension

Meanwhile the eleven disciples set out for Galilee, to the mountain where Jesus had arranged to meet them. When they saw him they fell down before him, though some hesitated. Jesus came up and spoke to them. He said, "All authority in heaven and on earth has been given to me. Go, therefore, make disciples of all the nations; baptise them in the name of the Father and of the Son and of the Holy Spirit, and teach them to observe all the commands I gave you. And know that I am with you always; yes, to the end of time."

Matthew 28:16-20

As he said this he was lifted up while they looked on, and a cloud took him from their sight. They were still staring into the sky when suddenly two men in white were standing near them and they said, "Why are you men from Galilee standing here looking into the sky? Jesus who has been taken up from you into heaven, this same Jesus will come back in the same way as you have seen him go there."

Acts 1:9-11

The Descent of the Holy Spirit

When Pentecost day came round, they had all met in one room, when suddenly they heard what sounded like a powerful wind from heaven, the noise of which filled the entire house in which they were sitting; and something appeared to them that seemed like tongues of fire; these separated and came to rest on the head of each of them. They were all filled with the Holy Spirit, and began to speak foreign languages as the Spirit gave them the gift of speech.

Now there were devout men living in Jerusalem from every nation under heaven, and at this sound they all assembled, each one bewildered to hear these men speaking his own language. They were amazed and astonished. "Surely", they said, "all these men speaking are Galileans? How does it happen that each of us hears them in his own native language? Parthians, Medes and Elamites; people from Mesopotamia, Judaea and Cappadocia, Pontus and Asia, Phrygia and Pamphylia, Egypt and the parts of Libya round Cyrene; as well as visitors from Rome – Jews and proselytes alike – Cretans and Arabs; we hear them preaching in our own language about the marvels of God." Everyone was amazed and unable to explain it; they asked one another what it all meant. Some, however, laughed it off. "They have been drinking too much new wine," they said.

Acts 2:1-13

The Assumption of the Blessed Virgin Mary into Heaven

I will tell you something that has been secret: that we are not all going to die, but we shall all be changed. This will be instantaneous, in the twinkling of an eye, when the last trumpet sounds. It will sound, and the dead will be raised, imperishable, and we shall be changed as well, because our present perishable nature must put on imperishability and this mortal nature must put on immortality.

When this perishable nature has put on imperishability, and when this mortal nature has put on immortality, then the words of scripture will come true: Death is swallowed up in victory. Death, where is your victory? Death, where is your sting? Now the sting of death is sin, and sin gets its power from the Law. So let us thank God for giving us the victory through our Lord Jesus Christ.

1 Corinthians 15:51-57

The Coronation of the Blessed Virgin Mary

After that I saw a huge number, impossible to count, of people from every nation, race, tribe and language; they were standing in front of the throne and in front of the Lamb, dressed in white robes and holding palms in their hands. They shouted aloud, "Victory to our God, who sits on the throne, and to the Lamb!" And all the angels who were standing in a circle round the throne, surrounding the elders and the four animals, prostrated themselves before the throne, and touched the ground with their foreheads, worshipping God with these words, "Amen. Praise and glory and wisdom and thanksgiving and honour and power and strength to our God for ever and ever. Amen"...

Now a great sign appeared in heaven: a woman, adorned with the sun, standing on the moon, and with the twelve stars on her head for a crown.

Apocalypse 7:9-12; 12:1

THE STATIONS OF THE CROSS

by Saint Alphonsus Liguori C.Ss.R.

PLENTIFUL REDEMPTION

From the earliest centuries of the Christian era, pilgrims to the Holy Land would retrace the steps that Our Lord took as he made his way to Golgotha, the place of his crucifixion. As time went by, and travel to Jerusalem became difficult and even dangerous, Christians replicated the sites of this Via Dolorosa in other places, and so the devotion known as the Stations of the Cross spread abroad. Now they are a familiar feature of Catholic churches throughout the world.

The actual number of stations has varied over the years, but in the eighteenth century the number was finally fixed at fourteen. In some places in recent years a fifteenth station has been added, commemorating Jesus' resurrection.

The Stations of the Cross may be followed either alone or with others. There are many forms of this devotion, which can aid us to remember and think anew about the Lord's great love and all that he has done for us. The version that is provided here is based on the meditations of St Alphonsus Liguori, the founder of the Redemptorist Congregation.

Prayer before the Altar

O Jesus Christ my Lord, with what great love you passed over the painful road which led you to death; and I, how often have I abandoned you. But now I love you with my whole soul, and because I love you I am sincerely sorry for having offended you. My Jesus, pardon me, and permit me to accompany you in this journey. You are going to die for love of me, and it is my wish also, my dearest Redeemer, to die for love of you. My Jesus, in your love I wish to live, in your love I wish to die.

First Station

JESUS IS CONDEMNED TO DEATH

We adore you, O Christ, and we praise you.
Because by your holy Cross you have redeemed the world.

Consider how Jesus, after having been scourged and crowned with thorns, was unjustly condemned by Pilate to die on the Cross.

Our Lord stands in silence condemned to death. False witnesses have accused him; judges in bad faith have condemned him; a friend has betrayed him, still he remains silent. "Harshly dealt with, he bore it humbly, never opening his mouth; like a lamb before its shearer never opening its mouth."

Lord, it was not Pilate; no, it was my sins that condemned you to die. I beseech you by the merits of this sorrowful journey, to assist me in my journey towards eternity.

I love you Jesus, my love, above all things: I repent with my whole heart for having offended you. Never permit me to separate myself from you again. Grant that I may love you always, and then do with me what you will.

At the cross her station keeping,
stood the mournful mother weeping,
close to Jesus to the last.

Second Station
JESUS RECEIVES THE CROSS

We adore you, O Christ, and we praise you.
Because by your holy Cross you have redeemed the world.

Consider how Jesus, in making this journey with the Cross on his shoulders, thought of us, and offered for us to his Father the death he was about to undergo.

Jesus begins his sorrowful journey. Burdened with the world's sin, still he thinks of each one of us. Embracing the Cross he does not complain of his fate. But as scripture says, "For my part I made no resistance, I offered my back to those who struck me, I did not cover my face against insult and spittle."

My loving Jesus, by the merits of carrying your Cross, give me the necessary help to carry mine with perfect patience and resignation.

I love you Jesus, my love, above all things: I repent with my whole heart for having offended you. Never permit me to separate myself from you again. Grant that I may love you always, and then do with me what you will.

Through her heart, his sorrow sharing,
all his bitter anguish bearing,
now at length the sword has pass'd.

Third Station
JESUS FALLS THE FIRST TIME

We adore you, O Christ, and we praise you.
Because by your holy Cross you have redeemed the world.

Consider this first fall of Jesus under his Cross. His flesh was torn by the scourges, his head was crowned with thorns; he had lost a great quantity of blood. So weakened he could scarcely walk, he yet had to carry this great load upon his shoulders. The guards struck him violently and he fell several times.

Jesus falls at the feet of his tormentors. Yet his longing for our salvation drives him on. He did not need the blows of the soldiery to flog him to Calvary. The love of his Sacred Heart drove him on; the Holy Spirit drove him on; the longing of the eternal Father to win us to heaven drove him on.

Lord, how heavily my sins must weigh upon your Sacred Heart. By the merits of this first fall, deliver me from the misfortune of falling into mortal sin.

I love you Jesus, my love, above all things: I repent with my whole heart for having offended you. Never permit me to separate myself from you again. Grant that I may love you always, and then do with me what you will.

Oh, how sad and sore distress'd
was that mother highly blest,
of the sole-begotten One.

Fourth Station
JESUS IS MET BY HIS BLESSED MOTHER

We adore you, O Christ, and we praise you.
Because by your holy Cross you have redeemed the world.

Consider the meeting of the Son and the Mother, which took place on this journey. Their looks became like so many arrows to wound those hearts which loved each other so tenderly.

Jesus beholds the loving face of Mary amidst the mockeries around him. But now he is hardly recognisable, so disfigured did he look. Without beauty, without majesty she saw him, "A thing despised and rejected by men, and the Lord has laid upon him the sins of us all."

My Jesus, by the sorrow you experienced in this meeting, grant me the grace of a devoted love for your Holy Mother. And do you my Queen, who were overwhelmed with sorrow, obtain for me a continual and tender remembrance of the Passion of your Son.

I love you Jesus, my love, above all things: I repent with my whole heart for having offended you. Never permit me to separate myself from you again. Grant that I may love you always, and then do with me what you will.

Christ above in torment hangs;
she beneath beholds the pangs
of her dying glorious Son.

Fifth Station
The Cross is laid upon Simon of Cyrene

We adore you, O Christ, and we praise you.
Because by your holy Cross you have redeemed the world.

Consider how his cruel tormentors, seeing Jesus was on the point of expiring, and fearing he would die on the way, whereas they wished him to die the shameful death of the Cross, constrained Simon of Cyrene to carry the Cross behind our Lord.

A stranger is forced to carry the Cross of Jesus. And yet in doing so, faith came to Simon and his family, for scripture names him, "Simon the father of Alexander and Rufus" who became well known to Christ's followers.

Lord Jesus, you invite all your people to take part with you in carrying the Cross and, like Simon of Cyrene, bring blessings upon themselves and upon others. I will try more willingly to unite my crosses and trials to your Sacred Passion; help me by your grace.

I love you Jesus, my love, above all things: I repent with my whole heart for having offended you. Never permit me to separate myself from you again. Grant that I may love you always, and then do with me what you will.

Is there one who would not weep,
whelm'd in miseries so deep,
Christ's dear mother to behold?

Sixth Station
VERONICA WIPES THE FACE OF JESUS

We adore you, O Christ, and we praise you.
Because by your holy Cross you have redeemed the world.

Consider how the holy woman named Veronica, seeing Jesus so ill-used, and bathed in sweat and blood, wiped his face with a towel, on which was left the impression of his holy countenance.

This was indeed a gracious reward for Veronica's compassion. Yet in this meeting there is a lesson for us all. For whenever out of love we minister to the needy, we receive an increase of grace, and the image and likeness of Christ grows in our souls.

Lord, my soul was once beautiful, when I received your grace in Baptism. But I have so often disfigured it by my sins. You alone, my Redeemer, can restore it to its former beauty. Do this by your Passion, O Jesus.

I love you Jesus, my love, above all things: I repent with my whole heart for having offended you. Never permit me to separate myself from you again. Grant that I may love you always, and then do with me what you will.

Can the human heart refrain
from partaking in her pain,
in that mother's pain untold?

Seventh Station
JESUS FALLS THE SECOND TIME

We adore you, O Christ, and we praise you.
Because by your holy Cross you have redeemed the world.

Consider the second fall of Jesus under the Cross: a fall which renews the pain of all the wounds in his head and body.

Again, Jesus falls beneath the weight of the Cross. Yet again he staggers to his feet and continues along the road to Calvary.

Lord, how many times have you pardoned me, and how many times have I fallen again and begun again to offend you. By the merits of this second fall, give me the help necessary to persevere in your grace until death. Grant that in all temptations which assail me I may always commend myself to you.

I love you Jesus, my love, above all things: I repent with my whole heart for having offended you. Never permit me to separate myself from you again. Grant that I may love you always, and then do with me what you will.

Bruised, derided, cursed, defiled,
she beheld her tender child,
all with bloody scourges rent.

Eighth Station
THE WOMEN OF JERUSALEM MOURN FOR OUR LORD

We adore you, O Christ, and we praise you.
Because by your holy Cross you have redeemed the world.

Consider how these women wept with compassion at seeing Jesus in such a pitiable state, streaming with blood as he walked along. "Daughters of Jerusalem," said he, "weep not for me, but for yourselves and for your children."

These courageous women mourned for him as he passed by. And supporting him in their grief they openly confessed their faith in his name, fearless of what might happen to them.

Lord Jesus, by the example of this meeting, let me always confess my faith in you as my Lord and my God, careless of any danger or derision it may bring me.

I love you Jesus, my love, above all things: I repent with my whole heart for having offended you. Never permit me to separate myself from you again. Grant that I may love you always, and then do with me what you will.

For the sins of his own nation,
saw him hang in desolation,
till his spirit forth he sent.

Ninth Station
JESUS FALLS THE THIRD TIME

We adore you, O Christ, and we praise you.
Because by your holy Cross you have redeemed the world.

Consider the third fall of Jesus Christ. His weakness was extreme, and the cruelty of his executioners excessive, who tried to hasten his steps when he could scarcely move.

Jesus was but a few steps from Calvary. Yet before he gained the very spot where he was to be crucified, again he fell to the ground. As scripture says of our Holy Redeemer, "My throat is dried up as parched clay, and in the dust of death you have laid me."

My loving Jesus, by the merits of this third fall, never allow me to remain discouraged beneath the weight and repetition of my sins. Grant me confidence in your forgiveness, and a firm purpose of amendment.

I love you Jesus, my love, above all things: I repent with my whole heart for having offended you. Never permit me to separate myself from you again. Grant that I may love you always, and then do with me what you will.

O thou mother! fount of love!
Touch my spirit from above,
make my heart with thine accord.

Tenth Station
JESUS IS STRIPPED OF HIS GARMENTS

We adore you, O Christ, and we praise you.
Because by your holy Cross you have redeemed the world.

Consider the violence with which Jesus was stripped by the executioners. His inner garments adhered to his torn flesh, and they dragged them off so roughly that the skin came with them. Pity your Saviour so cruelly treated.

Our Lord stands exposed to the gaze of the jeering crowd. He is made to look a fool for my sake. He who as God's creating Word rightly possesses all things, now possesses nothing.

My most innocent Jesus, by the merits of the ridicule that you bore, grant me readiness to be considered a fool for your sake. Strip me of all sinful desires for worldly things. But above all, never allow me to be stripped of your grace.

I love you Jesus, my love, above all things: I repent with my whole heart for having offended you. Never permit me to separate myself from you again. Grant that I may love you always, and then do with me what you will.

Make me feel as thou hast felt;
make my soul to glow and melt
with the love of Christ my Lord.

Eleventh Station
JESUS IS NAILED TO THE CROSS

We adore you, O Christ, and we praise you.
Because by your holy Cross you have redeemed the world.

Consider how Jesus, having been placed upon the Cross, extended his hands, and offered to his eternal Father the sacrifice of his life for our salvation.

Our Saviour is crucified, and in the company of two thieves. As scripture had foretold, he was taken for a sinner, while he was praying all the time for sinners. As they fastened him with nails, he prayed for us all: "Father, forgive them, for they know not what they do."

Lord, by the merits of your prayer on Calvary, grant me real sorrow for all my sins. Not only because of the punishment they deserve, but still more because of the suffering they have caused you, who love me so much.

I love you Jesus, my love, above all things: I repent with my whole heart for having offended you. Never permit me to separate myself from you again. Grant that I may love you always, and then do with me what you will.

Holy Mother, pierce me through,
in my heart each wound renew
of my Saviour crucified.

Twelfth Station
JESUS DIES ON THE CROSS

We adore you, O Christ, and we praise you.
Because by your holy Cross you have redeemed the world.

Consider how Jesus, being consumed with anguish after three hours' agony on the Cross, abandoned himself to the weight of his body, bowed his head and died.

How completely dependent we are on that holy Cross: for the grace of God's friendship; for forgiveness of sins; for hope of heaven hereafter. On Calvary, his life of sacrifice has reached its conclusion, "It is finished; Father, into your hands I commit my spirit."

My dying Jesus, since you are so deserving of all my love, may your love henceforward be my first concern. By the merits of your Cross, unite my heart more firmly to your holy will. I commit my life into your hands.

I love you Jesus, my love, above all things: I repent with my whole heart for having offended you. Never permit me to separate myself from you again. Grant that I may love you always, and then do with me what you will.

Let me share with thee his pain
who for all my sins was slain,
who for me in torments died.

Thirteenth Station
Jesus is taken down from the Cross

We adore you, O Christ, and we praise you.
Because by your holy Cross you have redeemed the world.

Consider how, after our Lord had died, two of his disciples, Joseph and Nicodemus, took him down from the Cross, and placed him in the arms of his sorrowful Mother.

Mary at last has possession of her Son. Now when his enemies can do no more, they leave him to her in contempt. How deeply now she felt the force of Simeon's words, "And your own soul a sword shall pierce."

O Mother of sorrows, for the love of your Son, accept me as your servant and pray for me. And do you my Redeemer, since you have died for me, grant that I may love you always, for I wish but you and nothing more.

I love you Jesus, my love, above all things: I repent with my whole heart for having offended you. Never permit me to separate myself from you again. Grant that I may love you always, and then do with me what you will.

Let me mingle tears with thee,
mourning him who mourn'd for me,
all the days that I may live.

Fourteenth Station
JESUS IS PLACED IN THE SEPULCHRE

We adore you, O Christ, and we praise you.
Because by your holy Cross you have redeemed the world.

Consider how the disciples, accompanied by his holy Mother, carried the body of Jesus to bury it. They closed the tomb, and all came sorrowfully away.

Jesus is left alone to rest in peace. And yet he is not alone, for the Father is always with him. He came from the Father into the world, and now he has left the world and gone to the Father.

My buried Jesus, grant that I too may find your peace at life's end. And by the merits of your own resurrection on the third day, make me rise in glory with you at the last day, to be always united with you in heaven, to praise you and love you for ever.

I love you Jesus, my love, above all things: I repent with my whole heart for having offended you. Never permit me to separate myself from you again. Grant that I may love you always, and then do with me what you will.

By the cross with thee to stay,
there with thee to weep and pray,
is all I ask of thee to give.

MY GOD, I LOVE YOU

A treasury of prayers by
Saint Alphonsus Liguori C.Ss.R.

Compiled by Richard Reid C.Ss.R.

PLENTIFUL REDEMPTION

Saint Alphonsus Liguori founded the Congregation of the Most Holy Redeemer ("The Redemptorists") in 1732. He was passionate about taking the Gospel of Jesus to people who were poor and abandoned in society, and helping them experience it as *good* news. His hope for his congregation was that it would continue this mission; today Redemptorists are active across the world, and they settled in Britain in 1843.

Perhaps the least-known thing about Saint Alphonsus is that he is a Doctor of the Church, one of only thirty-three. As such, he is recognised as having something important to say to Christians "in any age of the Church".

Originally taught to pray by his mother, Saint Alphonsus is also a Doctor of Prayer. It is with great confidence, therefore, that we can allow his gentleness to lead us deeply and contemplatively in prayer.

I Love You
I love you, Jesus, my love.
I love you with all my heart.
I repent of having offended you.
Never permit me to offend you again.
Grant that I may love you always,
and then do with me what you will.

Love of the Lord
Yes, O Lord, I love you more
than all the honours of the world,
more than all its riches.
I love you more than everything I possess,
more than myself.
Let others seek what they will;
I will seek nothing but you alone,
my love, my all.
In you alone I find
all that I can seek or desire.

The Way to Holiness
To gain all,
we must give all.
To possess God,
we must leave all that is not God.
Then, indeed, we can say to him:
My Jesus, I have left all for you:
now give yourself all to me.
Let others speak of riches and pleasures,
but let us turn to God,
and from deep in our heart
say to him:
My God and my all!

There are three steps on the road to holiness:

   to be aware of our defects
   and to try to overcome them;

among things which are good,
always to choose that which is
most pleasing to God;
to receive from the hands of God
with peace of mind and thanksgiving
even things which are displeasing to us.

O my Jesus, my love, my all,
teach me to know from which
things I ought to detach myself,
and what I must do to please you.
O my beloved Redeemer,
behold this day I give myself
all to you without reserve.

My God, I Love You

Lord, let me not complain
when I find myself deprived
of consolation, for I do not
deserve it; nor can I claim it.
It is enough for me to know
that you never reject anyone
who loves you. It is enough
for me to say with truth:
My God, I love you, I love you.

On Being Lukewarm

O Lord, have mercy on me.
I find myself without love,
without confidence
and without good desires.
O my Jesus, abandon me not.
Reach out your hand
and draw me from the depths
of the lukewarm life
into which I have fallen.

O Holy Virgin, pray to Jesus for me.

Helps to Holiness
Resolutions:
Let us then fix our minds on the ways of God.
Let us resolve to meditate each day
on the passion of our Lord Jesus Christ.
Let us resign ourselves in peace
to God's plan for us.
Let us endeavour, in the time remaining to us,
to give all to God.
Jesus has given himself to us;
may God help us to give ourselves to him.

Jesus, my saviour, help me.
I am resolved truly to love you,
and to leave all to please you.
Help me to free myself from everything
that hinders me from belonging wholly to you
who have loved me so much.

By your prayers, O mother Mary,
which are so powerful with God,
obtain for me this grace
to belong wholly to God.

Preparation for Death
Behold me, my God, ready to embrace the death
you have destined for me. From this moment
I accept it. O my Jesus, I unite the suffering
of my death to the pain and agony which you
my Saviour, endured in your death.

I accept the time, whether it be soon,
or after many years. I accept the manner,
whether with warning or suddenly.
In everything, I resign myself to your will.
Give me strength to suffer all with patience.

I thank you, my God, for the gift of faith.
I thank you for many lights and graces
with which you have drawn me to your love.

I do not deserve to hear those words:
"Well done, good and faithful servant:
enter the joy of your Lord."

But your death gives me hope
that I shall be admitted to heaven,
to love you eternally, and with all my being.

I love you with all my heart;
I love you more than myself.
Grant that I may love you always,
then do with me what you will.

Holy Mary, Mother of God, pray for me
now and at the hour of my death.
Jesus, Mary and Joseph be with me
at the hour of my death.

Trust
O my Jesus, you know my weakness.
You have promised to help
those who trust in you.
O Lord, I love you;
in you I trust.
Give me strength and make me belong
completely to you.

O sweet Mary, my advocate,
in you also I place my trust.

The Will of God
Receive, O God,
the gift of my entire will
and of my liberty.
I do not deserve
that you should accept this gift;
so often have I been unfaithful,
but I hear you command me
to love you with all my heart,
and therefore, I am sure you will accept it.

I resign myself wholly to your will.
Make me love you,
and then dispose of me
and all that is mine
as it pleases you.
I am in your hands;
do what you know to be best
for my salvation.

O Mother of God, do you obtain for me
holy perseverance.

O Jesus, my beloved Lord,
I seek for nought but thee!
My God, to thee I give myself –
do what thou wilt with me.

The Good Shepherd
O my saviour, worthy of all my love,
behold at your feet a lost sheep.
I have strayed from you
but you have not abandoned me.
You have left no means untried
to recover me.
What would have become of me

if you had not thought to seek me?
Unhappy me!
How long I have lived far from you?

Now through your mercy,
I trust I am in your grace.
Formerly I fled from you;
now I desire nothing but to love you.

Bind me fast with chains of holy love;
and cease not to seek me
as long as I live on this earth.

O Mary, advocate of sinners,
obtain for me holy perseverance.

In God Alone is True Peace Found

O my God, help me to disengage myself
from all the snares which draw me from you.
Grant me the grace to seek nothing but you;
and to desire nothing but to love you, and give you pleasure.
For love of you, I now renounce all earthly pleasures:
I renounce also all spiritual consolations.
I desire nothing but to do your will,
and to give you pleasure.
O Mother of God,
recommend me to your Son, who denies you nothing.

God of Love

God of love, O infinite lover, worthy of infinite love,
tell me what more can you devise to make us love you.
Was it not enough for you to become human,
to subject yourself to all our miseries?
Was it not enough for you to shed
all your blood for us in torments?

And then to die consumed with pain upon a cross,
destined for the worst of criminals?
Finally you reduced yourself to hiding
beneath the species of bread and wine,
to become our food, and so to be joined with each of us.

Tell me, I repeat, what more can you devise
to make us love you?
But now, I love you above all things.
I love you more than myself,
and I consecrate to you all my affections.
May you, who have already given me this desire,
also give me the strength to accomplish it.
My Jesus, I desire nothing from you but yourself.
Now that you have drawn me to your love,
I renounce everything.
I cling to you; you alone are enough for me.

Jesus on the Cross
Jesus on the cross! Here is proof of the love of a God.
This is the last appearance of the Incarnate Word on earth.
The first was in a stable, the last is on a cross.
Both manifest his infinite love and charity toward human beings.

Passion of Jesus
Eternal Word!
You spent thirty-three years in sweat and hardship.
You gave your blood and your life for our salvation.
In short, you spared nothing to make us love you.
Then how can there be people who know this
and yet do not love you?
O God, I am one of those ingrates.
I see the wrong I have done.
O my Jesus, have pity on me.
I offer you this ungrateful heart of mine –

ungrateful but repentant.
Yes, above every other evil, my dear Redeemer,
I repent of having despised you.
I repent, and I am sorry with all my heart.

My soul, you love a God who is bound like a criminal for you,
a God scourged like a slave for you,
a God made a mock-king for you.
Yes, my saviour, my God, I do love you.
Always remind me of everything you suffered for me,
so that I may never again forget to love you.

Ropes that bound Jesus, bind me to Jesus;
thorns that crowned Jesus, wound me with love for Jesus;
nails that pierced Jesus, nail me to the cross of Jesus;
that I may live and die united to Jesus.

Speaking to God

If you wish to please the loving heart of your God,
    take care to speak to God whenever you are able,
    continually and with the greatest confidence possible.
God is not reluctant to answer you in return.
God will not make himself heard by you in a voice that reaches
    your ears
    but rather in a voice that only your heart knows well.
Leave off conversations with creatures and speak one-on-one with
    your God:
"I will lead her into the desert and speak to her heart."

God will then speak to you with such inspiration,
such inner light,
with such demonstrations of his bounty,
with such sweet touches of the heart,
with tokens of forgiveness,
with such experiences of peace,
with such hope of paradise,

with such inner joy,
with such sweetness of grace,
with such loving and close embraces,
with such a voice of love that is well understood
by those whom God loves and who seek nothing
for themselves save God alone.

On Prayer
Let us pray, then, and let us always be asking for grace,
if we wish to be saved.
Let prayer be our most delightful occupation;
let prayer be the exercise of our whole life.
And when we are asking for particular graces,
let us always pray for the grace
to continue to pray in the future;
because if we leave off praying, we shall be lost.
There is nothing easier than prayer.
What does it cost us to say:
"Lord, stand by me! Lord, help me! Give me your love."
What can be easier than this?

Prayer on Visiting the Blessed Sacrament
My Lord Jesus Christ,
I believe that you are really here in this sacrament.
Night and day you remain here, compassionate and loving.
You call, you wait for, you welcome,
everyone who comes to visit you.
Unimportant though I am, I adore you.
I thank you for all the wonderful graces you have given me.

But I thank you especially for having given me yourself
in this sacrament, for having asked your own Mother
to mother me, for having called me here to talk to you.
I am here before you today to do three things:
to thank you for these precious gifts;

to make up for all the disrespect that you receive in this sacrament
from those who offend you;
to adore you everywhere in the world
where you are present in this living bread
but are left abandoned and unloved.

My Jesus, I love you with all my heart.
I know I have displeased you often in the past – I am sorry.
With your help, I promise never to do it again.
I am only a miserable sinner,
but I consecrate myself to you completely.
I give you my will, my love, my desires, everything I own.
From now on, do what you please with me.
All I ask is that you love me,
that you keep me faithful to the end of my life.
I ask for the grace to do your will exactly as you want it done.

I pray for the souls in purgatory –
especially those who were close to you in this sacrament
and close to your Mother, Mary.
I pray for every soul hardened in sin.
My saviour, I unite my love to the love of your divine heart,
and I offer them both together to your Father.
I beg him to accept this offering in your name.

Spiritual Communion

My Jesus, I believe that you are really here
in the Blessed Sacrament.
I love you more than anything in the world,
and I hunger to feed on your flesh.
But since I cannot receive communion at this moment,
feed my soul at least spiritually.
I unite myself to you now,
as I do when I actually receive you.
Never let me drift away from you.

Crib

My dearest Jesus,
if it is true that ownership is acquired by gift,
then you are truly mine since the Father has given you to me.
You were indeed born for me; you were given to me.
As scripture says: "For a child has been born for us,
a son given to us."
Therefore I can justly say to you:
"My God and my all!"
And since you are mine,
everything that belongs to you is also mine.
Therefore your precious blood is all mine,
your grace is mine, your paradise is mine;
and since you are mine,
who can ever take you away from me?

Cross

Was it possible that God, the creator of all things,
would have been pleased to die for love of his creatures?
Yes, it is through faith that he has done so.
The earth, the heavens, and all nature with astonishment
witnessed Jesus, the only begotten Son of God,
the Lord of the universe, die in intense pain and anguish,
like a criminal on a disgraceful cross.
Why?
For the love of humanity!
Lord, I have known your passion
and not only have I not loved you,
but I have frequently offended you.
Pardon me, I beg you, and remind me continually
of the death you have suffered for love of me,
so that I may never again offend you, but may always love you.
My crucified Jesus, I want to be yours alone now and forever,
and I will love no one else but you.

To the Holy Spirit

You are fire: enkindle in me your love.

You are light: enlighten my mind with the knowledge of eternal
things.

You are the dove: give me innocence of life.

You are the gentle breeze: disperse the storms of my passions.

You are the tongue: teach me how to bless you always.

You are the cloud: shelter me under the shadow of your protection.

You are the giver of all heavenly gifts: animate me,

I beseech you, with your grace;

sanctify me with your charity;

enlighten me with your wisdom;

adopt me by your goodness as your child,

and save me in your infinite mercy;

so that I may ever bless you, praise you, and love you;

first during this life on earth,

and then in heaven for all eternity.

Only One Thing is Necessary

O my God, help me to remember

that time is short, eternity is long.

What good is all the greatness of this world at the hour of death?

To love you, my God, and save my soul is the one thing necessary.

Without you, there is no peace, no joy.

My God, I need fear nothing but sin.

For to lose you, my God, is to lose all.

O my God, help me to remember –

that to gain all I must leave all,

that in loving you I have all good things.

BEAUTIFUL AND BRUISED

A Prayer
for Each Day of the Week

by Denis McBride C.Ss.R.

PLENTIFUL REDEMPTION

The prayer life of those who follow Christ is not limited to times of public assembly; we pray every day, to keep in contact with the Lord and to stay in contact with the best in ourselves. Our Lord is present not only in sacred space but also in our secret places, where we can be quiet and alone. Wherever that secret place is, there God awaits us.

Personal prayer can take many forms. As in the great book of the Psalms, it can be a scream or an endless groan, a grievance for some slight or hurt; it may be an angry complaint or an accusation; it could be a thank-you note for a loved one or for a special grace that has been granted; it could be delicious praise, shyly made. The great tradition of the Psalms teaches us that we can pray *always*, no matter what. Whatever mood or condition we are in, whatever is happening in our life, however we are feeling, we keep in touch with the God who is slow to anger and rich in graciousness. Nothing about us needs to be excluded from prayer.

Prayer, of course, is not just about ourselves, transfixed by our own agenda. We are expected to have a place in our prayer and in our lives for those who are poor or lonely, for those who feel rejected or forgotten, for all the people who feel hurt by life and have no one to support them. Prayer is not only being open to God about ourselves but bothering God about the people on the margins of our lives and of the world. As St John Vianney said: "Our dear God loves to be bothered."

Prayer pushes us out, beyond ourselves. And when we remind God of people or situations we believe deserve God's special attention, so we remind ourselves that these same people and situations also deserve *our* best attention. Prayer is not only aimed at God but reflects back to the deepest and best in ourselves: it is deep calling to deep.

The following prayers are a simple suggestion for opening ourselves daily to a larger world of need, one that will be truly blessed by our care and attention.

Sunday
This is the day the Lord has made;
let us rejoice and be glad in it.

We lift up our hearts to:
God the Father, to whom we pray;
God the Son, through whom we pray;
God the Holy Spirit, in whom we pray.

We pray for the Church throughout the world,
that God will preserve it in truth and in peace;
that its witness be faithful and its truth sincere;
its divisions healed and unity restored,
now and for evermore.

We pray for all those who are powerless
to influence their own future;
for all those who are oppressed
in body, in mind, or in spirit.
That whatever forces led them
to the confining place they now live,
the Spirit may lead them
out of the wasteland
and give them the courage and strength
to shape their lives anew.

We pray for all those who cannot resist temptation
and who, without intention, destroy their own lives
and bring distress and grief to their loved ones.
We pray for all those addicted to destructive behaviour:
that they may be granted the gift of insight
and the necessary power to choose life again
so they may enjoy peace and serenity in their souls.

We pray for ourselves:
that the Lord may not put us to the test
nor lead us to a time of trial,
but deliver us from all that is evil.

May the Lord mark us this day and all our days
with the blessing of his peace.
When we are tired and vulnerable,
may he enliven us with new purpose.
When we are unsure and distrustful,
may he fortify us with new confidence.
When we are depressed and weighed down,
may he raise us to new heights.
Amen.

Monday
How great is your name, O Lord our God,
through all the earth.

We give you heartfelt thanks, O Lord,
for the gift of life and the gift of faith.
We bless and praise you for all your goodness,
for the world you have made,
for the people you have created,
for the love of family and the joy of friendship.
Keep us kind in our outlook
and tender-hearted in our relationships
through Christ our Lord.

We pray for all who are marginalised in life,
for all who are excluded because of their race,
their religion, or their gender:
that they may know the loving embrace of the Lord
who offers them living water,
and experience the acceptance of the community.

We pray for all minorities in every land
who struggle to maintain their own customs
and safeguard their traditions:
that they may be seen as a blessing, not a threat;
a gift, not an embarrassment.

God and Father of all creation,
we bless your holy name,
which you revealed through the Word
you sent among us, your eternal gift,
Jesus Christ, our Lord and God.

He is the way:
through him may we know you and worship you.
He is the truth:
may he reveal your loving plans to us.
He is the life:
may he bring us to fullness of life.

May the God who revealed his fullness in Jesus
bless us and keep us close;
may he never withdraw his love from us,
but remember us as the brothers and sisters of Jesus.
This we pray through Christ our Lord.
Amen.

Tuesday
*The Lord is my light and my help;
whom shall I fear?*

For our beautiful and bruised earth
we pray to you, creator of all things.
Grant that we may reverence
everything we take for granted,
and learn to honour
what we now needlessly spoil.
Awaken in us a wonder for the earth
we have inherited from your providence.
May our care and attention
be partners in the growth of your world,
now and always.

We pray in thanksgiving for our families
and all those who love us in life.
As they have blessed and nurtured us with their love,
we pray that they may richly enjoy the gift that is life.
In their weakness, Lord, be their strength;
in their darkness, be their light;
in their sorrow, be their comfort and guide.

We pray for all who care for our health:
that the Lord will give skill, gentleness and patience
to doctors and nurses and all who minister to those who are sick,
that they may bring healing and comfort
to all who look to them for help.

We remember all those who feel defeated by life,
who believe that life has somehow passed them by;
we pray for all who are disfigured or scarred
in body, in mind, or in spirit;
for all those who are named and known
by their affliction or sin.

We pray for ourselves
that we may never undervalue
the power of love and attentiveness;
that we may never ignore the little people in life
who hunger to be noticed and counted.

May the Lord look upon us
with kindness and mercy;
may the Lord shine his radiance
upon us and all whom we cherish;
may the Lord keep us forever
in the embrace of his loving gaze.
Amen.

Wednesday
I will bless the Lord at all times,
his praise always on my lips.

We bless you, Lord, for the countless blessings
you have bestowed on us.

We pray for all who have had to quit home
because they were excluded and rejected.
For all who leave home as economic migrants,
unable to make a living where they first belonged.
That the Lord will guide their steps
to new pastures, to a place they can call home.

For all who are fleeing from danger;
for all who are homeless and hungry.
We pray for them
and all who work to bring them relief.
That the Lord in his kindness
may watch over refugees and exiles,
those separated from their loved ones,
young people who are lost,
and those who have left or run away from home.
We pray that they will arrive safely
at the place where they long to be.

We pray for all who welcome the stranger,
the itinerant, the outcast.
That they may know that their generosity
is truly blessed by the God of all mercies,
who will, one day, welcome them
into the kingdom prepared for them
because they have ministered
to the hidden Christ in their midst.

God be with us on every road we take,
on every sea we cross,

through every sky we fly.
May the one who is Alpha and Omega be with us
in our leaving and in our arriving,
in our rising and lying down to rest,
in our dreams of the night,
and especially in our last hours on earth.
Whoever we are, wherever we may be,
may the Lord never withhold
his loving hands from us.
Amen.

Thursday
I waited, I waited for the Lord
and he stooped down to me;
he heard my cry.

Stoop down, O Lord, and hear our cries
as we pray in confidence to you.
We pray for children,
that they may live in safety and security;
we pray for young people,
that you may deepen within them
a sense of their own dignity and purpose in life;
we pray for all adults,
that they may have the joy of a generous heart;
we pray for those who have grown old,
that they may look back in gratitude
and look forward in confidence and hope.

We pray for all who are forever overlooked and bypassed
and who feel wholly unwanted.
That the Lord may open the eyes and enlighten the minds
of his disciples today to extend a welcome
that will give new life to our neglected neighbours.

For those whose hurt encloses them in isolation
because they cannot find words for their sorrow;
for those who are depressed in spirit
and disheartened and discouraged by life.
We pray that the Lord may lift them out of sadness
and reconnect them with the joy of living
and of belonging to warm-hearted friends.

We remember all who are approaching death
and facing their last times.
That they may know the closeness of family,
and the support and love of good friends,
so that they may depart this world in peace.

May the Lord of the living and the dead
look upon us with resolute kindness
and grant us the comfort of his peace.
When we are confused, may he bring insight;
when we are broken, may he mend us and mind us;
when we are dying, may he console us
with the assurance of his loving embrace.
This we ask in the name of the one
who gave everything of himself to us,
Jesus Christ, our Lord.
Amen.

Friday
Out of the depths, I cry to you, O Lord.
Lord, hear my voice!

Father, we give you thanks and praise
for your everlasting love.
However much we turn from you,
you always seek us out
and welcome us back with joy.
Even when we grow dull and weary,

you smile on us and give us your blessing.
Thus we praise you, now and always.

We bring before you, Lord,
all whose grief and loss have distanced them
from your loving embrace;
all those whose hurt has isolated them
from believing in your constant care.
Grace them anew with signs of your love,
that they may come to know again
the lavishness and constancy of your love.

We pray for all who suffer in the cause of right,
for those who give their lives for a purpose
larger than their own safety and survival:
that their generosity of spirit may meet its own reward
in the fullness of everlasting life.

We pray for those who are afflicted by an unexpected death;
for those whose lives are cut short by accident;
for those who are killed through violence or terror or war;
for all who die out of due season.
That the Lord of all mercies
will make good their loss in this life
and gladden them with the glory of heaven.

We pray for those who mourn the loss
of those they have loved long and well:
that their sorrow may be free from hopeless grief
and from the agony of bitter regrets.
We pray that they may mourn in hope,
knowing that the one who is Alpha and Omega
embraces the living and the dead
in his loving compassion and purpose.

May the Lord of the living and the dead
give us the assurance of his everlasting kindness
in good times and in bad.
Amen.

Saturday
Before the beginning of the world
he chose us, chose us in Christ.

Father, we open our eyes and strain to see you;
we raise our voices in prayer
and hope you will hear our call.
We know you are ever with us
yet too often we seem to be alone.
Keep us open, Father, to the mystery which is you
and may we never be caught off guard
when you choose to surprise us.
We thank you that you are our God, now and for ever.

We pray for all those
who walk a road of loss and disappointment,
particularly those who have to face
the large absence of someone dear to them
or the death of a loved one.
That the Lord may join them on the road,
assuring them that their grief will not be everlasting,
but be overtaken by the power of God's abiding love.
We pray for an increase of hope
in our broken world.
That people may see signs
beyond the immediate horizons of struggle,
of deprivation, of violence.
We pray that God will continue to raise up
peacemakers in our communities,
women and men committed to building
human sanctuaries, holy places,
where poor people are honoured,
where crushed people are sheltered,
where lost people may find a home.

We pray for our own communities.
May they be places of welcome and care,

where sorrowing people find comfort,
where lonely people find fellowship,
where faithful people find grace.
Above all, may they be places of loving respect,
where each person is recognised and reverenced
as a child of the living God.

May the good Lord
walk with us and bear with us
in all our journeys through life.
May his presence enable us to face
whatever the future holds, whatever may await us.
May we hold fast to his reassurance
that he will attend us and abide with us,
even to the ends of the earth.
Amen.

LATIN TEXTS FOR THE MASS

Response to the Greeting
Et cum spiritu tuo.

I Confess
Confiteor Deo omnipotenti, et vobis, fratres,
quia peccavi nimis
cogitatione, verbo, opere et omissione:

(and striking their breast they say:)

mea culpa, mea culpa, mea maxima culpa.

(then they continue:)

Ideo precor beatam Mariam semper Virginem,
omnes Angelos et Sanctos,
et vos, fratres, orare pro me
ad Dominum Deum nostrum.

Glory to God
Gloria in excelsis Deo
et in terra pax hominibus bonæ voluntatis.
Laudamus te,
benedicimus te,
adoramus te,
glorificamus te,
gratias agimus tibi propter magnam gloriam tuam,
Domine Deus, Rex cælestis,
Deus Pater omnipotens.
Domine Fili unigenite, Iesu Christe,
Domine Deus, Agnus Dei, Filius Patris,
qui tollis peccata mundi, miserere nobis;
qui tollis peccata mundi,
   suscipe deprecationem nostram.
Qui sedes ad dexteram Patris, miserere nobis.
Quoniam tu solus Sanctus, tu solus Dominus,
   tu solus Altissimus,
Iesu Christe, cum Sancto Spiritu: in gloria Dei Patris.
Amen.

After the Readings
Deo gratias.

Before the Gospel
Dominus vobiscum.
Et cum spiritu tuo.
Lectio sancti Evangelii secundum N.
Gloria tibi, Domine.

At the End of the Gospel
Verbum Domini.
Laus tibi, Christe.

I Believe
Credo in unum Deum,
Patrem omnipotentem,
factorem cæli et terræ,
visibilium omnium et invisibilium.
Et in unum Dominum Iesum Christum,
Filium Dei Unigenitum,
et ex Patre natum ante omnia sæcula.
Deum de Deo, lumen de lumine, Deum verum de Deo vero,
genitum, non factum, consubstantialem Patri:
per quem omnia facta sunt.
Qui propter nos homines et propter nostram salutem
descendit de cælis.

(all bow during the next two lines)

Et incarnatus est de Spiritu Sancto
ex Maria Virgine, et homo factus est.
Crucifixus etiam pro nobis sub Pontio Pilato;
passus et sepultus est,
et resurrexit tertia die, secundum Scripturas,
et ascendit in cælum, sedet ad dexteram Patris.
Et iterum venturus est cum gloria, iudicare vivos et mortuos,
cuius regni non erit finis.
Et in Spiritum Sanctum, Dominum et vivificantem:
qui ex Patre Filioque procedit.
Qui cum Patre et Filio simul adoratur et conglorificatur:

qui locutus est per prophetas.
Et unam, sanctam, catholicam et apostolicam Ecclesiam.
Confiteor unum baptisma in remissionem peccatorum.
Et exspecto resurrectionem mortuorum,
et vitam venturi sæculi. Amen.

Response to the Offertory Prayers
Benedictus Deus in sæcula.

Response to "Pray brethren (brothers and sisters)…"
Suscipiat Dominus sacrificium de manibus tuis
ad laudem et gloriam nominis sui,
ad utilitatem quoque nostram
totiusque Ecclesiæ suæ sanctæ.

The Eucharistic Prayer
Opening Dialogue
Dominus vobiscum.
Et cum spiritu tuo.
Sursum corda.
Habemus ad Dominum.
Gratias agamus Domino Deo nostro.
Dignum et iustum est.

Holy, Holy
Sanctus, Sanctus, Sanctus Dominus Deus Sabaoth.
Pleni sunt cæli et terra gloria tua.
Hosanna in excelsis.
Benedictus qui venit in nomine Domini.
Hosanna in excelsis.

Memorial acclamations

1. **Mortem tuam annuntiamus, Domine,**
   et tuam resurrectionem confitemur, donec venias.

2. **Quotiescumque manducamus panem hunc**
   et calicem bibimus,
   mortem tuam annuntiamus, Domine, donec venias

3. **Salvator mundi, salva nos,**
   qui per crucem et resurrectionem tuam liberasti nos.

Our Father

Pater noster, qui es in cælis:
sanctificetur nomen tuum;
adveniat regnum tuum;
fiat voluntas tua, sicut in cælo, et in terra.
Panem nostrum cotidianum da nobis hodie;
et dimitte nobis debita nostra,
sicut et nos dimittimus debitoribus nostris;
et ne nos inducas in tentationem;
sed libera nos a malo.

Acclamation after the Our Father

Quia tuum est regnum,
et potestas, et gloria
in sæcula.

At the Peace

Pax Domini sit semper vobiscum.
Et cum spiritu tuo.

Lamb of God
Agnus Dei, qui tollis peccata mundi: miserere nobis.
Agnus Dei, qui tollis peccata mundi: miserere nobis.
Agnus Dei, qui tollis peccata mundi: dona nobis pacem.

Lord, I am not worthy…
Domine, non sum dignus ut intres sub tectum meum;
sed tantum dic verbo, et sanabitur anima mea.

At the conclusion
Dominus vobiscum.
Et cum spiritu tuo.
Benedicat vos omnipotens Deus,
Pater, et Filius, ✠ et Spiritus Sanctus.
Amen.
Ite, missa est.
Deo gratias.